FOR ORGANS, PIANOS & ELECTRONIC KEYBOARDS

E·Z PLAY TODAY 199 — JUMBO SONGBOOK

274 SONGS FOR ALL OCCASIONS

The E-Z Play® TODAY Jumbo Songbook has been especially created to offer the widest variety of musical selections for all occasions... and compiled in one convenient, easy-to-read volume.

In addition to the hundreds of pages of music, you'll also find a section in the front of this book devoted to note reading, chord accompaniment, organ registration and automatic rhythm. In the back of the book, for your reference, there is a glossary of music notation, terms, and note values. A chord speller chart for keyboard instruments and a guitar chord chart follow the glossary.

For quick cross-reference, all song arrangements in the E-Z Play TODAY Jumbo Songbook are listed by categories in the front of the book... and listed alphabetically in the back of the book.

For your continued playing enjoyment, dozens of songbooks are available in the E-Z Play TODAY music series. The entire series provides a play-on-sight repertoire filled with musical fun for everyone. A listing of these books can be found in the back of this book. Complete your music library today... see your local music dealer, or write directly to the National Sales Office of Hal Leonard Publishing Corporation.

CONTENTS

D1601779

HAL•LEONARD
CORPORATION
7777 W. BLUEMOUND RD. P.O. BOX 13819 MILWAUKEE, WI 53213

CATEGORICAL INDEX

NOTATION

All songs are written in the exclusive E-Z Play TODAY music notation.

- A STAFF is five lines with spaces between them. Each line or space represents a lettered note.

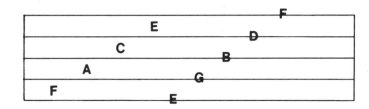

- Sometimes LEDGER LINES are added above or below the staff to accommodate additional notes.

LEDGER LINES

LEDGER LINES

- The lettered notes correspond to lettered keys on the keyboard guide. As notes move down the staff, the corresponding keys move down (to the left) on the keyboard. As the notes move up the staff, they move up (to the right) on the keyboard.

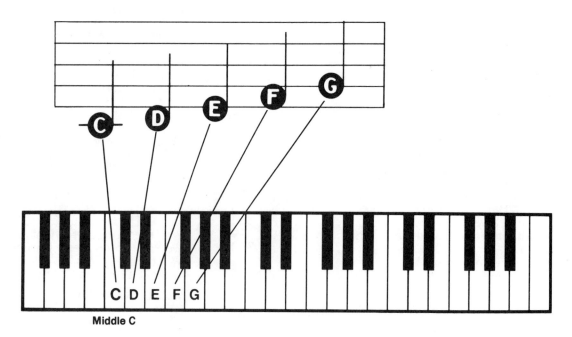

NOTE VALUES

- Each type of note has a specific TIME VALUE which is measured in rhythmic beats.

| QUARTER NOTE 1 Beat | HALF NOTE 2 Beats | DOTTED HALF NOTE 3 Beats | WHOLE NOTE 4 Beats |

- Each staff is divided by BAR LINES into sections called MEASURES. A DOUBLE BAR indicates the end of a song.

Measure   **Measure**

Bar Line   Bar Line   Double Bar Line

- A TIME SIGNATURE appears at the beginning of each song after the TREBLE CLEF sign.

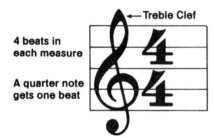

←Treble Clef

4 beats in each measure

A quarter note gets one beat

The **top number** indicates the number of rhythmic beats in each measure.

The **bottom number** indicates the type of note that receives one beat. 4 indicates a quarter note.

3 beats in each measure

A quarter note gets one beat

- Sometimes a note or notes appear at the beginning of a song which do not equal the number of beats indicated by the time signature. These are called PICK-UP NOTES, and the missing beats are written at the end of the song.

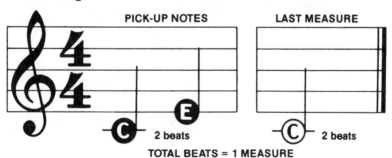

PICK-UP NOTES   **LAST MEASURE**

2 beats   2 beats

TOTAL BEATS = 1 MEASURE

- A TIE is a curved line that connects notes of the same pitch (notes on the same line or space). Play the first note and then hold for the total time of all tied notes.

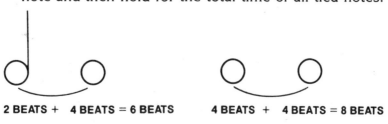

2 BEATS + 4 BEATS = 6 BEATS   4 BEATS + 4 BEATS = 8 BEATS

ACCOMPANIMENT

The arrangements in this book have been written for all types of chord accompaniment.

1 ONE BUTTON (Chord Organ) or ONE-KEY (Automatic) CHORDS

2 THREE-NOTE (Triad) CHORDS

3 CONVENTIONAL (Standard) KEYBOARD CHORD POSITIONS

4 GUITAR CHORDS

Chord names, called chord symbols, appear above the melody line as either a boxed symbol [C]

or as an alternate chord (C7)

or both
C7
[C]

1 CHORD ORGAN or ONE-KEY AUTOMATIC CHORDS —Play whichever name is on your instrument.

2 THREE-NOTE (Triad) CHORDS —If you've previously learned to play three-note triad chords, or if you wish to learn this system:

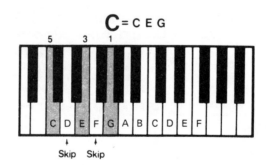

- Place your little finger on the key which has the same letter name as the chord.

- Skip a white key and place your middle finger on the next white key.

- Skip another white key and place your thumb on the next white key.

CHORD SYMBOLS WITH ARROWS

When triad chord symbols are made up of one or more black keys, a special chord notation with arrows is used. The following illustration will help you understand this system.

- Think of a chord as having three sections.

- Each section represents one note of the triad.

The placement of arrows in one or more "sections" to the right or the left of the chord name indicates which of the notes will be raised or lowered one half step. For example:

- Move a chord key **down** one half step when the arrow is placed to the **left** of the chord letter name.

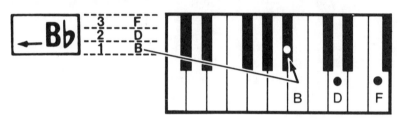

B is lowered one-half step.

- Move a chord key **up** when the arrow is placed to the **right** of the chord letter name.

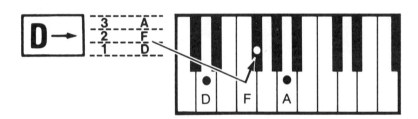

F is raised one-half step.

- If two or three arrows are shown, use the same procedure by altering the number of chord keys according to the direction of the arrows.

3 STANDARD CHORD POSITIONS—When playing standard chord positions, the positions (inversions) of the three-note and four-note chords is strictly a matter of your own choice. Usually, bass pedals are played with standard chord positions.

For your reference, a CHORD SPELLER of commonly used standard chord positions is included at the back of this book.

4 GUITAR CHORDS—Follow the boxed chord symbol, unless an alternate is indicated. Play the alternate chord whenever possible.

REGISTRATION

On most organs or electronic keyboards, there are various tabs or tonebars and/or controls which produce and/or enhance sounds. Some are called voice tabs . . . instrumental voices at different pitches. Some are general controls . . . such as Vibrato or Tremolo. A combination of tabs or tonebars and general controls is called REGISTRATION.

A registration number appears at the beginning of each song in this book.

● Match this number with the same number on the E-Z Play TODAY Registration Guide (opposite page).

● Set the voice tabs or tonebars and controls as indicated.

● If you wish to use special effect registrations such as Banjo or Hawaiian Guitar, consult your Owner's Manual.

Because registration has so many variables, one of which is personal imagination, the registrations suggested on the Registration Guide are generalized.

AUTOMATIC RHYTHM

The excitement created by an automatic rhythm will enhance your music regardless of which left-hand chord system you select. Here are a few hints for the most effective use of your rhythm unit:

● Experiment with the various rhythms available on your unit. Select a rhythm pattern that complements each song. Sometimes it's fun to create unusual or different moods by combining two or more rhythm patterns.

● Most rhythm units have a volume control which regulates the volume level of the percussion instruments. For Latin rhythms, the percussion instruments usually play a more prominent role than they do in a ballad type rhythm; therefore adjust the volume control accordingly.

● Every rhythm unit has a tempo (speed) control which regulates the speed of the selected rhythm pattern. As you first begin to learn a song, adjust the tempo control to a slower speed until you can play the song with ease and accuracy.

● The tempo light flashes at predetermined time intervals. Watch the light for the speed of the rhythm and also to determine when a rhythm pattern begins.

REGISTRATION GUIDE

Instrumental voices can be categorized into three groups: Strings, Reeds, and Horns. The names of these voices vary from one organ model to another. The following chart shows a variety of instrumental voice names listed in each of the categories.

E-Z Play TODAY registrations show instrumental voices by their general catgegory. Select the tabs that most closely resemble the tab names on your organ model.

Strings	Reeds	Horns
Violin	Clarinet	Trumpet
Cello	Oboe	Trombone
Viola	Bassoon	Brass
Violina	Saxophone	Kinura
String	Reed	Tuba
		Horn

E-Z Play TODAY Reg. No.	Tab Model Organs	Tonebar Model Organs
1 Open Flutes	Upper: Flutes (Tibias) 16', 4' Lower: Diapason 8' or Flute 8' Pedal: 16', 8' Vib/Trem: On, Normal	Upper: 80 0800 000 Lower: (00) 7600 000 Pedal: 4(0)5(0) Vib/Trem: On, Normal
2 Full Flutes	Upper: Flutes (Tibias) 16', 8', 4', 2' Lower: Diapason 8', Reed 8' Pedal: 16', 8' Vib/Trem: On, Normal	Upper: 80 8808 008 Lower: (00) 7503 000 Pedal: 4(0)6(0) Vib/Trem: On, Normal
3 Flute/String Ensemble	Upper: Flutes (Tibias) 8', 4', String 8' Lower: Diapason 8' Pedal: 16', 8' Vib/Trem: On, Normal	Upper: 40 4555 554 Lower: (00) 7503 333 Pedal: 5(0)5(0) Vib/Trem: On, Normal
4 Flute/Reed Ensemble	Upper: Flutes (Tibias) 8', 4', Reed 16' or 8' Lower: Flute 8', Reed 8' Pedal: 16', 8' Vib/Trem: On, Normal	Upper: 80 7766 006 Lower: (00) 7540 000 Pedal: 5(0)6(0) Vib/Trem: On, Normal
5 Flute/Reed/String Ensemble	Upper: Flutes (Tibias) 16', 8', 4', Reed 16' or 8', String 8' Lower: Diapason 8', String 8' Pedal: 16', 8' Vib/Trem: On, Normal	Upper: 80 8868 553 Lower: (00) 6634 221 Pedal: 5(0)6(0) Vib/Trem: On, Normal
6 Liturgical or Classical	Upper: Flutes (Tibias) 16', 8', 4', Reed 8', String 8' Lower: Diapason 8', Reed 8' Pedal: 16' Vib/Trem: Off	Upper: 80 8868 550 Lower: (00) 6604 020 Pedal: 6(0)4(0) Vib/Trem: Off
7 Jazz Ensemble	Upper: Flutes (Tibias) 16', 8', 5⅓', 2⅔' Lower: Diapason 8', Flute 8' Pedal: 8' or 16' Vib/Trem: Off or Slow	Upper: 88 5080 000 Lower: (00) 5633 320 Pedal: 4(0)6(0) Vib/Trem: Off or Celeste
8 Piano Solo	Upper: Piano or Flute (Tibia) 8' Lower: Diapason 8' Pedal: 8' or 16' Vib/Trem: On, Normal (lower only)	Upper: Piano Solo Lower: (00) 4302 010 Pedal: 4(0)3(0) Vib/Trem: On, Normal (lower only)
9 Reed Solo	Upper: Reed 16' or 8' Lower: Flute 8' Pedal: 16', 8' Vib/Trem: On, Small	Upper: 00 8080 840 Lower: (00) 5544 331 Pedal: 4(0)4(0) Vib/Trem: On, Small
10 String Solo	Upper: String 8' Lower: Flute 8' Pedal: 8' or 16' Vib/Trem: On, Small (delay)	Upper: 00 7888 888 Lower: (00) 7765 443 Pedal: 5(0)4(0) Vib/Trem: On, Small (delay)

Boola Boola

Registration 5

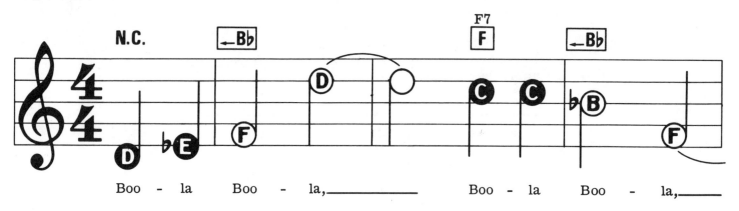

Boo - la Boo - la,_____ Boo - la Boo - la,_____

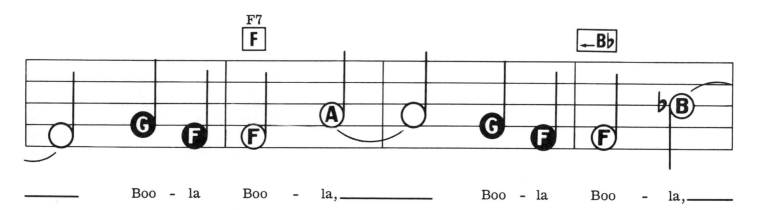

_____ Boo - la Boo - la,_____ Boo - la Boo - la,_____

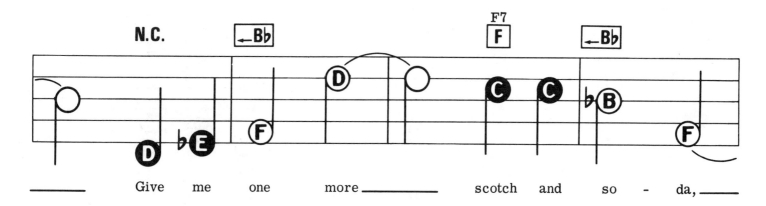

_____ Give me one more_____ scotch and so - da,_____

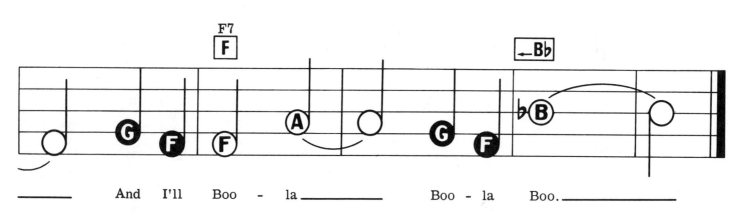

_____ And I'll Boo - la_____ Boo - la Boo._____

Far Above Cayuga's Waters

Registration 6

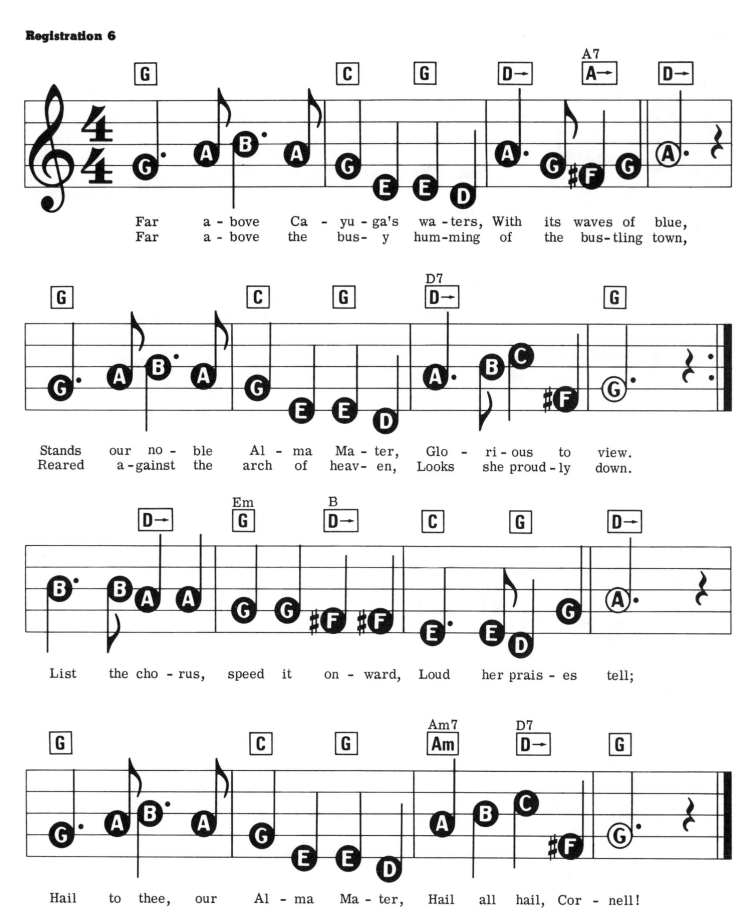

My College Gal

Registration 3

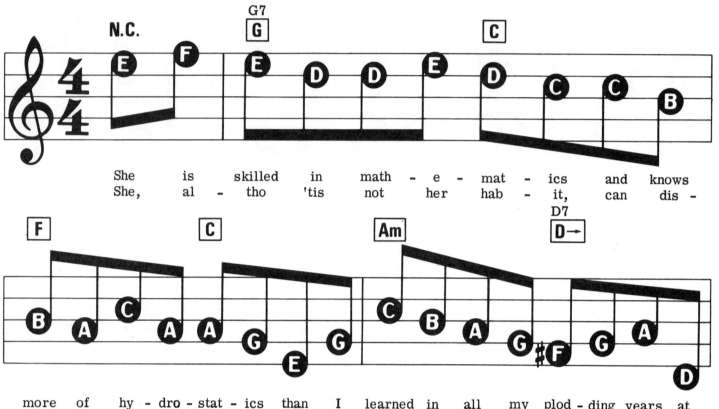

She is skilled in math - e - mat - ics and knows
She, al - tho 'tis not her hab - it, can dis -

more of hy - dro - stat - ics than I learned in all my plod - ding years at
sect a good sized rab - bit, Giv - ing you the name of each and ev - 'ry

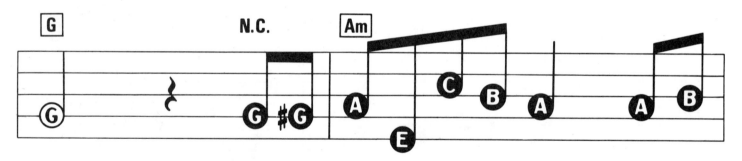

Yale.
bone.

She per - forms ex - per - i - ments with the
Much she knows of plant and tree on the

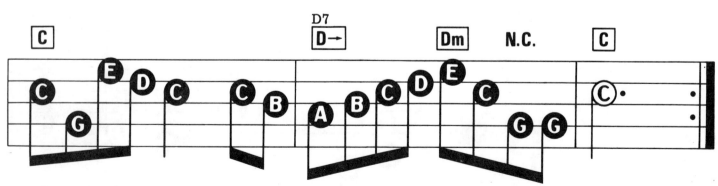

di - verse el - e - ments that would make her lit - tle broth - er's cheek turn pale.
land and on the sea, slight - ing not mean - while the all im - por - tant stone.

University Of Michigan Song

Registration 5

Hail to the vic - tors val - iant!

Hail to the con - qu'ring Her - oes!

Hail, hail_____ to Mich - i - gan, the

Cham - pions of the West!_____

Harvard March

Registration 4

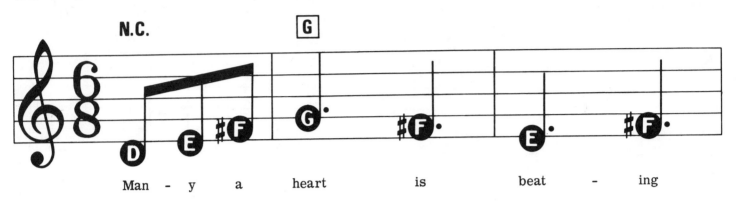

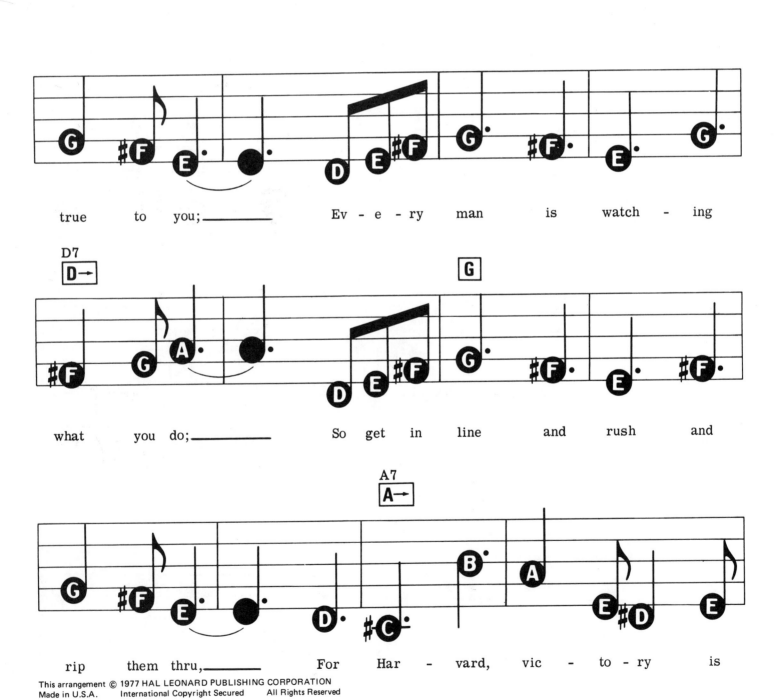

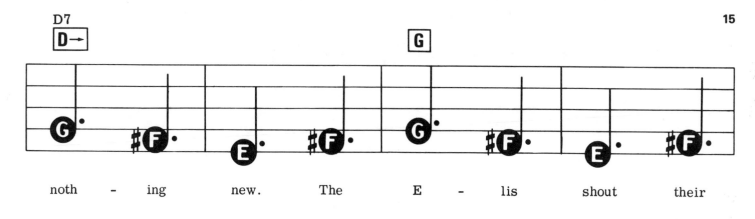

noth - ing new. The E - lis shout their

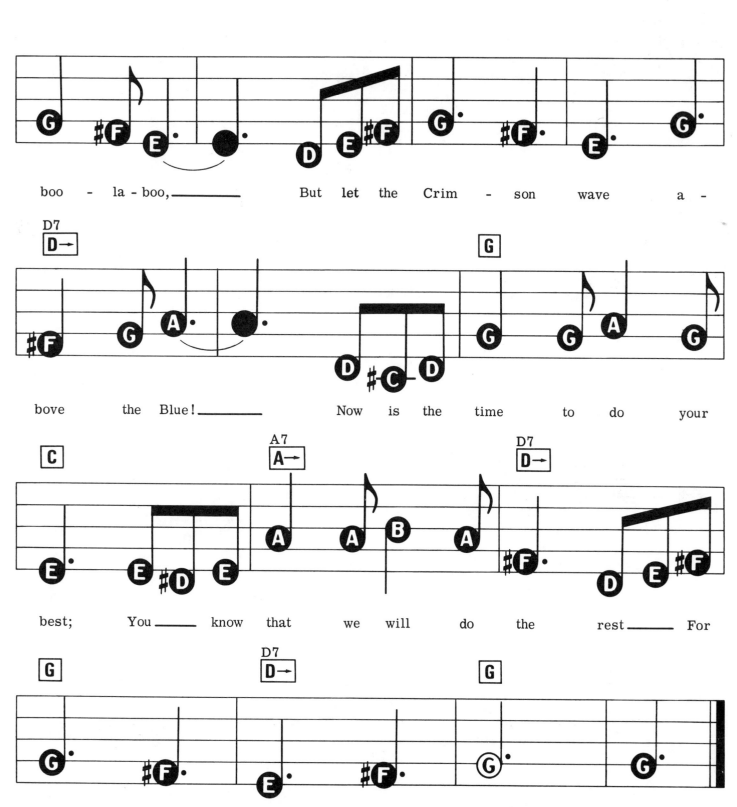

boo - la - boo, _____ But let the Crim - son wave a -

bove the Blue! _____ Now is the time to do your

best; You ____ know that we will do the rest ____ For

Har - vard, Har - vard, Har - vard!

Ta-Ra-Ra-Boom-De-Ay

Registration 5

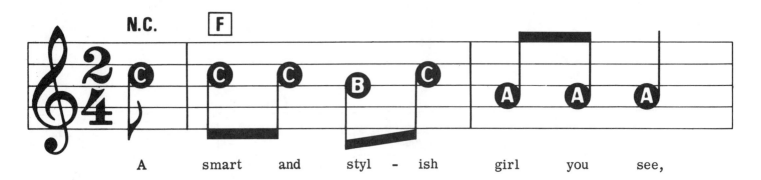

A smart and styl - ish girl you see,

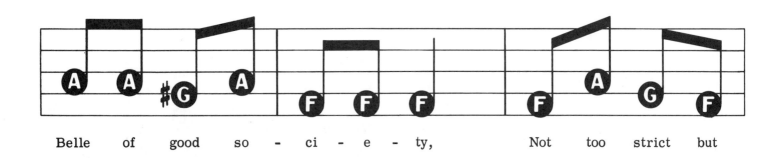

Belle of good so - ci - e - ty, Not too strict but

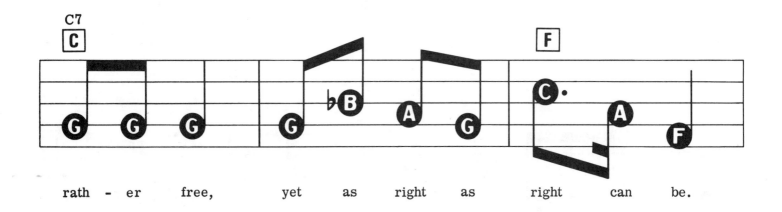

rath - er free, yet as right as right can be.

But the ver - y thing I'm told, that in your arms you'd like to hold,

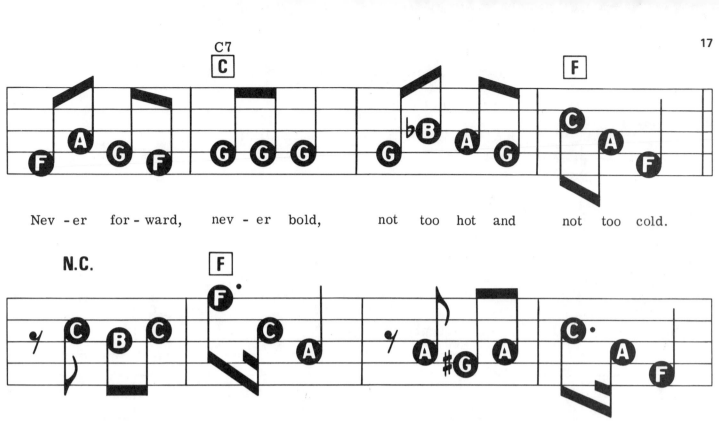

Nev-er for-ward, nev-er bold, not too hot and not too cold.

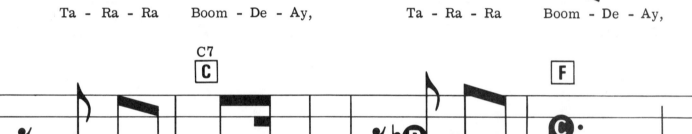

Ta - Ra - Ra Boom - De - Ay, Ta - Ra - Ra Boom - De - Ay,

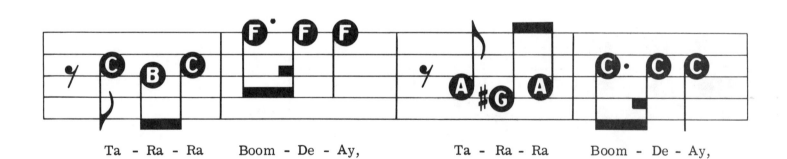

Ta - Ra - Ra Boom - De - Ay, Ta - Ra - Ra Boom - De - Ay,

Ta - Ra - Ra Boom - De - Ay, Ta - Ra - Ra Boom - De - Ay,

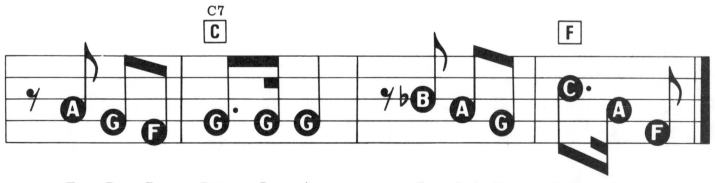

Ta - Ra - Ra Boom - De - Ay, Ta - Ra - Ra Boom - De - Ay.

The Dear Old Farm

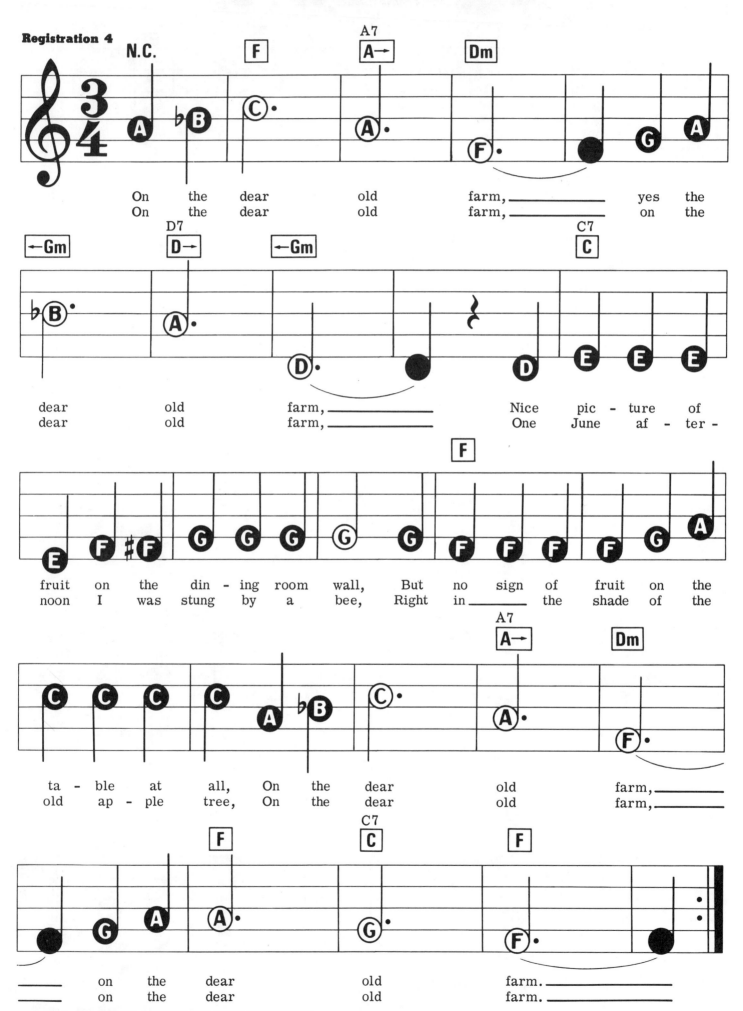

I Don't Mind If I Do

Registration 3

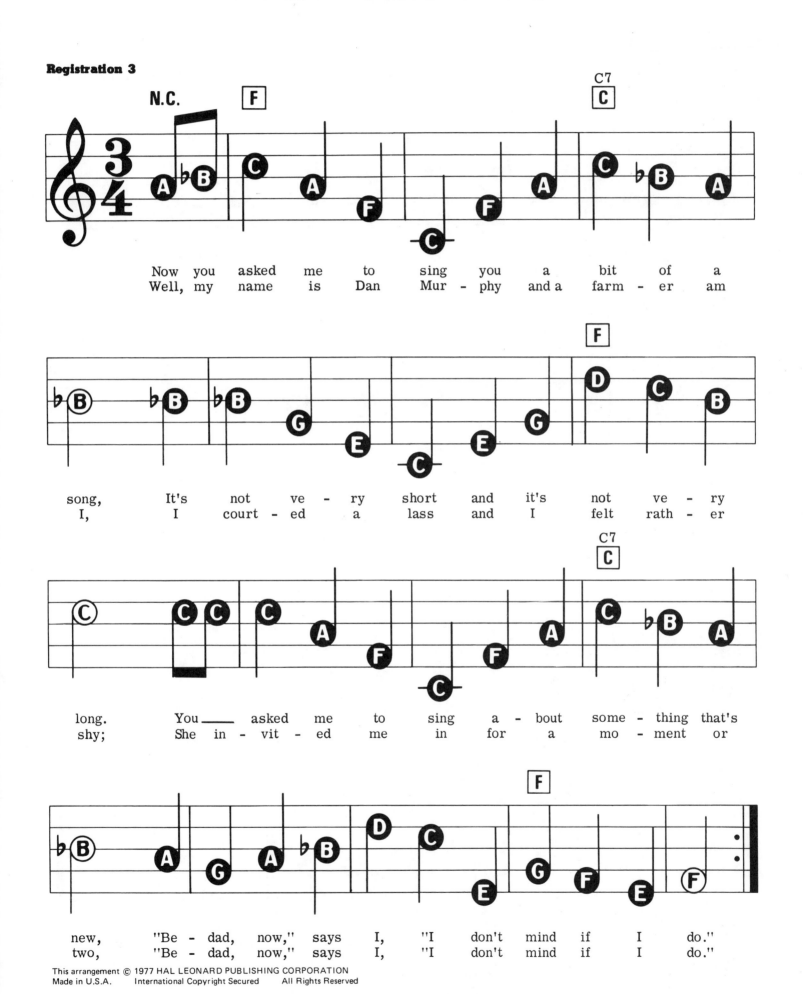

Now you asked me to sing you a bit of a
Well, my name is to Dan Mur - phy and a farm - er am

song, It's not ve - ry short and it's not ve - ry
I, I court - ed a lass and it I felt rath - er

long. You___ asked me to sing a - bout some - thing that's
shy; She in - vit - ed me in for a mo - ment or

new, "Be - dad, now," says I, "I don't mind if I do."
two, "Be - dad, now," says I, "I don't mind if I do."

I Married A Wife

Registration 5

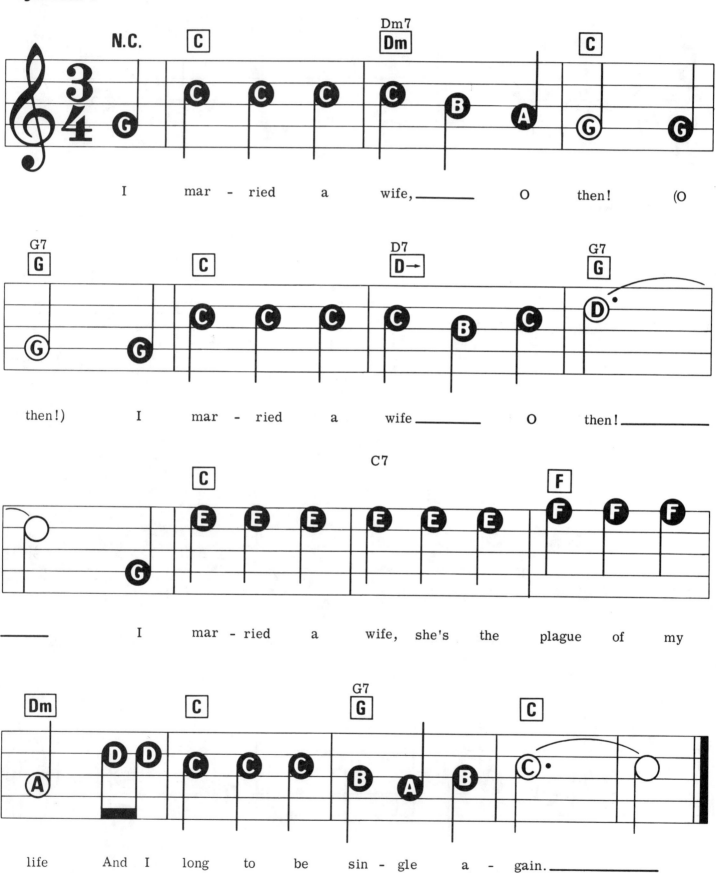

I'm Unlucky

Registration 3

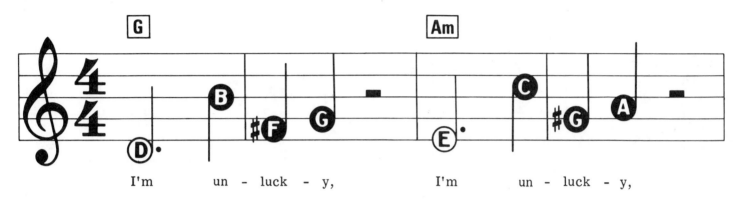

I'm un-luck-y, I'm un-luck-y,

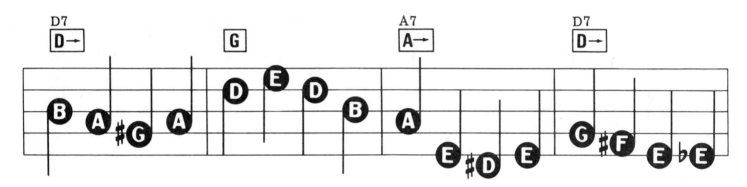

Born on Fri-day af-ter-noon up-on the thir-teenth day of June,____

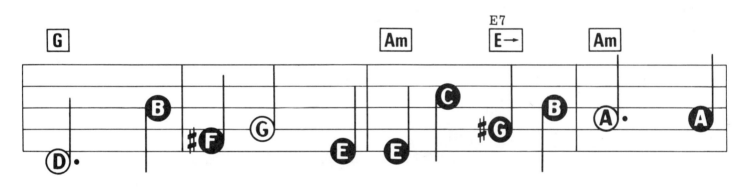

I'm un-luck-y, de-ny it no one can, For

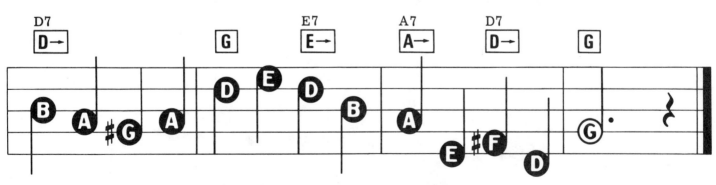

years I've beat all com-ers as the most un-luck-y man.

M-O-N-E-Y Spells Money

Registration 7

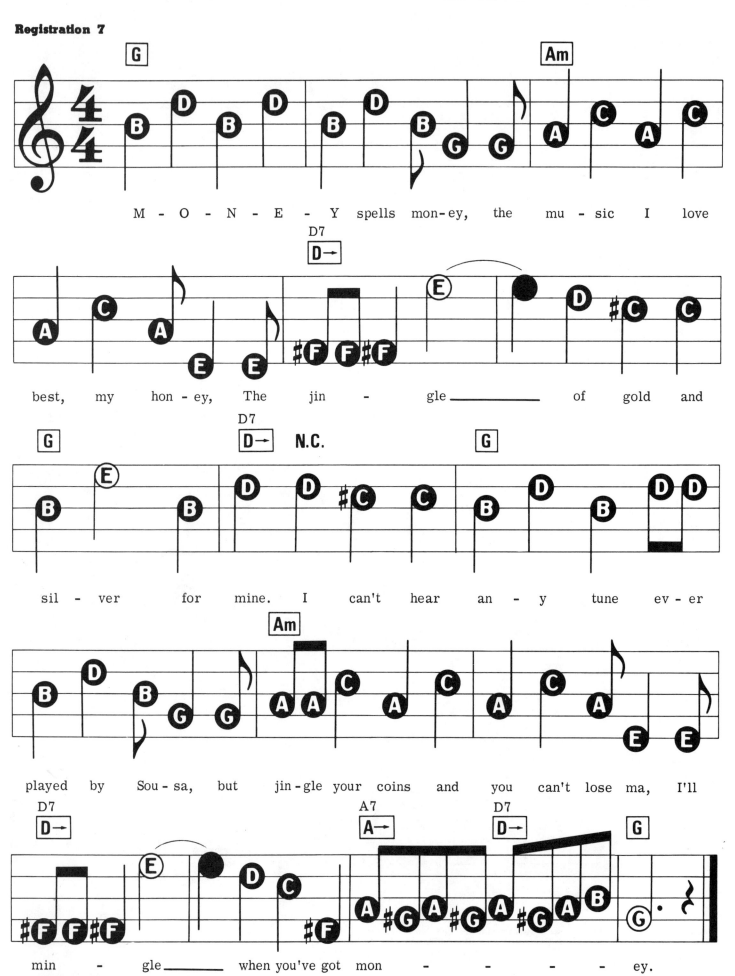

Oh, Dear What Can The Matter Be

Registration 2

Oh! Dear! What can the

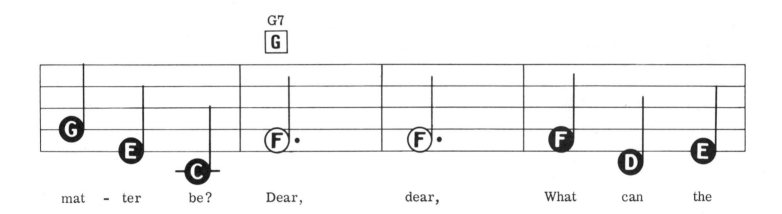

mat - ter be? Dear, dear, What can the

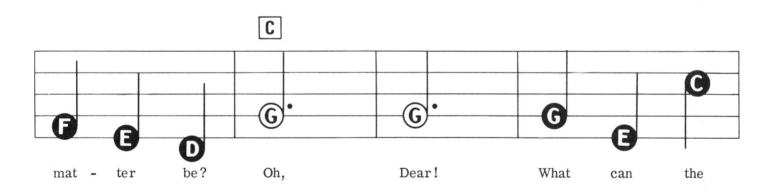

mat - ter be? Oh, Dear! What can the

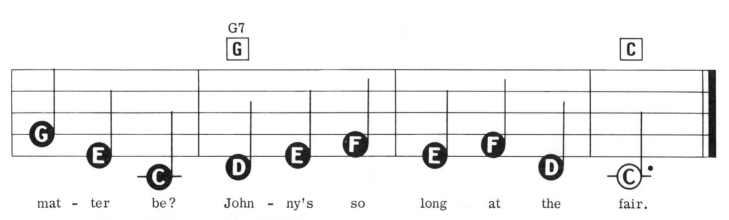

mat - ter be? John - ny's so long at the fair.

Nothin' From Nothin' Leaves You

Registration 2

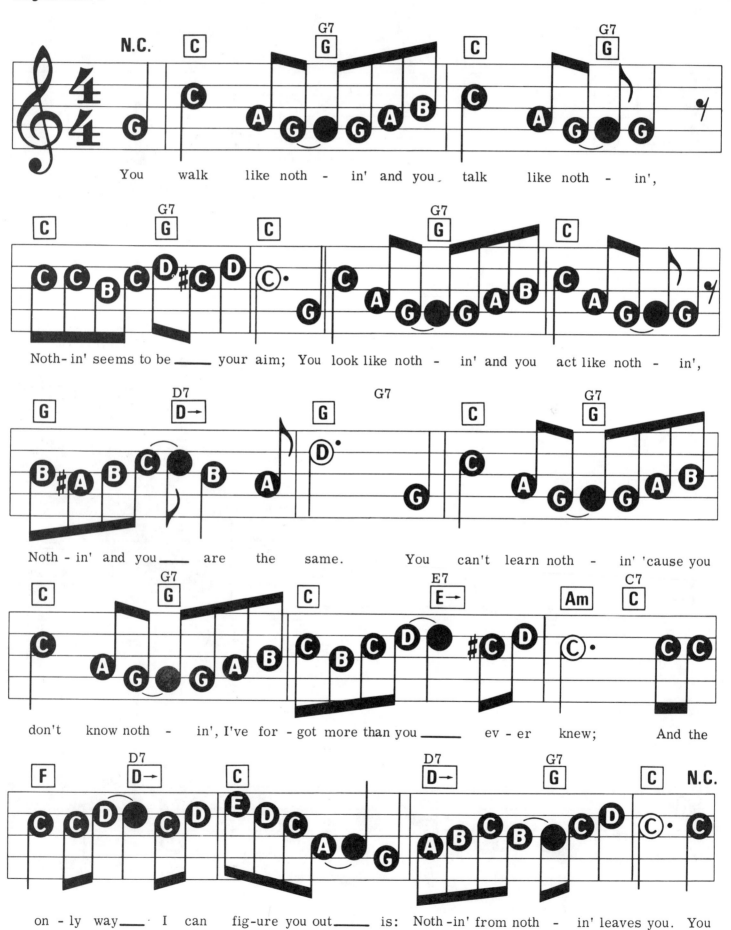

You walk like noth – in' and you talk like noth – in', Noth-in' seems to be _____ your aim; You look like noth – in' and you act like noth – in', Noth – in' and you _____ are the same. You can't learn noth – in' 'cause you don't know noth – in', I've for – got more than you _____ ev – er knew; And the on – ly way _____ I can fig-ure you out _____ is: Noth -in' from noth – in' leaves you. You

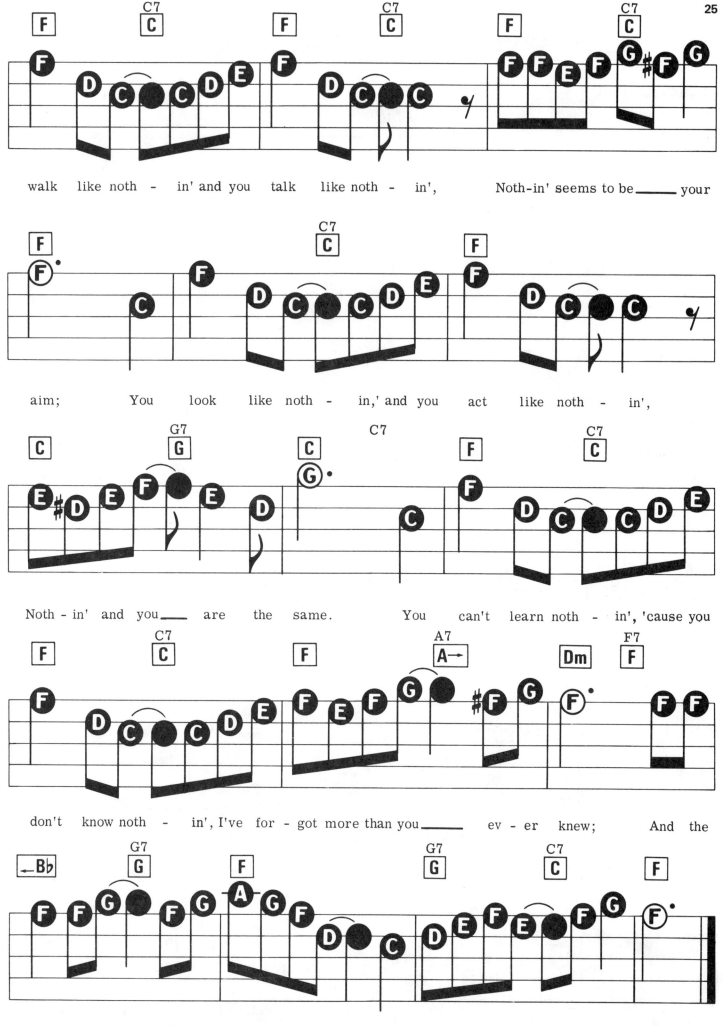

Robinson Crusoe's Isle

Registration 4

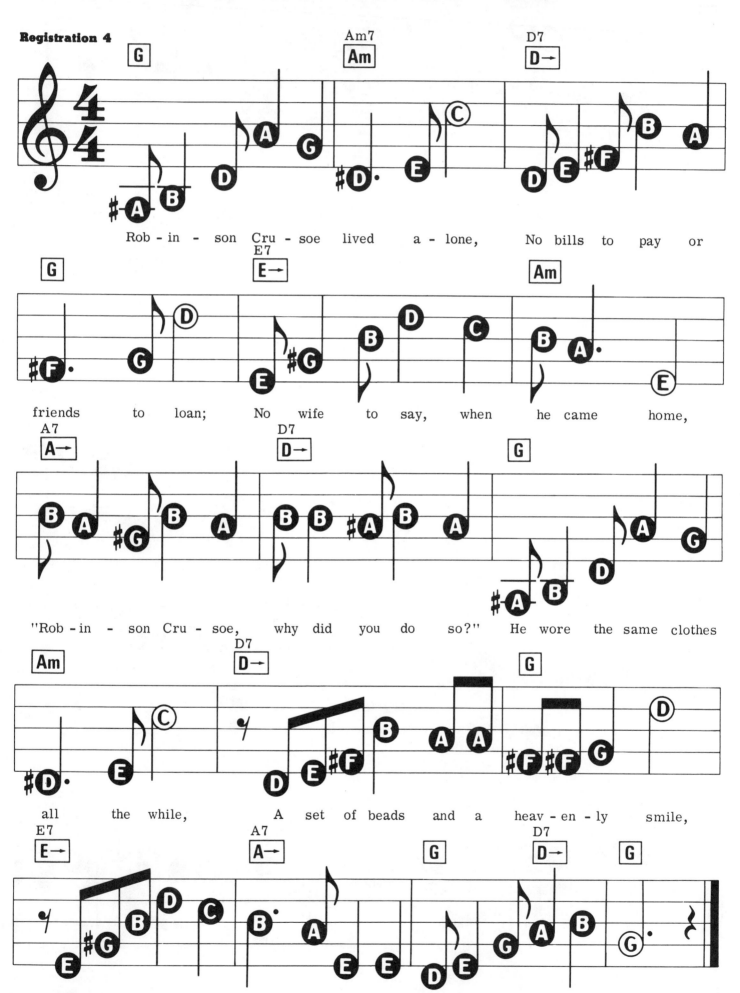

Rob - in - son Cru - soe lived a - lone, No bills to pay or friends to loan; No wife to say, when he came home, "Rob - in - son Cru - soe, why did you do so?" He wore the same clothes all the while, A set of beads and a heav - en - ly smile, They ve - ry sel - dom changed the style on Rob - in - son Cru - soe's Isle.

The Girl I Left Behind Me

Registration 4

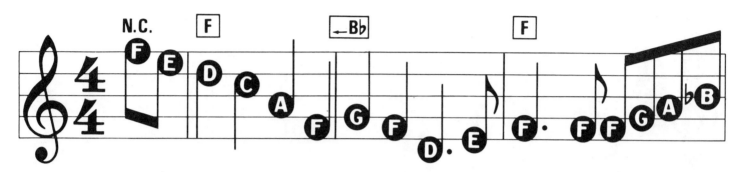

The___ dames of France are fond and free, and Flem - ish lips___ are___

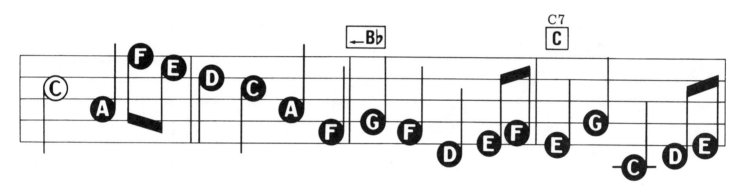

will - ing, and___ soft the maids of It - a - ly, and___ Span - ish eyes are___

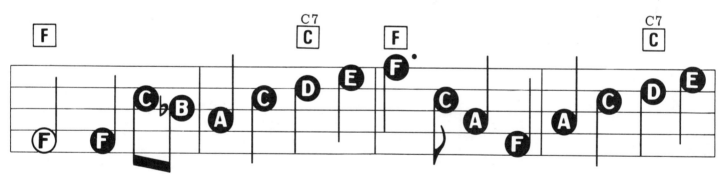

thrill - ing: Still___ though I bask be - neath their smile, their charms___ fail to

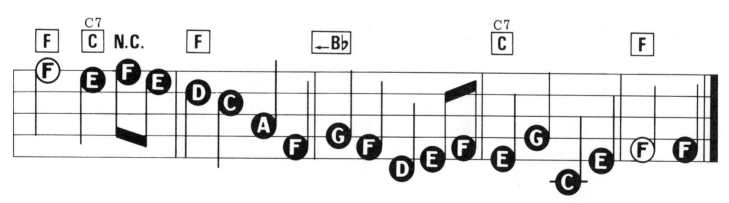

bind me, and my heart falls back to E - rin's Isle to the girl I left be - hind me.

America

Registration 5

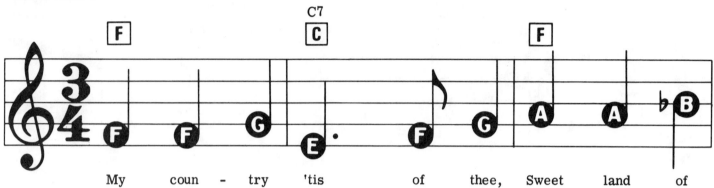

My coun - try 'tis of thee, Sweet land of

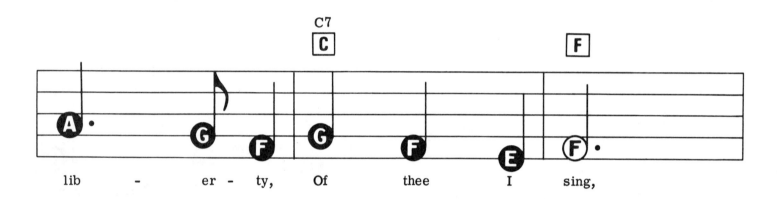

lib - er - ty, Of thee I sing,

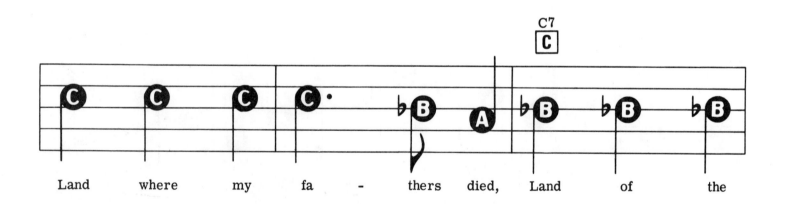

Land where my fa - thers died, Land of the

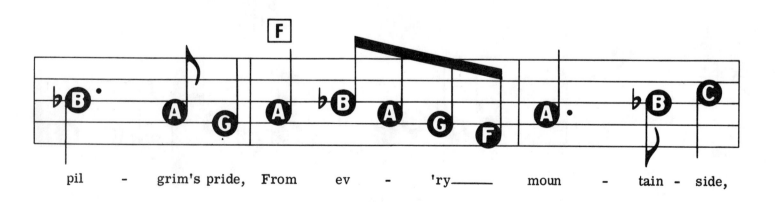

pil - grim's pride, From ev - 'ry___ moun - tain - side,

29

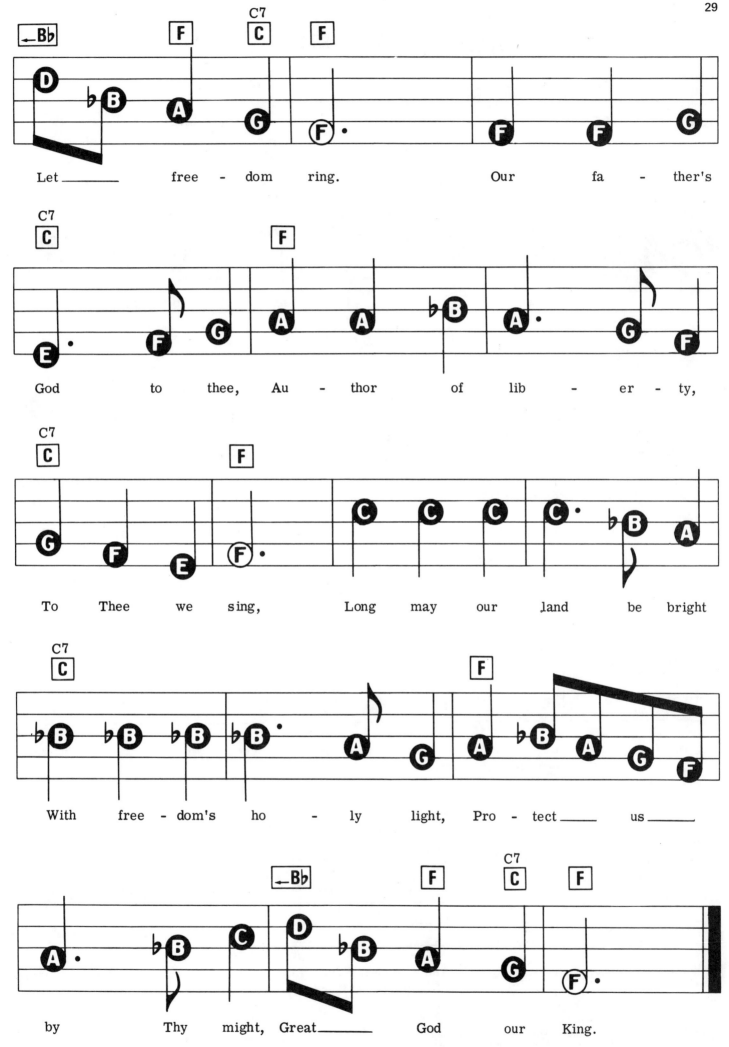

America The Beautiful

Registration 3

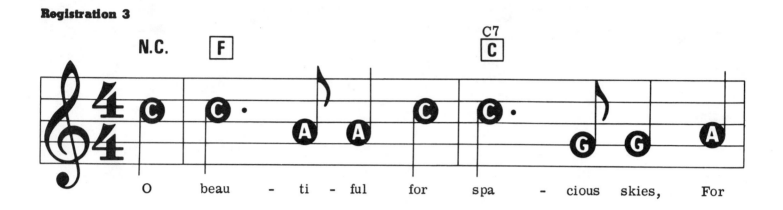

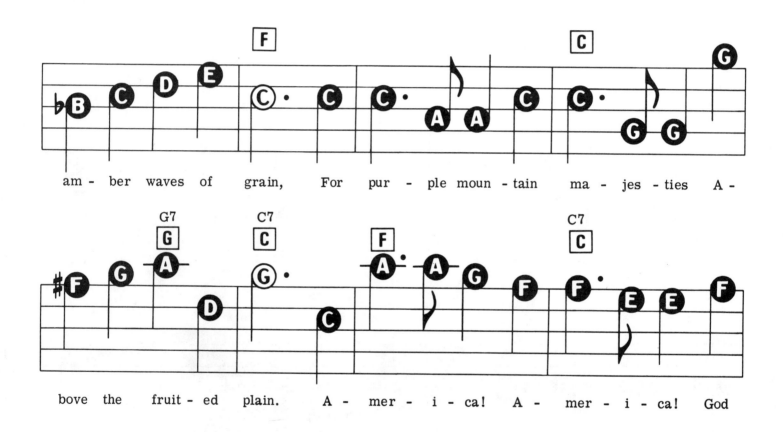

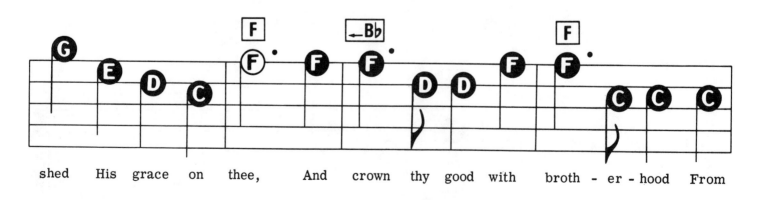

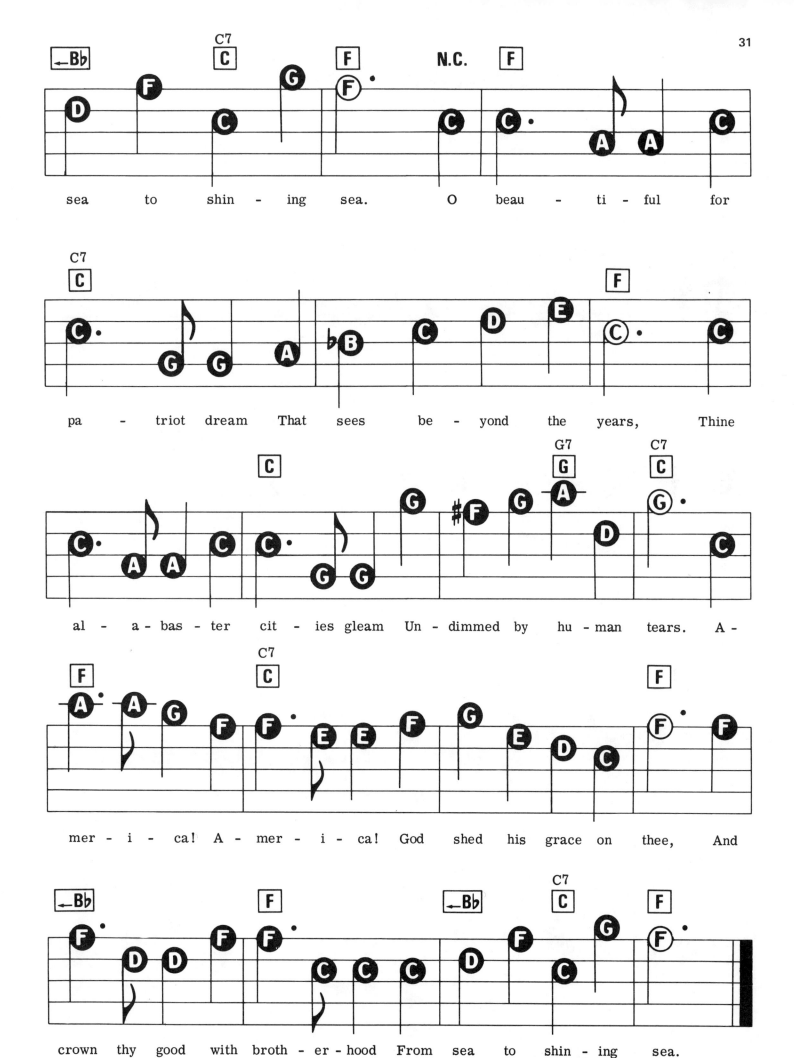

American Patrol

Registration 4

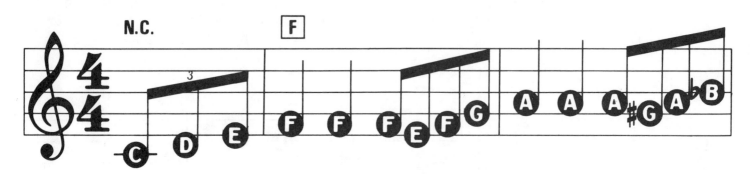

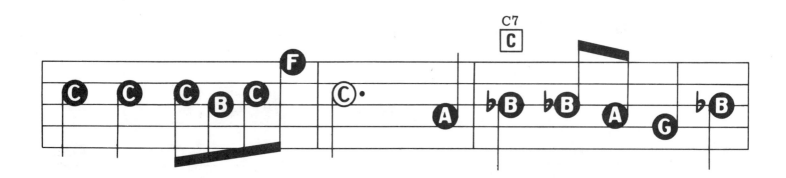

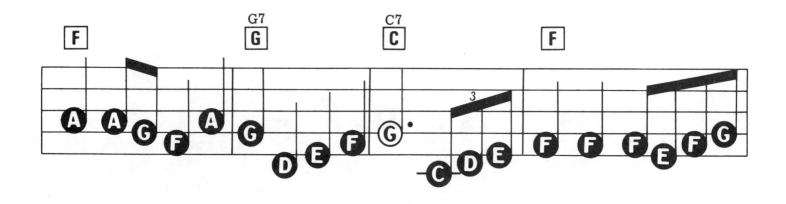

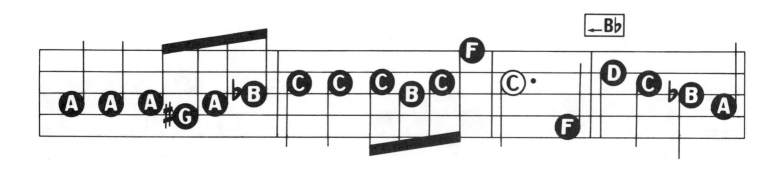

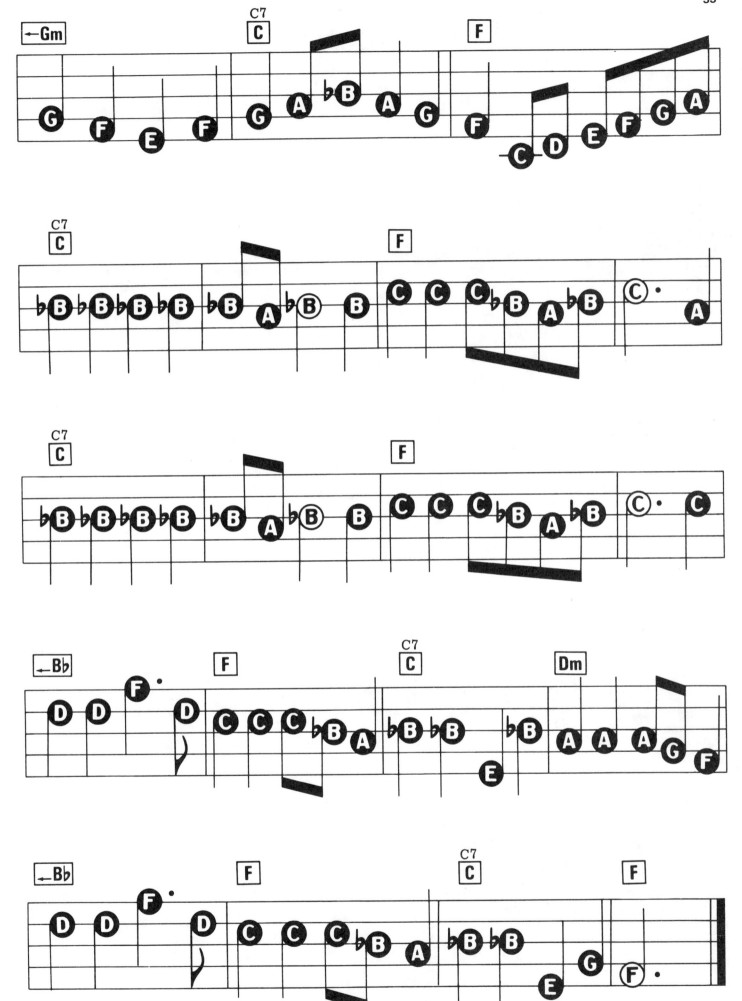

The Battle Cry Of Freedom

Registration 1

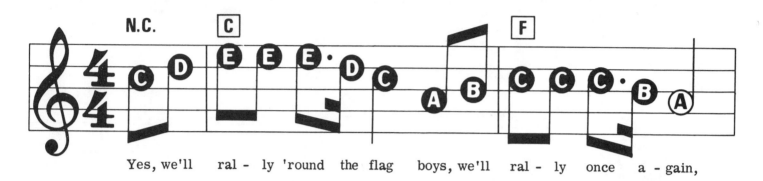

Yes, we'll ral - ly 'round the flag boys, we'll ral - ly once a - gain,

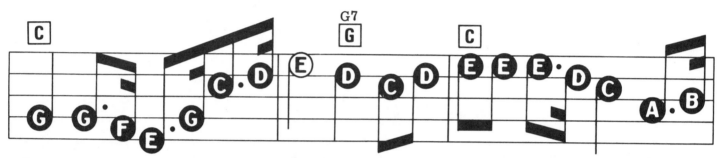

Shout - ing the bat - tle cry of free - dom; We will ral - ly from the hill - side, we'll

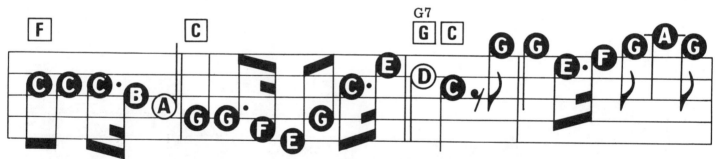

gath - er from the plain, Shout-ing the bat -tle cry of free - dom. The Un - ion for - ev - er, hur -

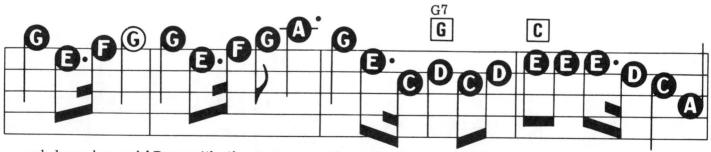

rah, boys, hur-rah! Down with the trai-tor, Up with the star; While we ral - ly 'round the flag, boys,

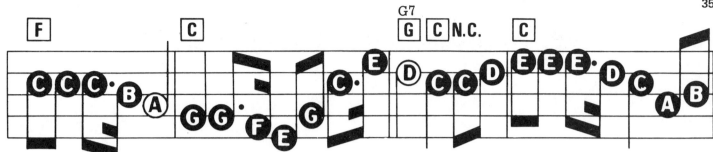

ral -ly once a-gain, Shout-ing the bat-tle cry of free-dom. We are spring-ing to the call of our

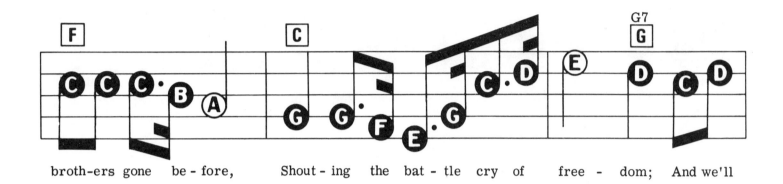

broth-ers gone be-fore, Shout - ing the bat - tle cry of free - dom; And we'll

fill the va -cant ranks with a mil-lion free men more, Shout-ing the bat-tle cry of free-dom. The

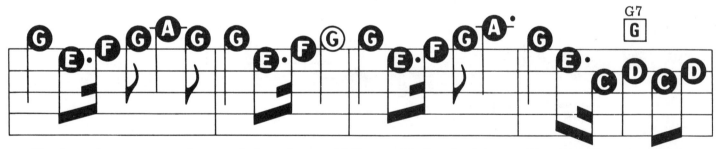

Un-ion for - ev - er, hur - rah, boys, hur -rah! Down with the trai-tor, Up with the star; While we

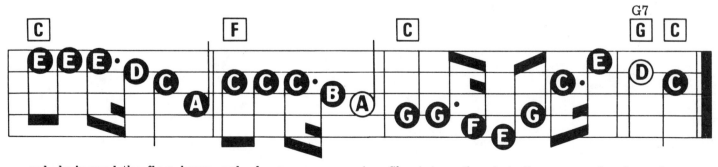

ral -ly 'round the flag, boys, ral - ly once a-gain, Shout-ing the bat-tle cry of free-dom.

Battle Hymn Of The Republic

Registration 5

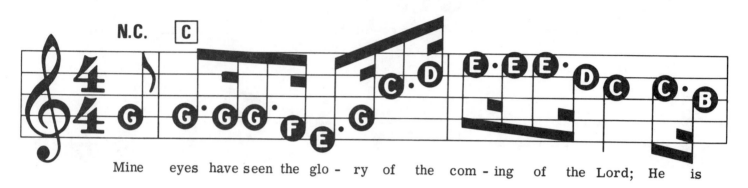

Mine eyes have seen the glo - ry of the com - ing of the Lord; He is

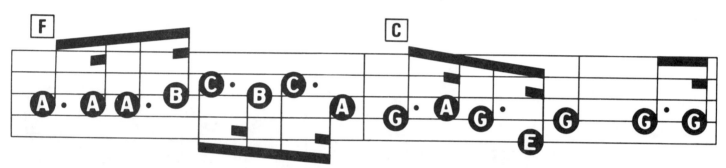

tramp - ling out the vin - tage where the grapes of wrath are stored; He hath

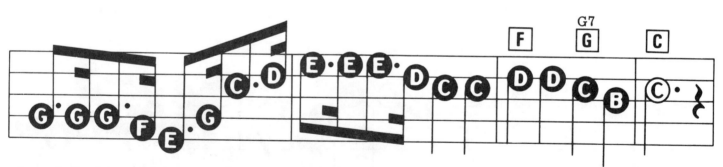

loosed the fate - ful light-ning of His ter - ri - ble swift sword, His truth is march-ing on.

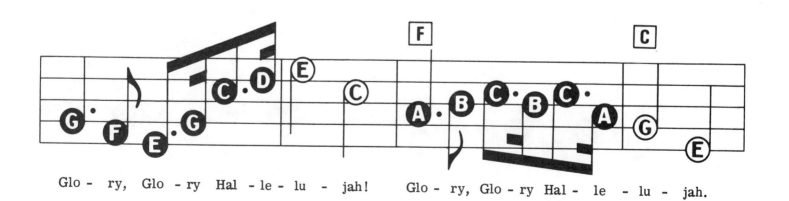

Glo - ry, Glo - ry Hal - le - lu - jah! Glo - ry, Glo - ry Hal - le - lu - jah.

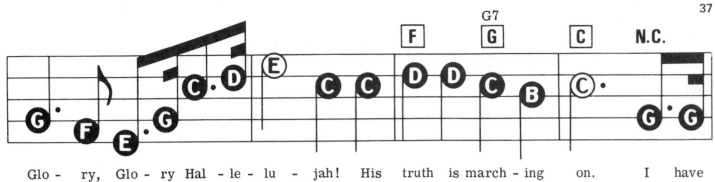

Glo - ry, Glo - ry Hal - le - lu - jah! His truth is march - ing on. I have

seen Him in the watch-fires of a hun-dred circ-ling camps, They have build-ed Him an al - tar in the

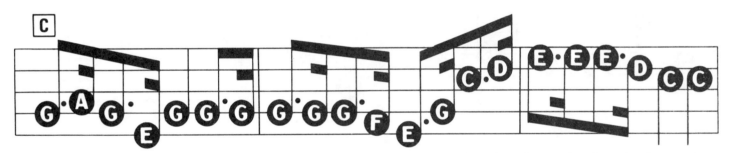

eve - ning dews and damps; I can read His right-eous sen-tence by the dim and flar-ing lamps, His

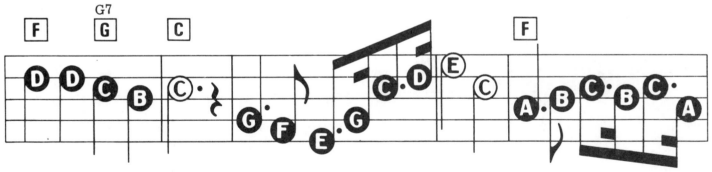

day is march-ing on. Glo - ry, Glo - ry Hal - le - lu - jah! Glo - ry, Glo - ry Hal - le -

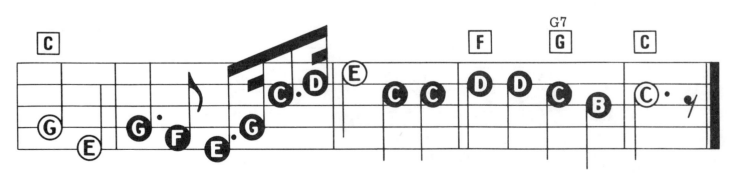

lu - jah! Glo - ry, Glo - ry Hal - le - lu - jah! His truth is march - ing on.

Caissons Song

Registration 2

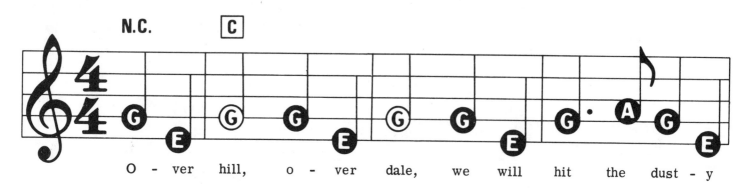

O - ver hill, o - ver dale, we will hit the dust - y

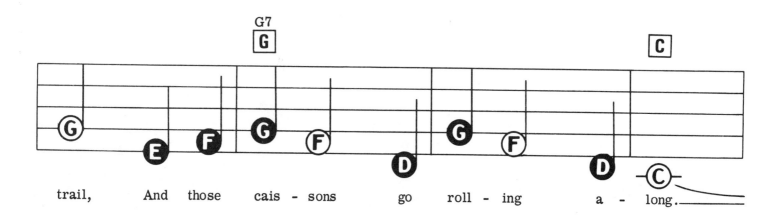

trail, And those cais - sons go roll - ing a - long.

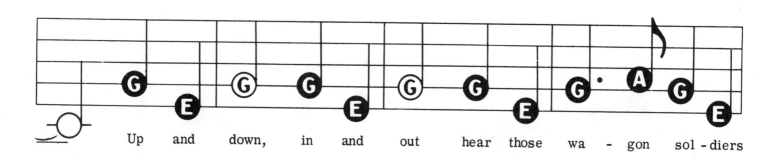

Up and down, in and out hear those wa - gon sol - diers

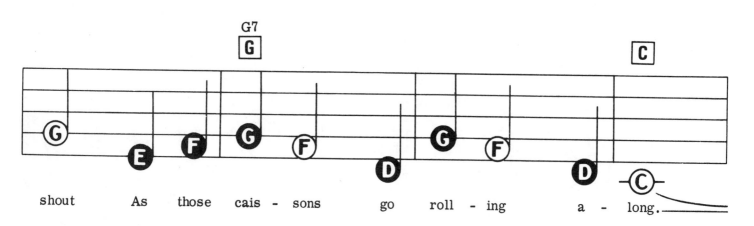

shout As those cais - sons go roll - ing a - long.

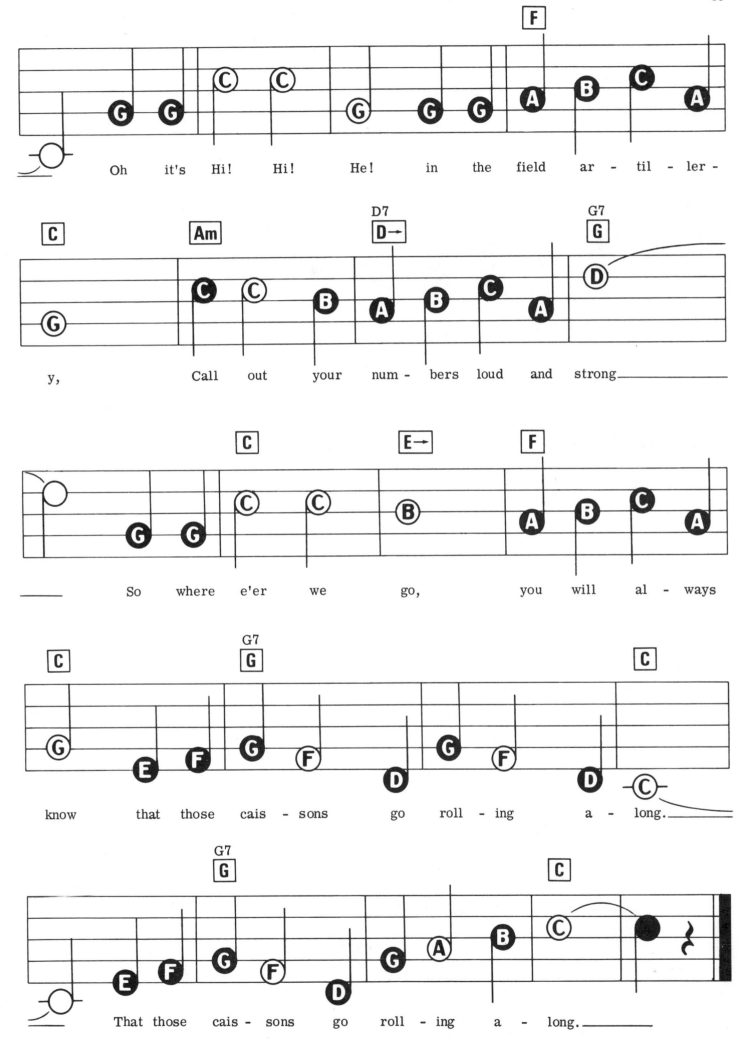

Dixie

Registration 9

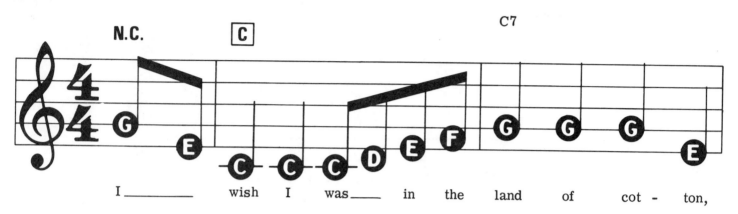

I _____ wish I was___ in the land of cot - ton,

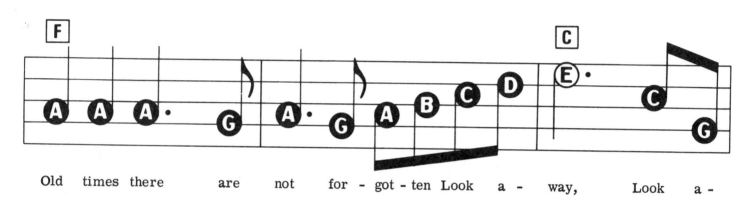

Old times there are not for - got - ten Look a - way, Look a -

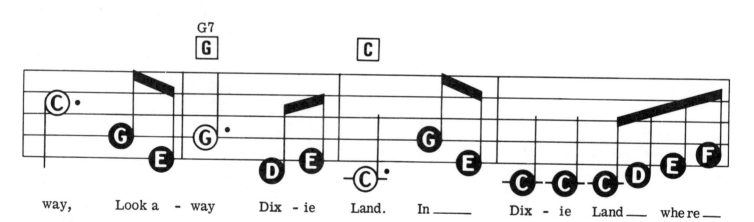

way, Look a - way Dix - ie Land. In ____ Dix - ie Land __ where __

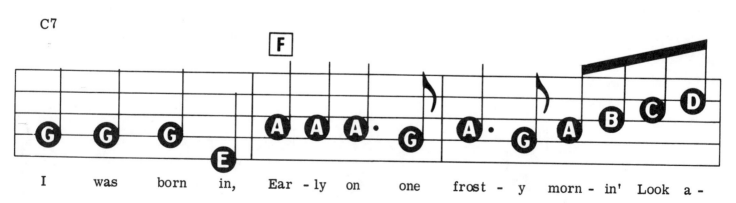

I was born in, Ear - ly on one frost - y morn - in' Look a -

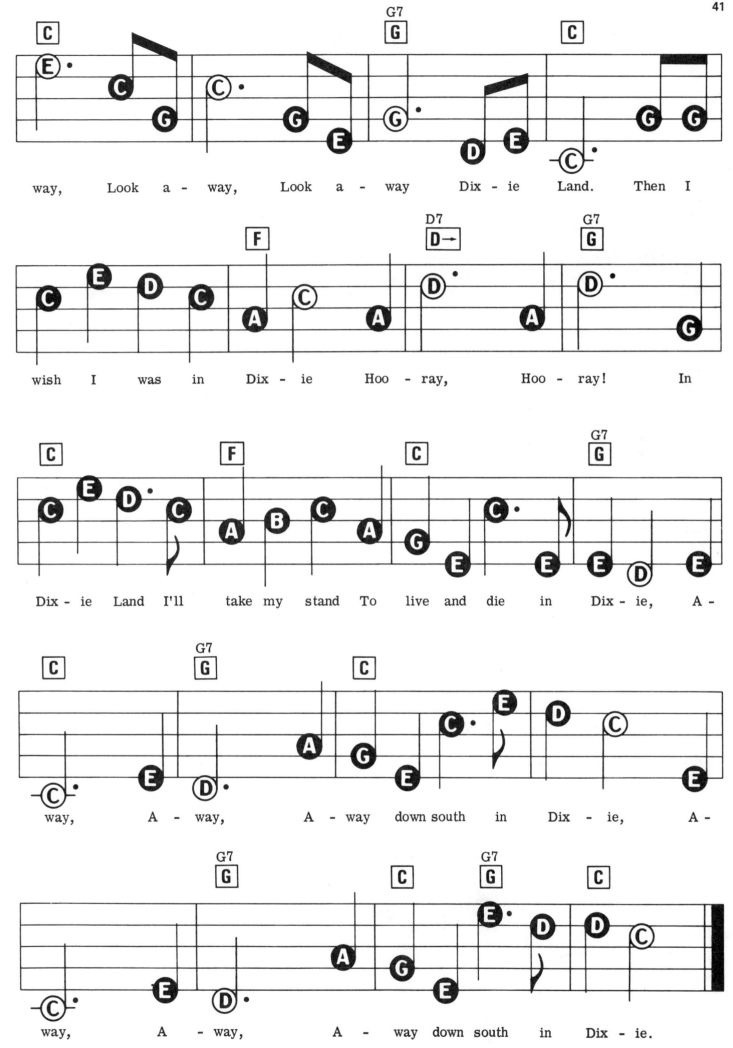

Home On The Range

Registration 4

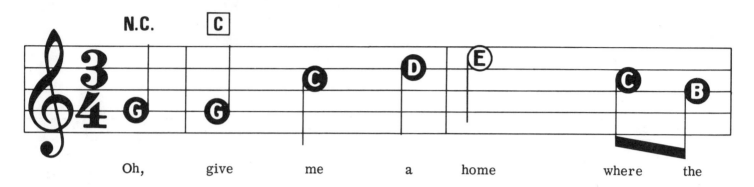

Oh, give me a home where the

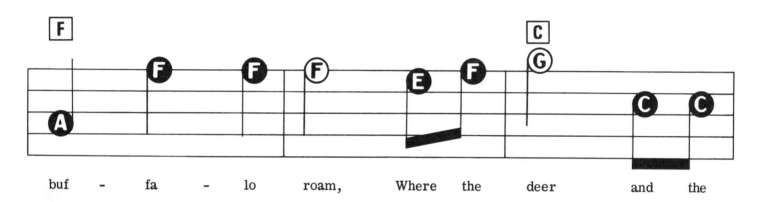

buf - fa - lo roam, Where the deer and the

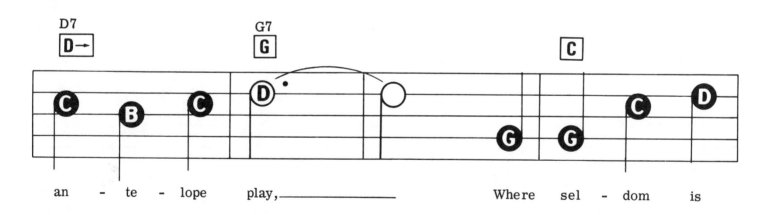

an - te - lope play,_____ Where sel - dom is

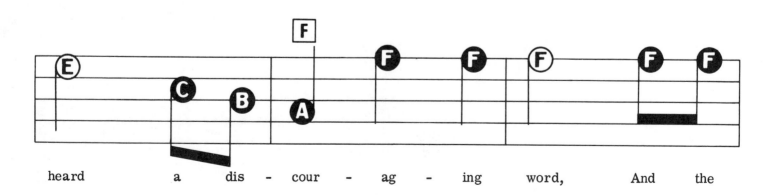

heard a dis - cour - ag - ing word, And the

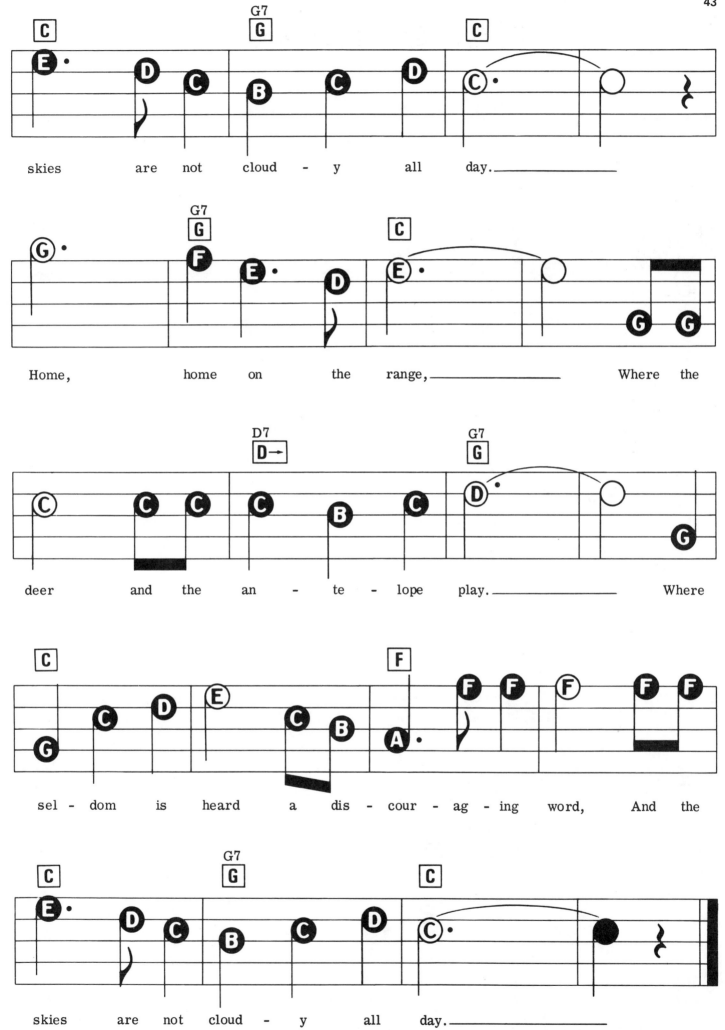

Marine's Hymn

Registration 1

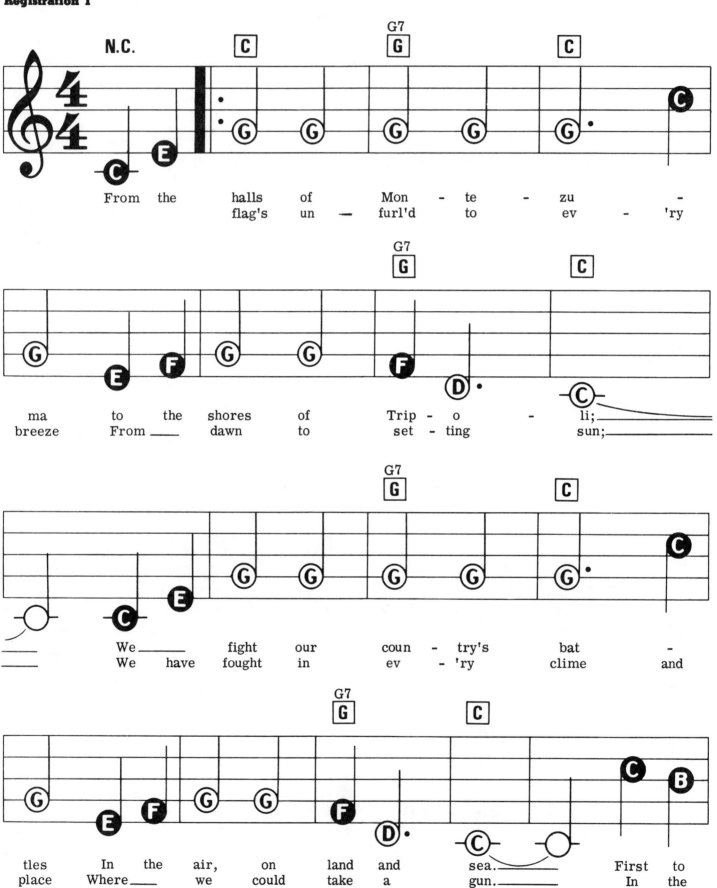

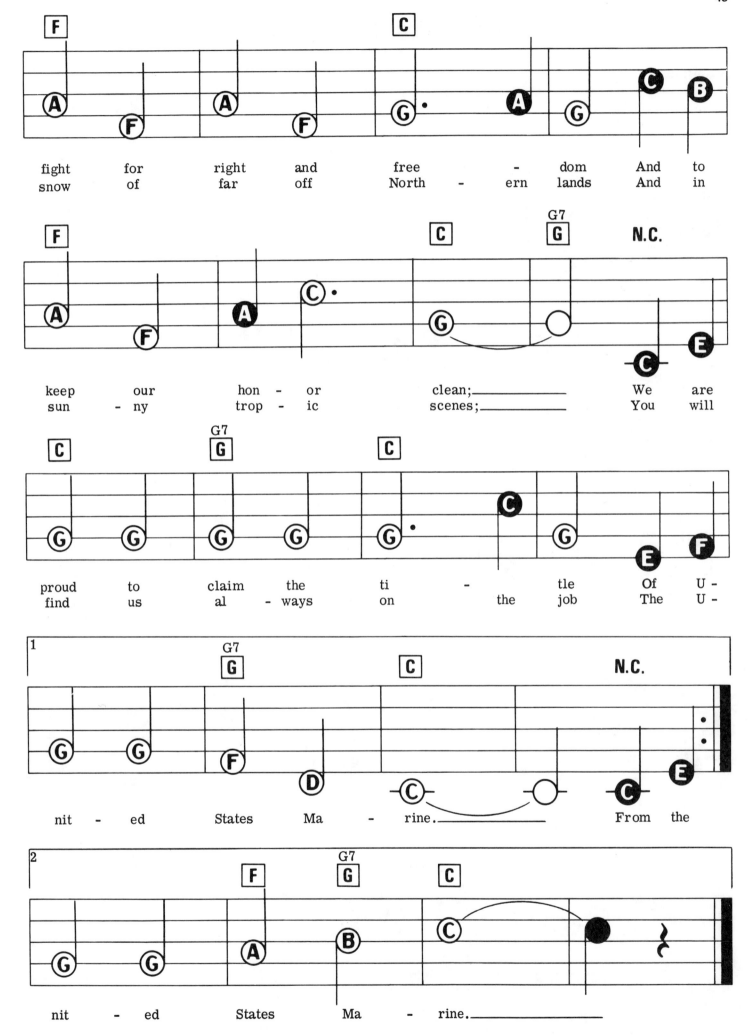

Our Director March

Registration 5

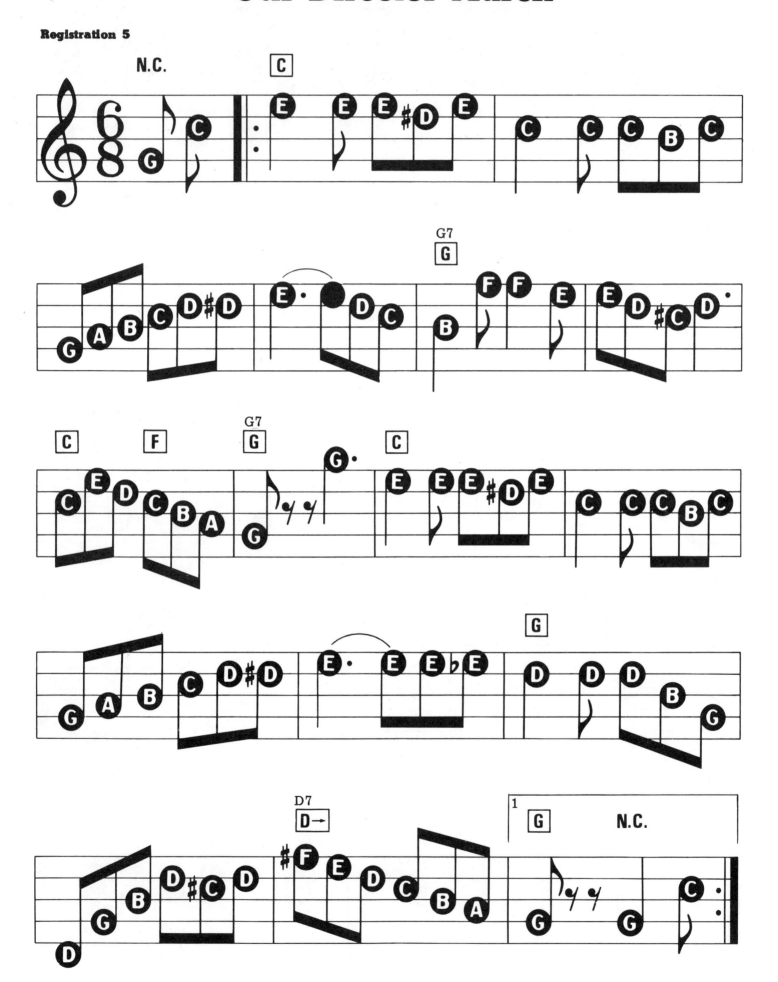

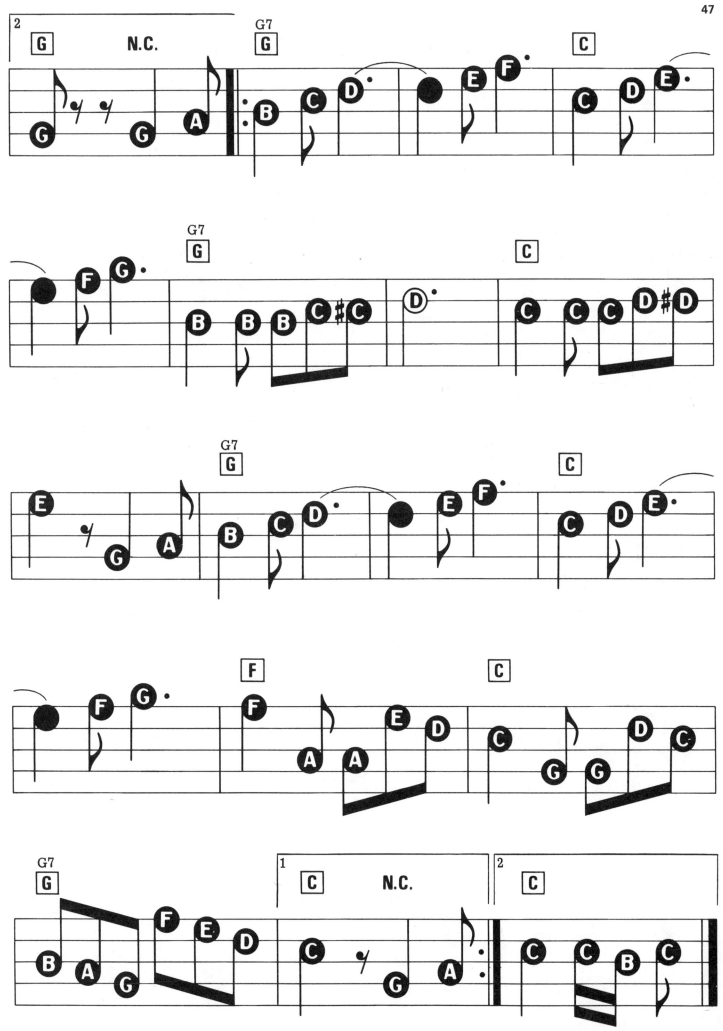

Scotland The Brave

Registration 4

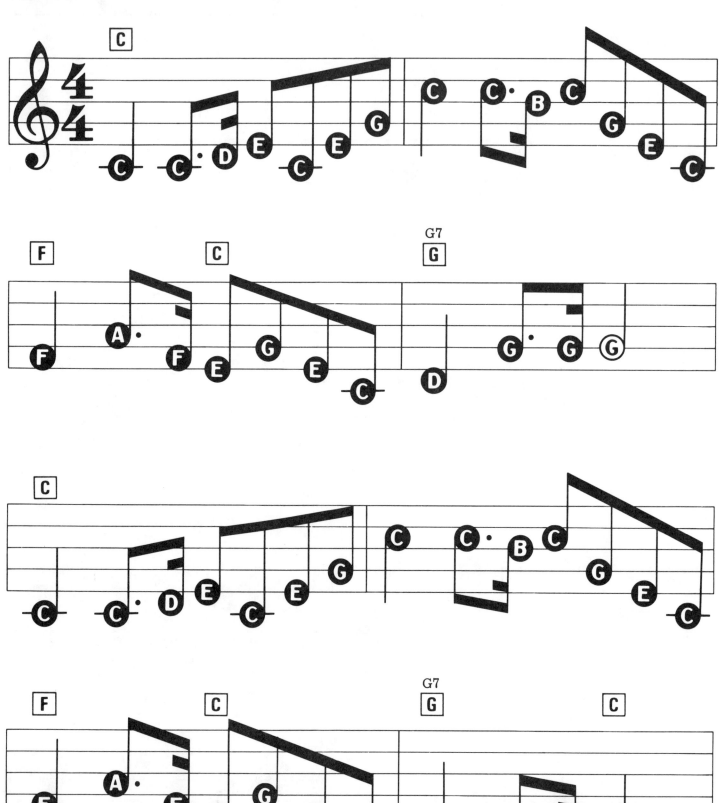

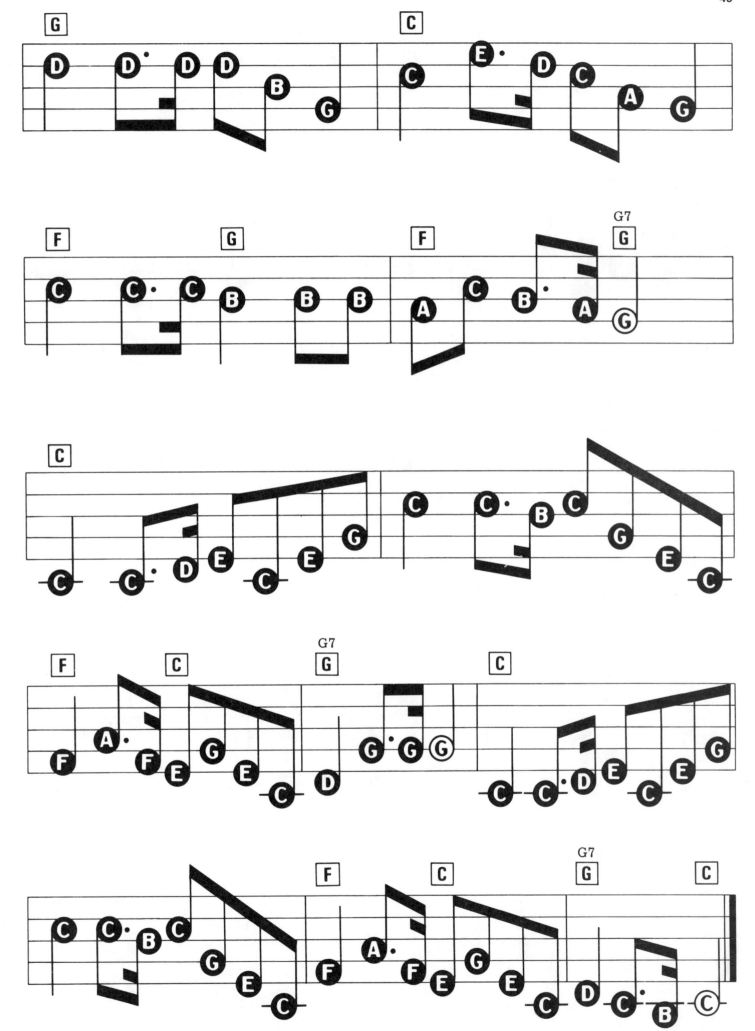

Star Spangled Banner

Registration 5

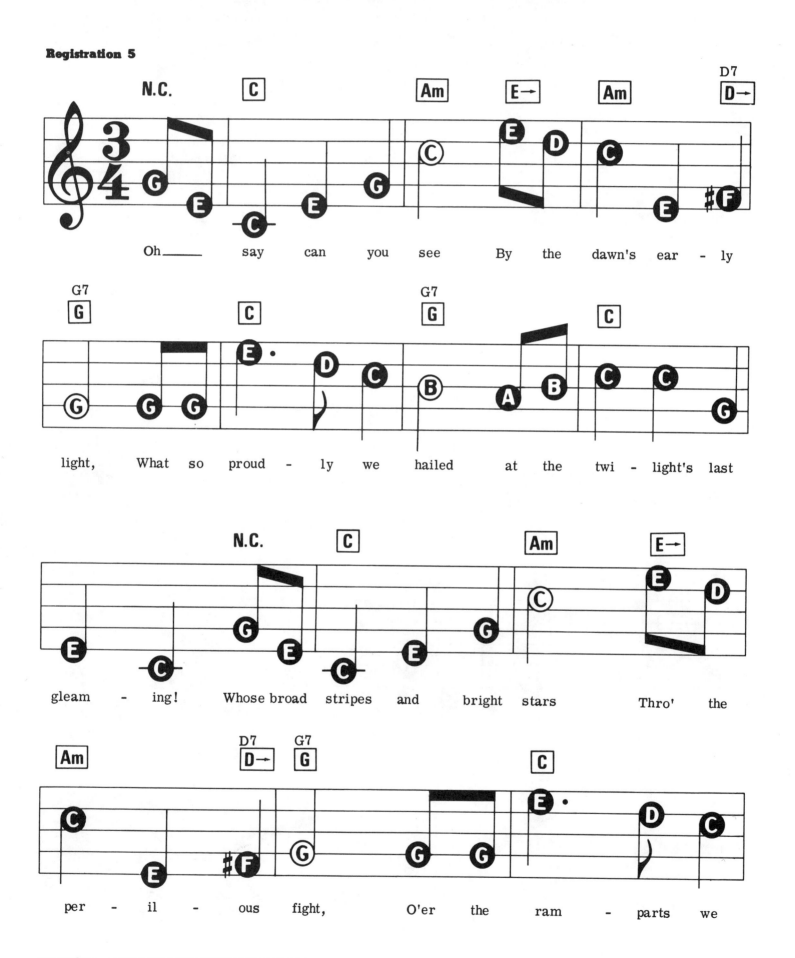

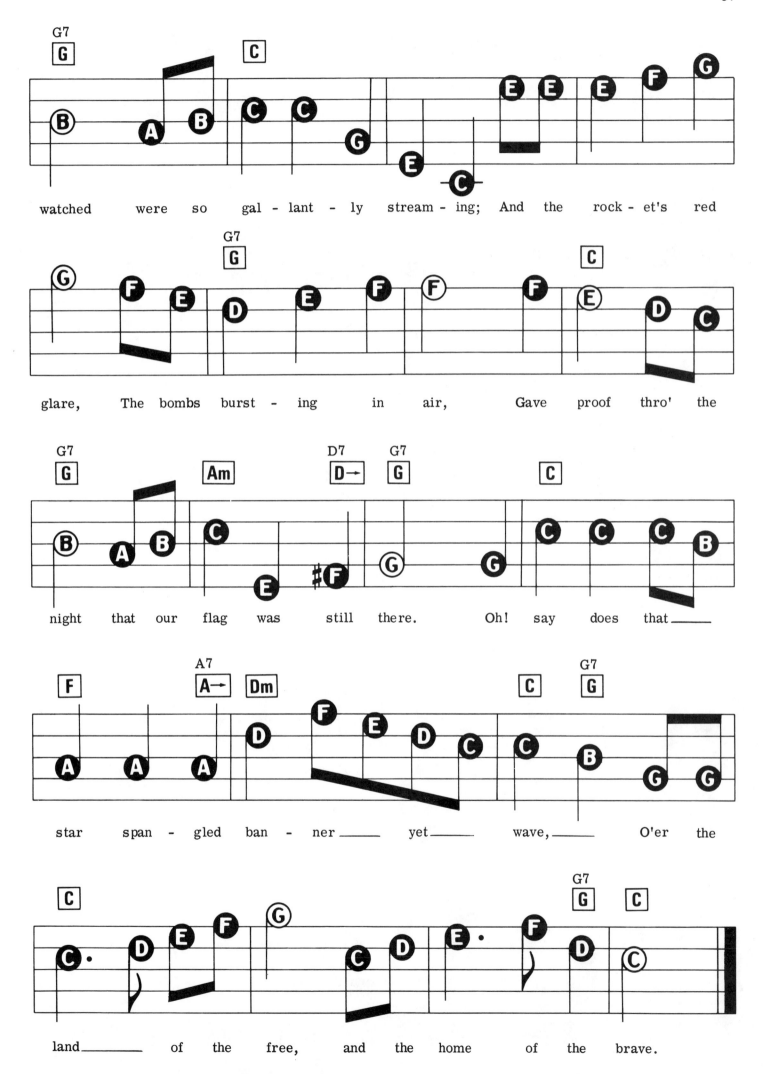

Stars And Stripes Forever

Registration 2

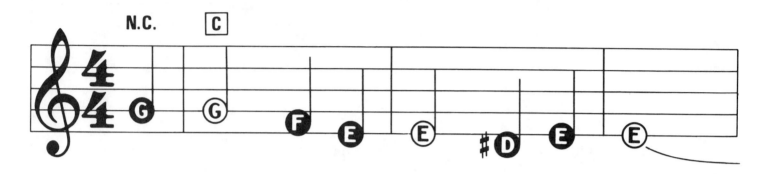

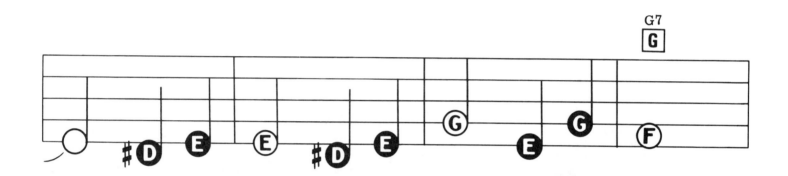

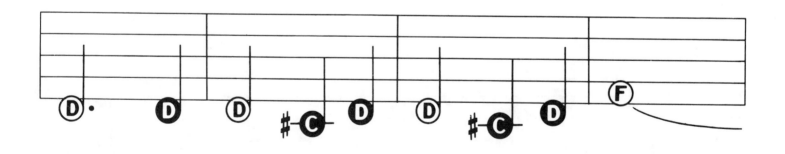

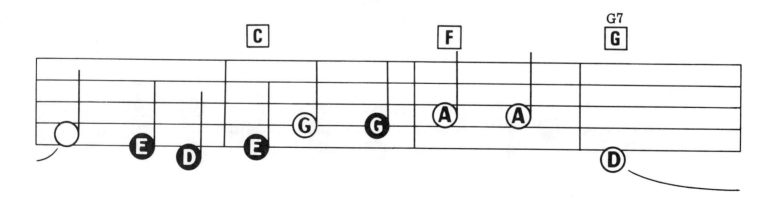

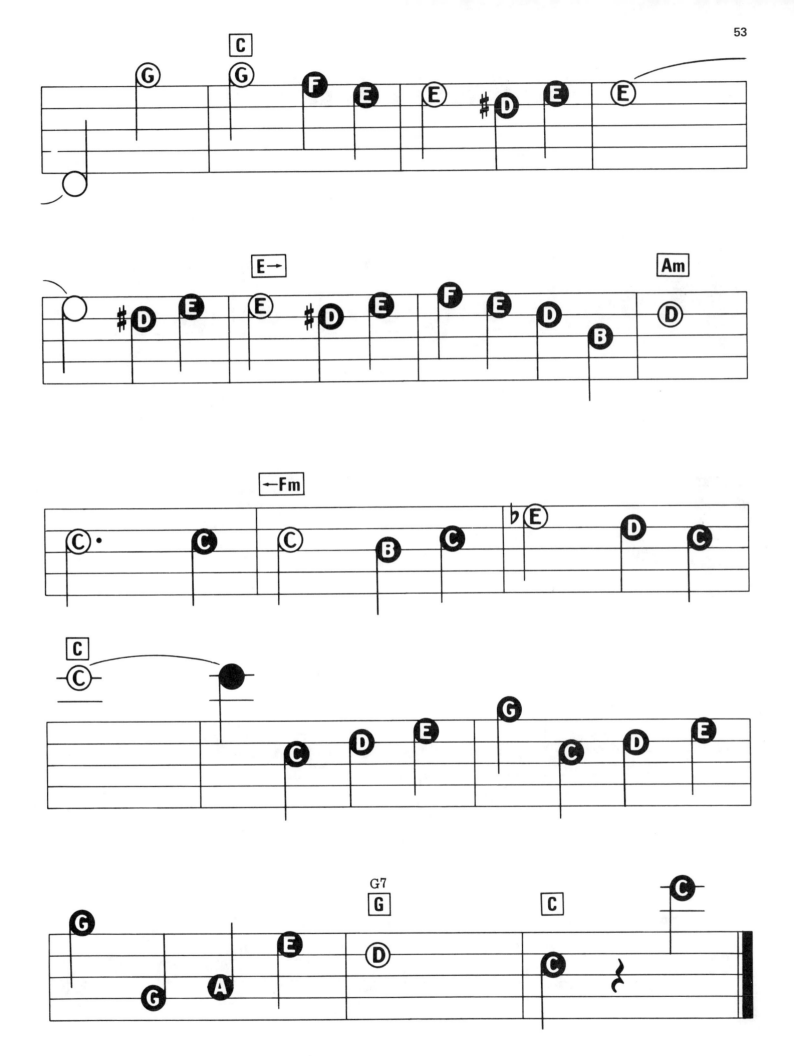

Washington Post March

Registration 5

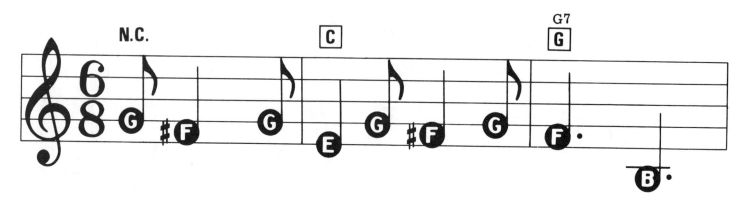

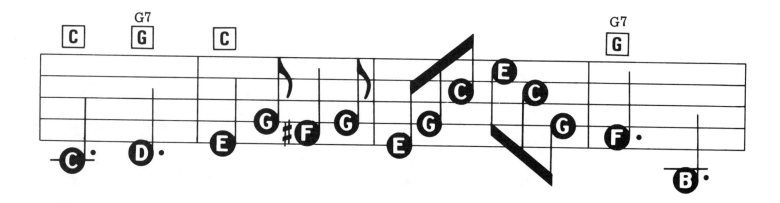

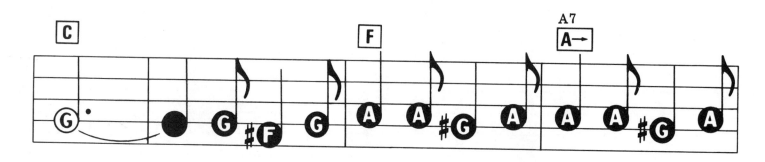

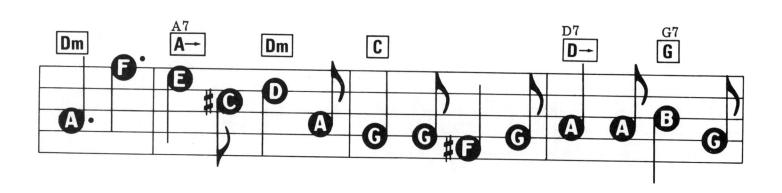

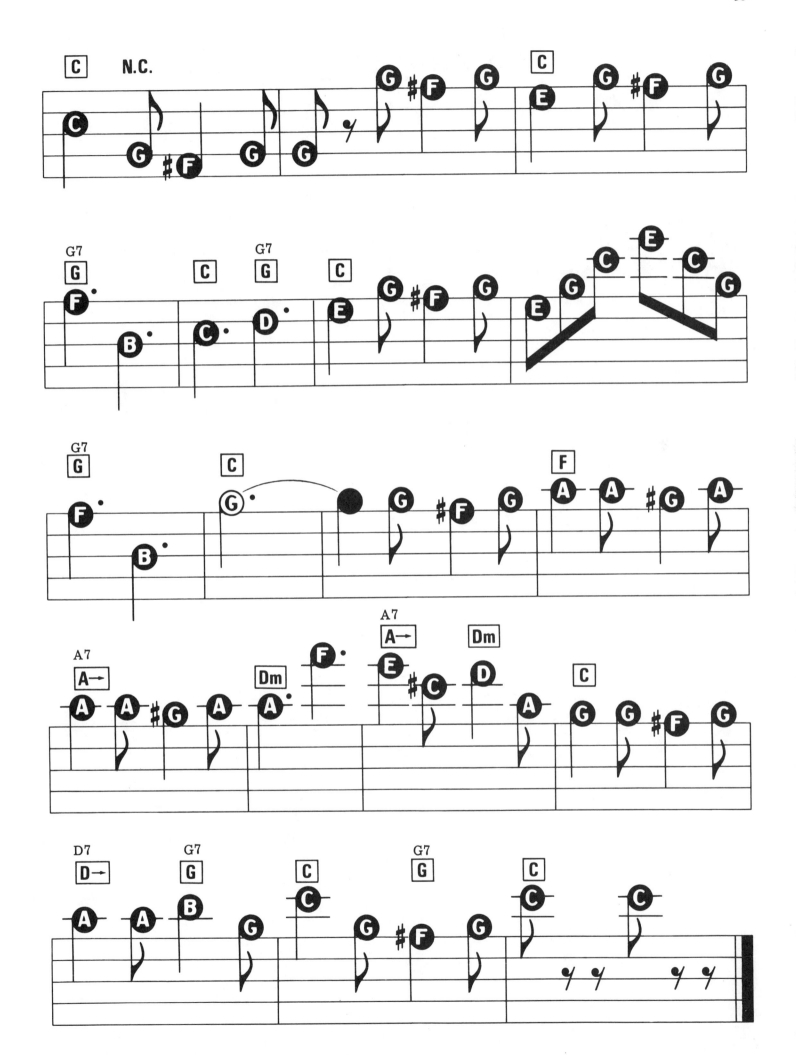

When Johnny Comes Marching Home Again

Registration 4

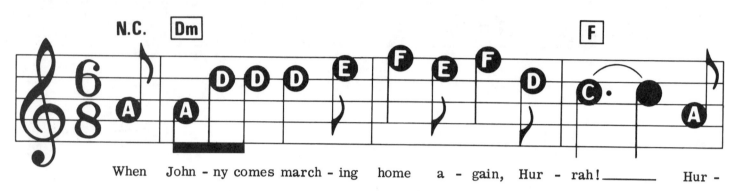

When John - ny comes march - ing home a - gain, Hur - rah!_____ Hur -

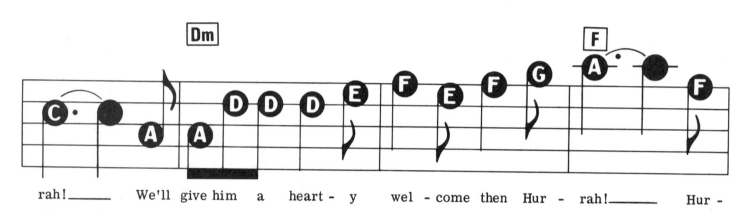

rah!_____ We'll give him a heart - y wel - come then Hur - rah!_____ Hur -

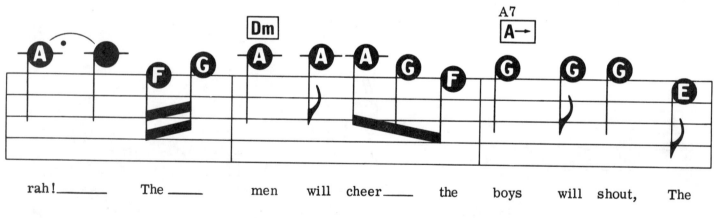

rah!_____ The ____ men will cheer____ the boys will shout, The

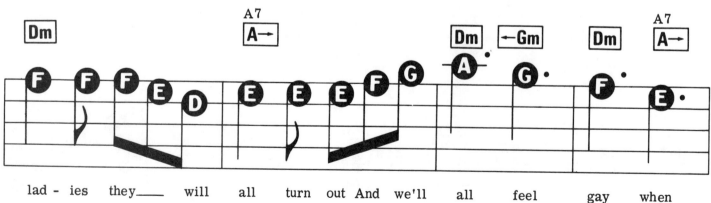

lad - ies they____ will all turn out And we'll all feel gay when

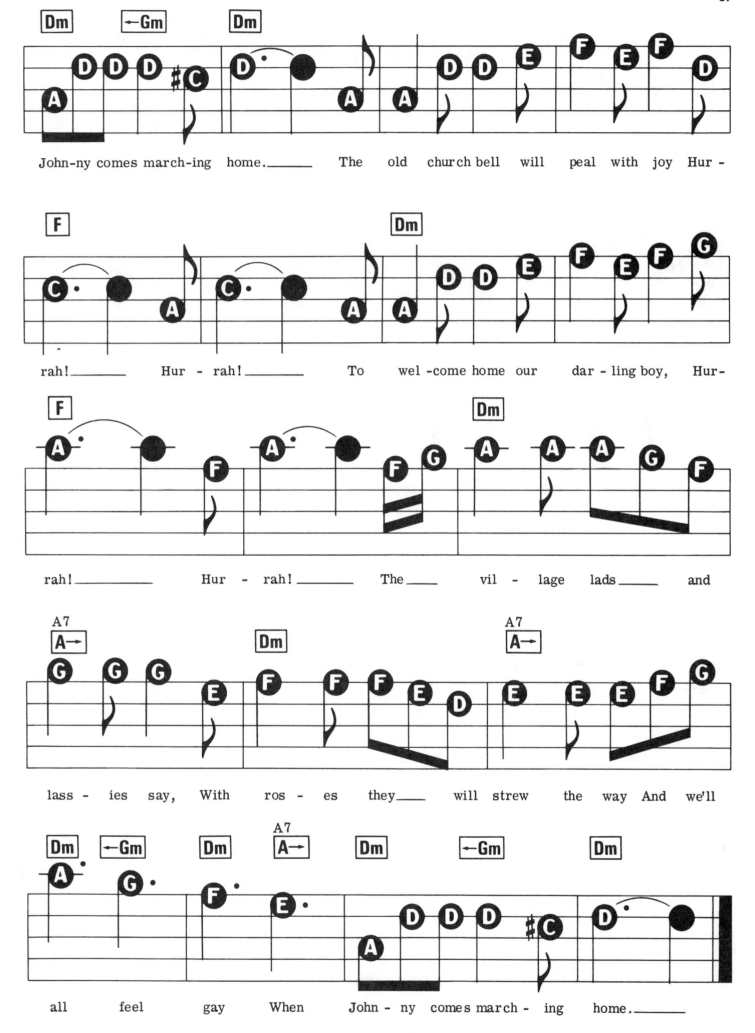

Yankee Doodle Dandy

Registration 9

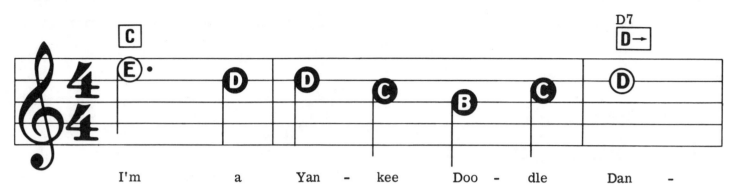

I'm a Yan - kee Doo - dle Dan -

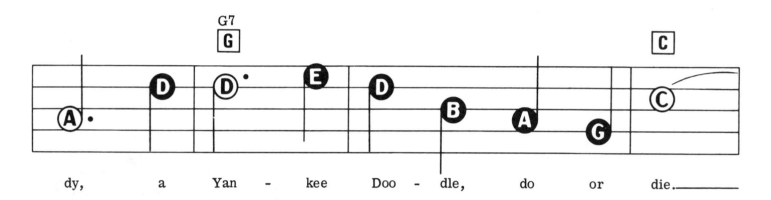

dy, a Yan - kee Doo - dle, do or die.

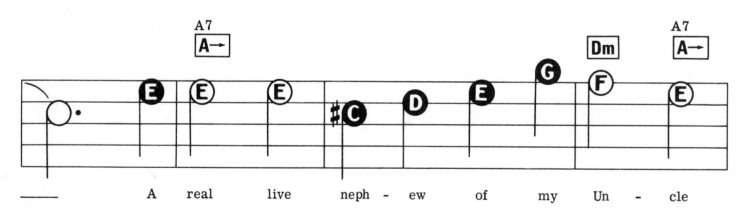

A real live neph - ew of my Un - cle

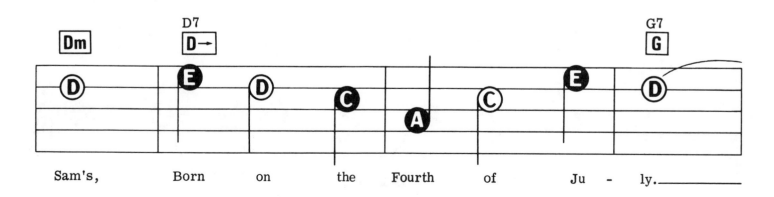

Sam's, Born on the Fourth of Ju - ly.

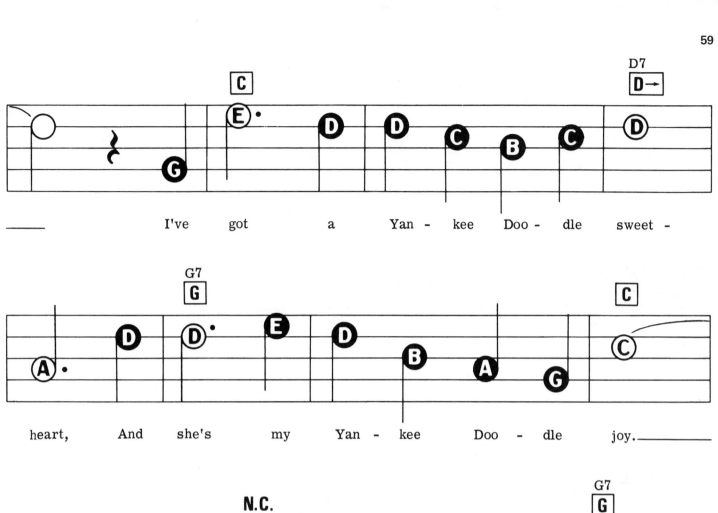

I've got a Yan - kee Doo - dle sweet -

heart, And she's my Yan - kee Doo - dle joy.

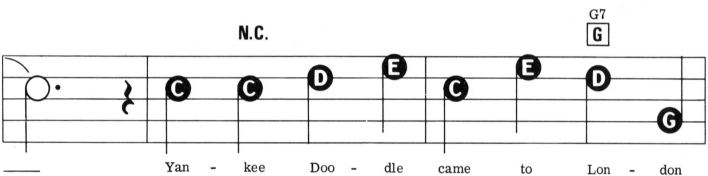

Yan - kee Doo - dle came to Lon - don

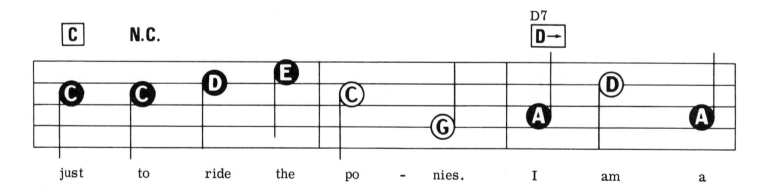

just to ride the po - nies. I am a

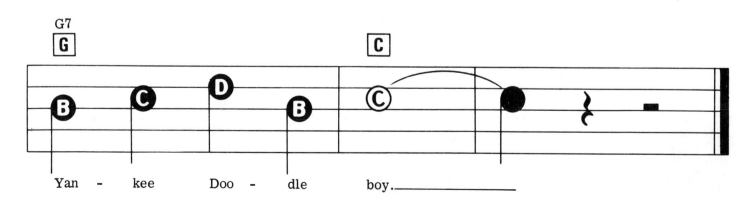

Yan - kee Doo - dle boy.

Yellow Rose Of Texas

Registration 3

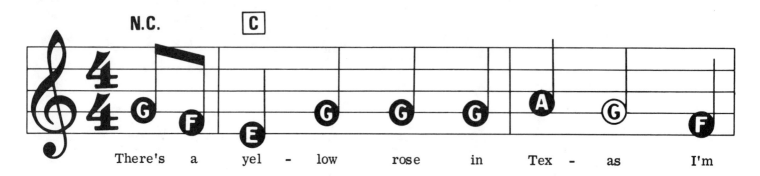

There's a yel - low rose in Tex - as I'm

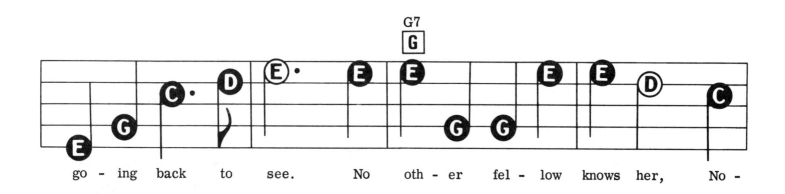

go - ing back to see. No oth - er fel - low knows her, No -

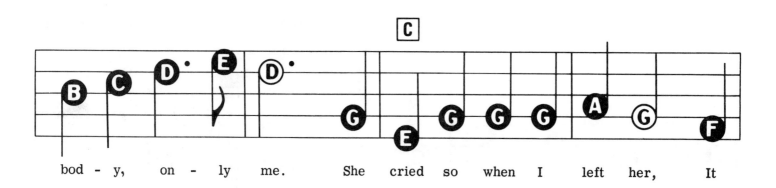

bod - y, on - ly me. She cried so when I left her, It

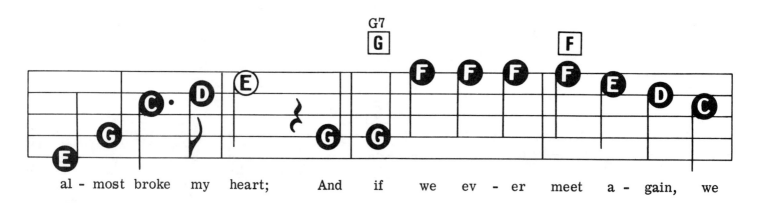

al - most broke my heart; And if we ev - er meet a - gain, we

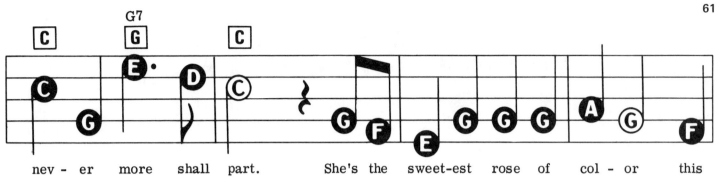

nev - er more shall part. She's the sweet-est rose of col - or this

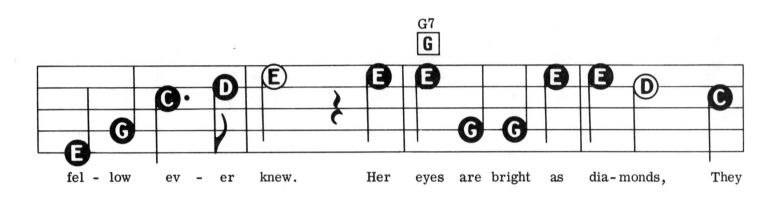

fel - low ev - er knew. Her eyes are bright as dia-monds, They

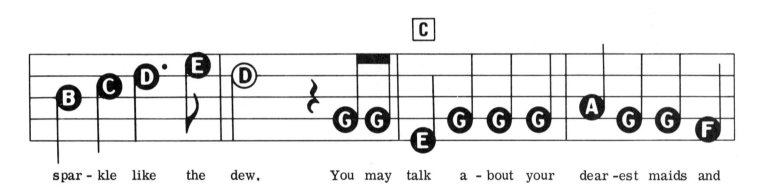

spar - kle like the dew. You may talk a - bout your dear -est maids and

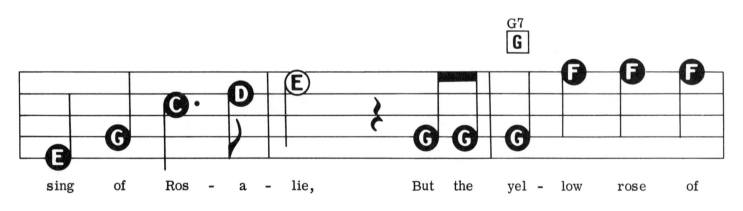

sing of Ros - a - lie, But the yel - low rose of

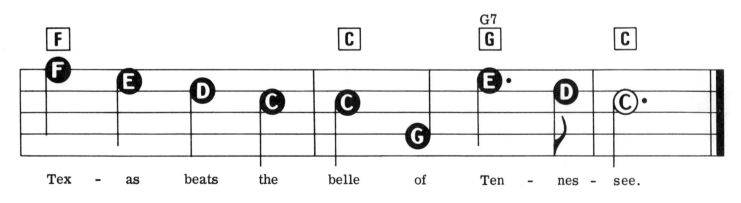

Tex - as beats the belle of Ten - nes - see.

You're A Grand Old Flag

Registration 2

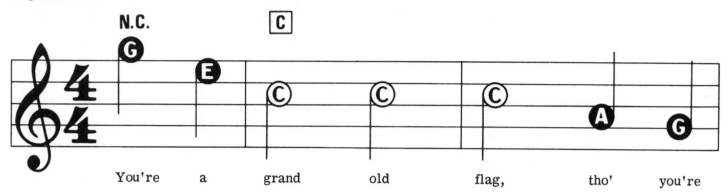

You're a grand old flag, tho' you're

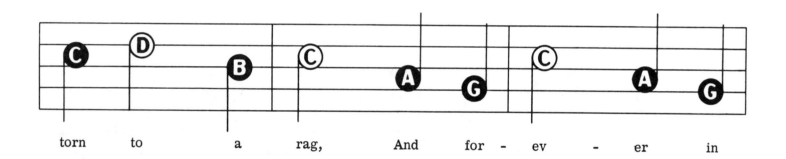

torn to a rag, And for - ev - er in

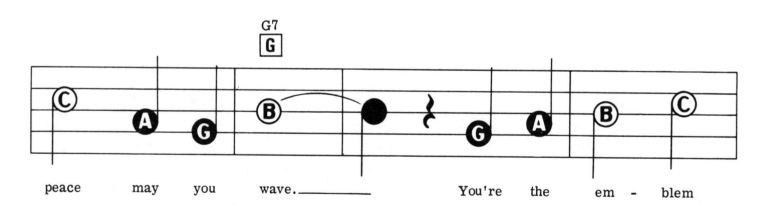

peace may you wave._____ You're the em - blem

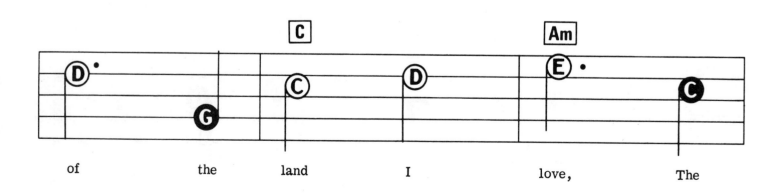

of the land I love, The

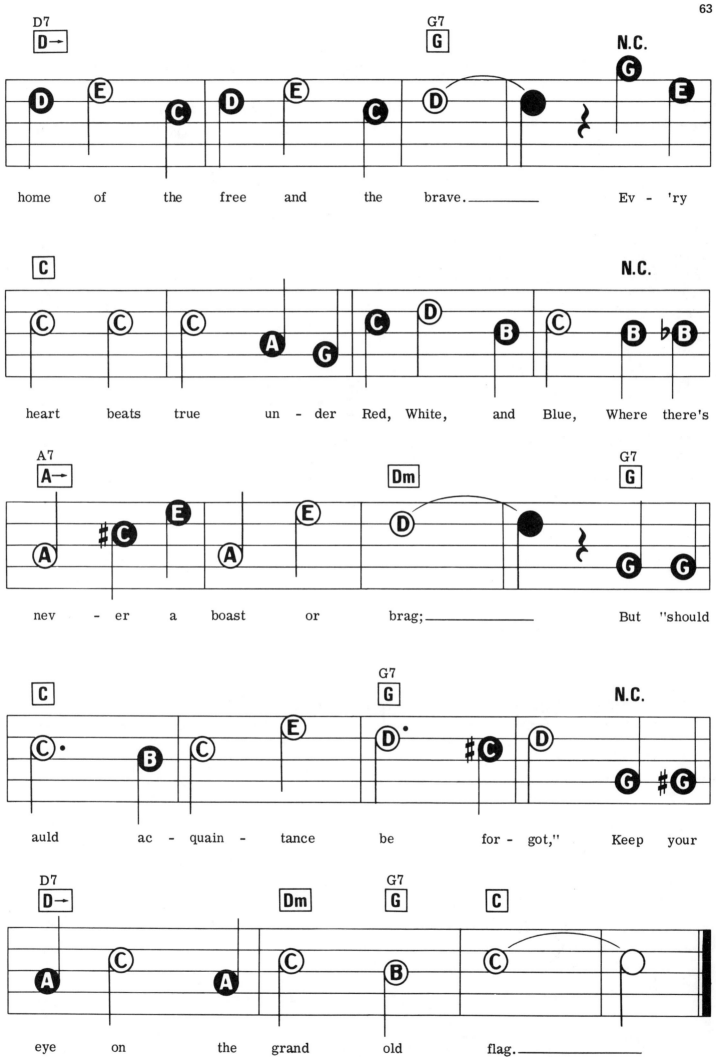

Ach, Du Lieber Augustin

Registration 4

German

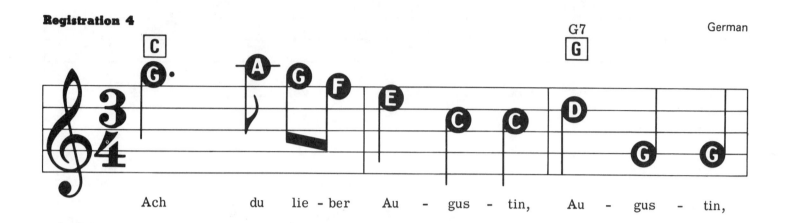

Ach du lie - ber Au - gus - tin, Au - gus - tin,

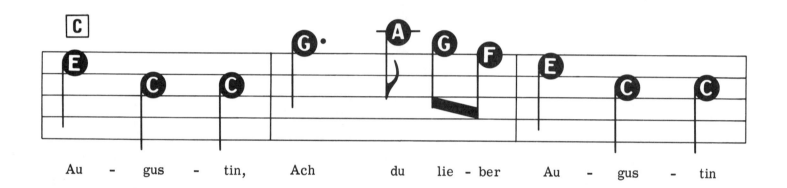

Au - gus - tin, Ach du lie - ber Au - gus - tin

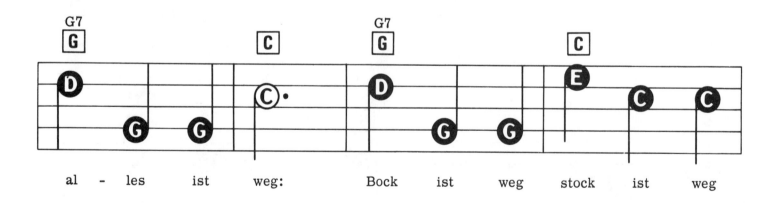

al - les ist weg: Bock ist weg stock ist weg

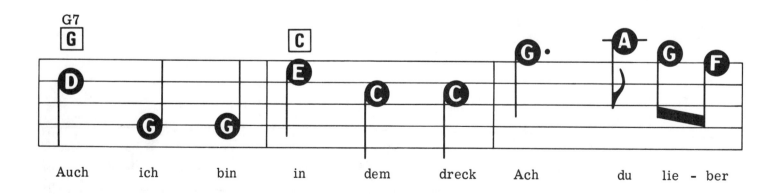

Auch ich bin in dem dreck Ach du lie - ber

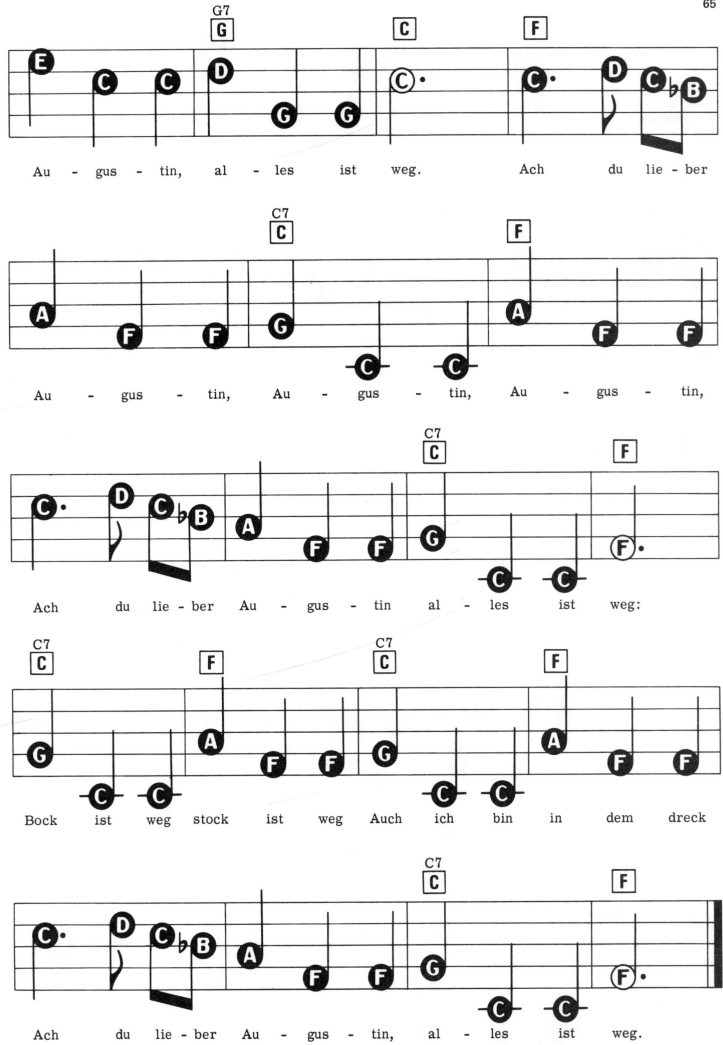

Believe Me If All Those Endearing Young Charms

Registration 9

Irish

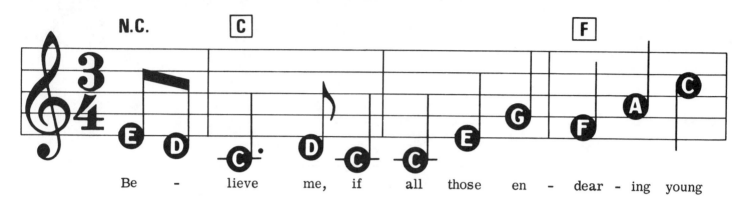

Be - lieve me, if all those en - dear - ing young

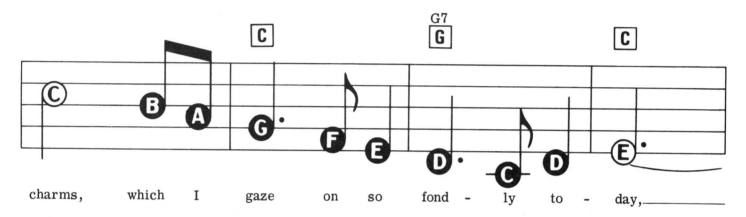

charms, which I gaze on so fond - ly to - day,_____

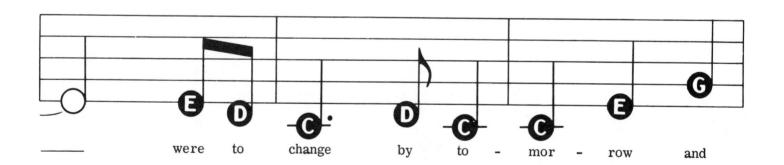

_____ were to change by to - mor - row and

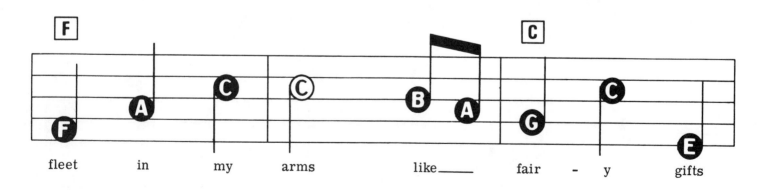

fleet in my arms like_____ fair - y gifts

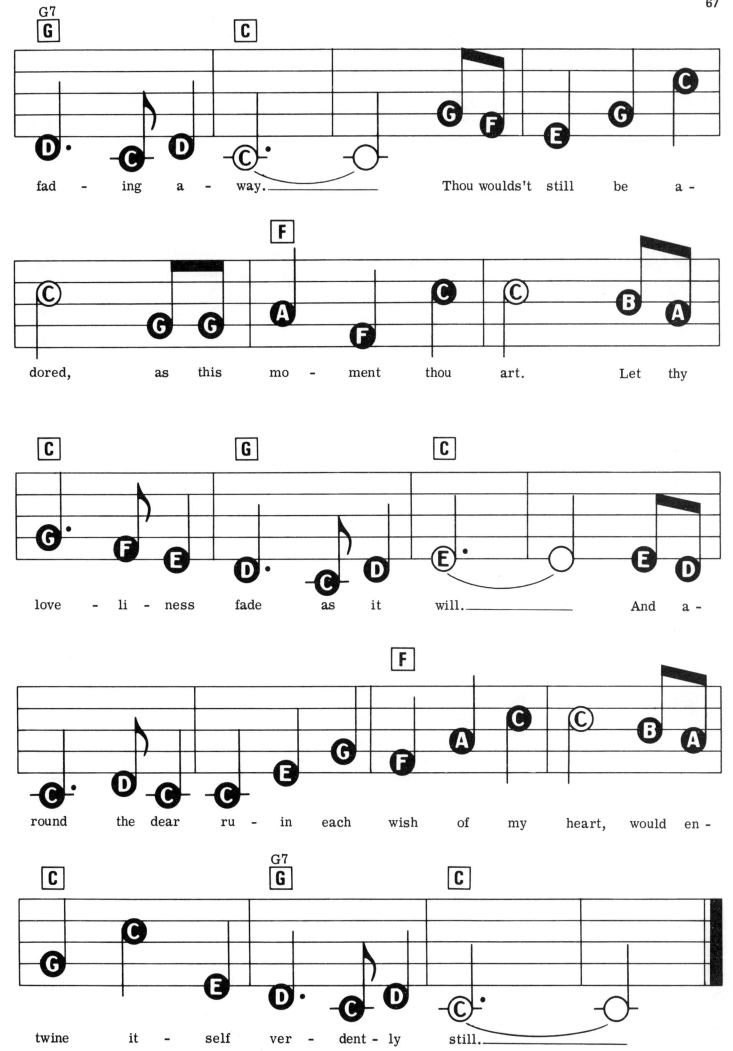

Blue Bells Of Scotland

Registration 2

Scottish

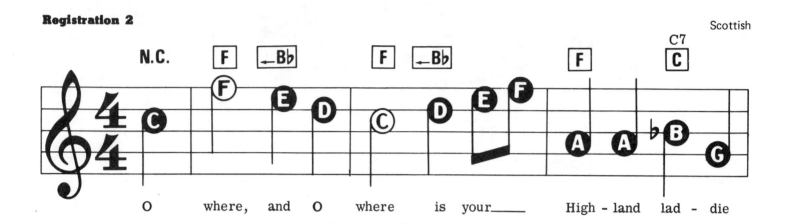

O where, and O where is your____ High - land lad - die

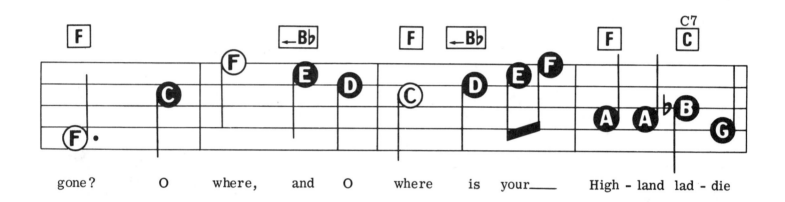

gone? O where, and O where is your____ High - land lad - die

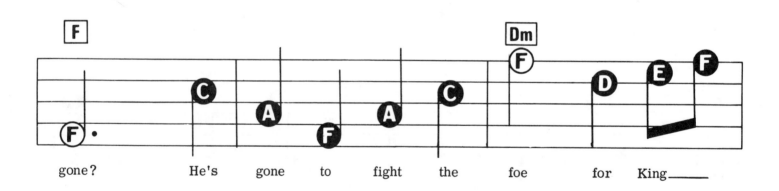

gone? He's gone to fight the foe for King____

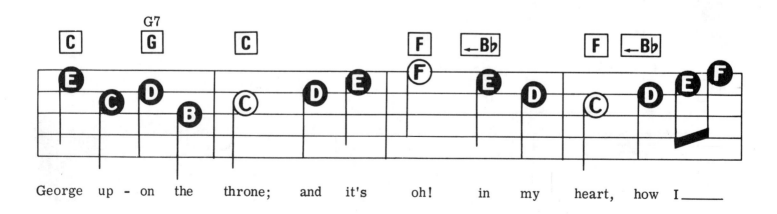

George up - on the throne; and it's oh! in my heart, how I____

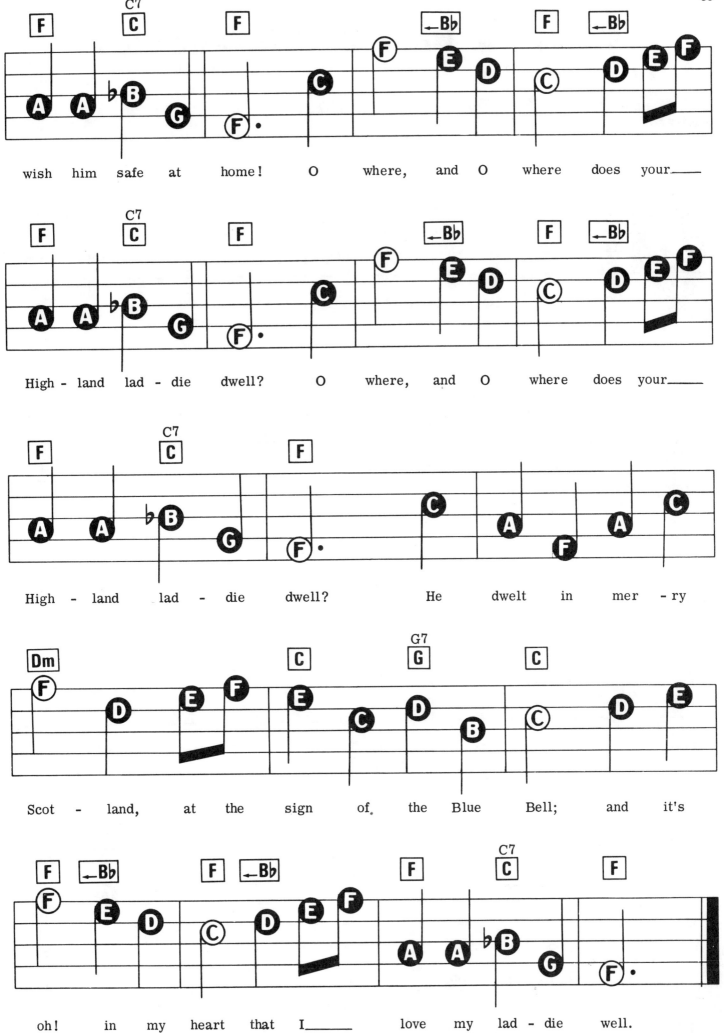

Carry Me Back To Old Virginny

Registration 3

American

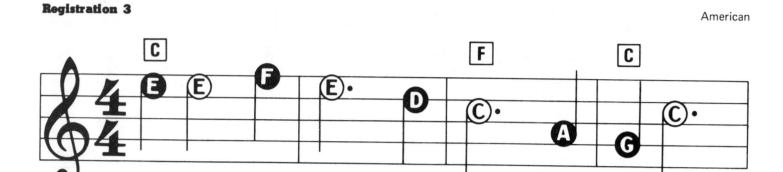

Car - ry me back to old Vir - gin - ny.

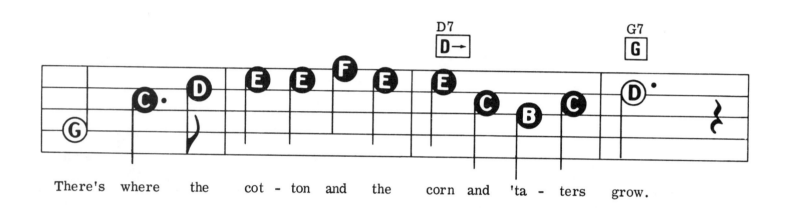

There's where the cot - ton and the corn and 'ta - ters grow.

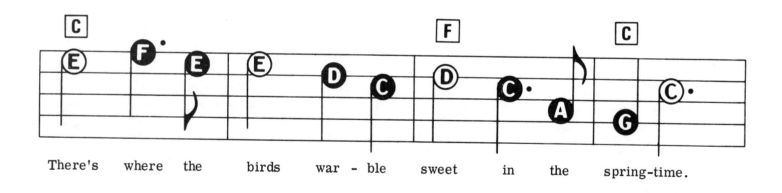

There's where the birds war - ble sweet in the spring-time.

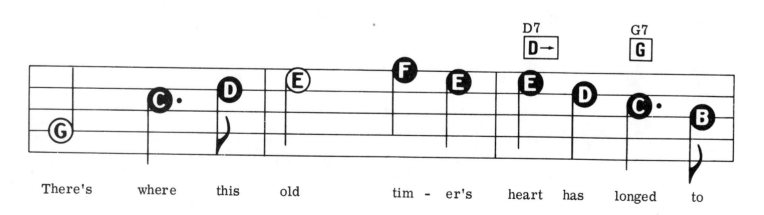

There's where this old tim - er's heart has longed to

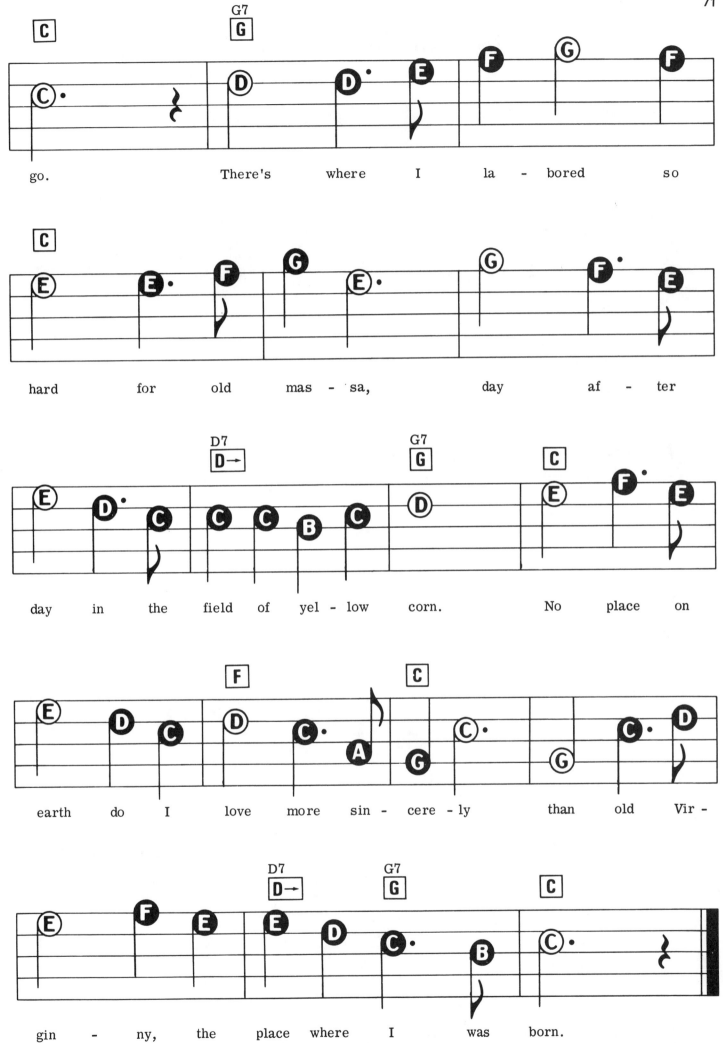

Cockels And Mussels

Registration 5

Irish

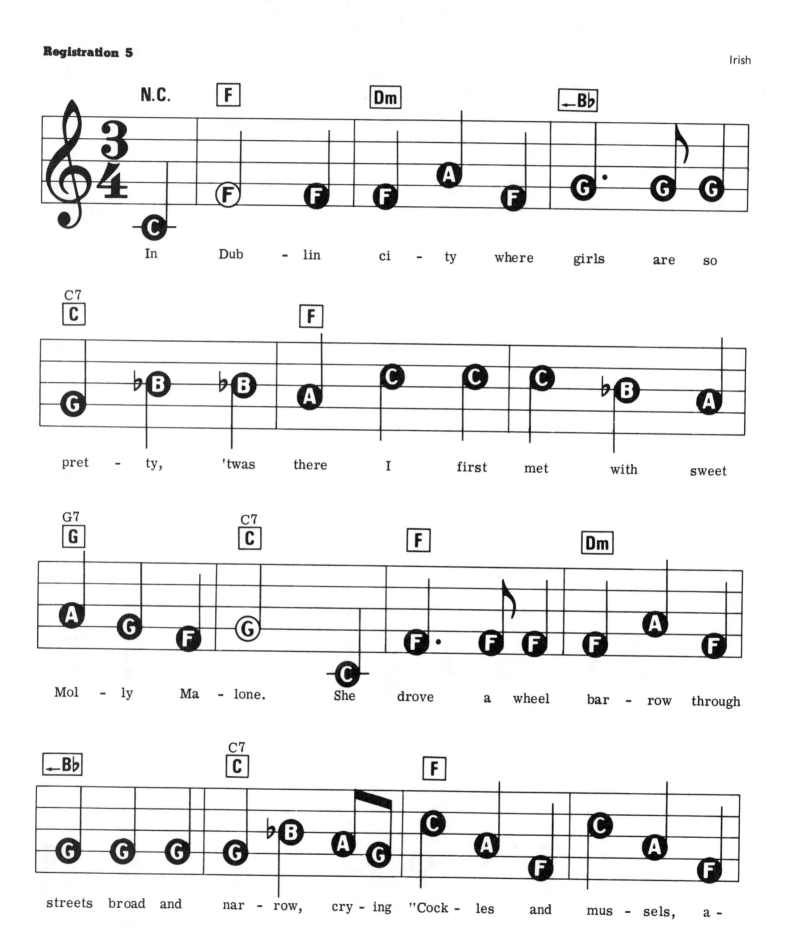

In Dub - lin ci - ty where girls are so pret - ty, 'twas there I first met with sweet Mol - ly Ma - lone. She drove a wheel bar - row through streets broad and nar - row, cry - ing "Cock - les and mus - sels, a -

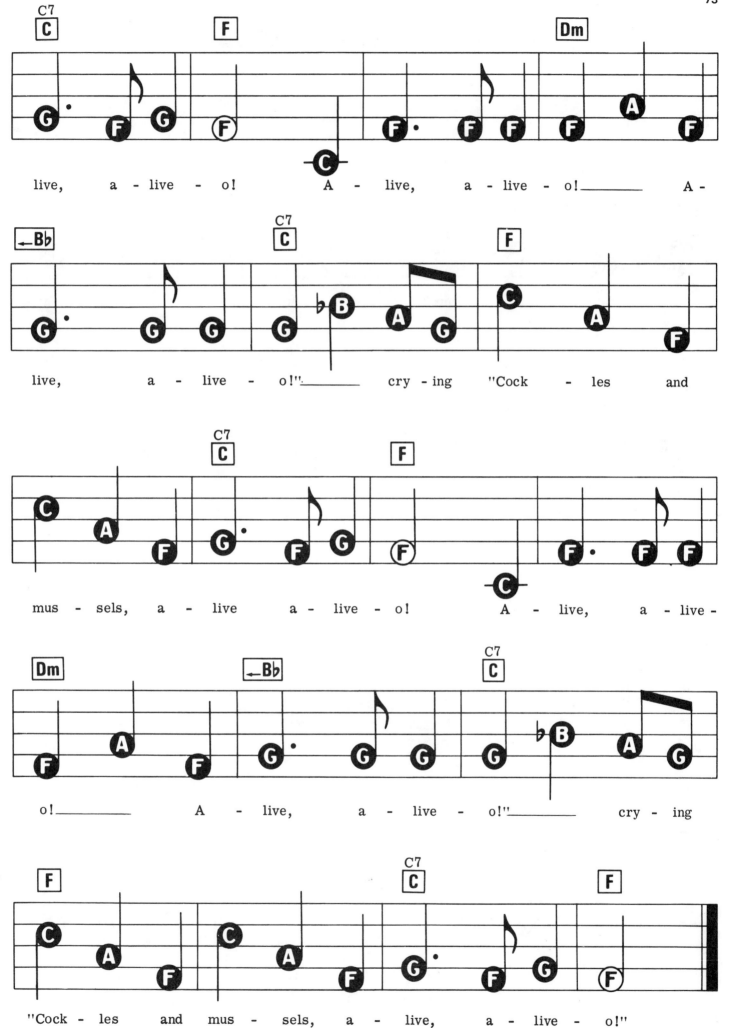

Come To The Sea
(Vieni Sul Mar!)

Registration 2

Italian

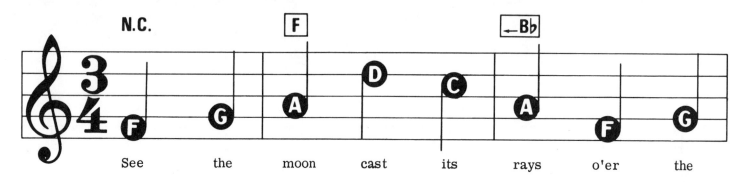

See the moon cast its rays o'er the

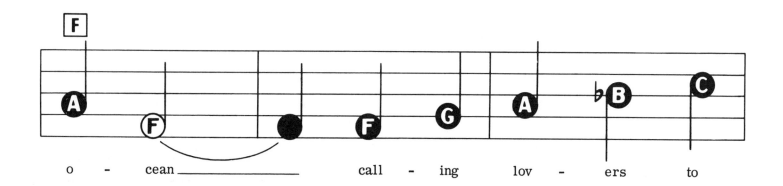

o - cean _____ call - ing lov - ers to

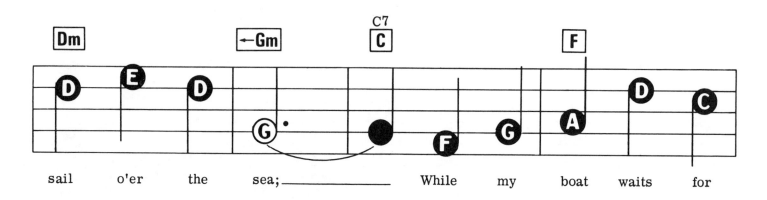

sail o'er the sea; _____ While my boat waits for

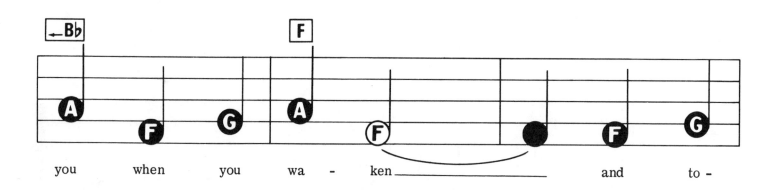

you when you wa - ken _____ and to -

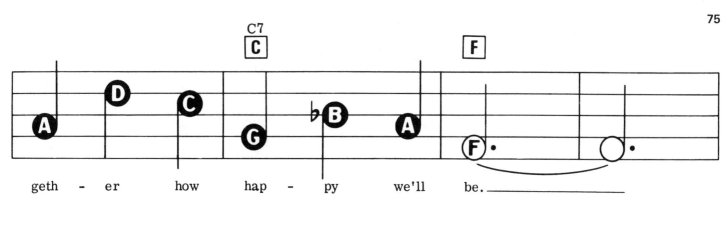

geth - er how hap - py we'll be. _____

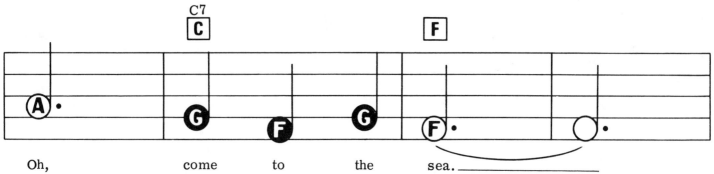

Oh, come to the sea. _____

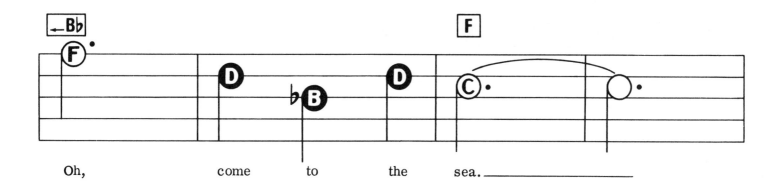

Oh, come to the sea. _____

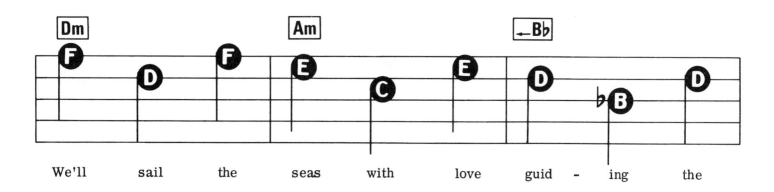

We'll sail the seas with love guid - ing the

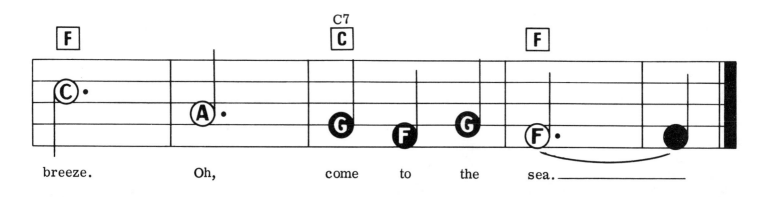

breeze. Oh, come to the sea. _____

Dark Eyes

Registration 10

Russian

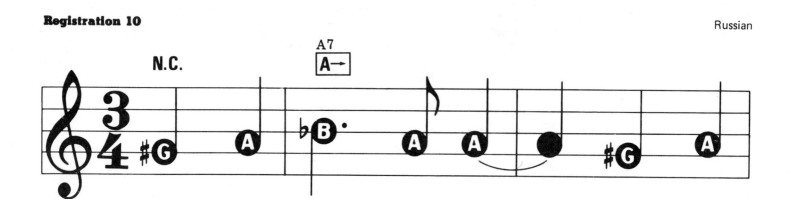

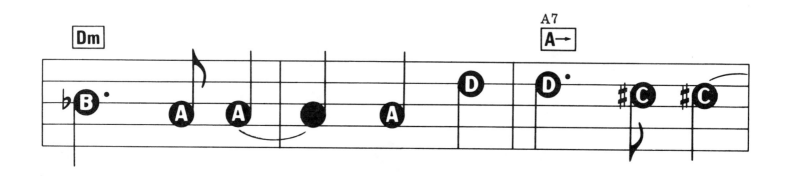

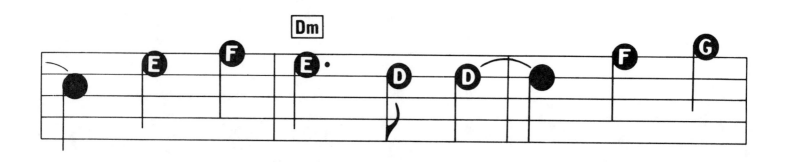

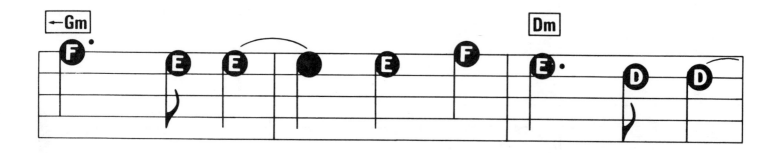

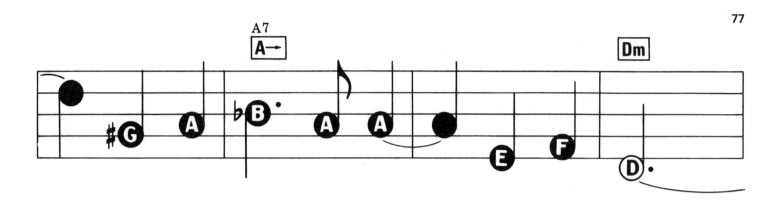

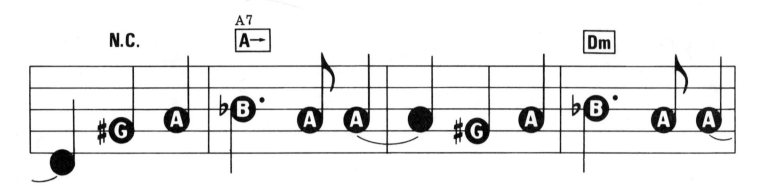

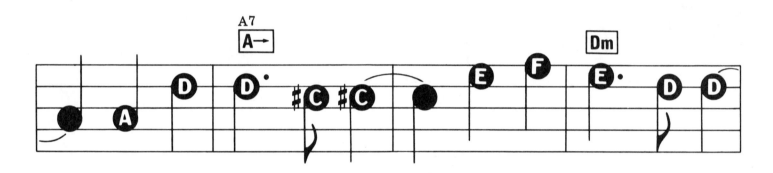

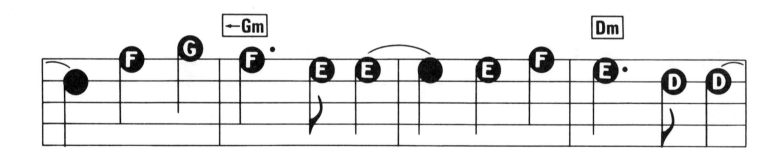

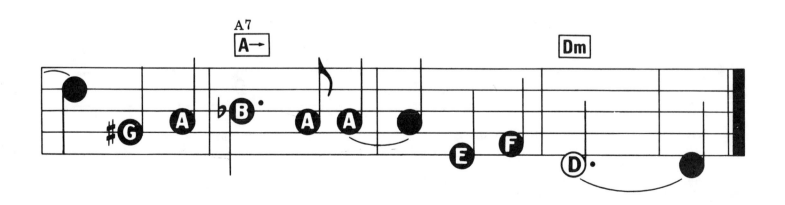

Du, Du Liegst Mir Im Herzen

Registration 4

German

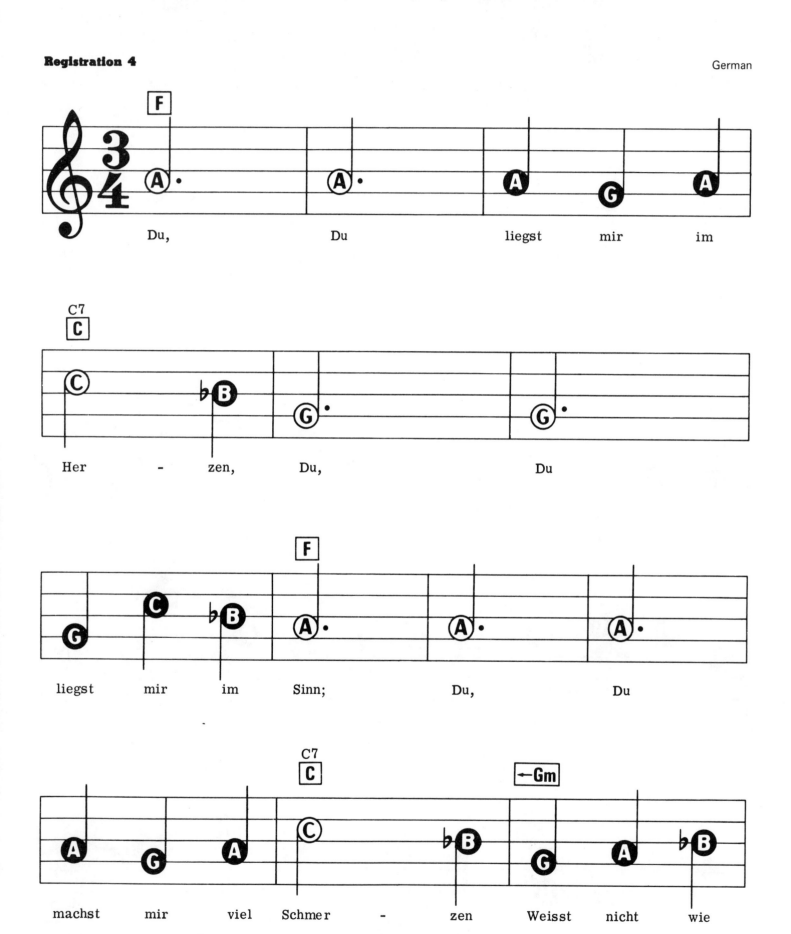

Du, Du liegst mir im
Her - zen, Du, Du
liegst mir im Sinn; Du, Du
machst mir viel Schmer - zen Weisst nicht wie

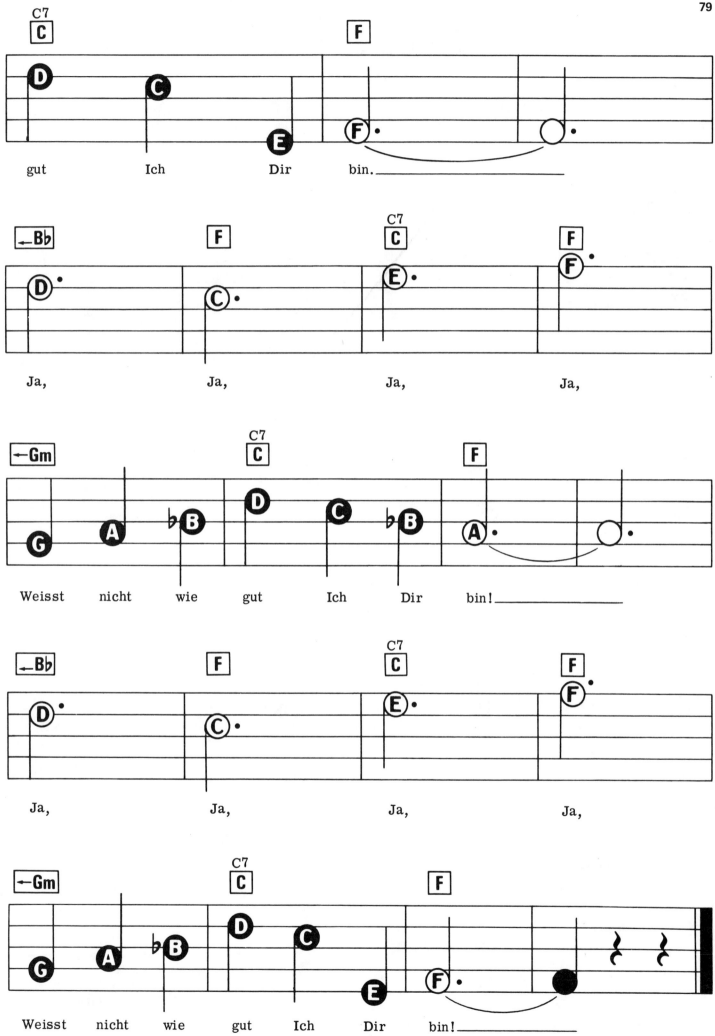

Frère Jacques

Registration 8

French

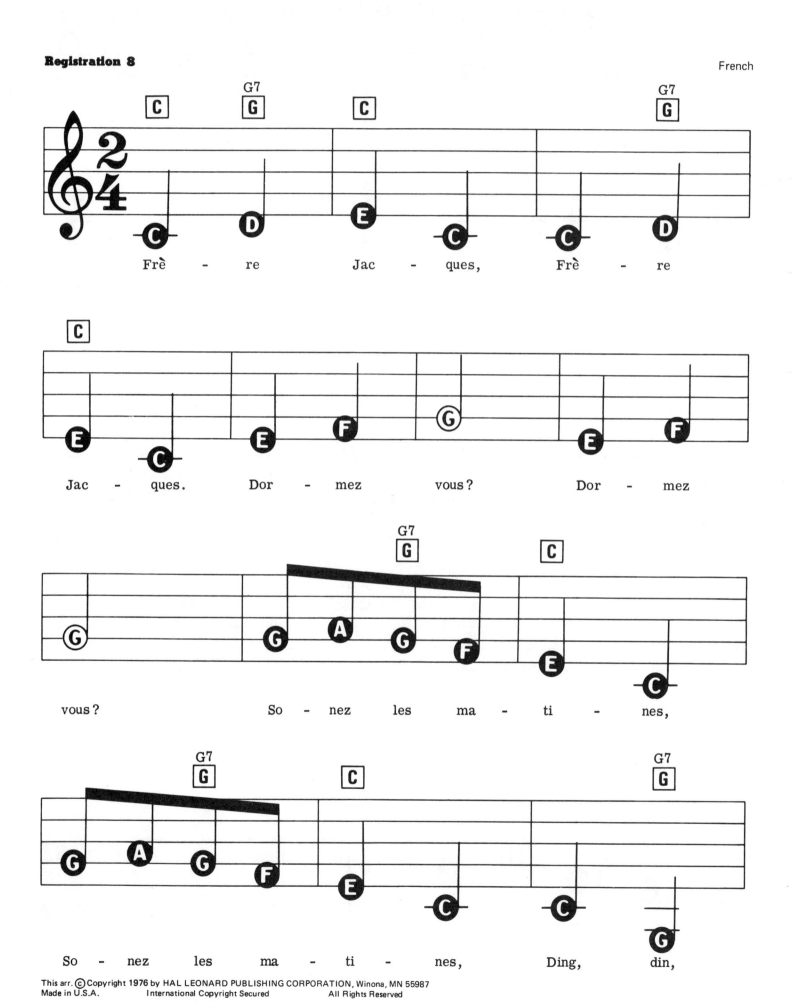

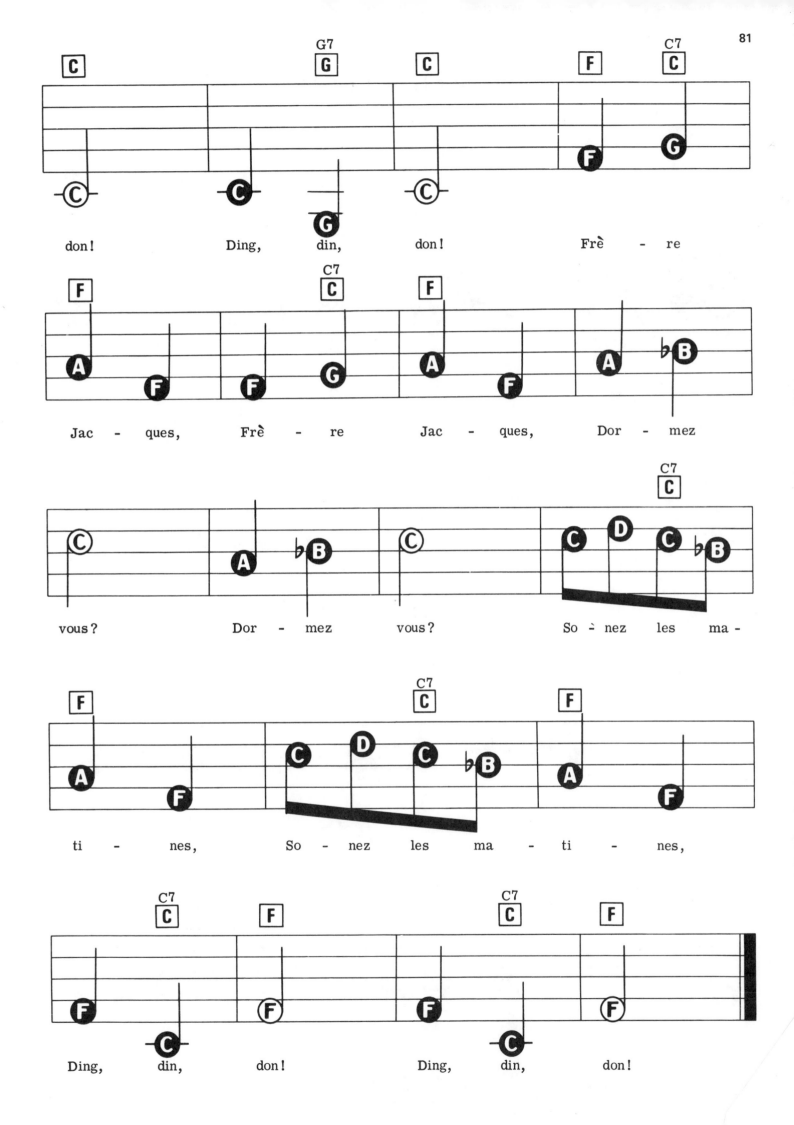

Havah Nagilah

Registration 10

Hebrew

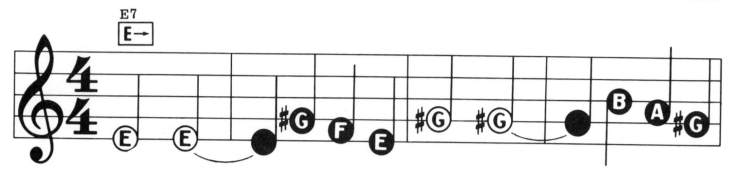

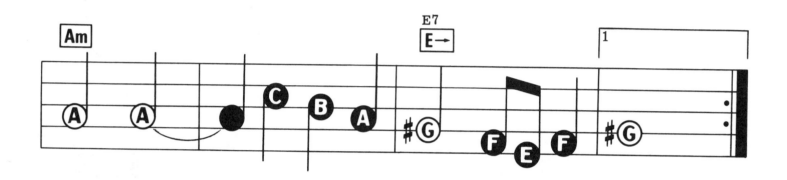

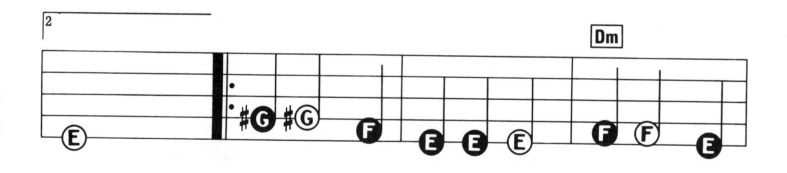

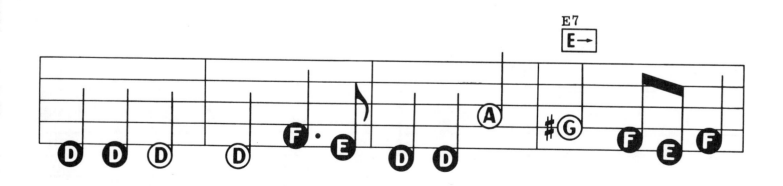

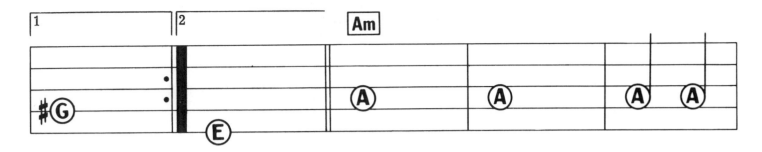
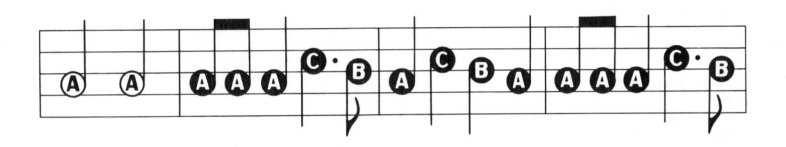
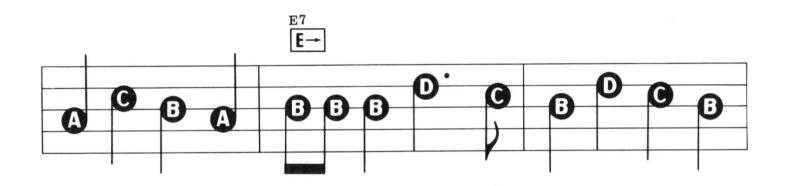
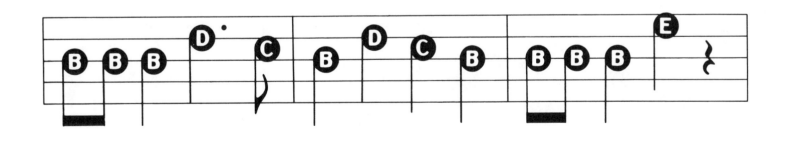
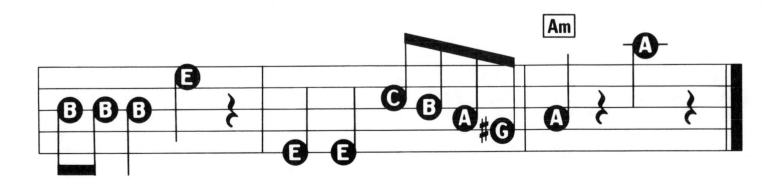

Hopak

Registration 2

Polish

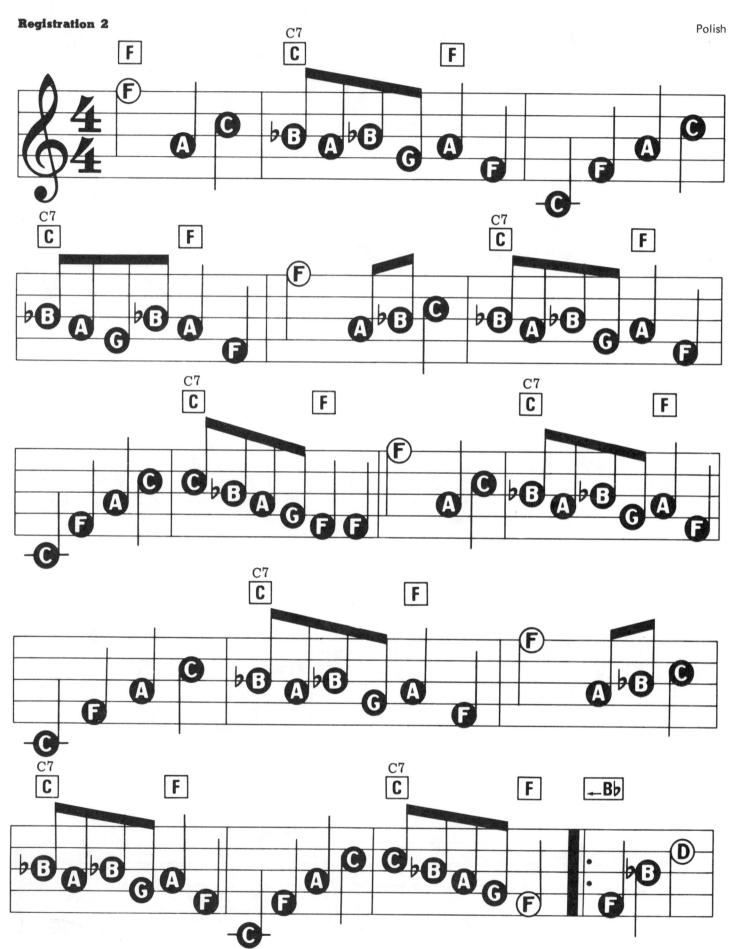

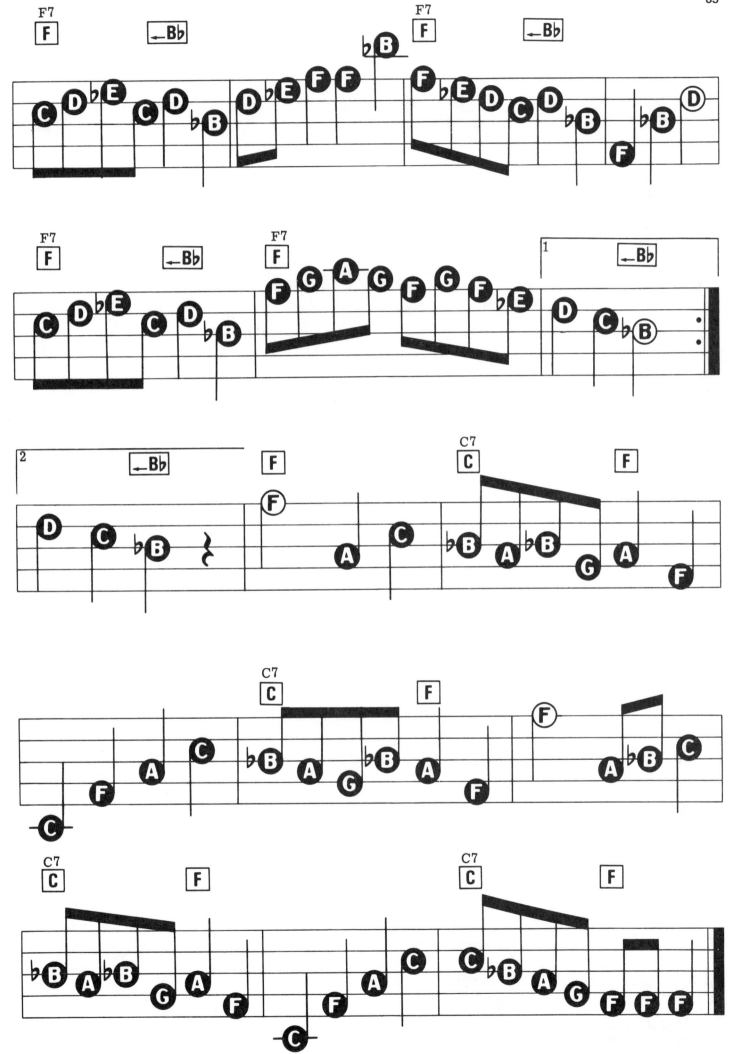

In The Gloaming

Registration 9

Scottish

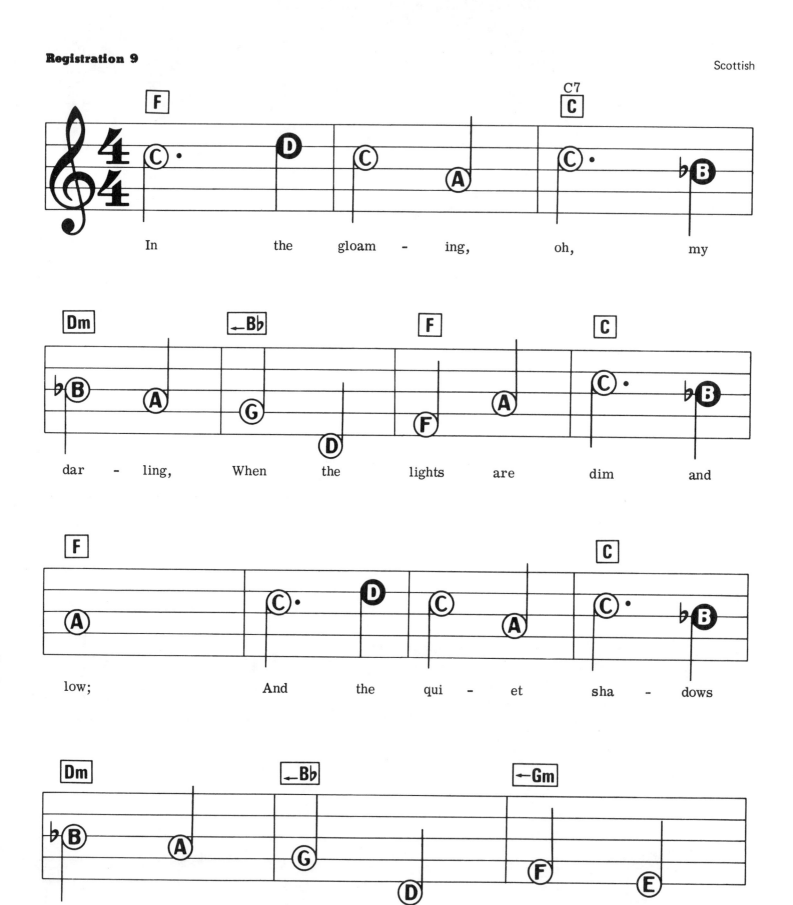

In the gloam - ing, oh, my

dar - ling, When the lights are dim and

low; And the qui - et sha - dows

fall - ing, Soft - ly come and

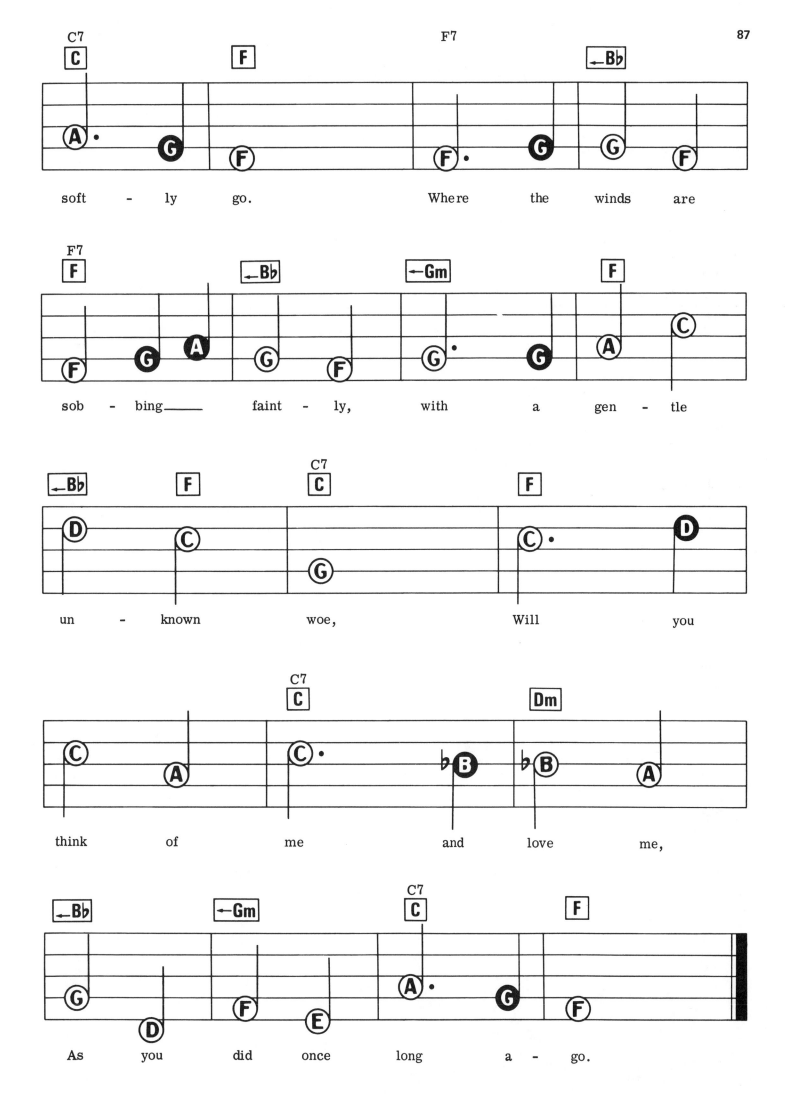

Irish Washerwoman

Registration 2

Irish

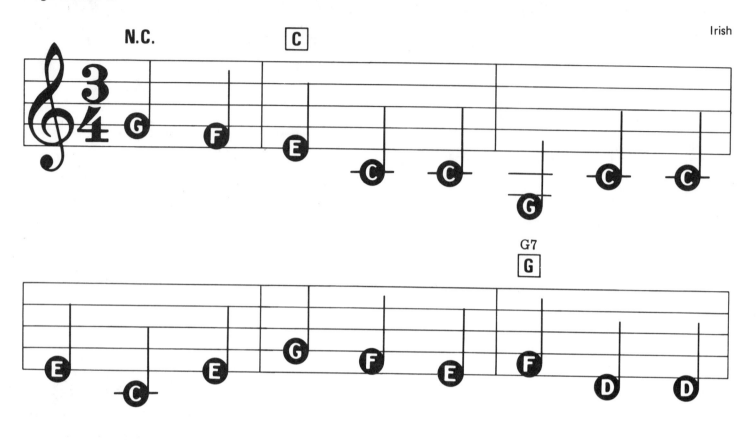

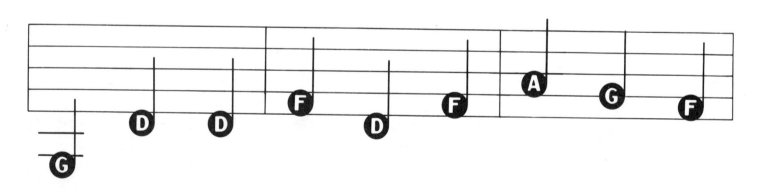

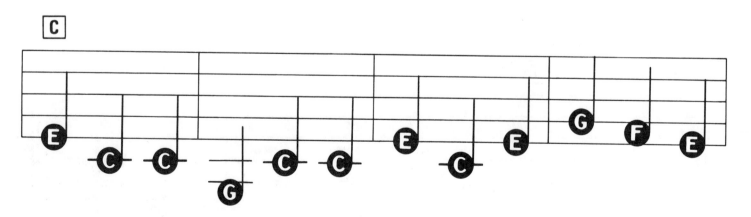

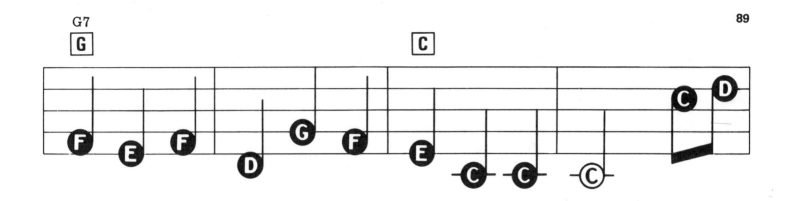

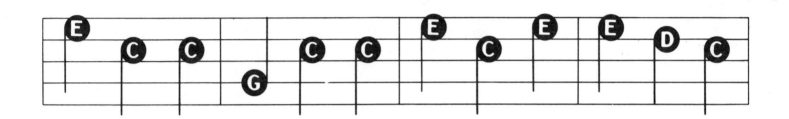

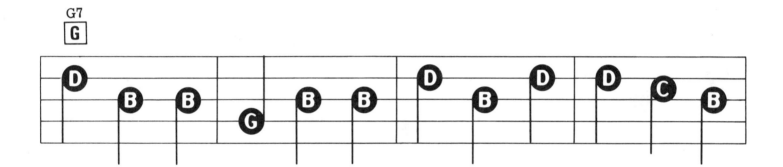

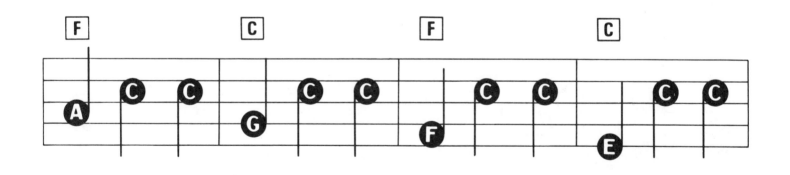

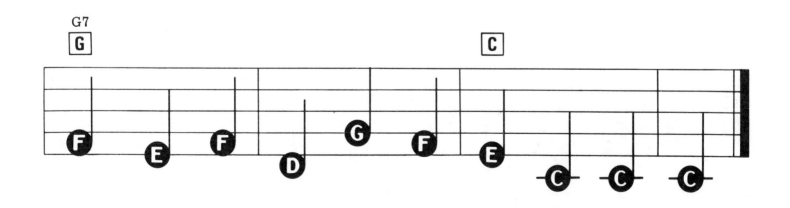

John Peel

Registration 4

English

N.C.

Do you know John Peel with his coat so gay? Do you

know John Peel at the break of day, Do you know John Peel when he's

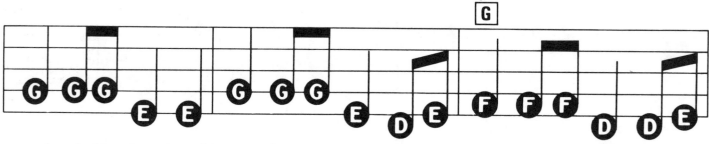

far, far a - way, With his hands and his horn in the morn - ing? For the

sound of his horn brought me from my bed, And the cry of the hounds which he

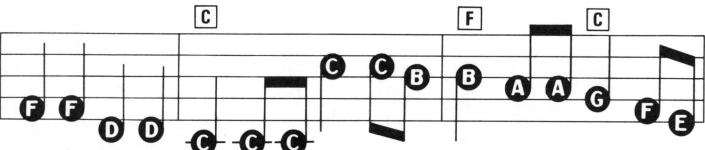

oft - times led; For Peel's view hal - loo would a - wak - en the dead, or the

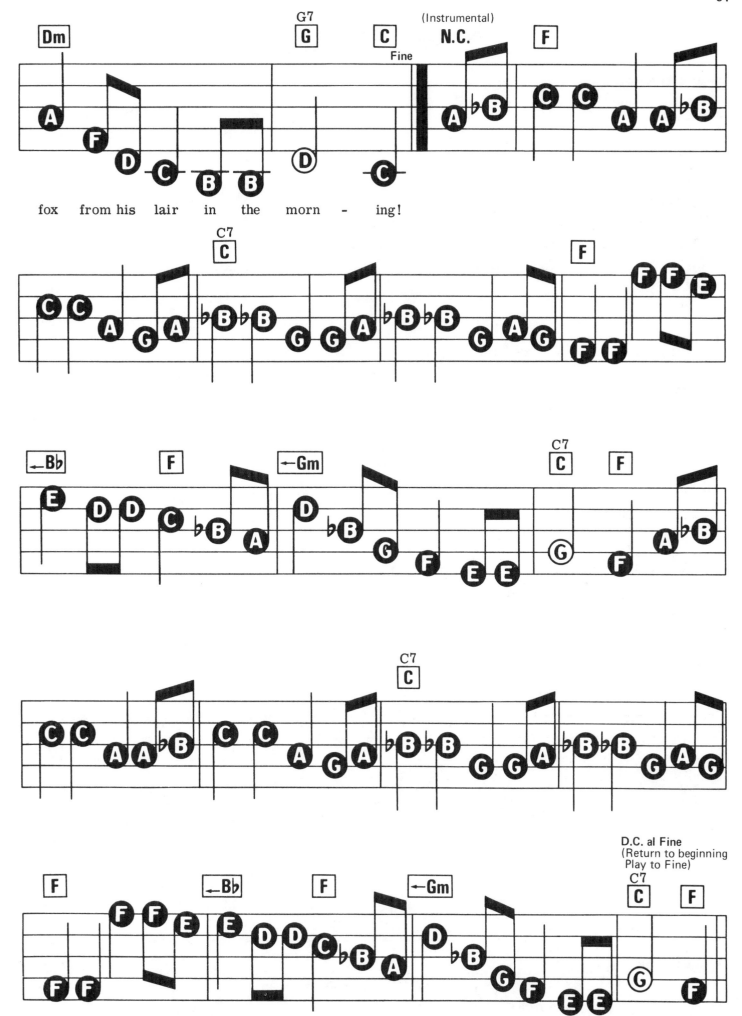

fox   from   his   lair   in   the   morn – ing!

Loch Lomond

Registration 9

Scottish

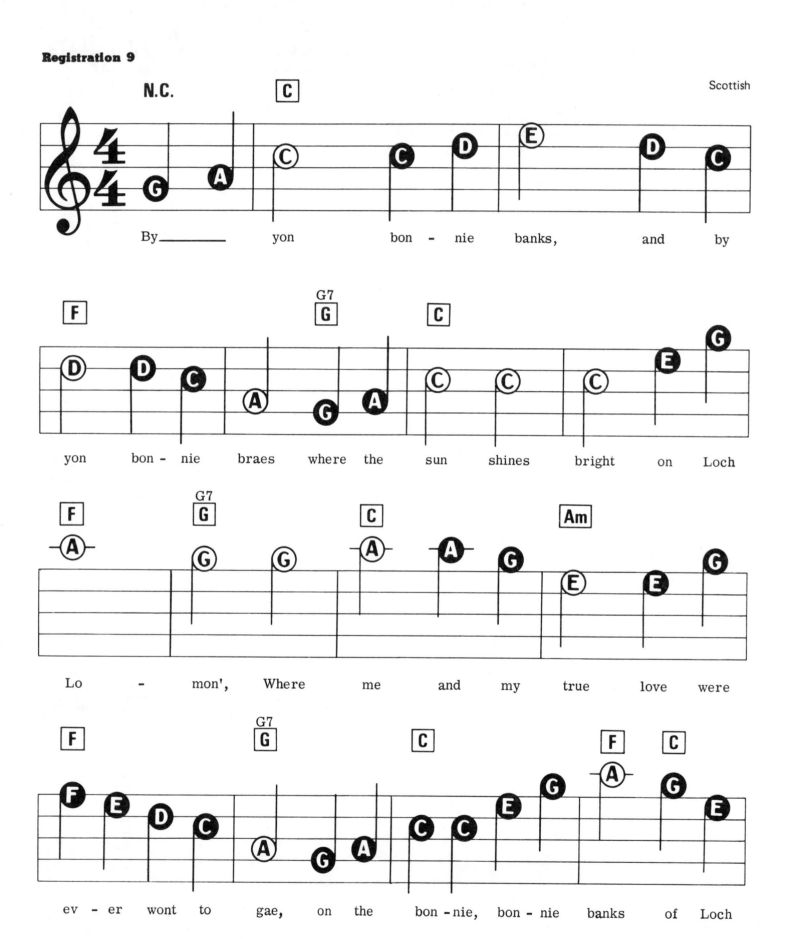

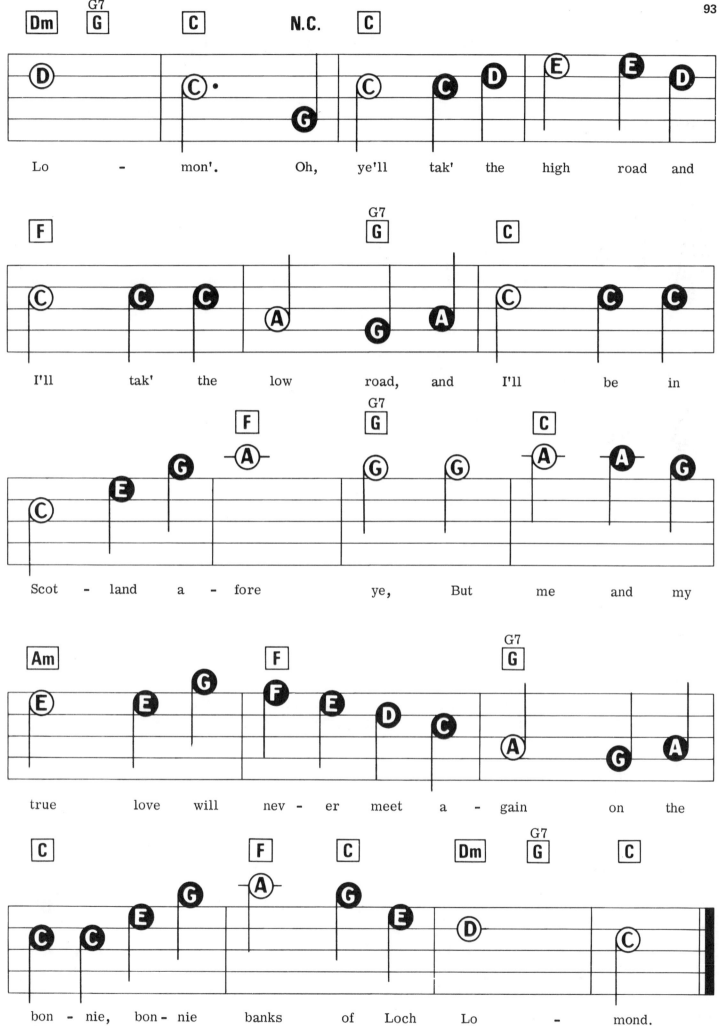

Maori Farewell Song

Registration 10

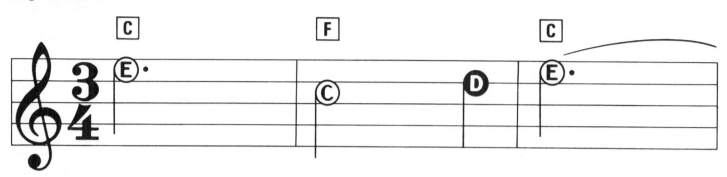

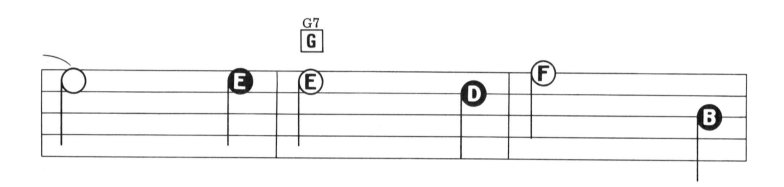

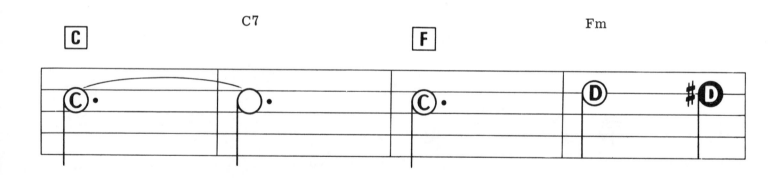

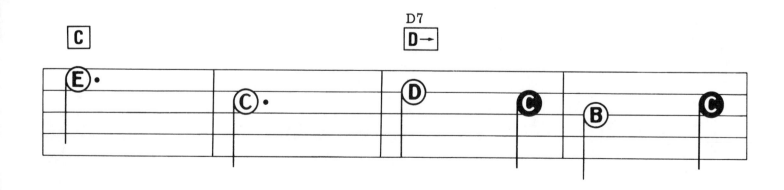

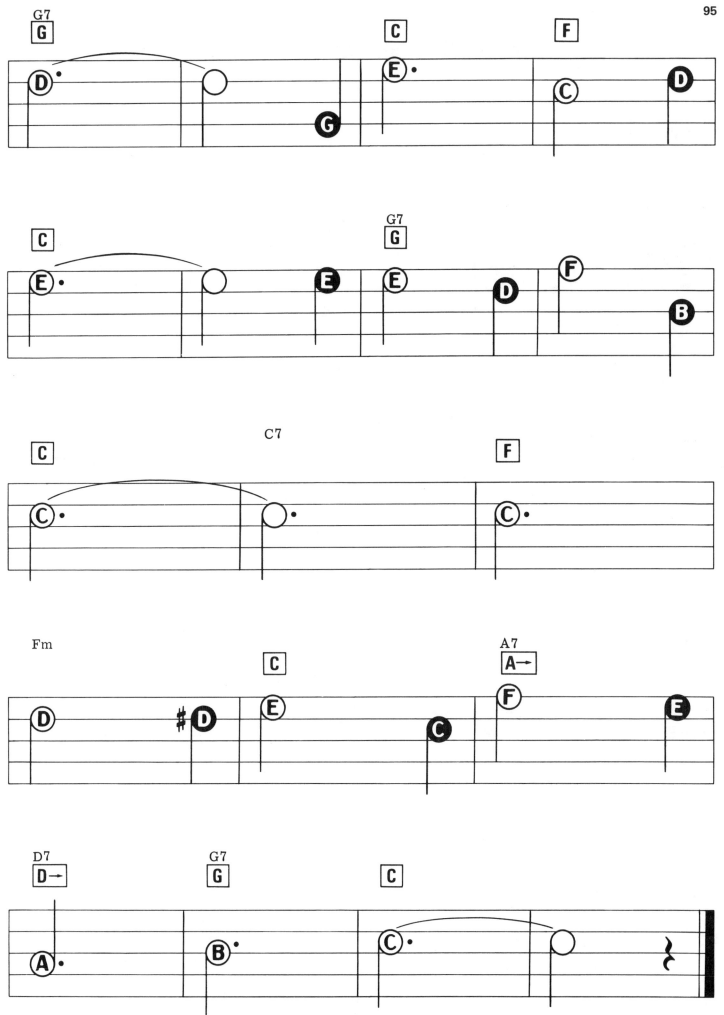

My Old Kentucky Home

Registration 5

American

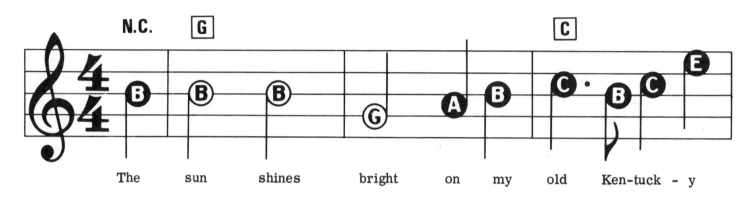

The sun shines bright on my old Ken-tuck-y

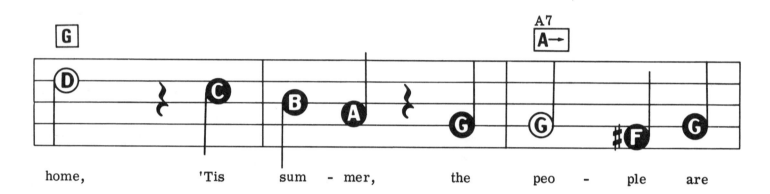

home, 'Tis sum - mer, the peo - ple are

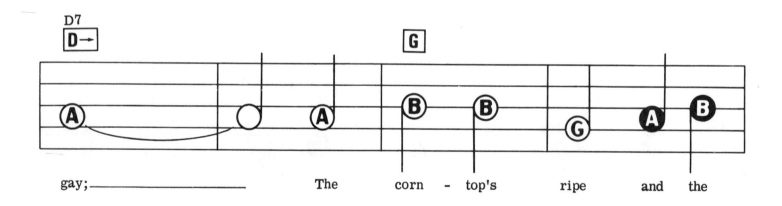

gay; The corn - top's ripe and the

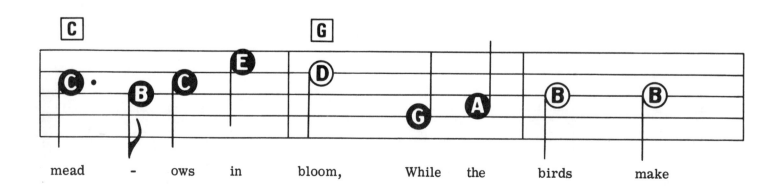

mead - ows in bloom, While the birds make

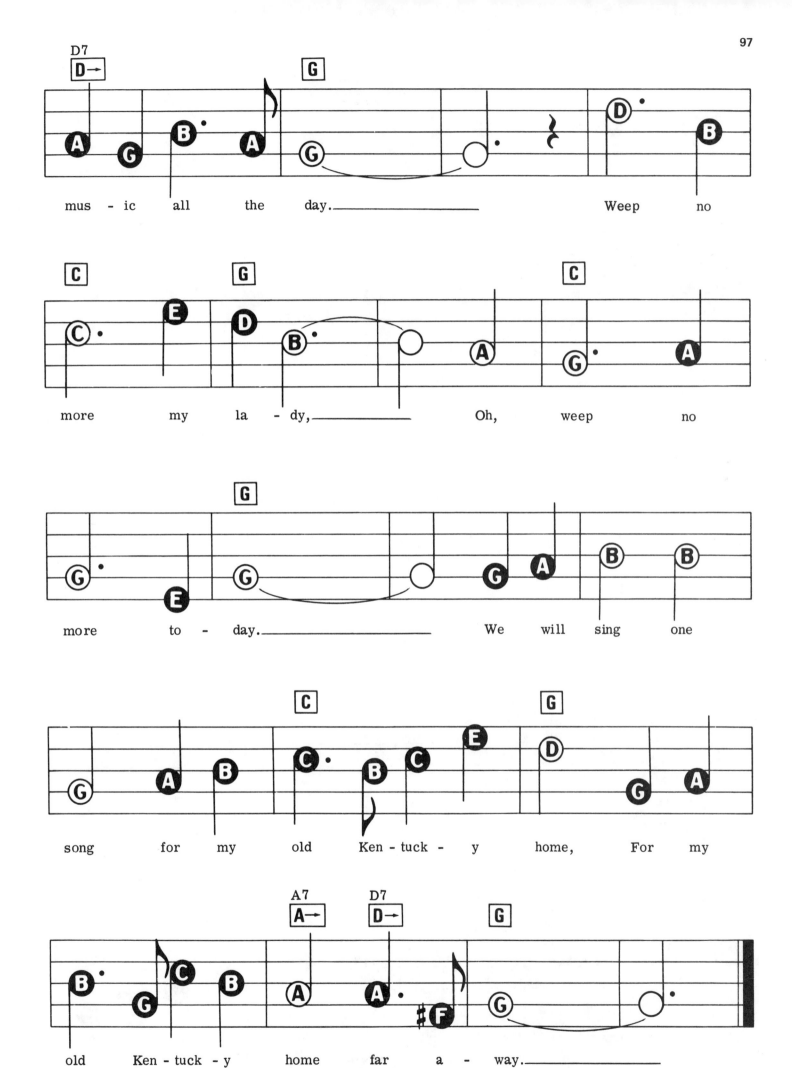

O Sole Mio

Registration 10

Italian

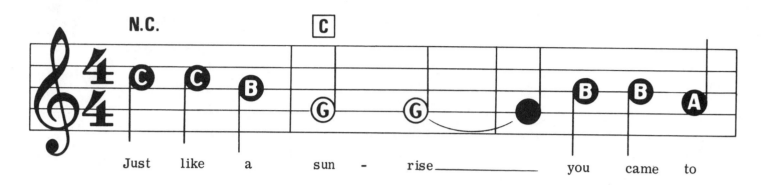

Just like a sun - rise _____ you came to

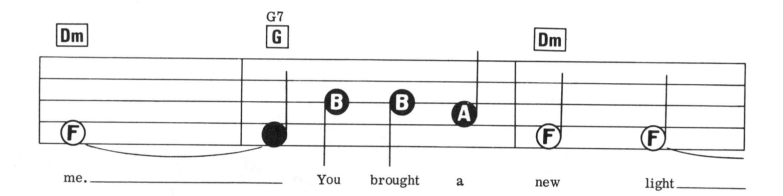

me. _____ You brought a new light _____

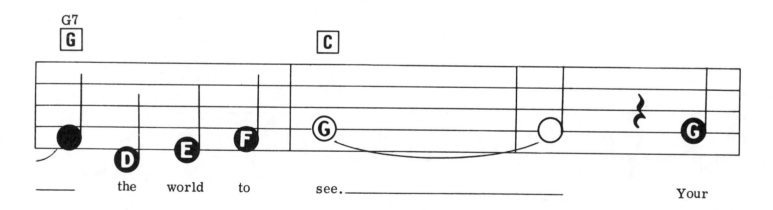

_____ the world to see. _____ Your

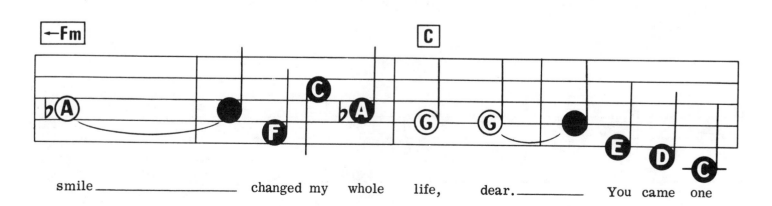

smile _____ changed my whole life, dear. _____ You came one

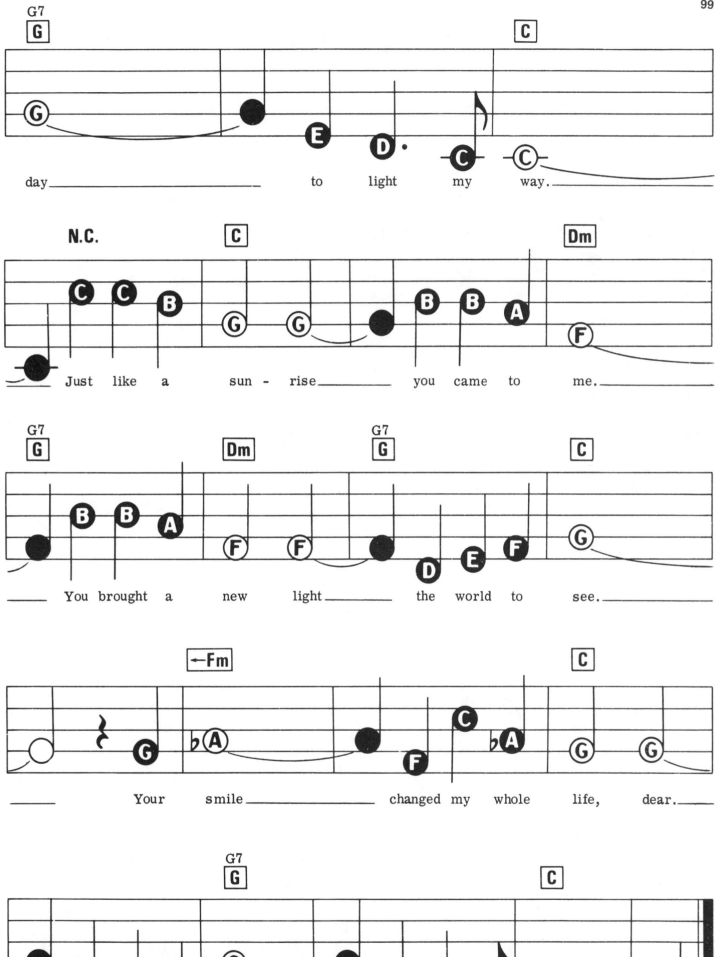

Santa Lucia

Registration 3

Italian

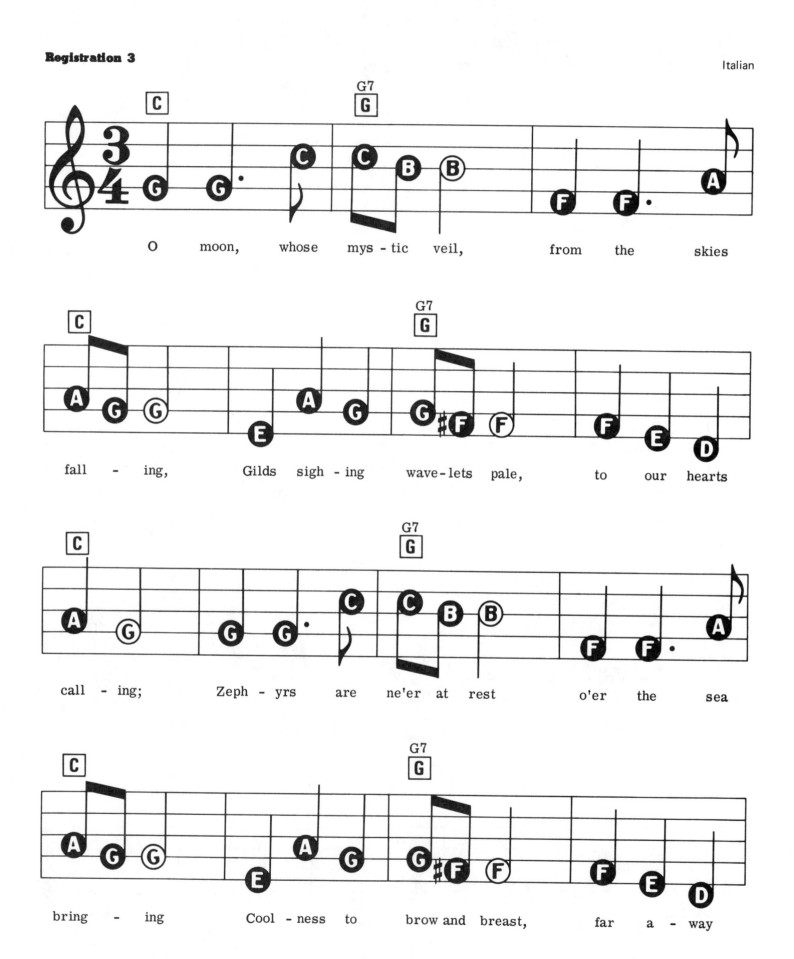

O moon, whose mys - tic veil, from the skies

fall - ing, Gilds sigh - ing wave-lets pale, to our hearts

call - ing; Zeph - yrs are ne'er at rest o'er the sea

bring - ing Cool - ness to brow and breast, far a - way

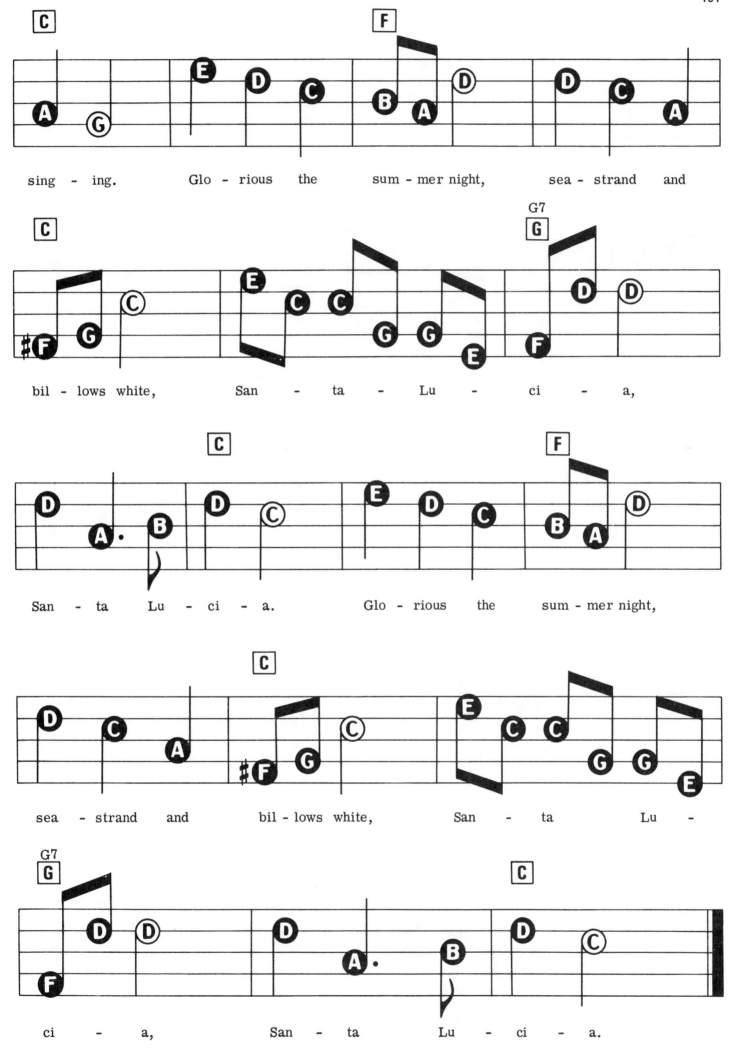

Wait For The Wagon

Registration 1

American

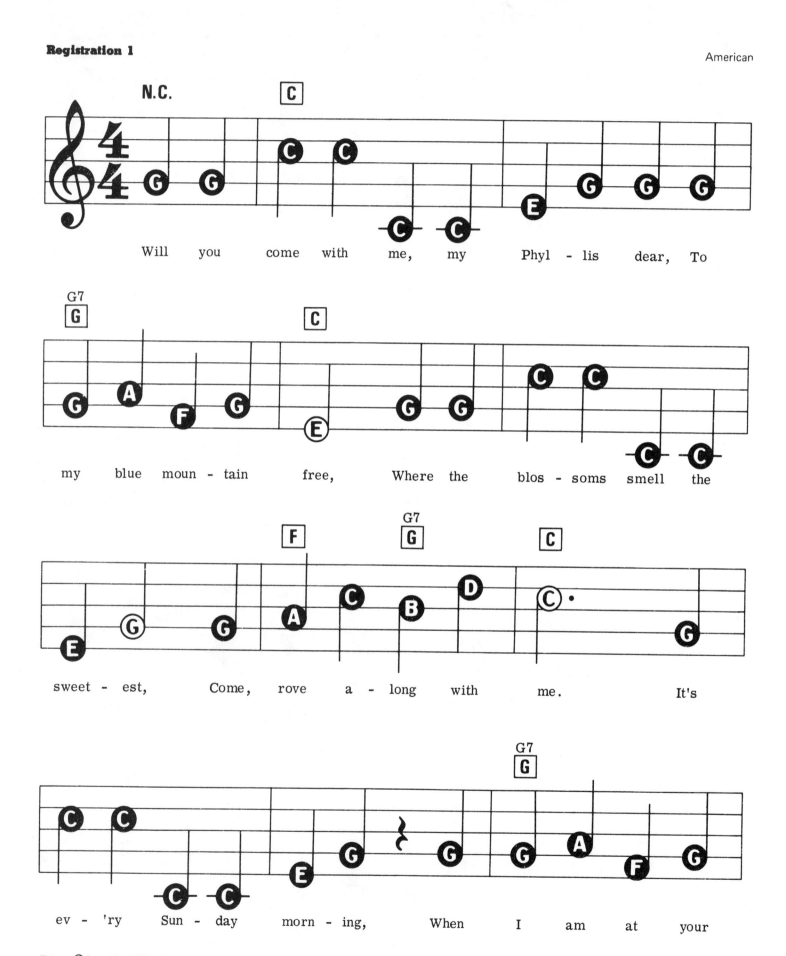

Will you come with me, my Phyl - lis dear, To my blue moun - tain free, Where the blos - soms smell the sweet - est, Come, rove a - long with me. It's ev - 'ry Sun - day morn - ing, When I am at your

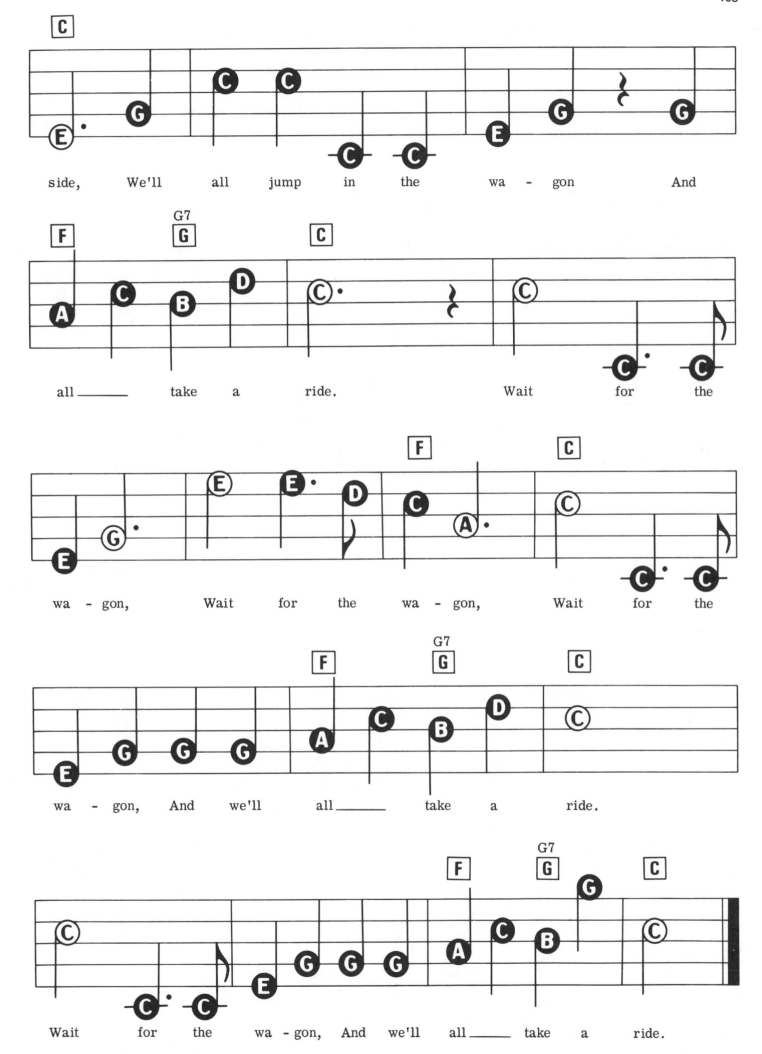

Wearing Of The Green

Registration 9

Irish

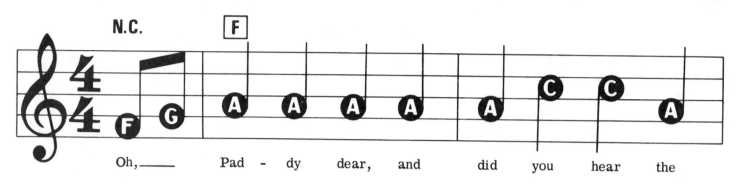

Oh,___ Pad - dy dear, and did you hear the

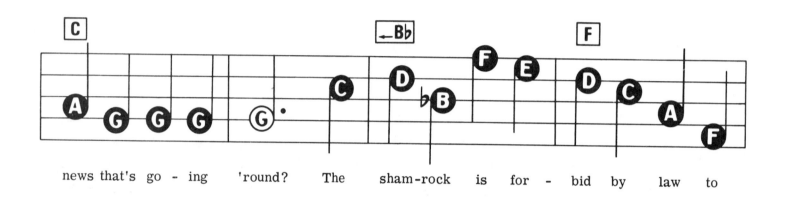

news that's go - ing 'round? The sham-rock is for - bid by law to

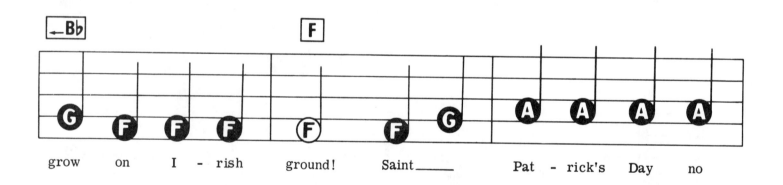

grow on I - rish ground! Saint___ Pat - rick's Day no

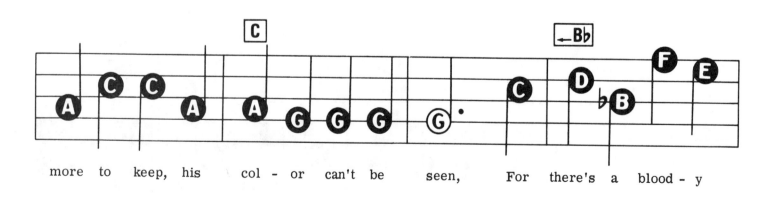

more to keep, his col - or can't be seen, For there's a blood - y

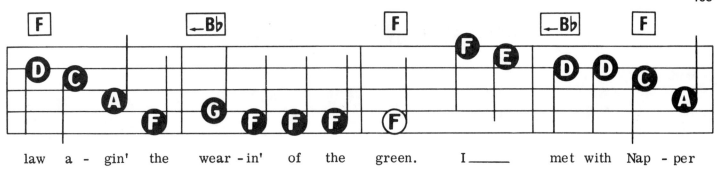

law a - gin' the wear - in' of the green. I ____ met with Nap - per

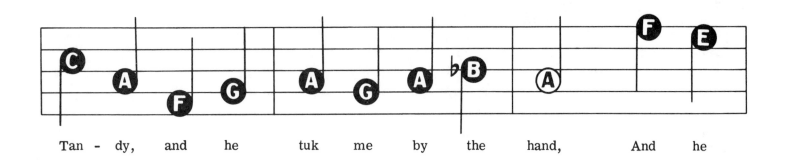

Tan - dy, and he tuk me by the hand, And he

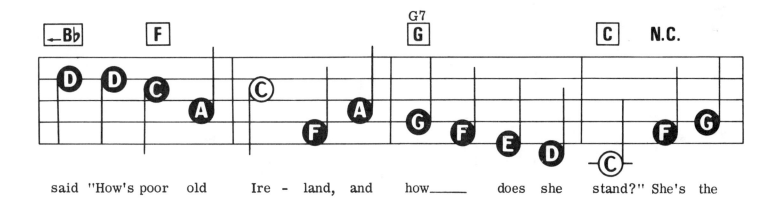

said "How's poor old Ire - land, and how ____ does she stand?" She's the

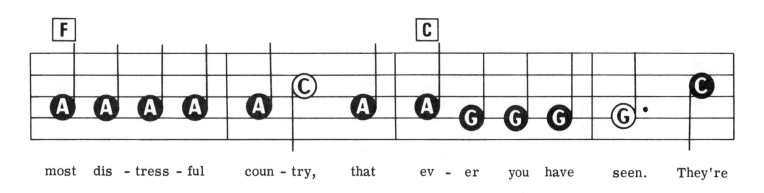

most dis - tress - ful coun - try, that ev - er you have seen. They're

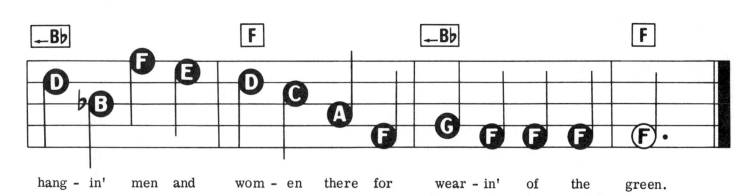

hang - in' men and wom - en there for wear - in' of the green.

Annie Laurie

Registration 9

Scottish

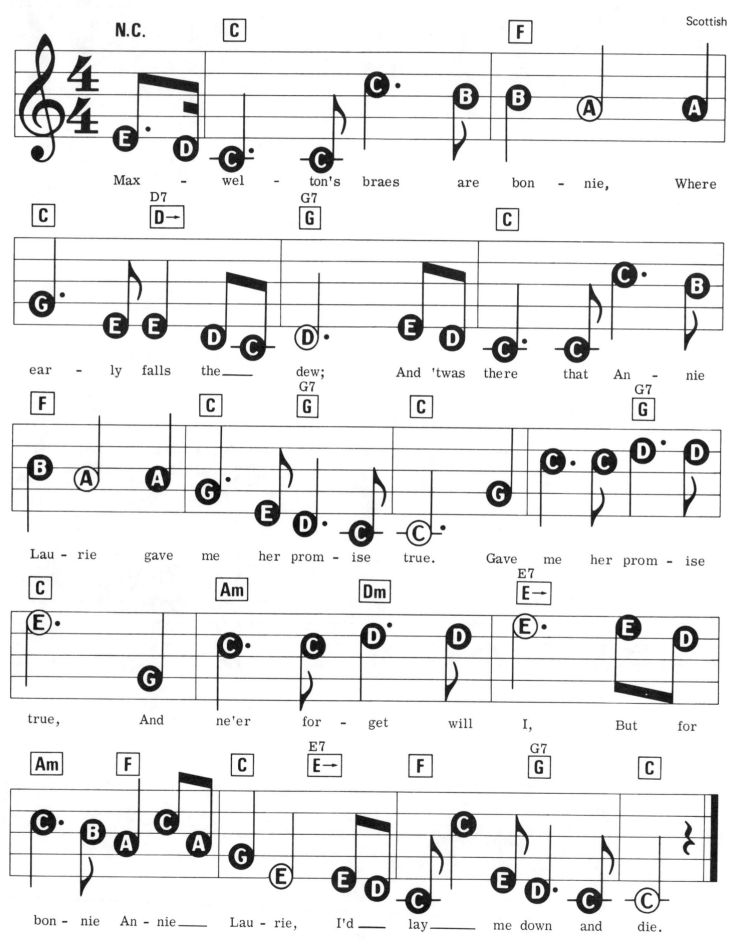

Max - wel - ton's braes are bon - nie, Where ear - ly falls the dew; And 'twas there that An - nie Lau - rie gave me her prom - ise true. Gave me her prom - ise true, And ne'er for - get will I, But for bon - nie An - nie Lau - rie, I'd lay me down and die.

Banana Boat

Registration 4

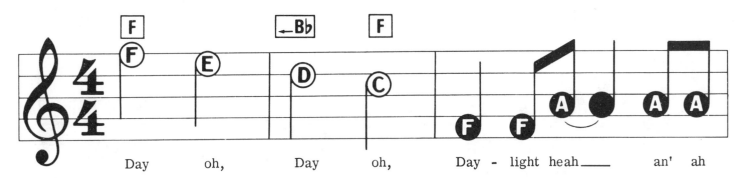

Day   oh,   Day   oh,   Day - light heah___   an' ah

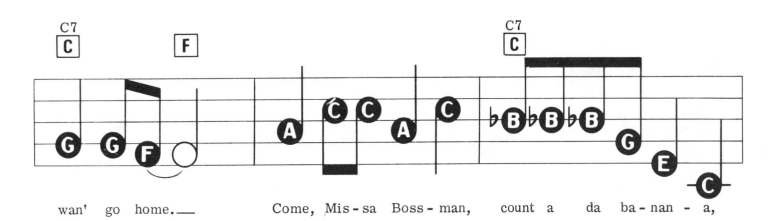

wan' go home.___   Come, Mis - sa Boss - man,   count a   da ba - nan - a,

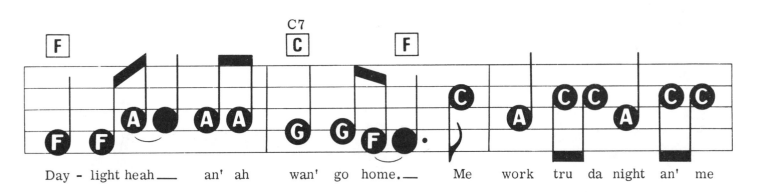

Day - light heah___   an' ah   wan' go home.___   Me   work   tru da night an' me

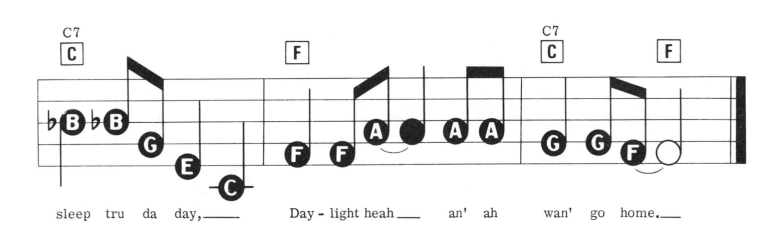

sleep tru da day,___   Day - light heah___   an' ah   wan' go home.___

Beautiful Isle Of Somewhere

Registration 5

Some-where the sun   is   shin - ing,   Some-where the song- birds
Some-where my love   lies   wait - ing,   Some-where my love   is

dwell.____ Hush then, thy sad   re - pin - ing,   God lives and all____ is   well.____
true.____ There'll be   no hes - i - ta - ting,   Once I am   safe____ with   you.____

Some - where,   Some - where,   Beau -ti - ful   Isle____   of   Some - where.
Some - where,   Some - where,   Beau -ti - ful   Isle____   of   Some - where.

Lord of   the   true, Where we   live   a - new,   Beau -ti - ful   Isle____   of   Some-where.
We'll find   our   rest,   We'll be   heav - en   blest,   Beau -ti - ful   Isle____   of   Some-where.

Beautiful Sea

Registration 10

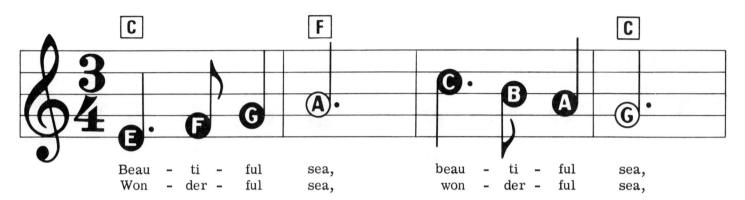

Beau – ti – ful sea, beau – ti – ful sea,
Won – der – ful sea, won – der – ful sea,

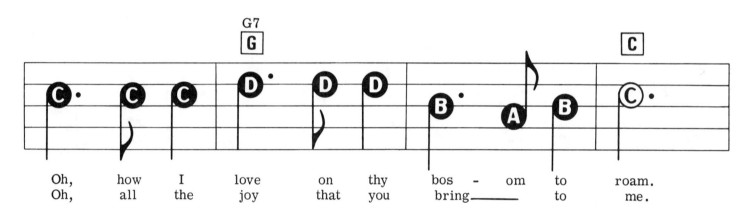

Oh, how I love on thy bos – om to roam.
Oh, all the love joy that you bring_____ to me.

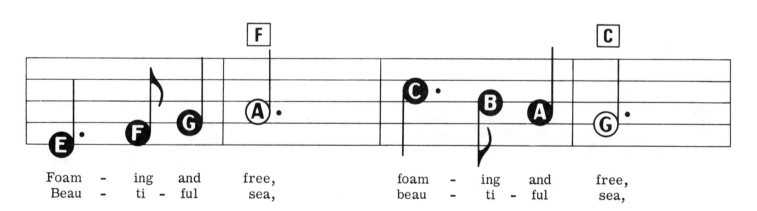

Foam – ing and free, foam – ing and free,
Beau – ti – ful sea, beau – ti – ful sea,

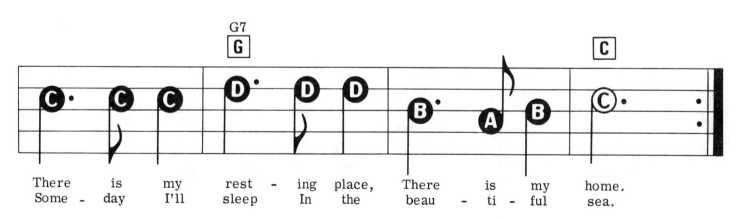

There is my rest – ing place, There is my home.
Some – day I'll sleep In the beau – ti – ful sea.

Crawdad Song

Registration 8

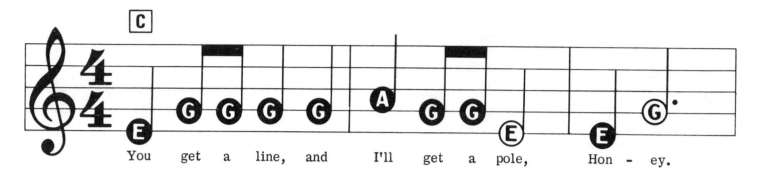

You get a line, and I'll get a pole, Hon - ey.

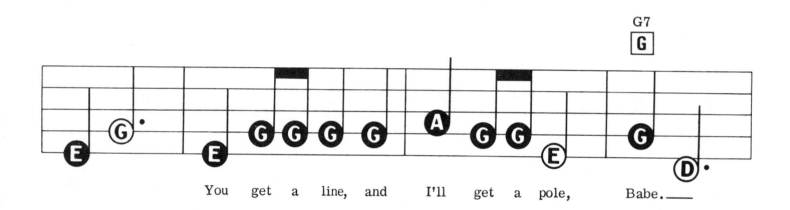

You get a line, and I'll get a pole, Babe.

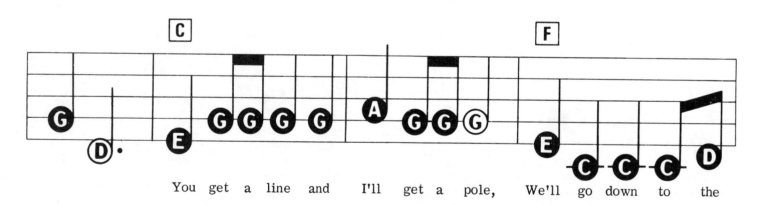

You get a line and I'll get a pole, We'll go down to the

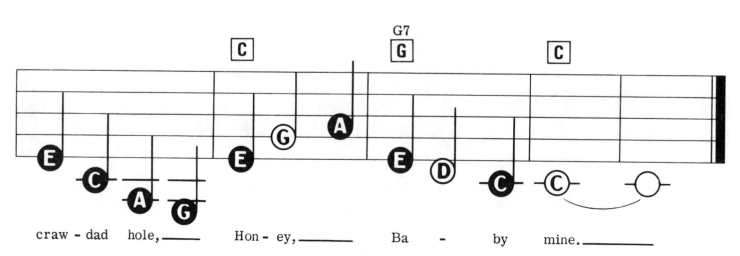

craw - dad hole, Hon - ey, Ba - by mine.

Immer Noch Ein Troepchen

Registration 5

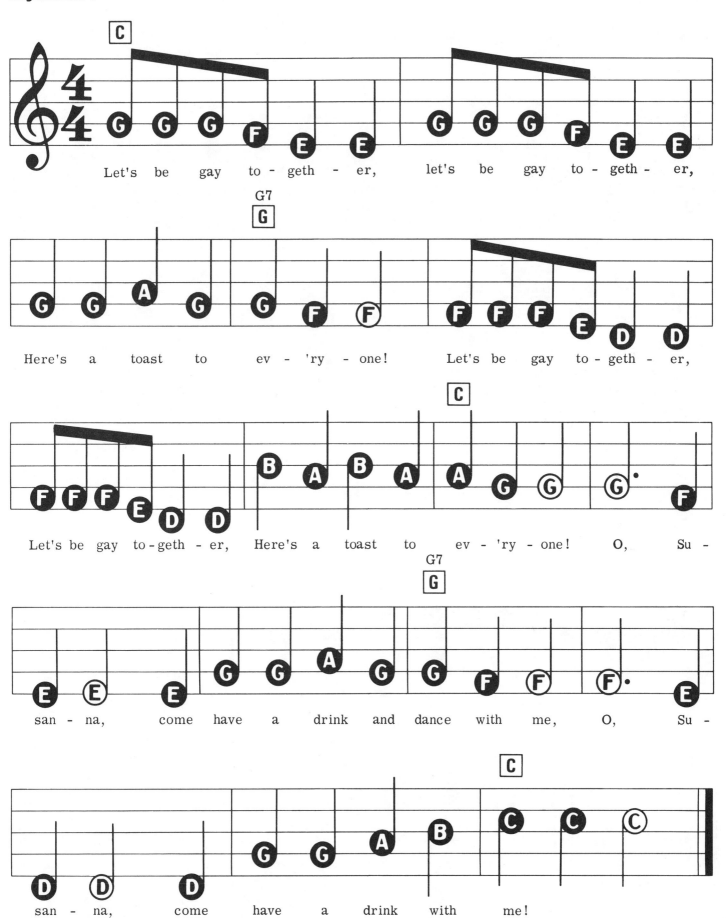

Let Him Go, Let Him Tarry

Registration 5

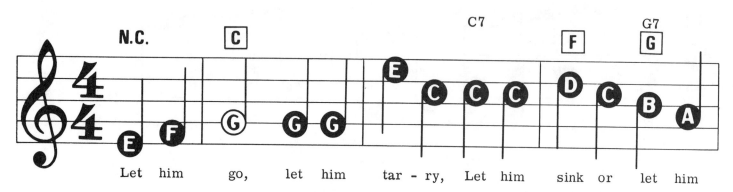

Let him go, let him tar - ry, Let him sink or let him

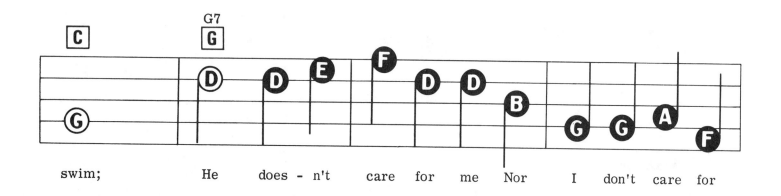

swim; He does - n't care for me Nor I don't care for

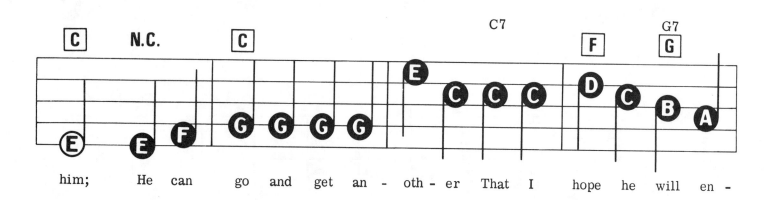

him; He can go and get an - oth - er That I hope he will en -

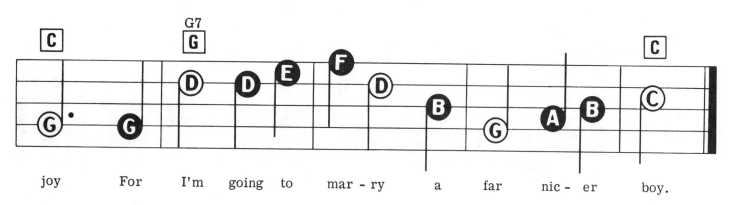

joy For I'm going to mar - ry a far nic - er boy.

Marianne

Registration 4

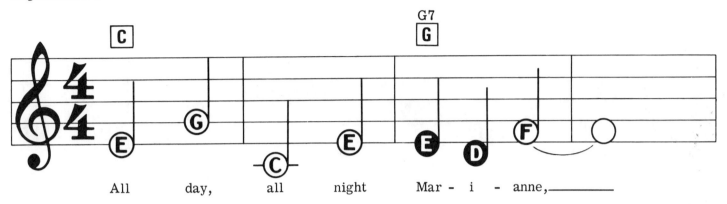

All day, all night Mar - i - anne,_____

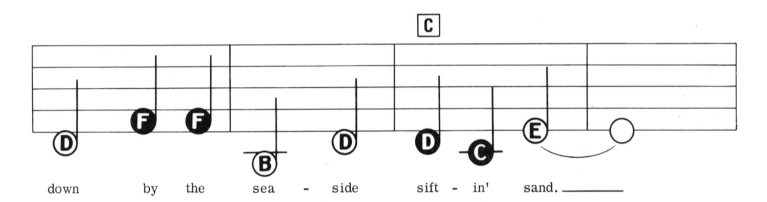

down by the sea - side sift - in' sand._____

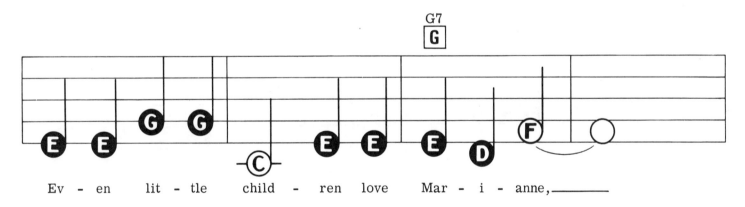

Ev - en lit - tle child - ren love Mar - i - anne,_____

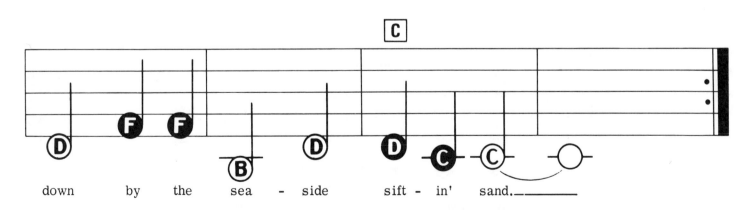

down by the sea - side sift - in' sand._____

Ring, Ring The Banjo

Registration 3

American

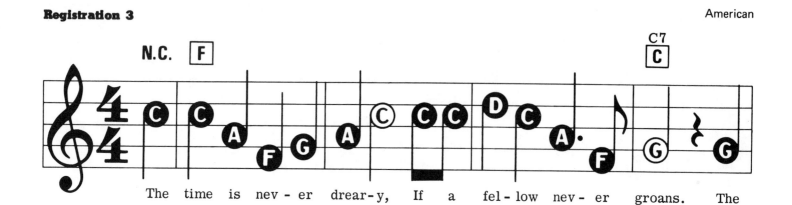

The time is nev - er drear-y, If a fel - low nev - er groans. The

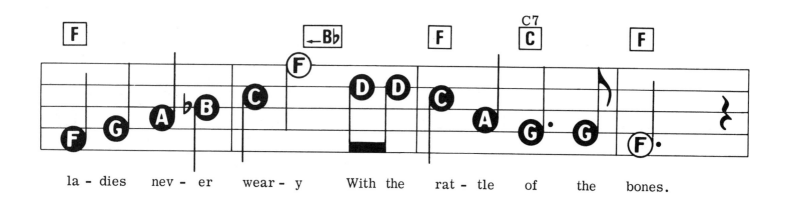

la - dies nev - er wear - y With the rat - tle of the bones.

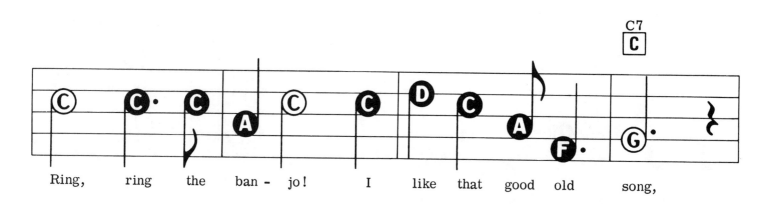

Ring, ring the ban - jo! I like that good old song,

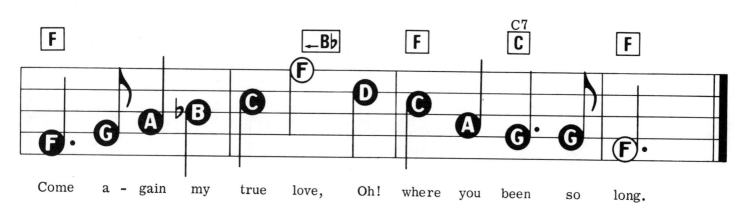

Come a - gain my true love, Oh! where you been so long.

Ballet Music

Franz Schubert

Registration 3

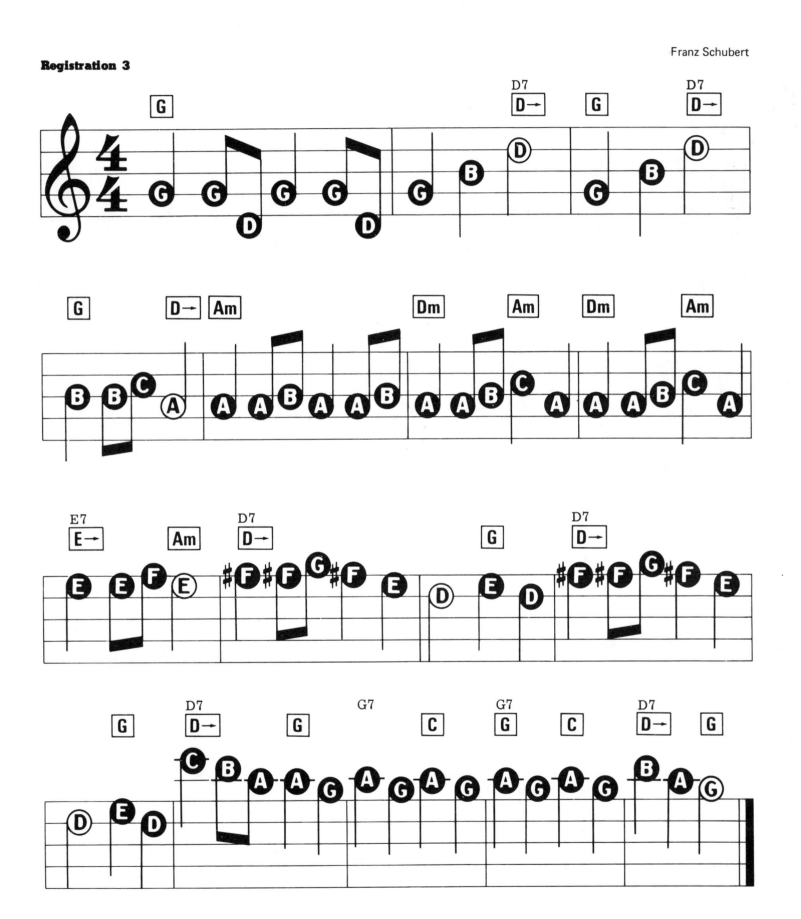

Andante Cantabile

Registration 6

Peter I. Tschaikowsky

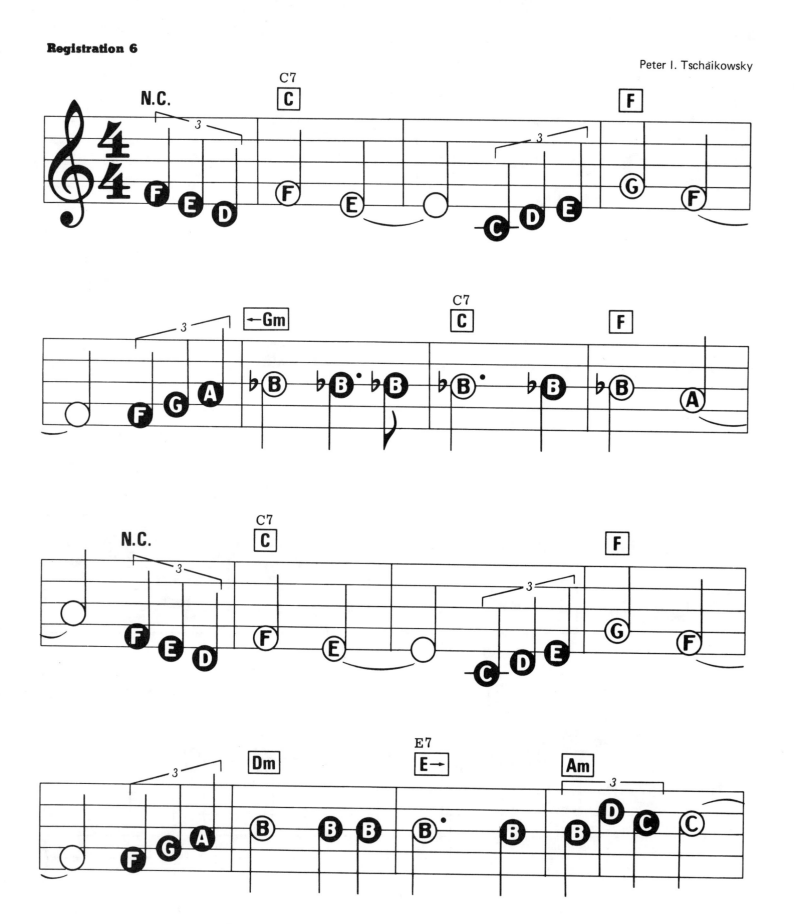

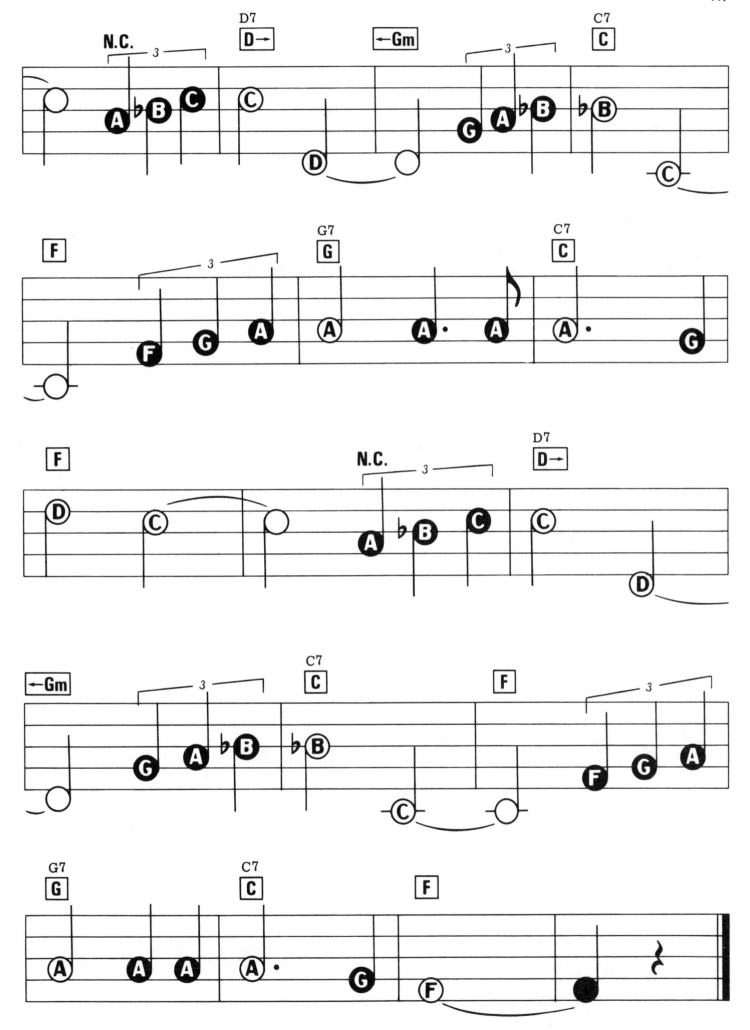

Artist Life

Registration 3

Johann Strauss

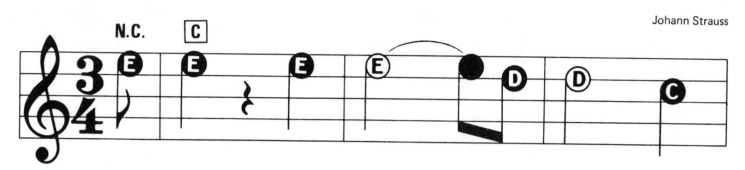

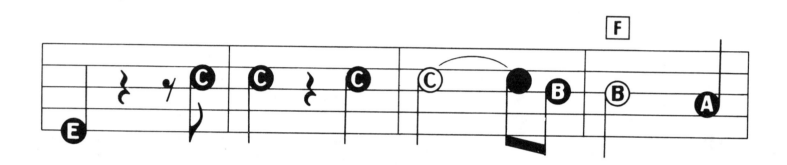

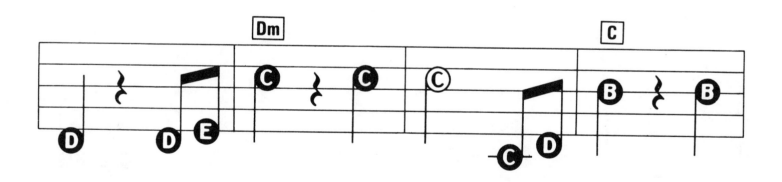

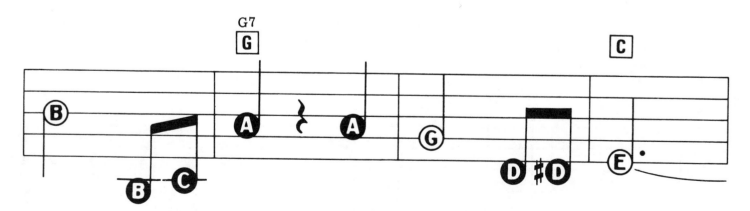

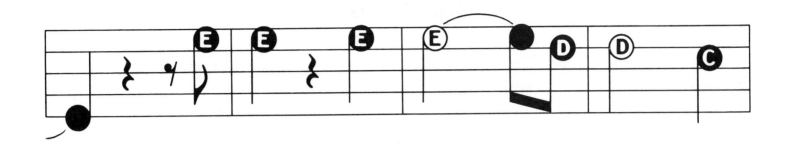

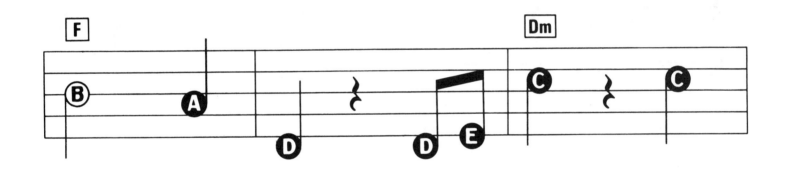

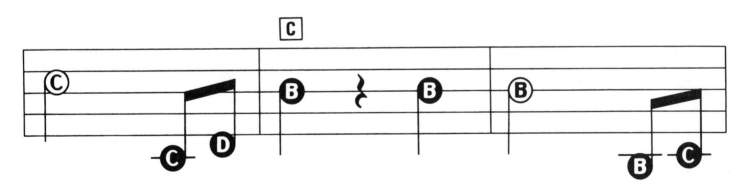

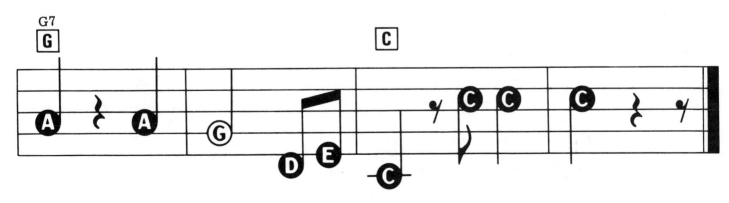

Brahm's Lullaby

Registration 10

Johannes Brahms

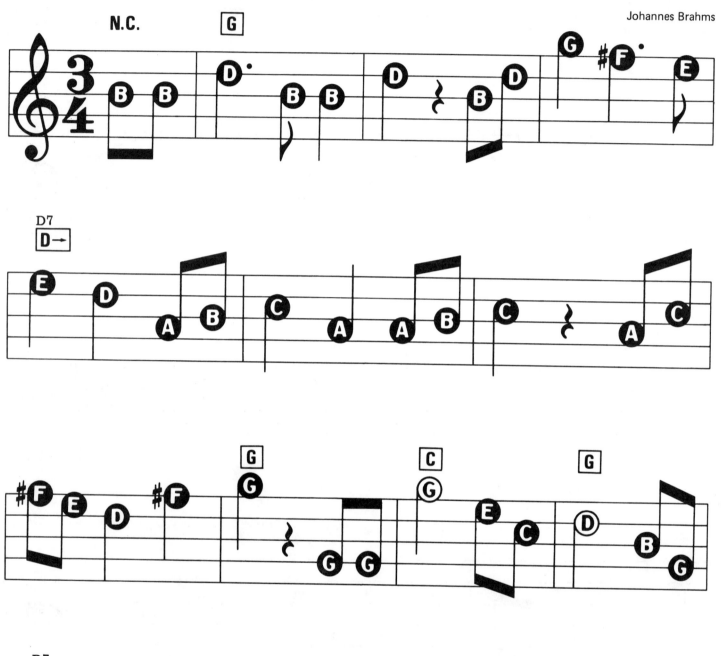

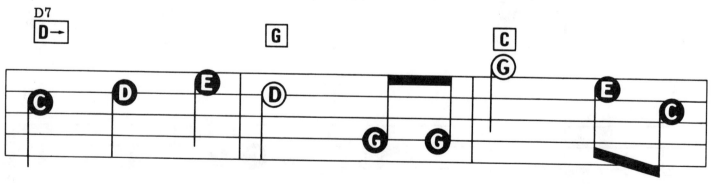

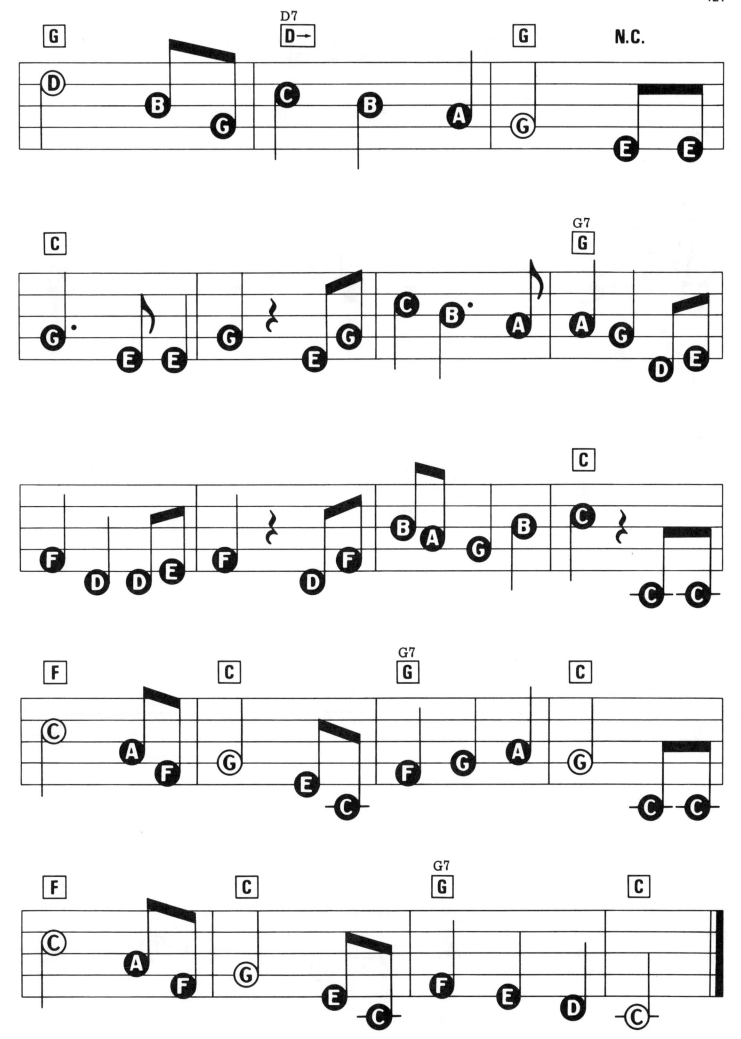

121

Capriccio Italien

Registration 5

Peter I. Tschaikowsky

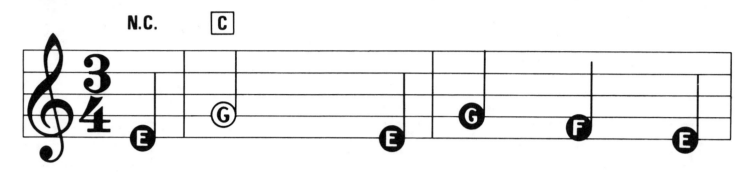

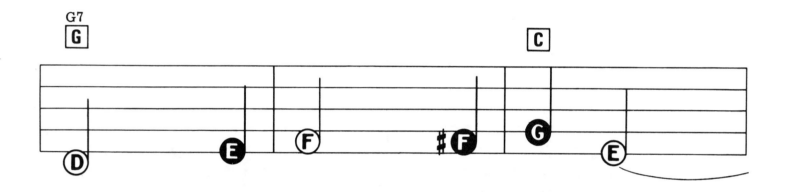

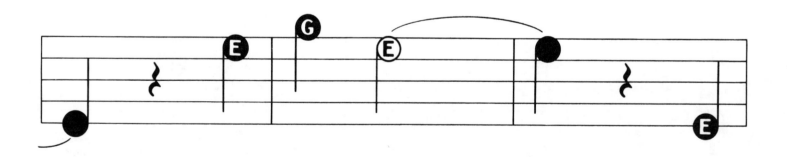

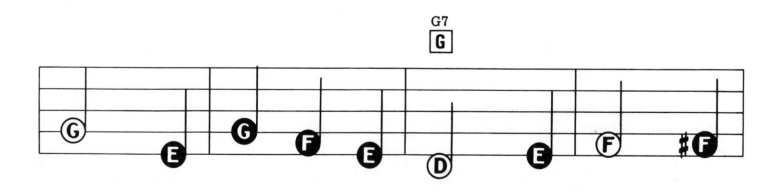

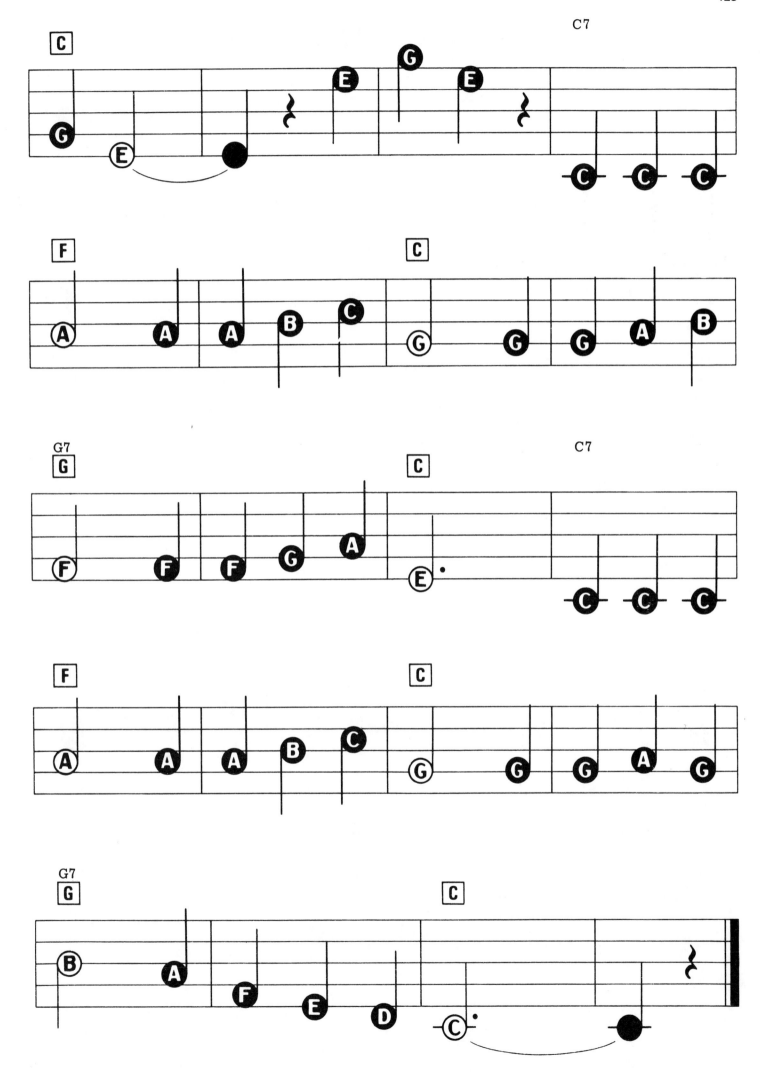

Chopin's Nocturne

Registration 6

Chopin

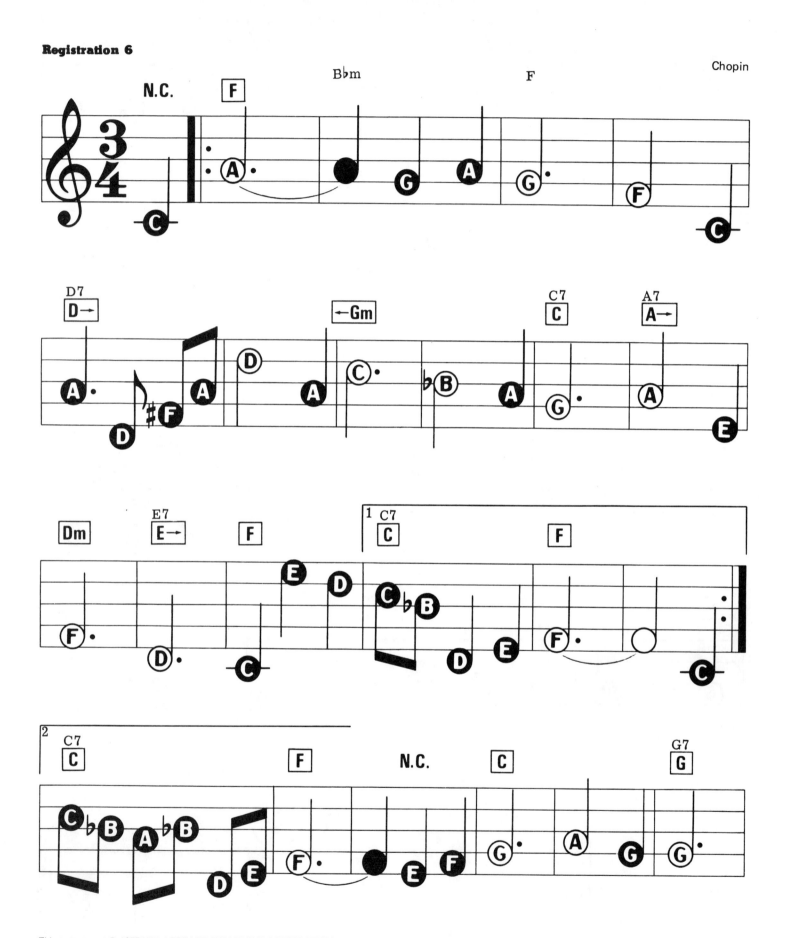

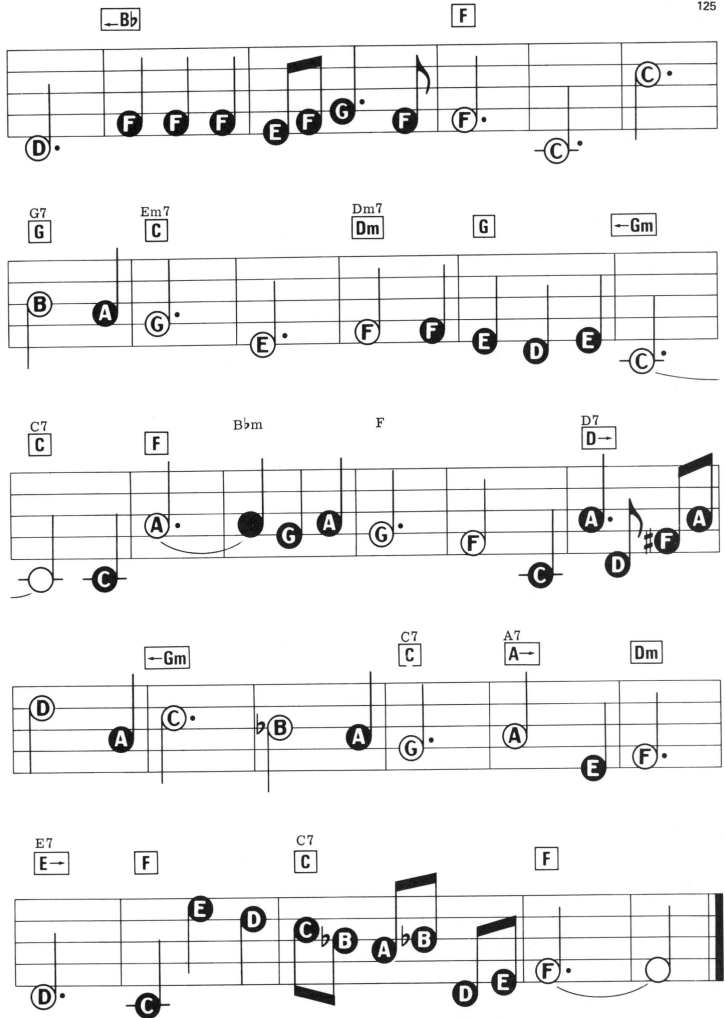

Fantasie Impromptu

Registration 1

Frederic Chopin

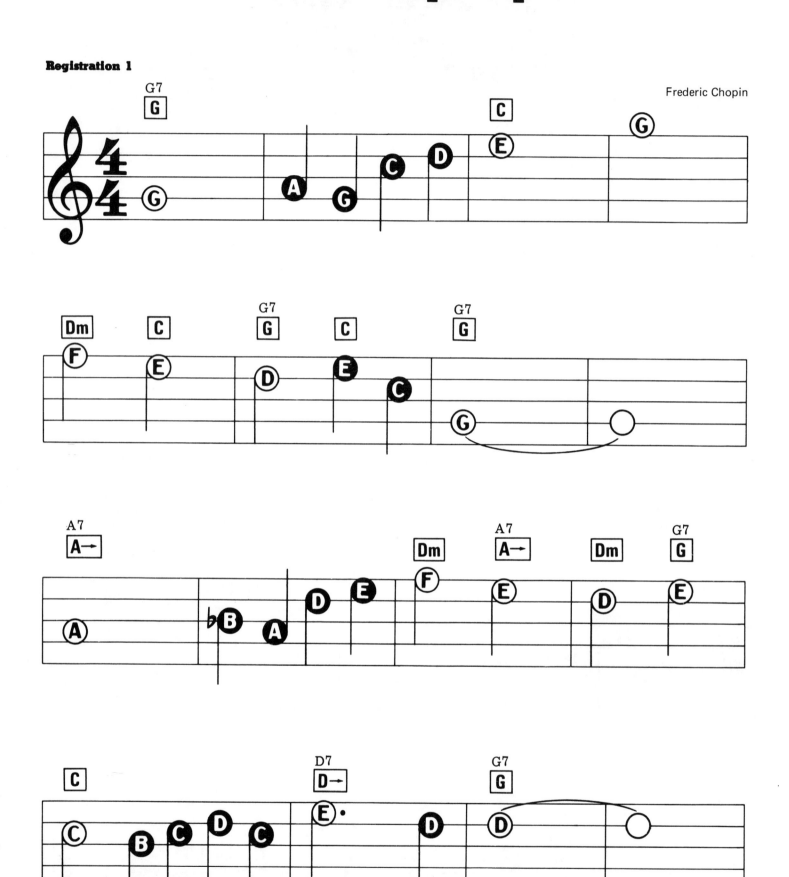

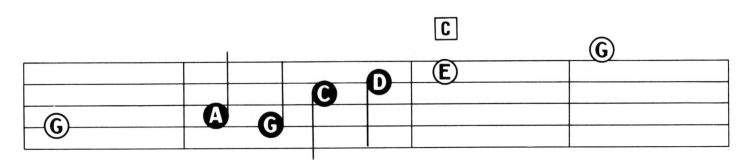

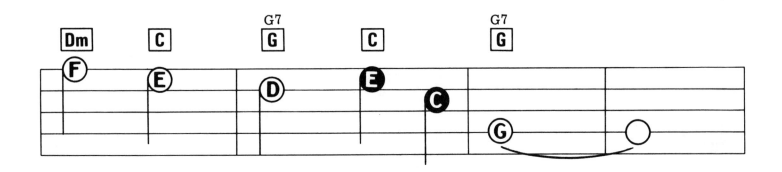

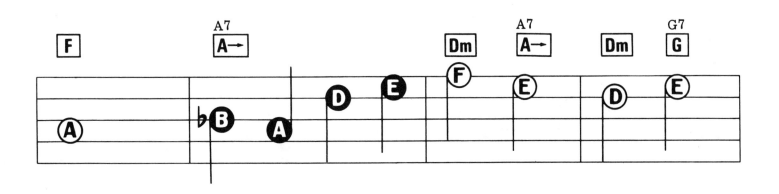

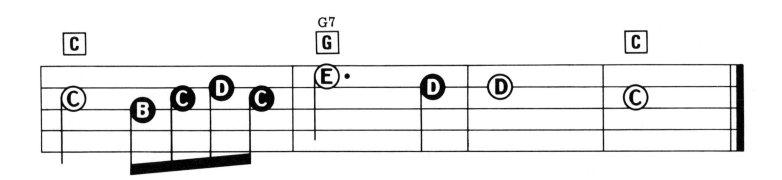

Humoresque

Registration 5

Anton Dvorak

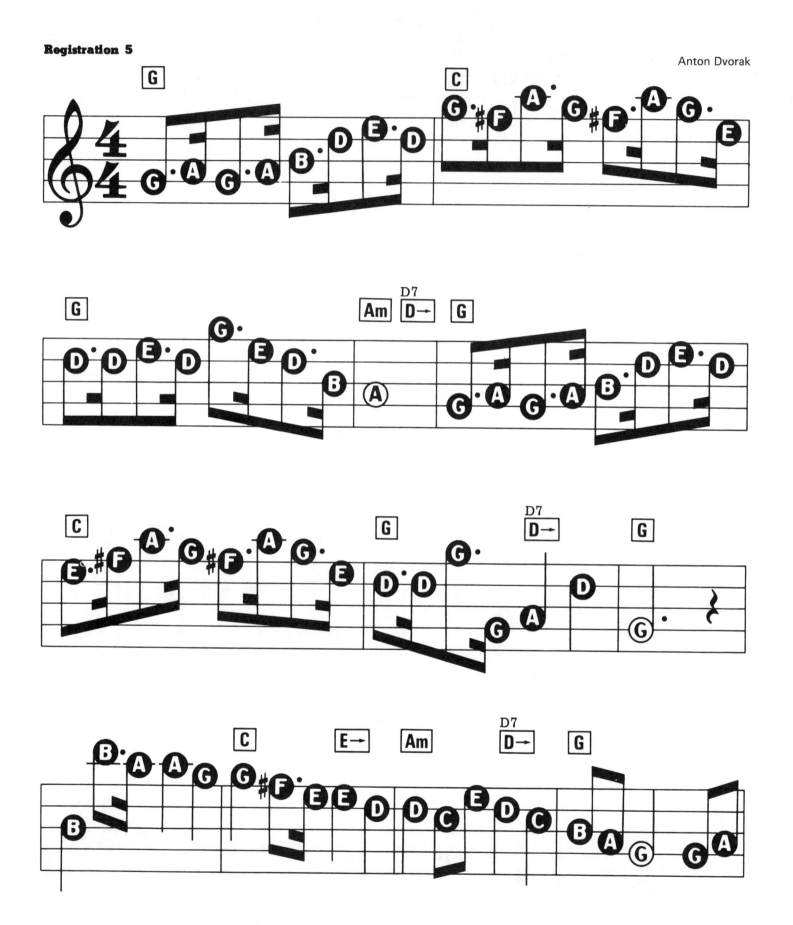

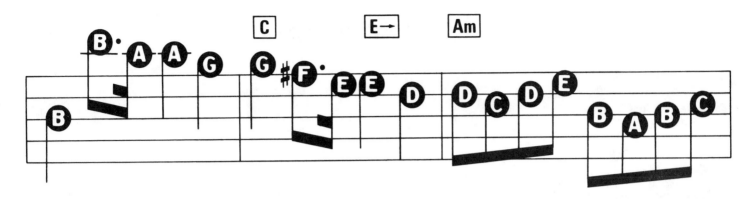

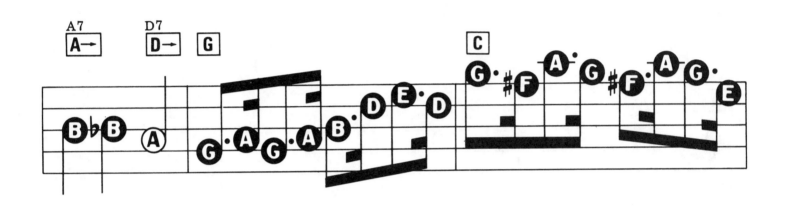

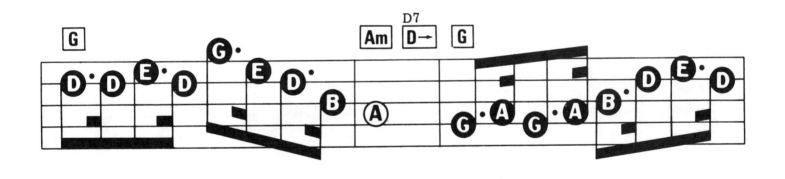

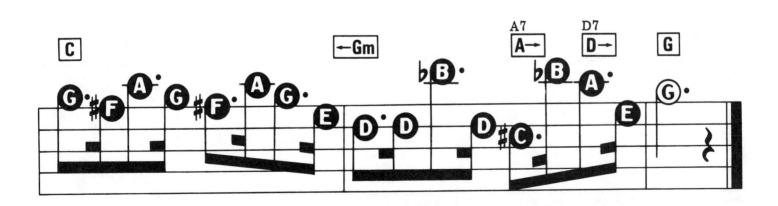

Liebestraum

Registration 1

Franz Liszt

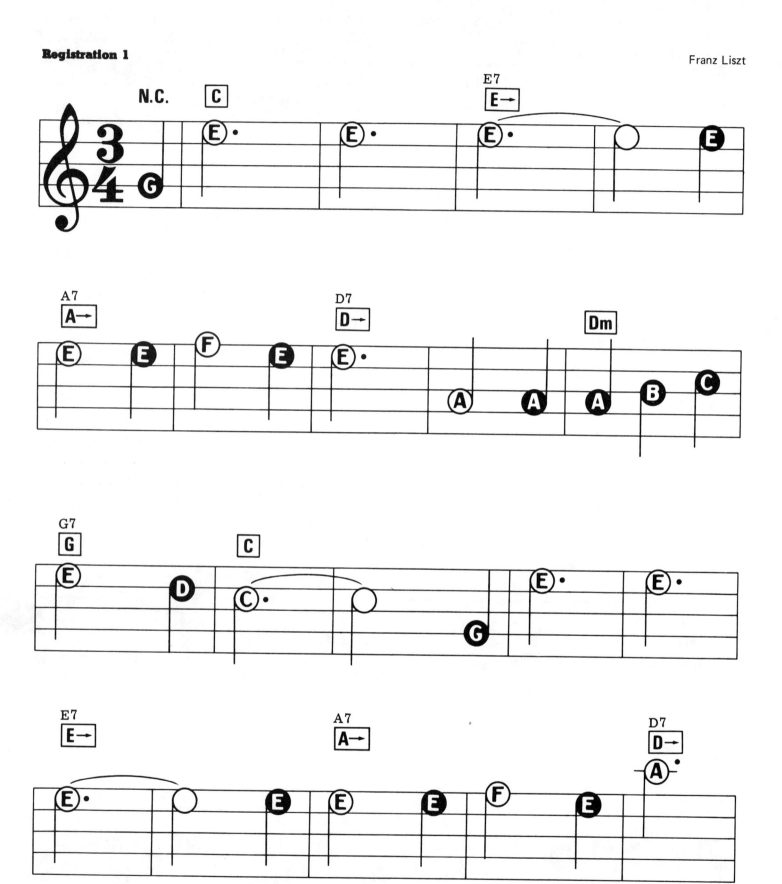

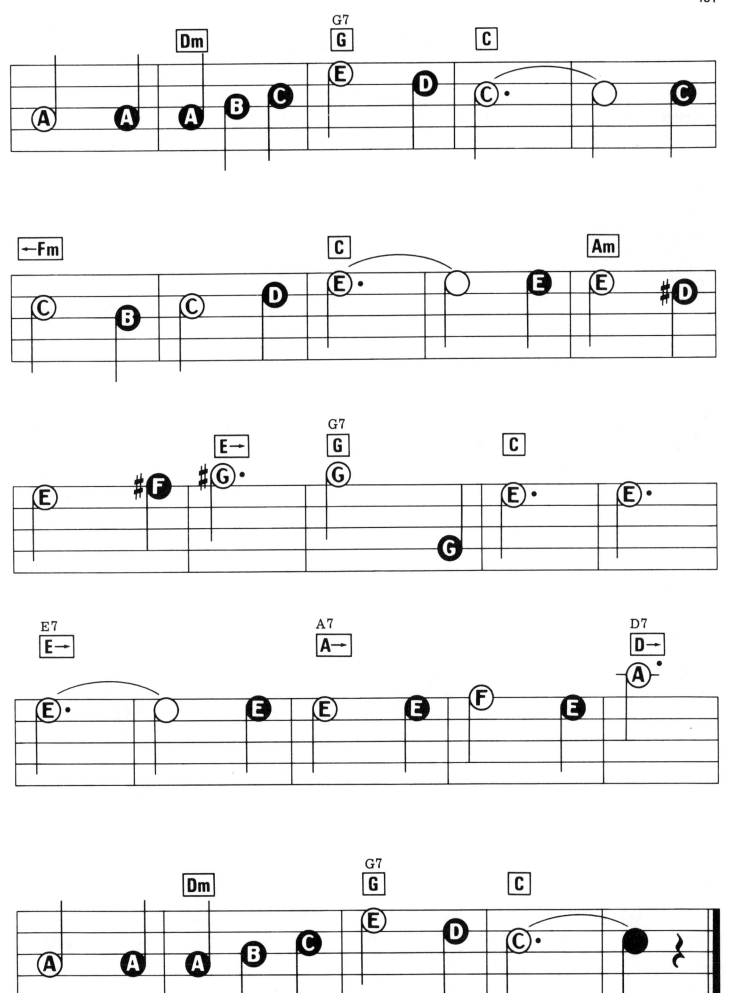

131

Mattinata

Registration 4

Ruggiero Leoncavallo

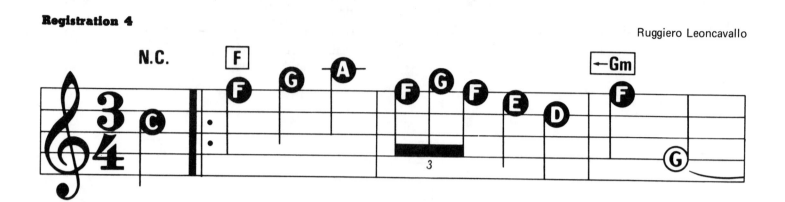

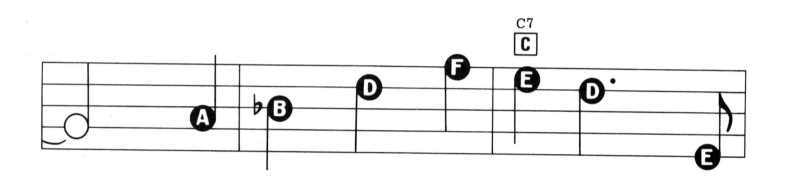

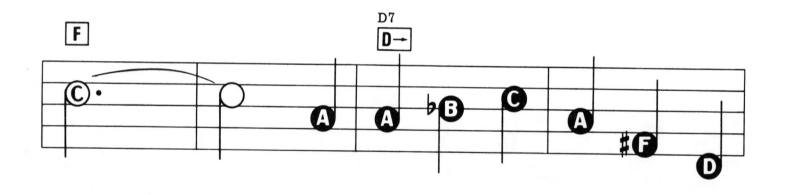

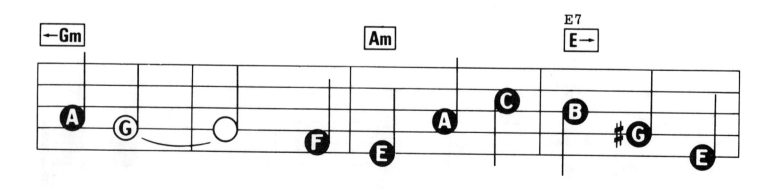

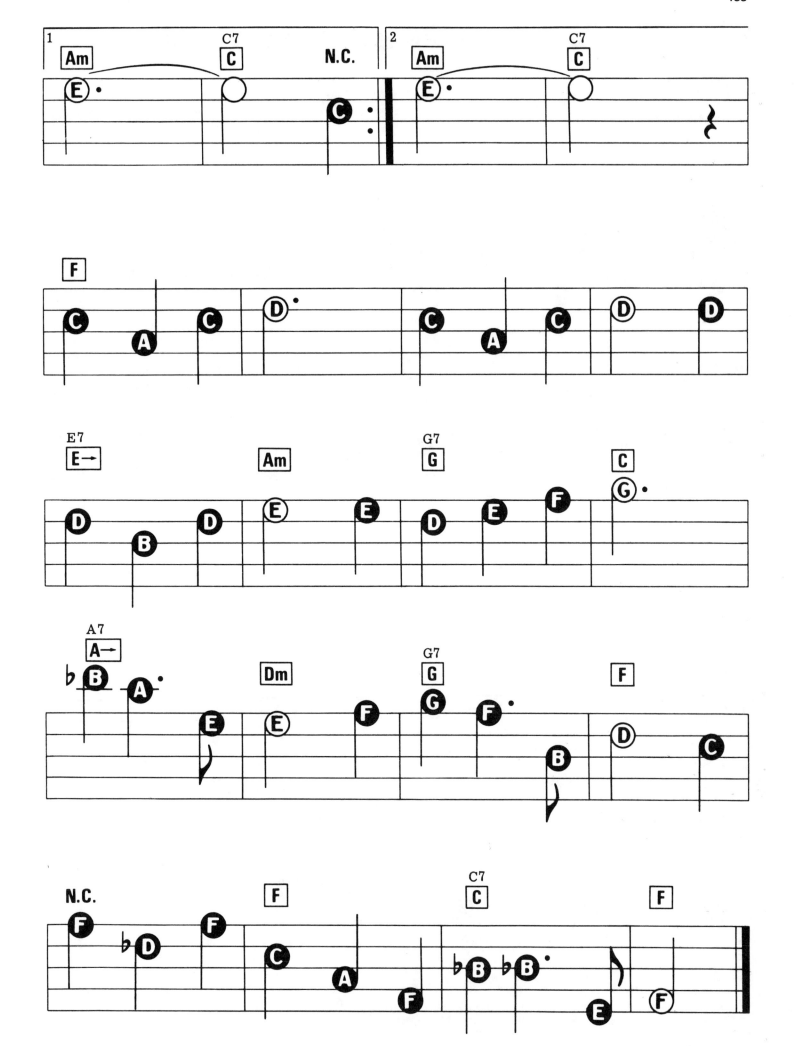

Poet And Peasant Overture

Registration 9

Franz Von Suppe

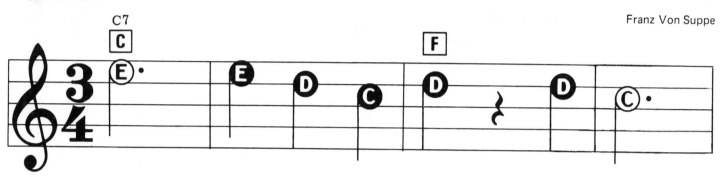

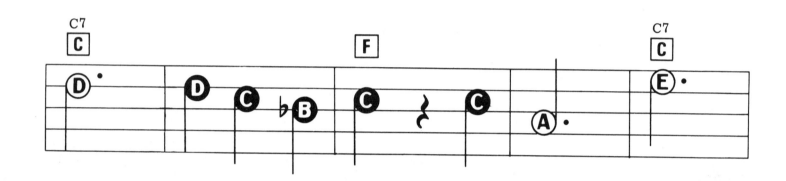

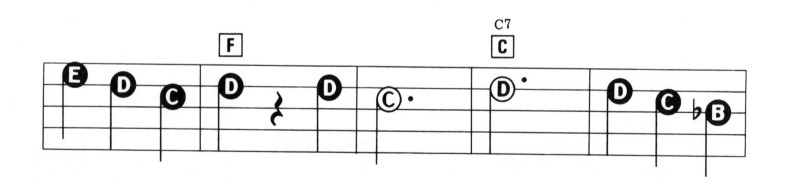

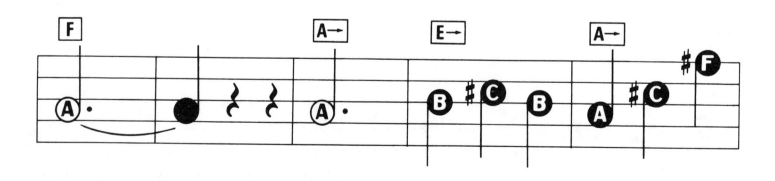

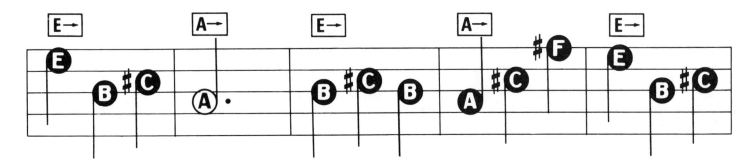

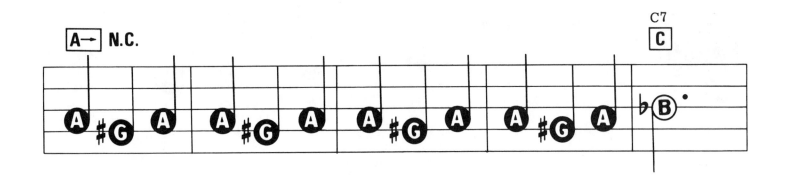

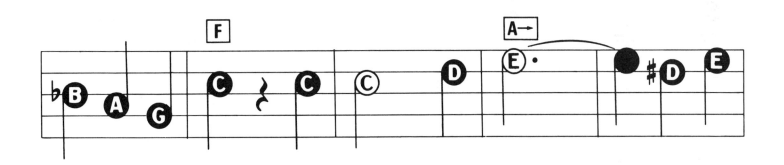

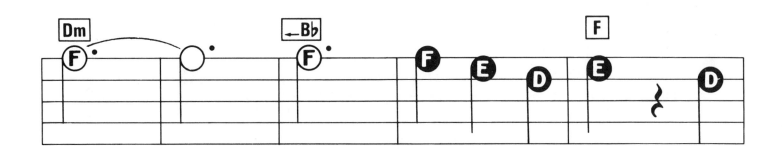

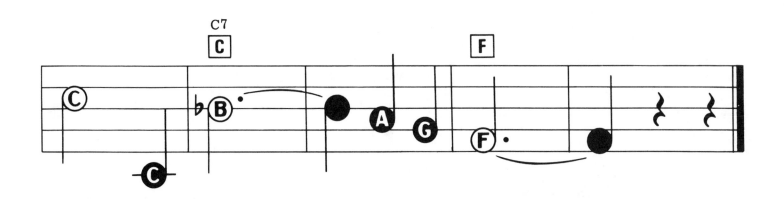

Reverie

Registration 8

Achille Claude Debussy

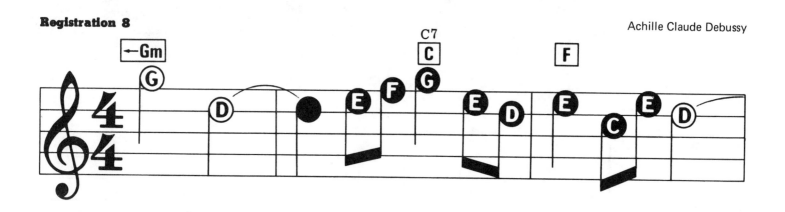

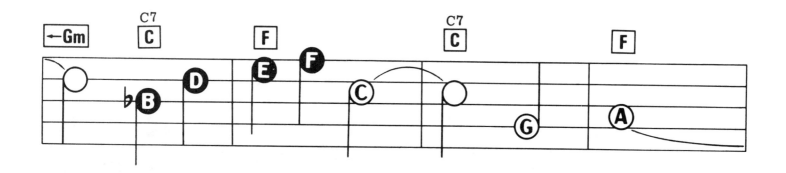

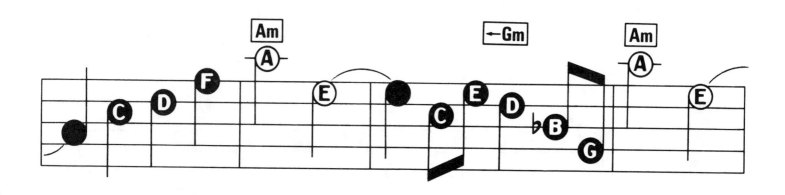

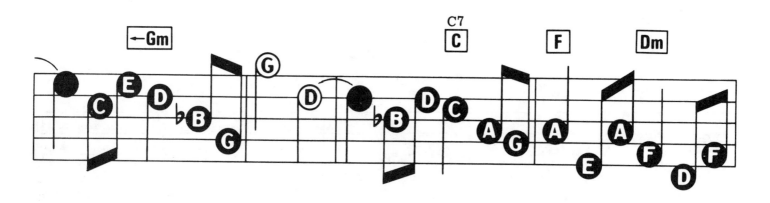

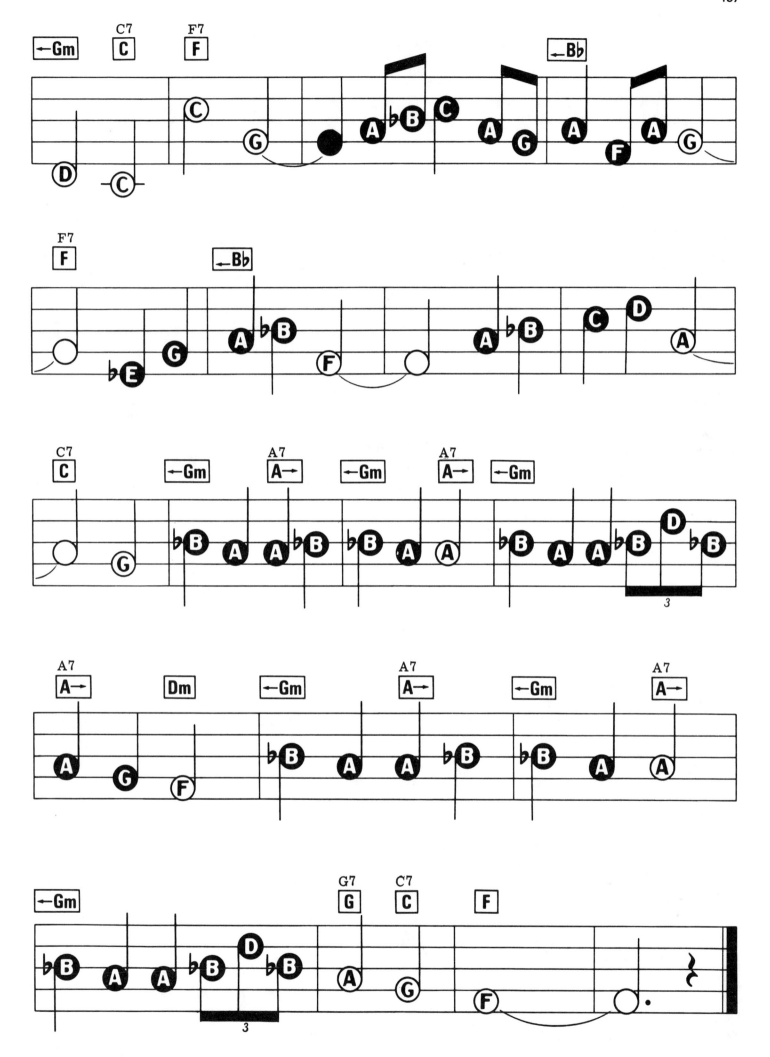

Romeo And Juliet

Registration 3

Charles Gounod

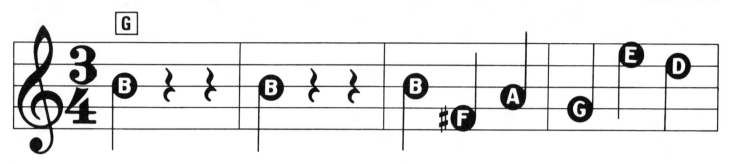

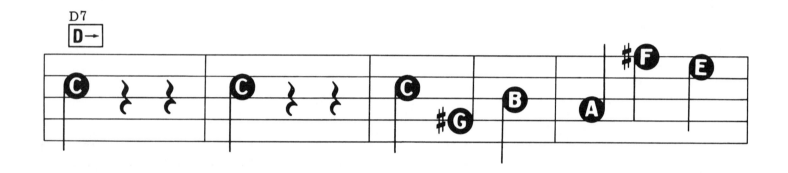

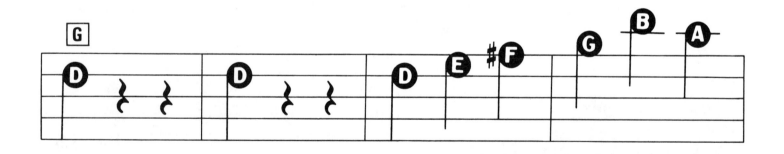

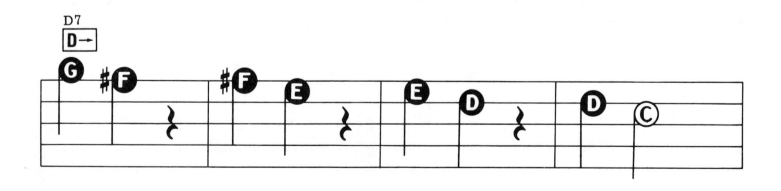

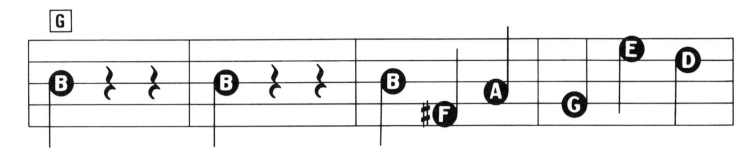

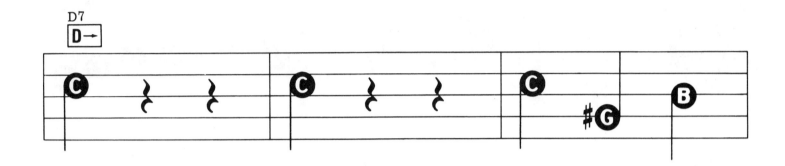

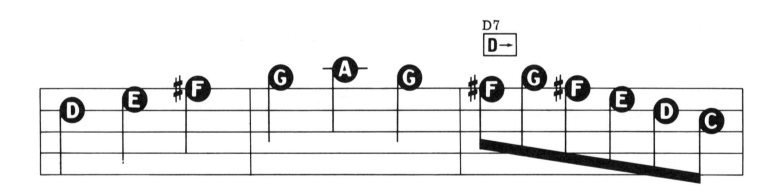

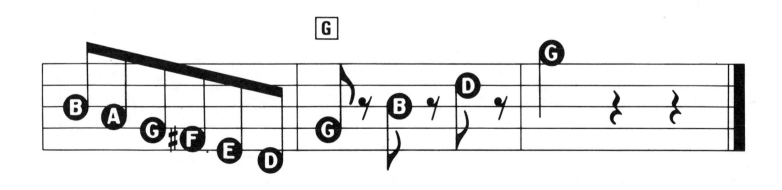

Serenade

Franz Schubert

Registration 4

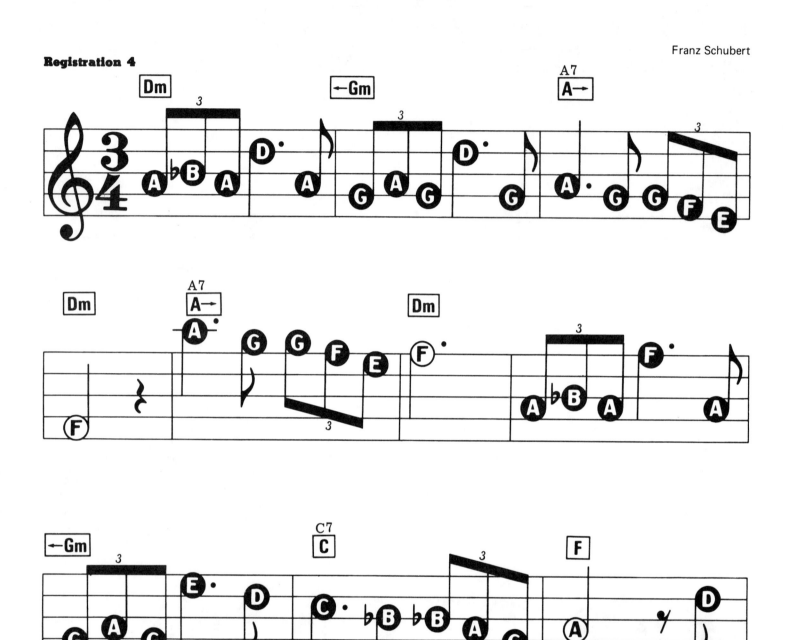

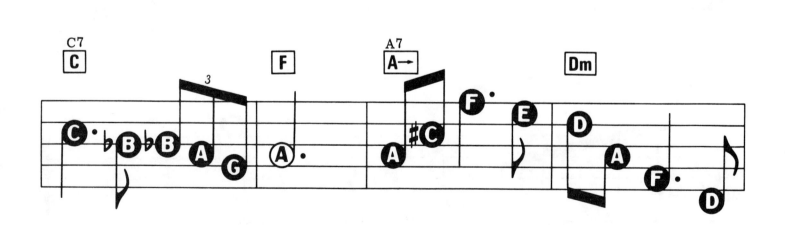

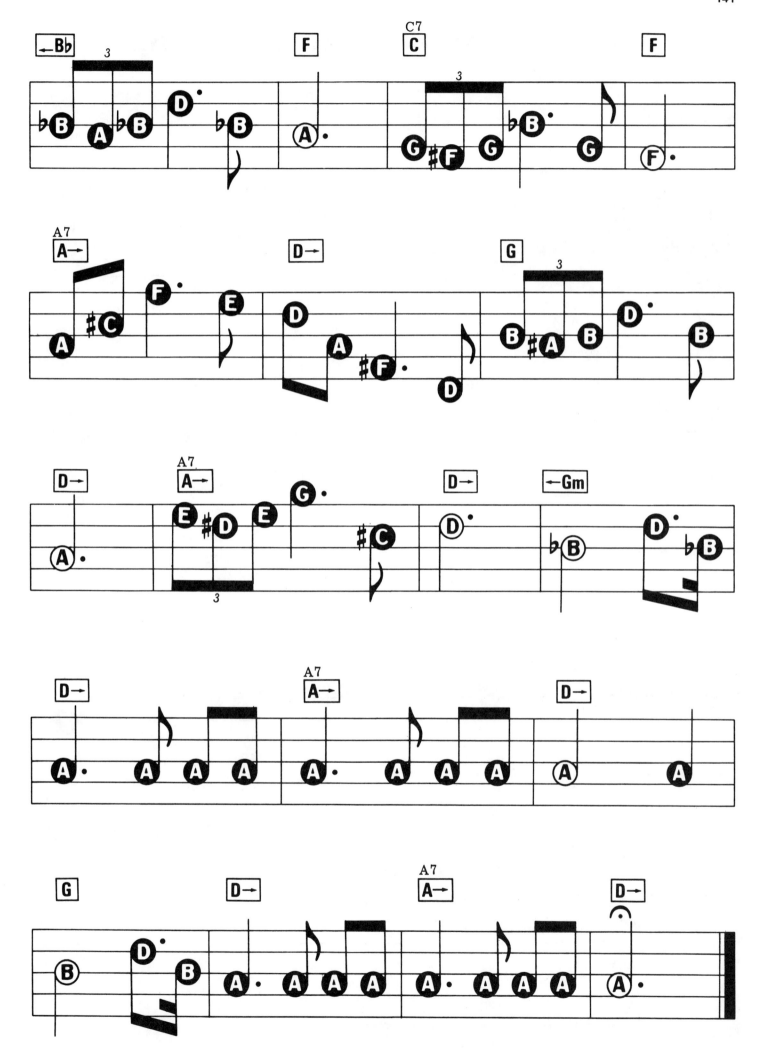

Tales From The Vienna Woods

Registration 4

Johann Strauss

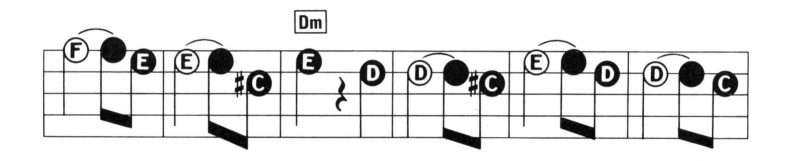

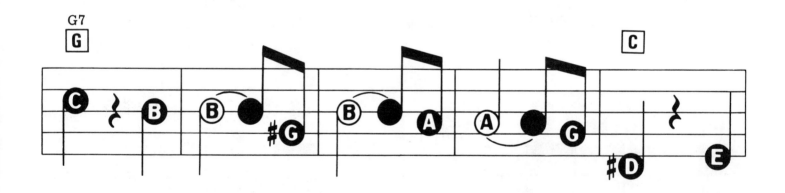

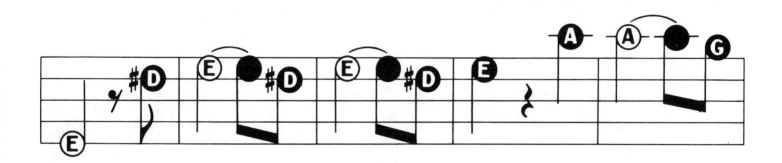

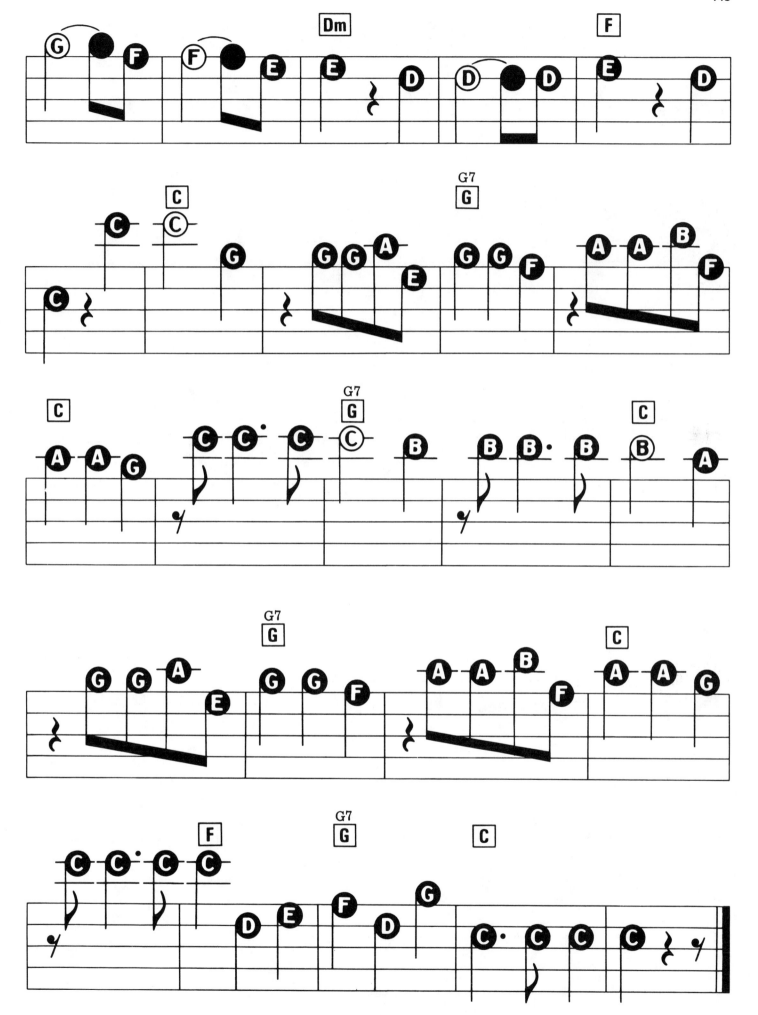

Valse Bleue

Registration 3

Alfred Margis

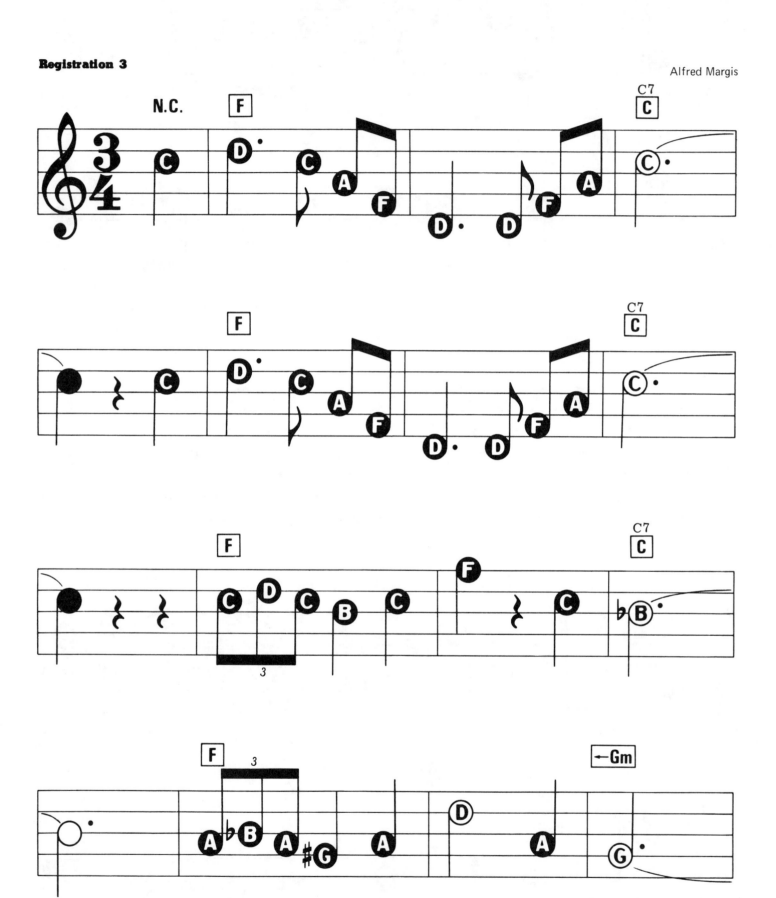

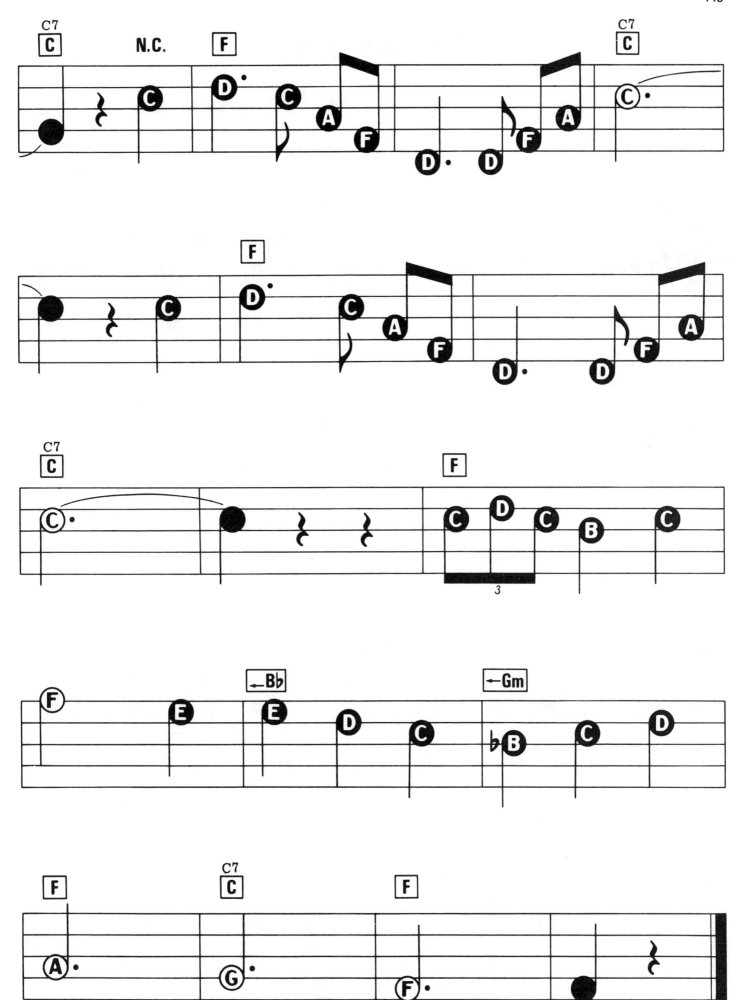

Vienna Life

Johann Strauss

Registration 5

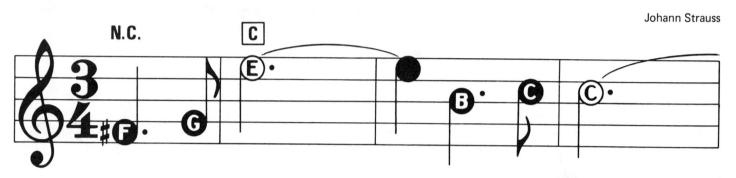

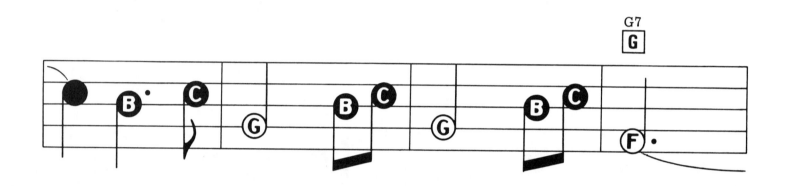

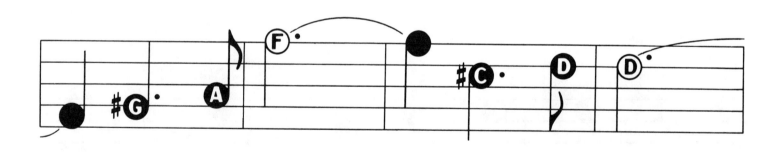

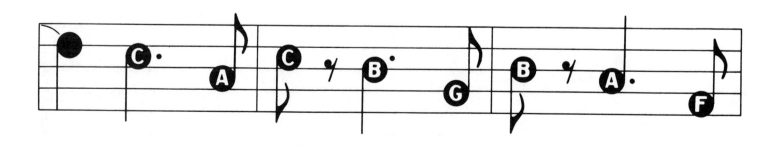

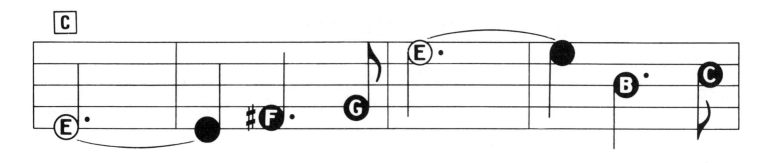

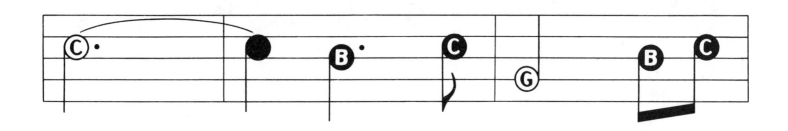

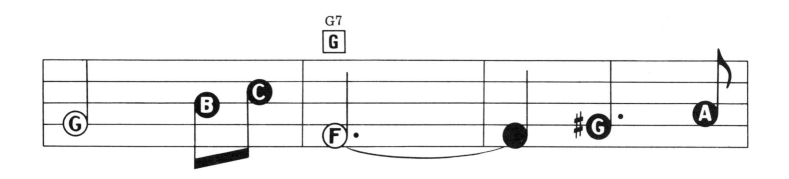

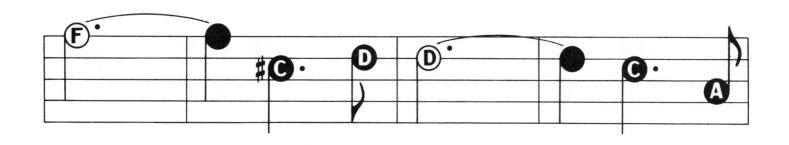

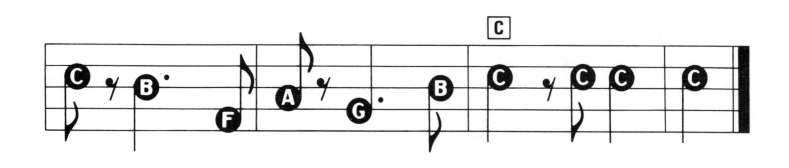

Barcarolle

Registration 4

Offenbach

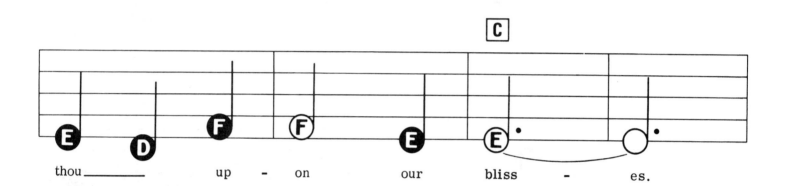

Love - ly night, O night   of love, smile

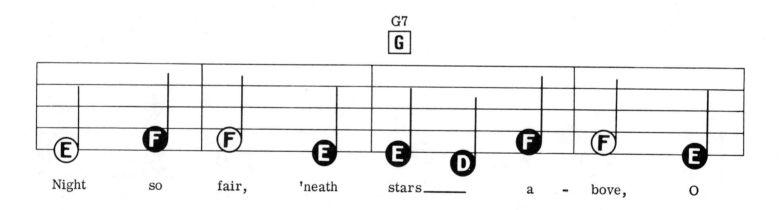

thou   up - on our bliss - es.

Night so fair, 'neath stars   a - bove, O

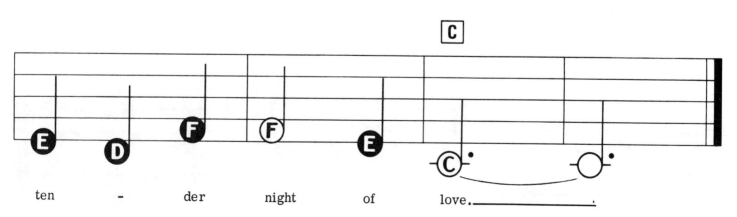

ten - der night of love.

Dance Of The Hours

A. Ponchielli

Registration 5

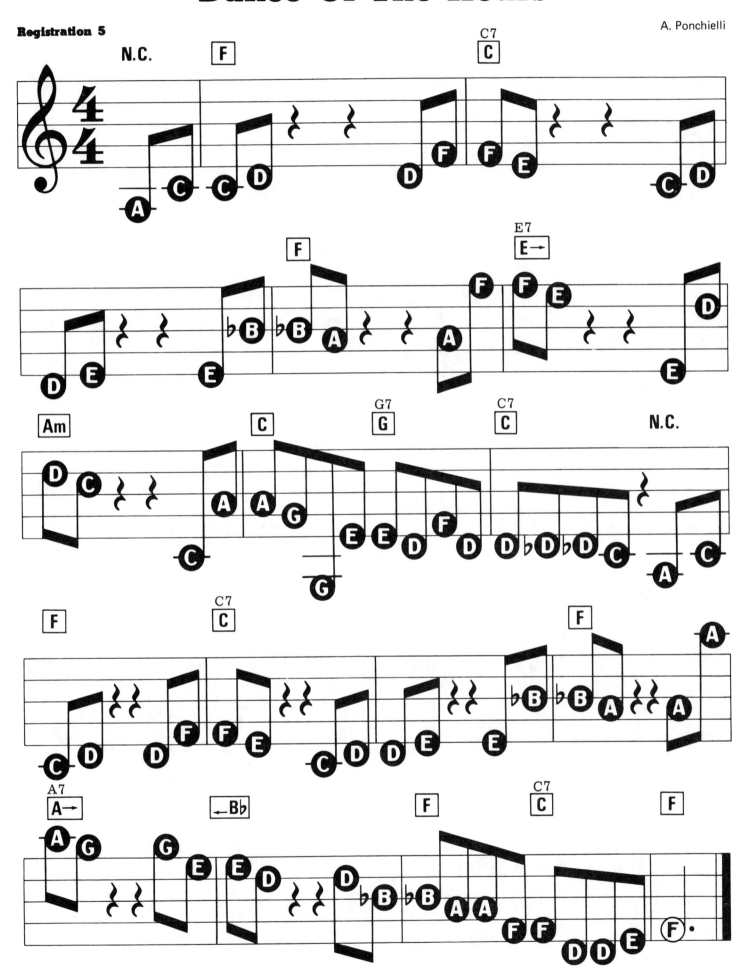

Fur Elise

Registration 8

Ludvig von Beethoven

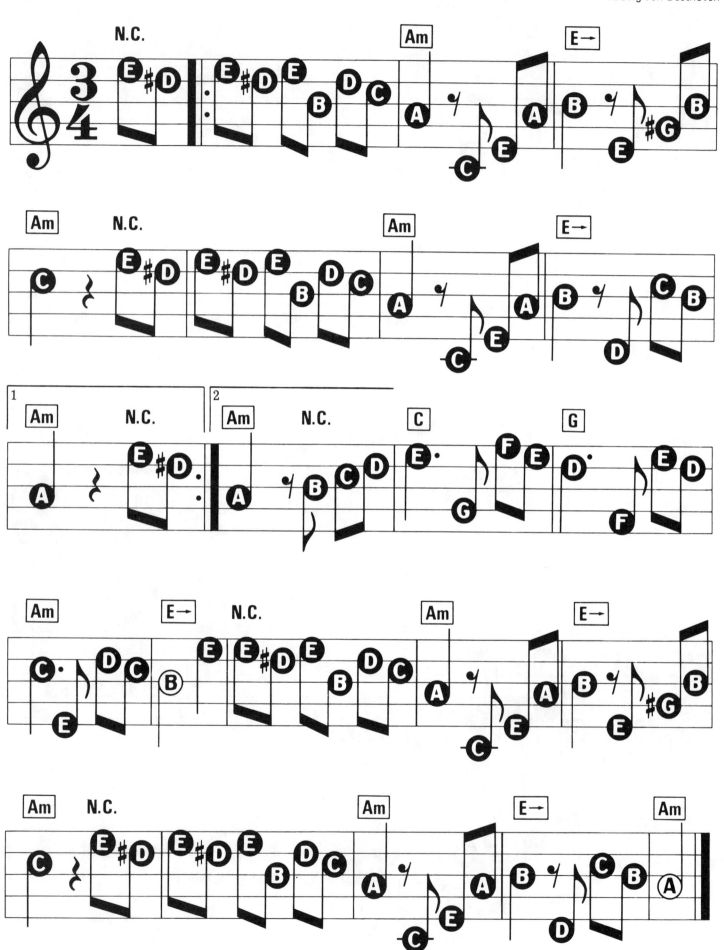

Il Bacio

Registration 5

Luigi Arditi

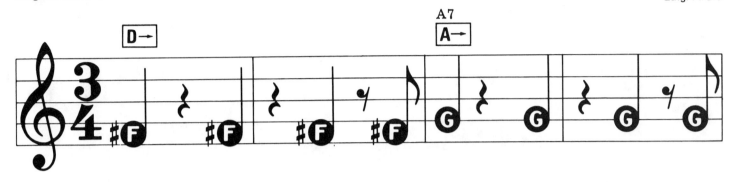

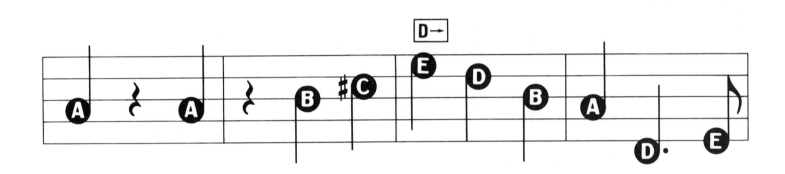

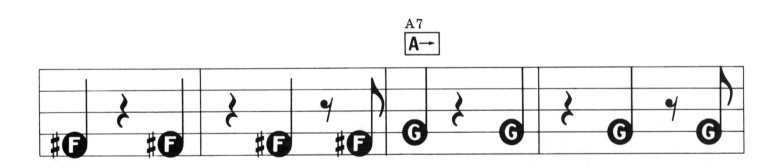

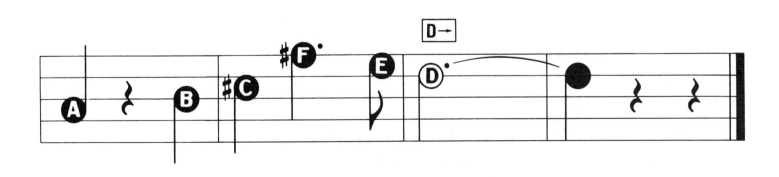

Prelude

Registration 8

Chopin

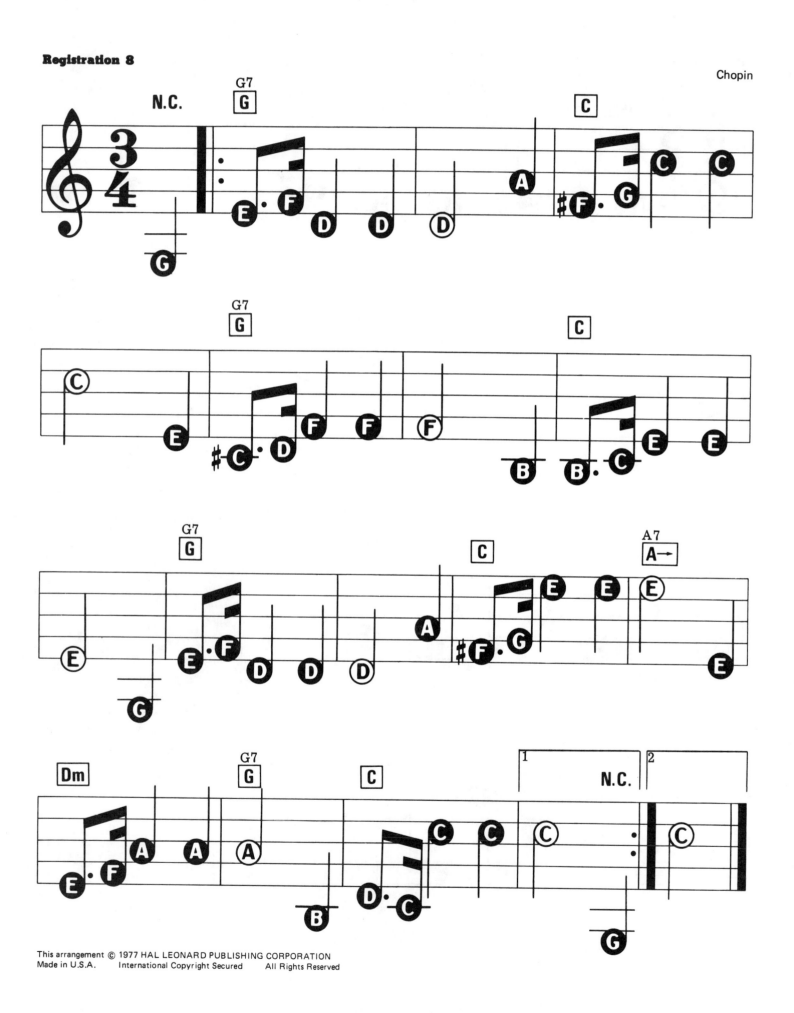

Theme From Polovetzian Dance

Registration 9

Alexander Borodin

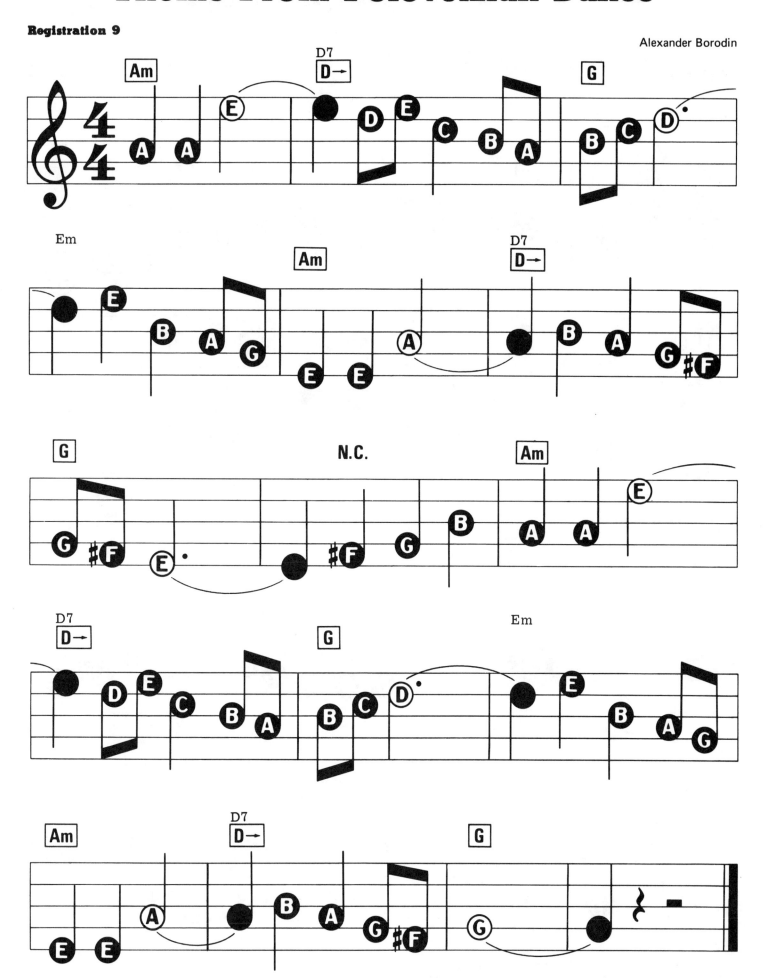

Theme From The Surprise Symphony

Registration 5

Jasef Haydn

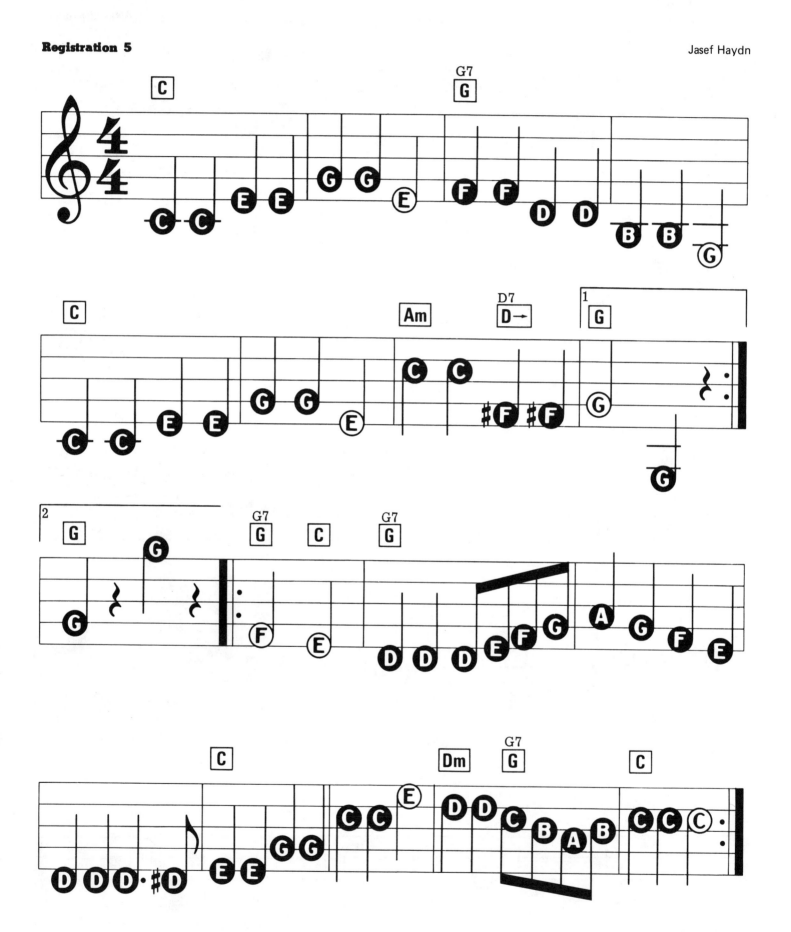

Unfinished Symphony

Registration 3

Franz Schubert

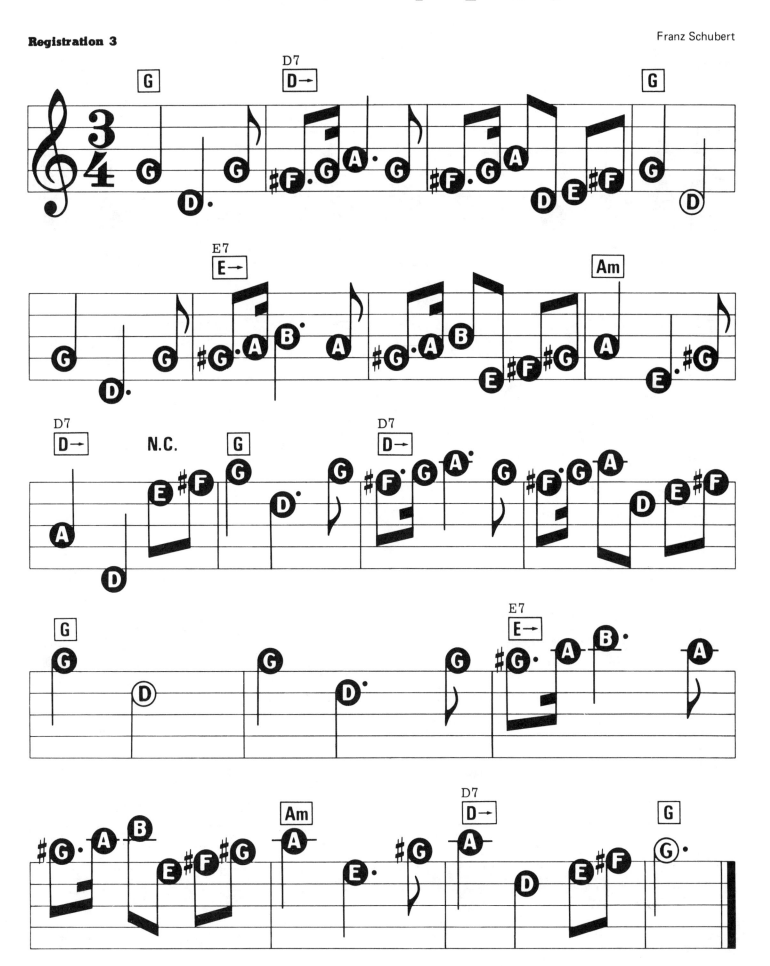

All Through The Night

Registration 6

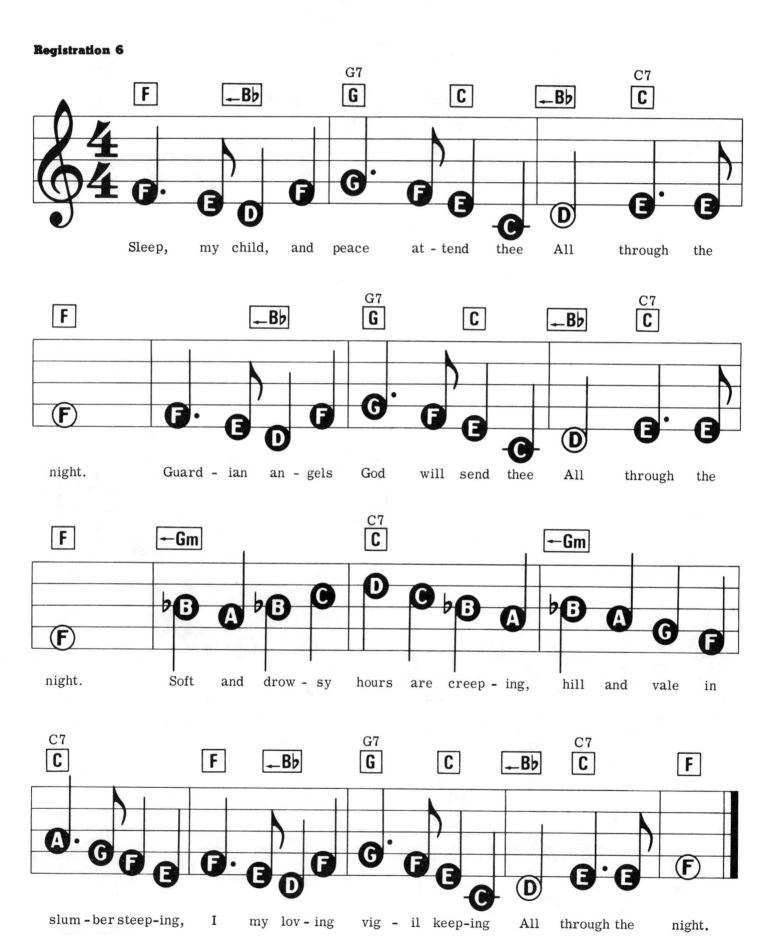

Beautiful Savior
(King Of Creation)

Registration 6

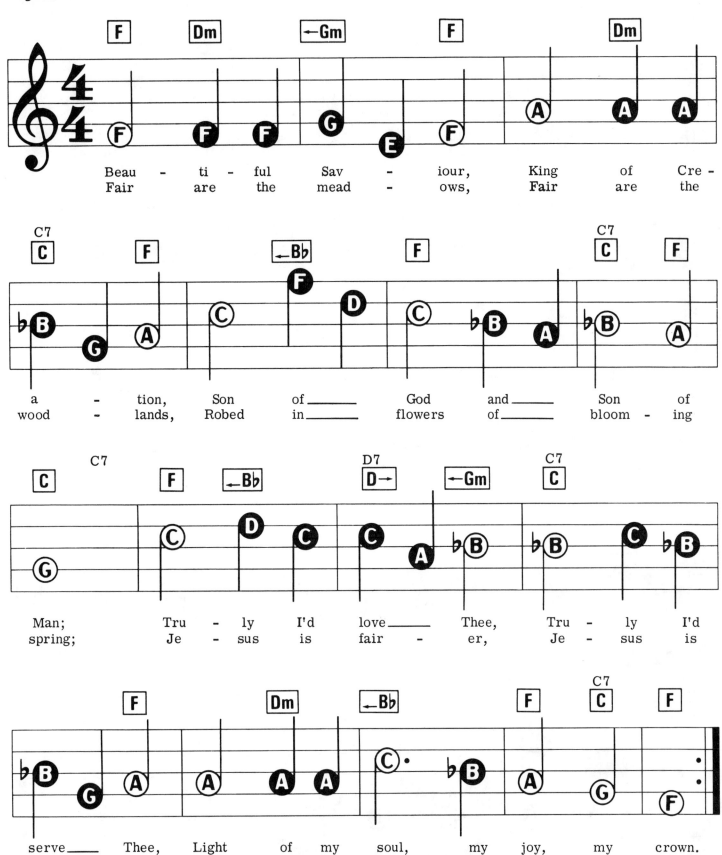

Christ The Lord Is Risen Today

Registration 3

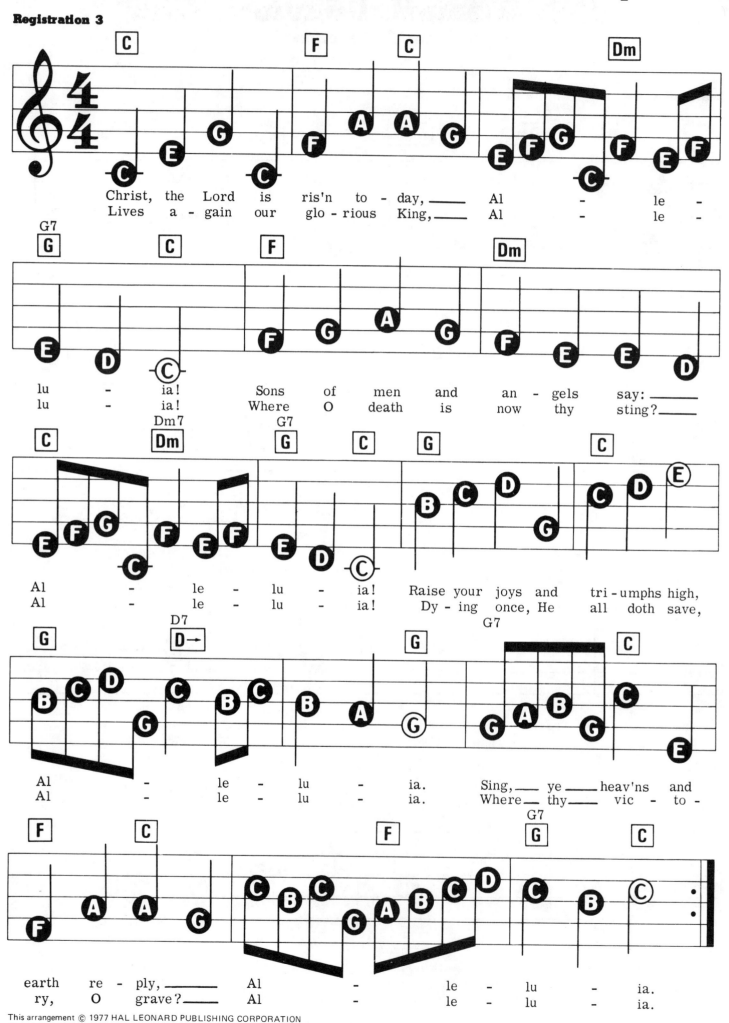

Christ, the Lord is ris'n to-day, ___ Al - le -
Lives a-gain our glo-rious King, ___ Al - le -

lu - ia! Sons of men and an - gels say: ___
lu - ia! Where O death is now thy sting? ___

Al - le - lu - ia! Raise your joys and tri-umphs high,
Al - le - lu - ia! Dy - ing once, He all doth save,

Al - le - lu - ia. Sing, ___ ye ___ heav'ns and
Al - le - lu - ia. Where ___ thy ___ vic - to -

earth re - ply, ___ Al - le - lu - ia.
ry, O grave? ___ Al - le - lu - ia.

Come, Thou Almighty King

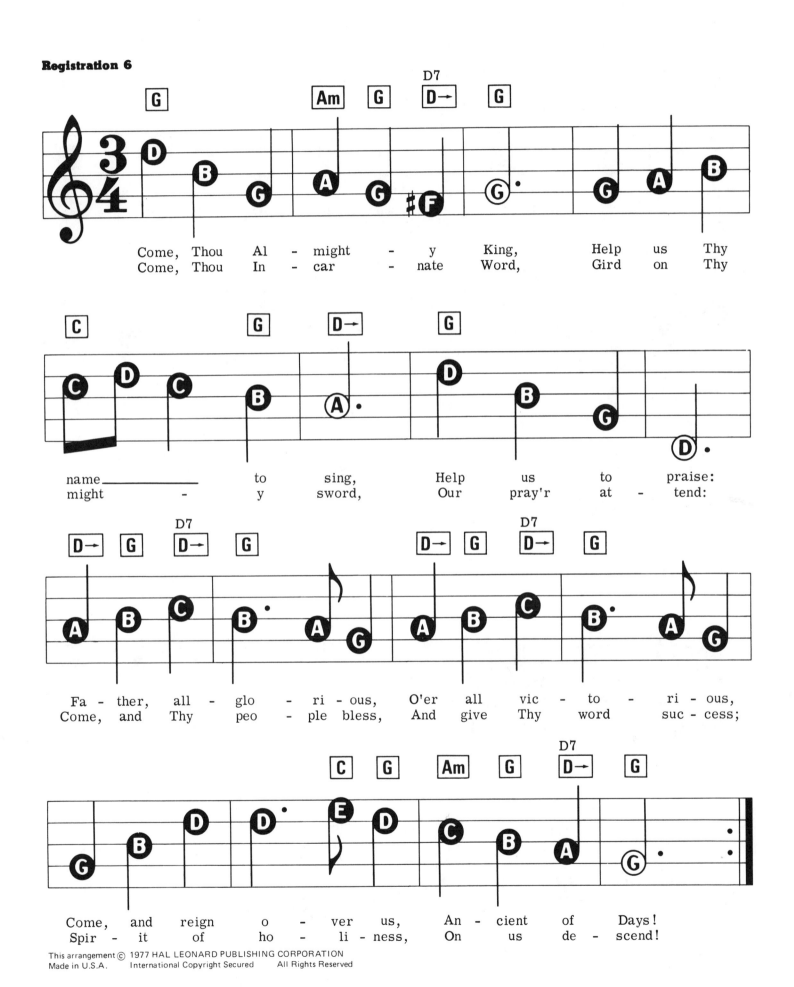

Go Tell It On The Mountain

Registration 4

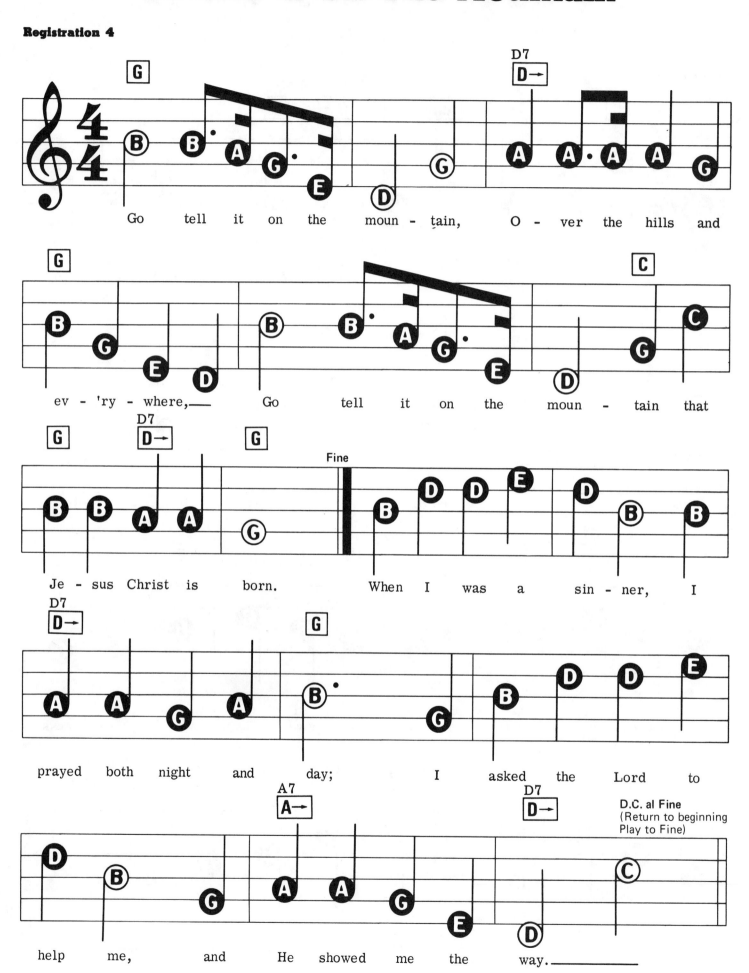

Holy, Holy, Holy

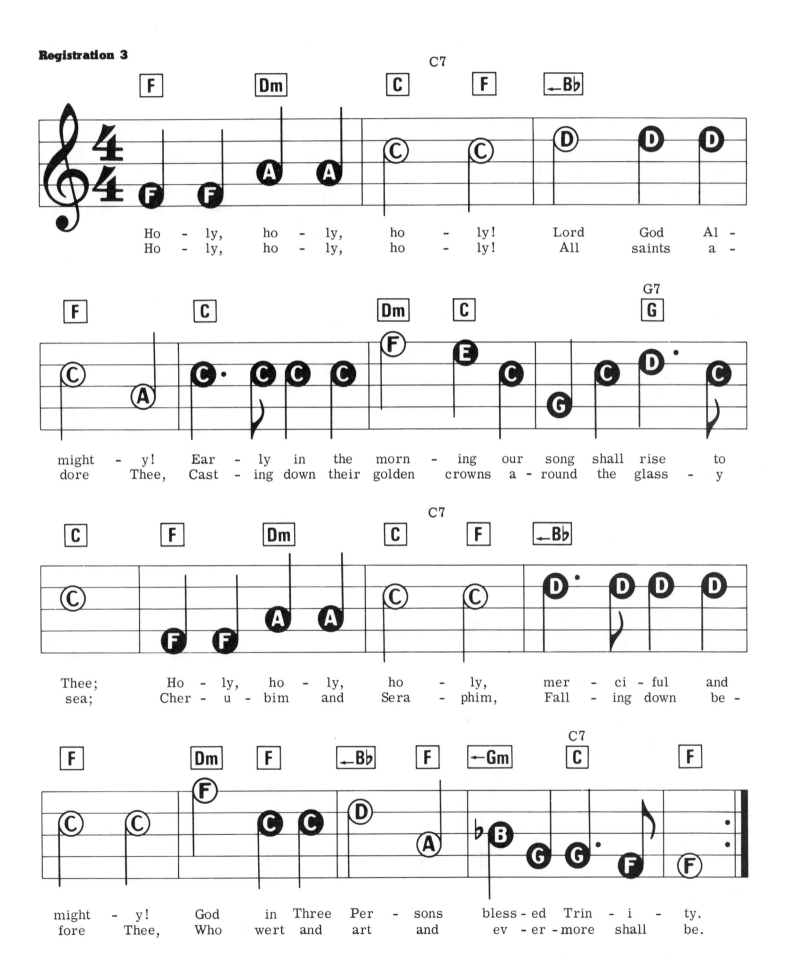

Jesus Loves Me

Registration 6

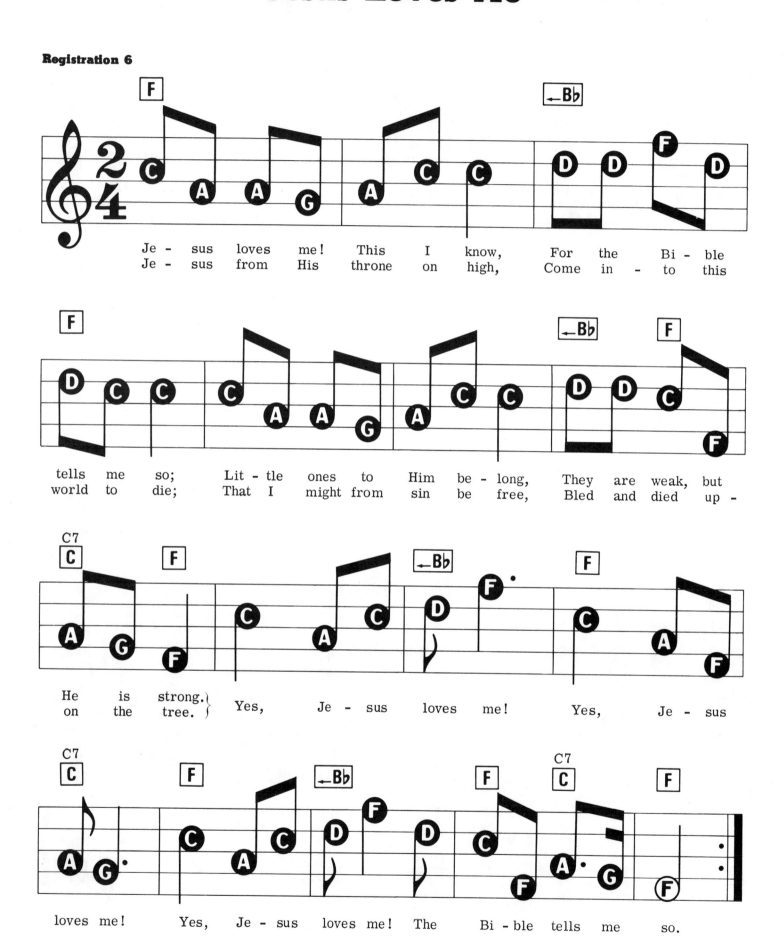

Just A Closer Walk With Thee

Registration 6

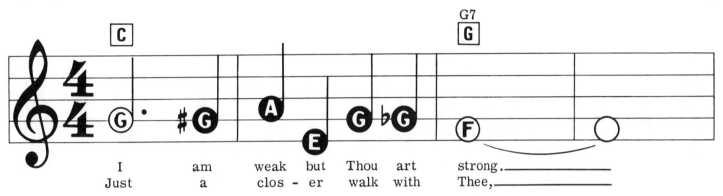

I am weak but Thou art strong._____
Just a clos - er walk with Thee,_____

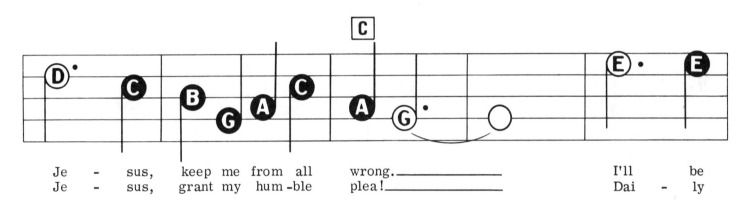

Je - sus, keep me from all wrong._____ I'll be
Je - sus, grant my hum -ble plea!_____ Dai - ly

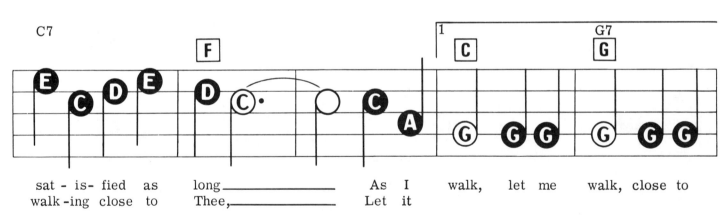

sat - is- fied as long_____ As I walk, let me walk, close to
walk -ing close to Thee,_____ Let it

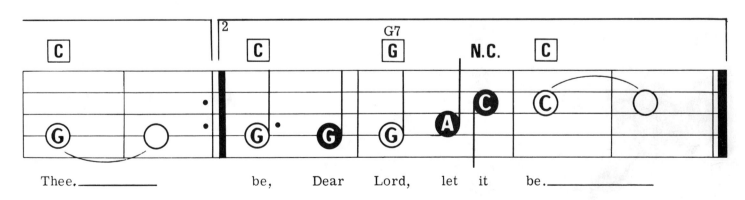

Thee._____ be, Dear Lord, let it be._____

Just A-Wearyin' For You

Registration 1

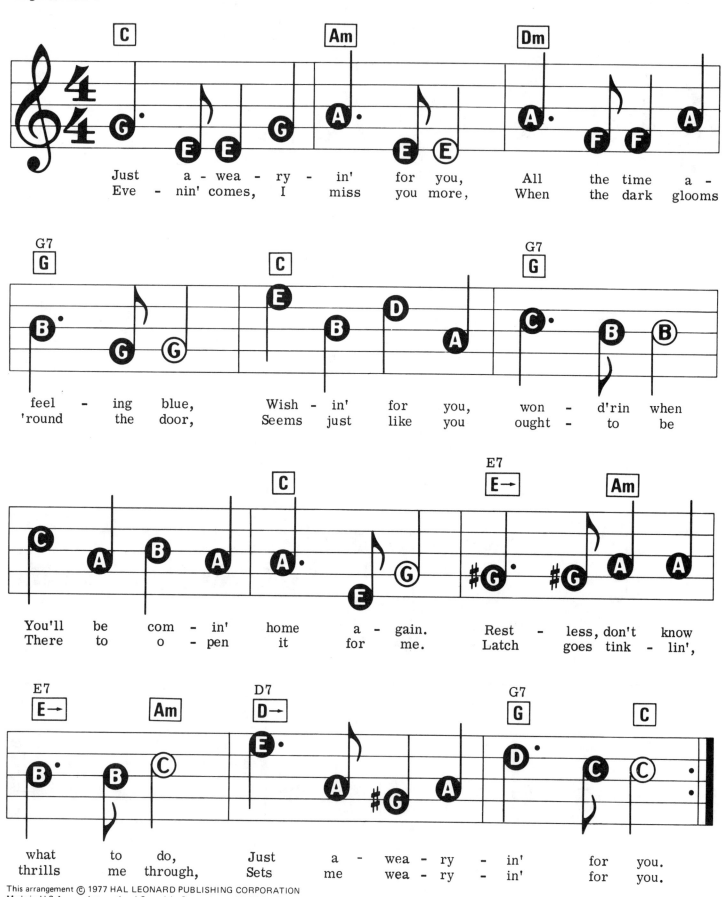

O Lord, I Am Not Worthy

Registration 4

Abide With Me

Registration 3

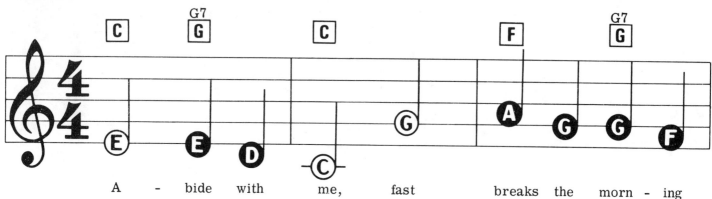

A - bide with me, fast breaks the morn - ing

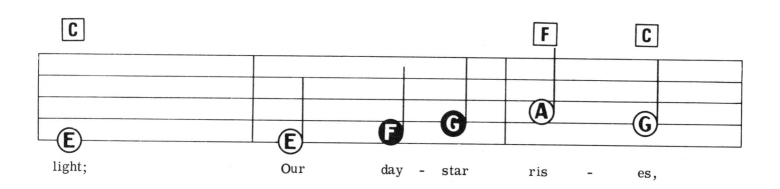

light; Our day - star ris - es,

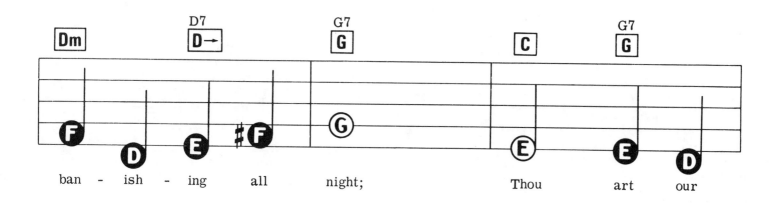

ban - ish - ing all night; Thou art our

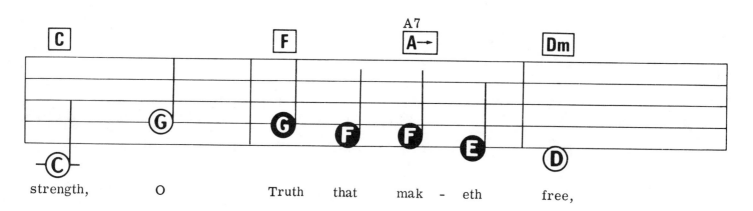

strength, O Truth that mak - eth free,

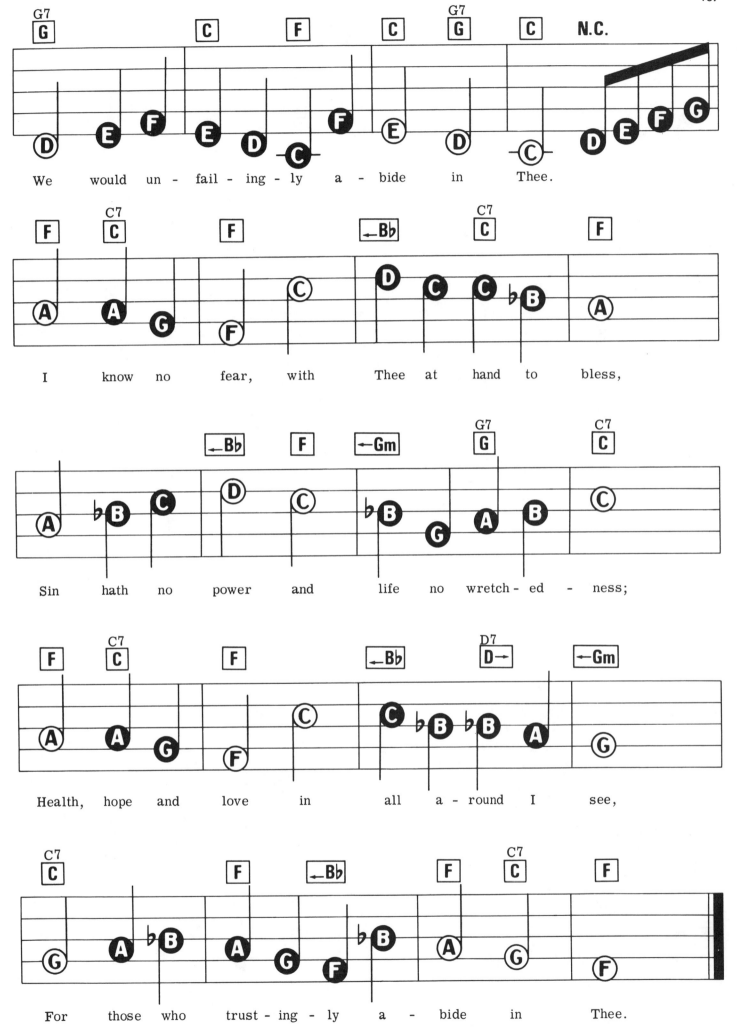

Ave Maria

Registration 6

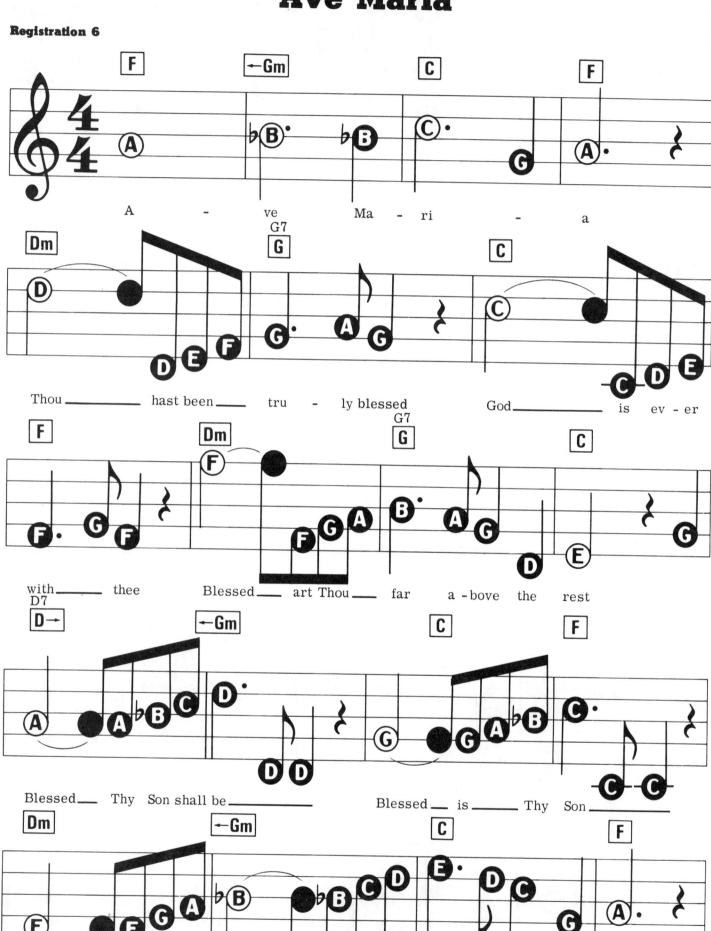

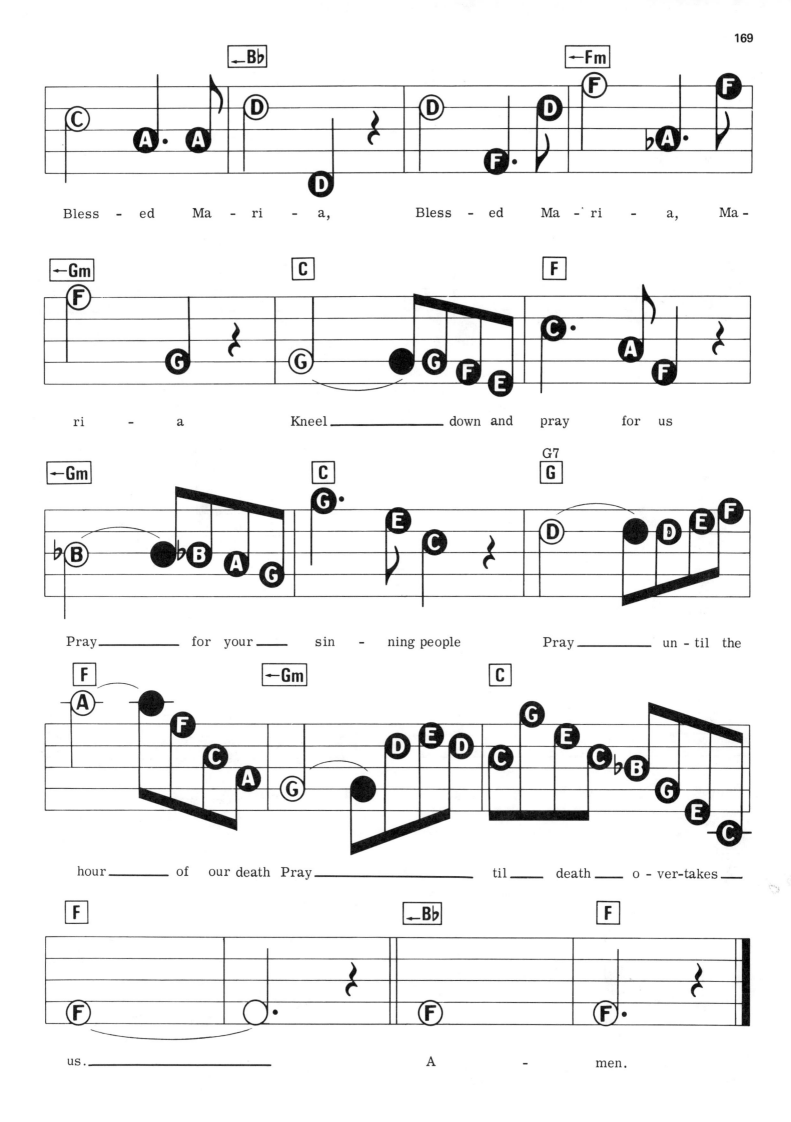

Blessed Assurance

Registration 6

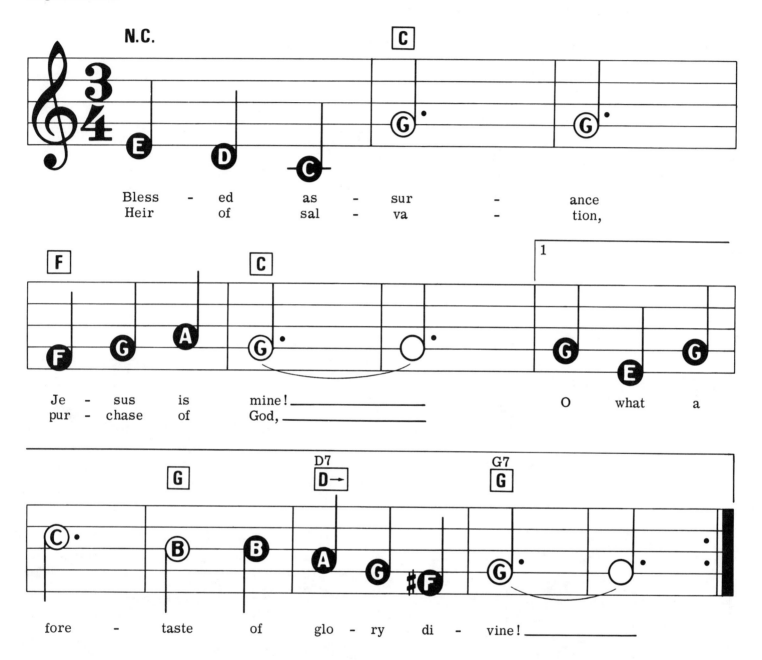

Bless - ed as - sur - ance
Heir of sal - va - tion,

Je - sus is mine! O what a
pur - chase of God,

fore - taste of glo - ry di - vine!

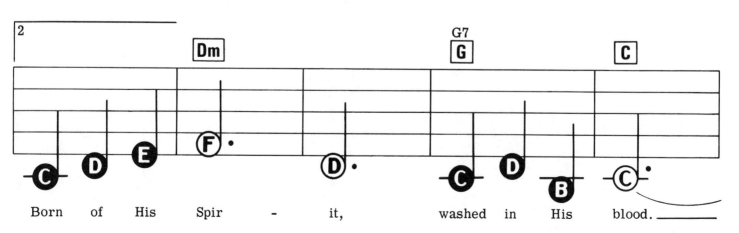

Born of His Spir - it, washed in His blood.

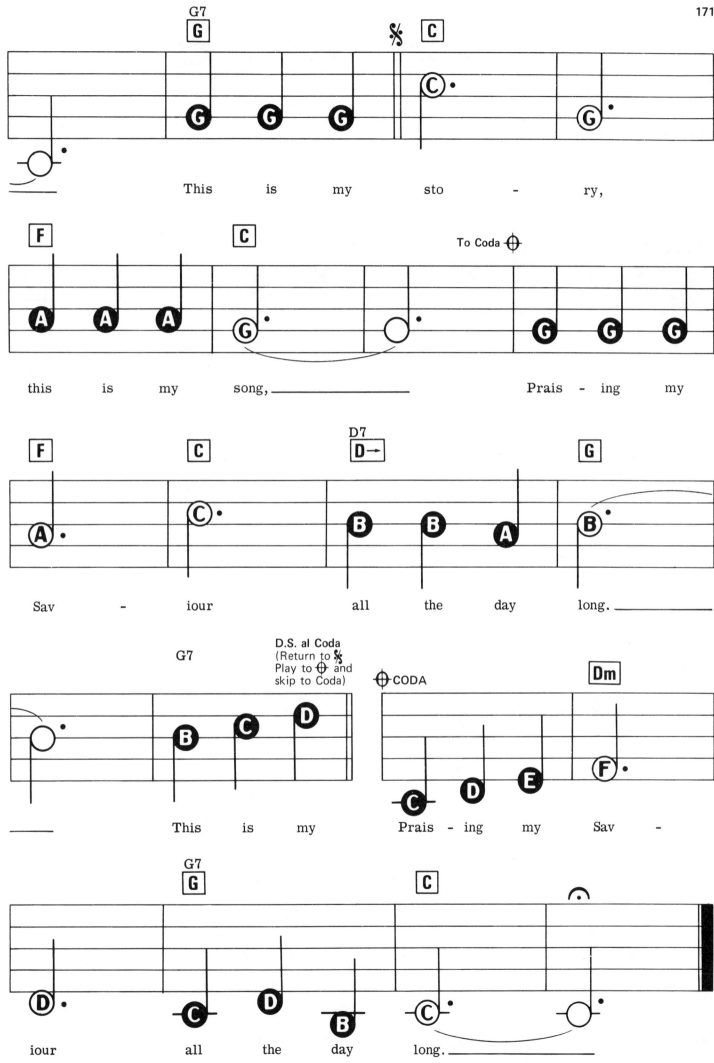

Blest Be The Tie That Binds

Registration 4

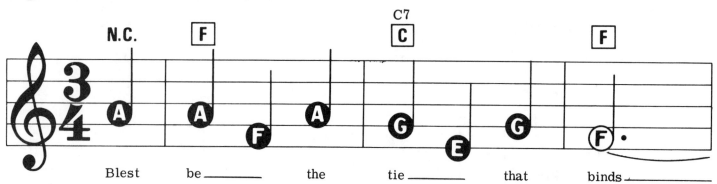

Blest be ____ the tie ____ that binds ____

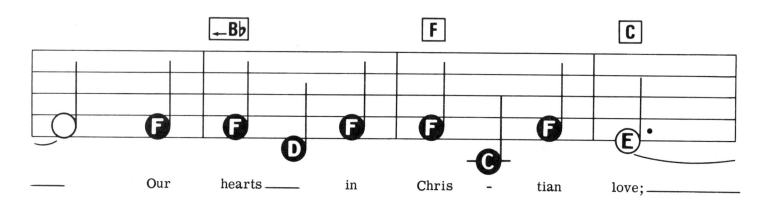

____ Our hearts ____ in Chris - tian love; ____

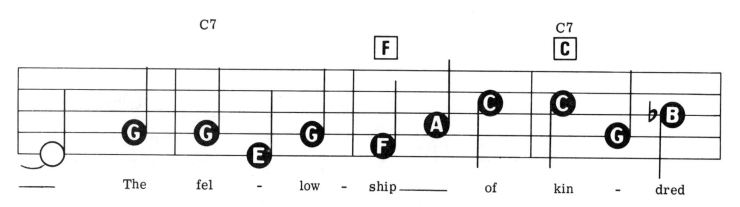

____ The fel - low - ship ____ of kin - dred

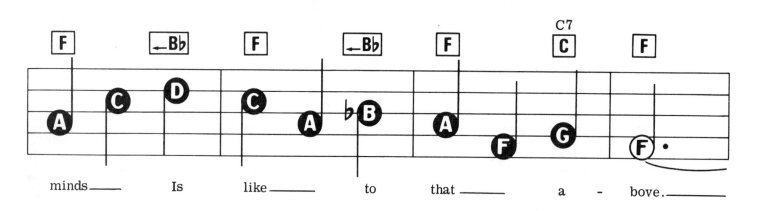

minds ____ Is like ____ to that ____ a - bove. ____

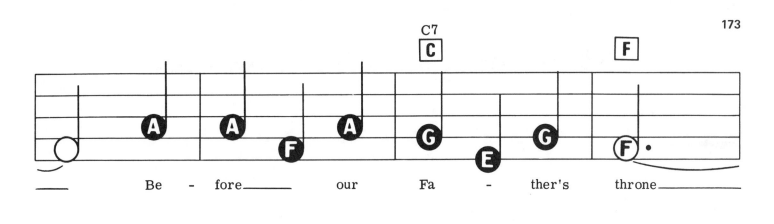

Be - fore____ our Fa - ther's throne____

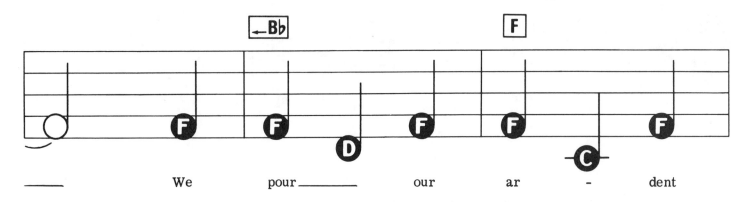

____ We pour____ our ar - dent

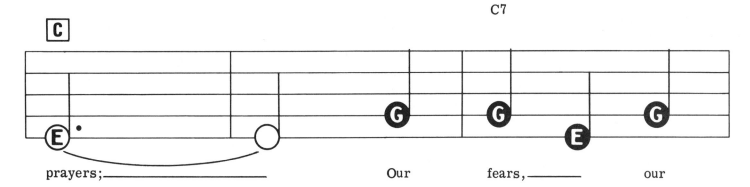

prayers;____ Our fears,____ our

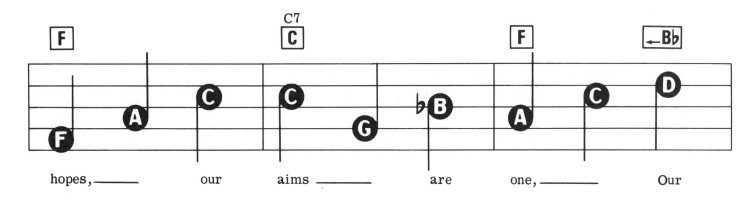

hopes,____ our aims ____ are one,____ Our

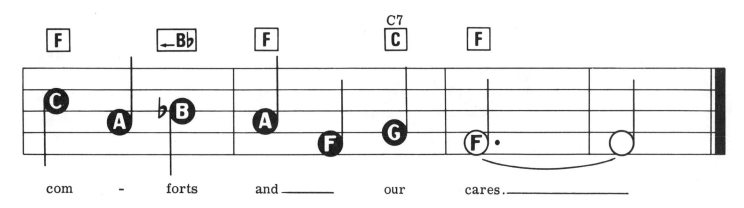

com - forts and ____ our cares.____

The Church In The Wildwood

Registration 6

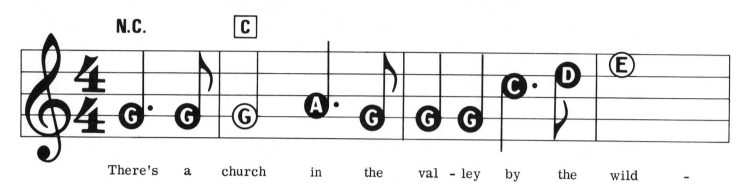

There's a church in the val - ley by the wild -

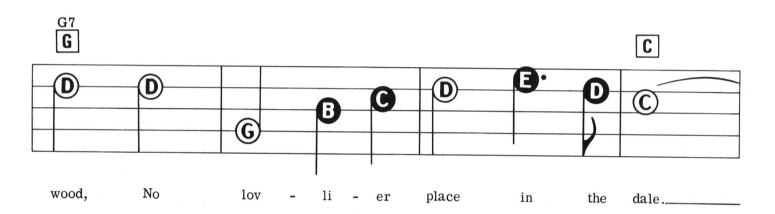

wood, No lov - li - er place in the dale.____

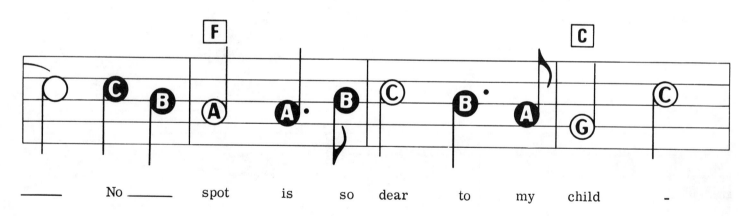

____ No ____ spot is so dear to my child -

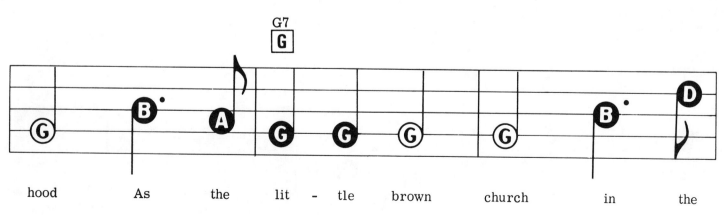

hood As the lit - tle brown church in the

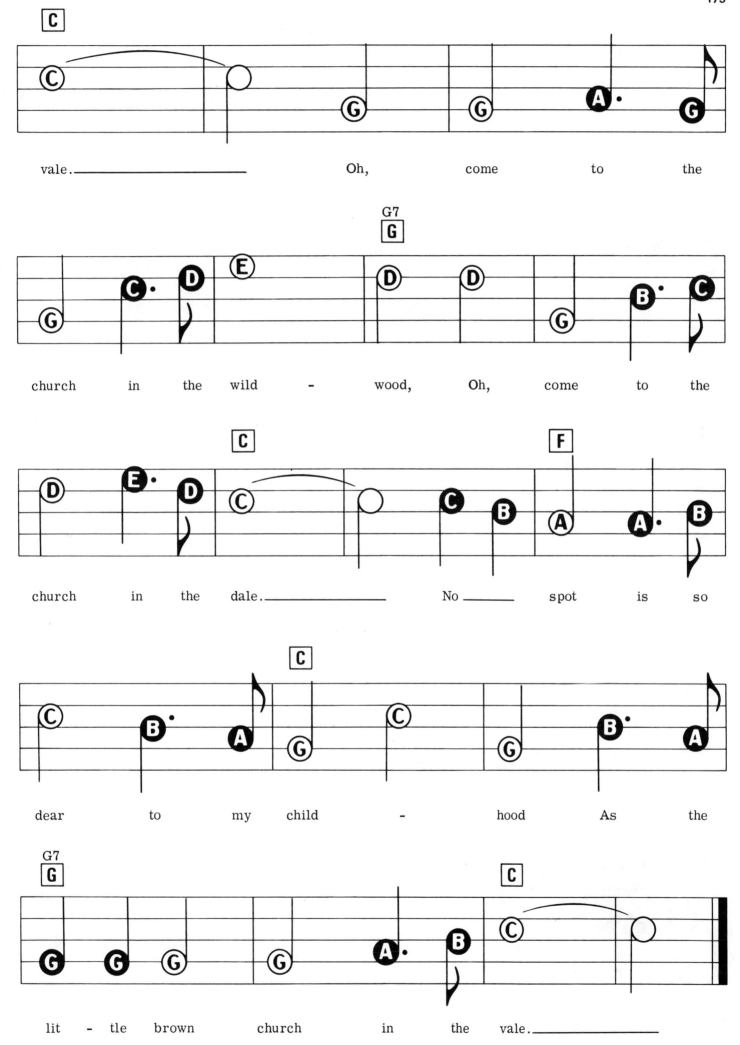

Cleanse Me

Registration 2

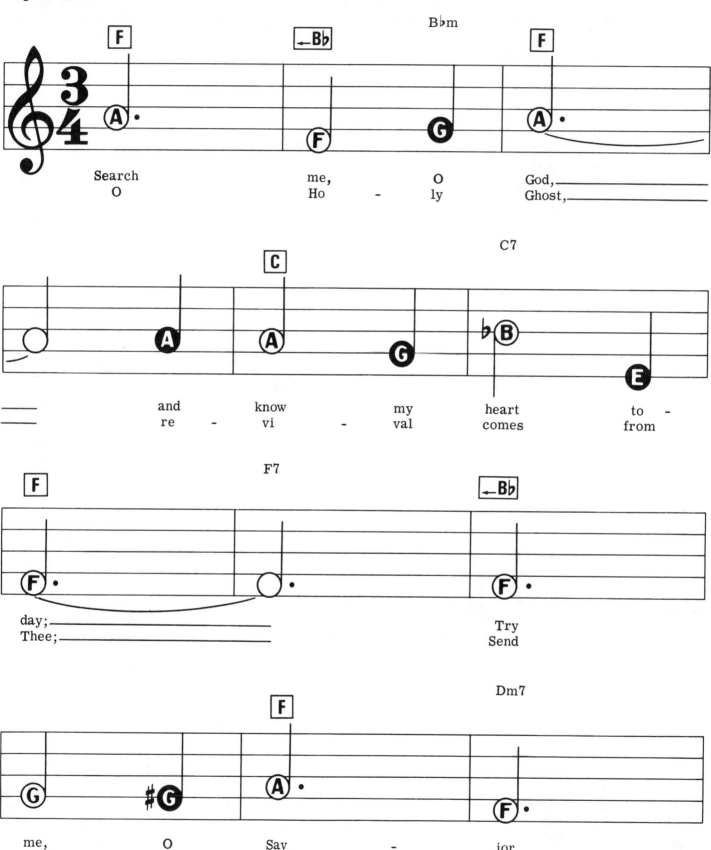

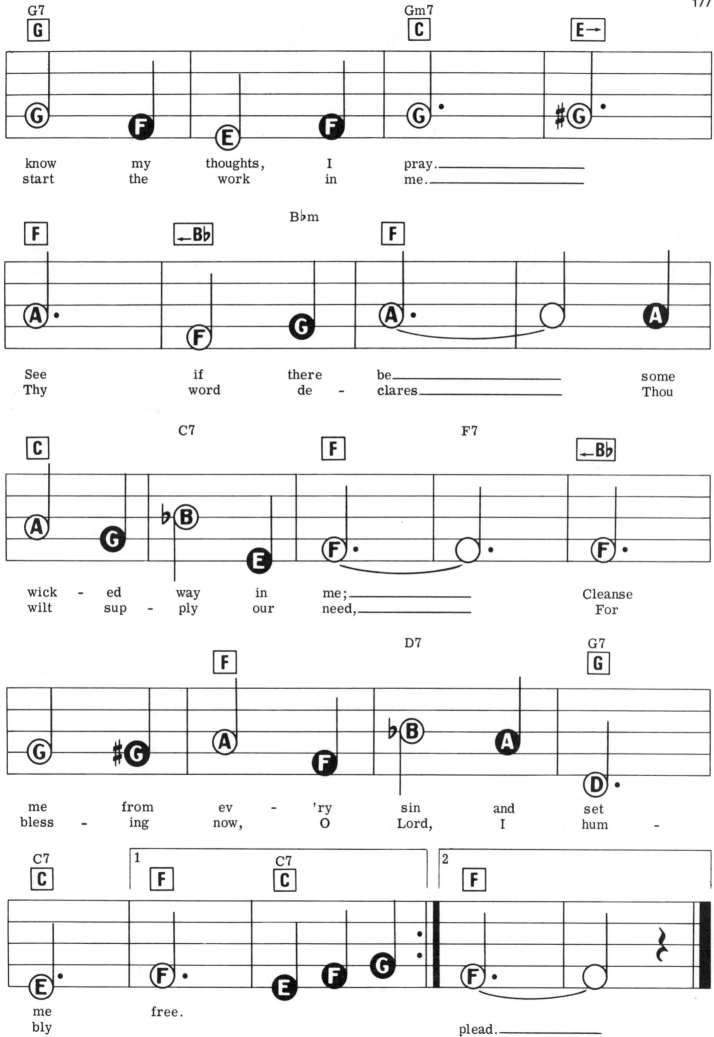

Crown Him With Many Crowns

Registration 6

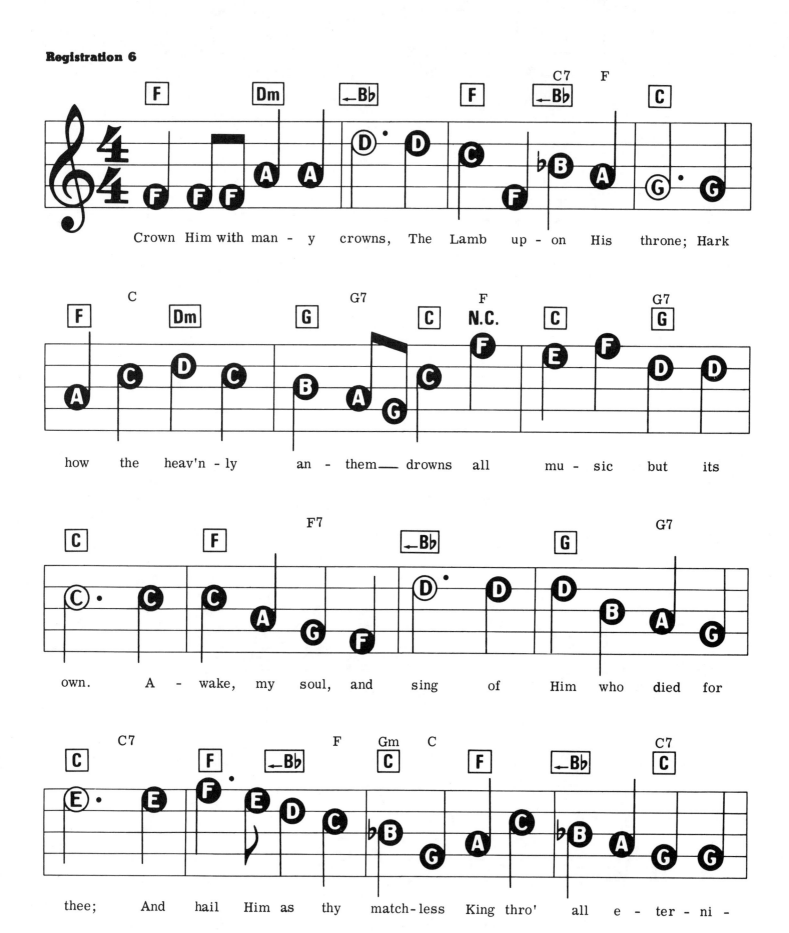

179

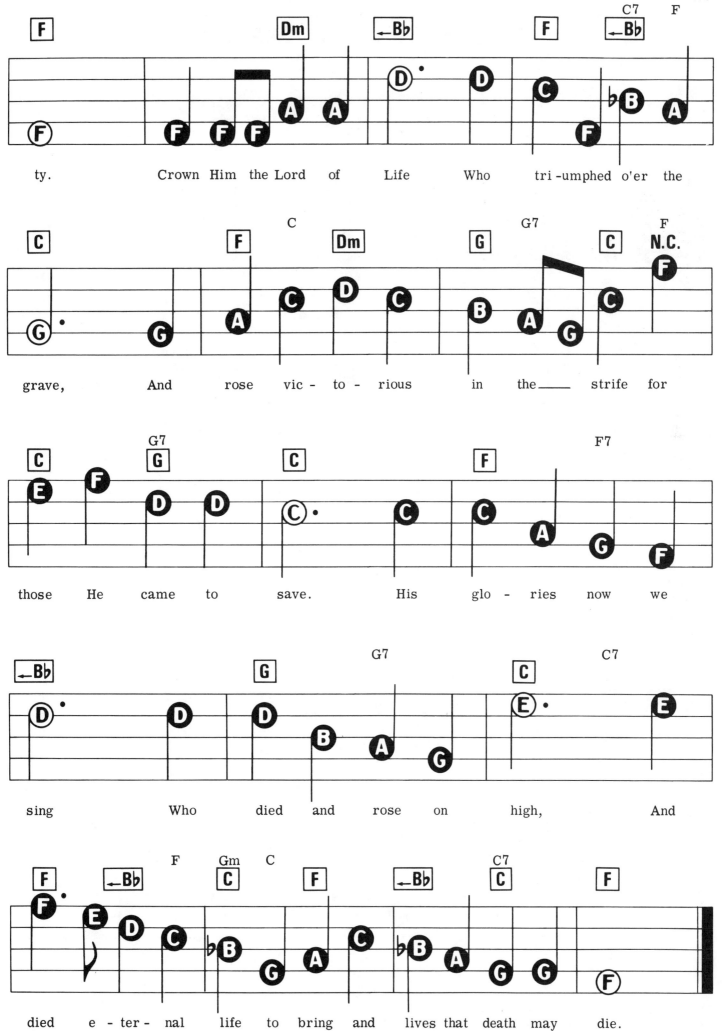

Fairest Lord Jesus

Registration 5

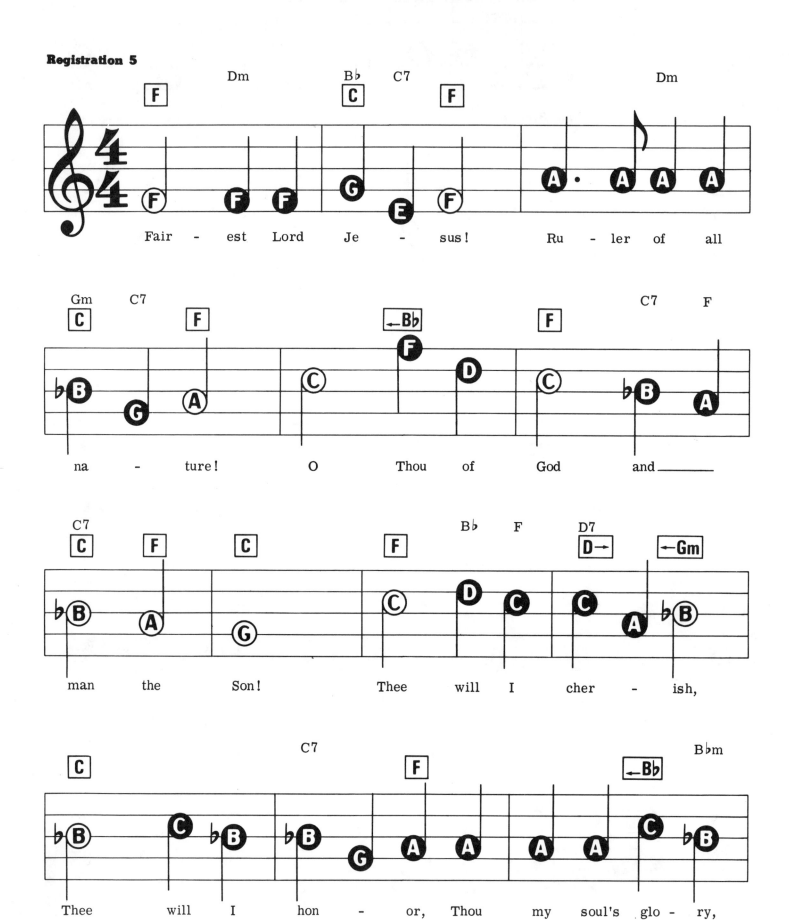

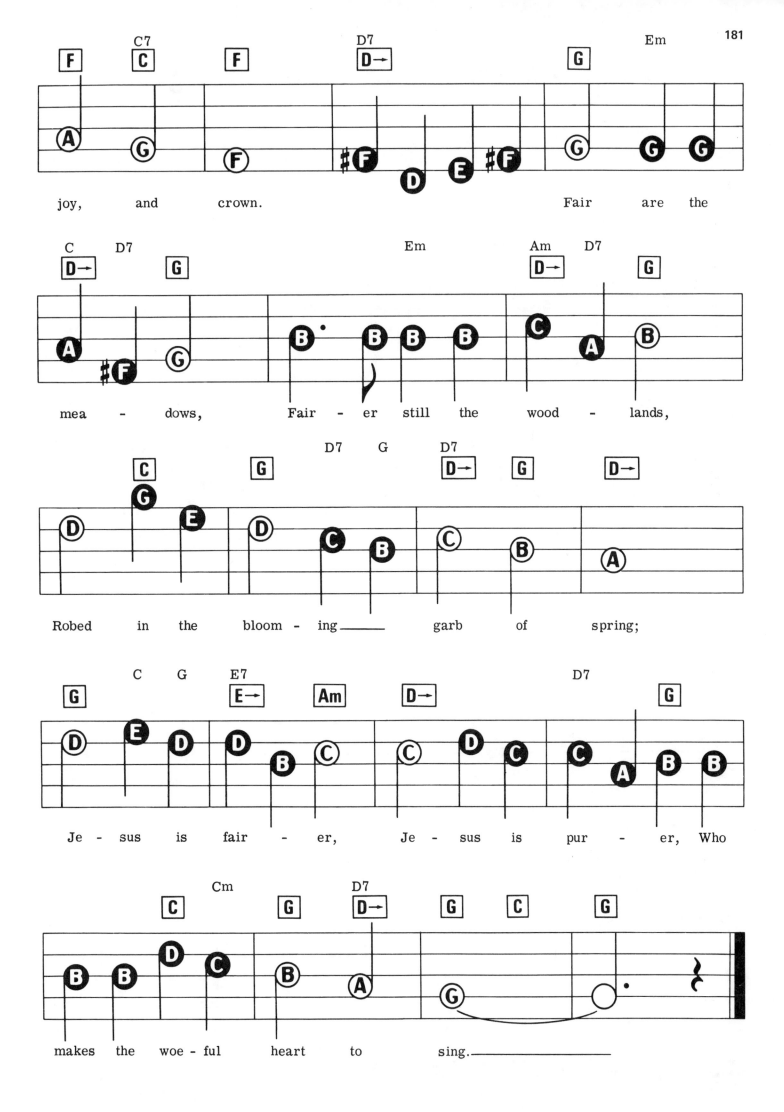

Give Me That Old Time Religion

Registration 5

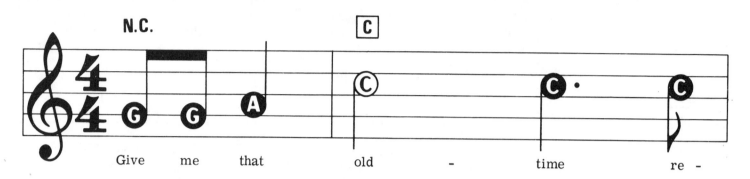

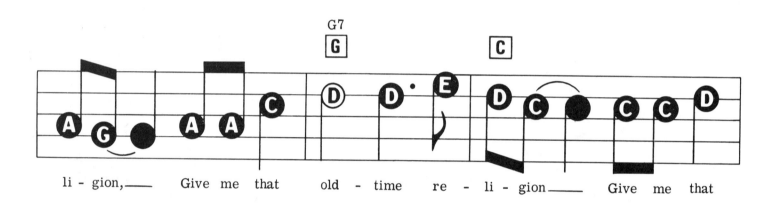

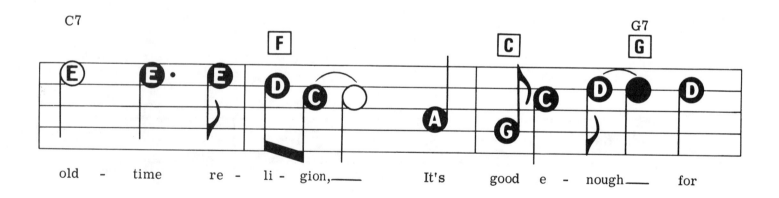

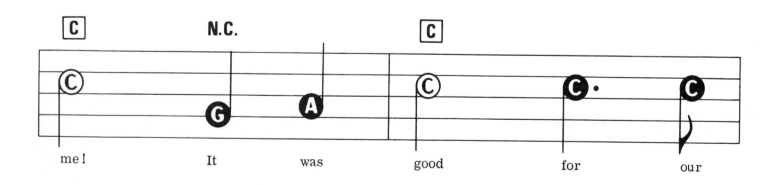

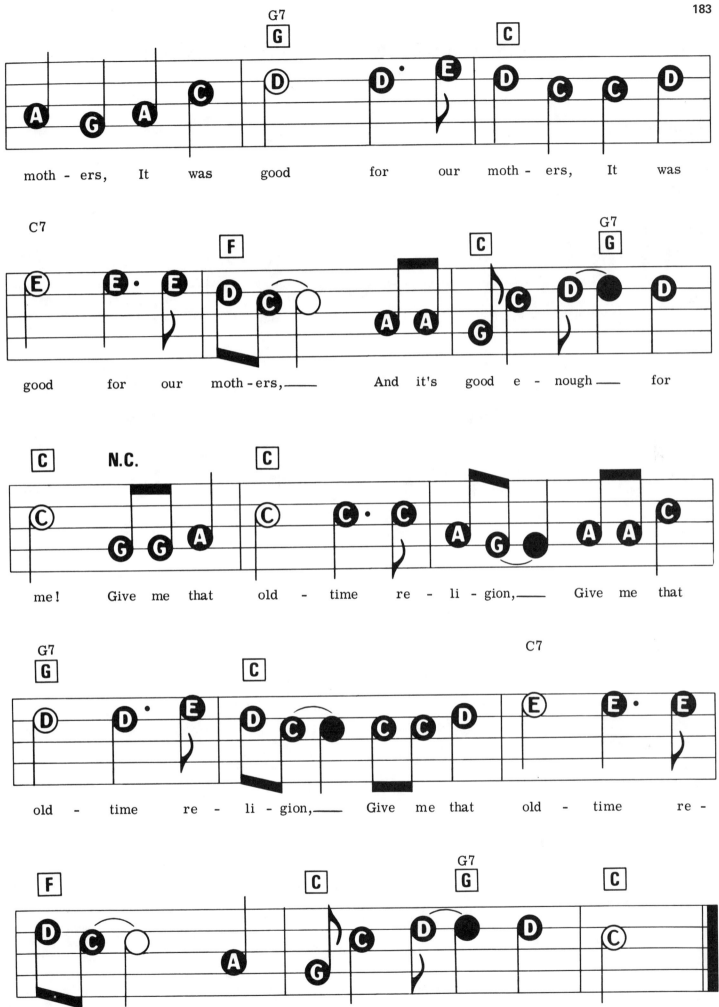

In The Sweet Bye And Bye

Registration 1

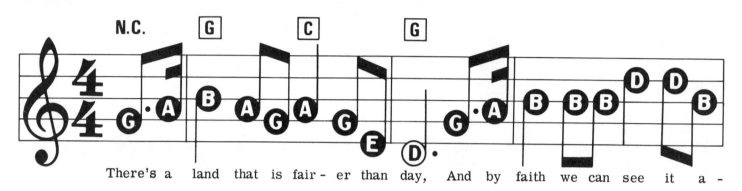

There's a land that is fair - er than day, And by faith we can see it a -

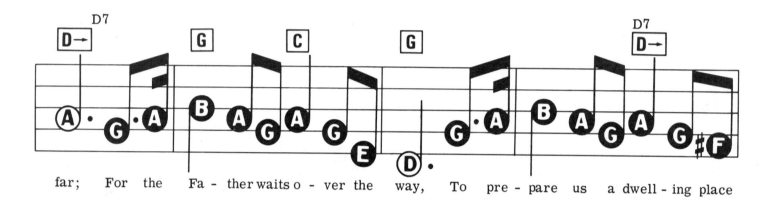

far; For the Fa - ther waits o - ver the way, To pre - pare us a dwell - ing place

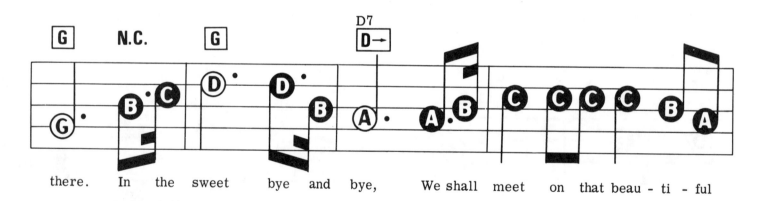

there. In the sweet bye and bye, We shall meet on that beau - ti - ful

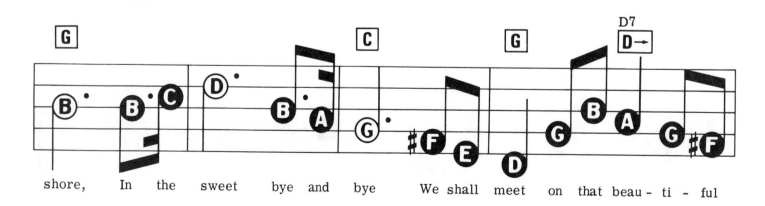

shore, In the sweet bye and bye We shall meet on that beau - ti - ful

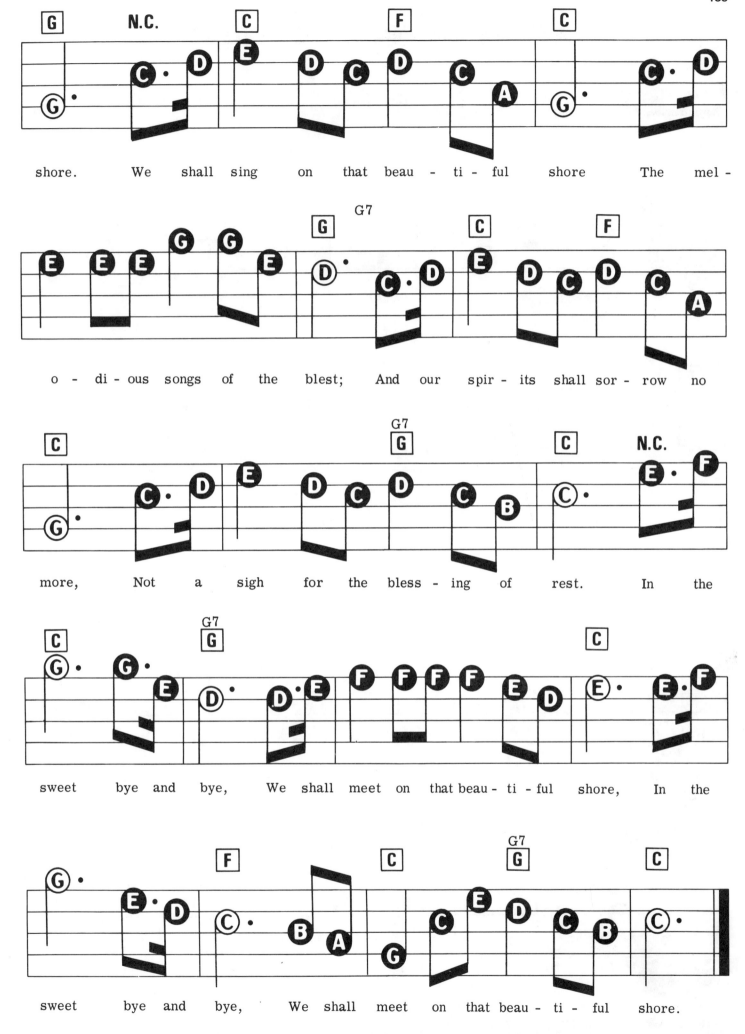

Jesus, Lover Of My Soul

Registration 3

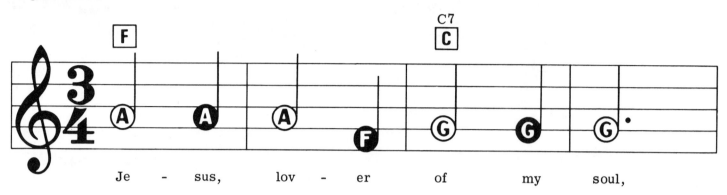

Je - sus, lov - er of my soul,

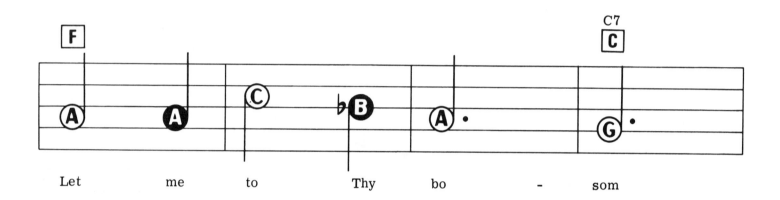

Let me to Thy bo - som

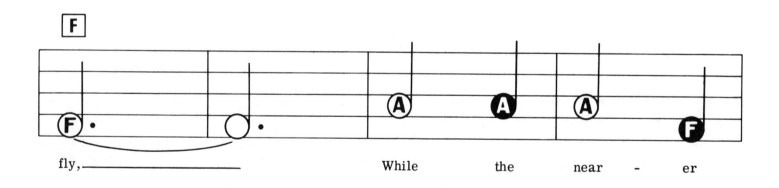

fly,⸺ While the near - er

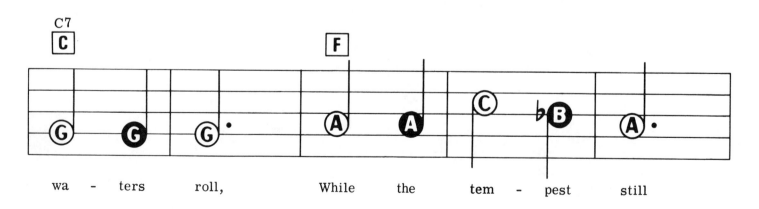

wa - ters roll, While the tem - pest still

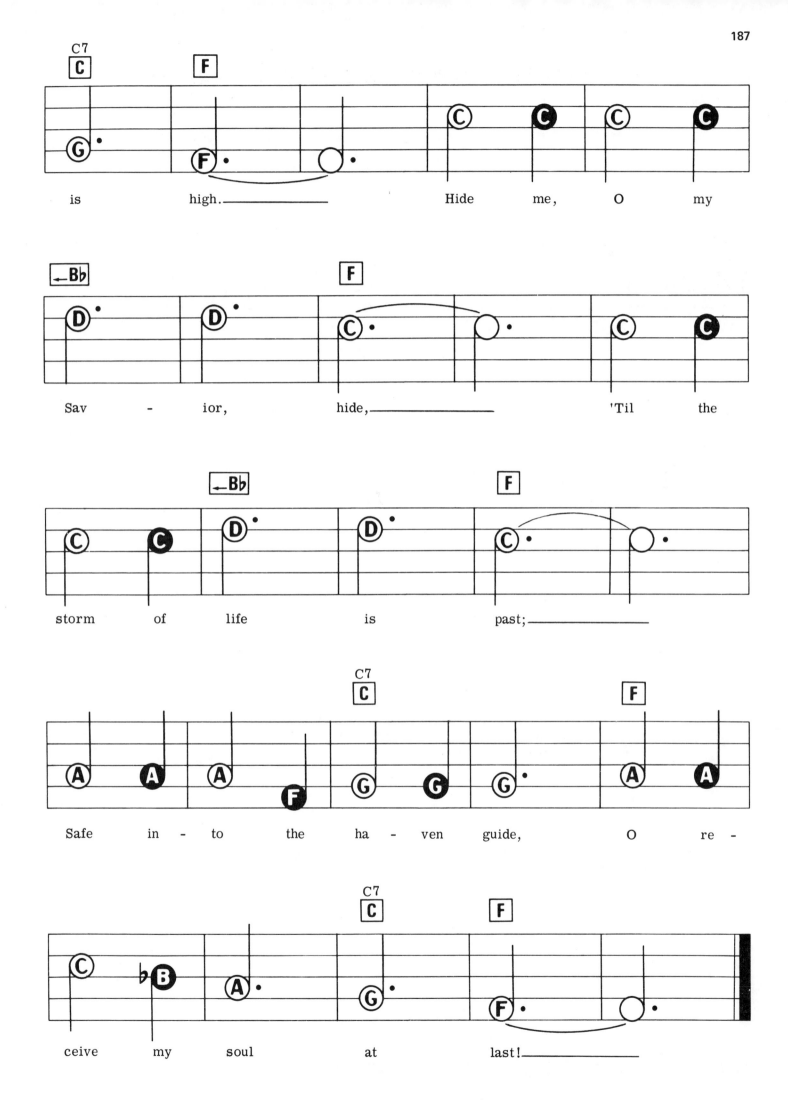

Joshua Fit The Battle Of Jericho

Registration 6

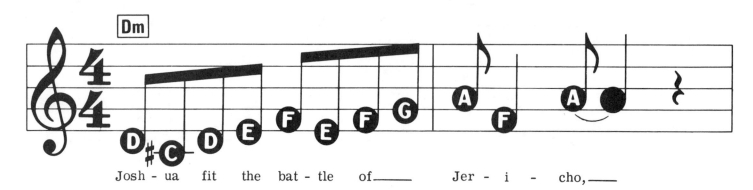

Josh - ua fit the bat - tle of____ Jer - i - cho,____

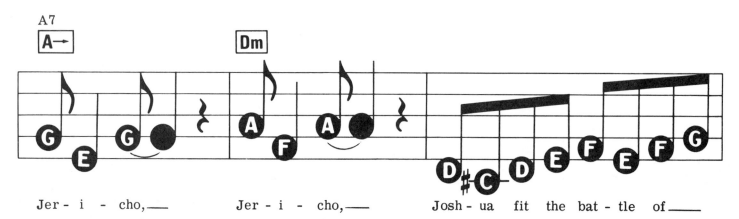

Jer - i - cho,____ Jer - i - cho,____ Josh - ua fit the bat - tle of____

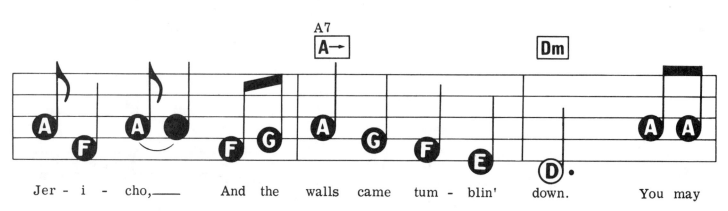

Jer - i - cho,____ And the walls came tum - blin' down. You may

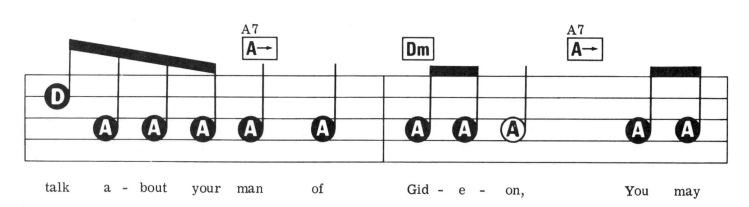

talk a - bout your man of Gid - e - on, You may

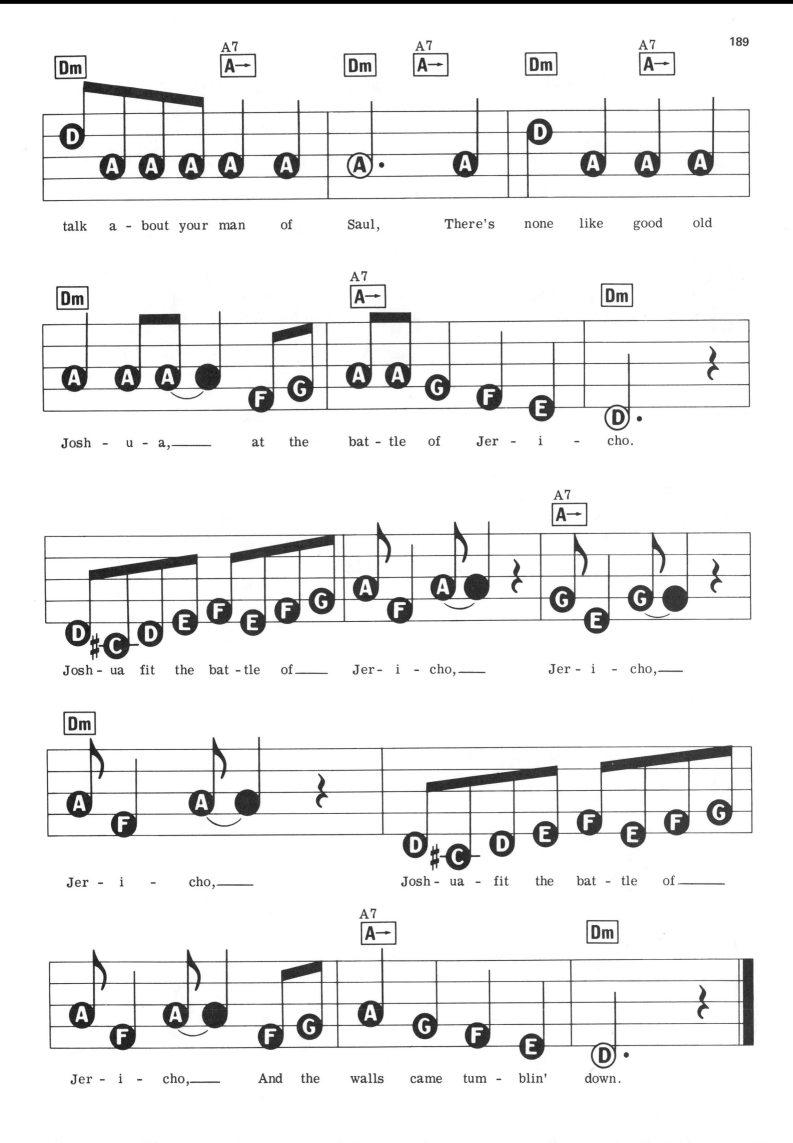

Nearer, My God, To Thee

Registration 2

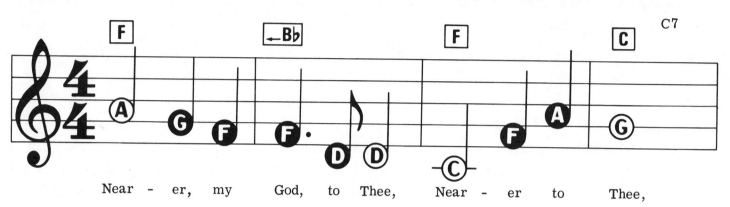

Near - er, my God, to Thee, Near - er to Thee,

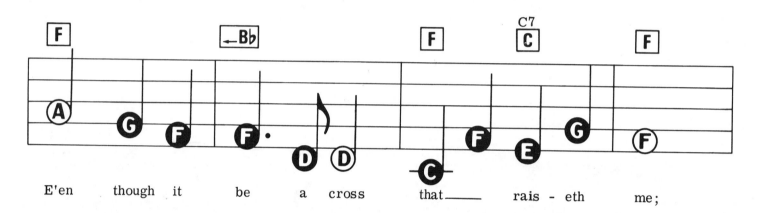

E'en though it be a cross that___ rais - eth me;

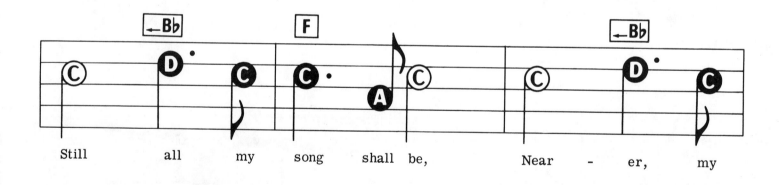

Still all my song shall be, Near - er, my

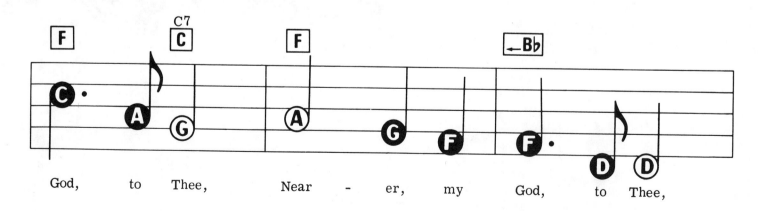

God, to Thee, Near - er, my God, to Thee,

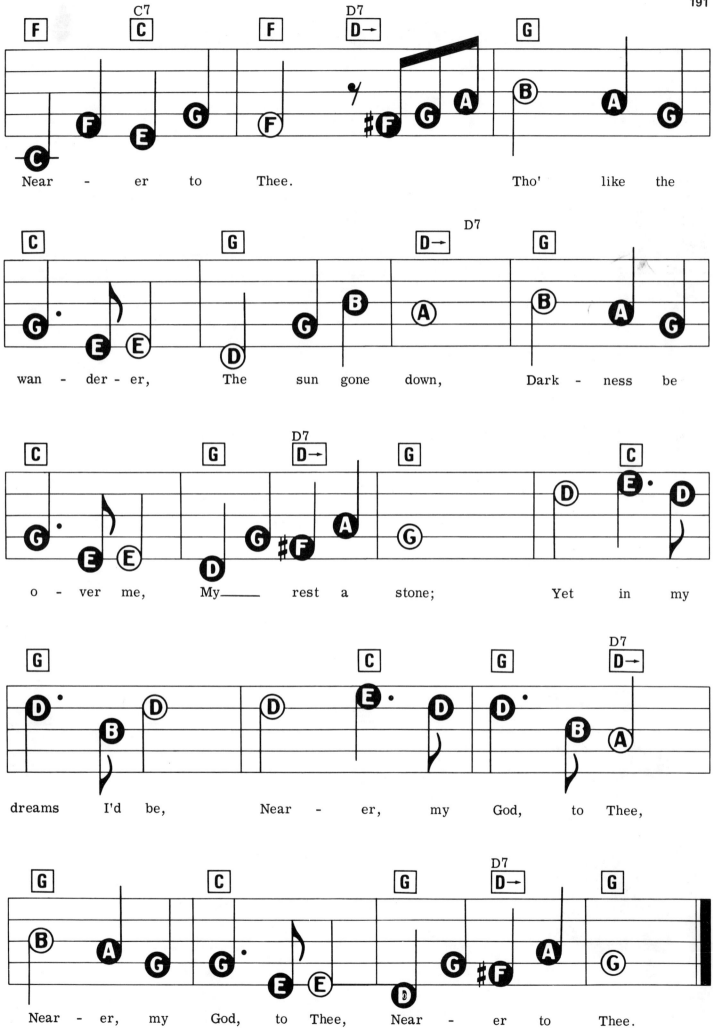

Nobody Knows The Trouble I've Seen

Registration 6

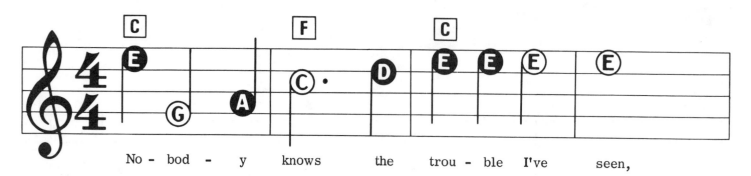

No - bod - y knows the trou - ble I've seen,

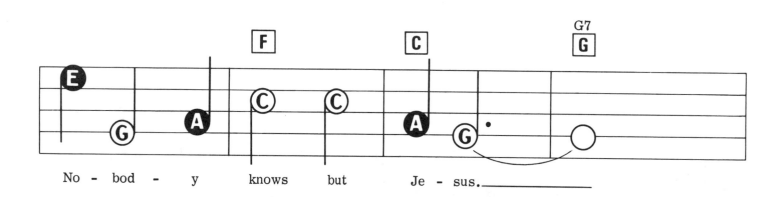

No - bod - y knows but Je - sus.

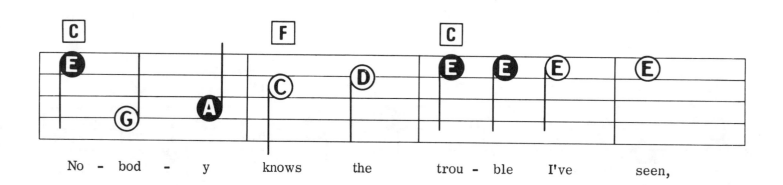

No - bod - y knows the trou - ble I've seen,

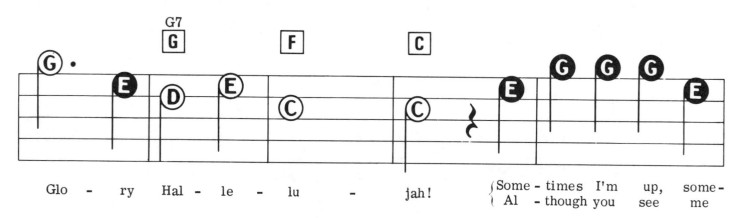

Glo - ry Hal - le - lu - jah! Some - times I'm up, some -
Al - though you see me

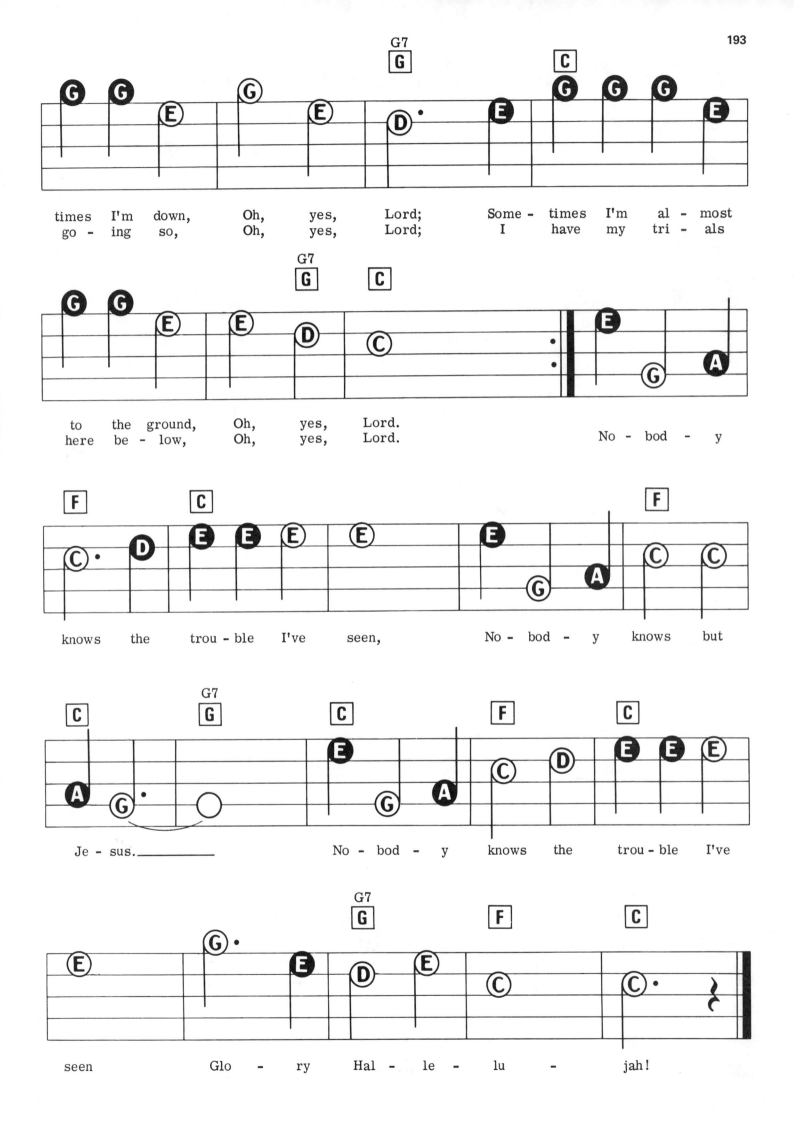

Onward, Christian Soldiers

Registration 6

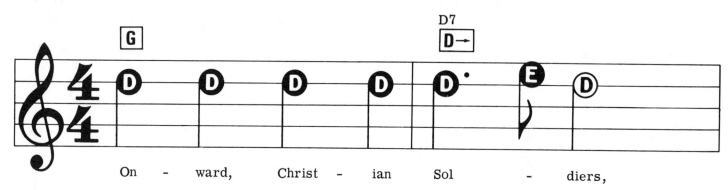

On - ward, Christ - ian Sol - diers,

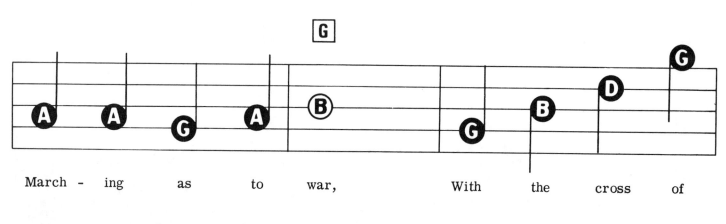

March - ing as to war, With the cross of

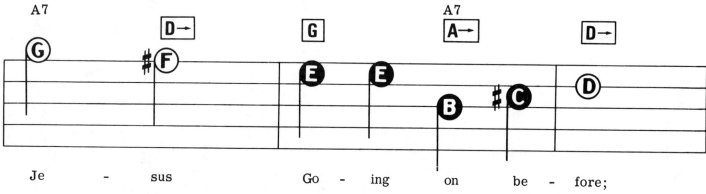

Je - sus Go - ing on be - fore;

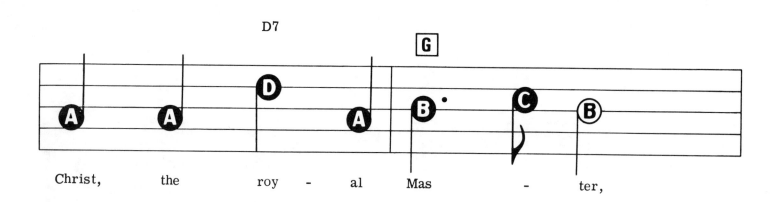

Christ, the roy - al Mas - ter,

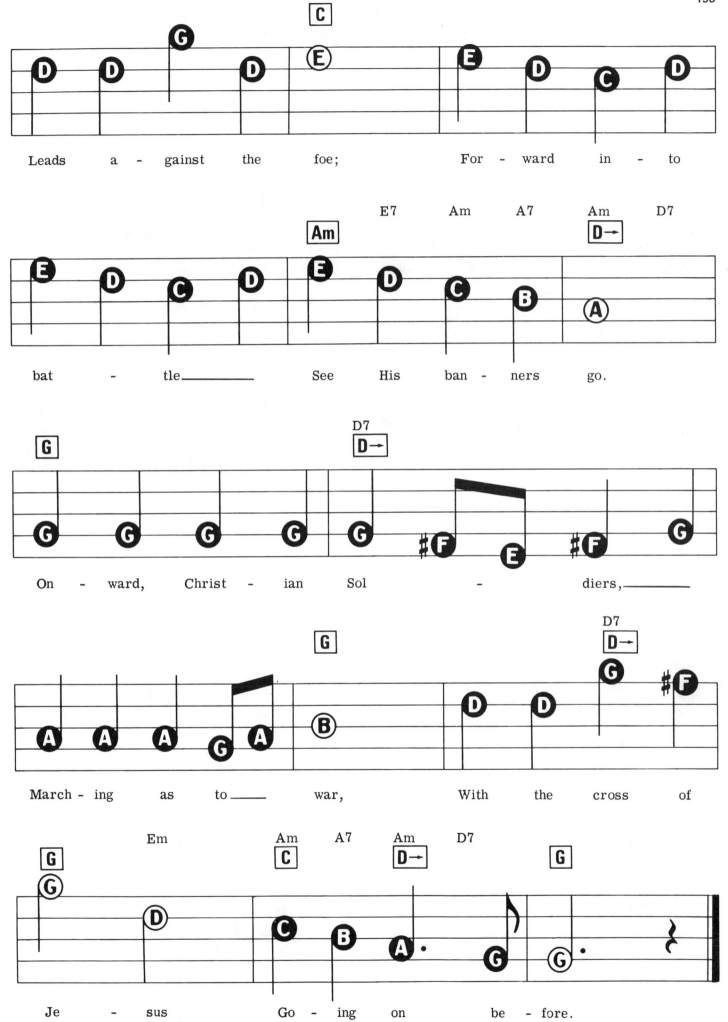

Pass Me Not, O Gentle Saviour

Registration 1

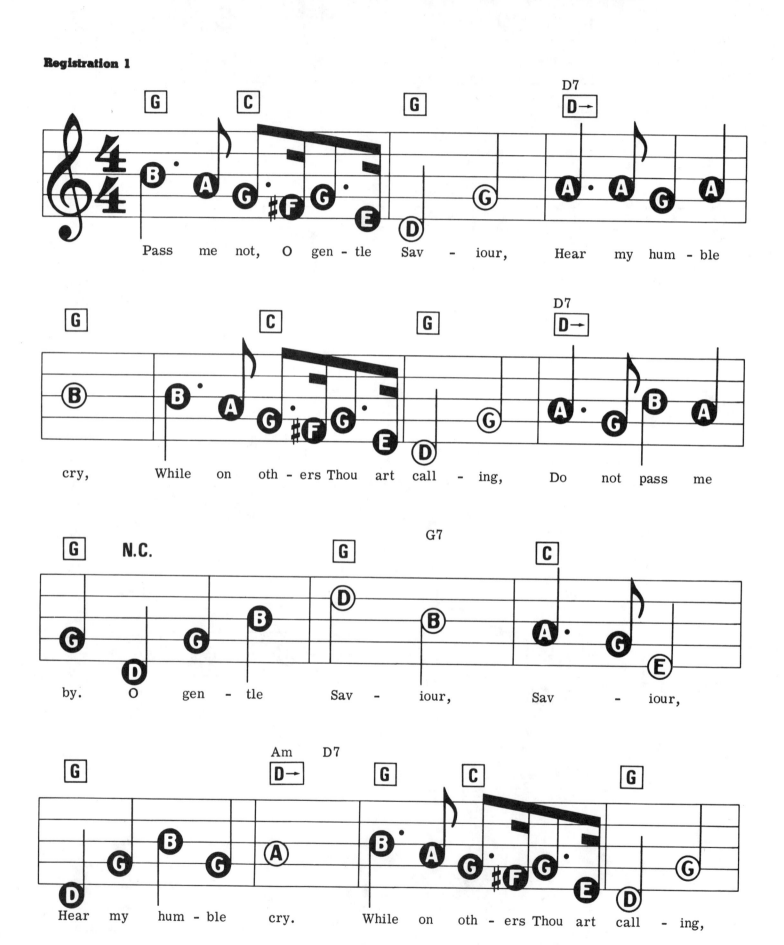

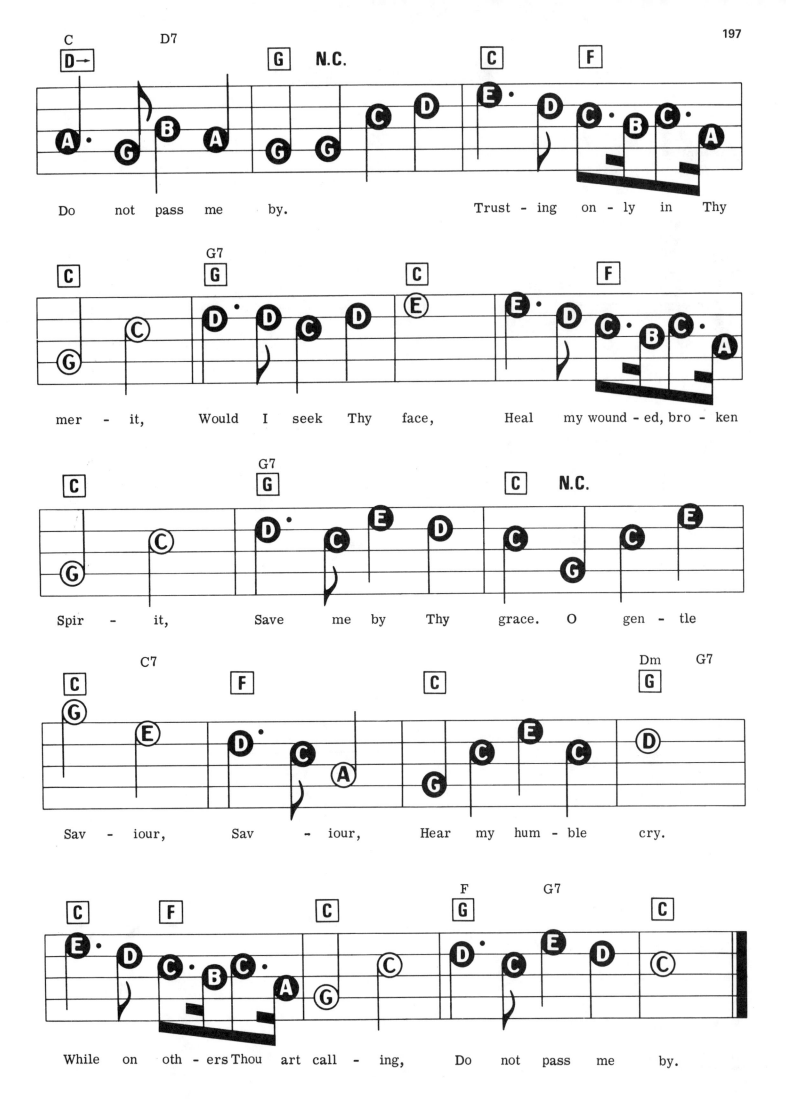

Rock Of Ages

Registration 6

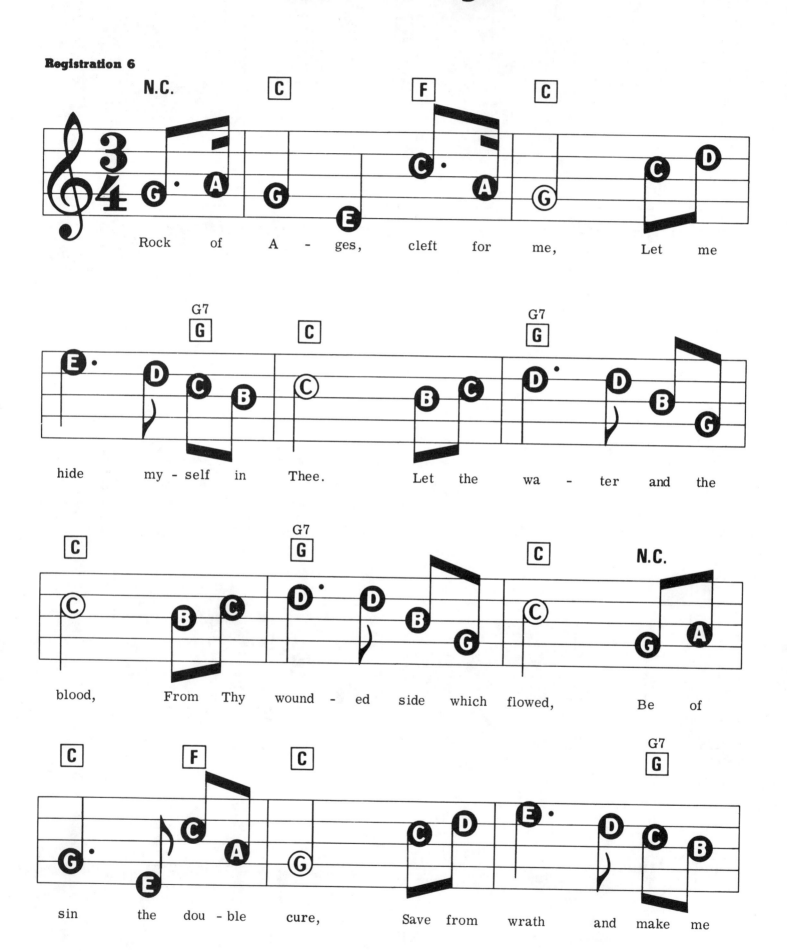

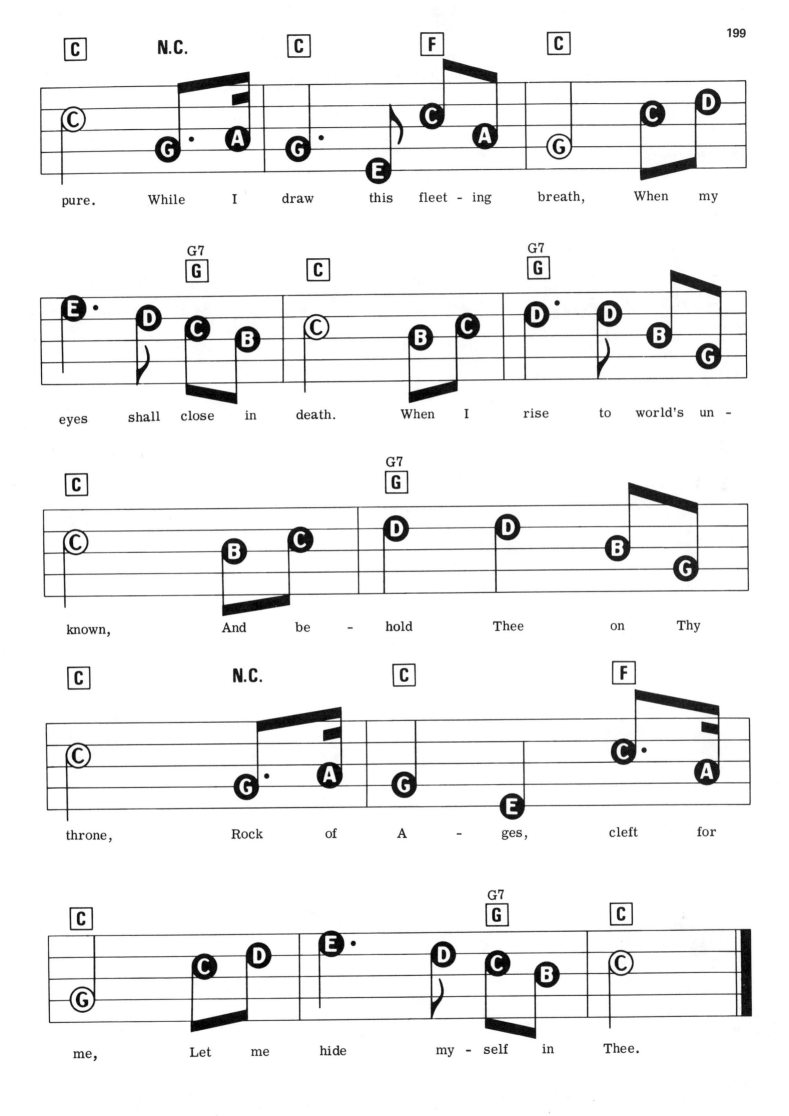

Saviour, Like A Shepherd Lead Us

Registration 4

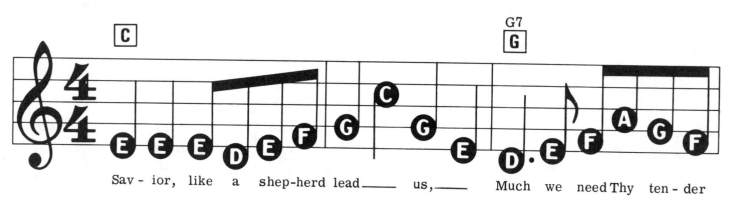

Sav - ior, like a shep-herd lead_____ us,_____ Much we need Thy ten - der

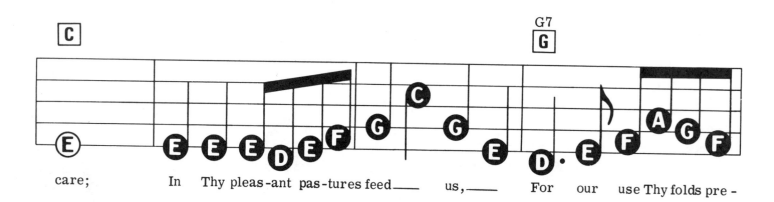

care; In Thy pleas-ant pas-tures feed_____ us,_____ For our use Thy folds pre -

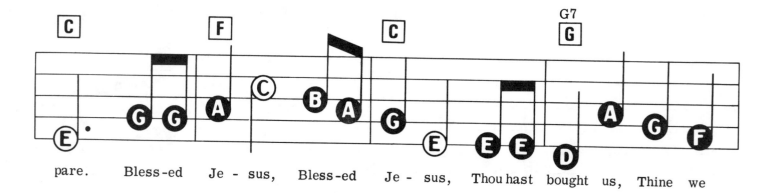

pare. Bless-ed Je - sus, Bless-ed Je - sus, Thou hast bought us, Thine we

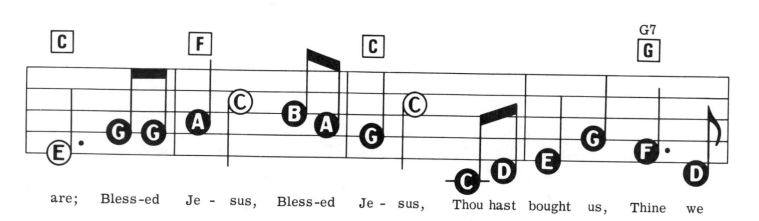

are; Bless-ed Je - sus, Bless-ed Je - sus, Thou hast bought us, Thine we

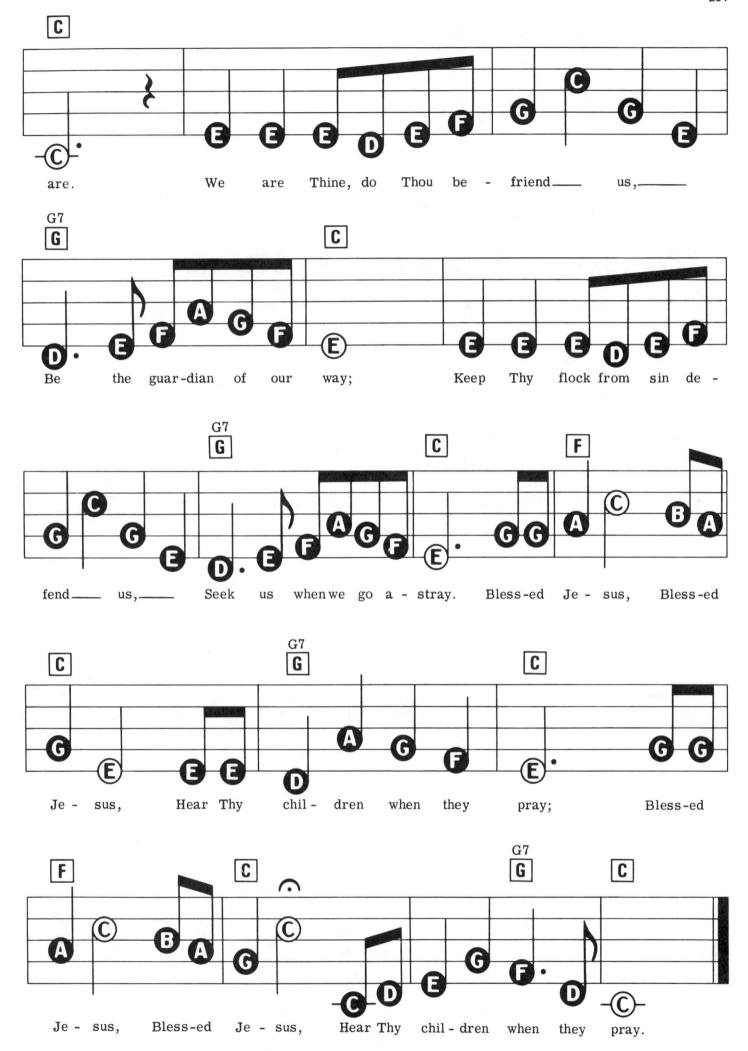

Shall We Gather At The River?

Registration 6

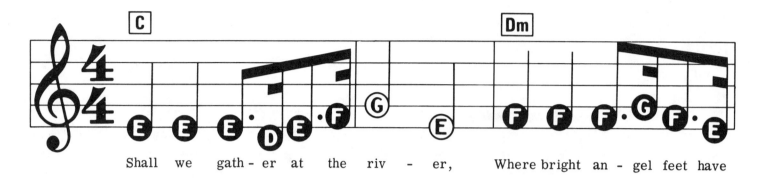

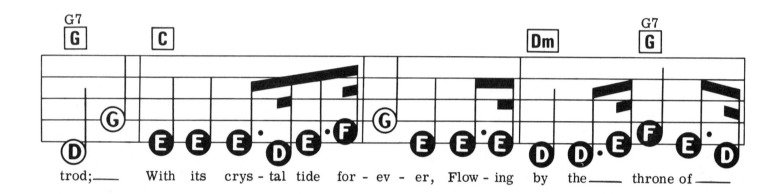

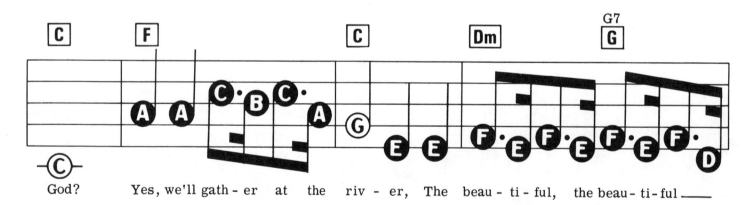

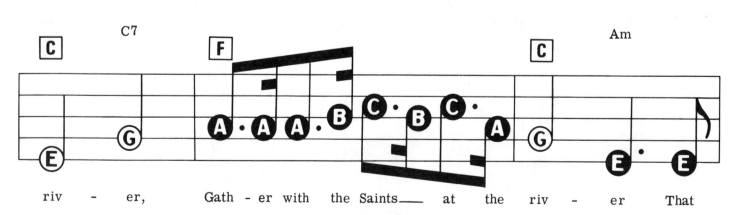

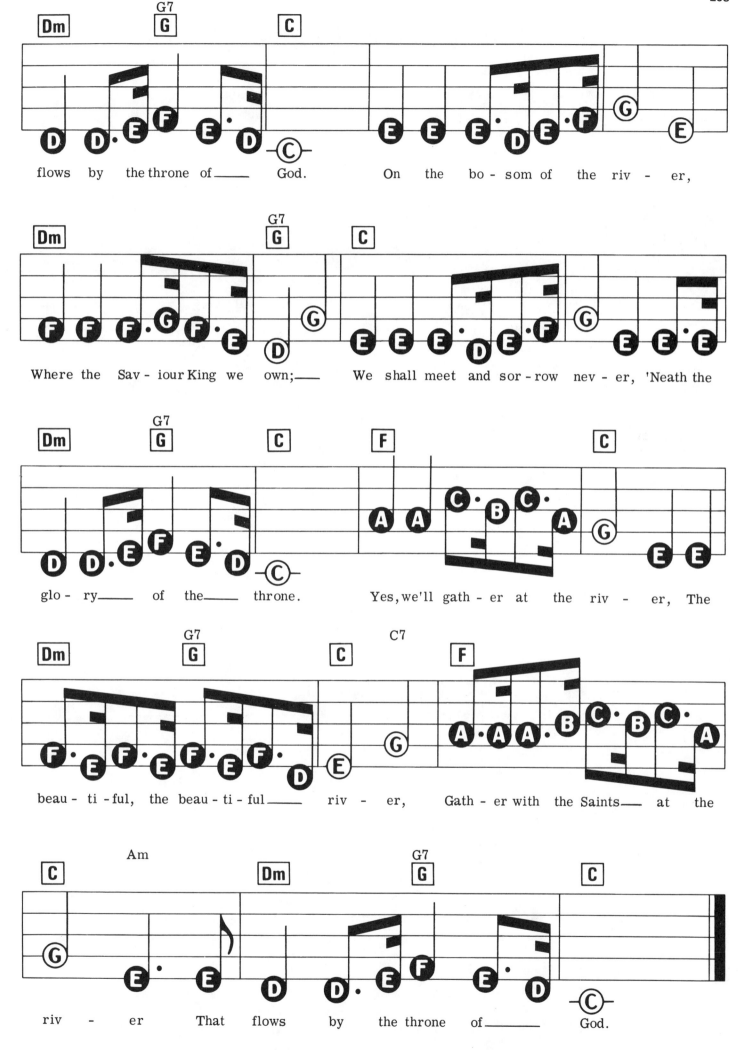

Softly And Tenderly

Registration 2

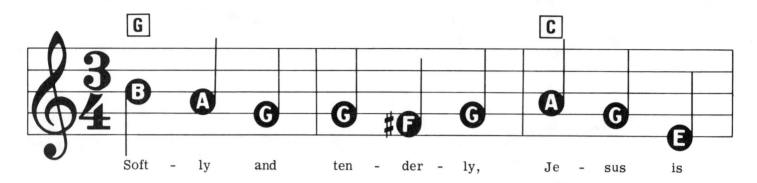

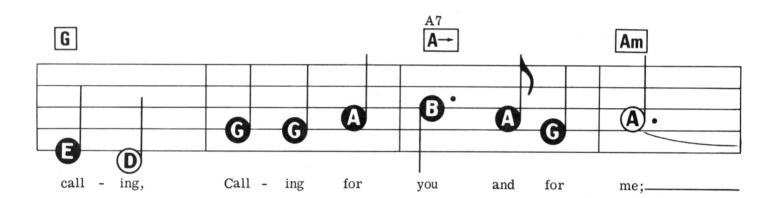

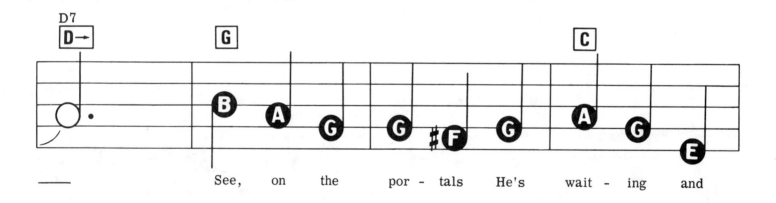

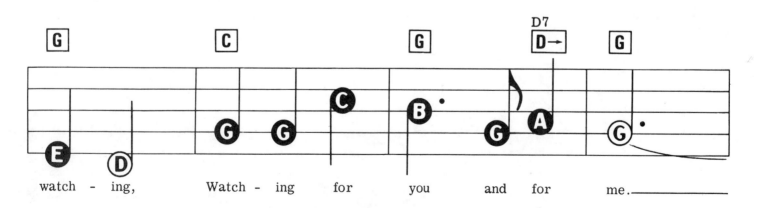

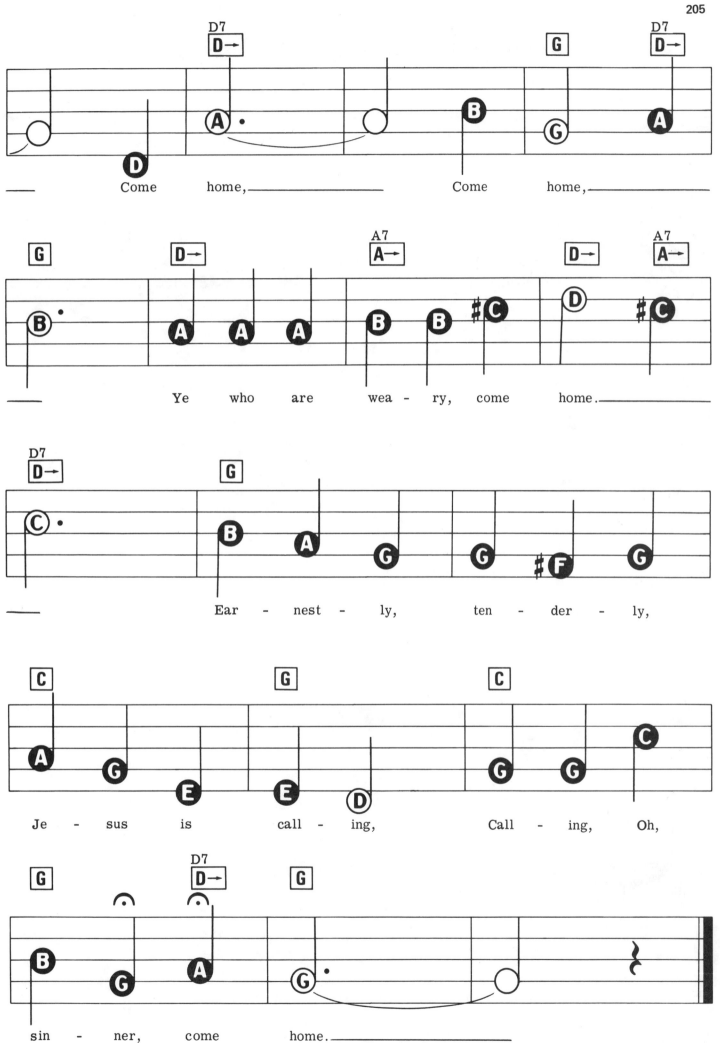

Swing Low, Sweet Chariot

Registration 5

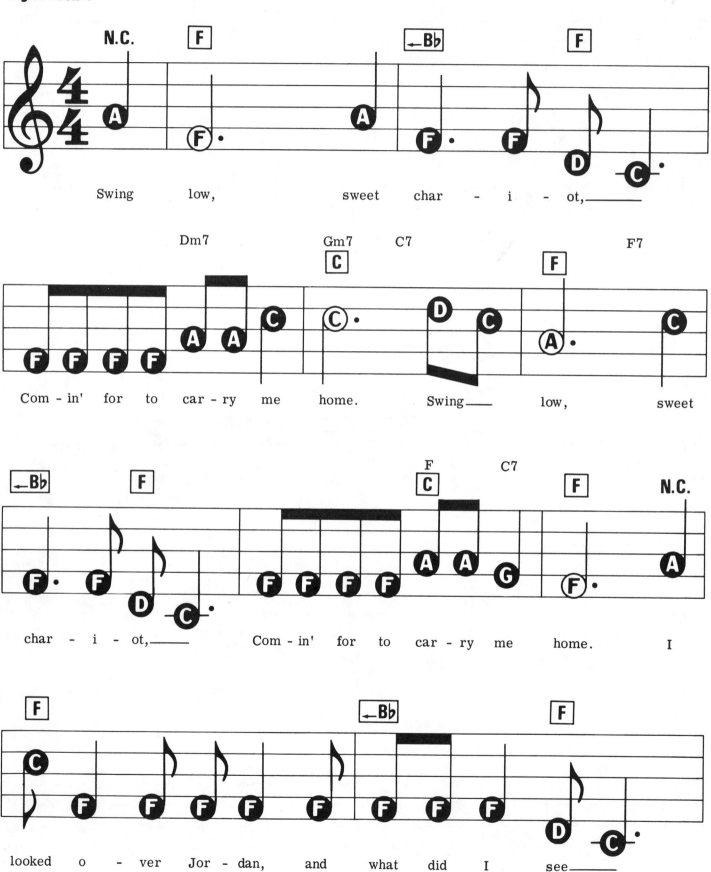

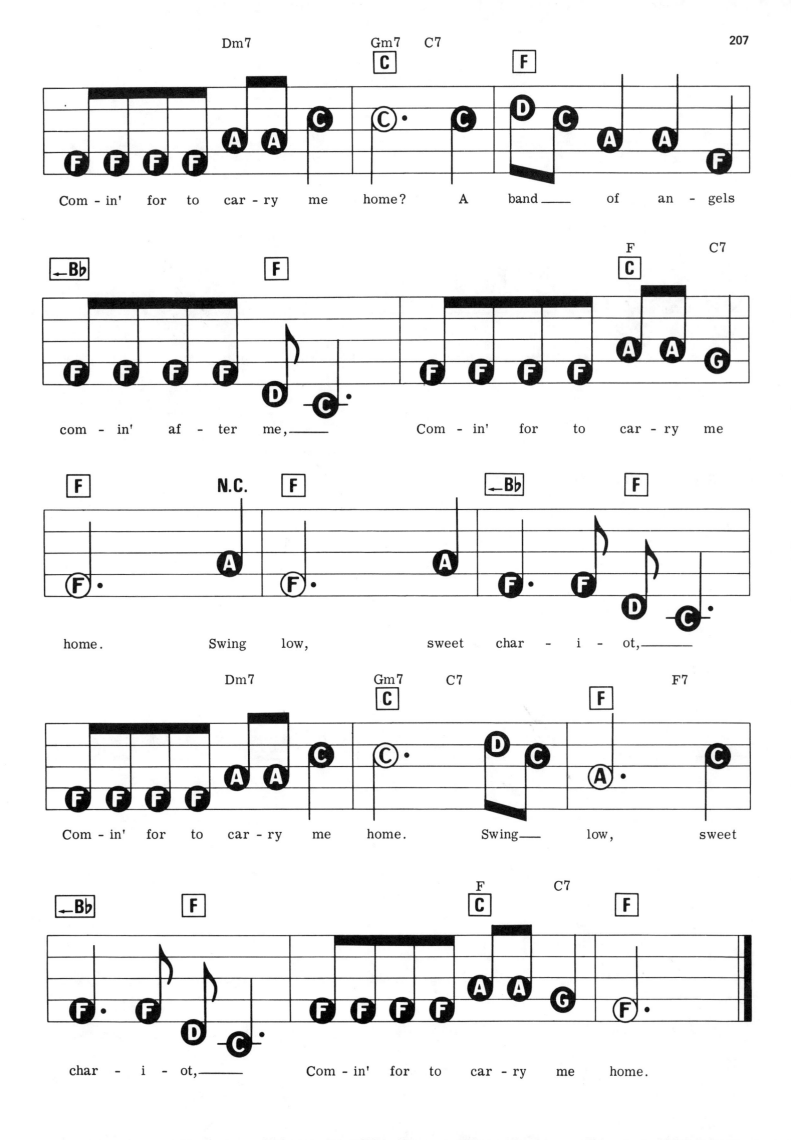

Were You There?

Registration 6

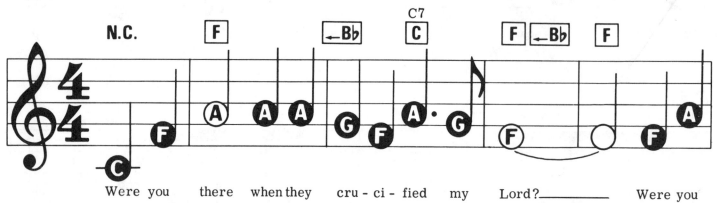

Were you there when they cru-ci-fied my Lord?_____ Were you

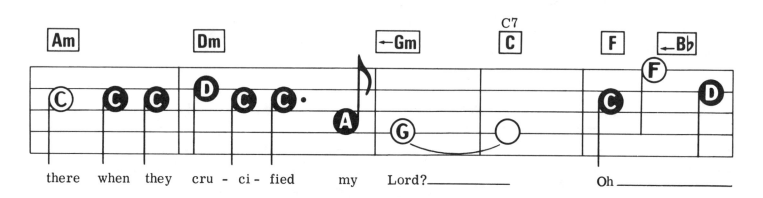

there when they cru-ci-fied my Lord?_____ Oh _____

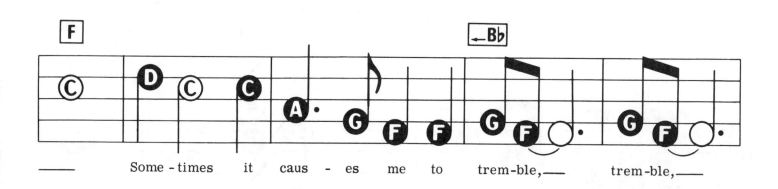

_____ Some-times it caus-es me to trem-ble,_____ trem-ble,_____

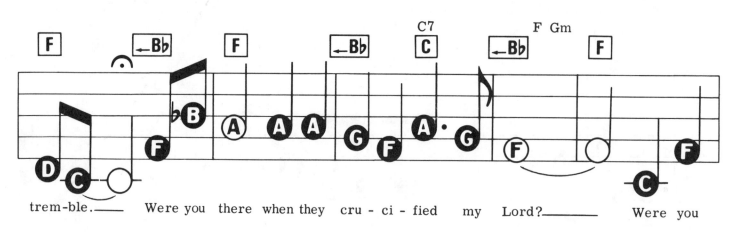

trem-ble._____ Were you there when they cru-ci-fied my Lord?_____ Were you

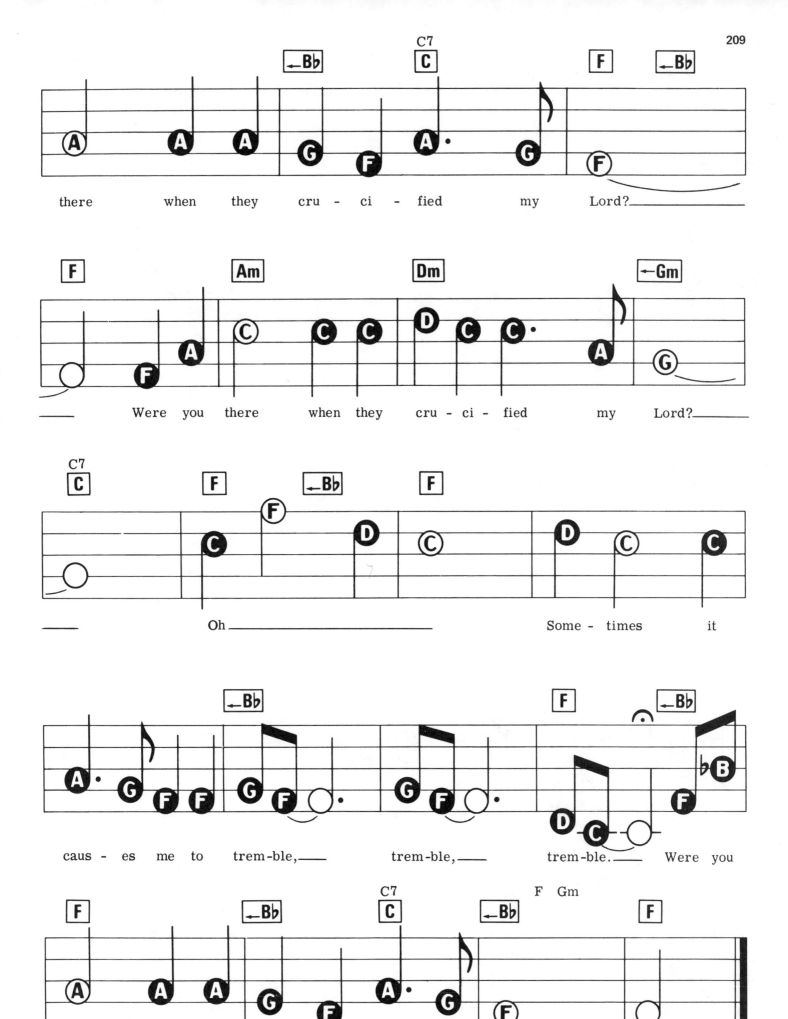

What A Friend We Have In Jesus

Registration 3

What a friend we have in Je - sus, All our sins and griefs to

bear, What a priv - i - lege to car - ry,

Ev - 'ry-thing to God in pray'r. Oh, what peace we of - ten for - feit,

Oh, what need-less pain we bear, All be - cause we do not

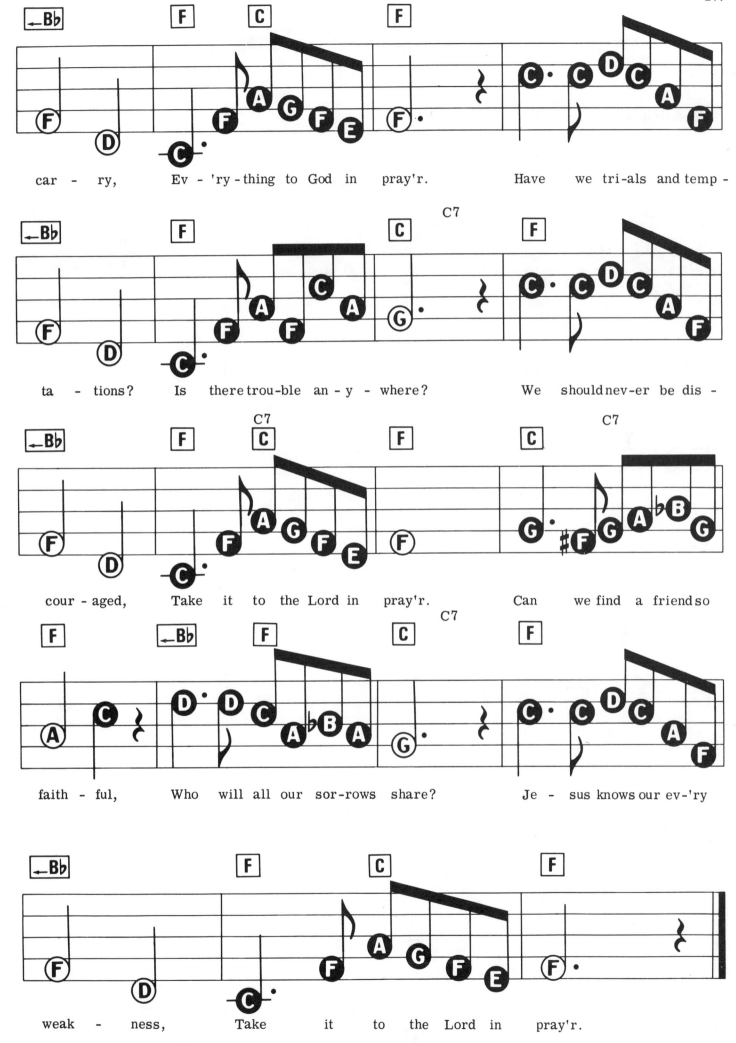

Whispering Hope

Registration 10

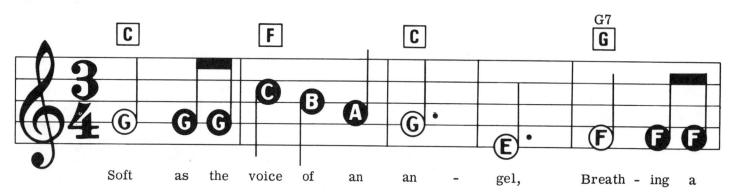

Soft as the voice of an an - gel, Breath - ing a

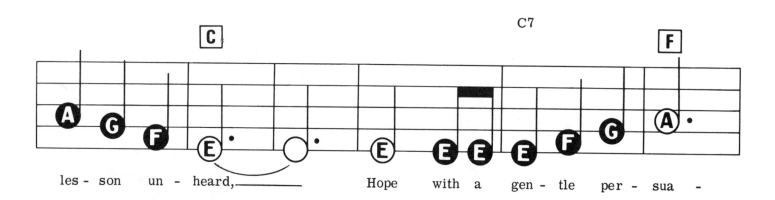

les - son un - heard,_____ Hope with a gen - tle per - sua -

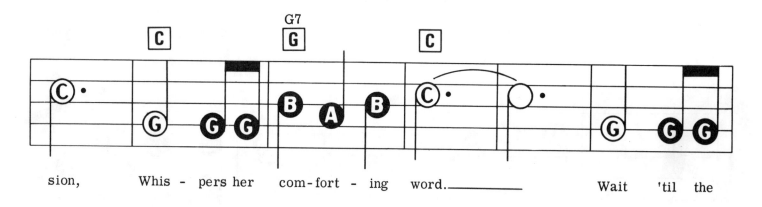

sion, Whis - pers her com - fort - ing word._____ Wait 'til the

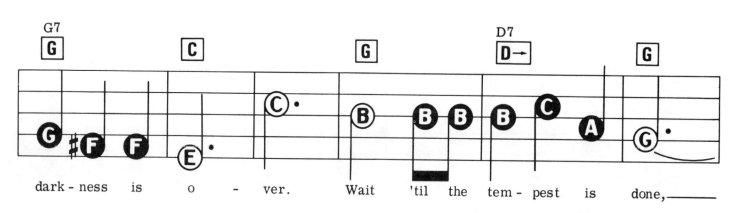

dark - ness is o - ver. Wait 'til the tem - pest is done,_____

213

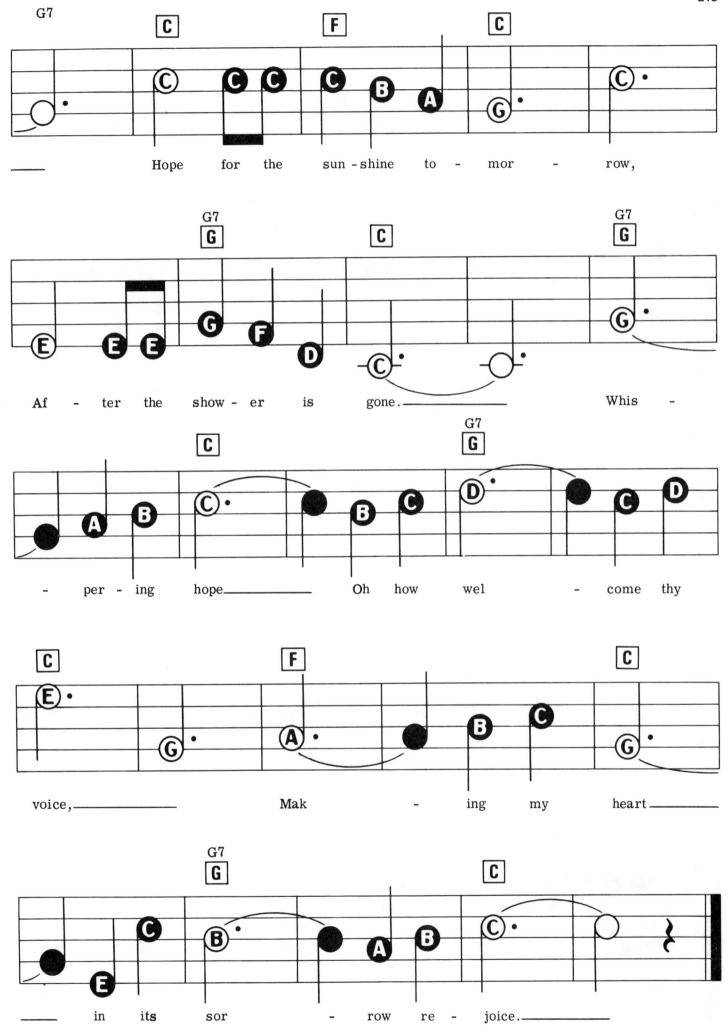

Adios Muchachos

Registration 5

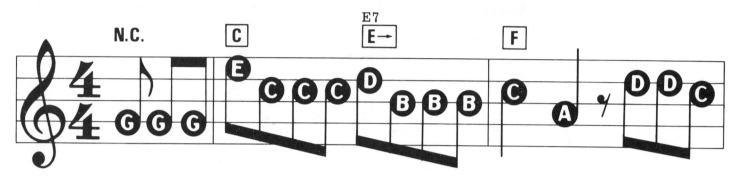

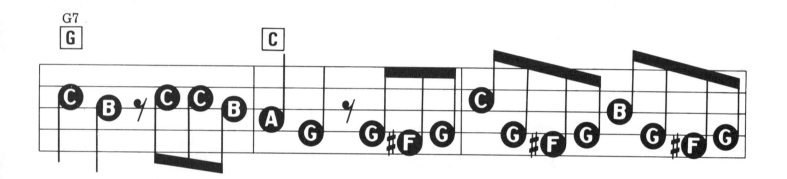

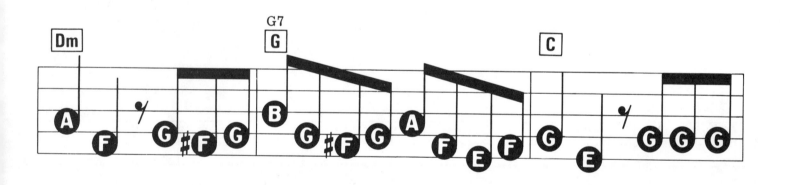

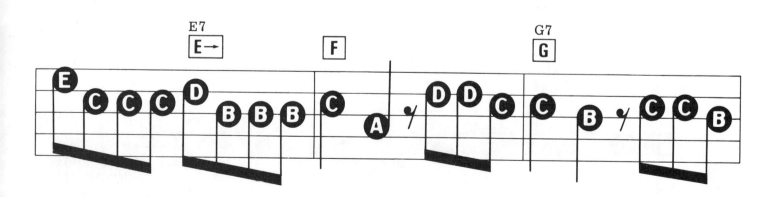

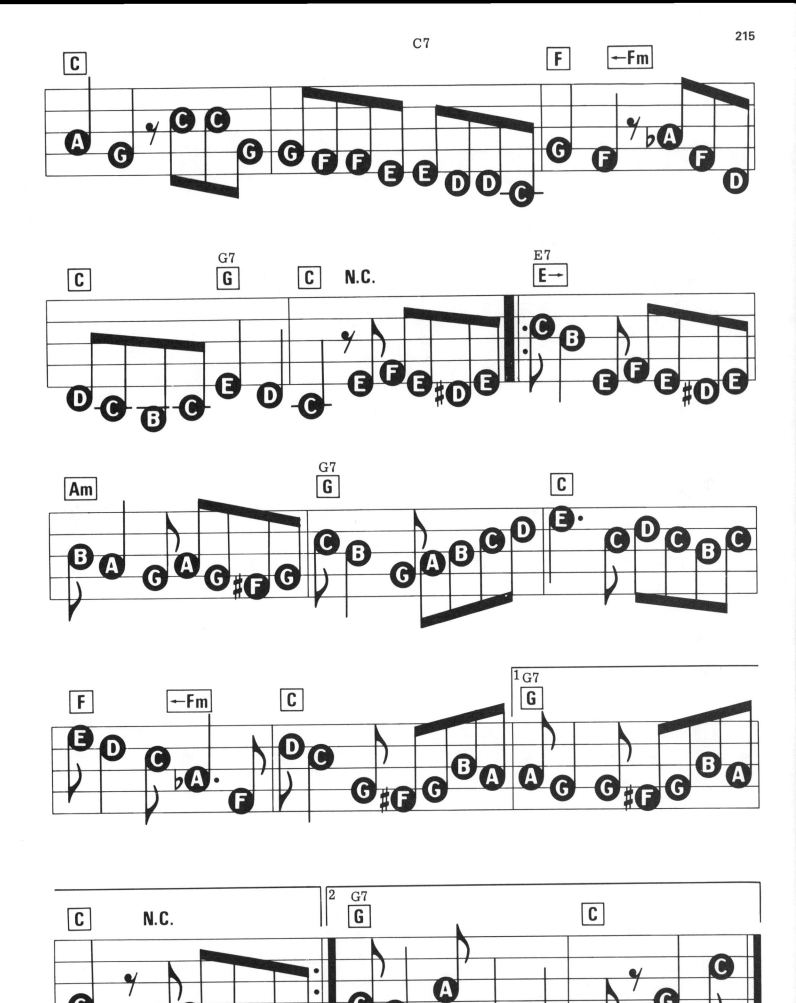

Cielito Lindo

Registration 4

Mexican

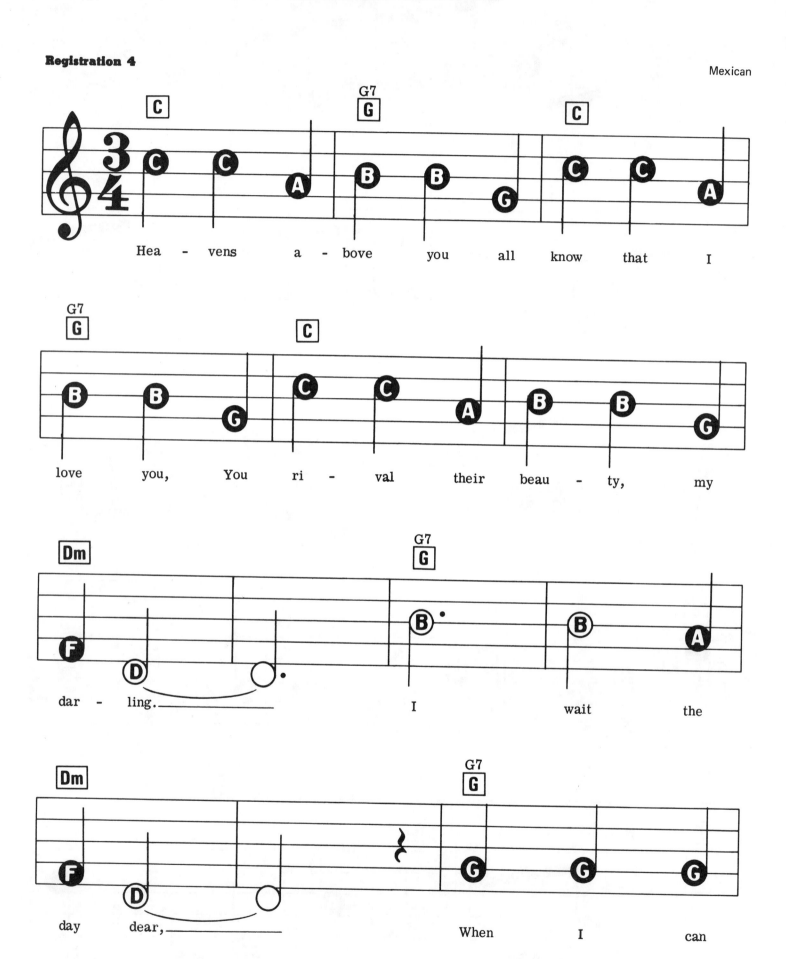

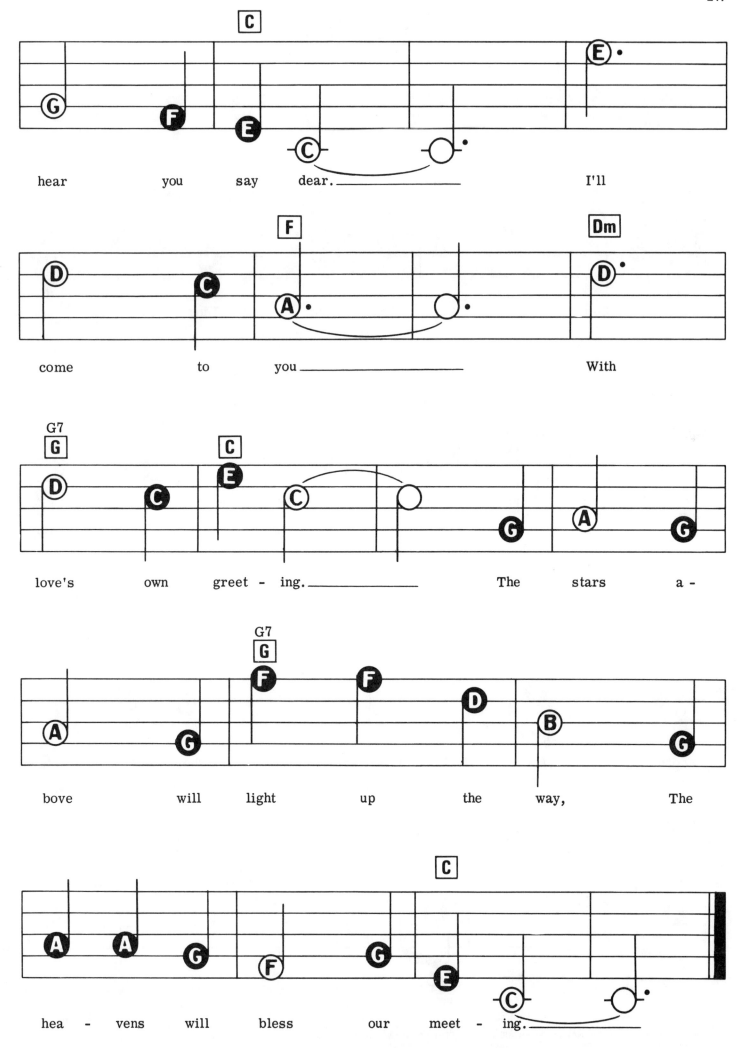

Juanita

Registration 10

Spanish

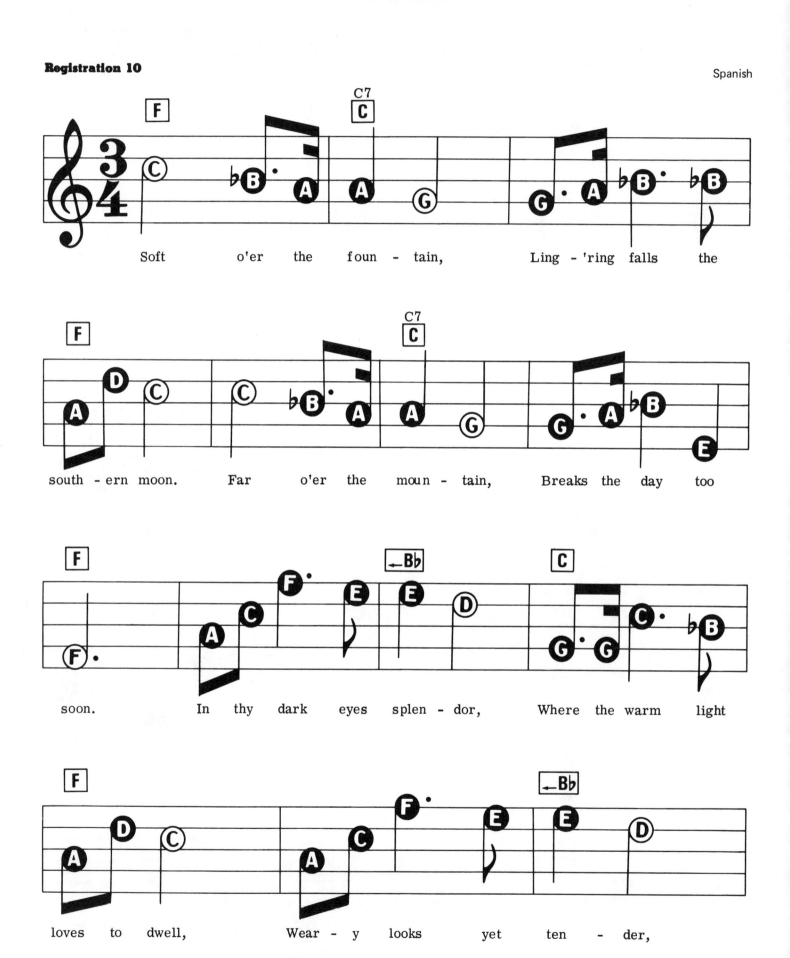

Soft o'er the foun - tain, Ling - 'ring falls the

south - ern moon. Far o'er the moun - tain, Breaks the day too

soon. In thy dark eyes splen - dor, Where the warm light

loves to dwell, Wear - y looks yet ten - der,

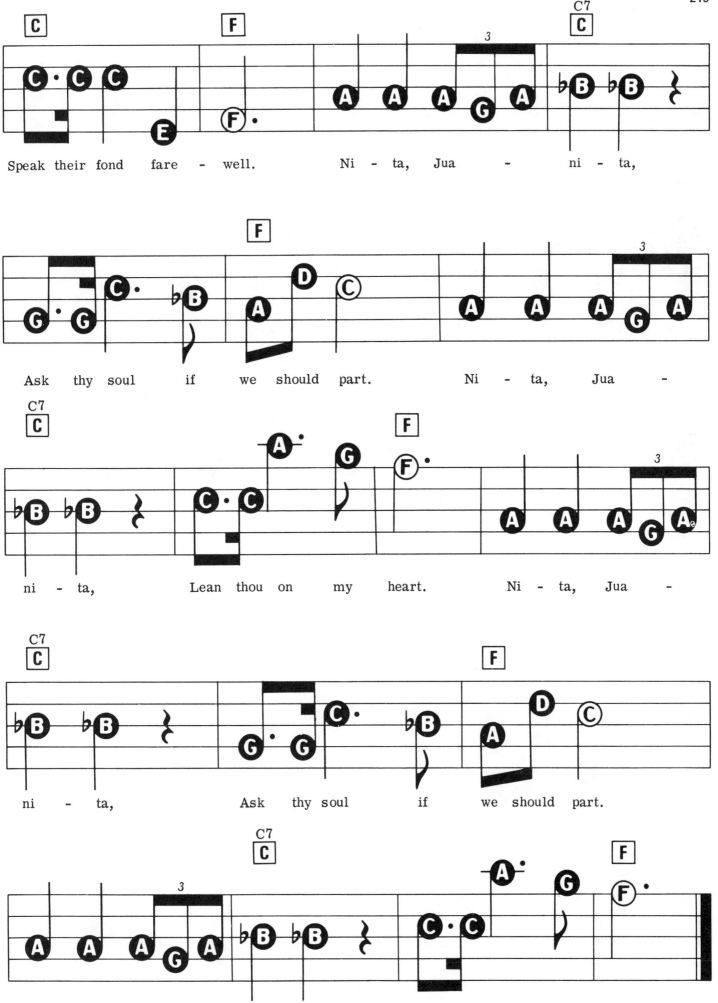

La Golondrina

Registration 2

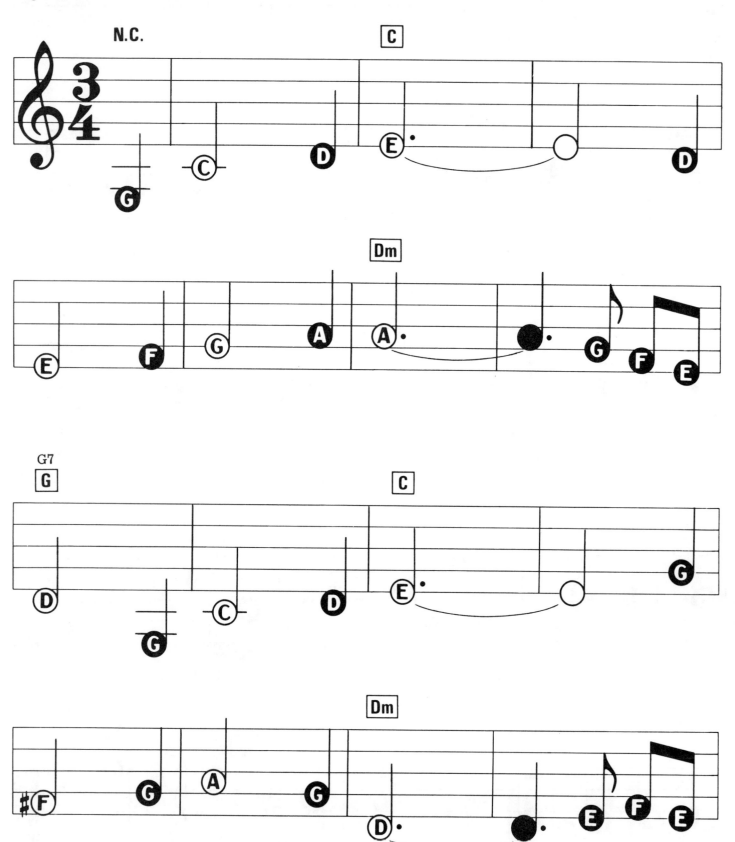

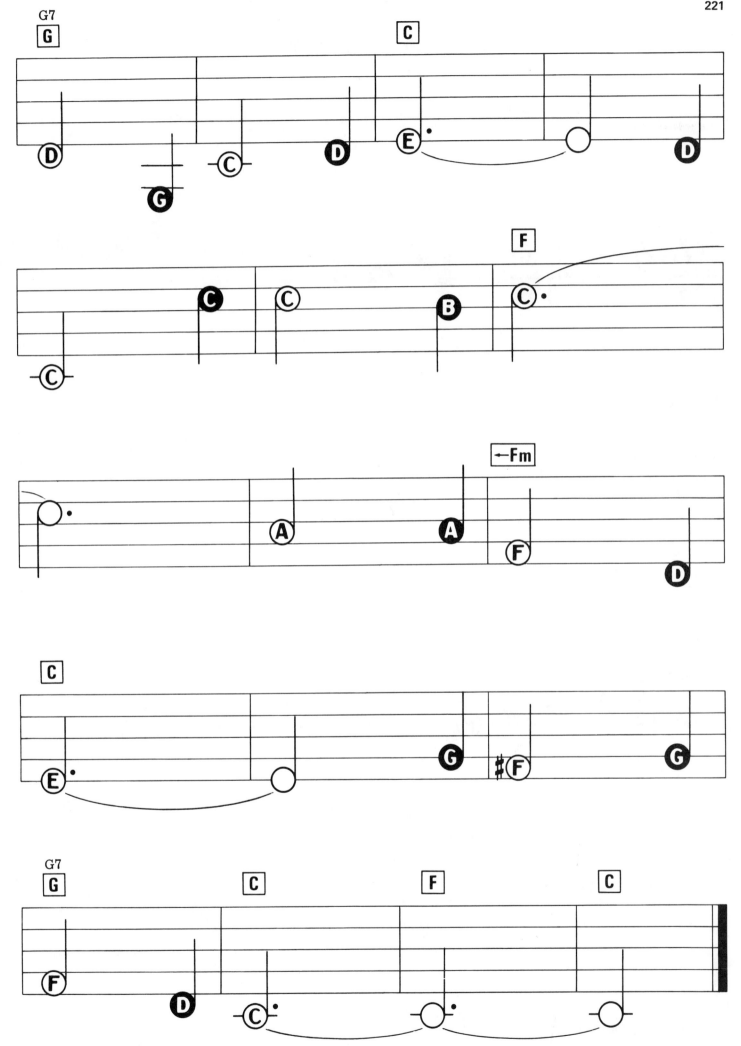

La Paloma

Registration 3

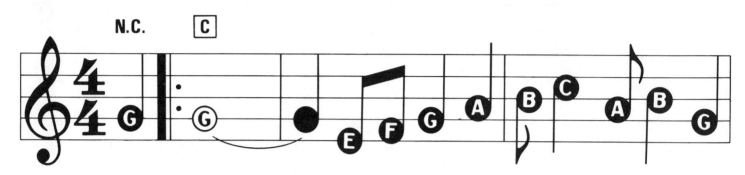

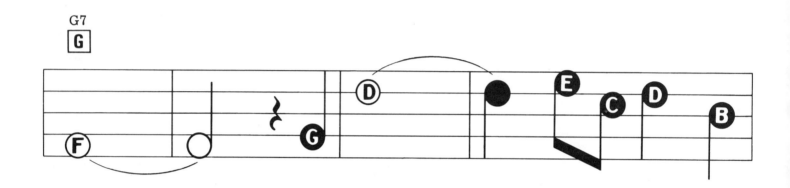

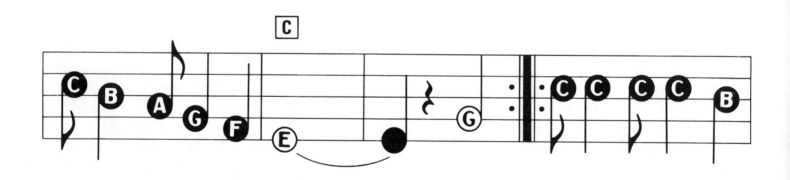

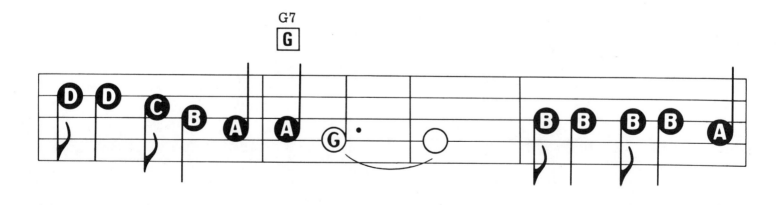

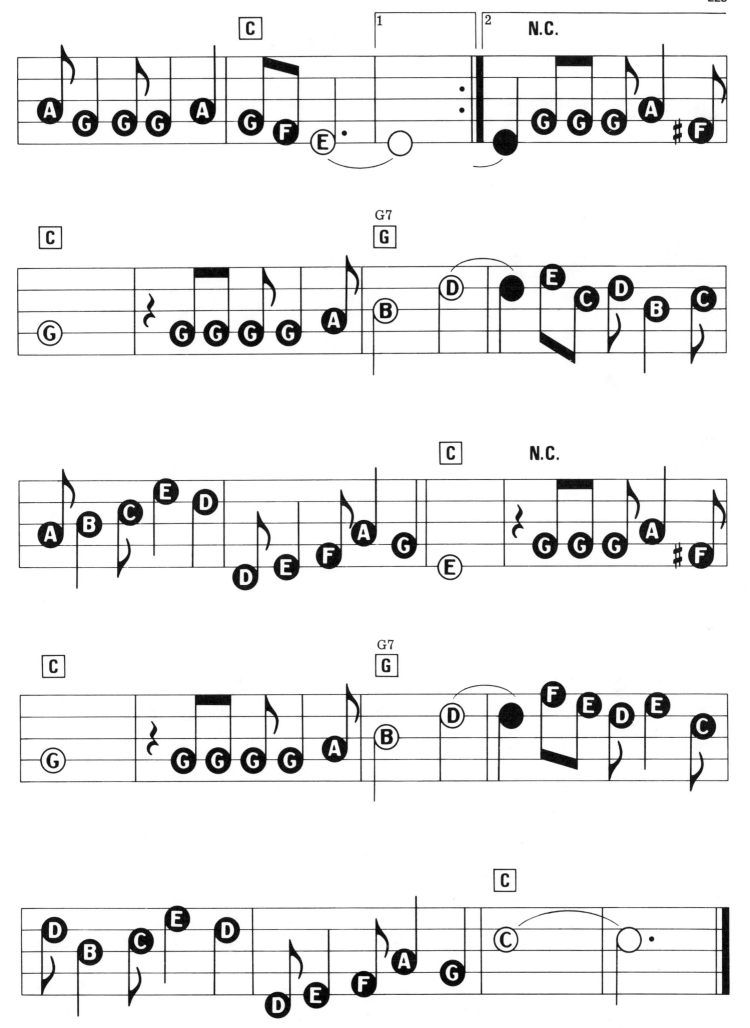

Toreador Song

Registration 1

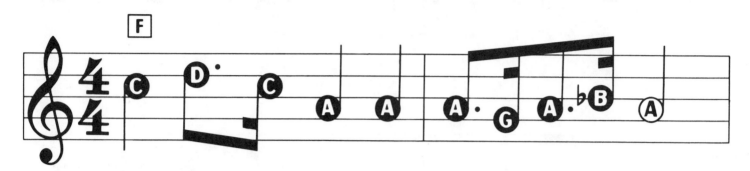

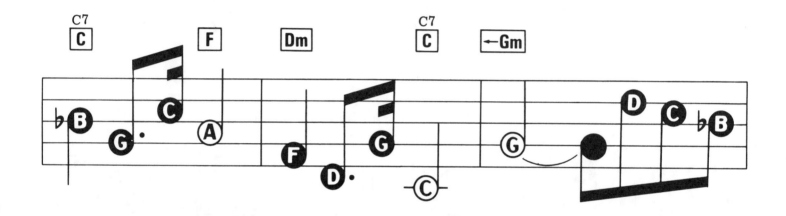

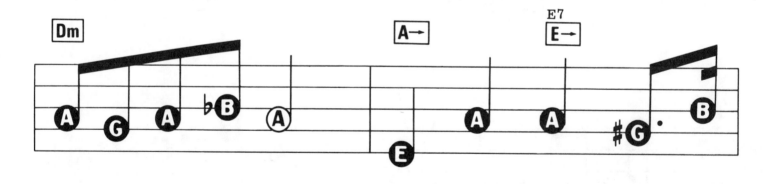

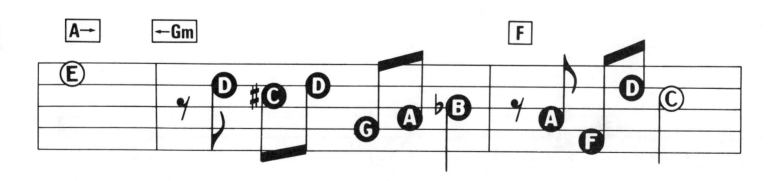

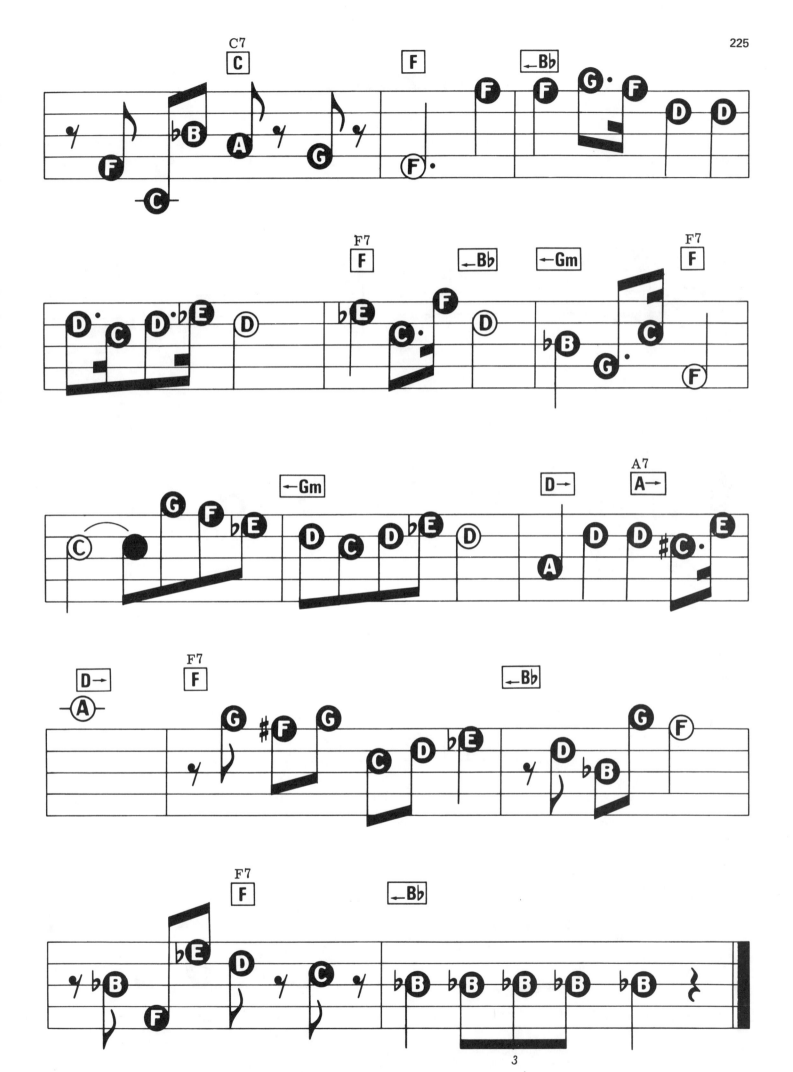

Finale

Registration 3

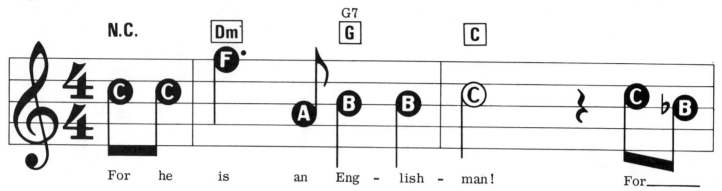

For he is an Eng - lish - man! For_____

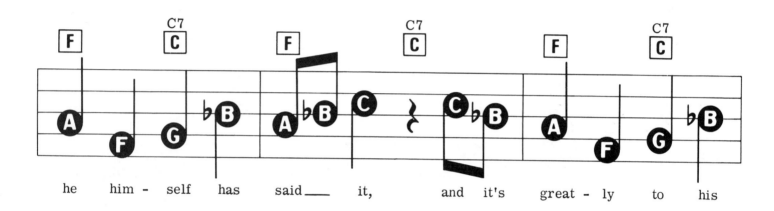

he him - self has said____ it, and it's great - ly to his

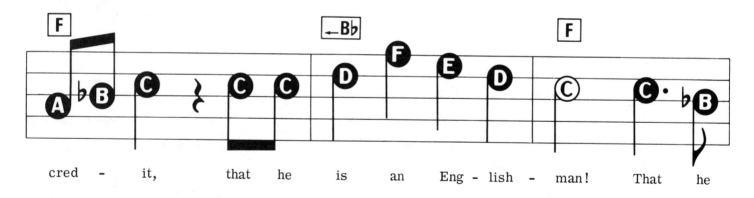

cred - it, that he is an Eng - lish - man! That he

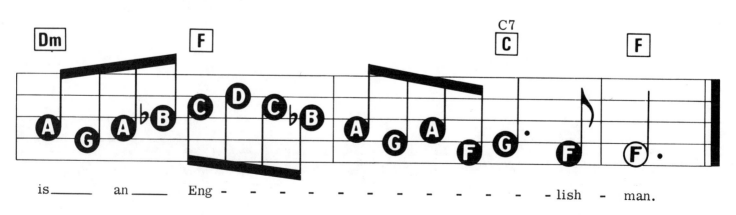

is____ an____ Eng - - - - - - - - - - lish - man.

When I Was A Lad

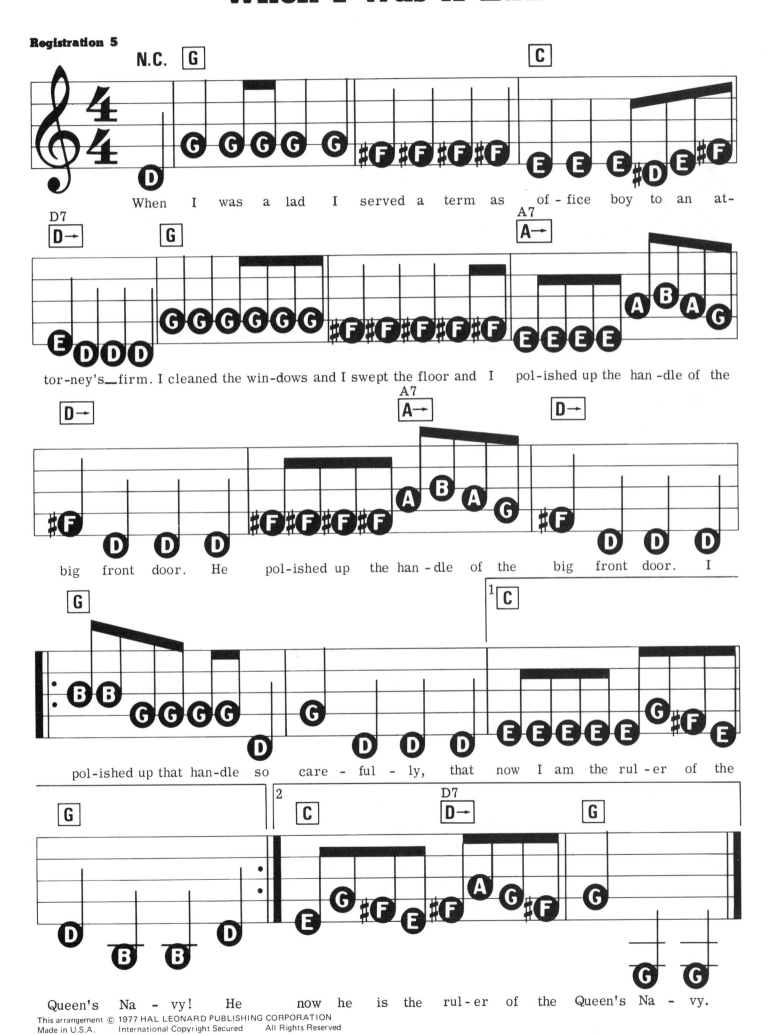

Hear The Waltz

Registration 10

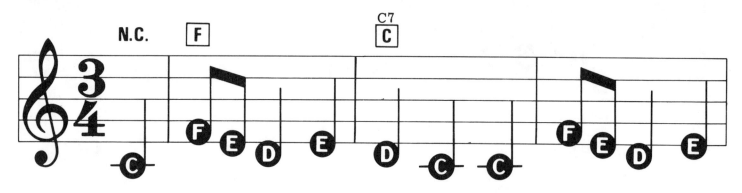

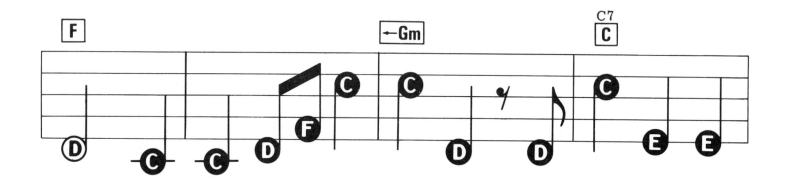

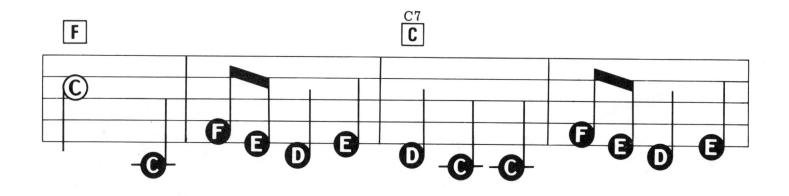

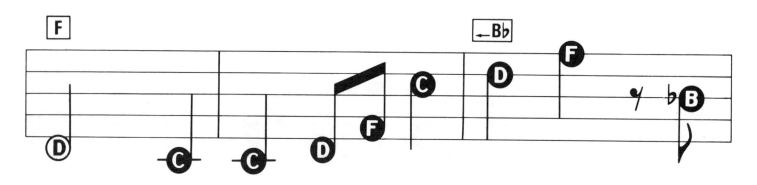

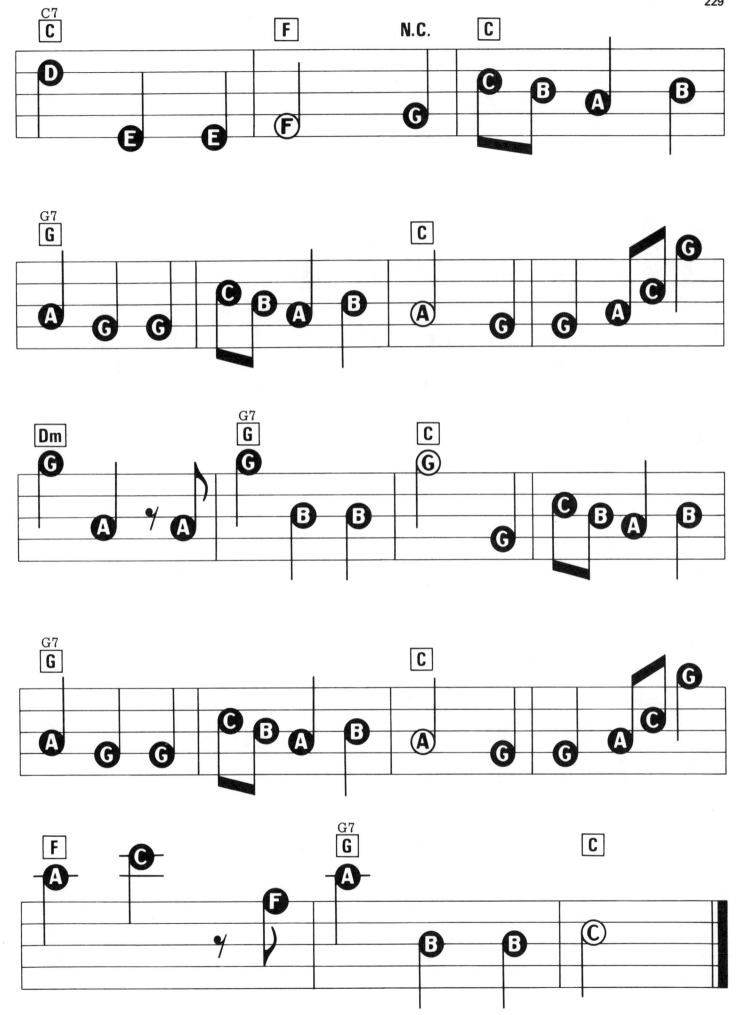

I'm Called Little Buttercup

Registration 5

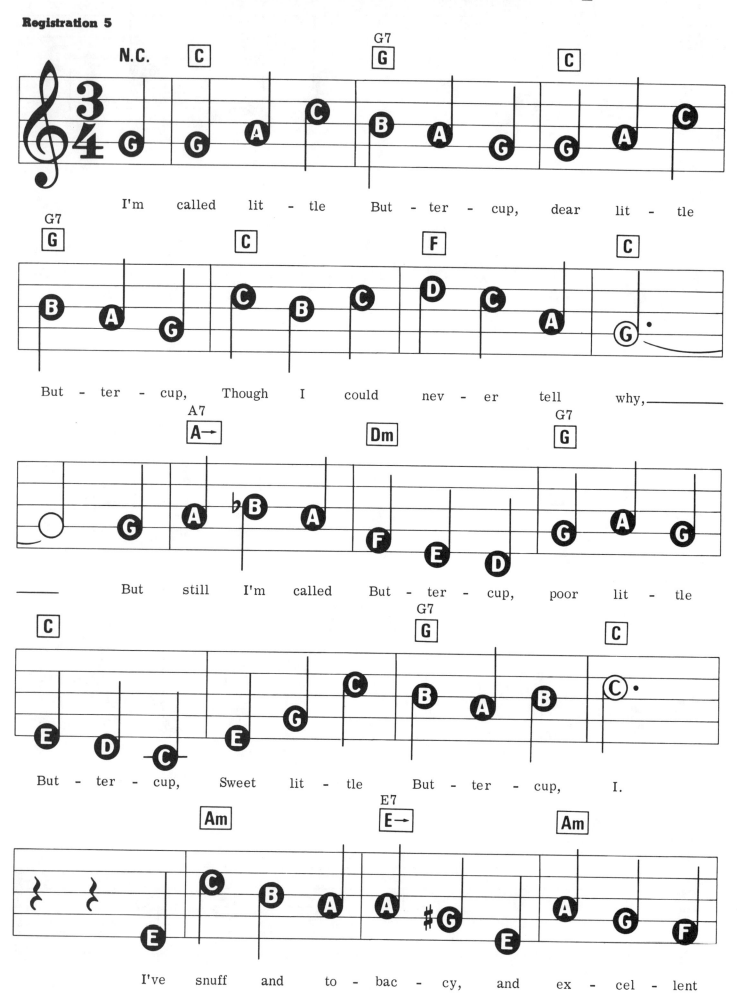

I'm called lit - tle But - ter - cup, dear lit - tle But - ter - cup, Though I could nev - er tell why, _____ But still I'm called But - ter - cup, poor lit - tle But - ter - cup, Sweet lit - tle But - ter - cup, I. I've snuff and to - bac - cy, and ex - cel - lent

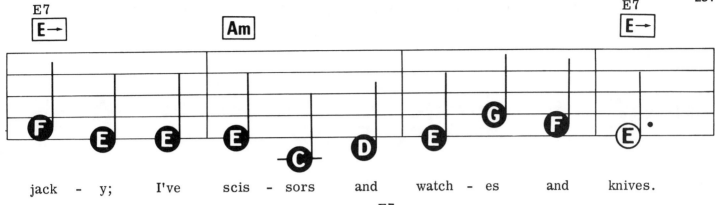

jack - y; I've scis - sors and watch - es and knives.

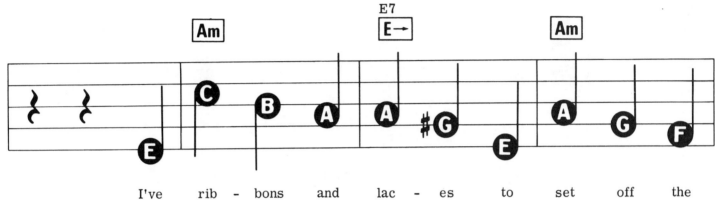

I've rib - bons and lac - es to set off the

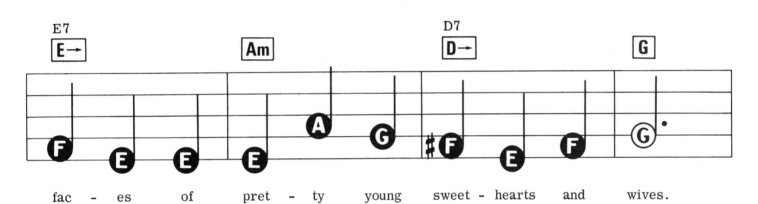

fac - es of pret - ty young sweet - hearts and wives.

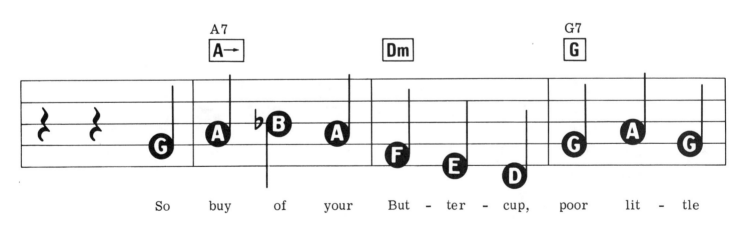

So buy of your But - ter - cup, poor lit - tle

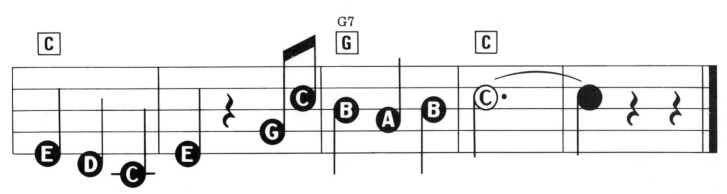

But - ter - cup, come, of your But - ter - cup buy._____

Tit Willow

Registration 4

On a tree by a riv-er a lit-tle tom-tit sang____

"Wil-low, tit-wil-low, tit-wil-low!"_____ And I

said to him, "Dick-y-bird why do you sit sing-ing

"Wil-low, tit-wil-low, tit-wil-low"?_____ "Is it

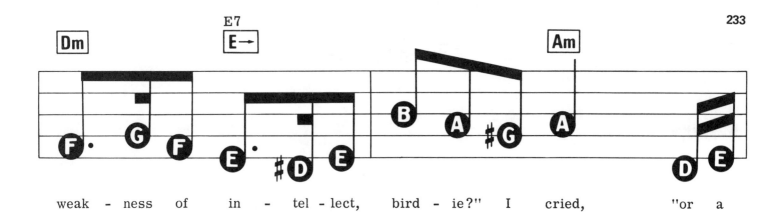

weak - ness of in - tel - lect, bird - ie?" I cried, "or a

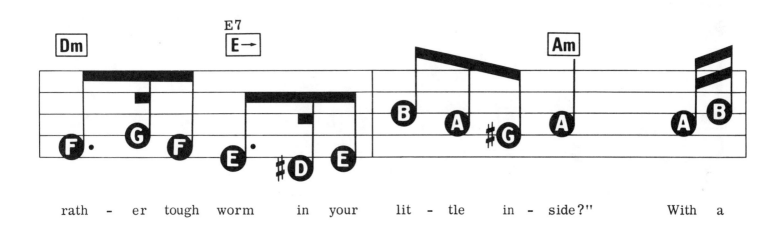

rath - er tough worm in your lit - tle in - side?" With a

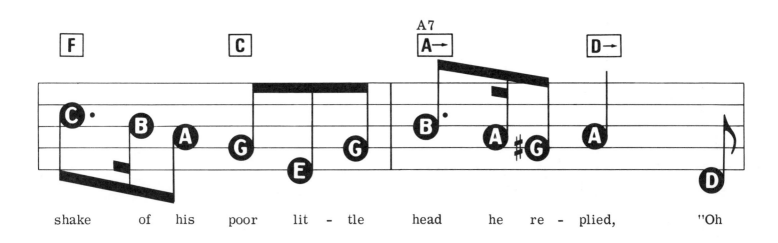

shake of his poor lit - tle head he re - plied, "Oh

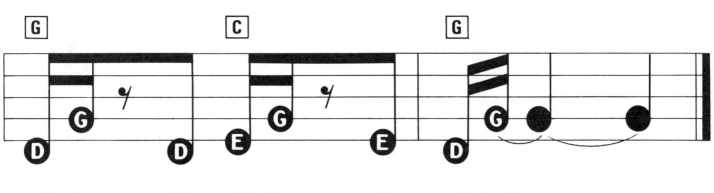

wil - low, tit - wil - low, tit - wil - low!"_____

Toyland

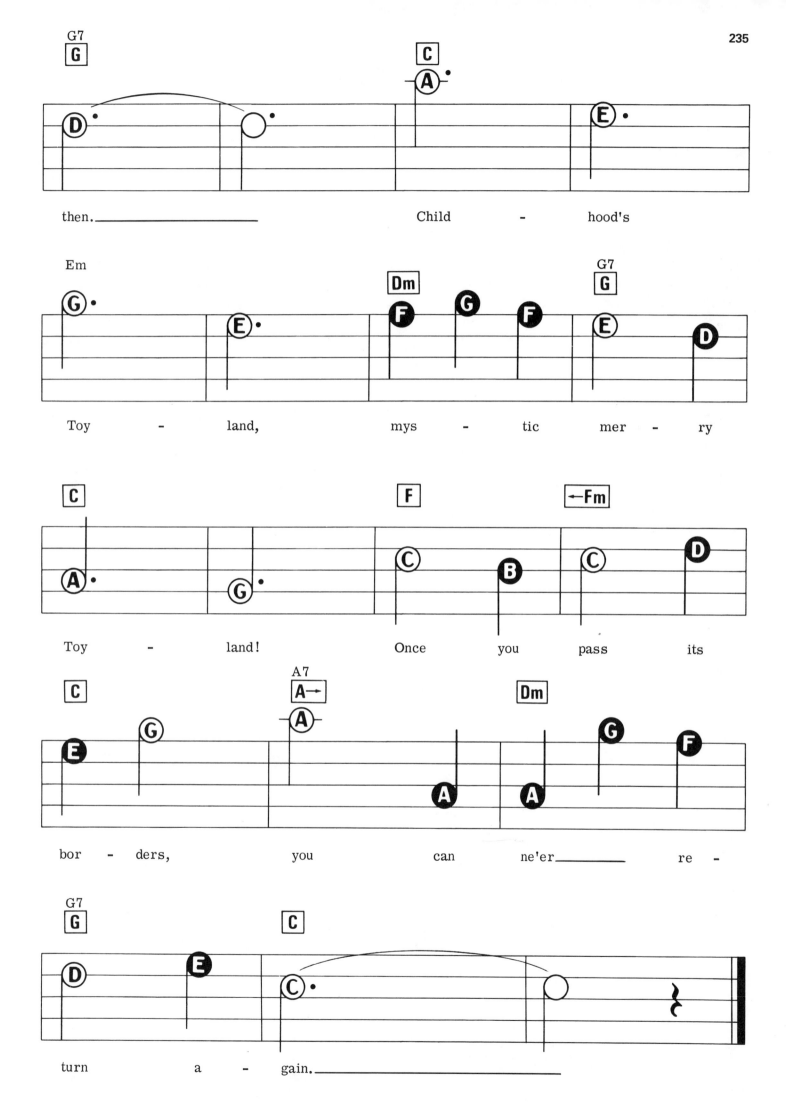

A Wandering Minstrel

Registration 5

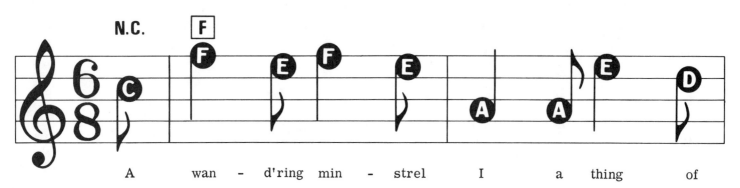

A wan - d'ring min - strel I a thing of

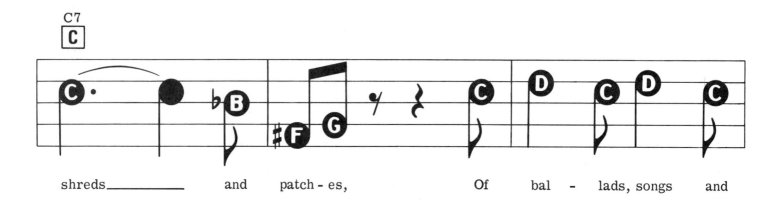

shreds_____ and patch - es, Of bal - lads, songs and

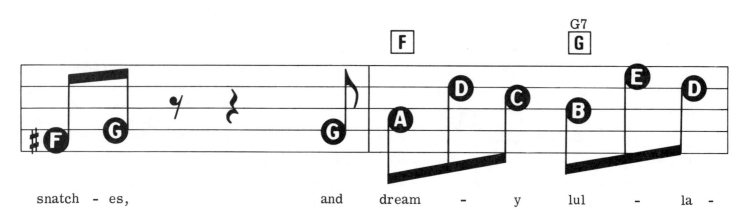

snatch - es, and dream - y lul - la -

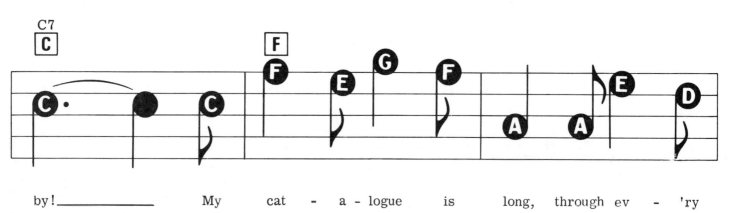

by!_____ My cat - a - logue is long, through ev - 'ry

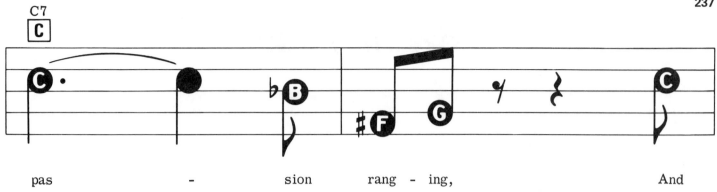

pas - - sion rang - ing, And

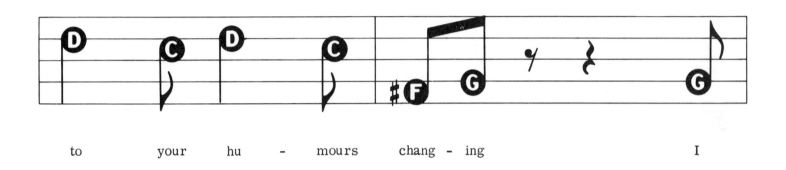

to your hu - mours chang - ing I

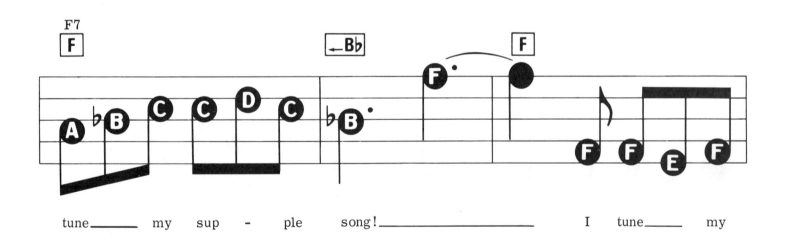

tune_____ my sup - ple song!_____ I tune_____ my

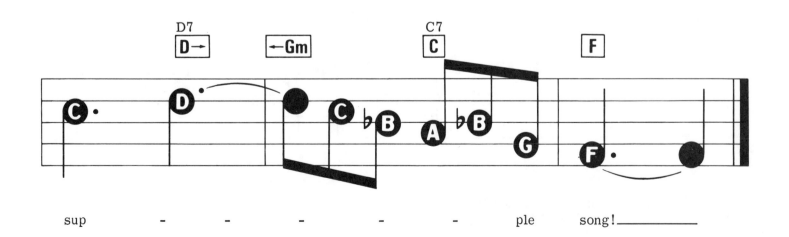

sup - - - - - ple song!_____

Barbara Polka

Registration 3

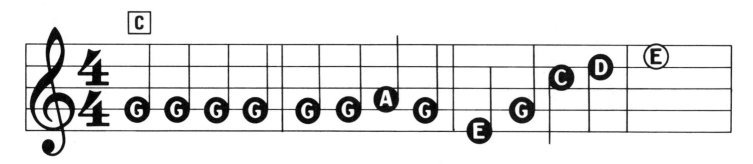

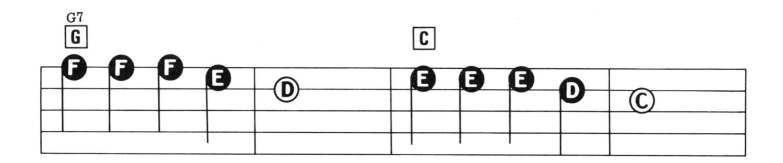

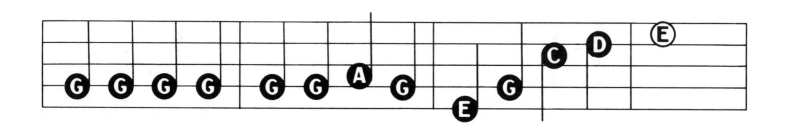

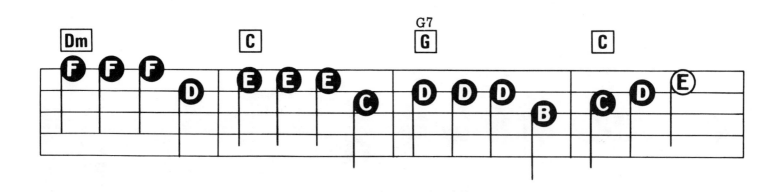

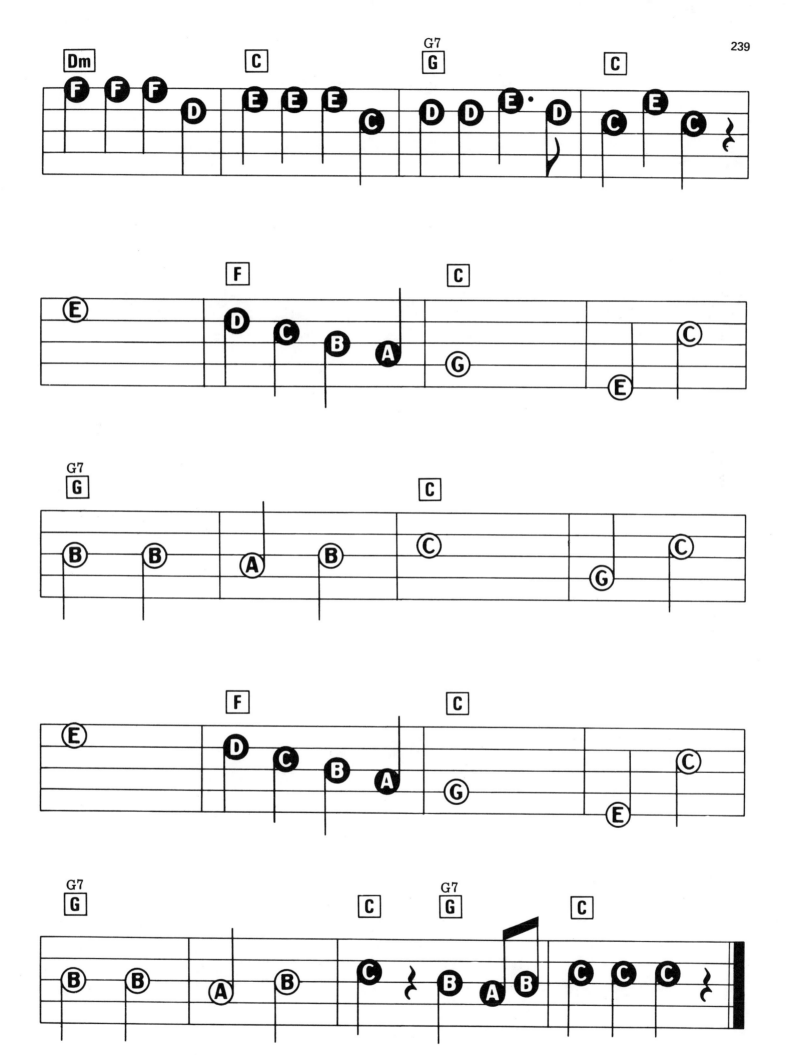

Can Can Polka

Registration 5

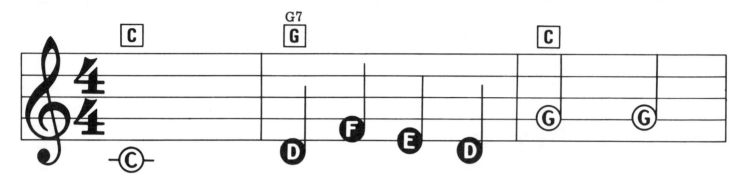

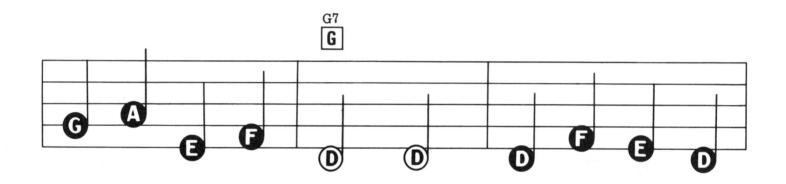

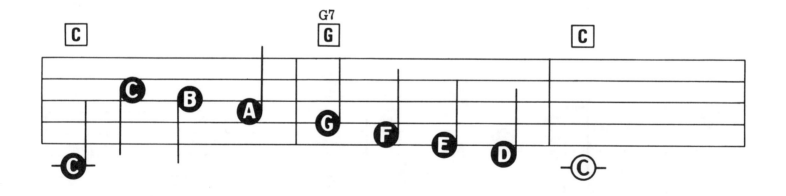

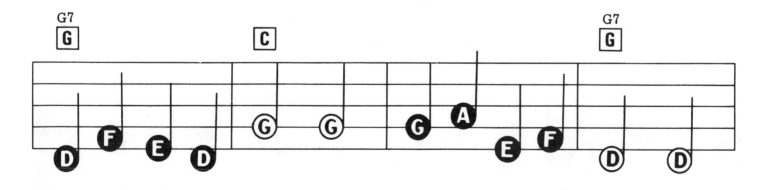

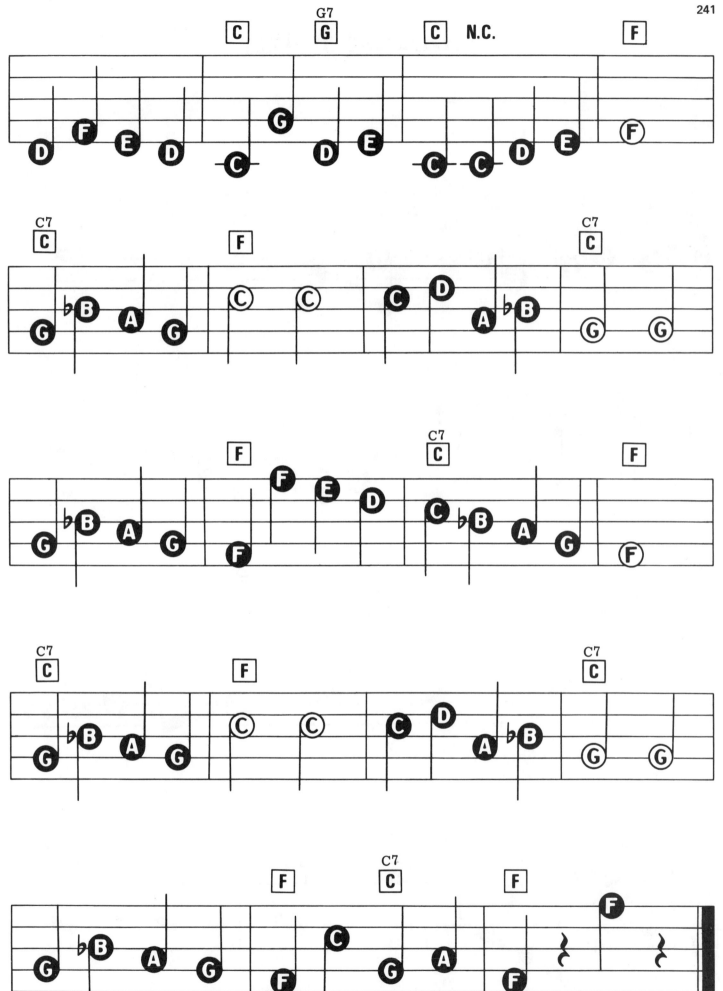

Clarinet Polka

Registration 9

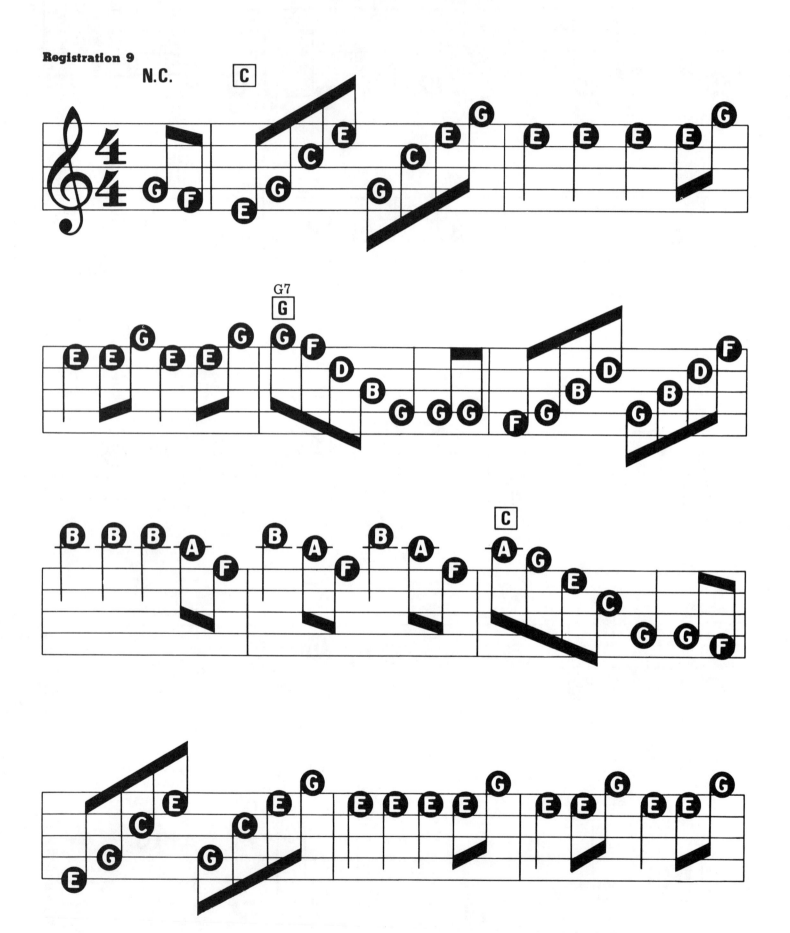

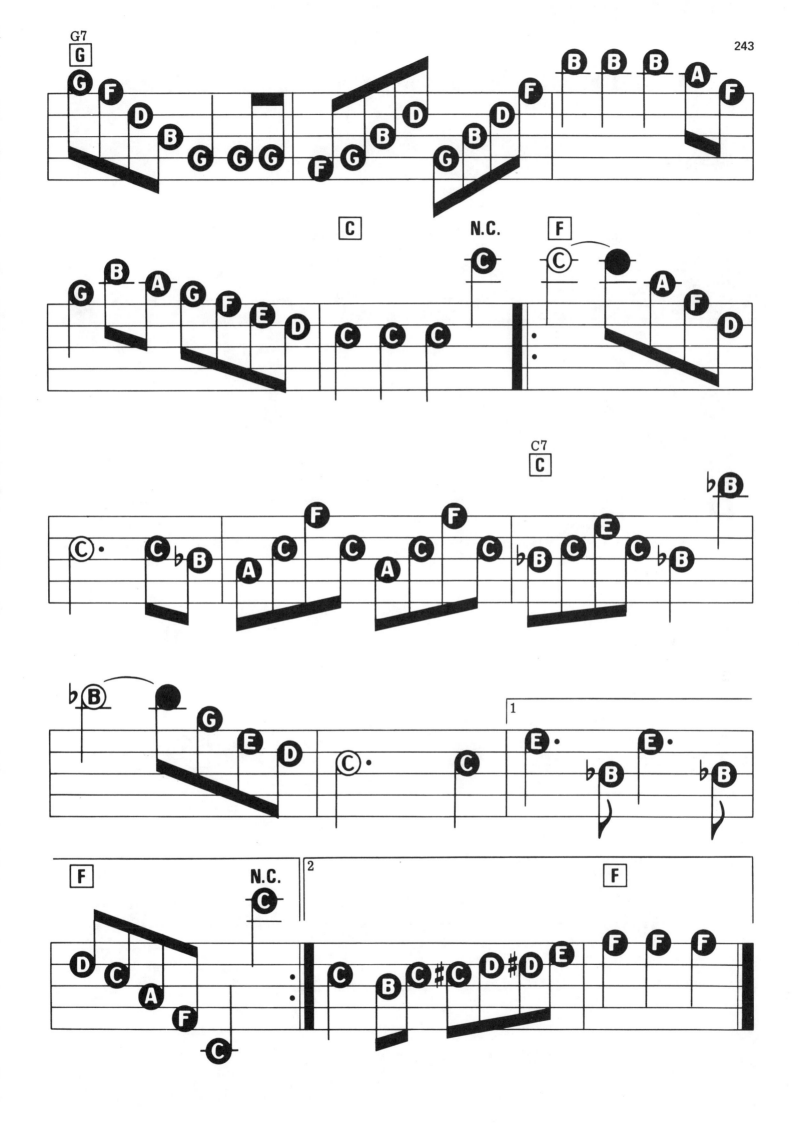

Columbia, The Gem Of The Ocean

Registration 4

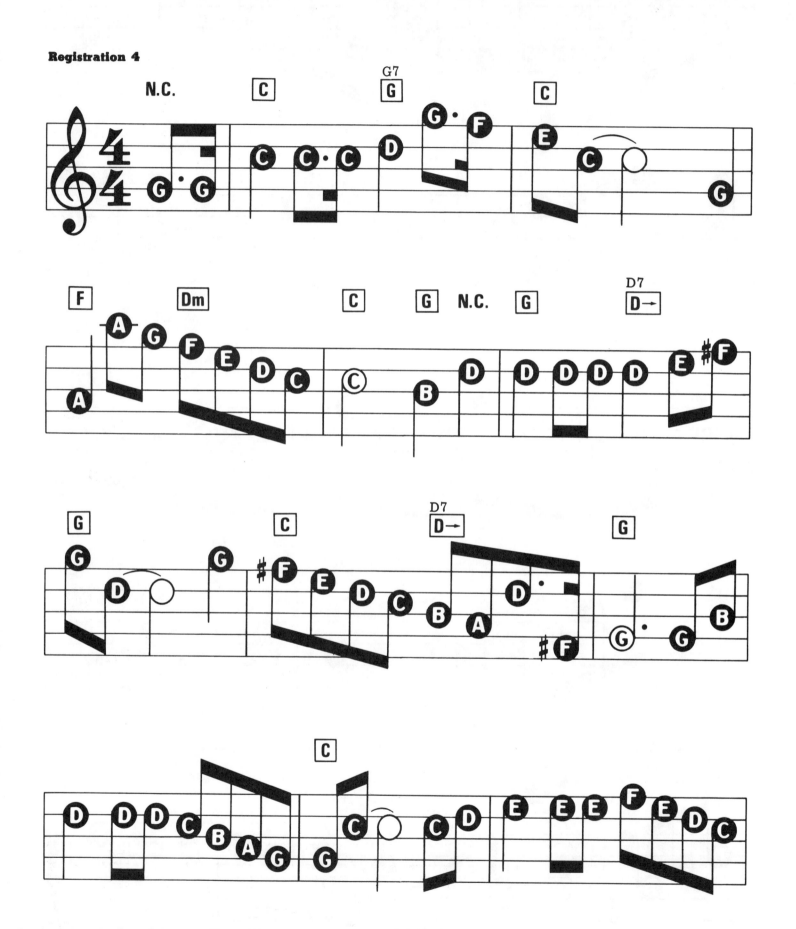

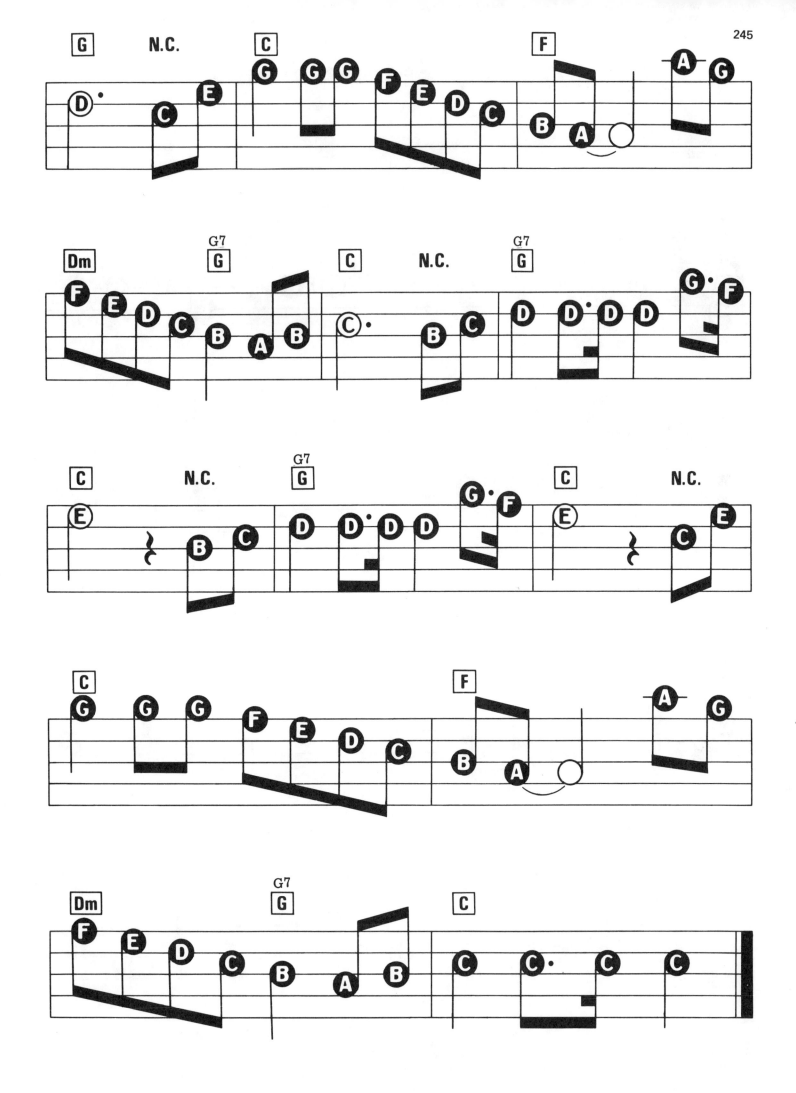

Friendly Fellows Polka

Registration 3

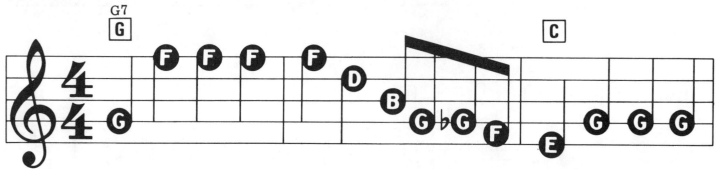

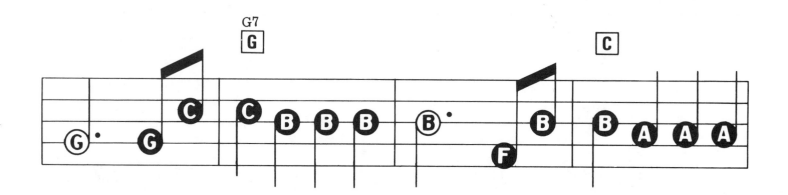

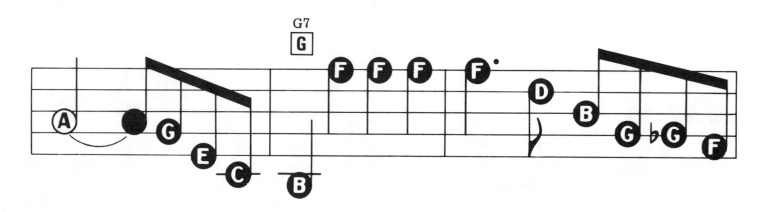

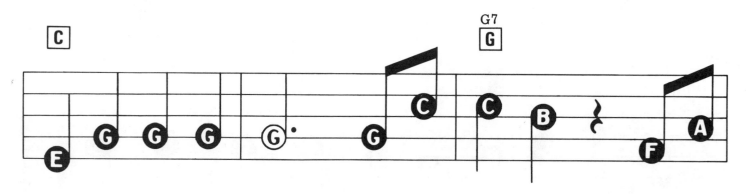

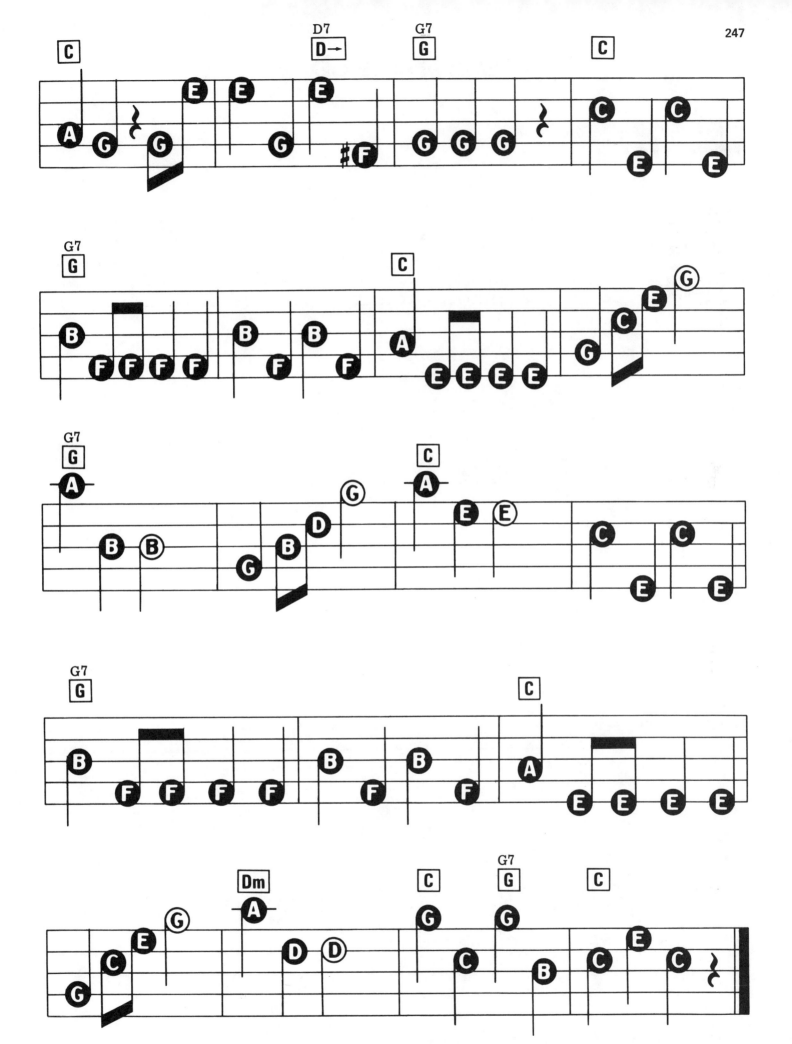

Helena Polka

Registration 9

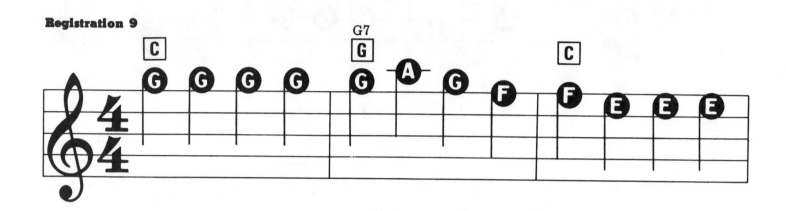

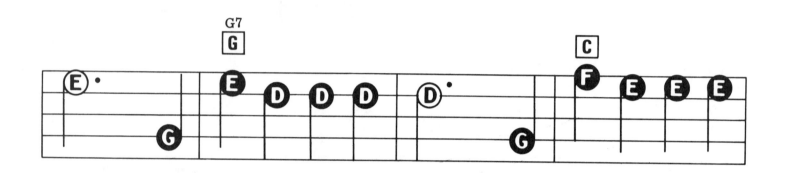

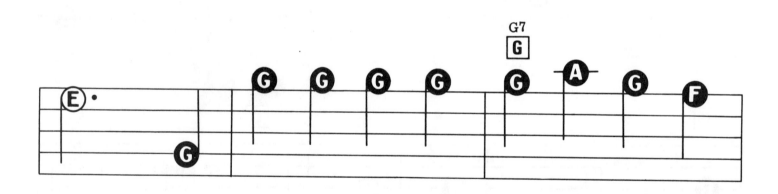

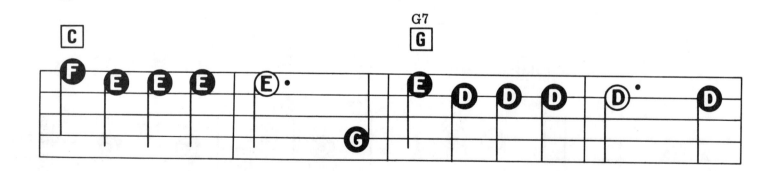

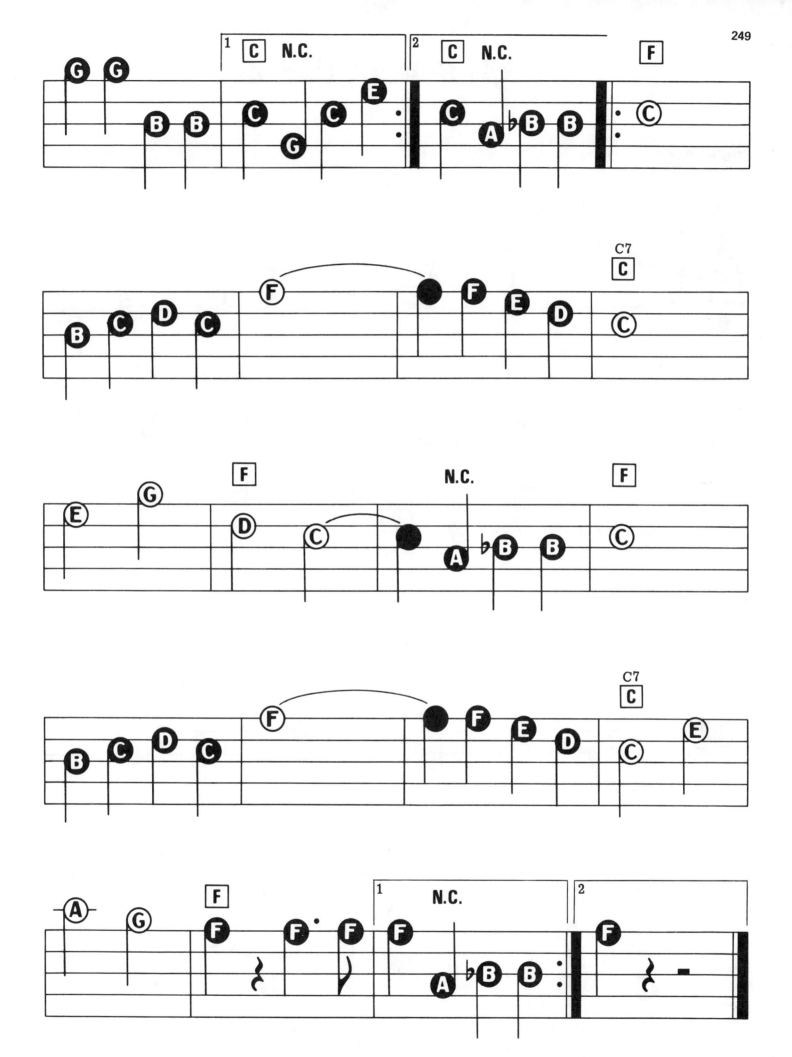

High School Cadets

Registration 2

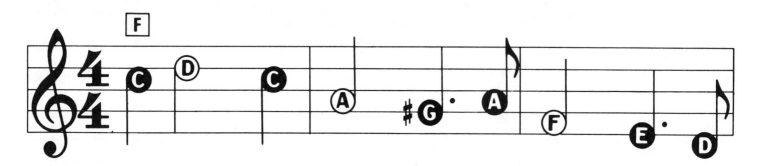

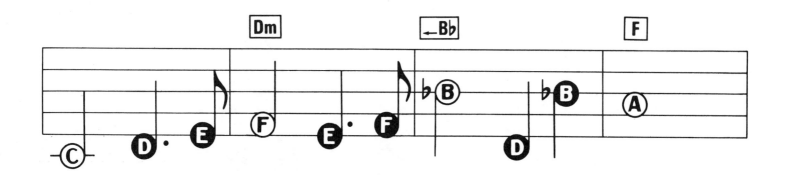

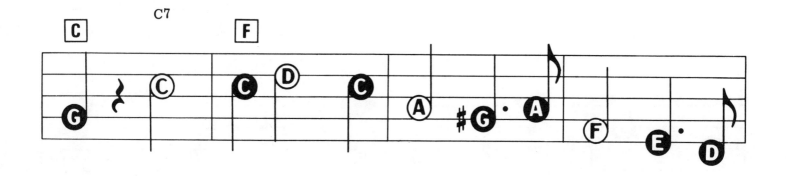

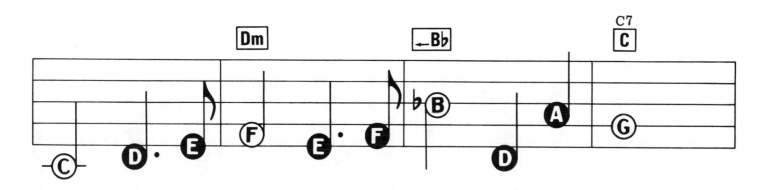

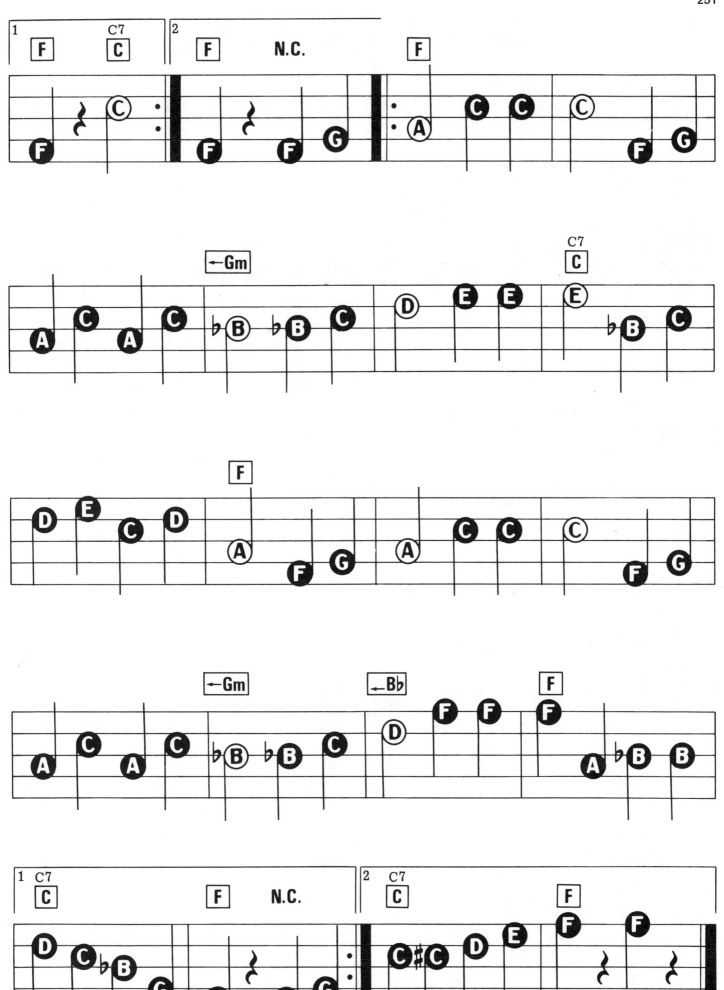

The Jolly Coppersmith

Registration 4

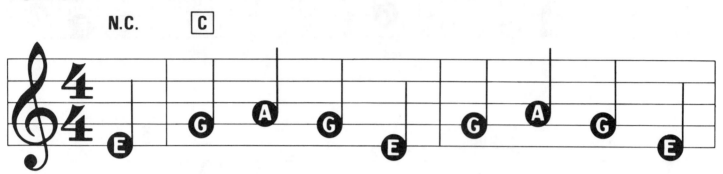

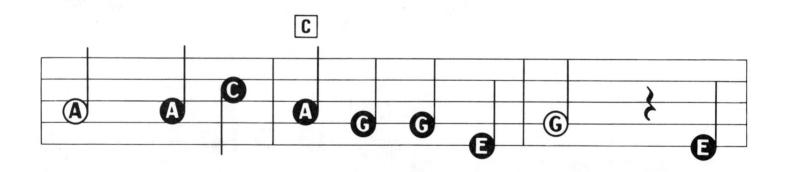

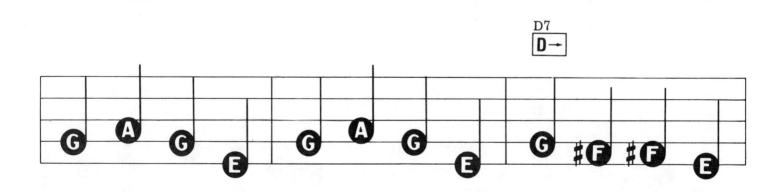

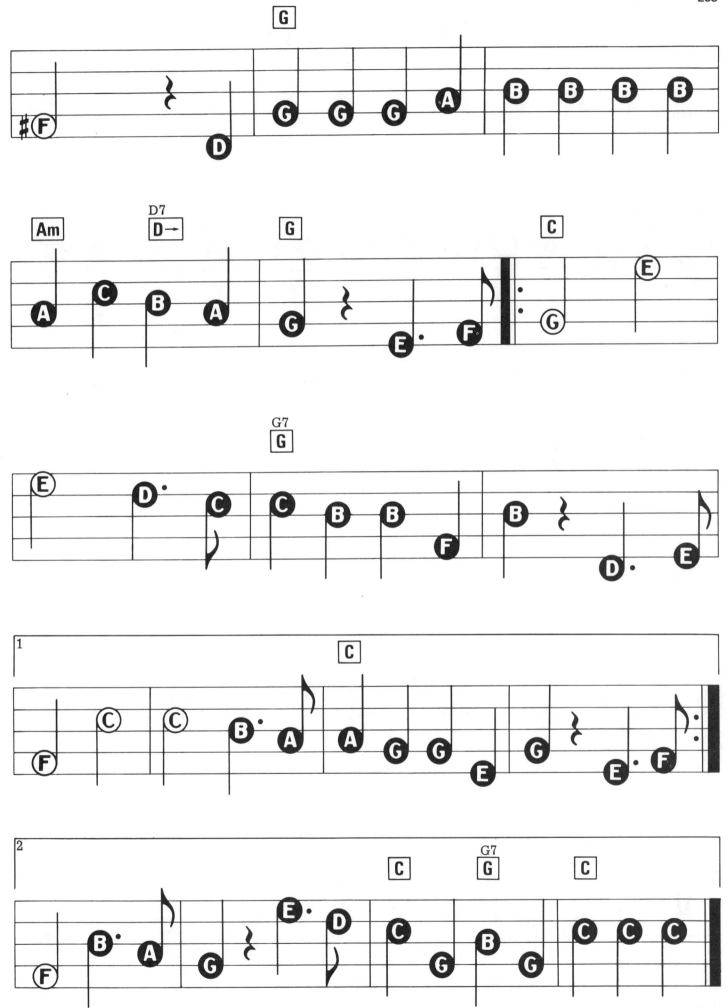

Julida Polka

Registration 4

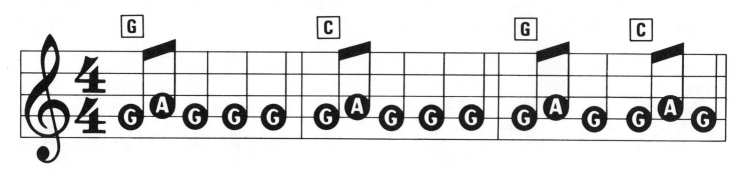

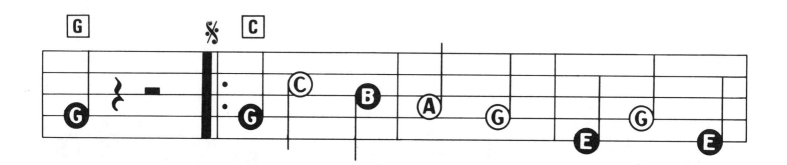

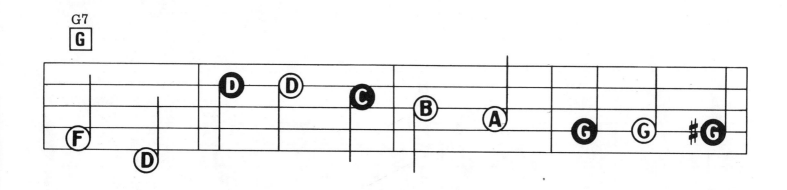

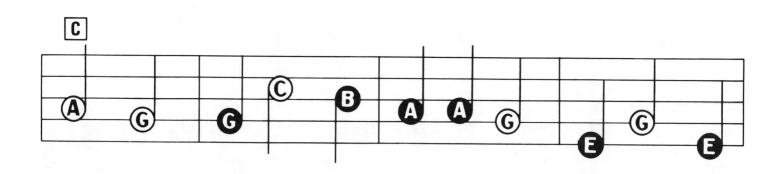

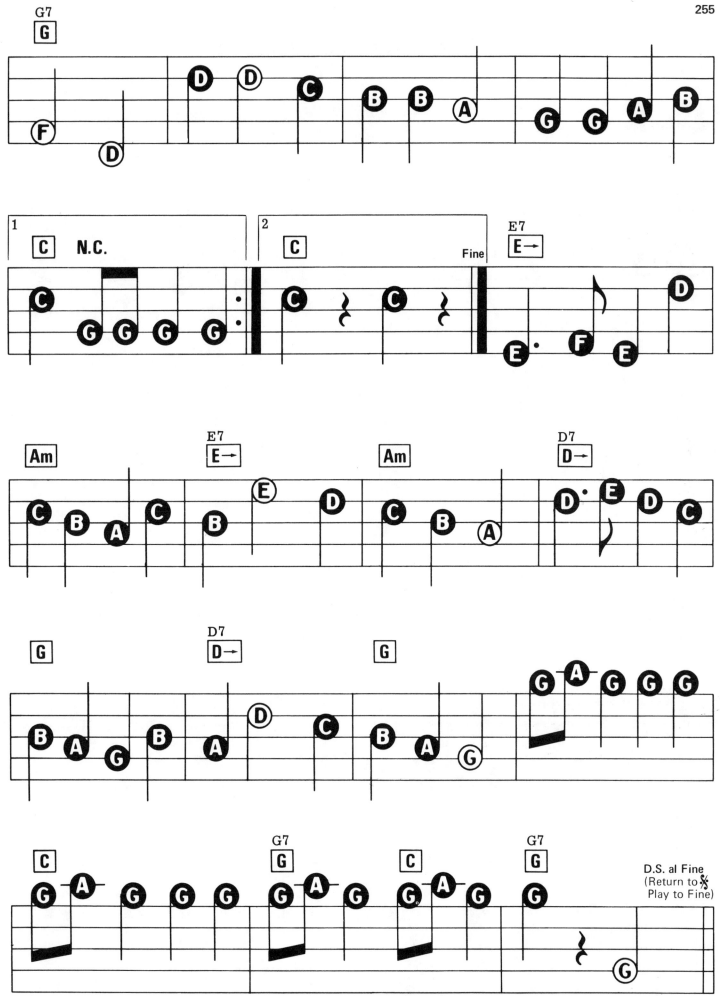

King Cotton March

Registration 5

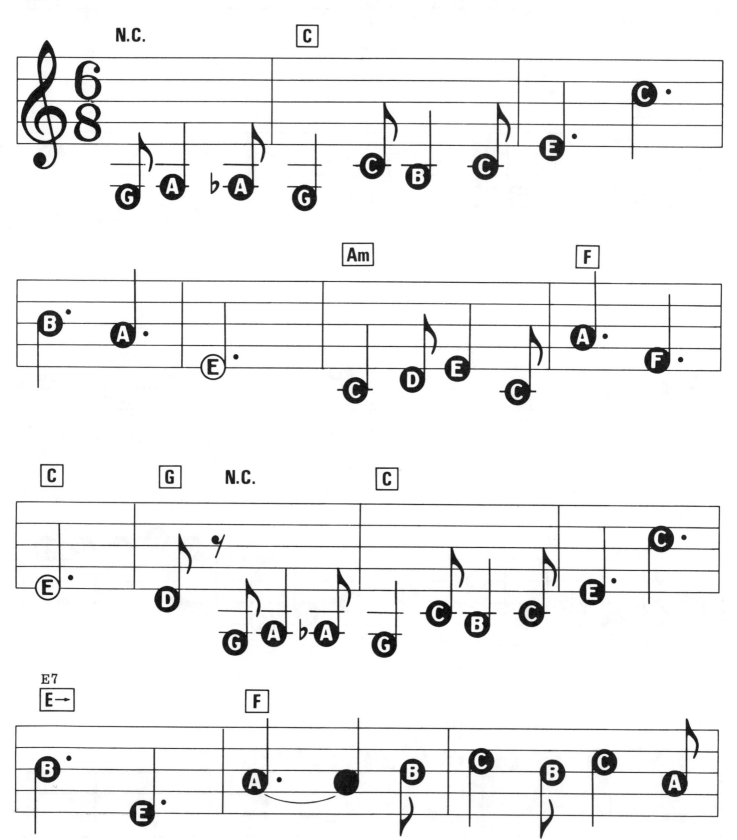

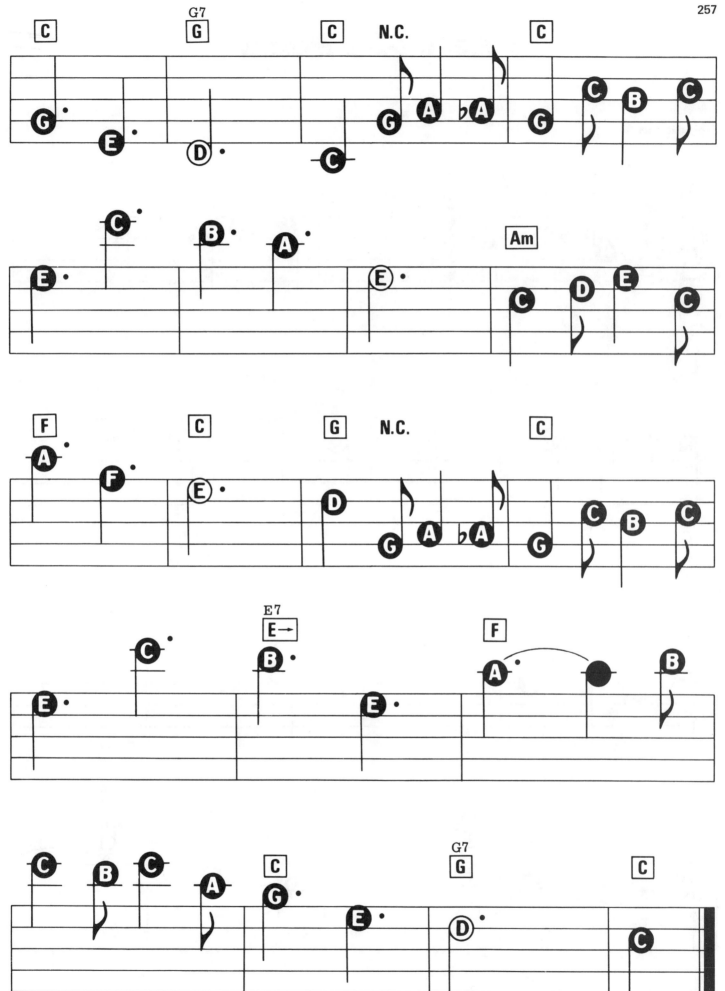

La-La-La Polka

Registration 8

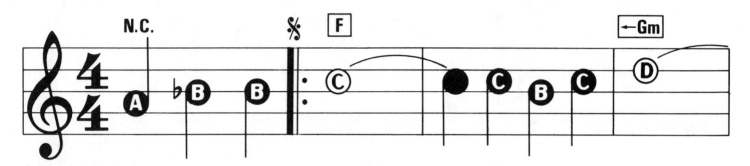

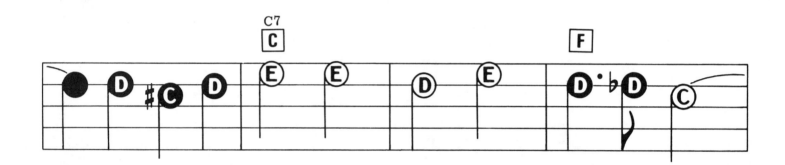

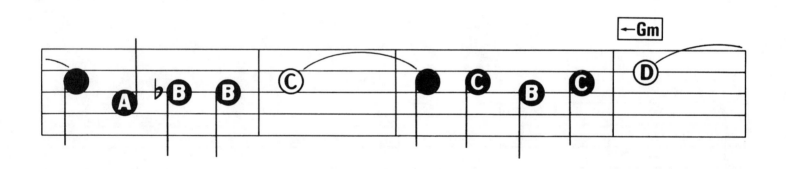

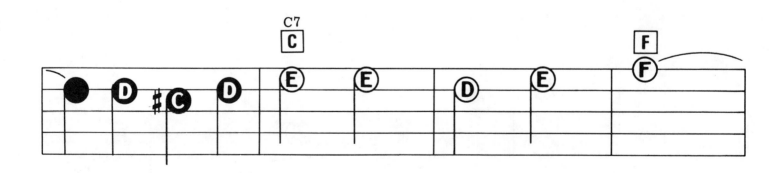

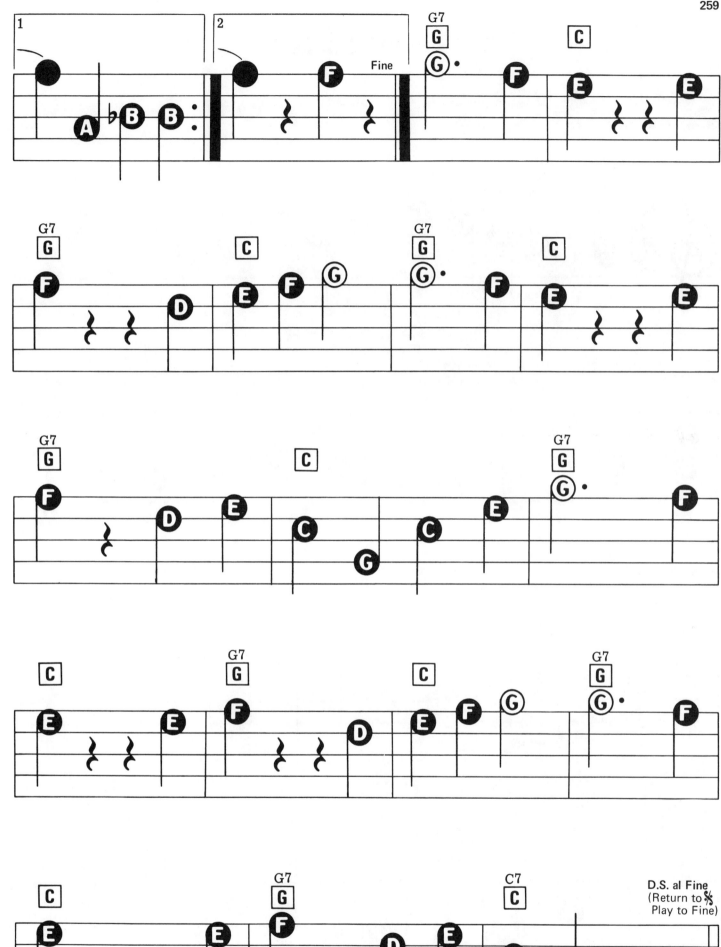

La Sorella

Registration 1

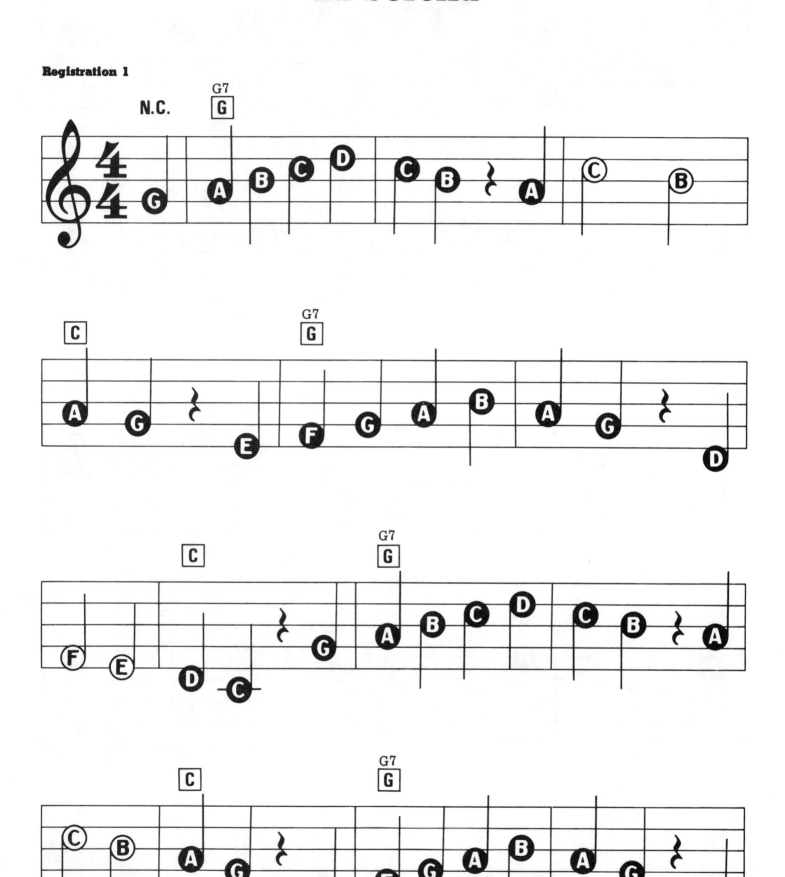

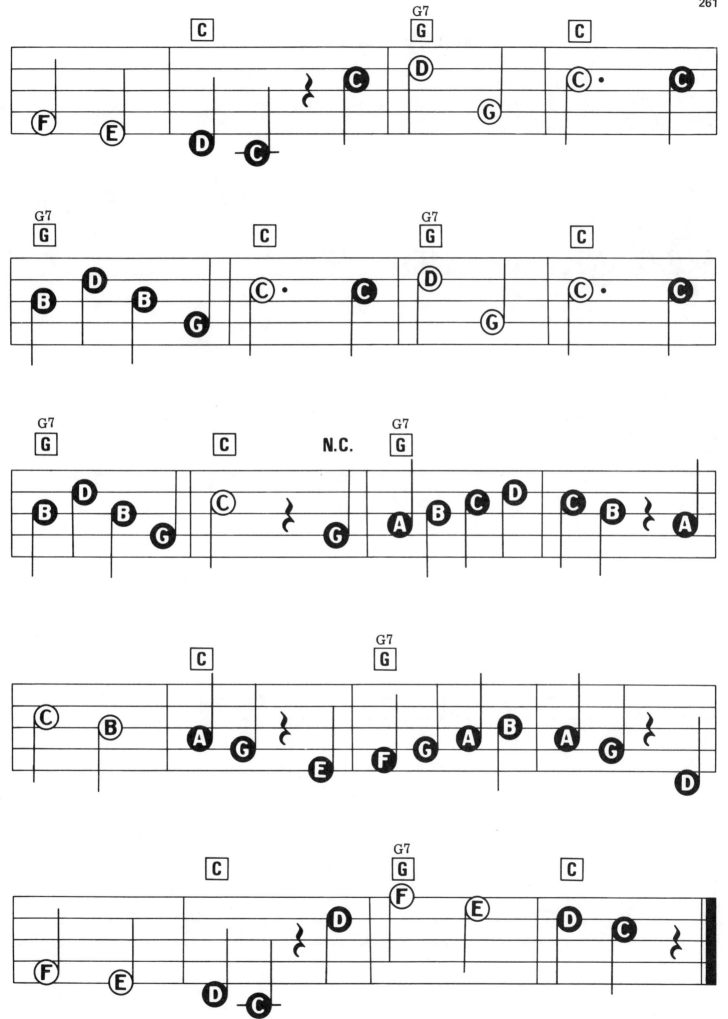

Liberty Bell March

Registration 3

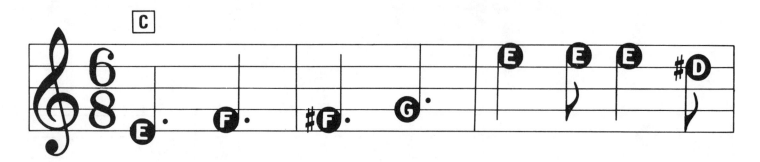

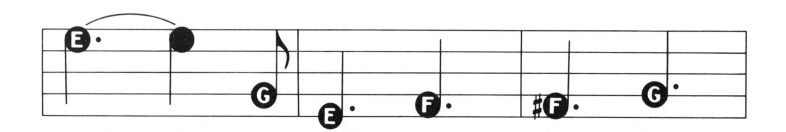

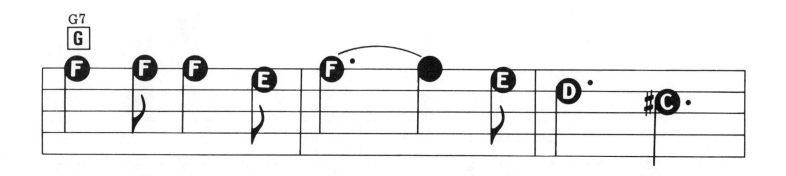

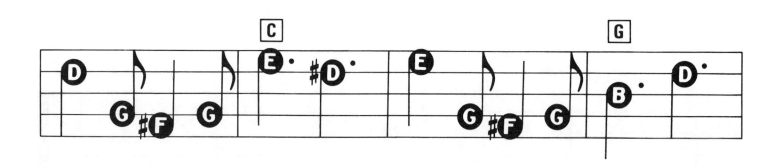

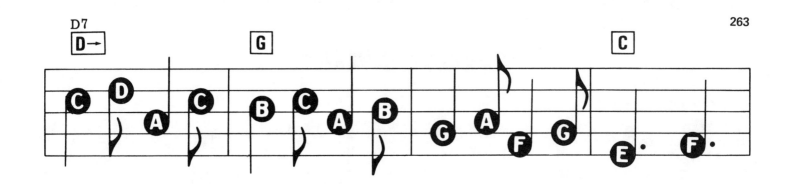

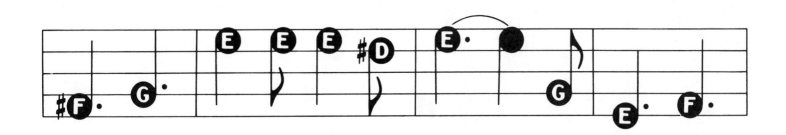

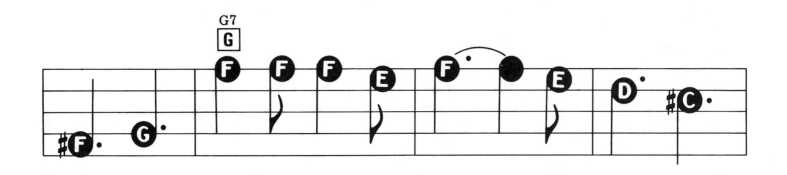

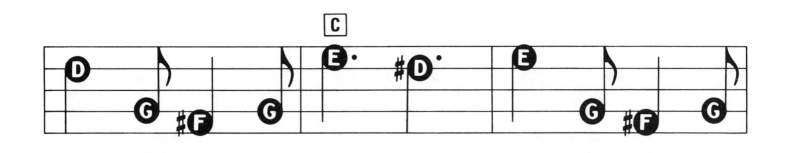

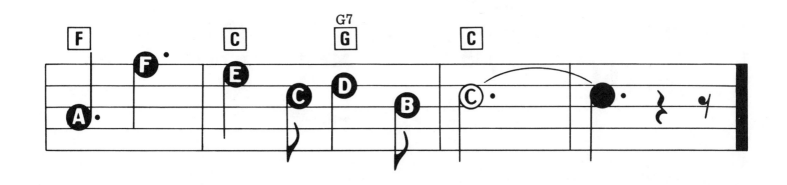

Lucia Polka

Registration 4

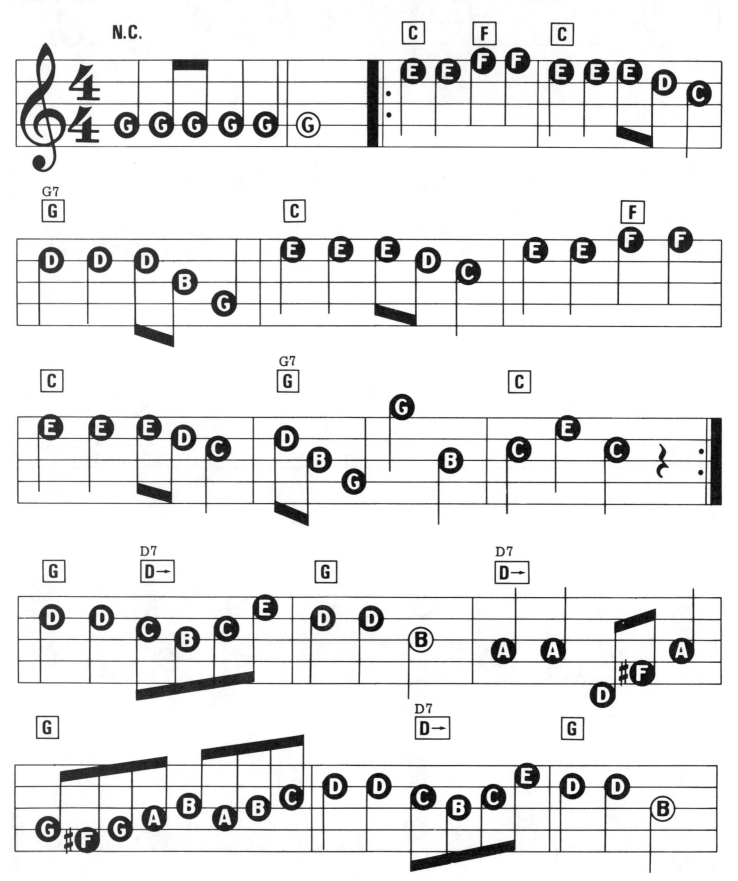

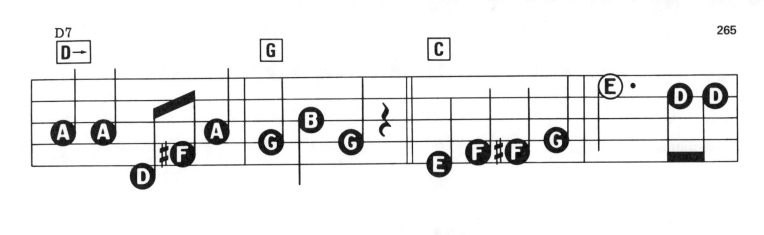

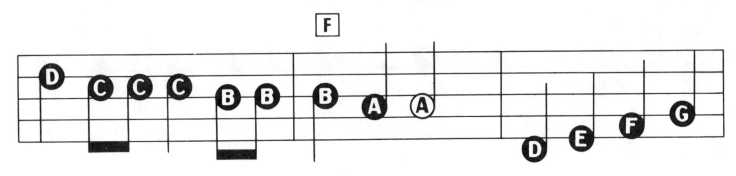

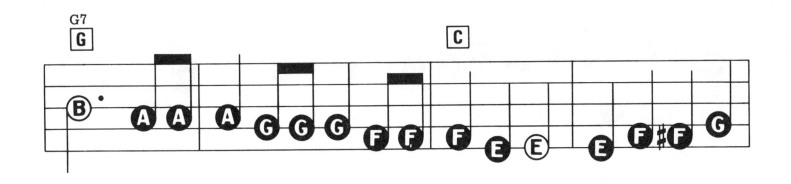

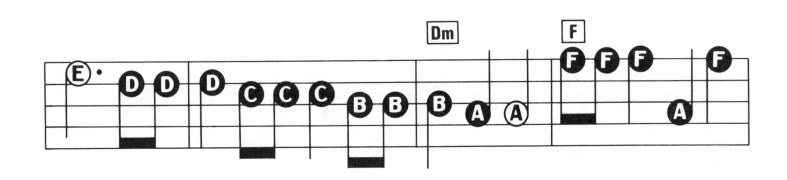

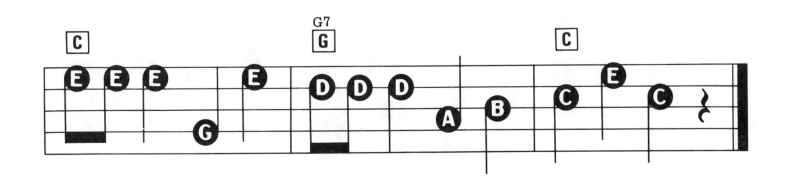

Mademoiselle From Armentiers

Registration 2

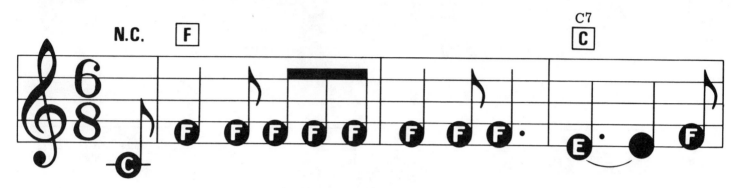

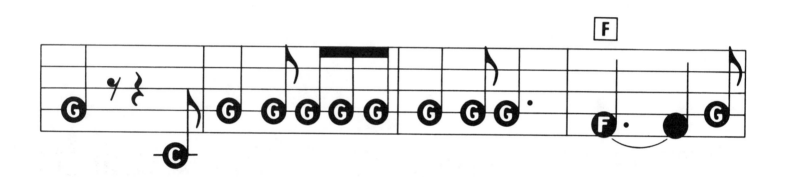

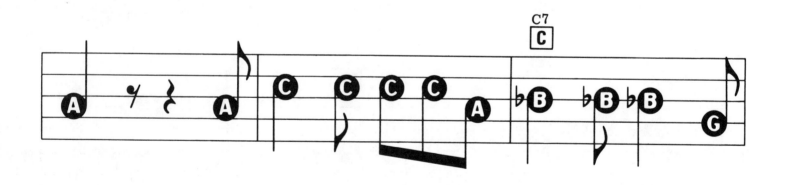

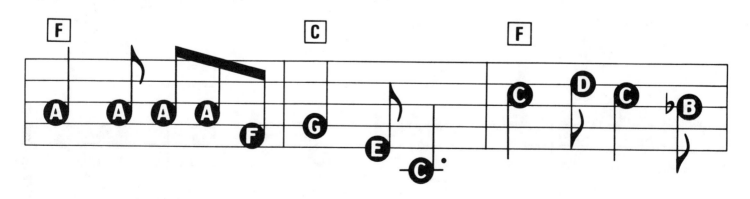

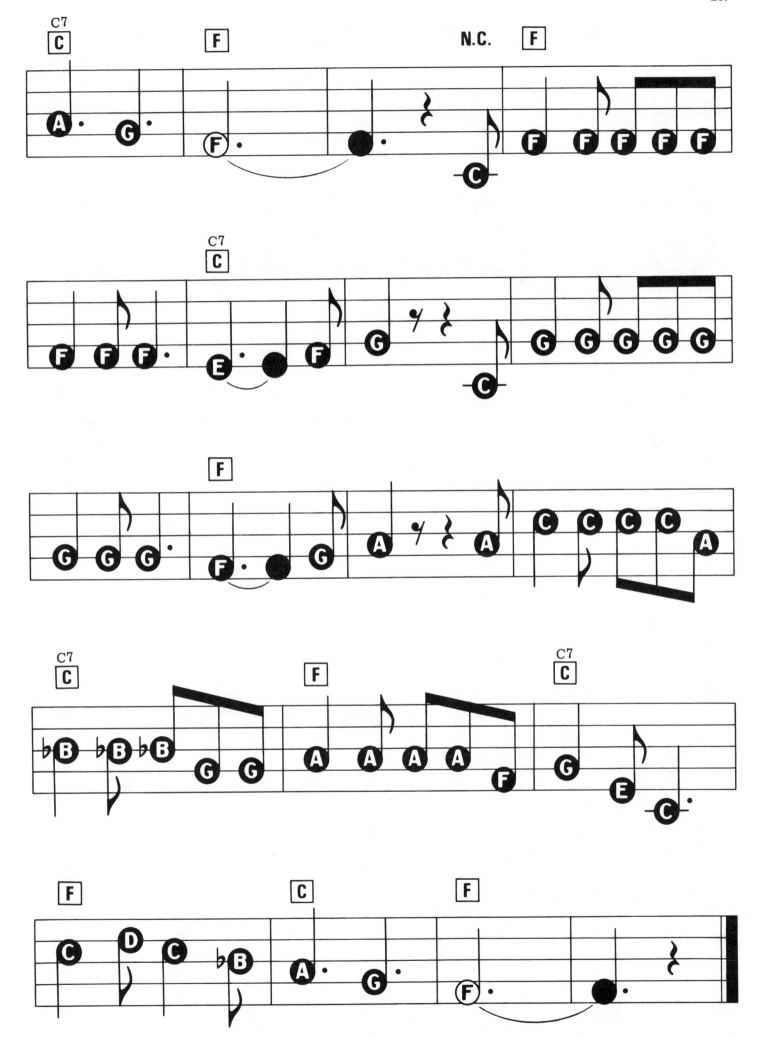

Martha Polka

Registration 4

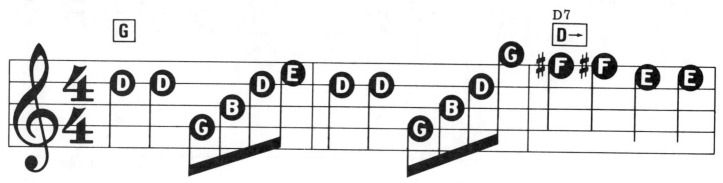

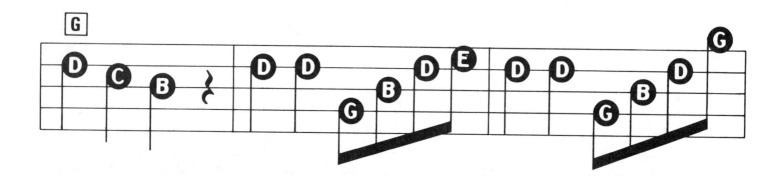

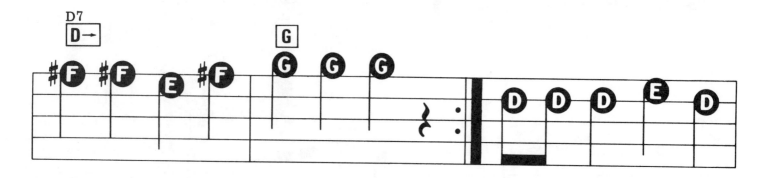

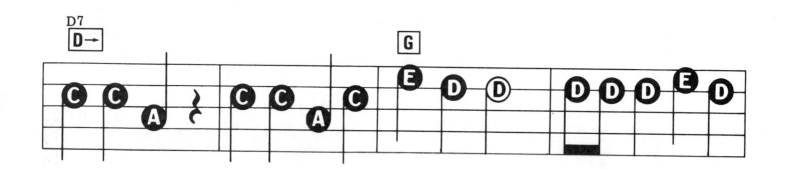

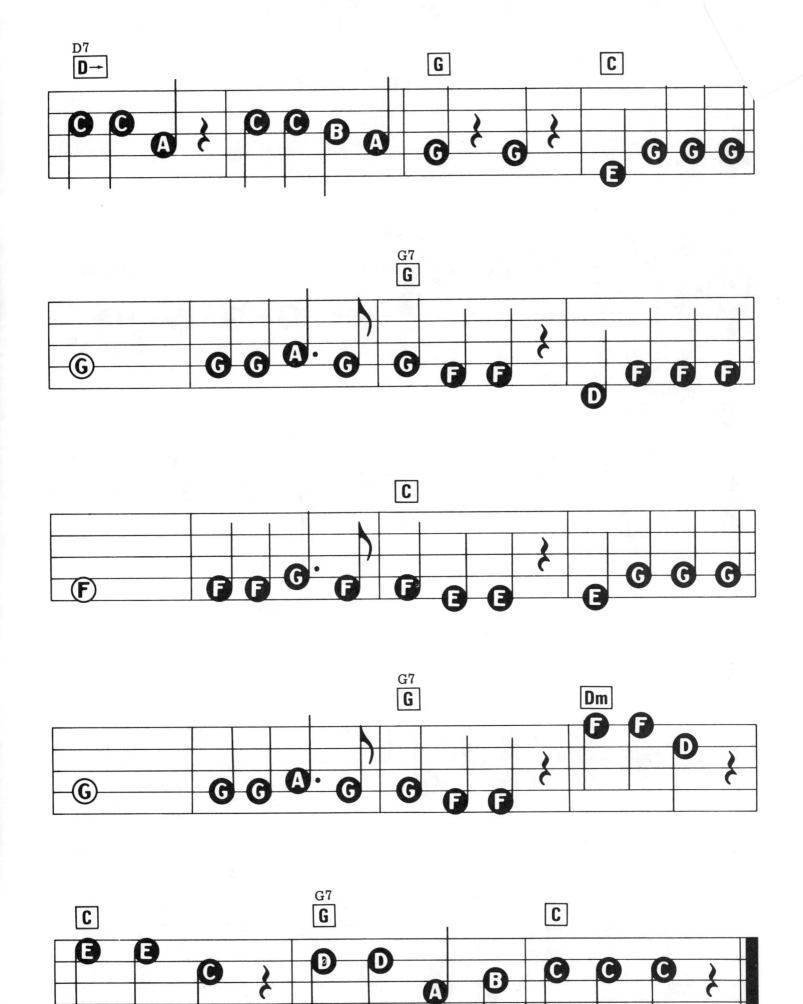

Pizzicato Polka

Registration 10

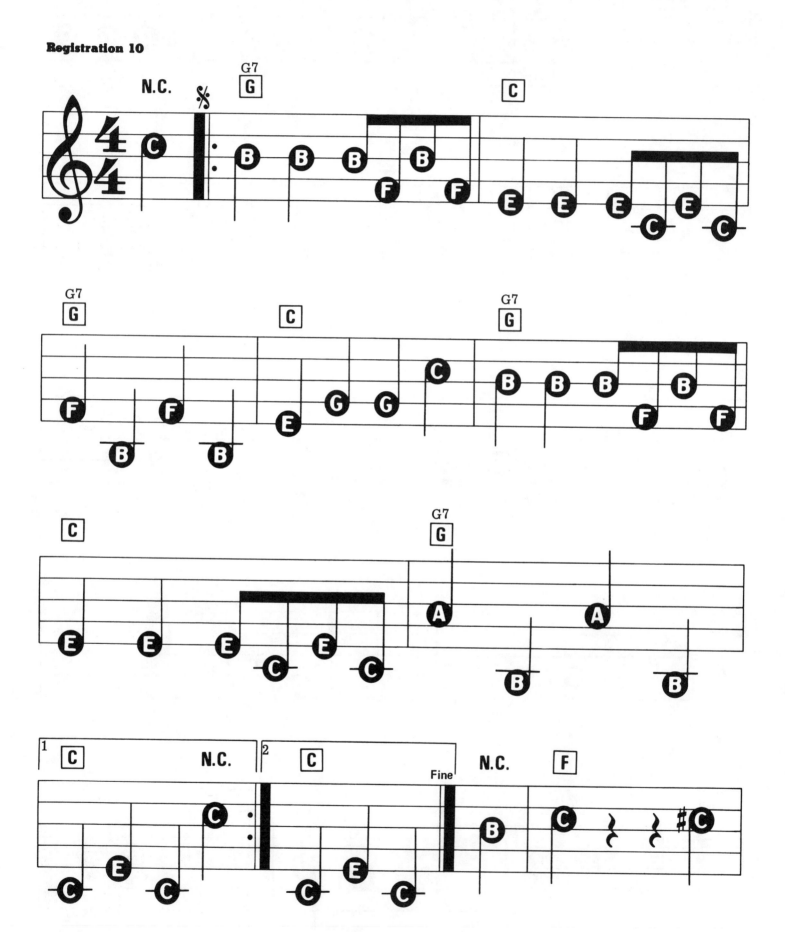

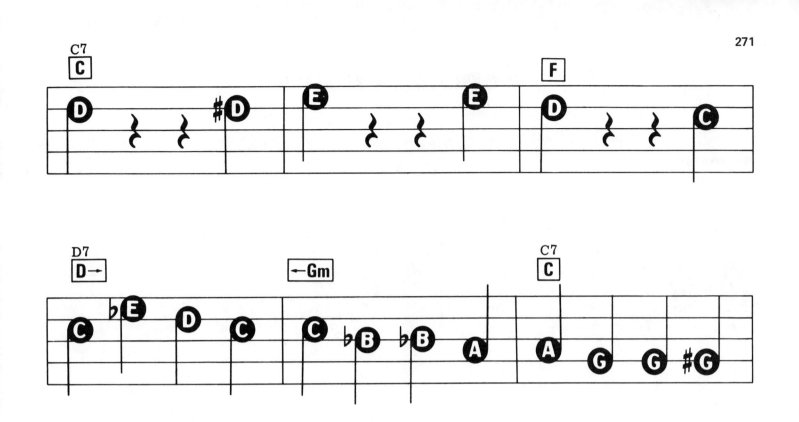

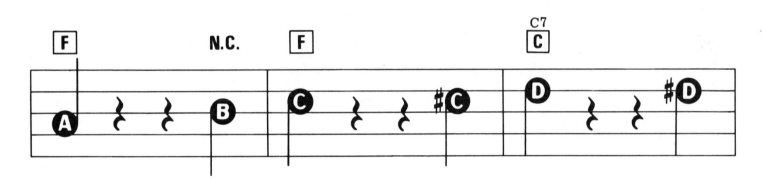

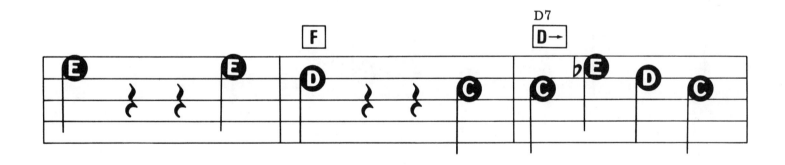

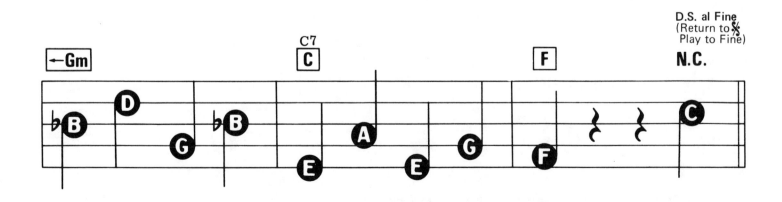

Semper Fidelis

Registration 5

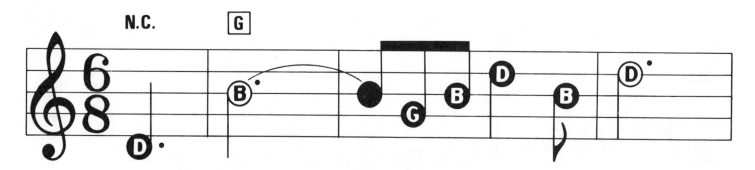

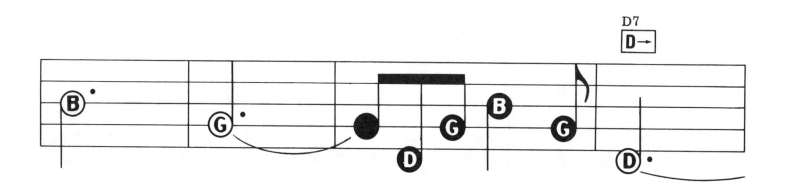

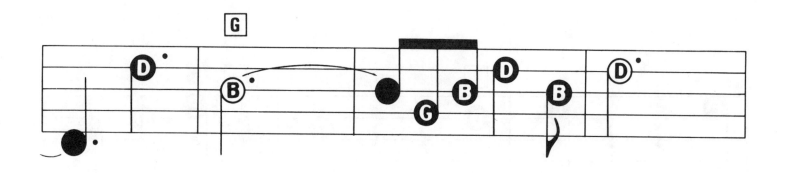

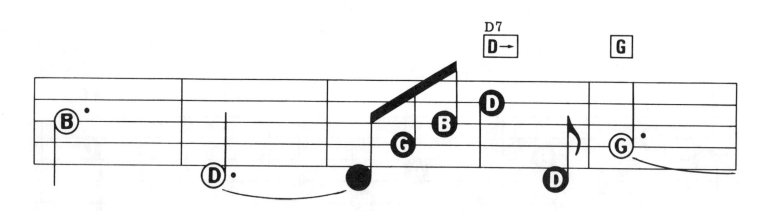

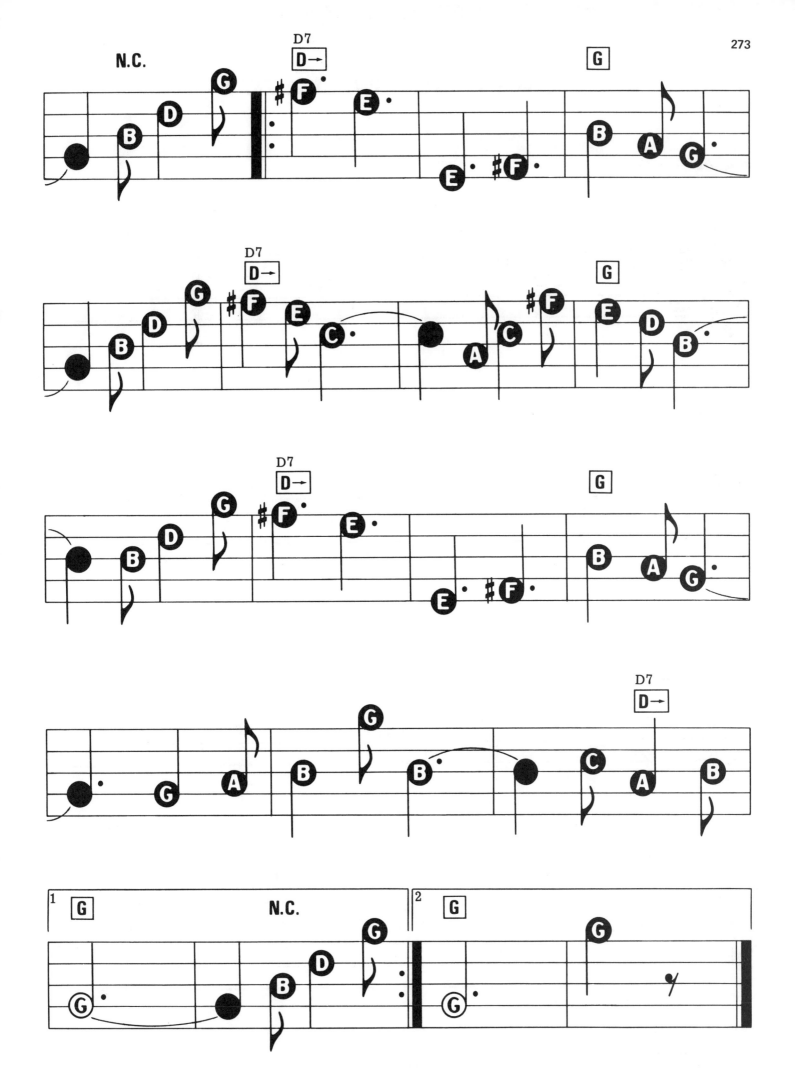

Sharpshooters March

Registration 4

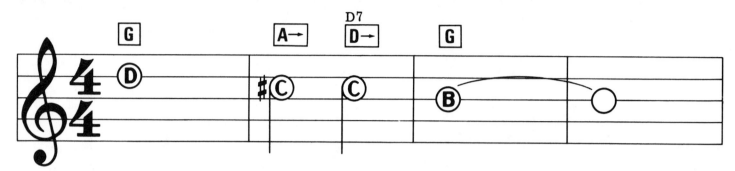

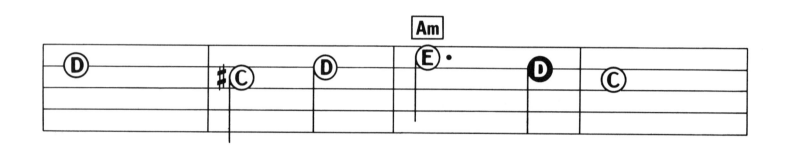

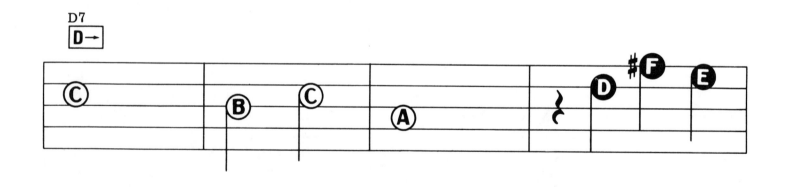

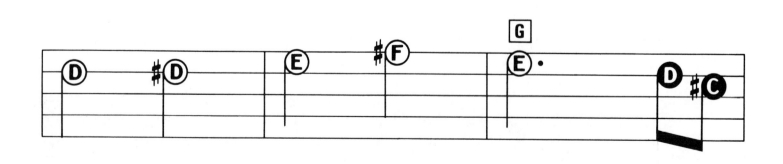

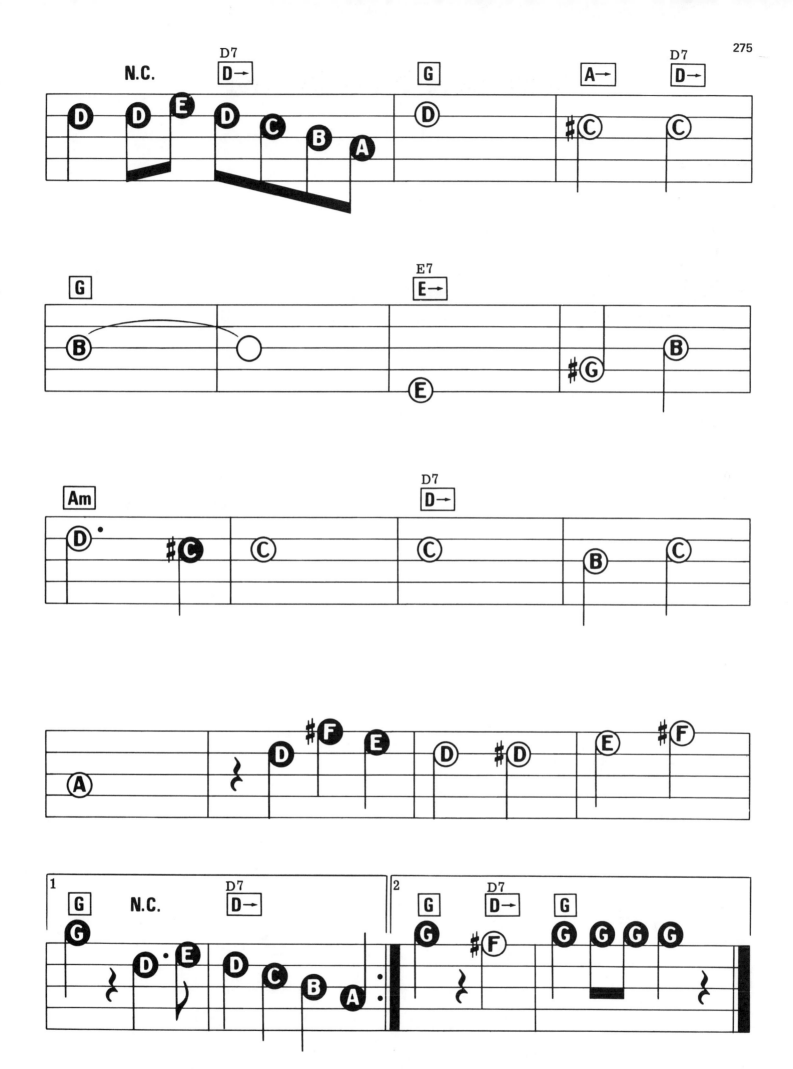

Thunder And Blazes

Registration 5

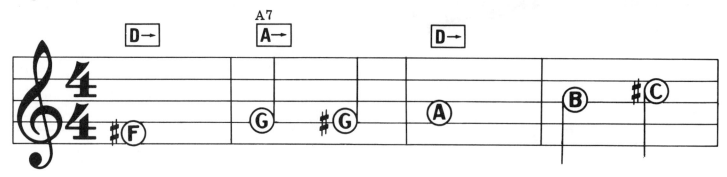

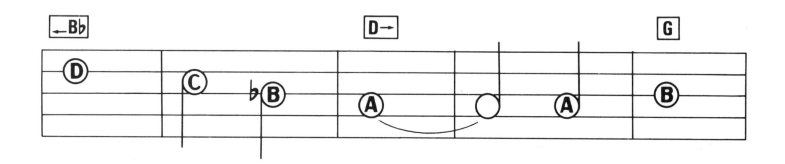

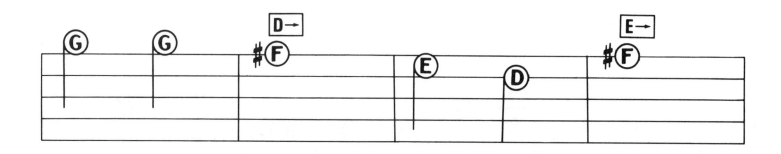

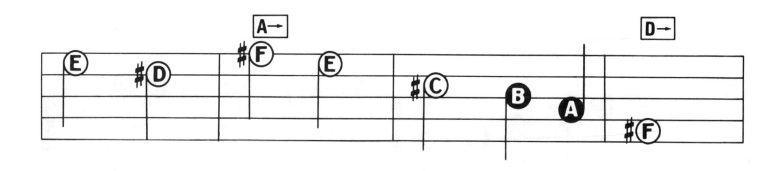

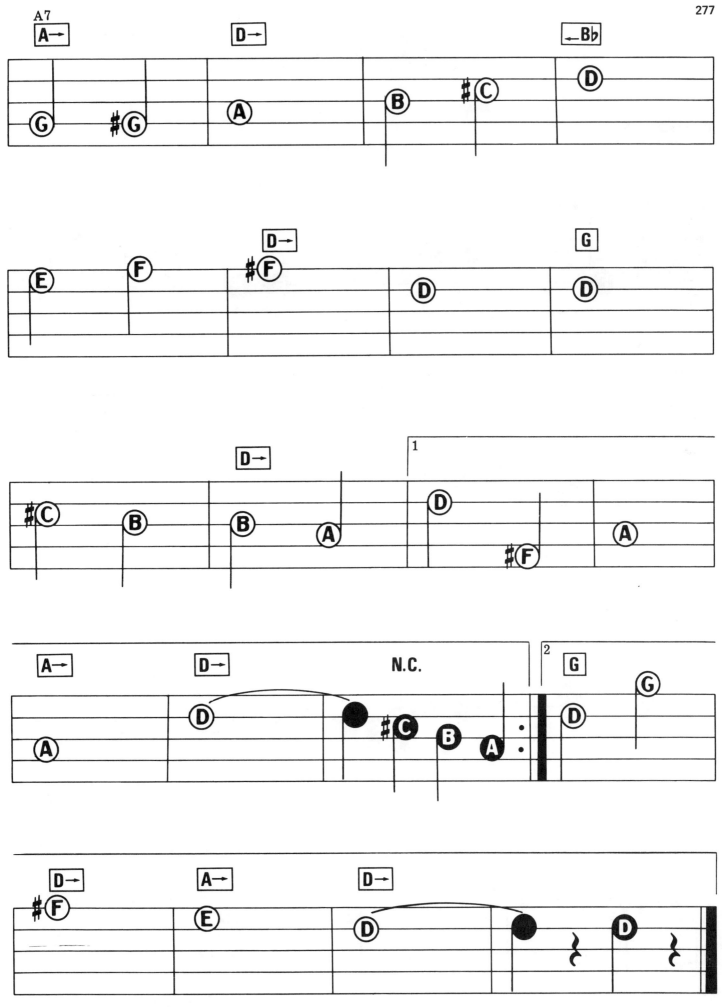

Tinker Polka

Registration 3

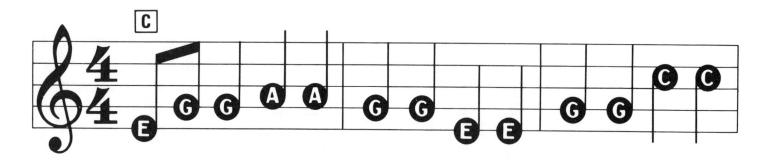

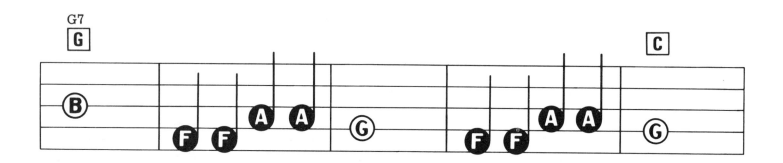

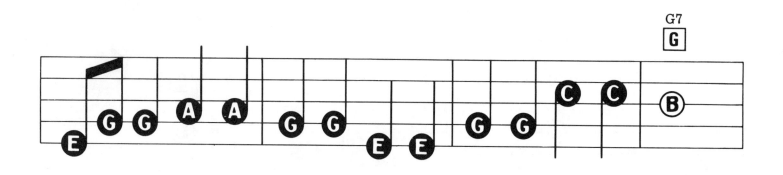

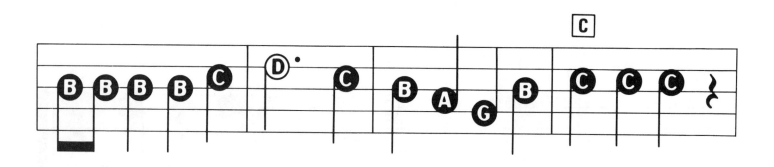

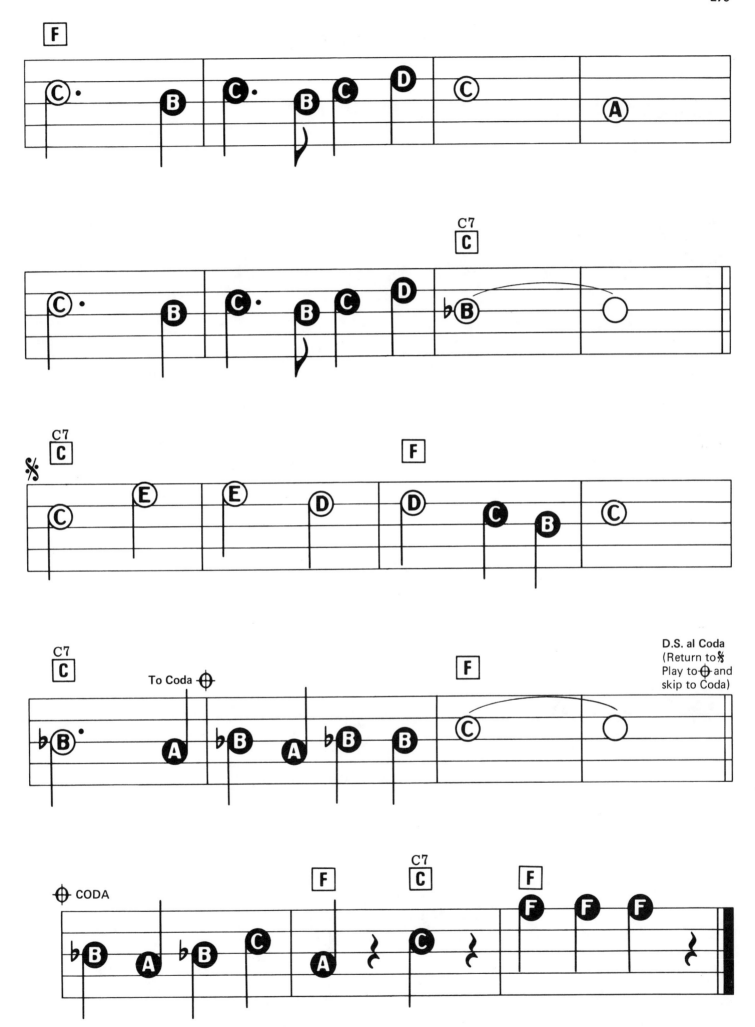

The Bowery

Registration 4

Dolores Waltz

Registration 2

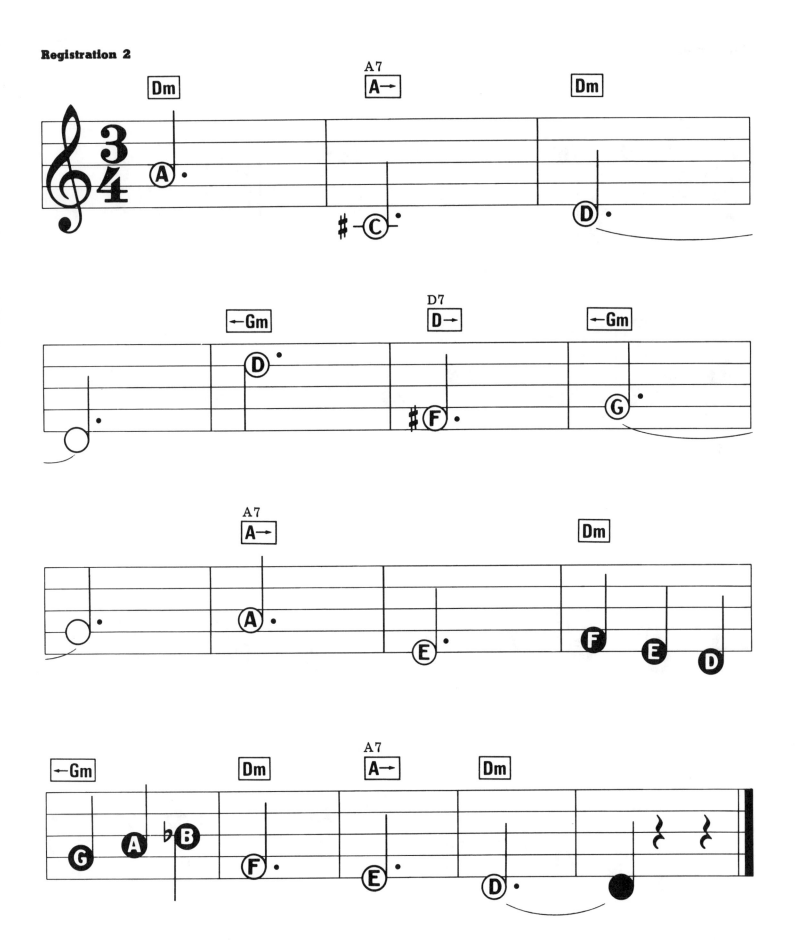

Estudiantina

Registration 3

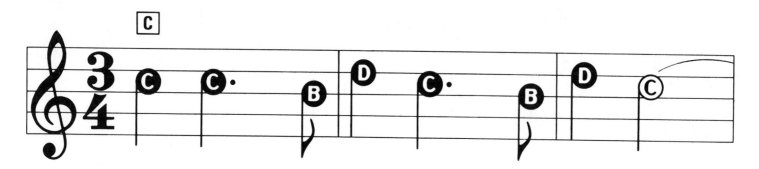

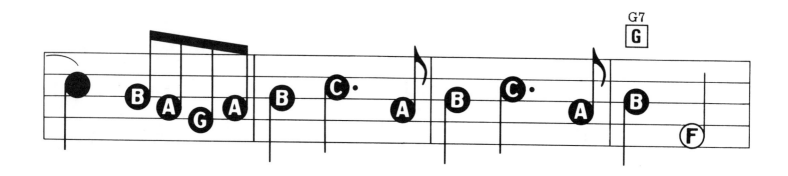

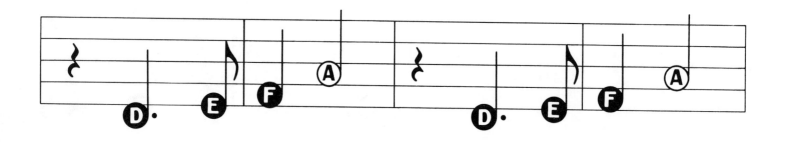

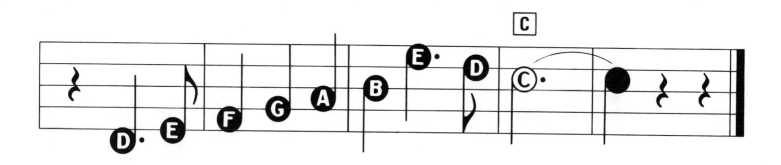

Marguerite Waltz

Registration 5

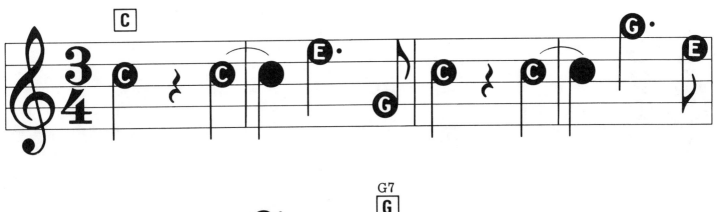

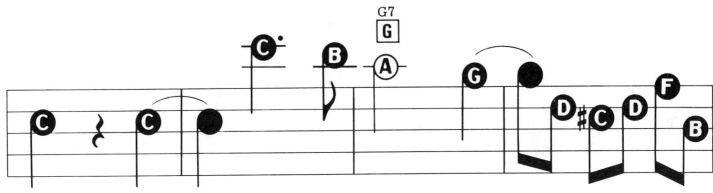

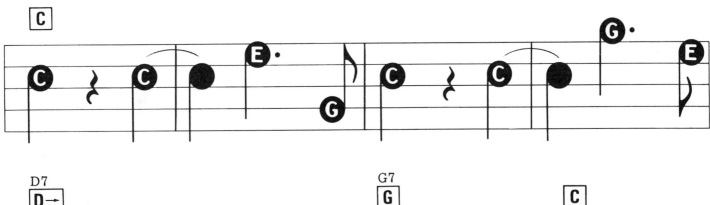

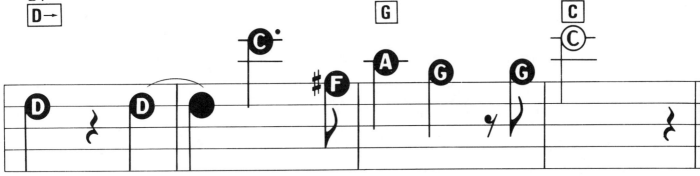

My Dear Marquis

Registration 4

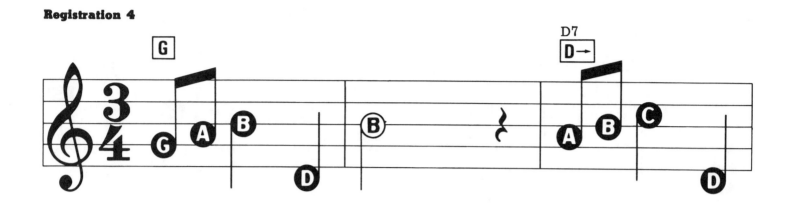

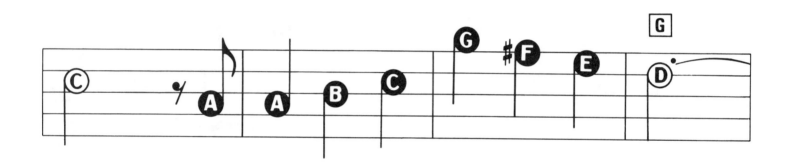

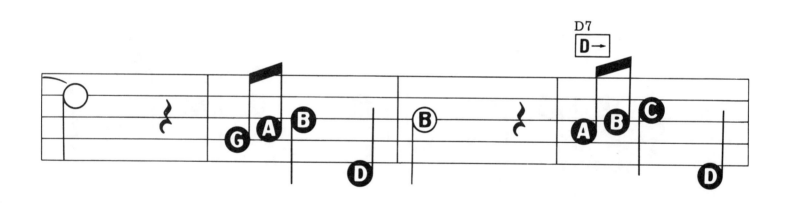

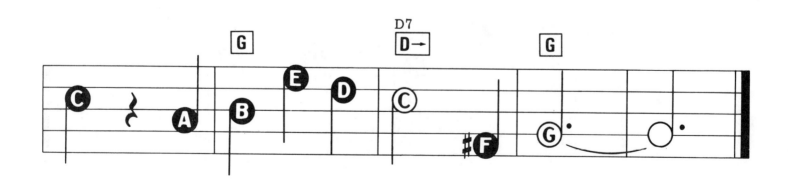

Treasure Waltz

Registration 4

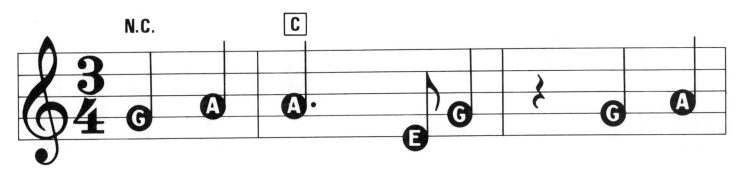

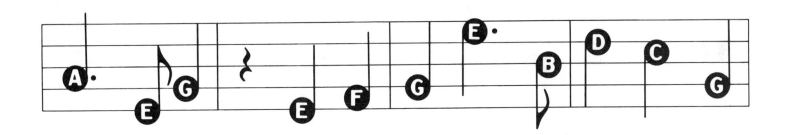

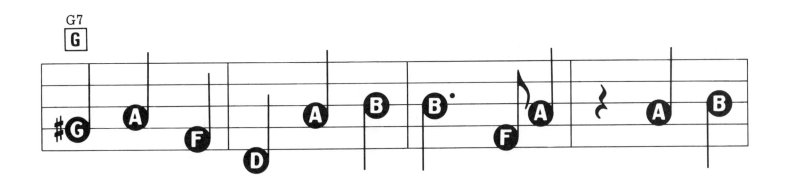

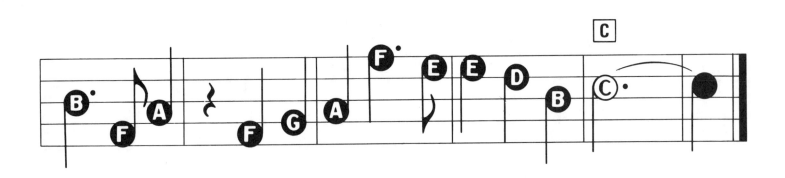

Wine, Women And Song

Registration 3

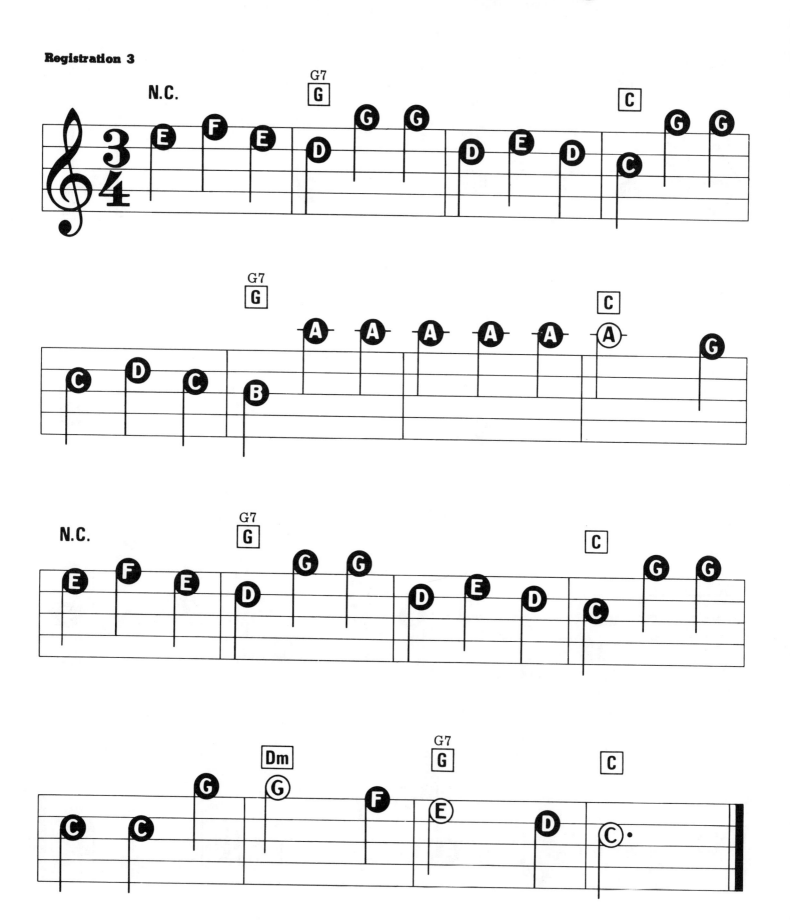

Waltz Of The Flowers

Registration 6

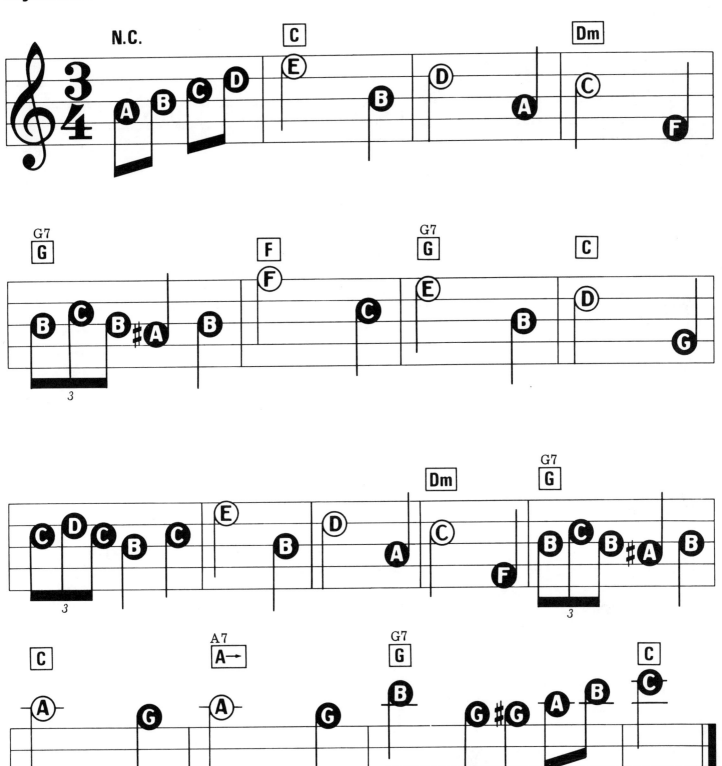

After The Ball

Registration 5

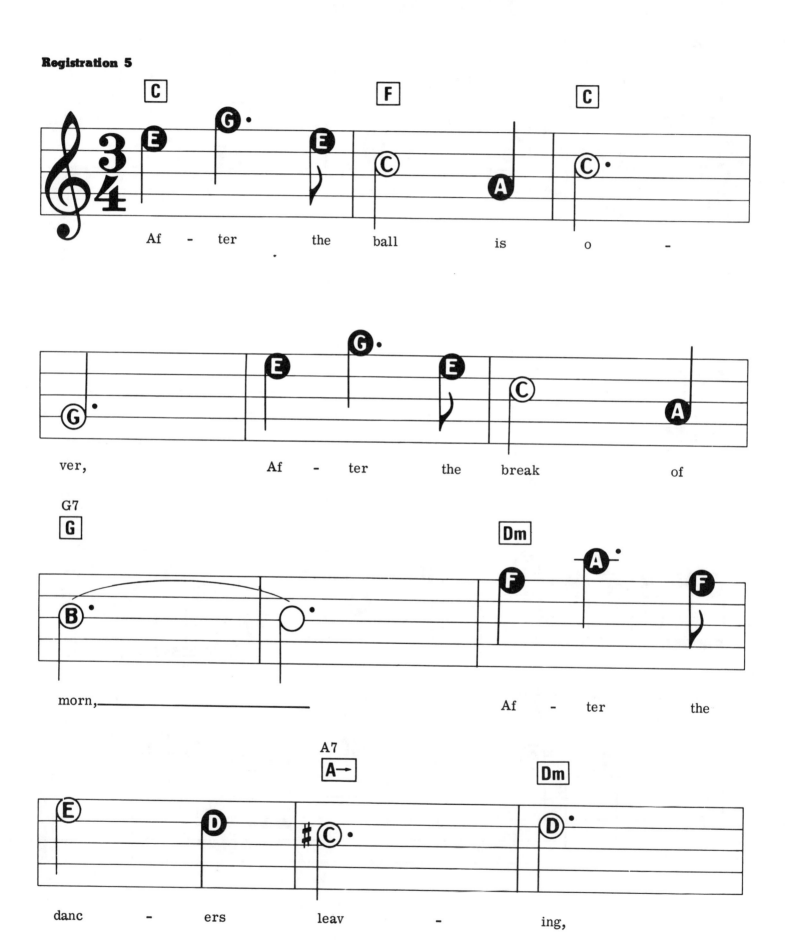

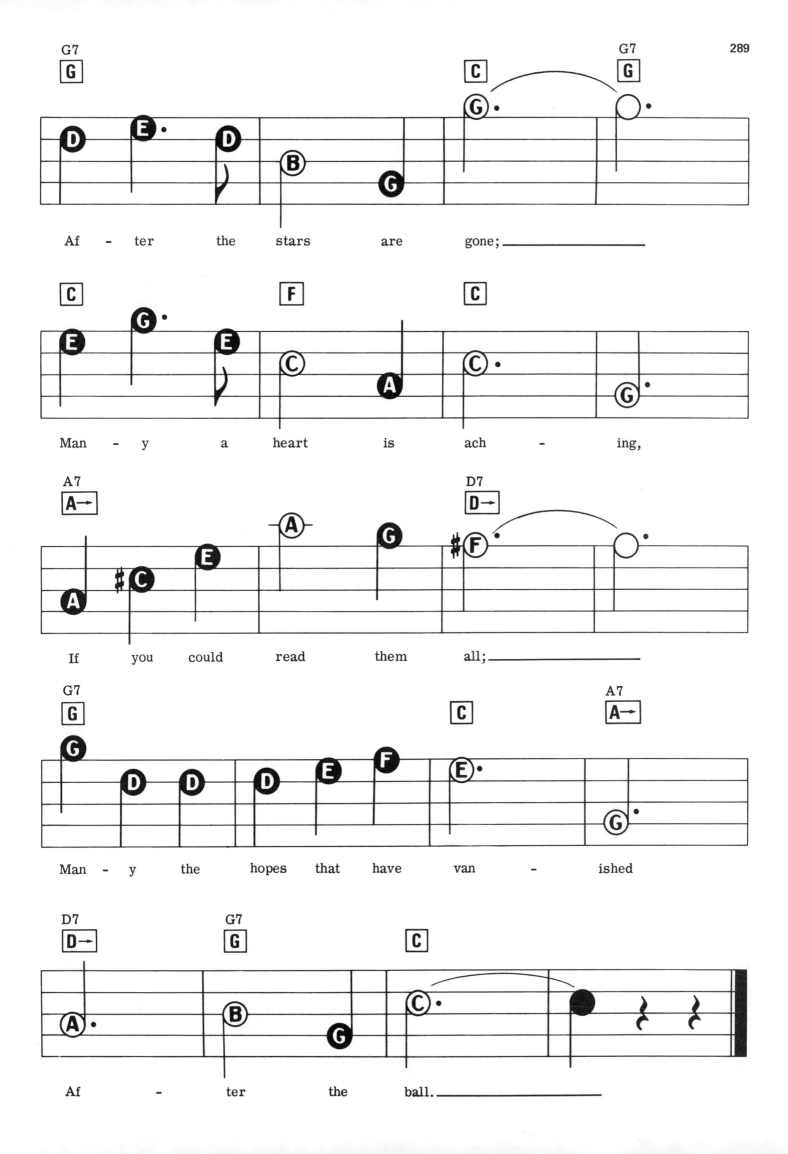

Blue Danube Waltz

Registration 2

Johann Strauss

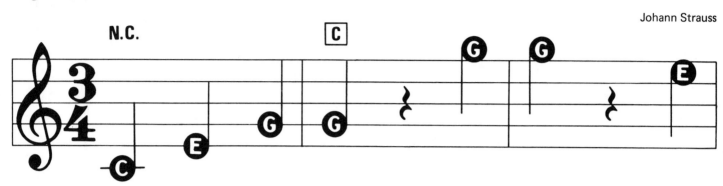

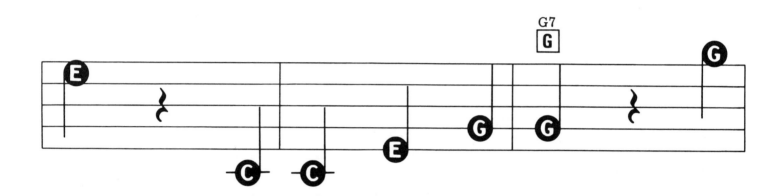

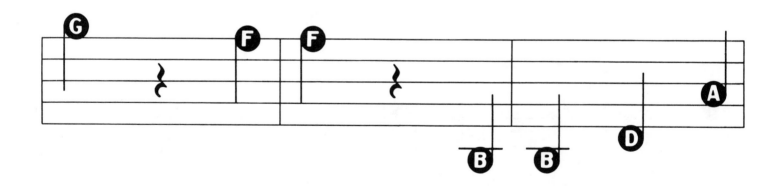

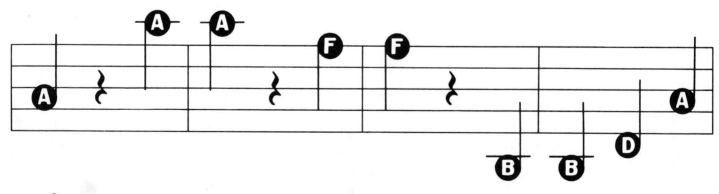

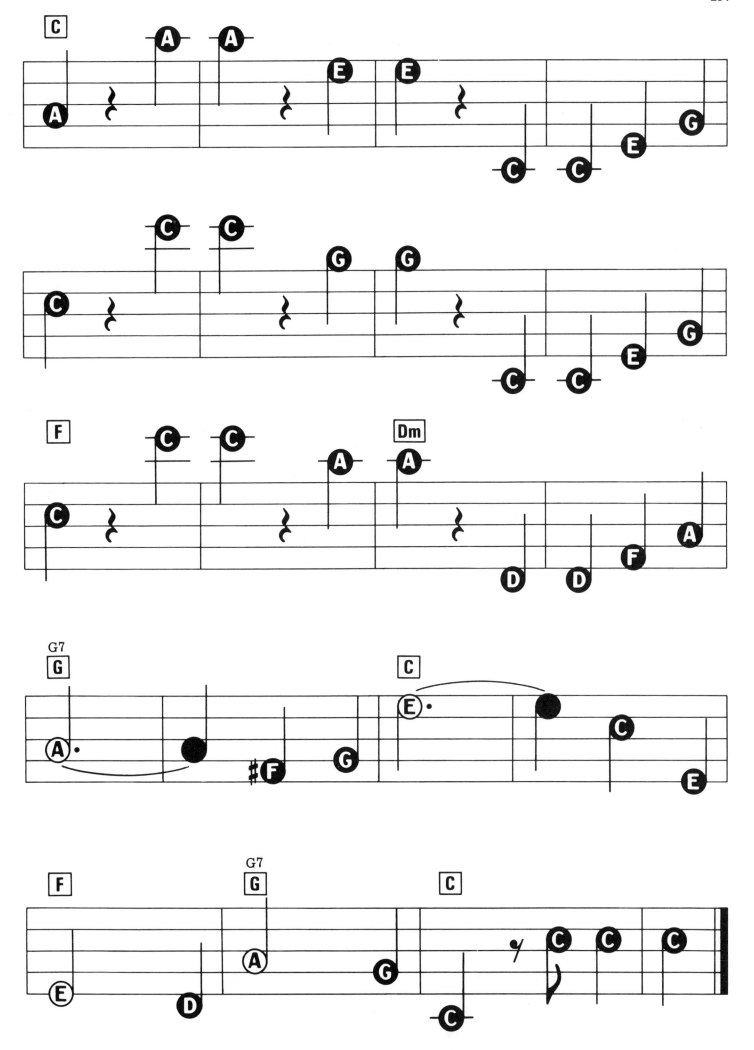

Ciribiribin

Registration 9

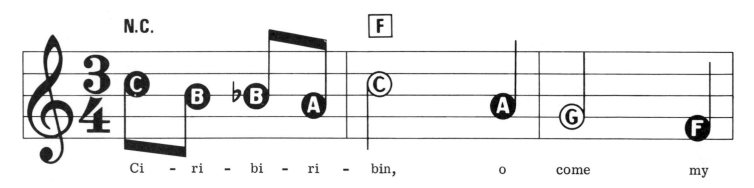

Ci - ri - bi - ri - bin,   o come   my

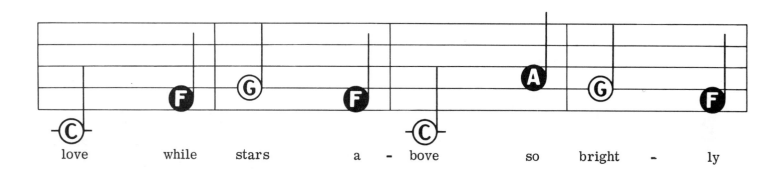

love   while   stars   a - bove   so   bright - ly

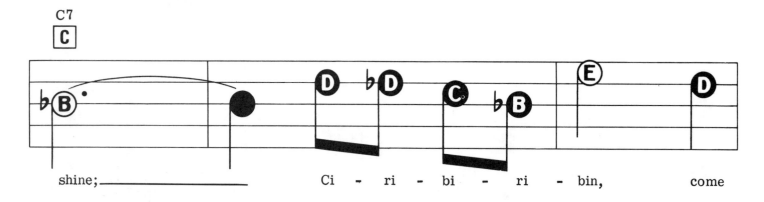

shine;_____   Ci - ri - bi - ri - bin,   come

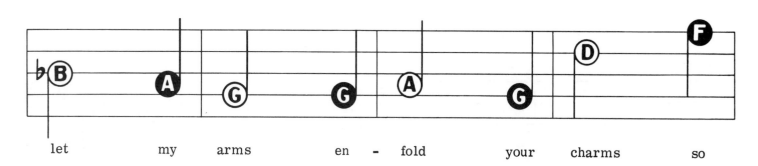

let   my   arms   en - fold   your   charms   so

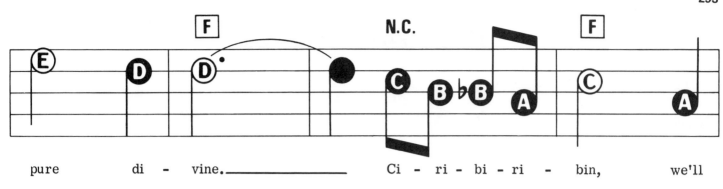

pure   di — vine._____   Ci — ri — bi — ri — bin,   we'll

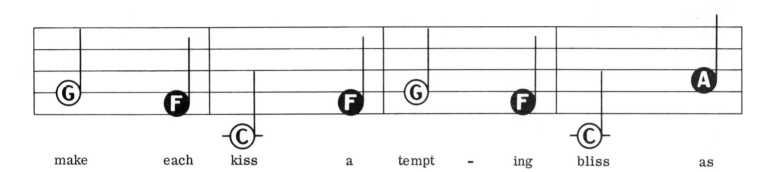

make   each   kiss   a   tempt — ing   bliss   as

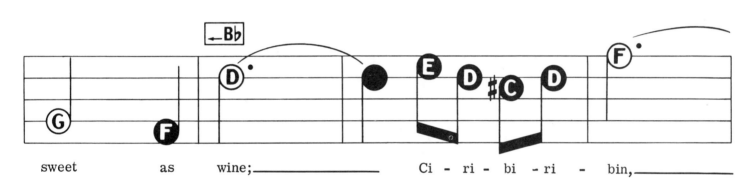

sweet   as   wine;_____   Ci — ri — bi — ri — bin,_____

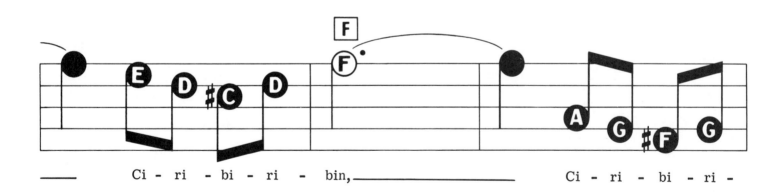

_____   Ci — ri — bi — ri — bin,_____   Ci — ri — bi — ri —

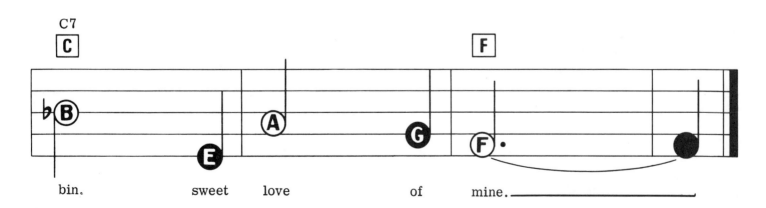

bin.   sweet   love   of   mine._____

Danube Waves

Registration 8

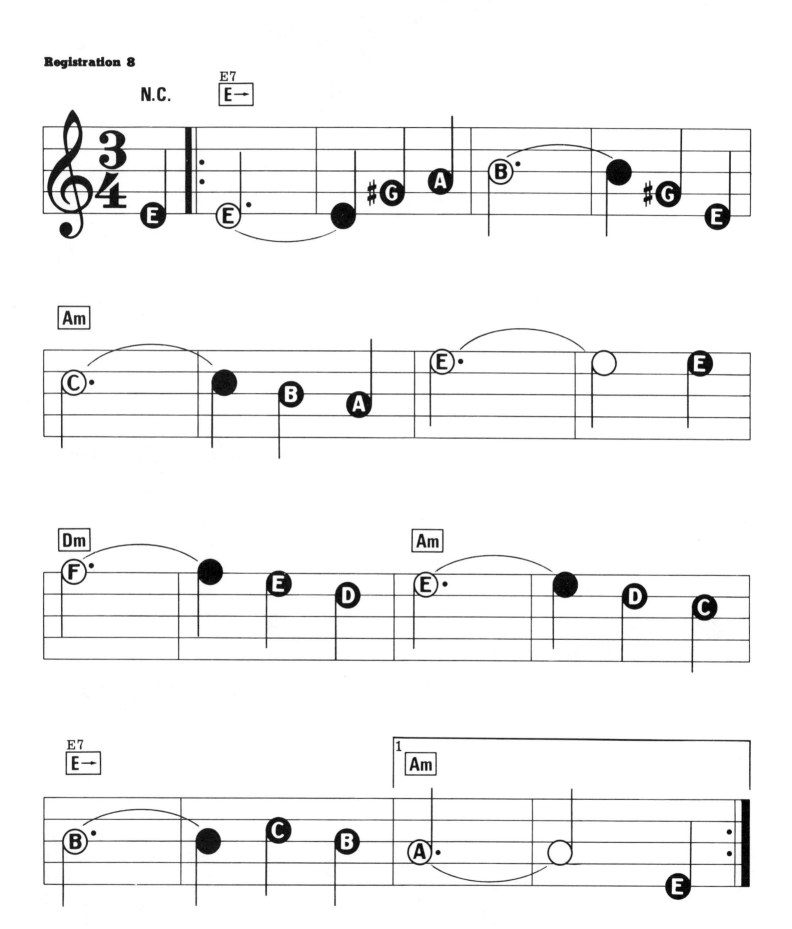

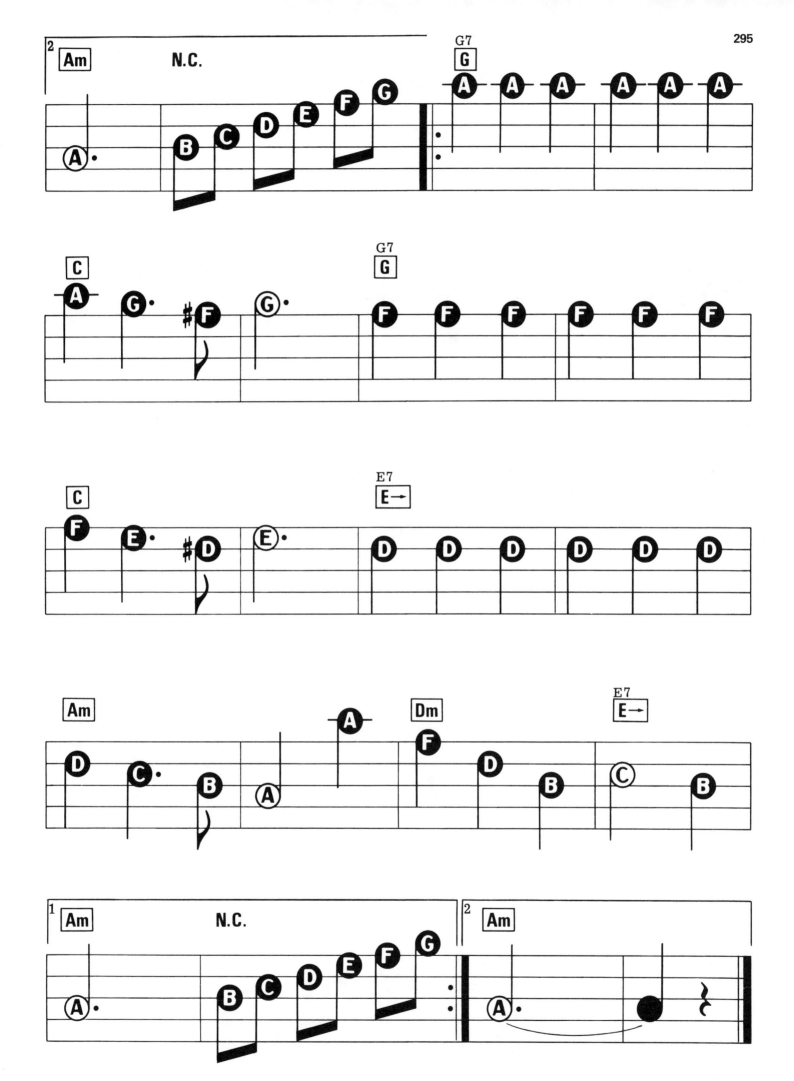

Emperor Waltz

Registration 3

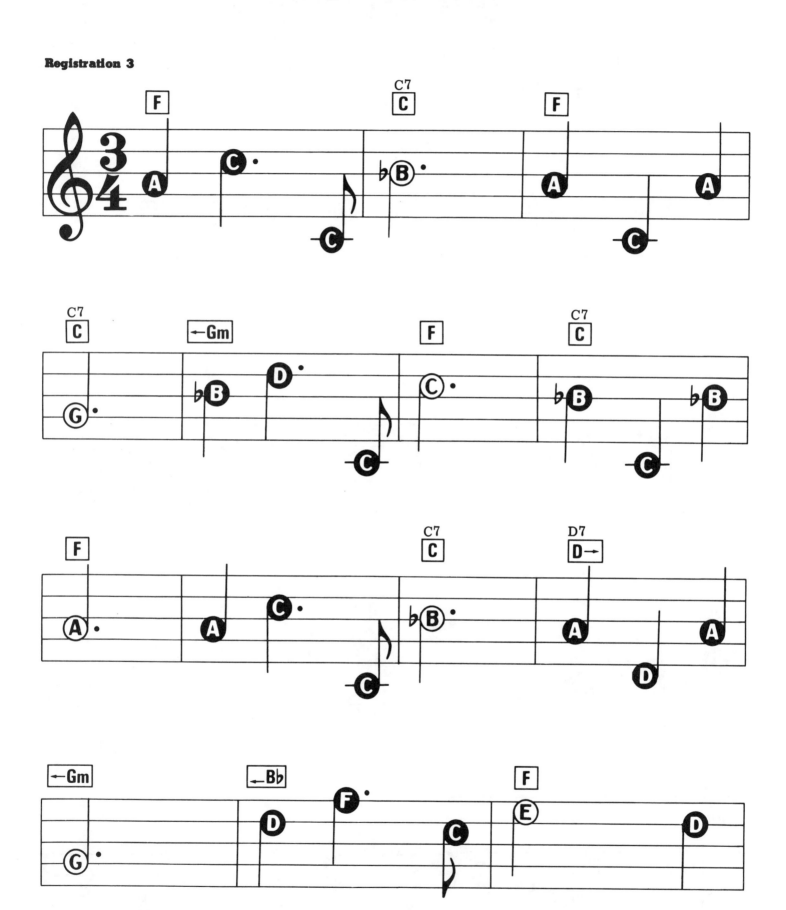

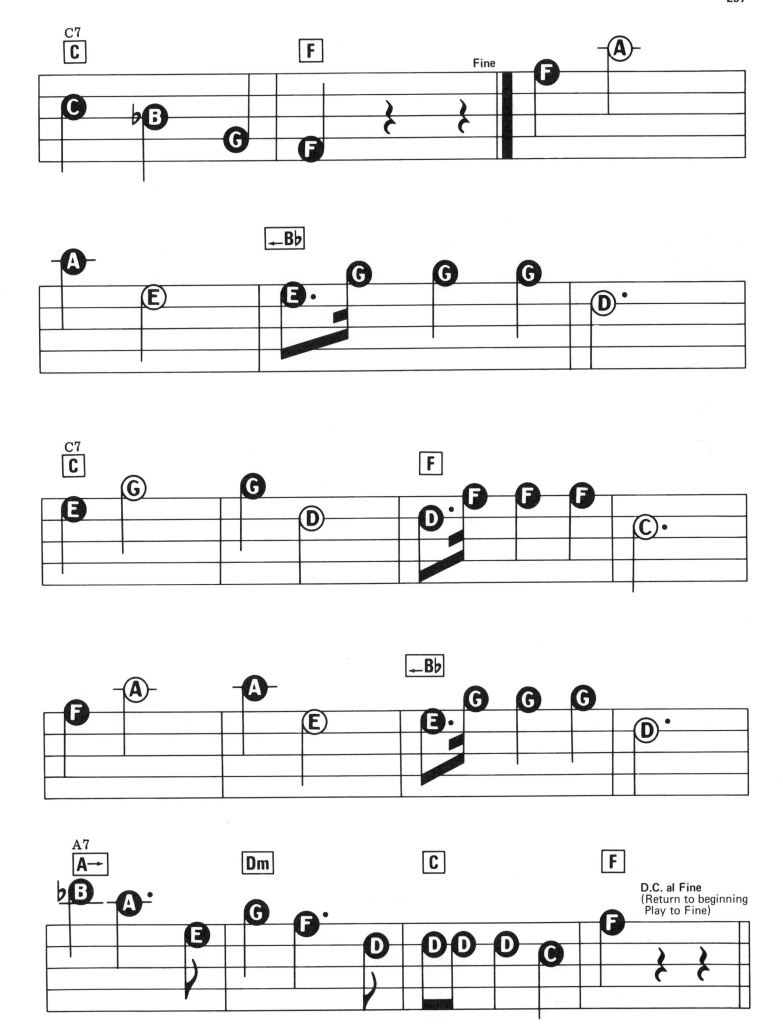

Fascination

Registration 10

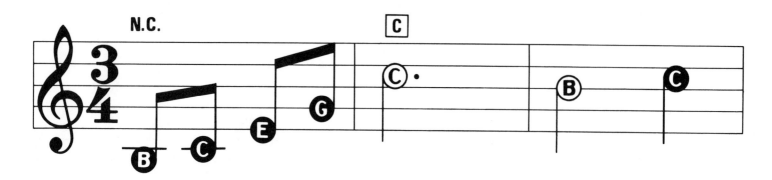

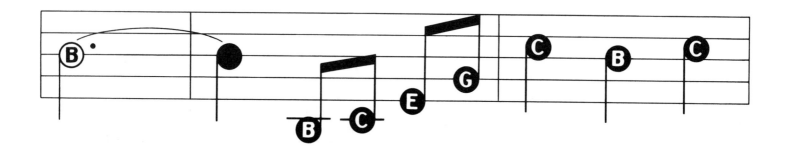

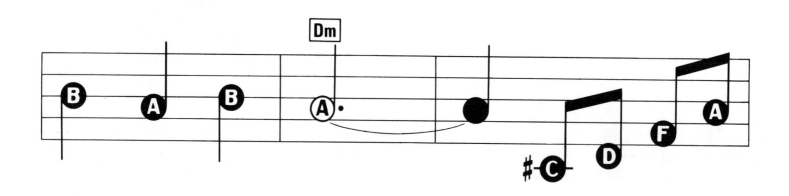

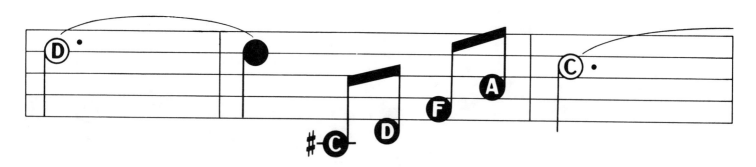

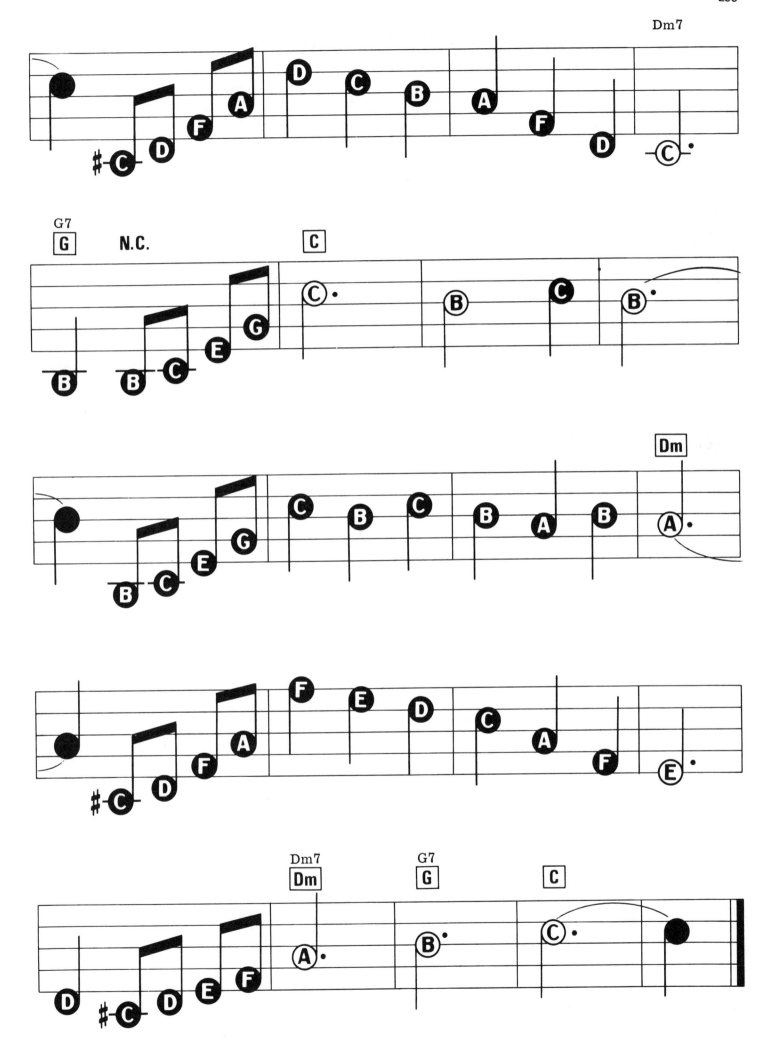

Melody Of Love

Registration 10

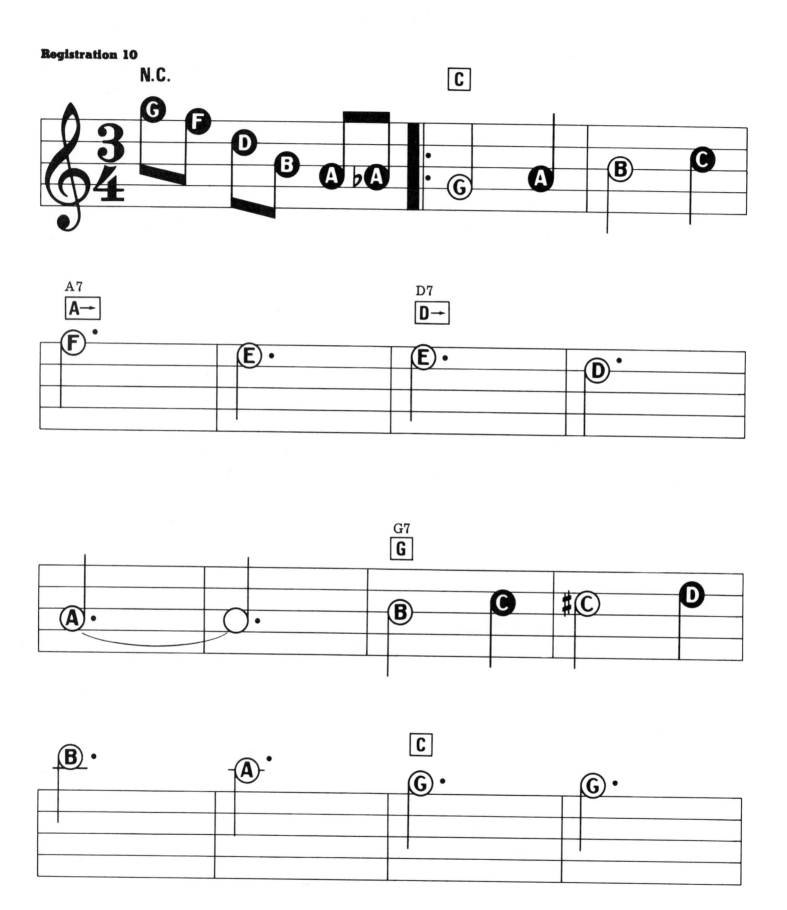

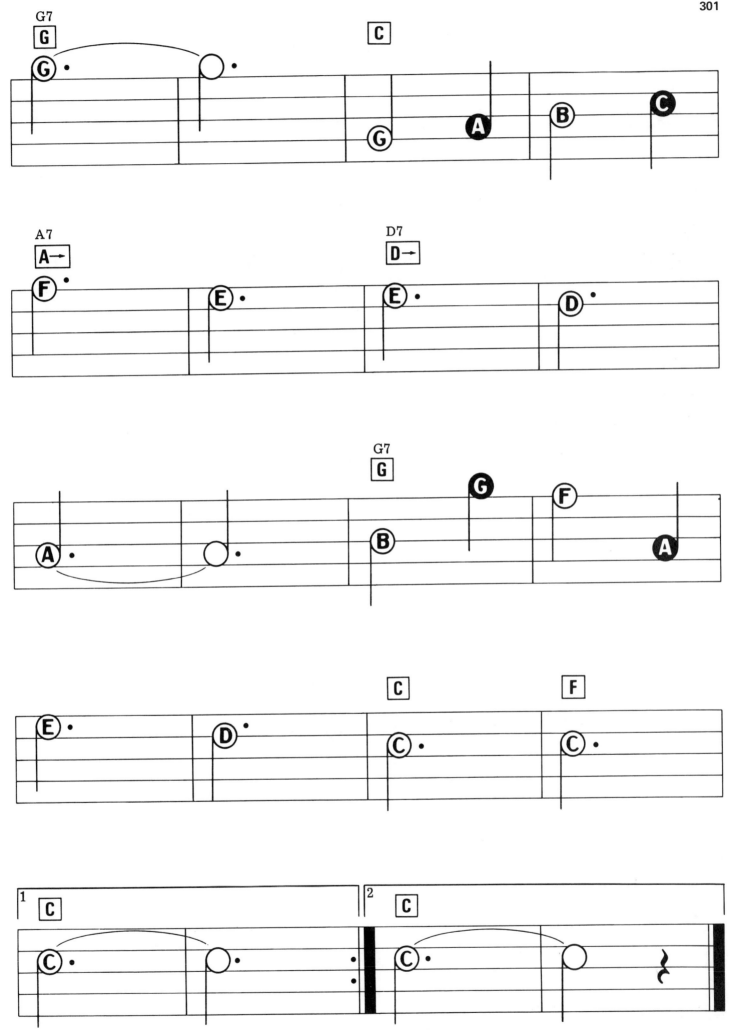

Over The Waves

Registration 3

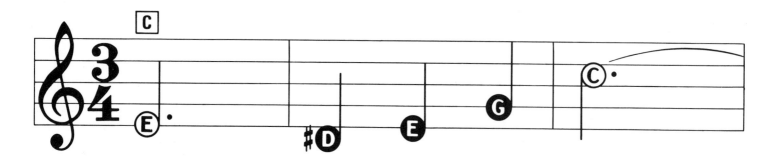

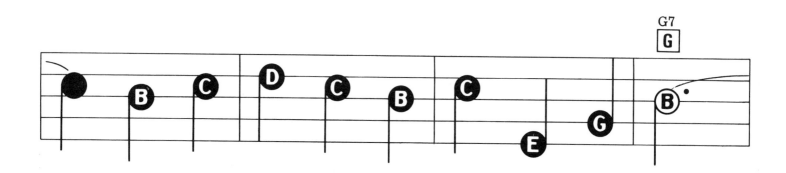

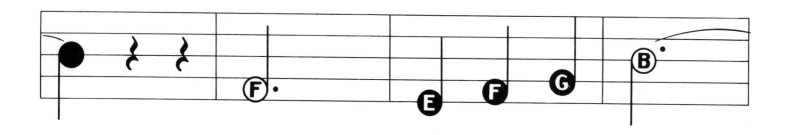

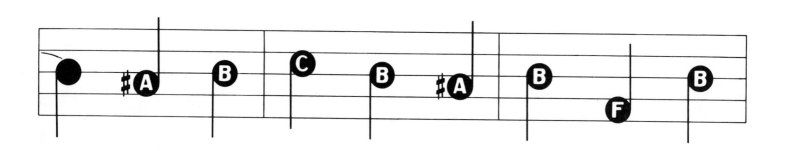

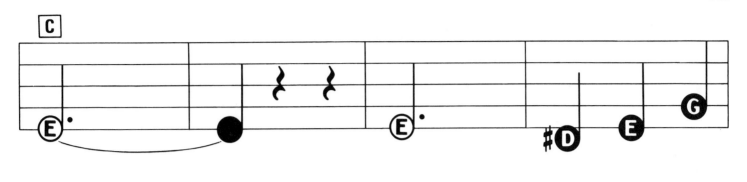

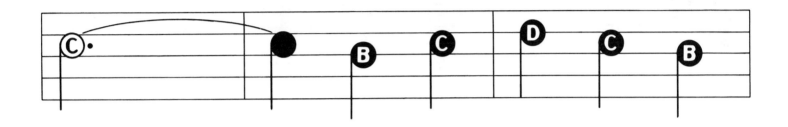

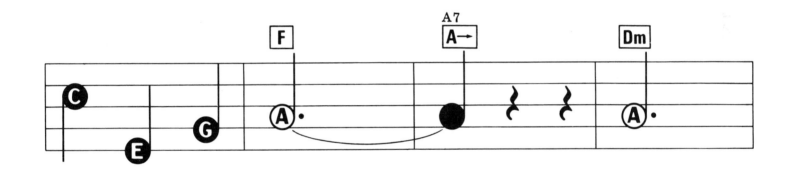

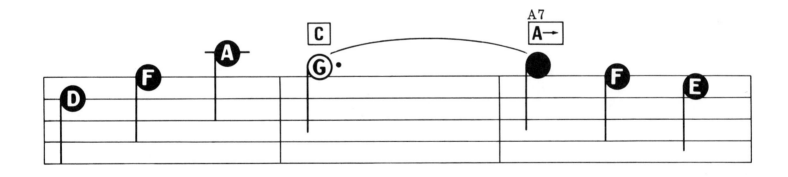

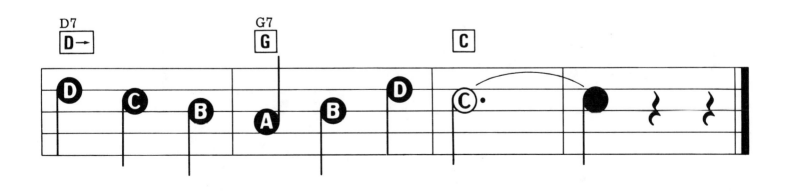

Roses From The South

Registration 5

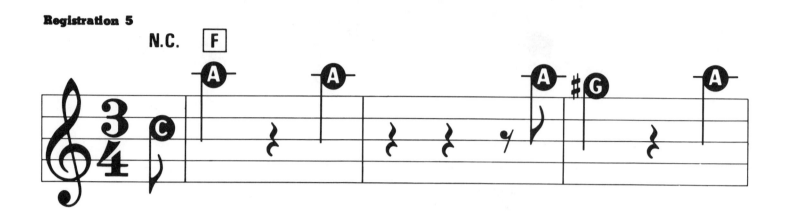

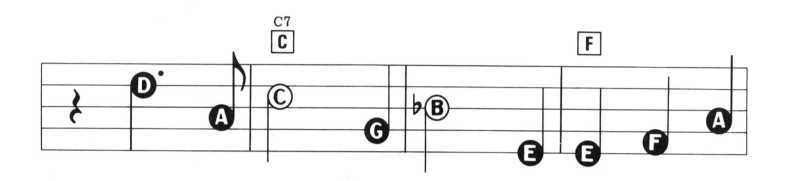

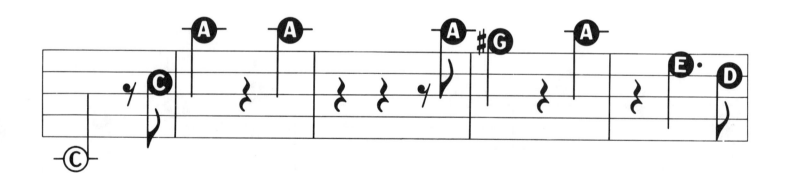

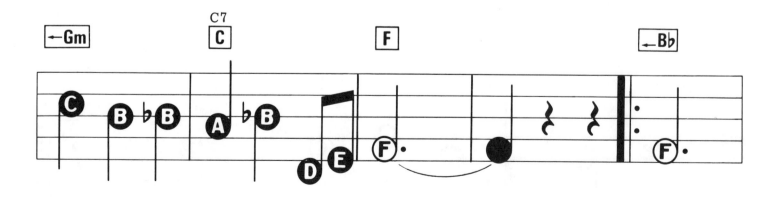

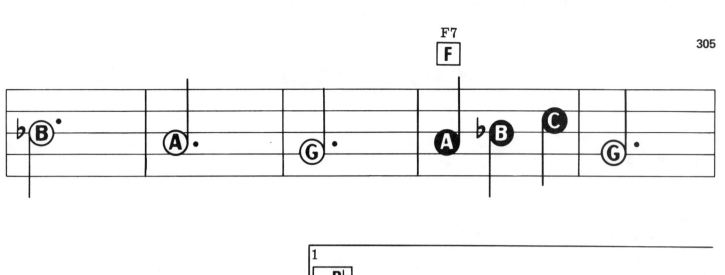

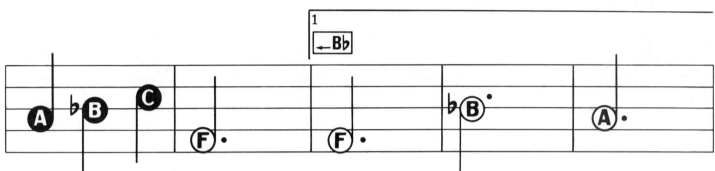

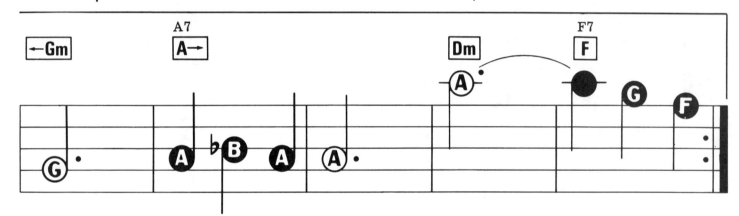

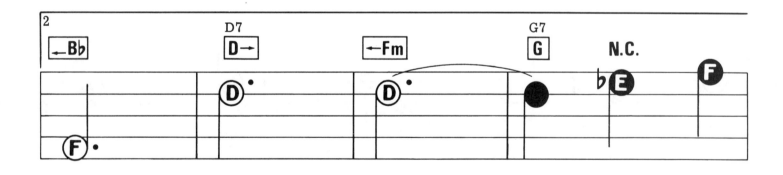

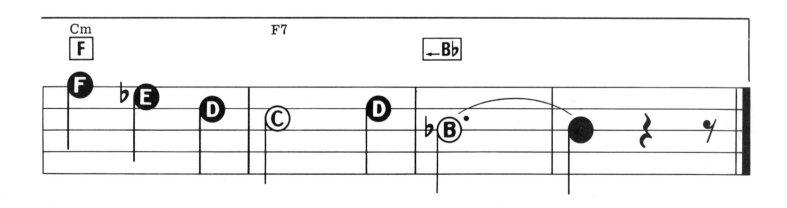

Sailing, Sailing

Registration 5

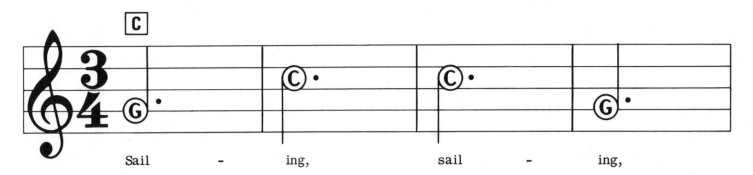

Sail - ing, sail - ing,

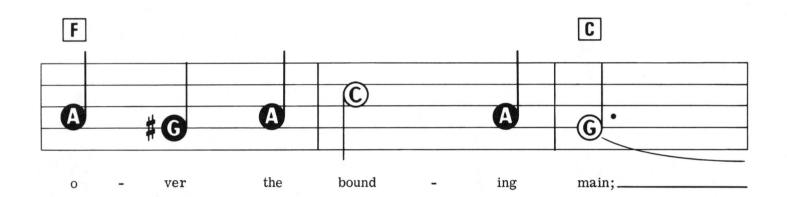

o - ver the bound - ing main;

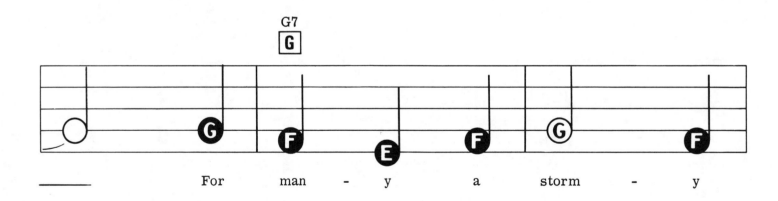

For man - y a storm - y

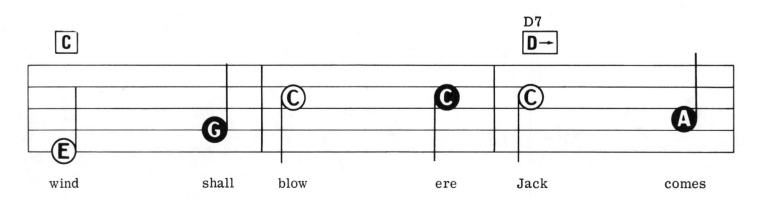

wind shall blow ere Jack comes

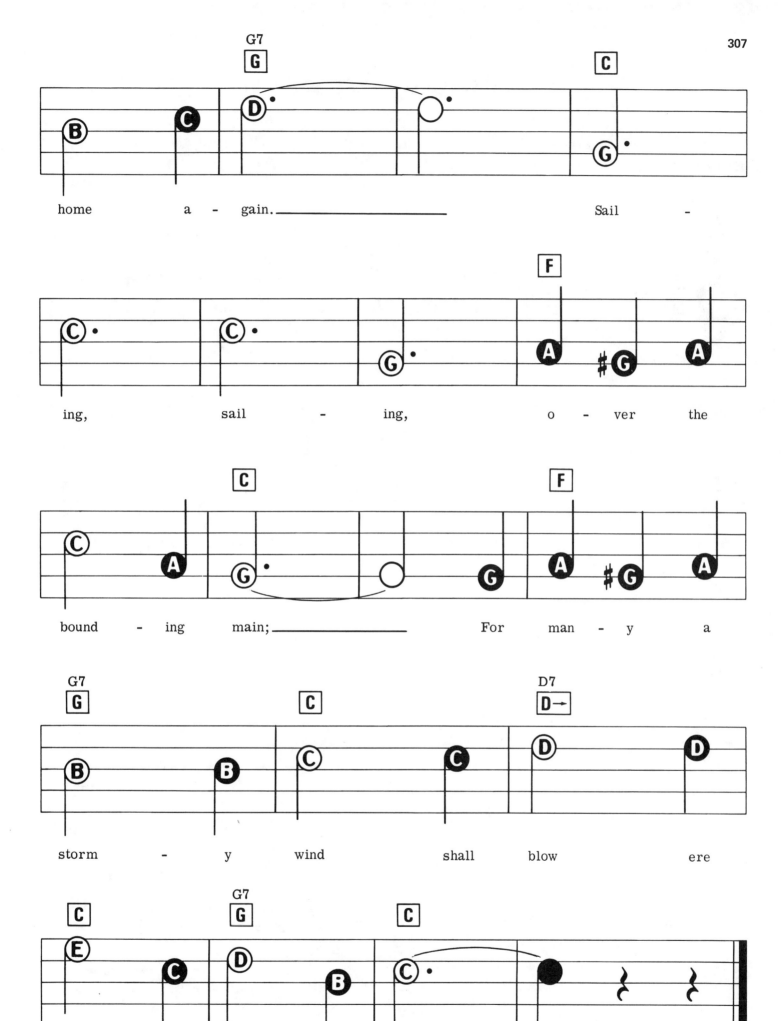

Skaters Waltz

Registration 5

Emil Waldteufel

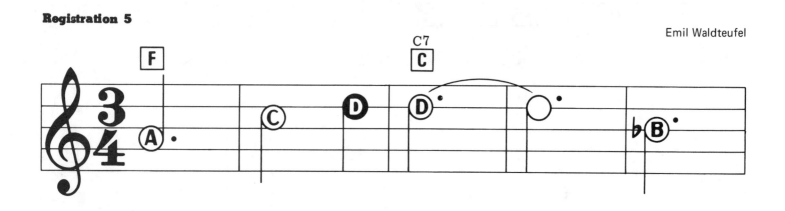

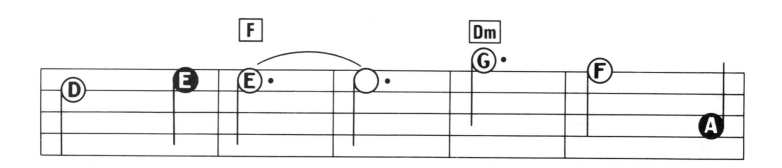

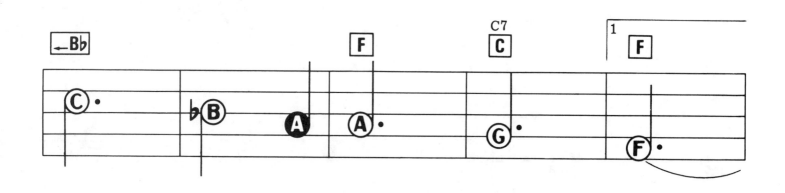

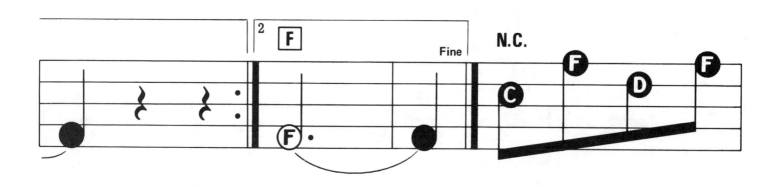

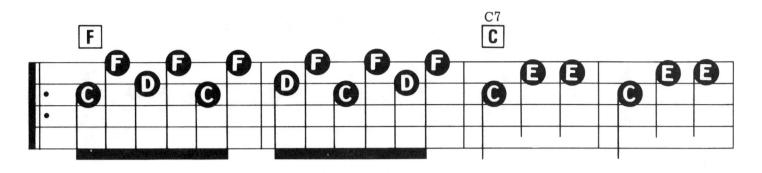

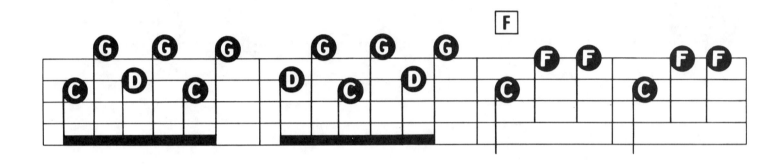

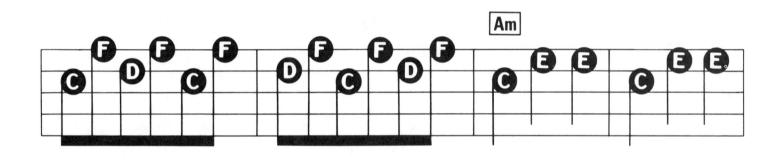

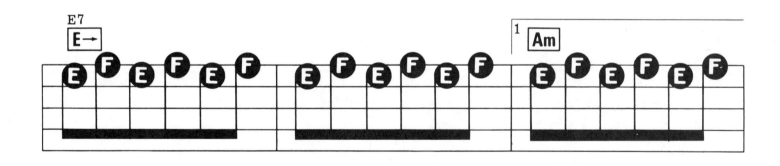

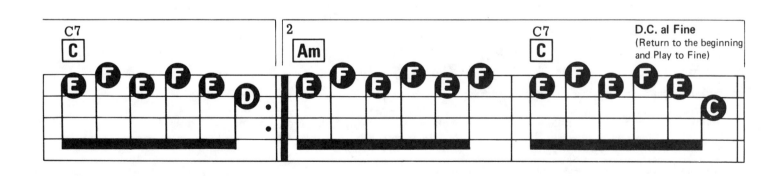

That Viennese Waltz

Registration 3

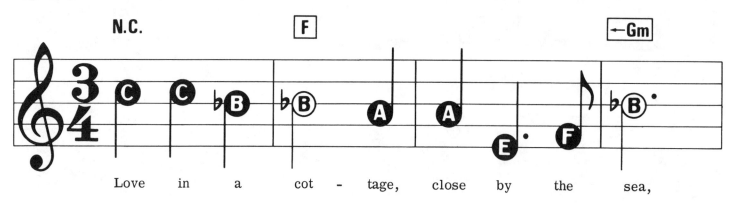

Love in a cot - tage, close by the sea,

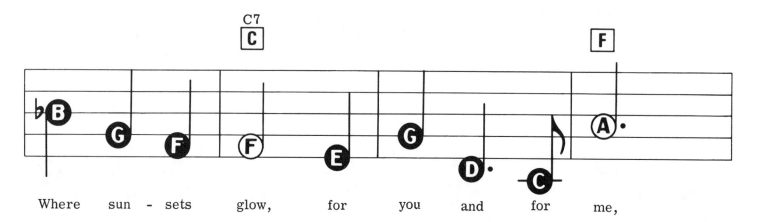

Where sun - sets glow, for you and for me,

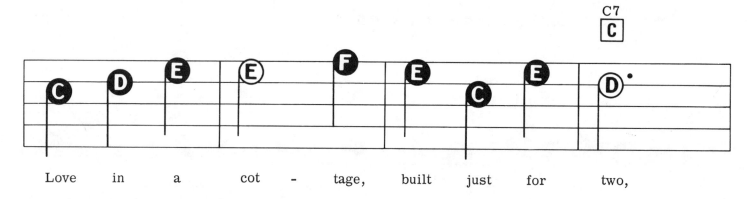

Love in a cot - tage, built just for two,

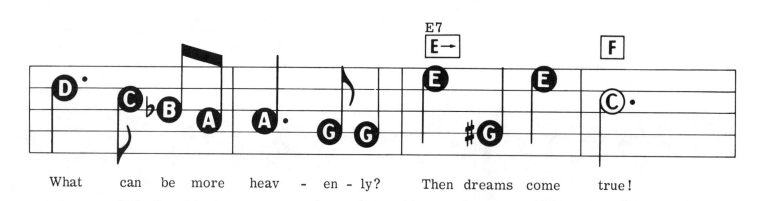

What can be more heav - en - ly? Then dreams come true!

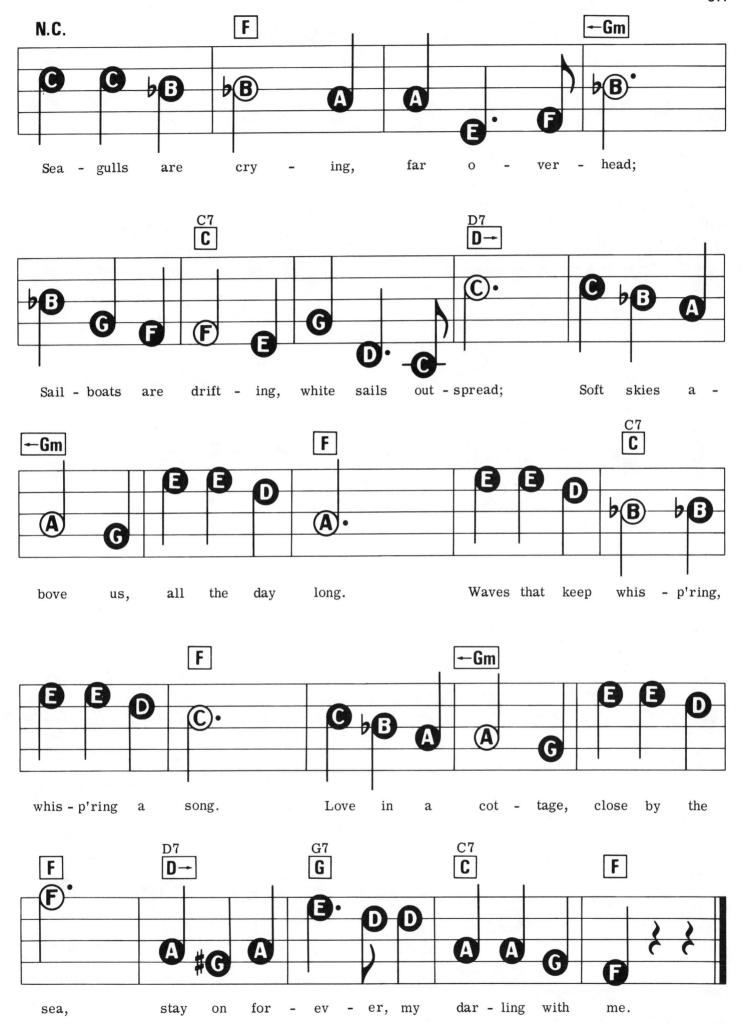

Viva L'Amour

Registration 3

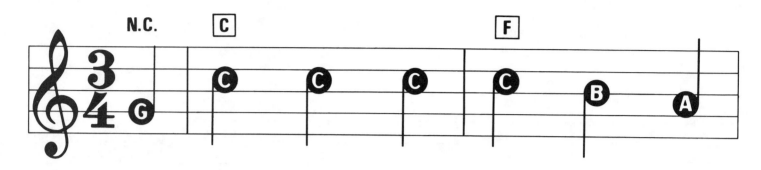

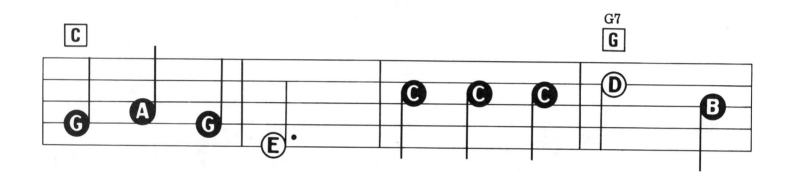

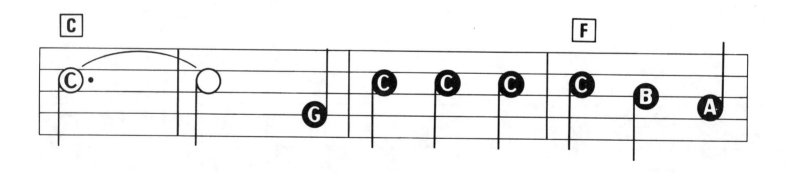

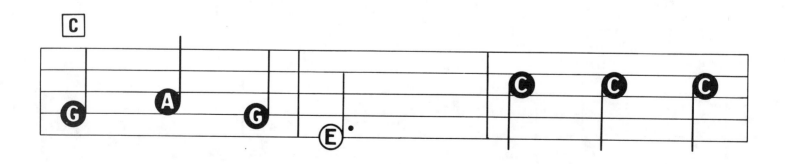

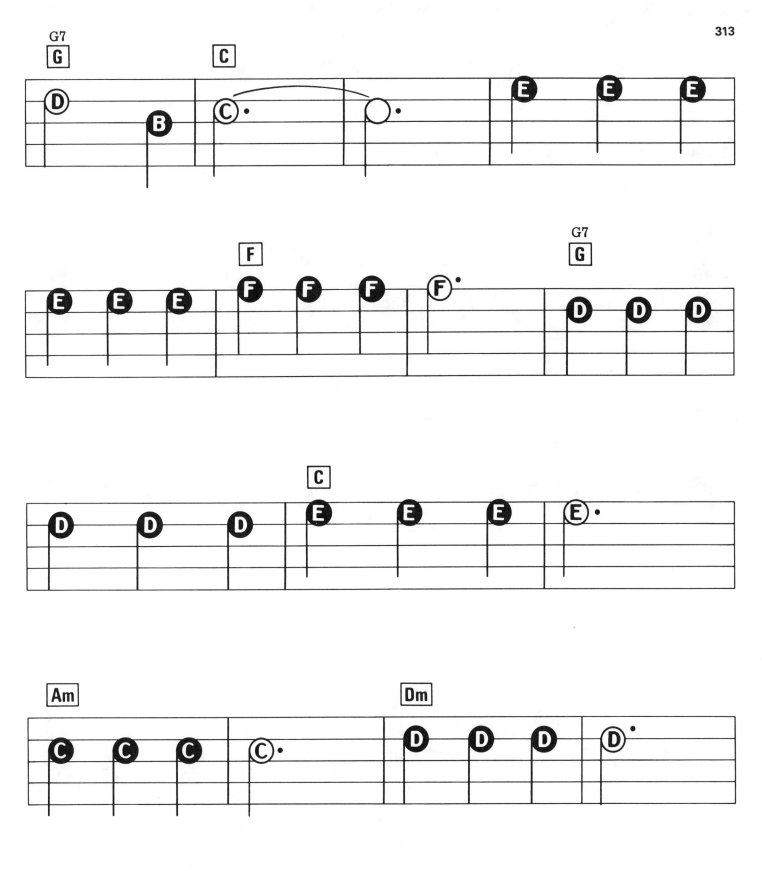

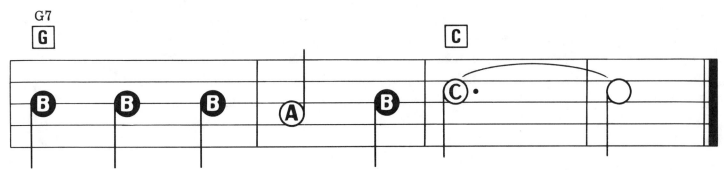

The Waltz Dream

Registration 9

Oscar Strauss

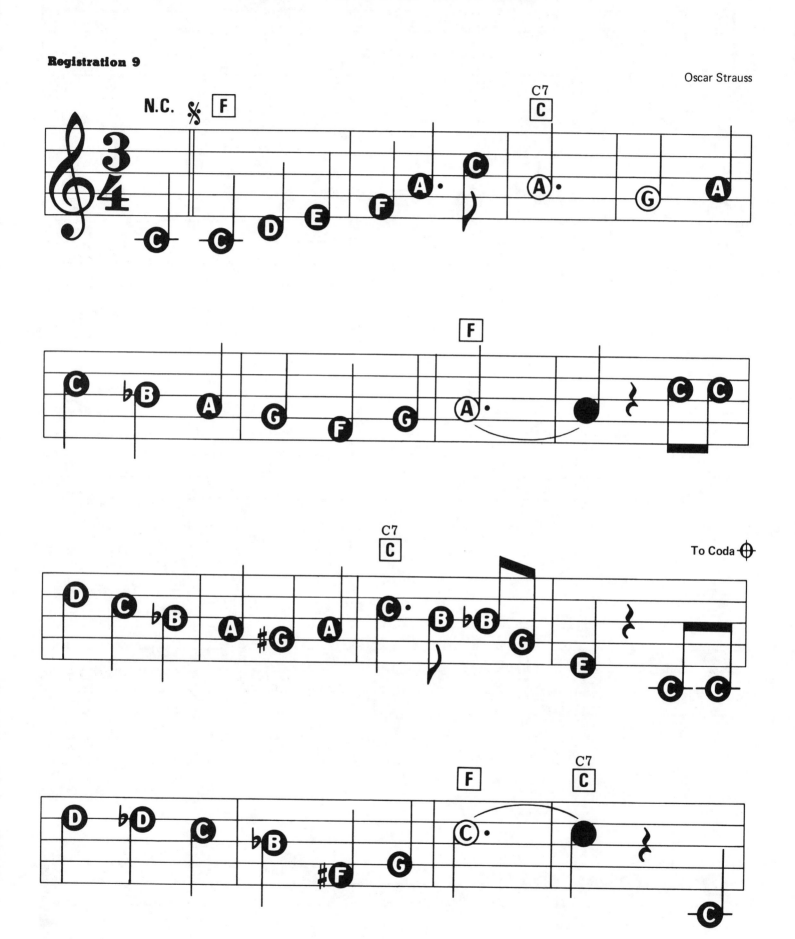

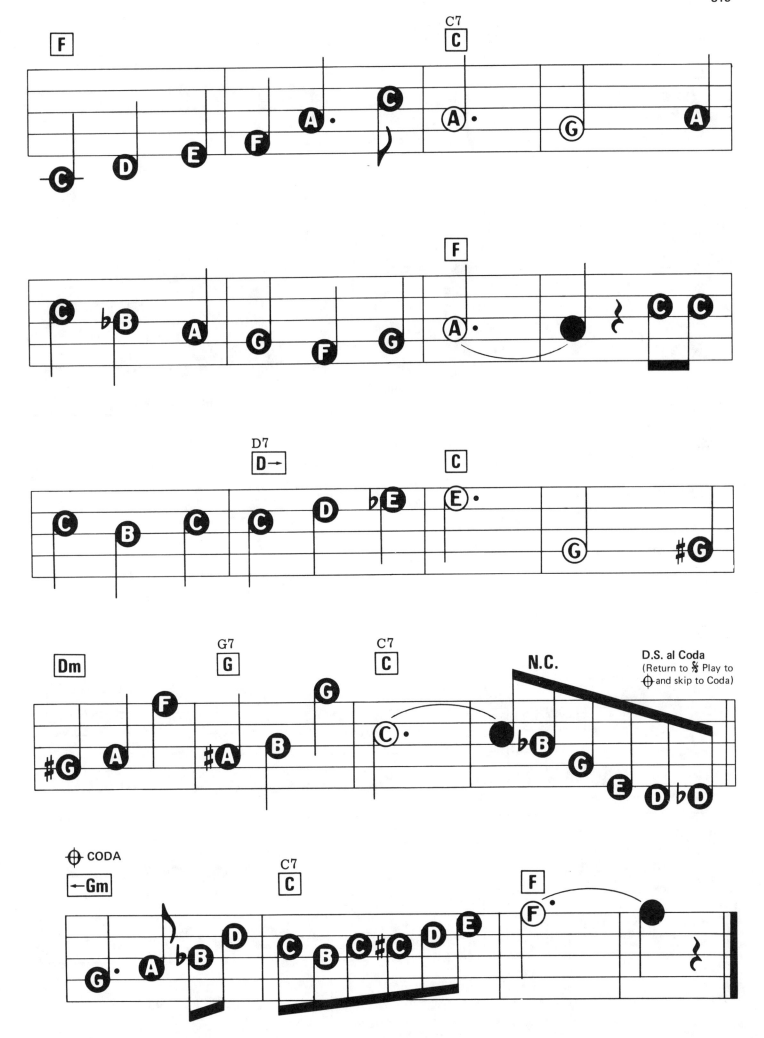

Alouette

Registration 3

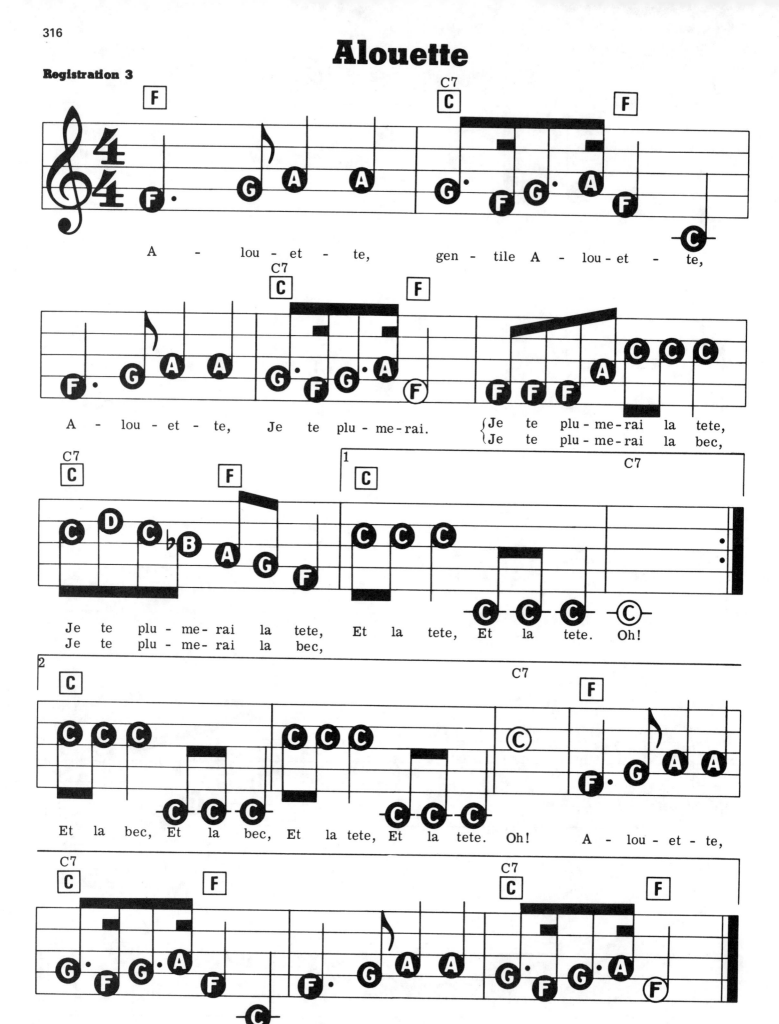

Goodnight Ladies

Registration 3

Hail, Hail The Gang's All Here

Registration 5

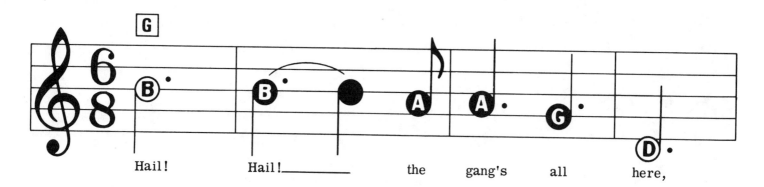

Hail! Hail!_____ the gang's all here,

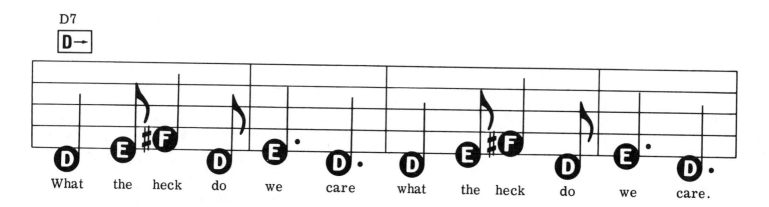

What the heck do we care what the heck do we care.

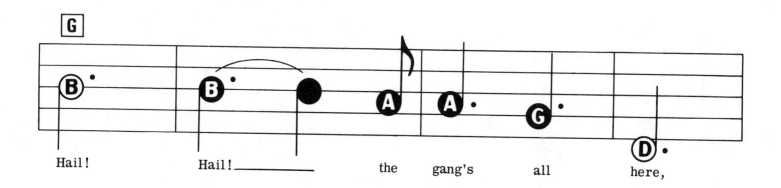

Hail! Hail!_____ the gang's all here,

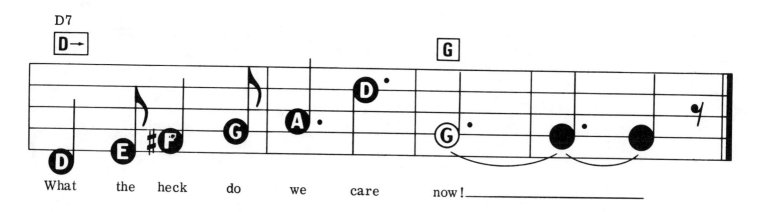

What the heck do we care now!_____

A Hot Time In The Old Town Tonight

Registration 7

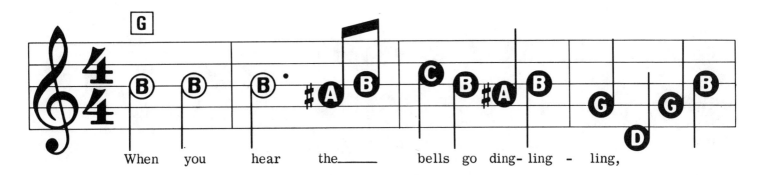

When you hear the___ bells go ding-ling - ling,

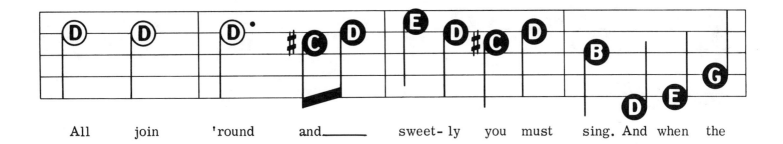

All join 'round and___ sweet-ly you must sing. And when the

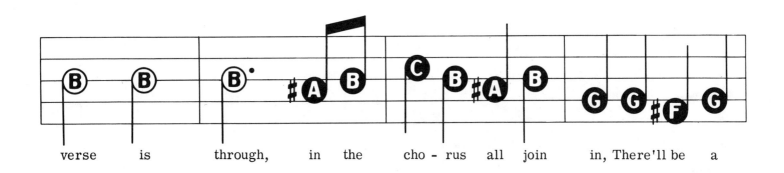

verse is through, in the cho - rus all join in, There'll be a

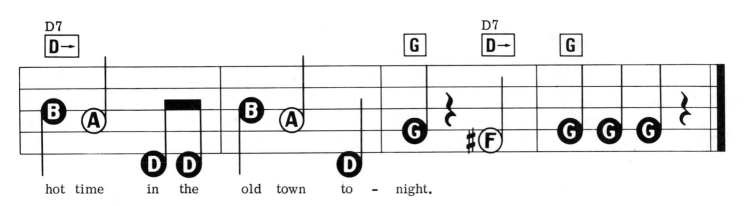

hot time in the old town to - night.

In The Evenin' By The Moonlight

Registration 2

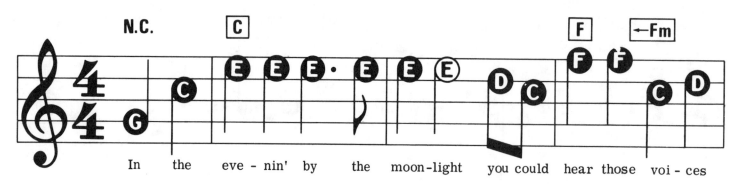

In the eve - nin' by the moon-light you could hear those voi - ces

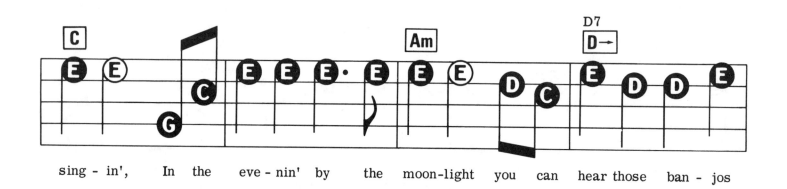

sing - in', In the eve - nin' by the moon-light you can hear those ban - jos

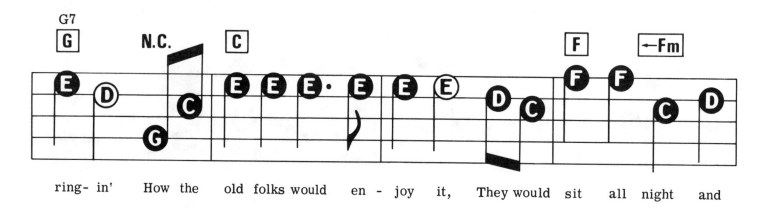

ring- in' How the old folks would en - joy it, They would sit all night and

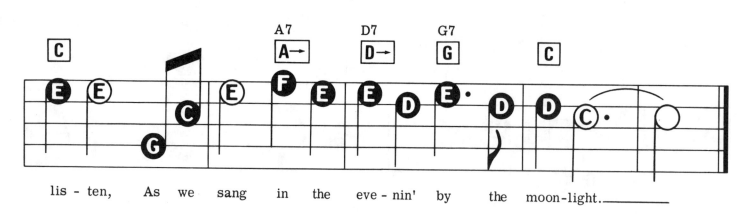

lis - ten, As we sang in the eve - nin' by the moon-light._____

Li'l Liza Jane

Registration 9

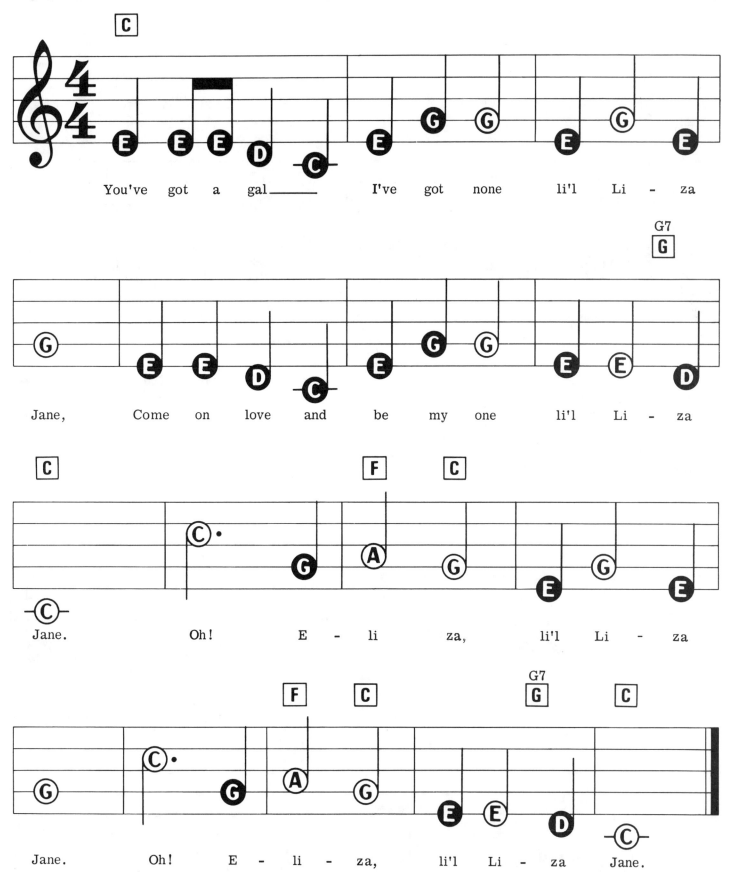

Registration 8

The Old Gray Mare

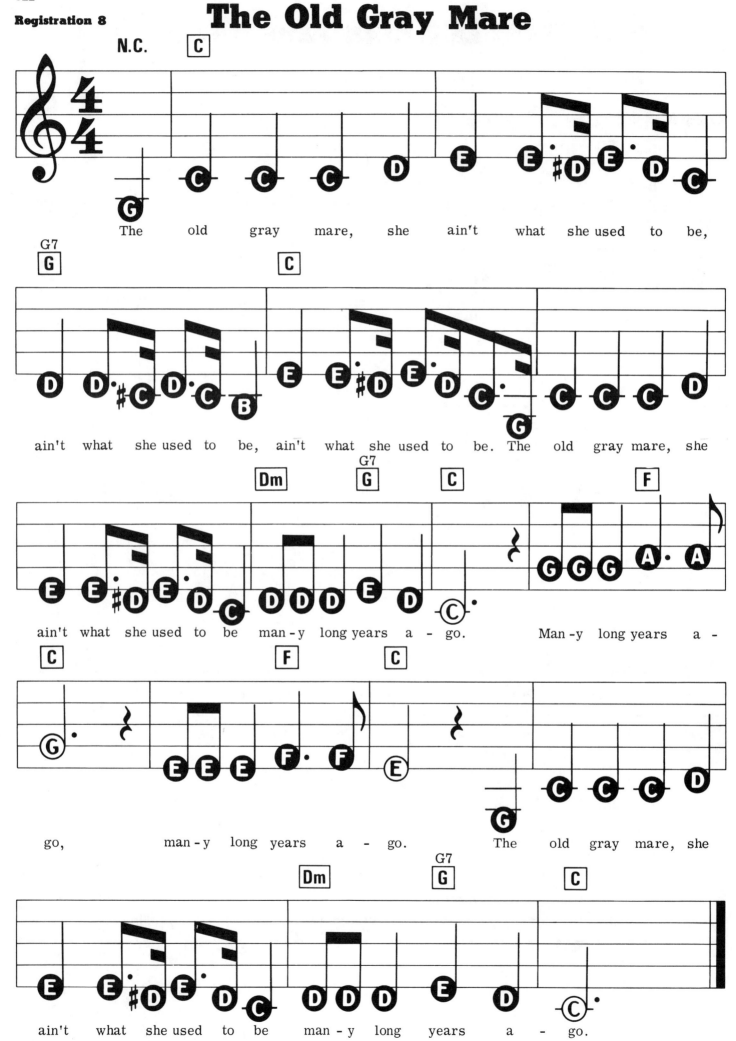

The Old Oaken Bucket

Registration 3

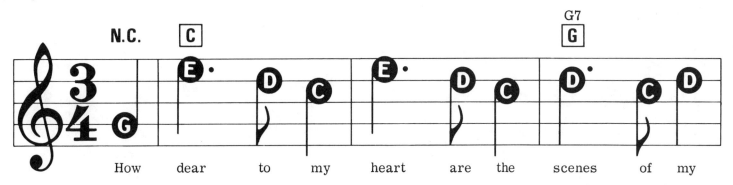

How dear to my heart are the scenes of my

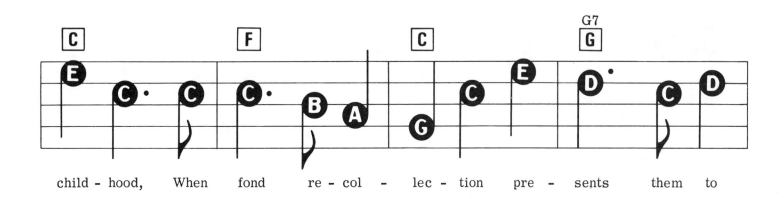

child - hood, When fond re - col - lec - tion pre - sents them to

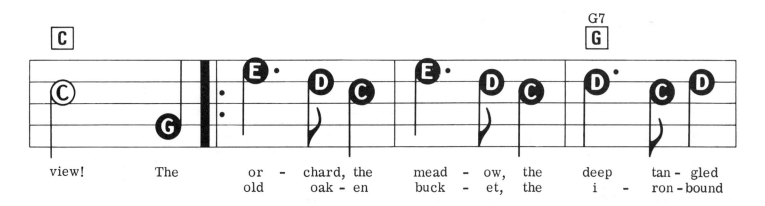

view! The or - chard, the mead - ow, the deep tan - gled
old oak - en buck - et, the i - ron - bound

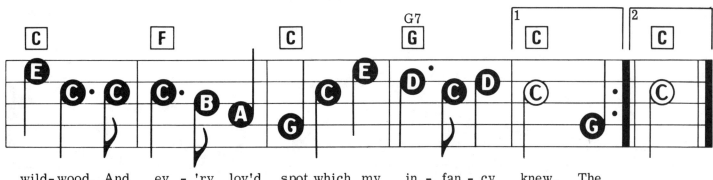

wild-wood, And ev - 'ry lov'd spot which my in - fan - cy knew. The
buck - et, the moss - cov - ered buck - et that hung in the well.

Polly Wolly Doodle

Registration 4

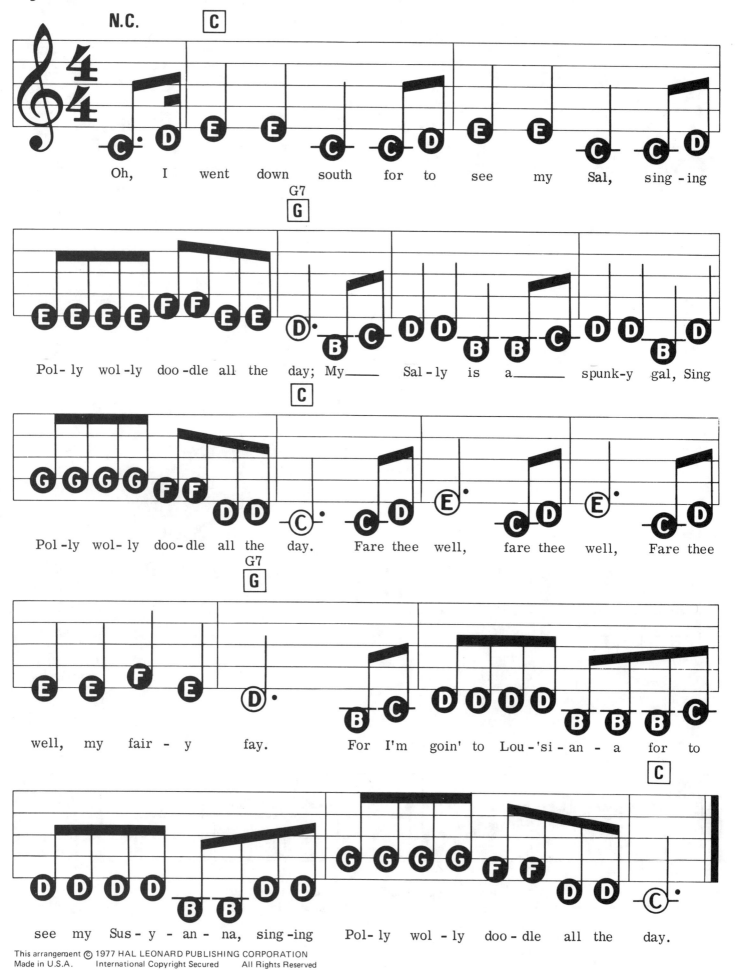

When You Were Sweet Sixteen

Registration 10

When first I saw the love-light in your eye, And
love you as I nev-er lov'd be-fore, Since

heard thy voice like sweet-est mel-o-dy, Speak
first I met you on the vil-lage green; Come

words of love to my en-rap-tur'd soul, The
to me, or my dream of love is o'er, I

world had naught but joy in store for me. I

love you as I lov'd you, When you were sweet, When you were sweet six-teen.

The Band Played On

Registration 5

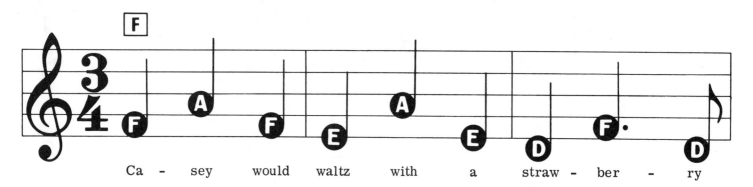

Ca - sey would waltz with a straw - ber - ry

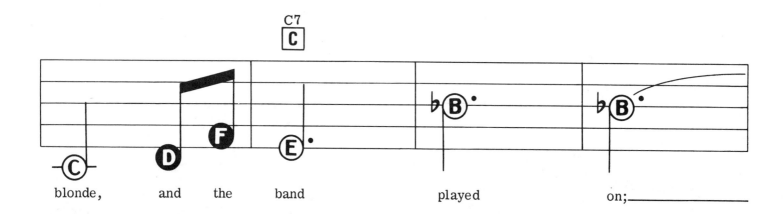

blonde, and the band played on;

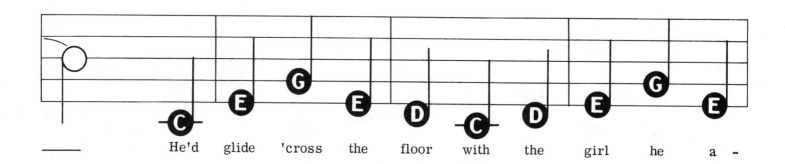

He'd glide 'cross the floor with the girl he a -

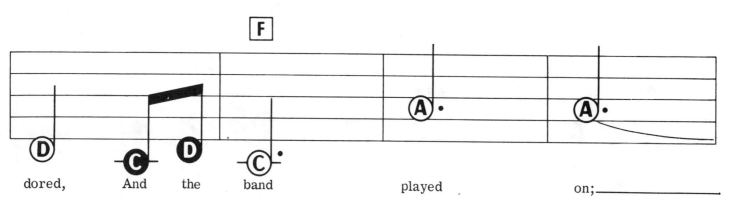

dored, And the band played on;

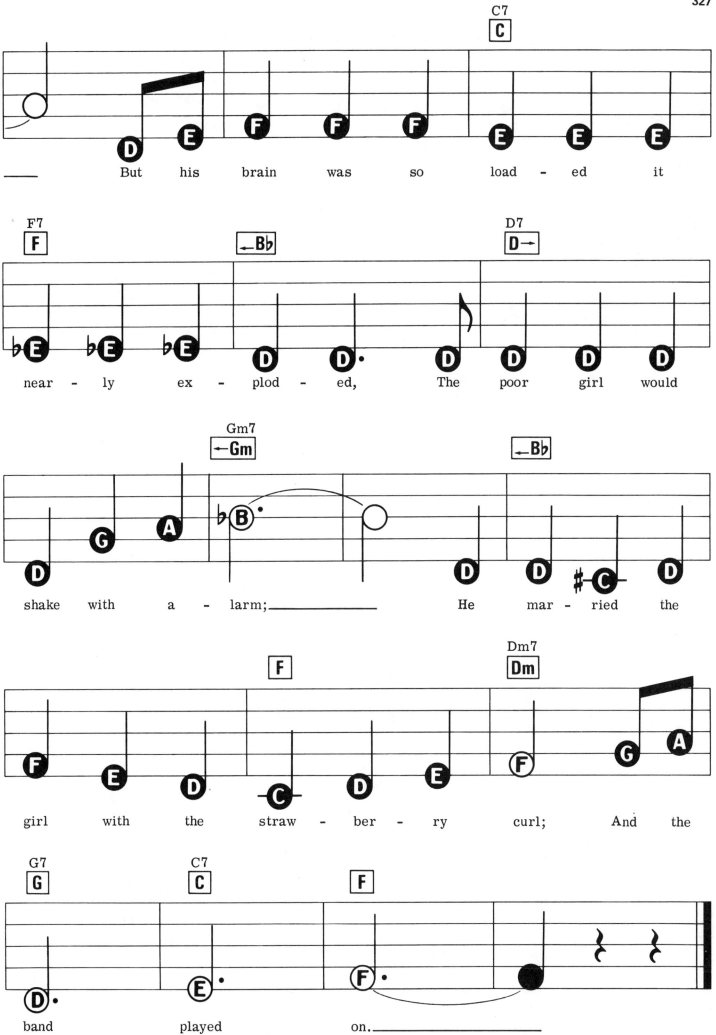

Beautiful Dreamer

Registration 5

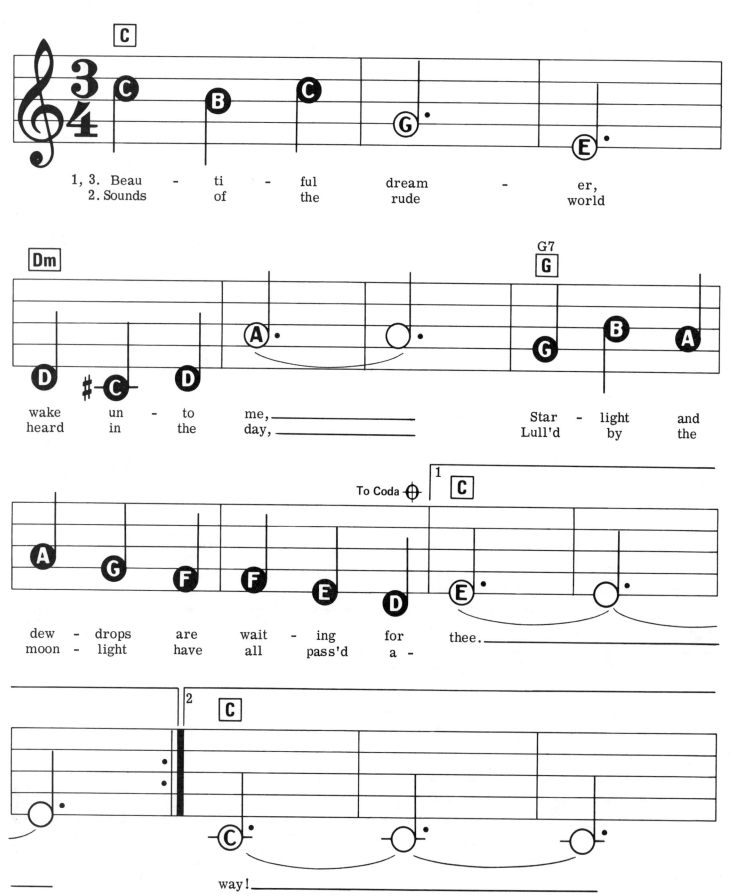

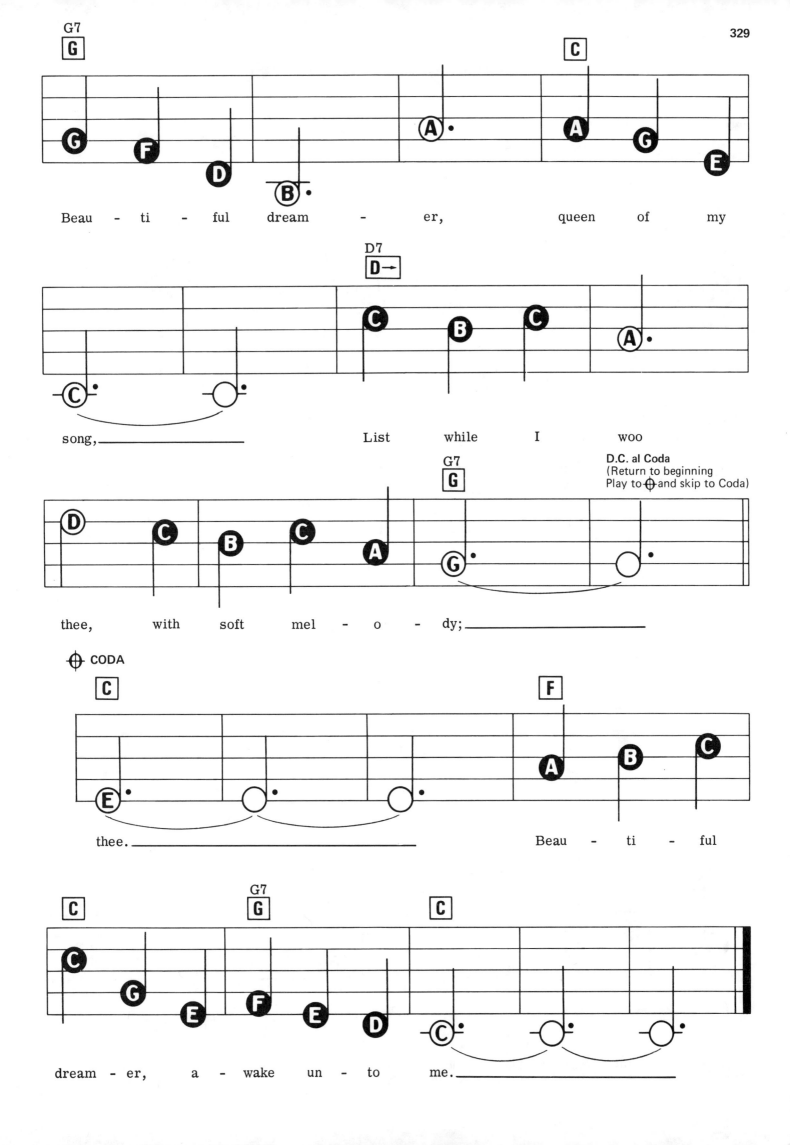

Bicycle Built For Two

Registration 2

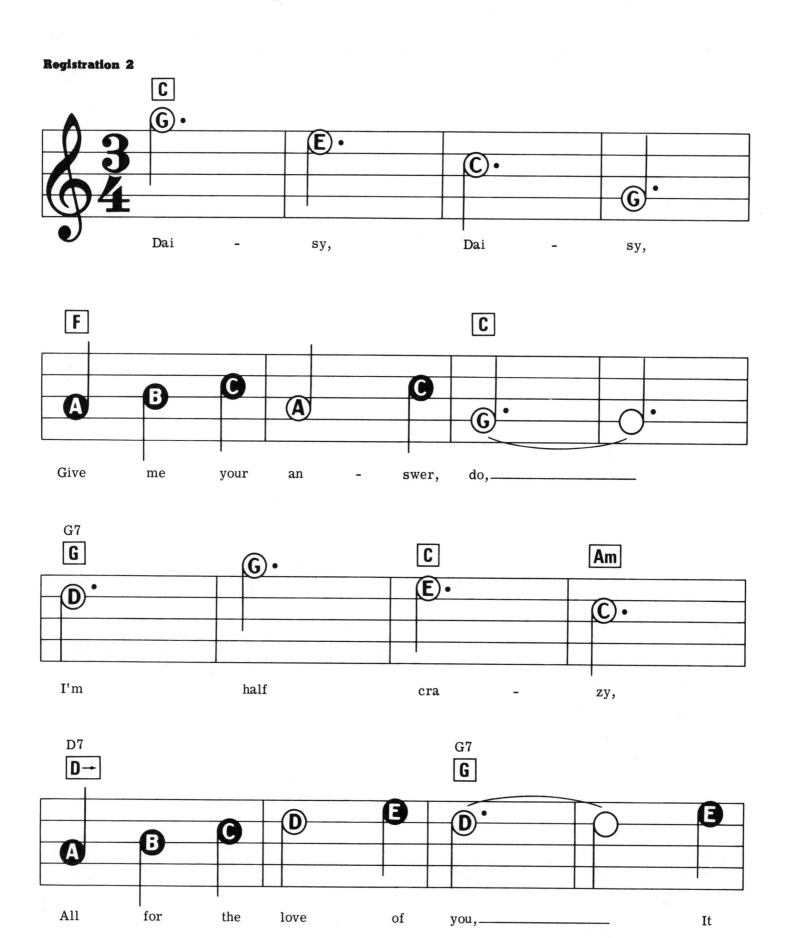

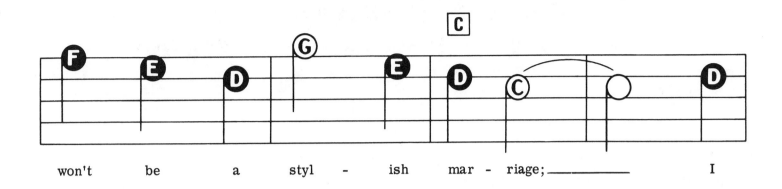

won't   be   a   styl - ish   mar - riage;_____   I

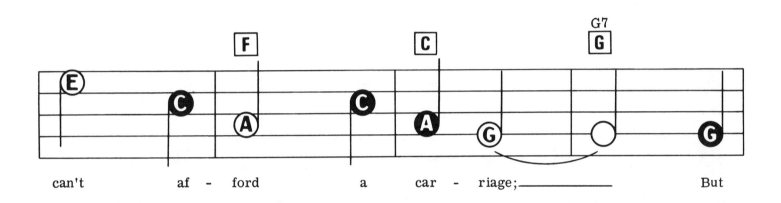

can't   af - ford   a   car - riage;_____   But

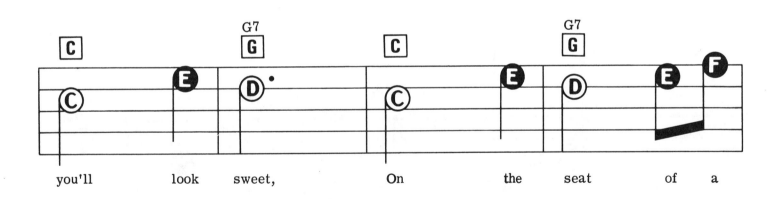

you'll   look   sweet,   On   the   seat   of   a

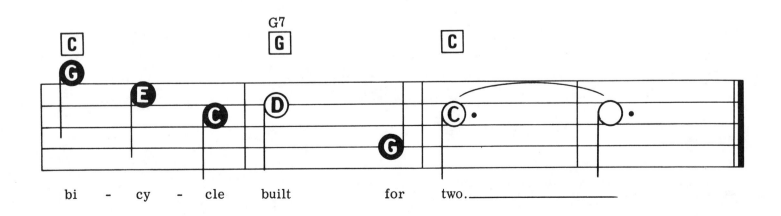

bi - cy - cle   built   for   two._____

Bill Bailey, Won't You Please Come Home

Registration 7

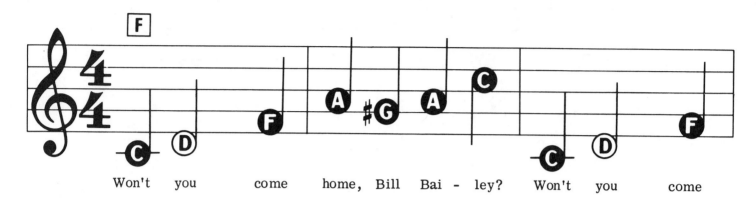

Won't you come home, Bill Bai - ley? Won't you come

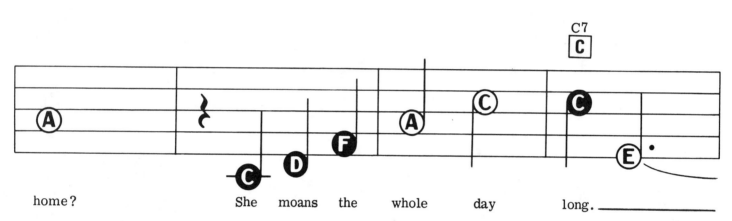

home? She moans the whole day long. _____

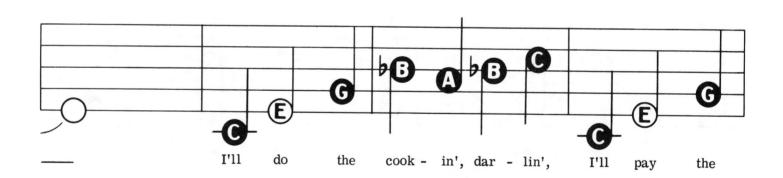

I'll do the cook - in', dar - lin', I'll pay the

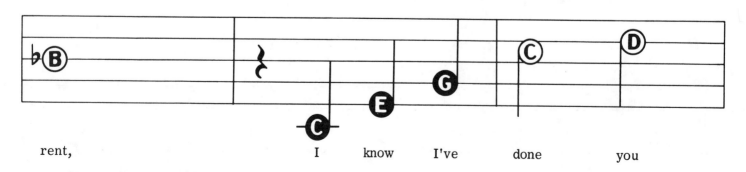

rent, I know I've done you

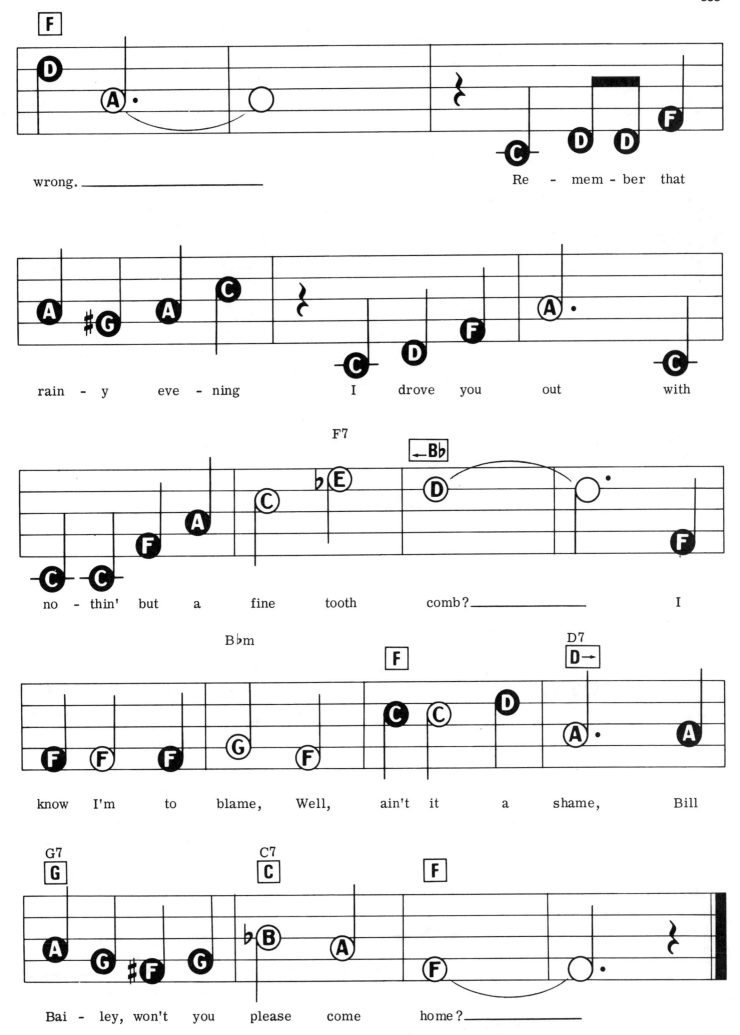

A Bird In A Gilded Cage

Registration 10

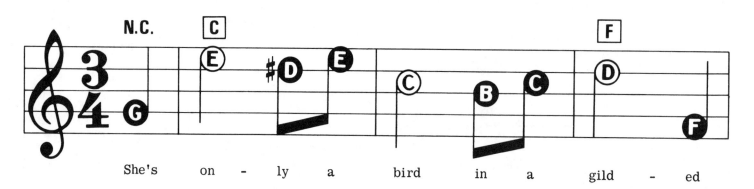

She's on - ly a bird in a gild - ed

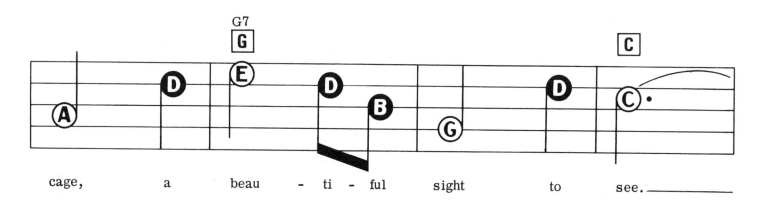

cage, a beau - ti - ful sight to see. ___

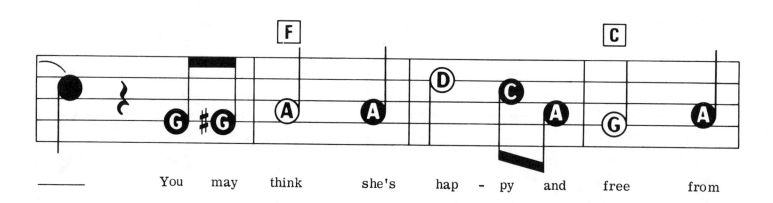

___ You may think she's hap - py and free from

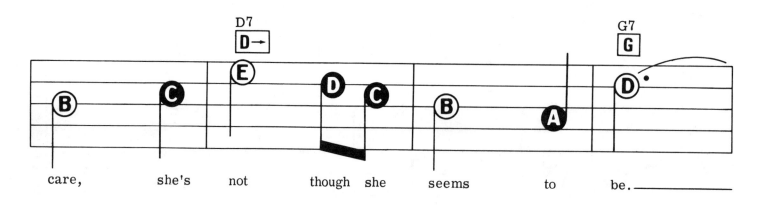

care, she's not though she seems to be. ___

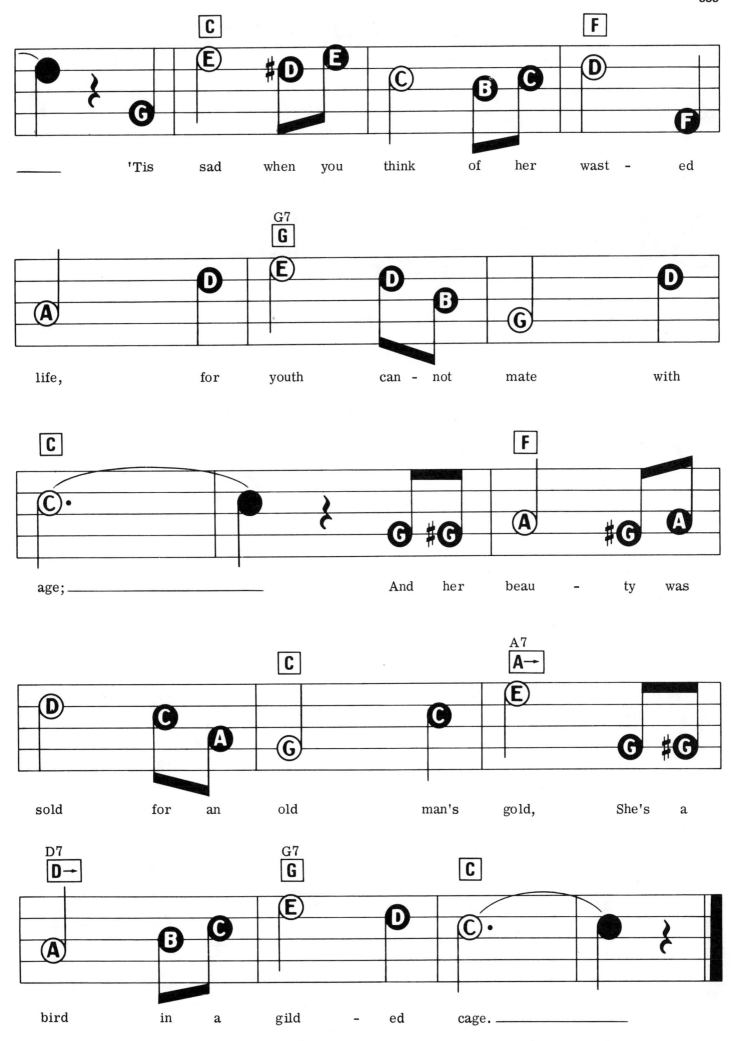

_____ 'Tis sad when you think of her wast - ed

life, for youth can - not mate with

age; _____ And her beau - ty was

sold for an old man's gold, She's a

bird in a gild - ed cage. _____

Blue Tail Fly

Registration 4

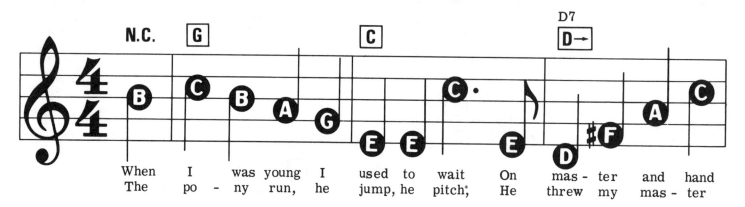

When I was young I used to wait On mas-ter and hand
The po - ny run, he jump, he pitch; On He threw my mas-ter

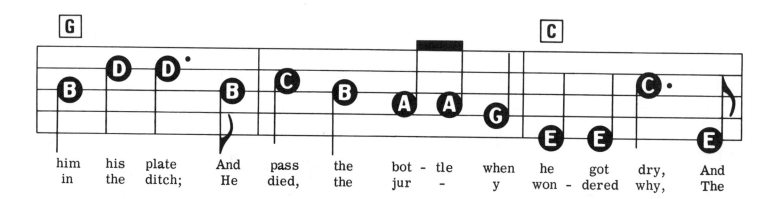

him his plate; And pass the bot - tle when he got dry, And
in the ditch; He died, the jur - y won - dered why, The

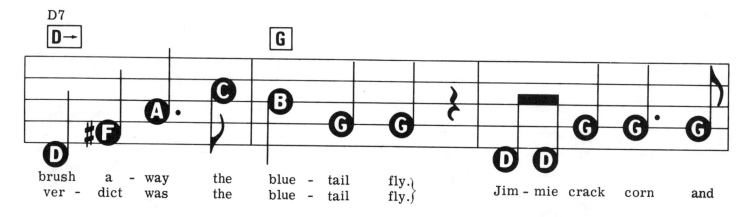

brush a - way the blue - tail fly.}
ver - dict was the blue - tail fly.}
Jim - mie crack corn and

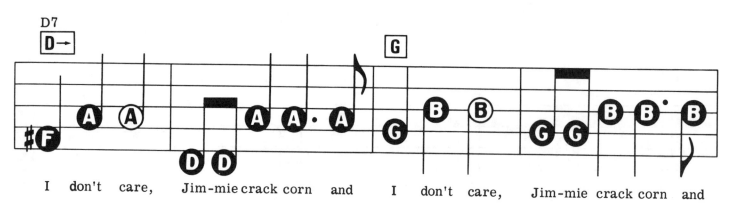

I don't care, Jim-mie crack corn and I don't care, Jim-mie crack corn and

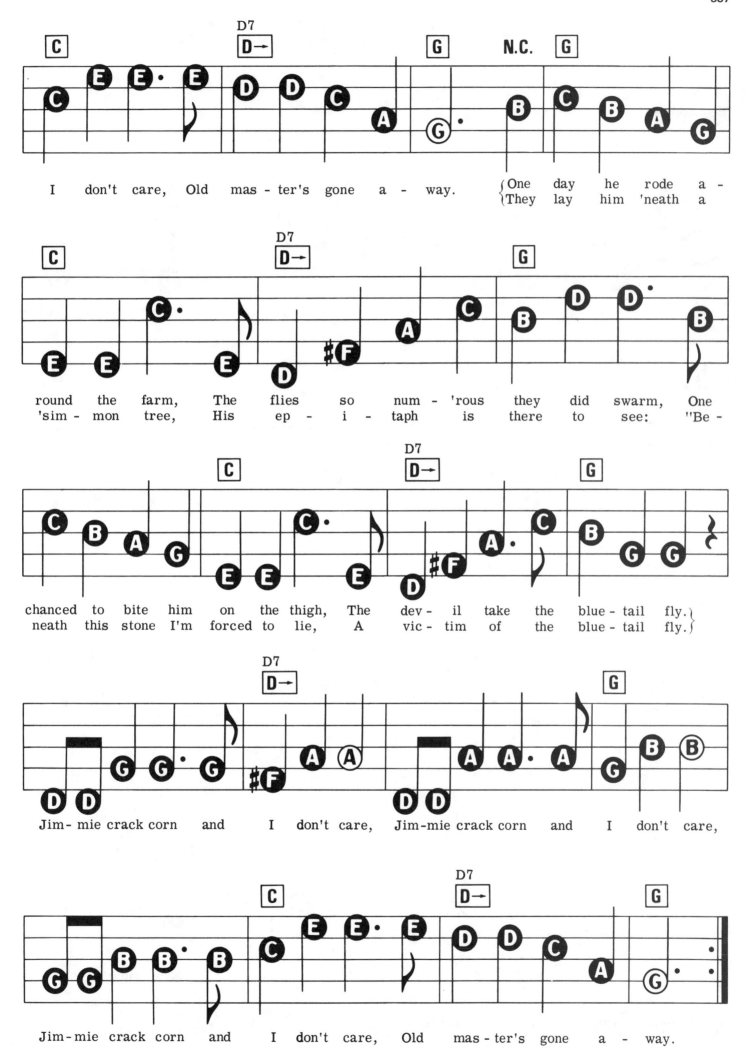

Comin' Through The Rye

Registration 9

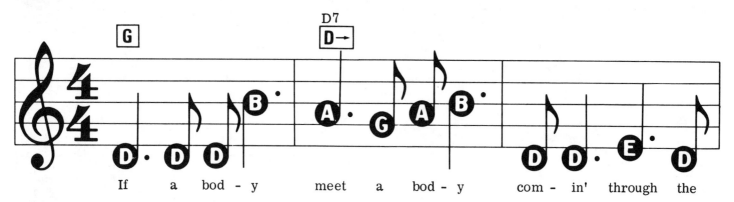

If a bod - y meet a bod - y com - in' through the

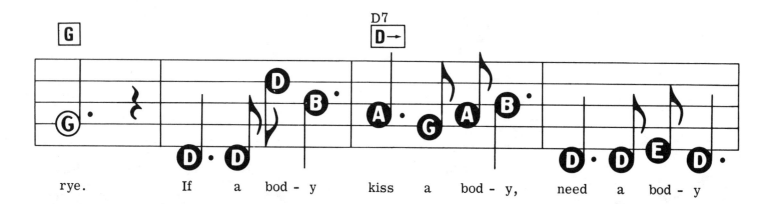

rye. If a bod - y kiss a bod - y, need a bod - y

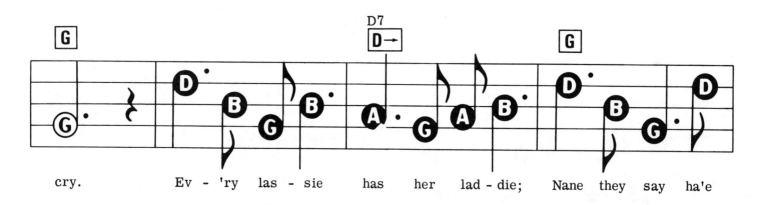

cry. Ev - 'ry las - sie has her lad - die; Nane they say ha'e

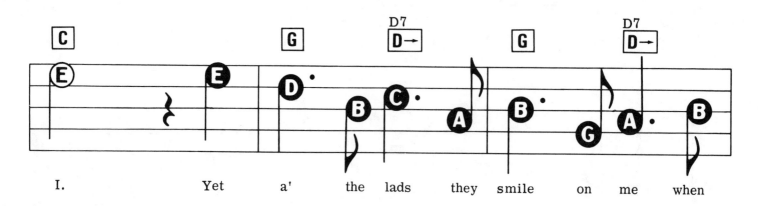

I. Yet a' the lads they smile on me when

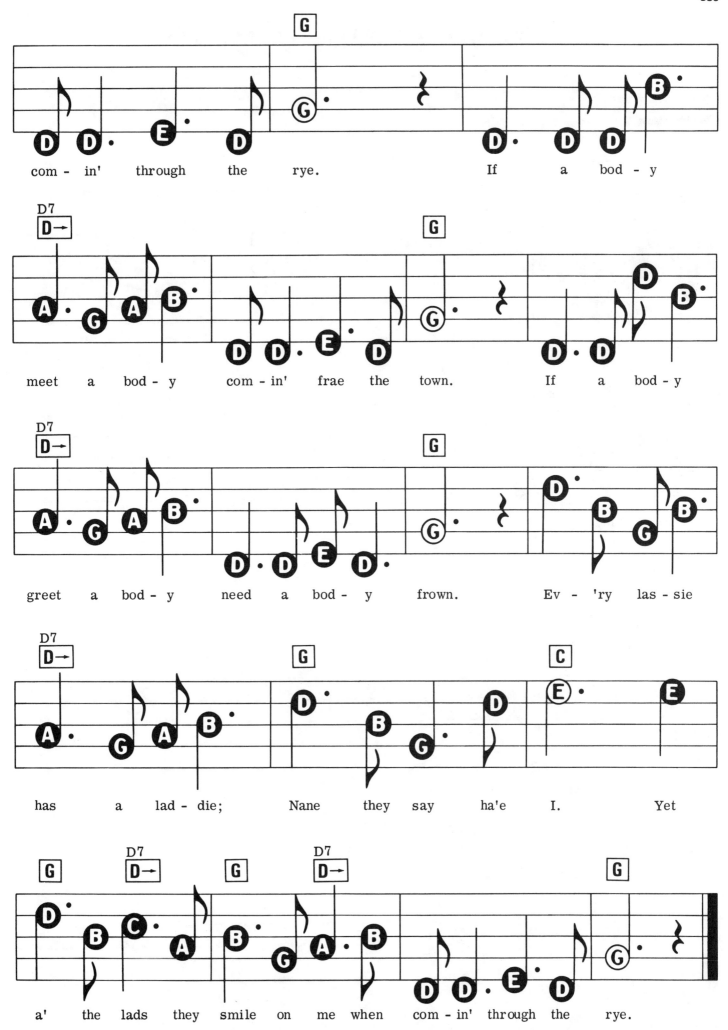

Down In The Valley

Registration 8

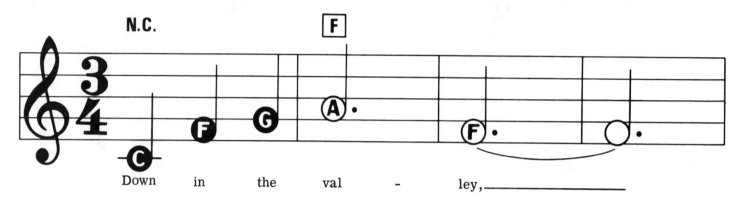

Down in the val - ley, _____

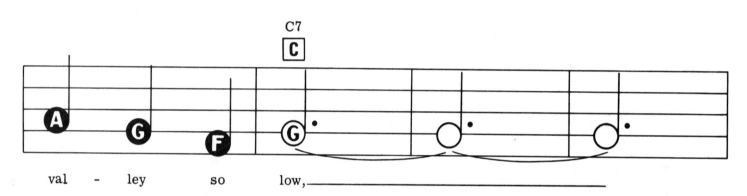

val - ley so low, _____

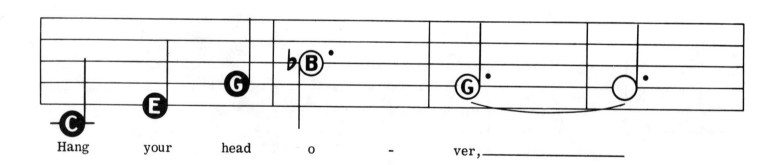

Hang your head o - ver, _____

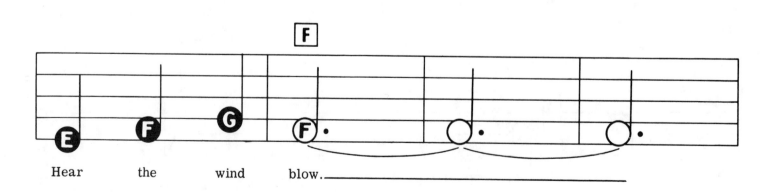

Hear the wind blow. _____

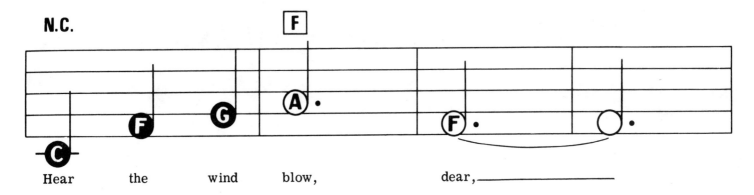

Hear the wind blow, dear,_____

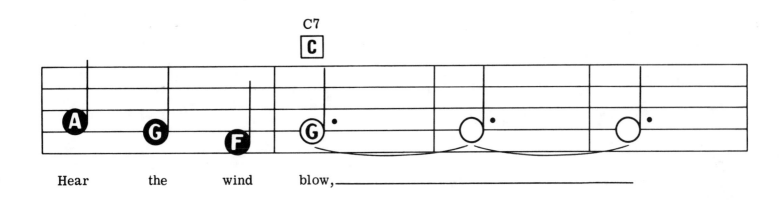

Hear the wind blow,_____

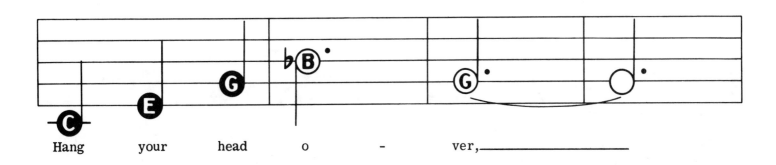

Hang your head o - ver,_____

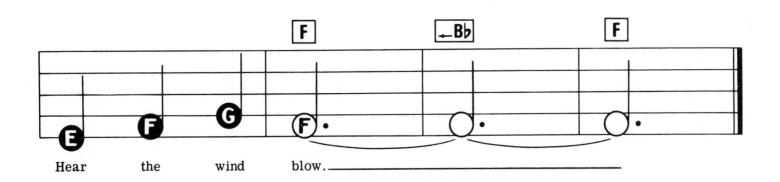

Hear the wind blow._____

For He's A Jolly Good Fellow

Registration 4

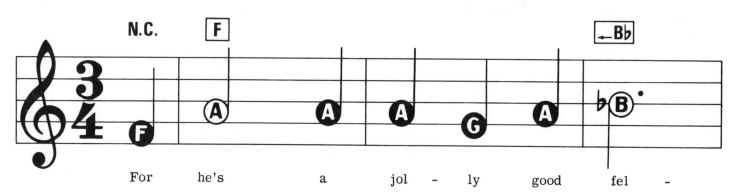

For he's a jol - ly good fel -

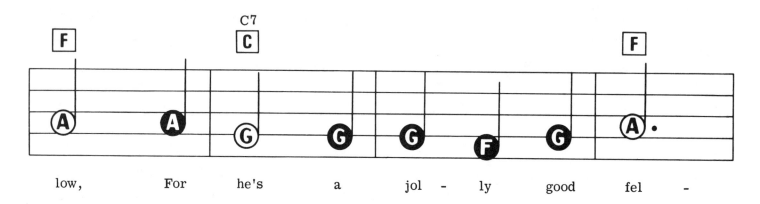

low, For he's a jol - ly good fel -

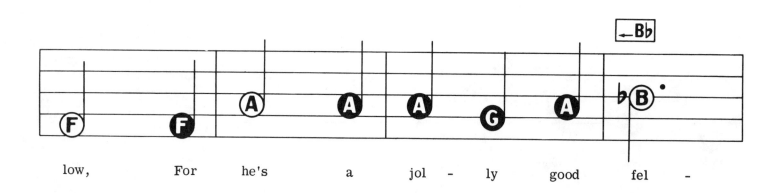

low, For he's a jol - ly good fel -

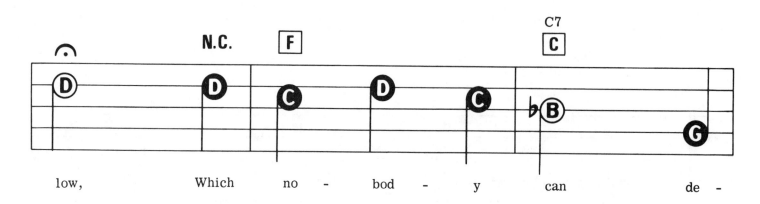

low, Which no - bod - y can de -

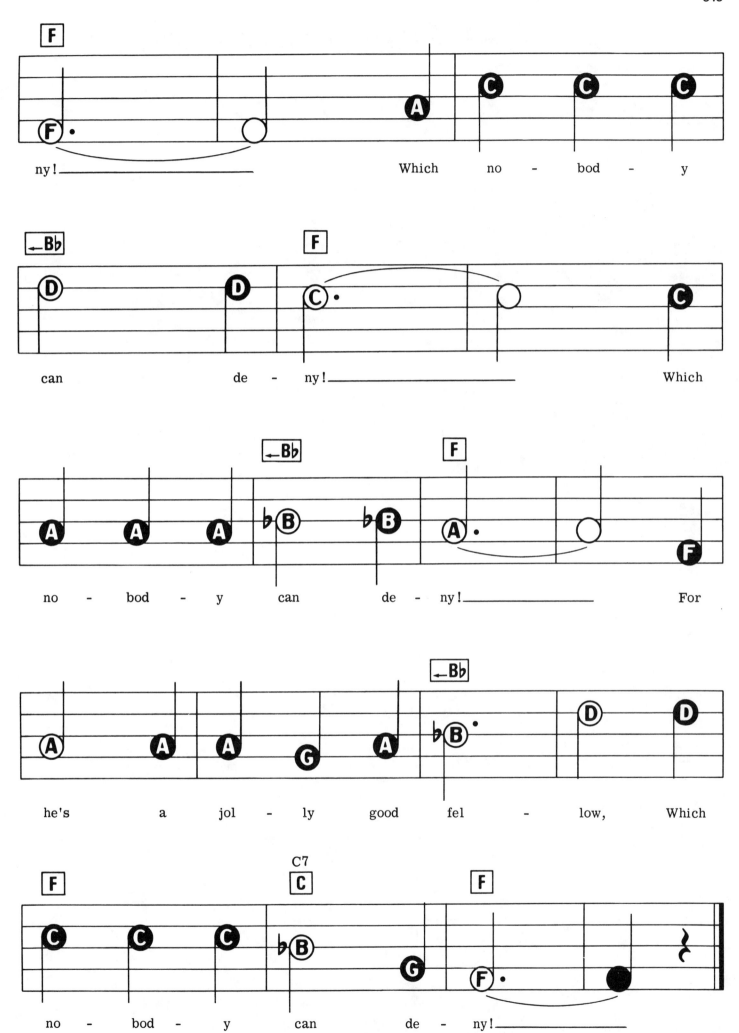

Frankie And Johnny

Registration 3

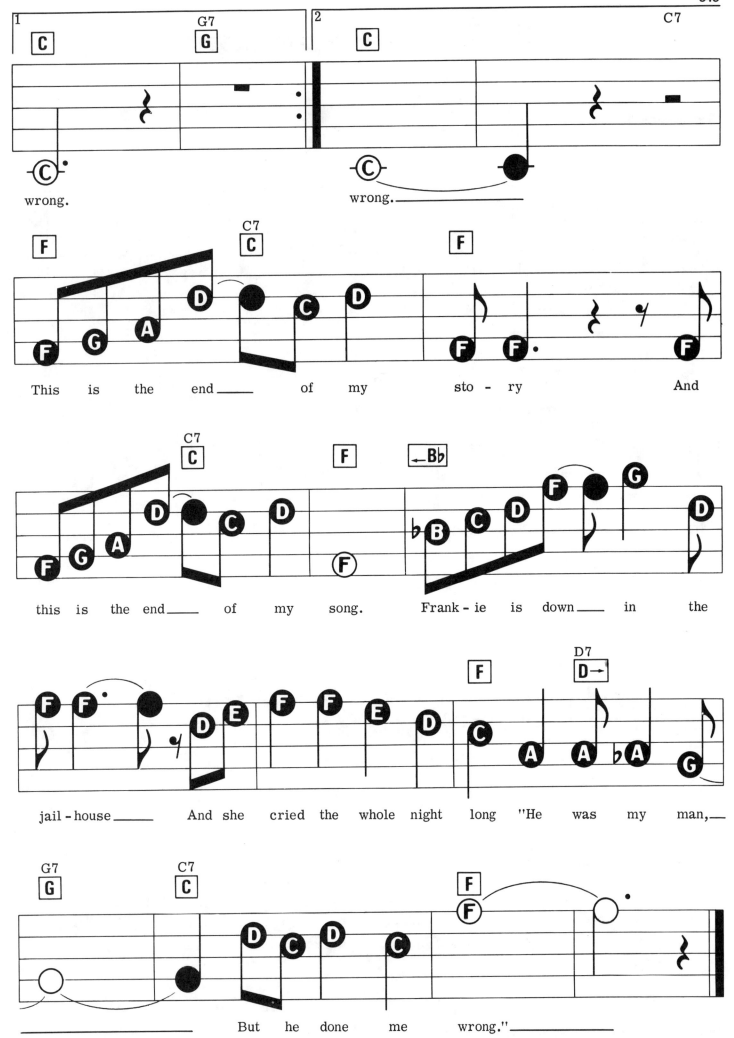

Git Along Home, Cindy

Registration 3

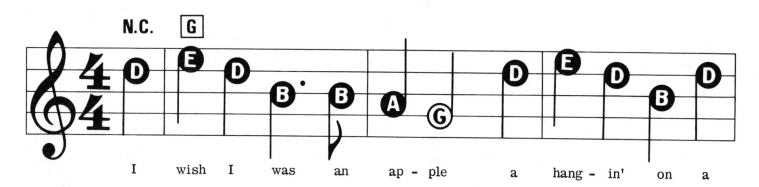

I wish I was an ap - ple a hang - in' on a

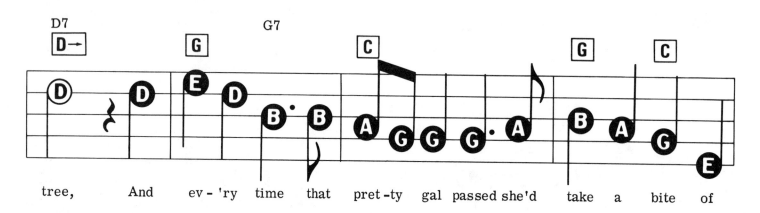

tree, And ev - 'ry time that pret - ty gal passed she'd take a bite of

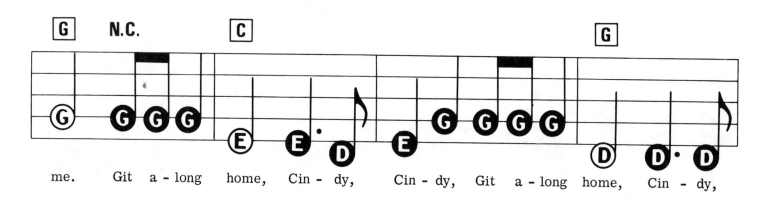

me. Git a - long home, Cin - dy, Cin - dy, Git a - long home, Cin - dy,

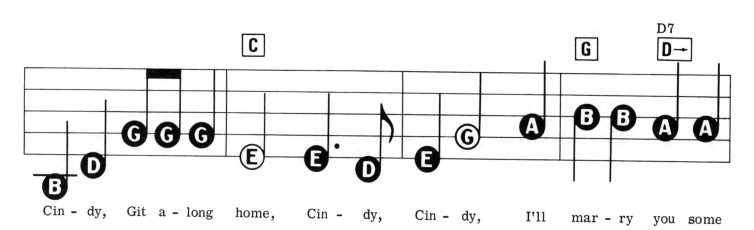

Cin - dy, Git a - long home, Cin - dy, Cin - dy, I'll mar - ry you some

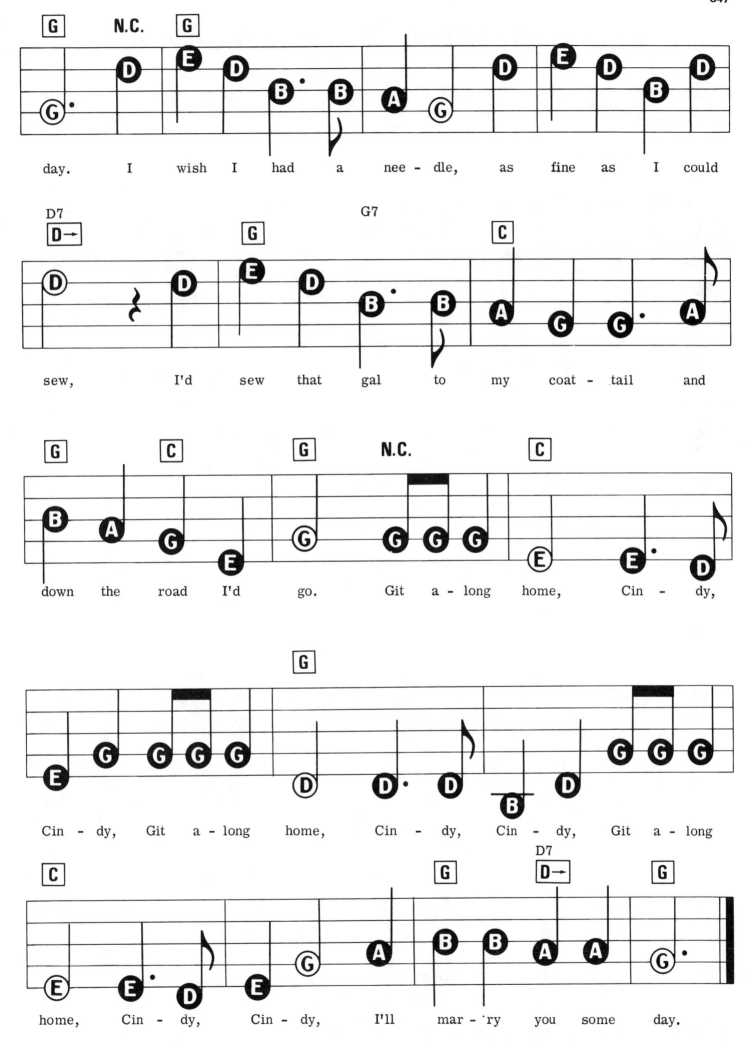

Give My Regards To Broadway

Registration 2

Words and Music by
George M. Cohan

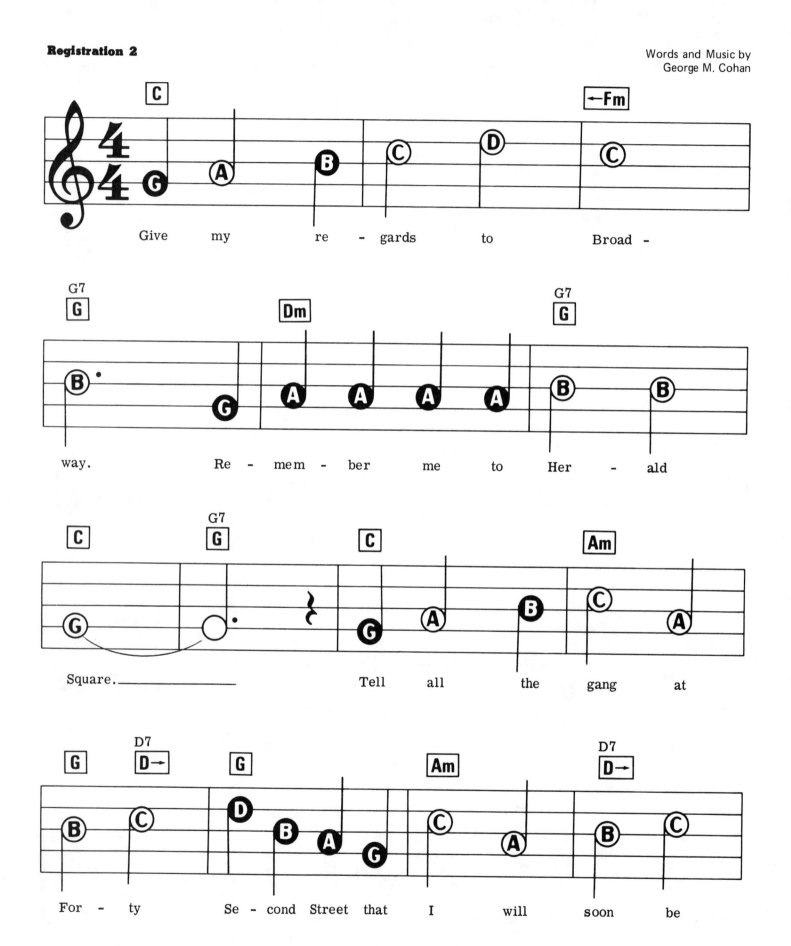

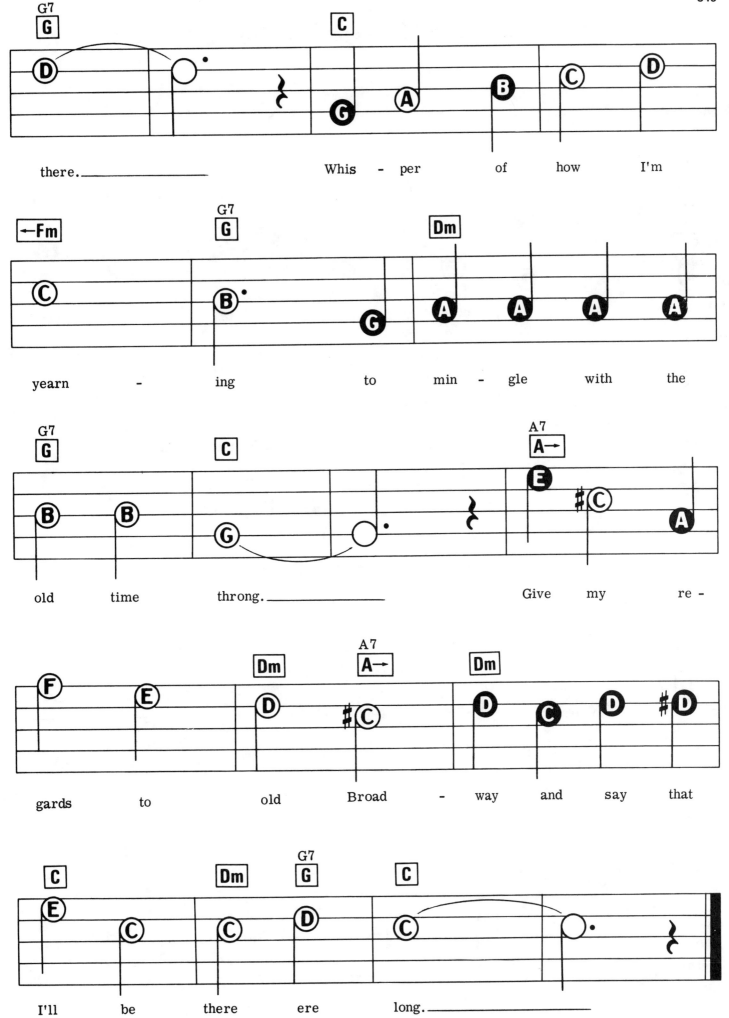

Home Sweet Home

Registration 9

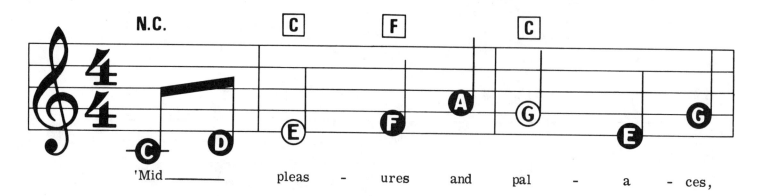

'Mid_____ pleas - ures and pal - a - ces,

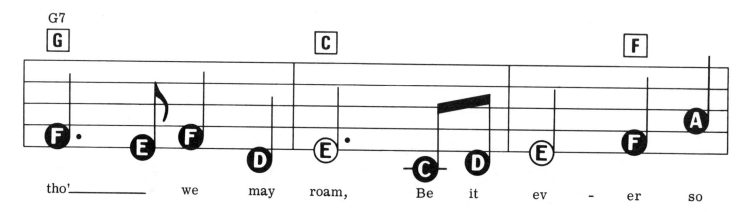

tho'_____ we may roam, Be it ev - er so

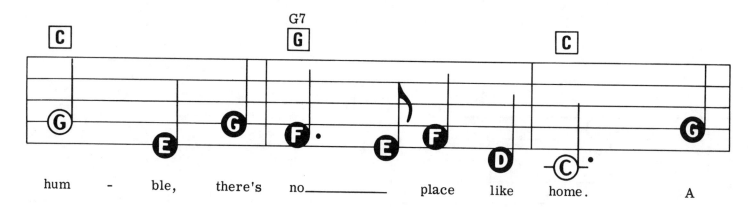

hum - ble, there's no_____ place like home. A

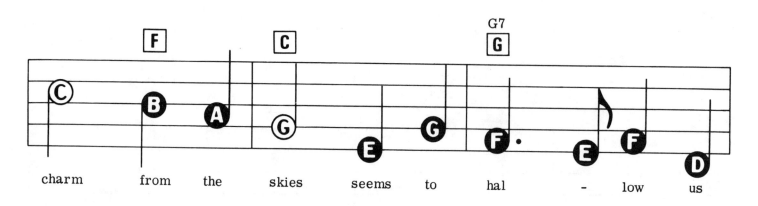

charm from the skies seems to hal - low us

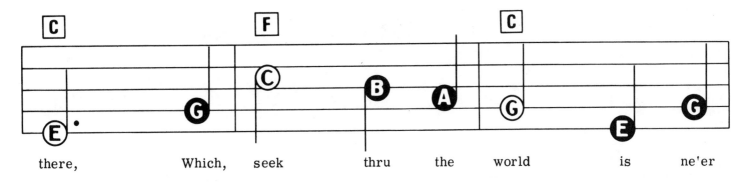

there, Which, seek thru the world is ne'er

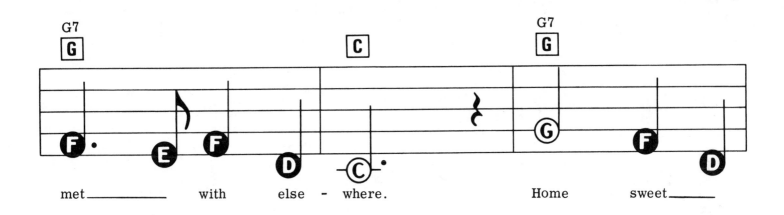

met_____ with else - where. Home sweet_____

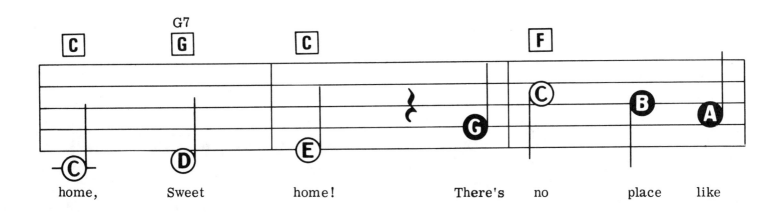

home, Sweet home! There's no place like

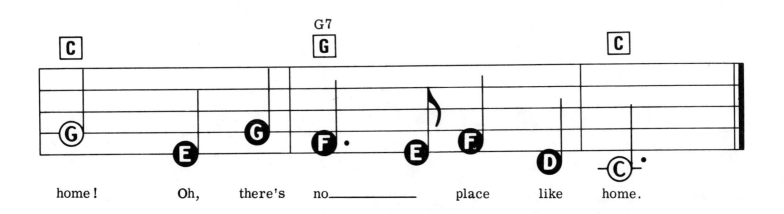

home! Oh, there's no_____ place like home.

Ida

Registration 3

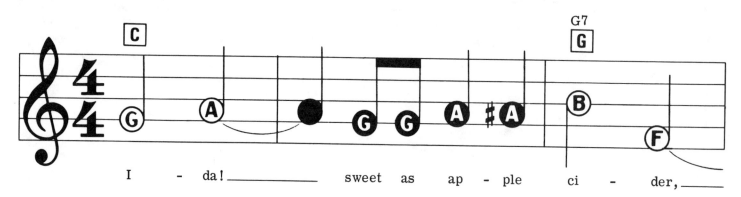

I - da! _____ sweet as ap - ple ci - der, _____

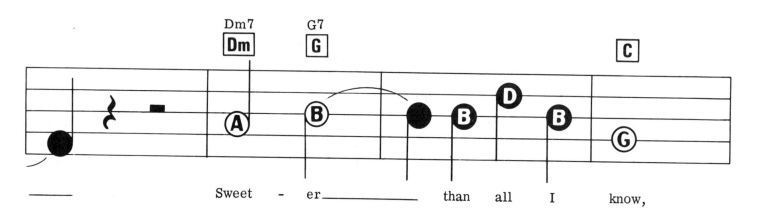

_____ Sweet - er _____ than all I know,

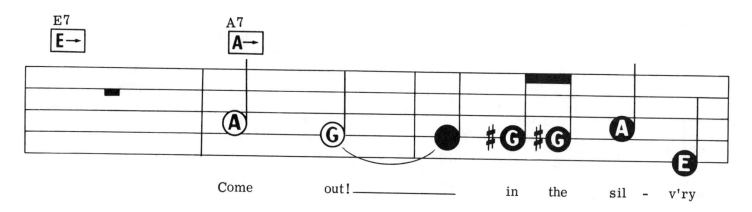

Come out! _____ in the sil - v'ry

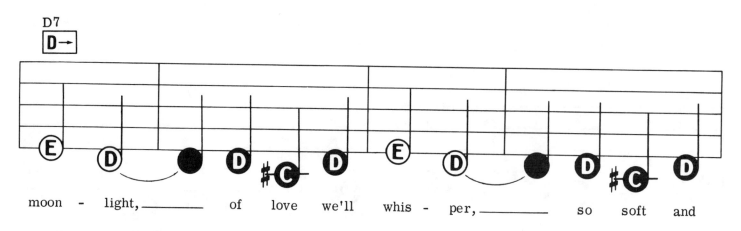

moon - light, _____ of love we'll whis - per, _____ so soft and

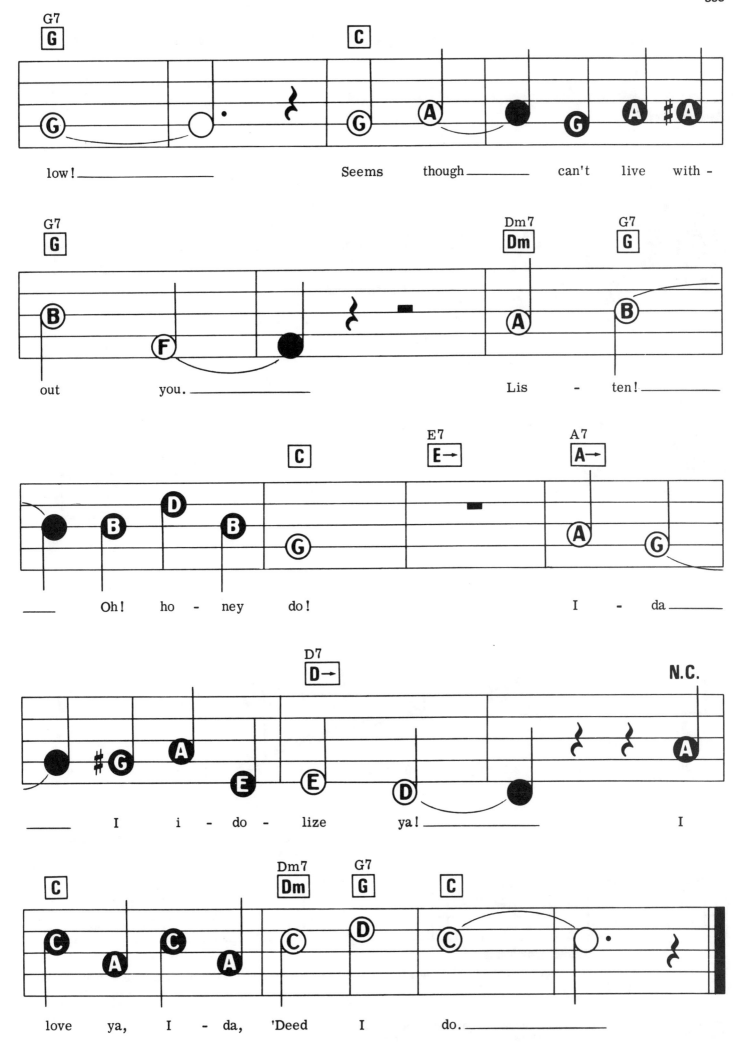

I'll Take You Home Again, Kathleen

Registration 1

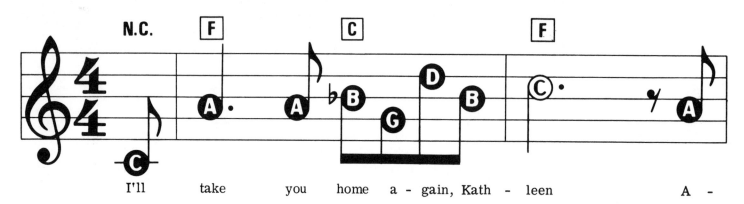

I'll take you home a - gain, Kath - leen A -

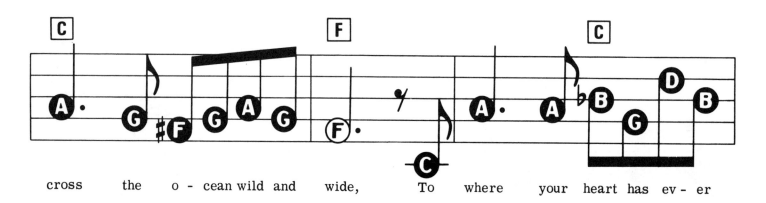

cross the o - cean wild and wide, To where your heart has ev - er

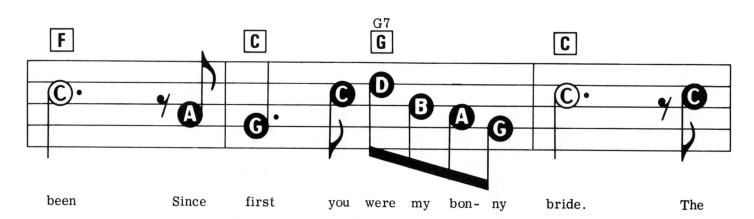

been Since first you were my bon - ny bride. The

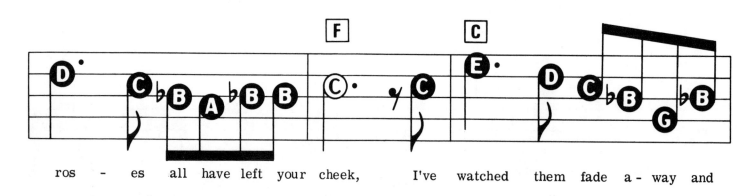

ros - es all have left your cheek, I've watched them fade a - way and

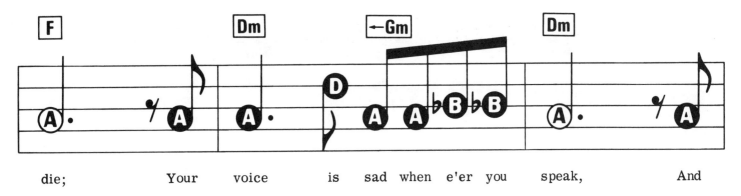

die;   Your   voice   is   sad when e'er you   speak,   And

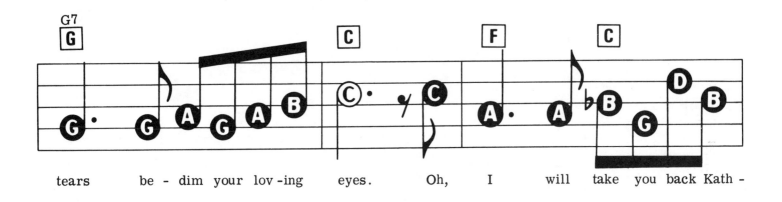

tears   be - dim your lov -ing   eyes.   Oh,   I   will   take   you back Kath -

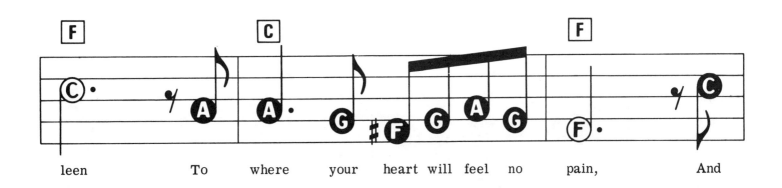

leen   To   where   your   heart will feel   no   pain,   And

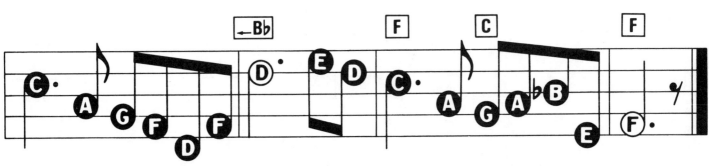

when   the fields are fresh and green,   I'll___   take   you   to your home a - gain.

In My Merry Oldsmobile

Registration 4

Words and Music by Vincent P. Bryan and
Gus Edwards

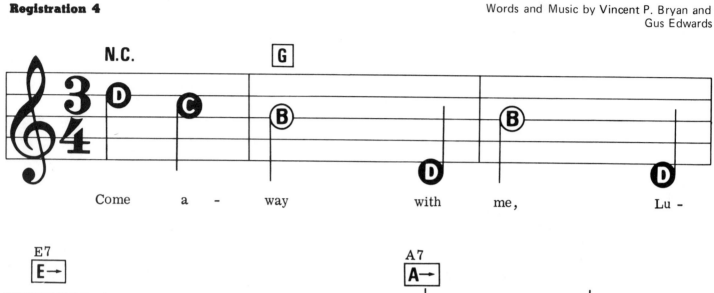

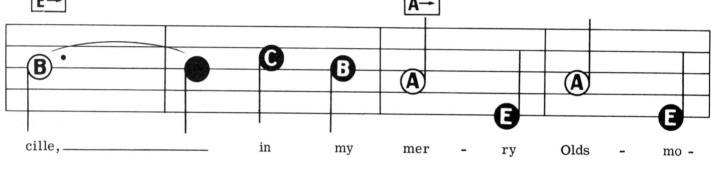

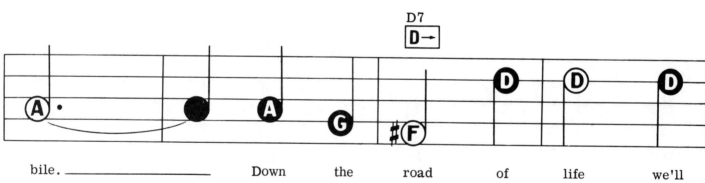

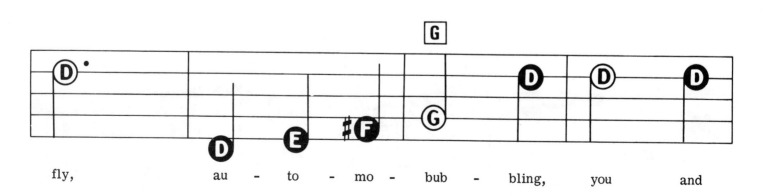

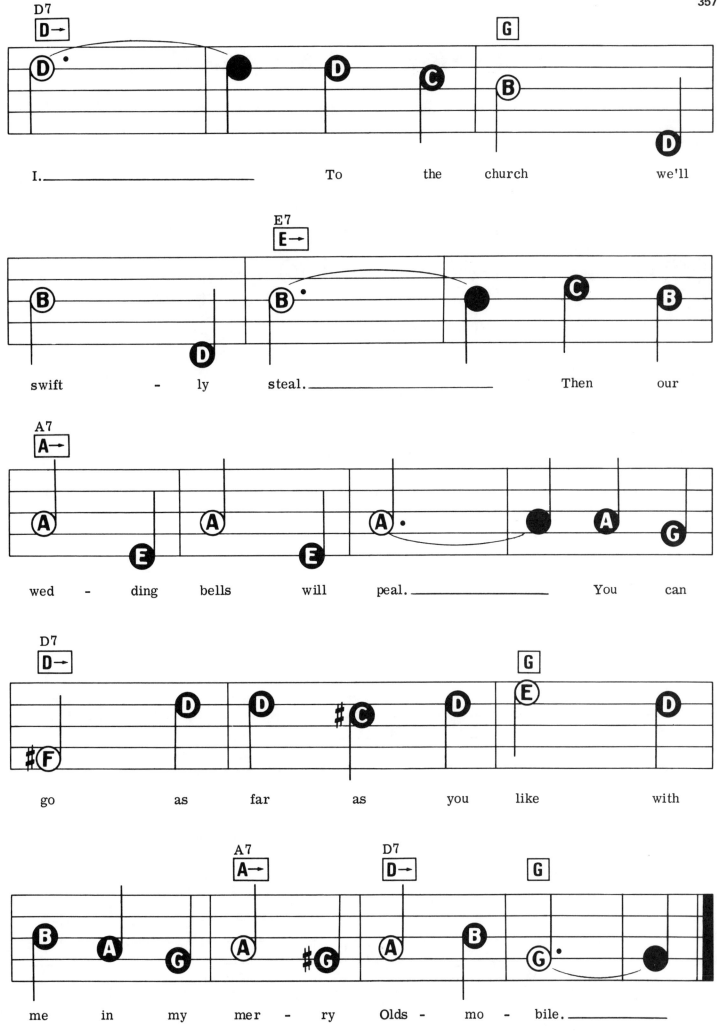

In The Good Old Summertime

Registration 5

Words and Music by Ren Shields and
George Evans

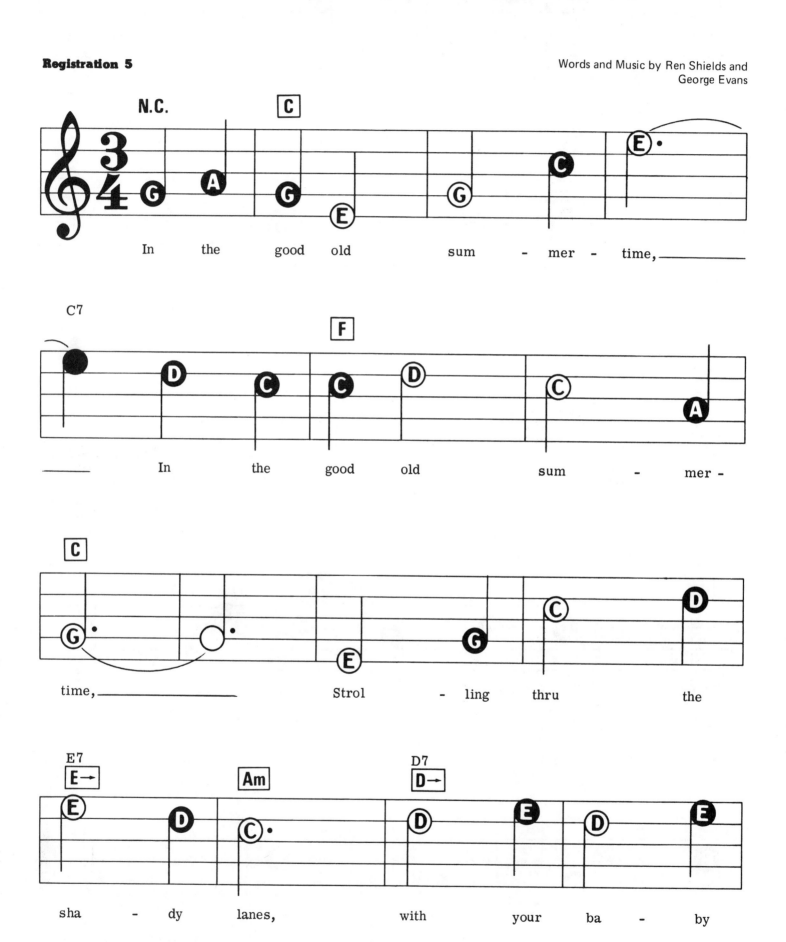

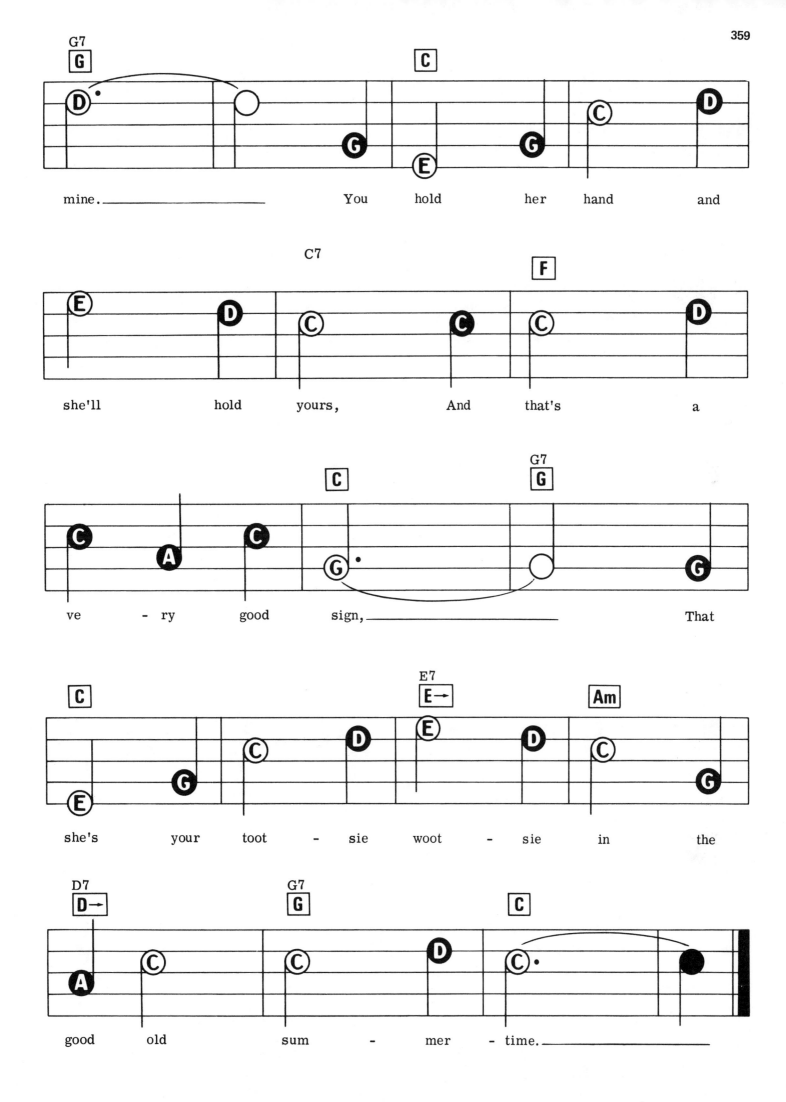

In The Shade Of The Old Apple Tree

Registration 3

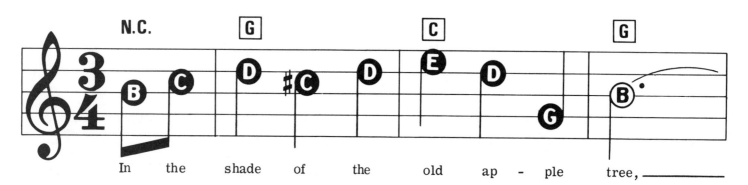

In the shade of the old ap - ple tree, _____

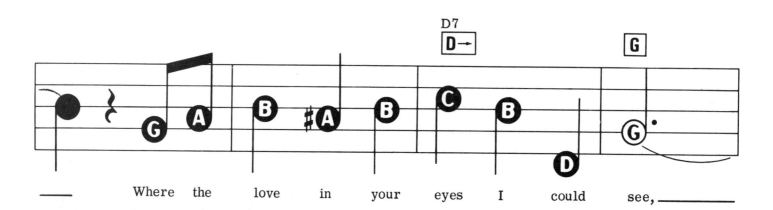

_____ Where the love in your eyes I could see, _____

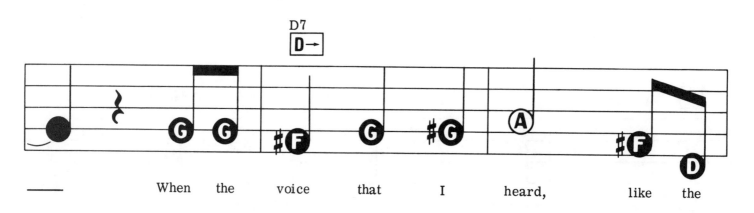

_____ When the voice that I heard, like the

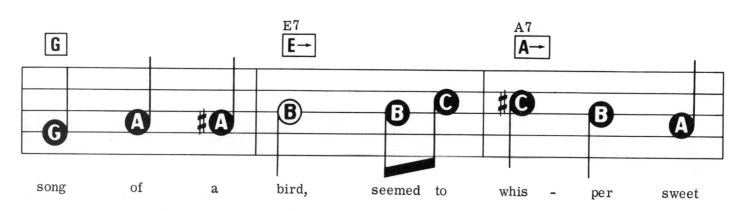

song of a bird, seemed to whis - per sweet

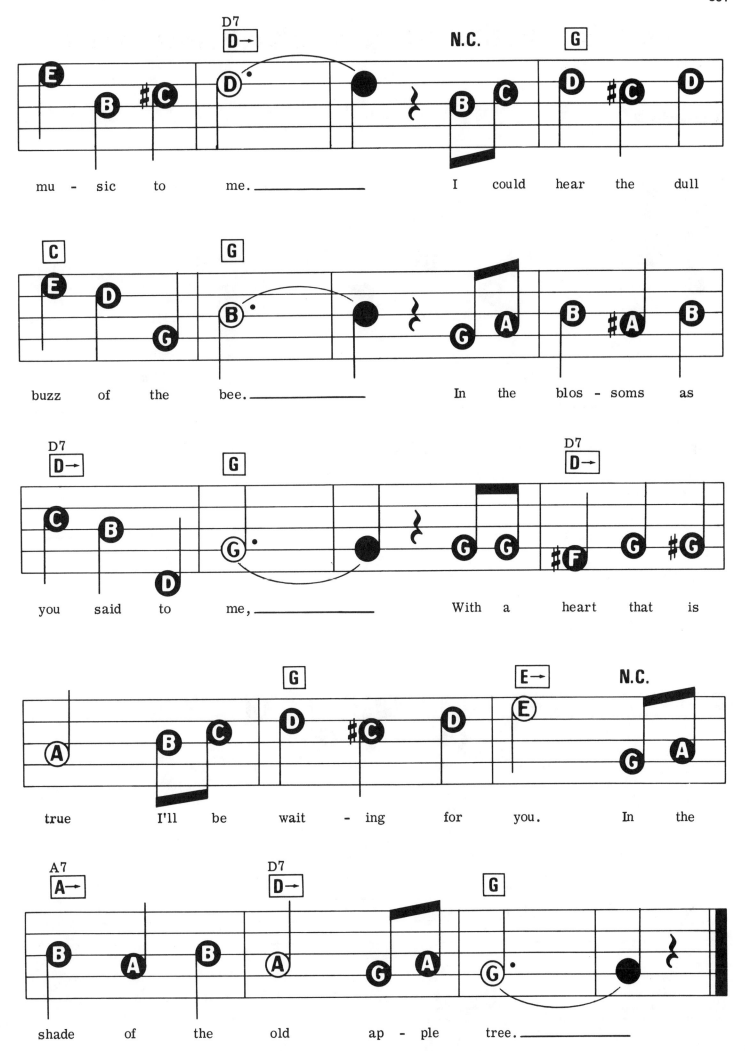

I've Been Working On The Railroad

Registration 5

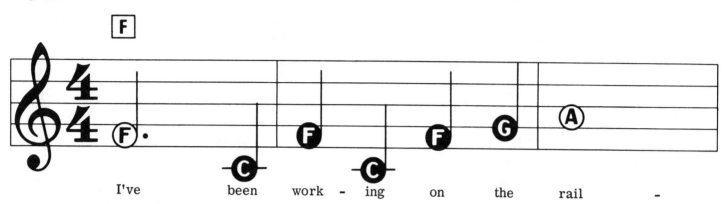

I've been work - ing on the rail -

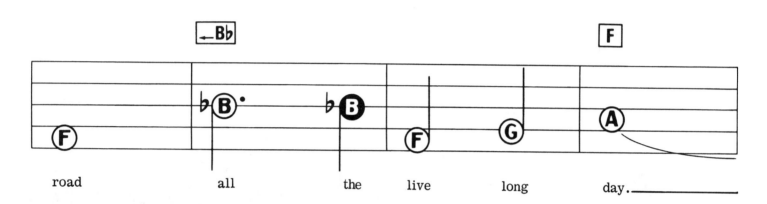

road all the live long day.

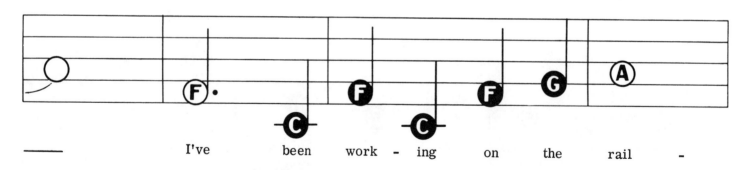

I've been work - ing on the rail -

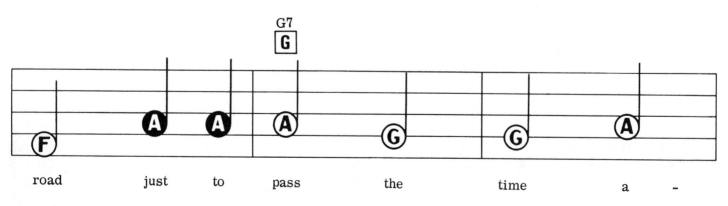

road just to pass the time a -

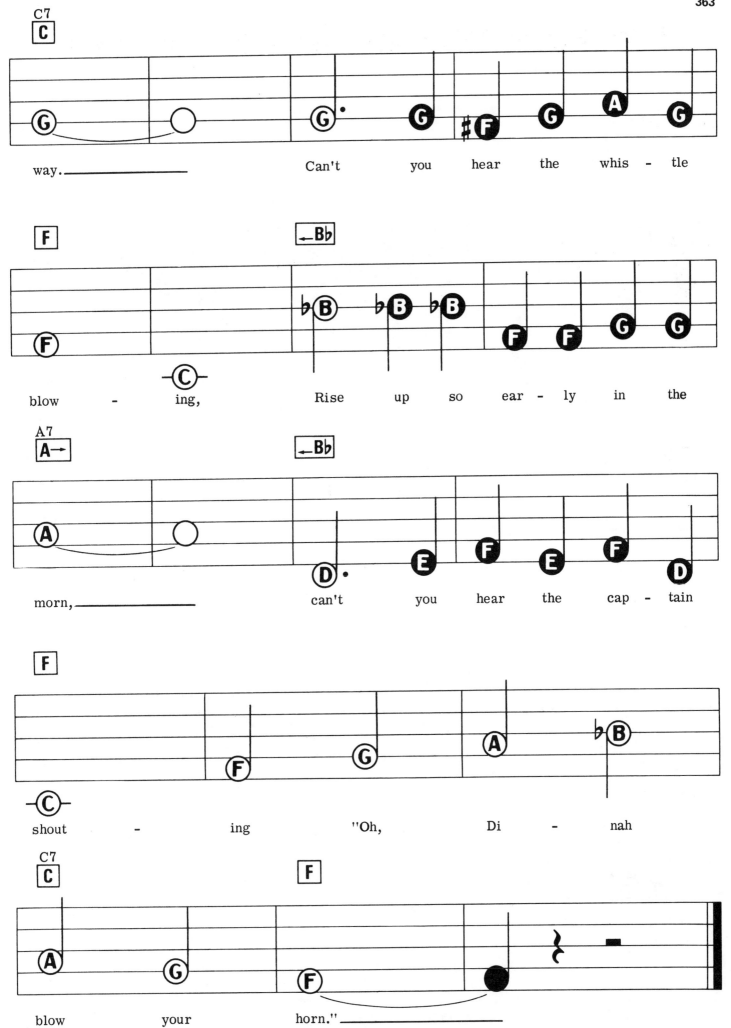

Jeannie With The Light Brown Hair

Registration 9

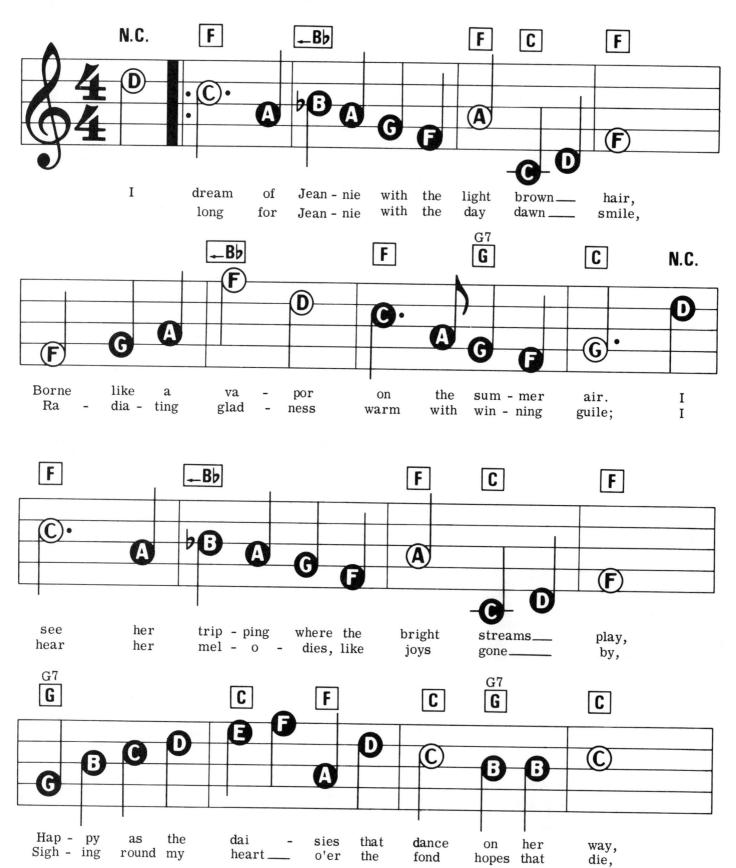

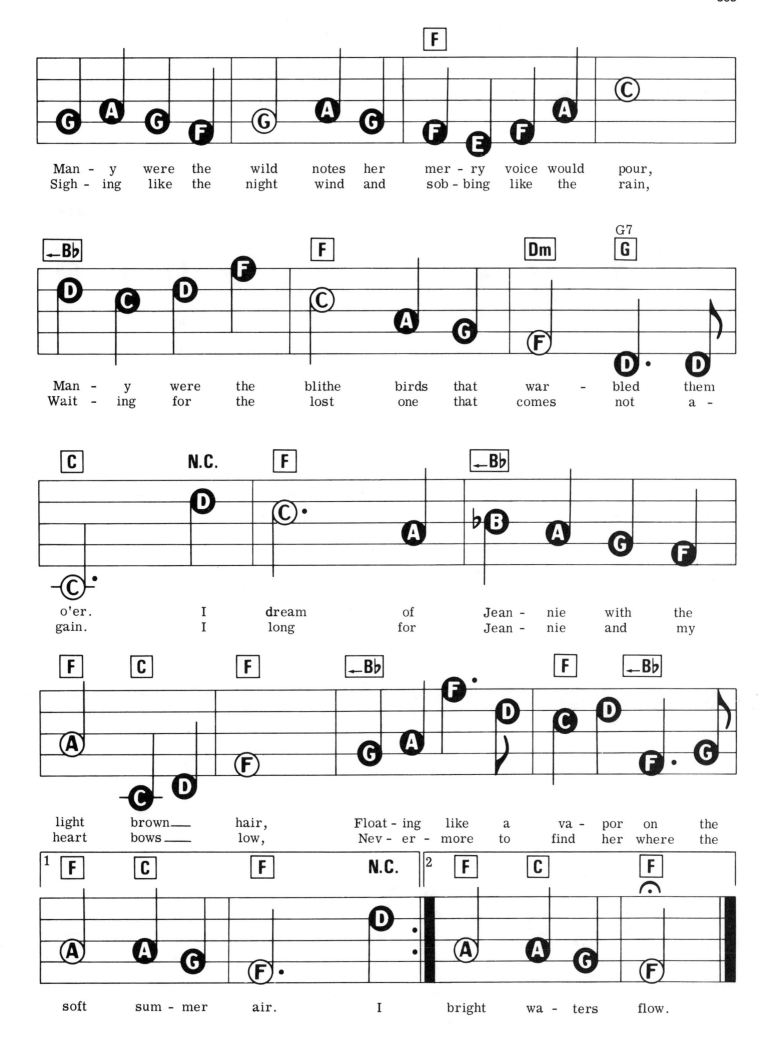

Little Brown Jug

Registration 2

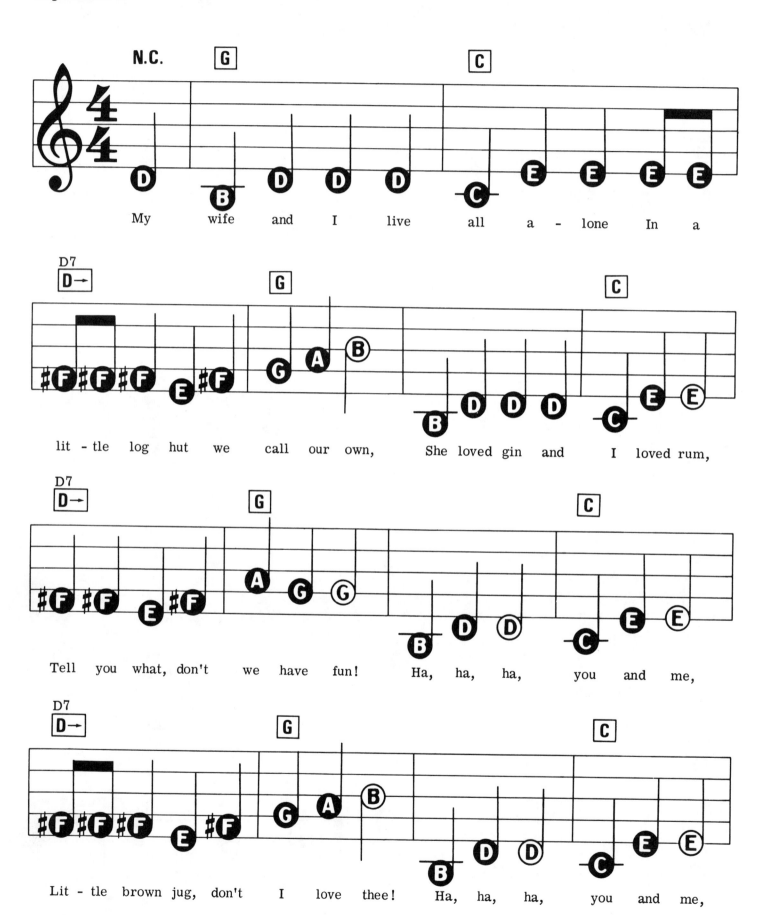

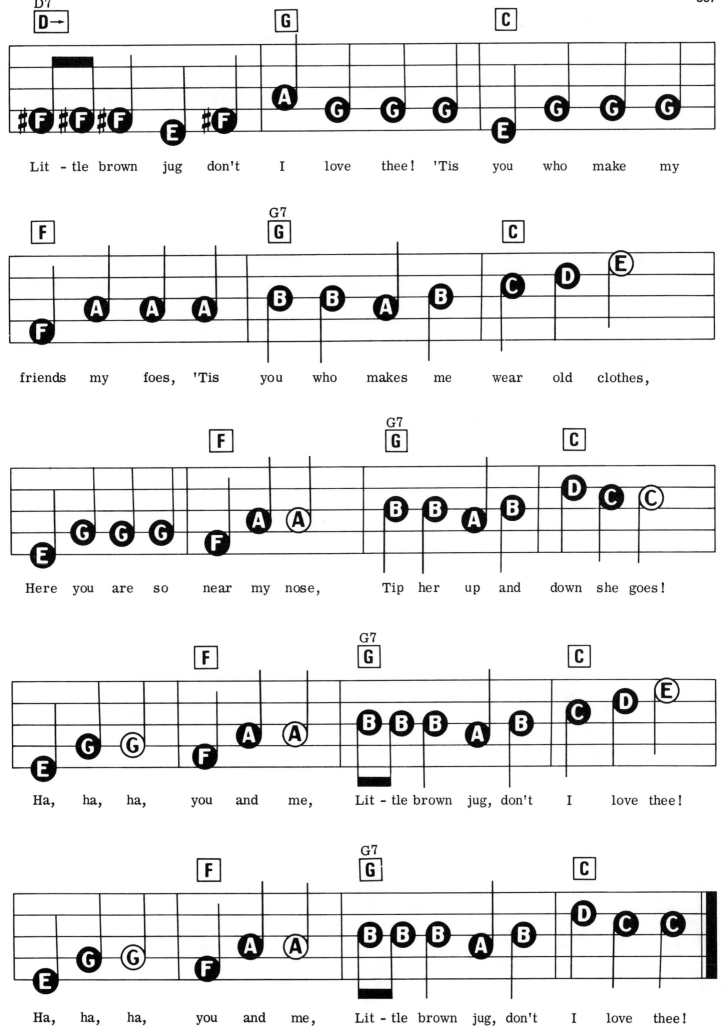

Listen To The Mocking Bird

Registration 2

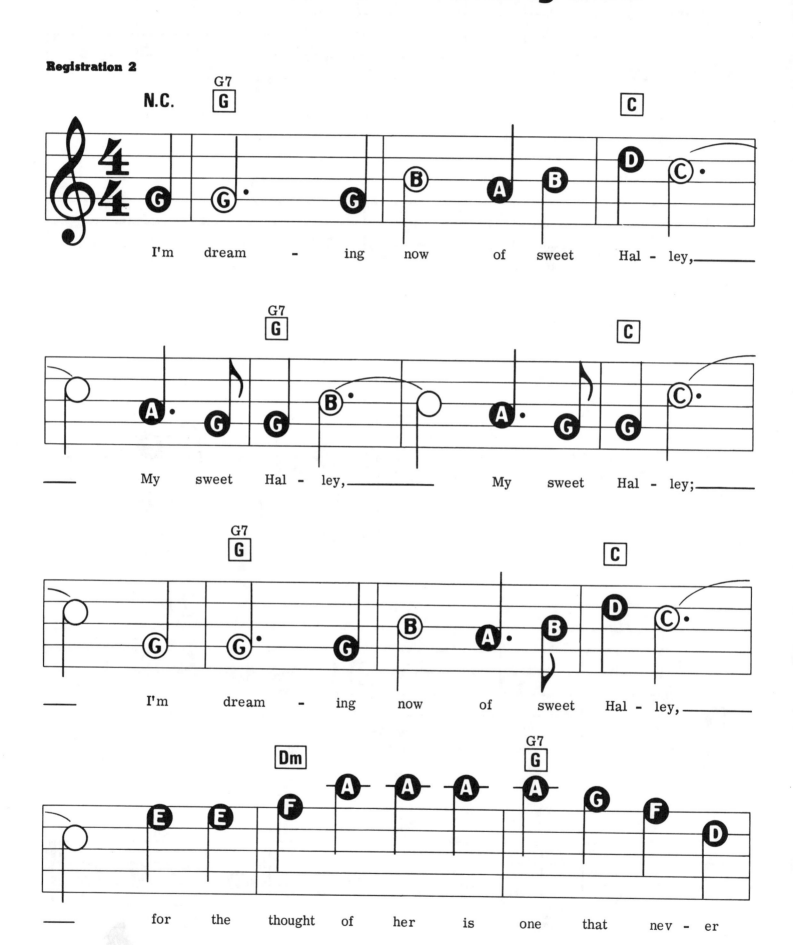

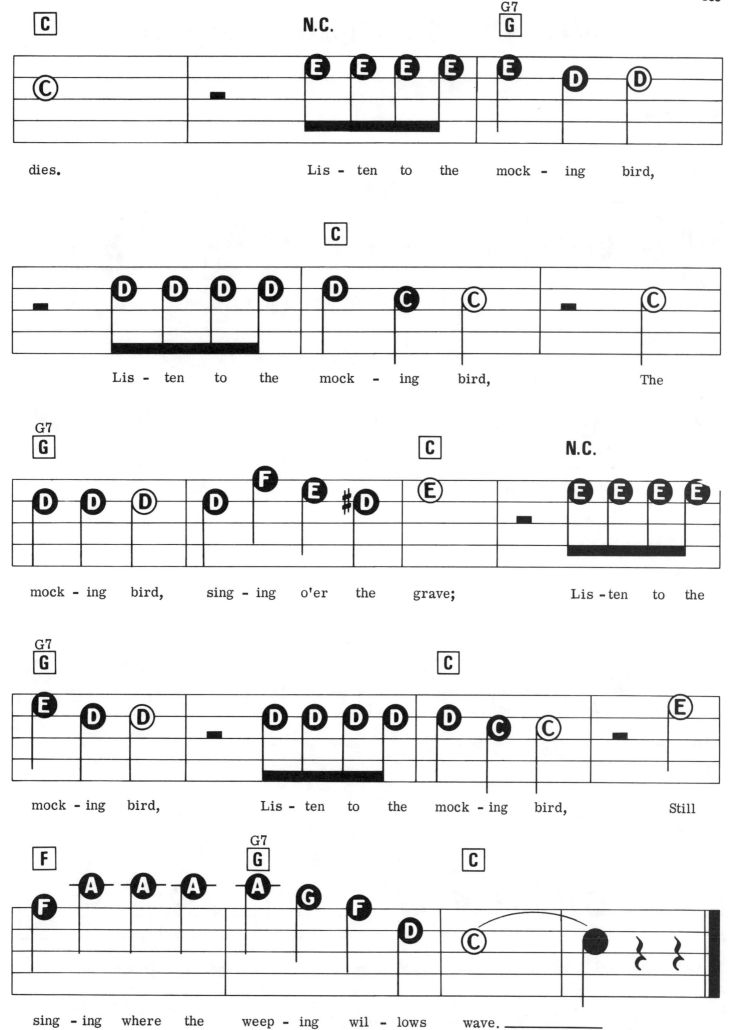

Man On The Flying Trapeze

Registration 5

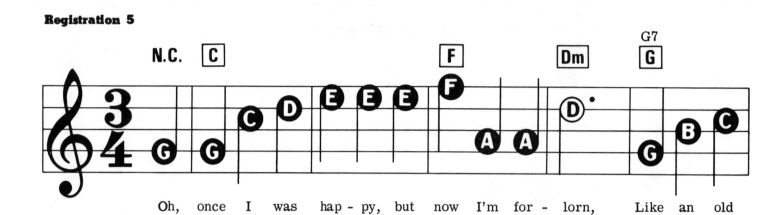

Oh, once I was hap-py, but now I'm for-lorn, Like an old

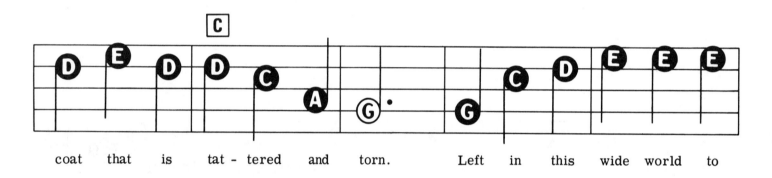

coat that is tat-tered and torn. Left in this wide world to

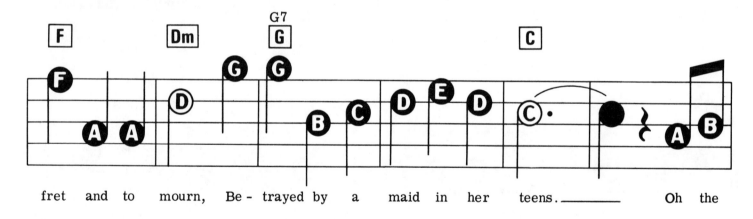

fret and to mourn, Be-trayed by a maid in her teens._____ Oh the

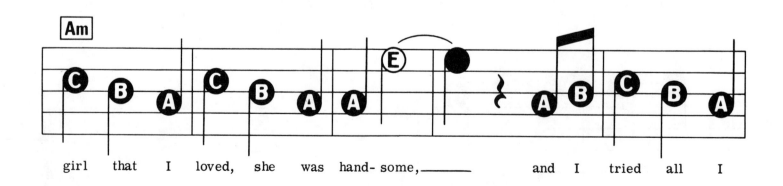

girl that I loved, she was hand-some,_____ and I tried all I

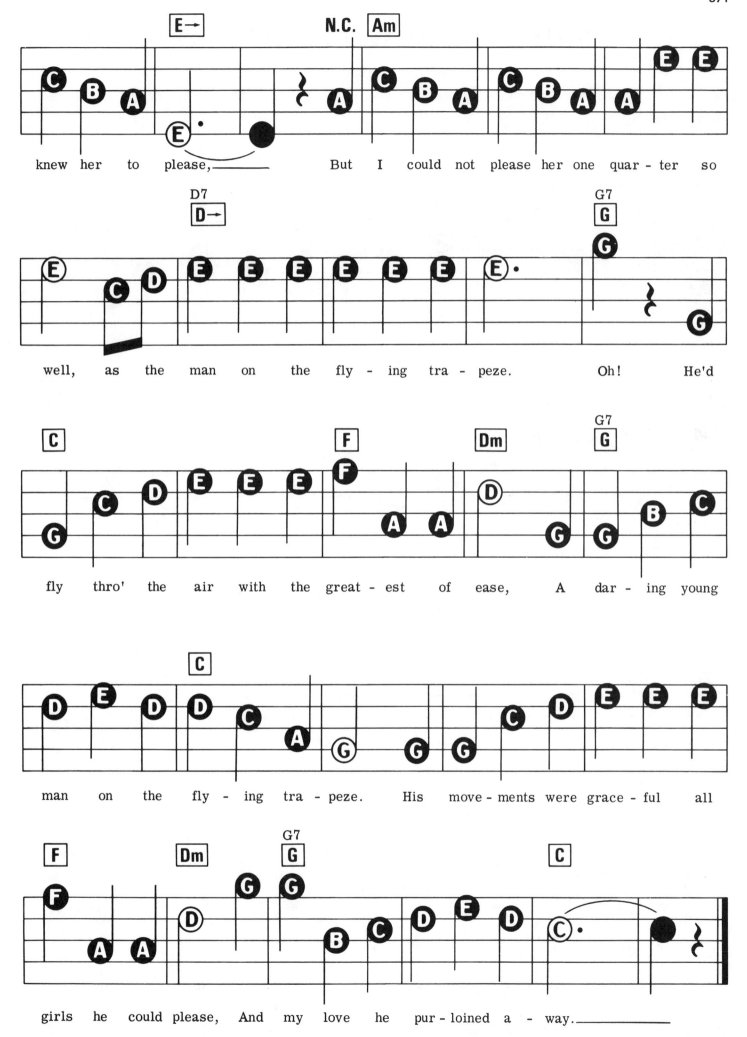

Mary's A Grand Old Name

Registration 5

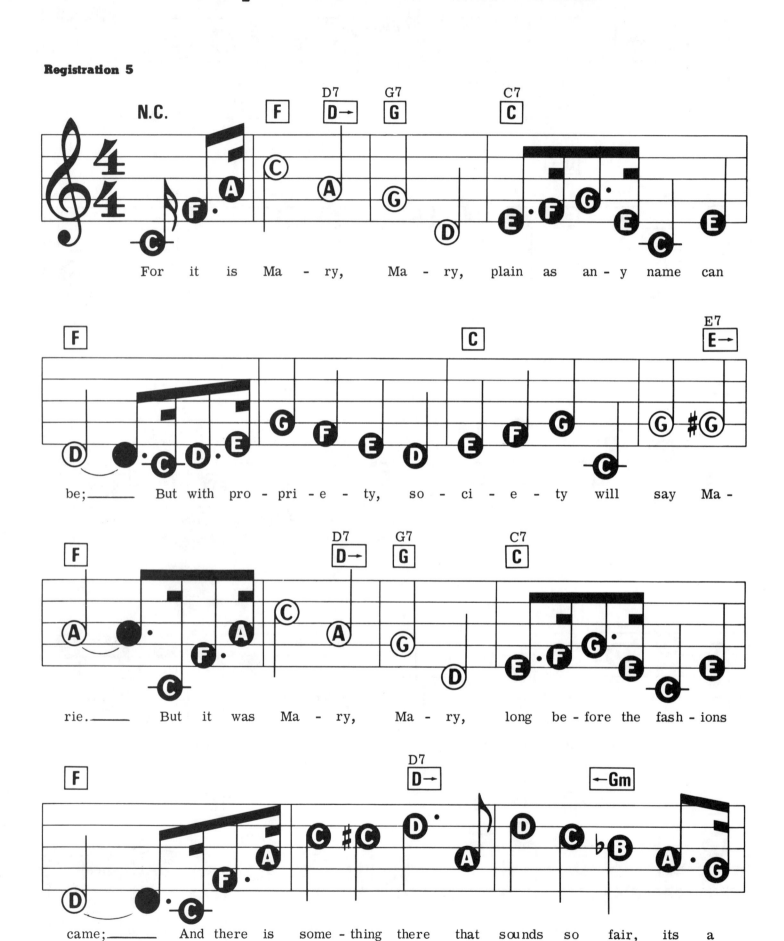

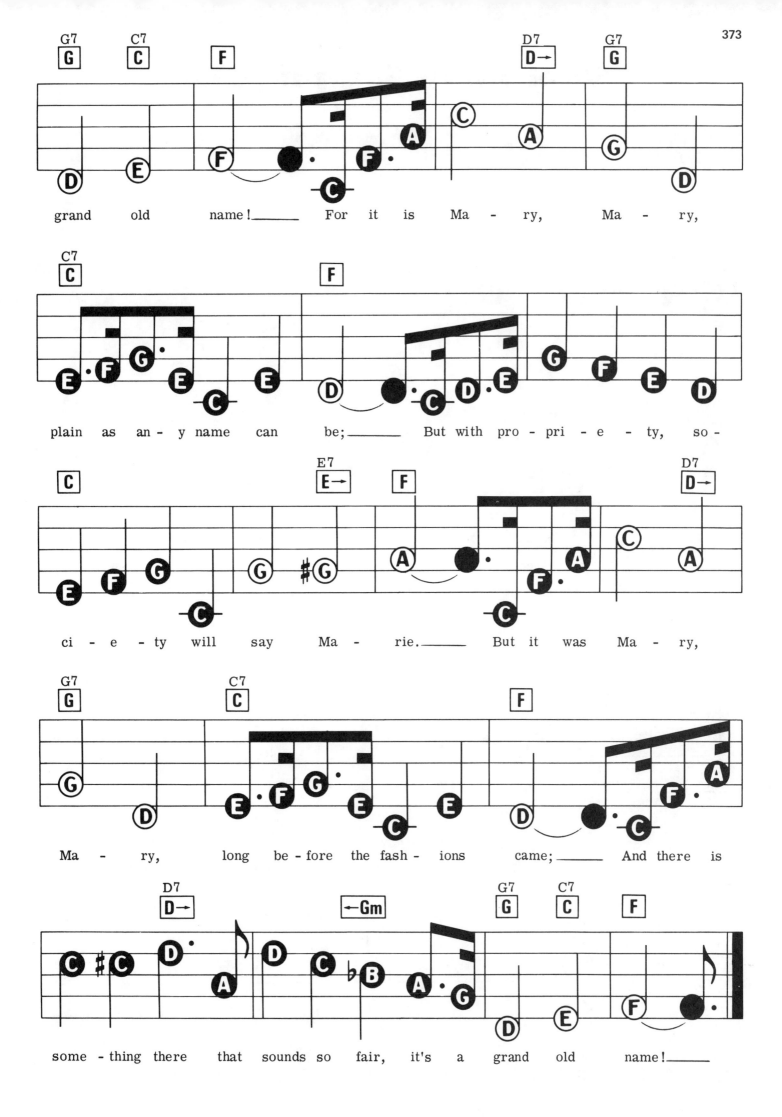

Meet Me In St. Louis, Louis

Registration 9

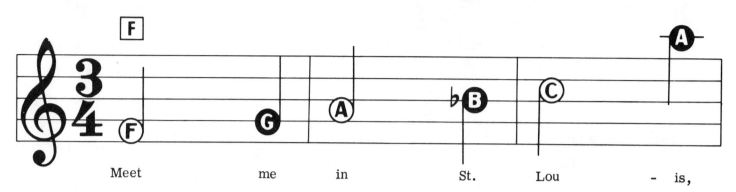

Meet   me   in   St.   Lou - is,

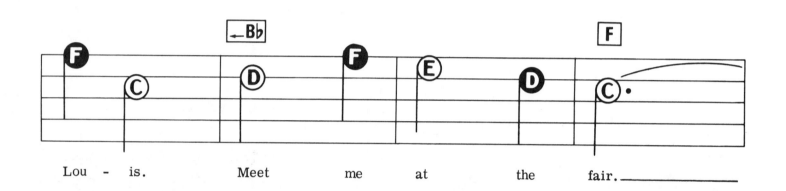

Lou - is.   Meet   me   at   the   fair._____

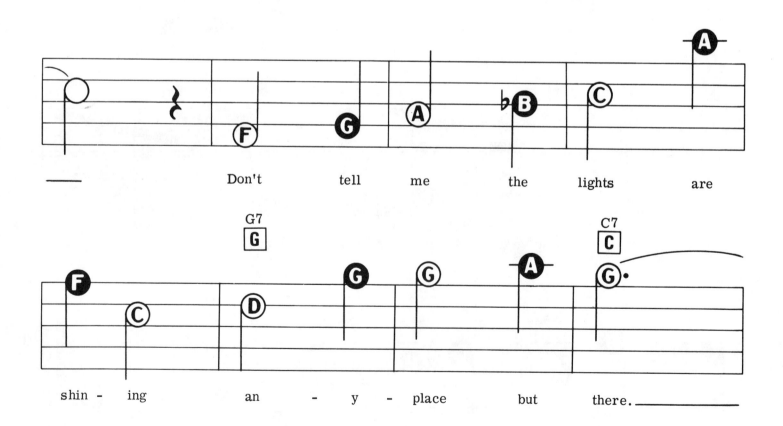

_____   Don't   tell   me   the   lights   are

shin - ing   an - y - place   but   there._____

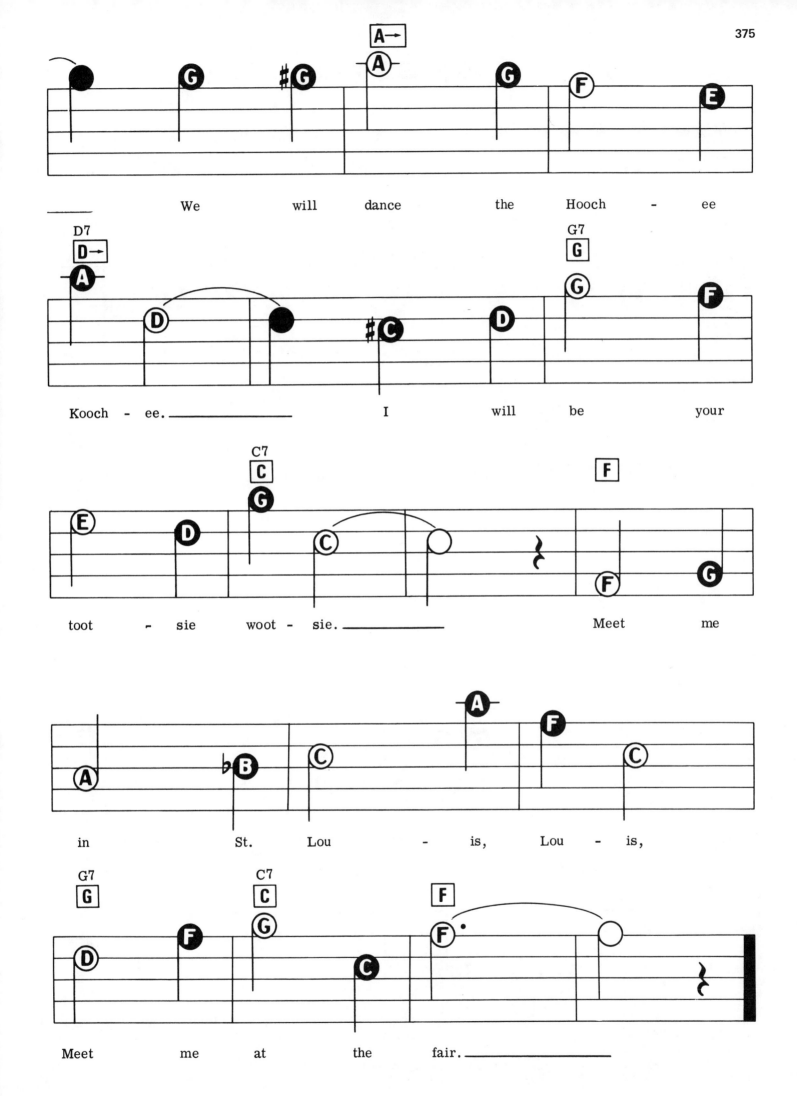

We will dance the Hooch - ee

Kooch - ee. _____ I will be your

toot - sie woot - sie. _____ Meet me

in St. Lou - is, Lou - is,

Meet me at the fair. _____

My Bonnie

Registration 3

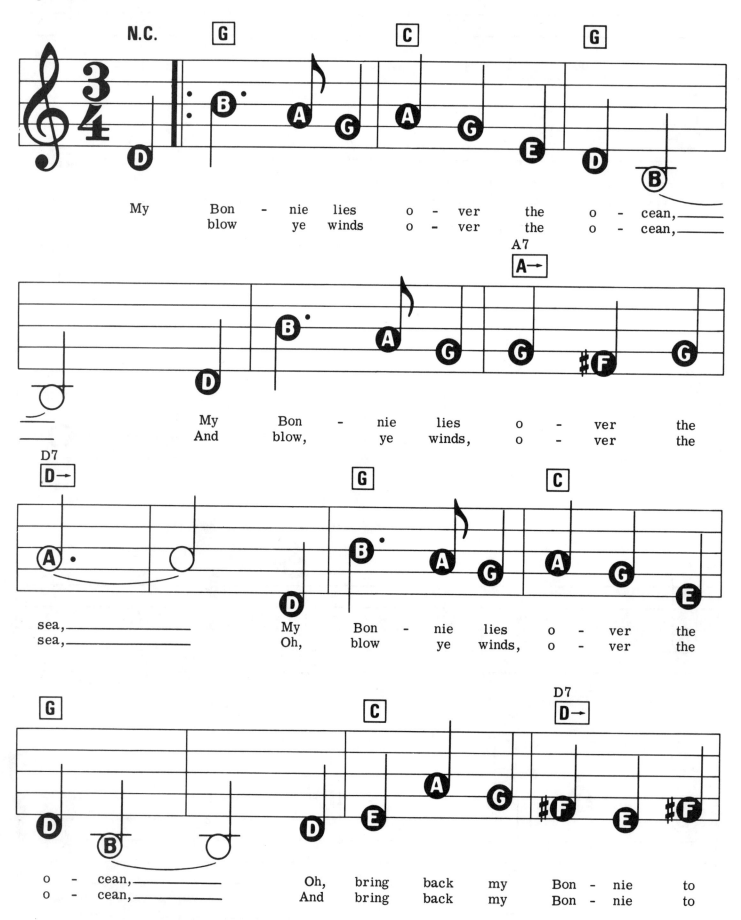

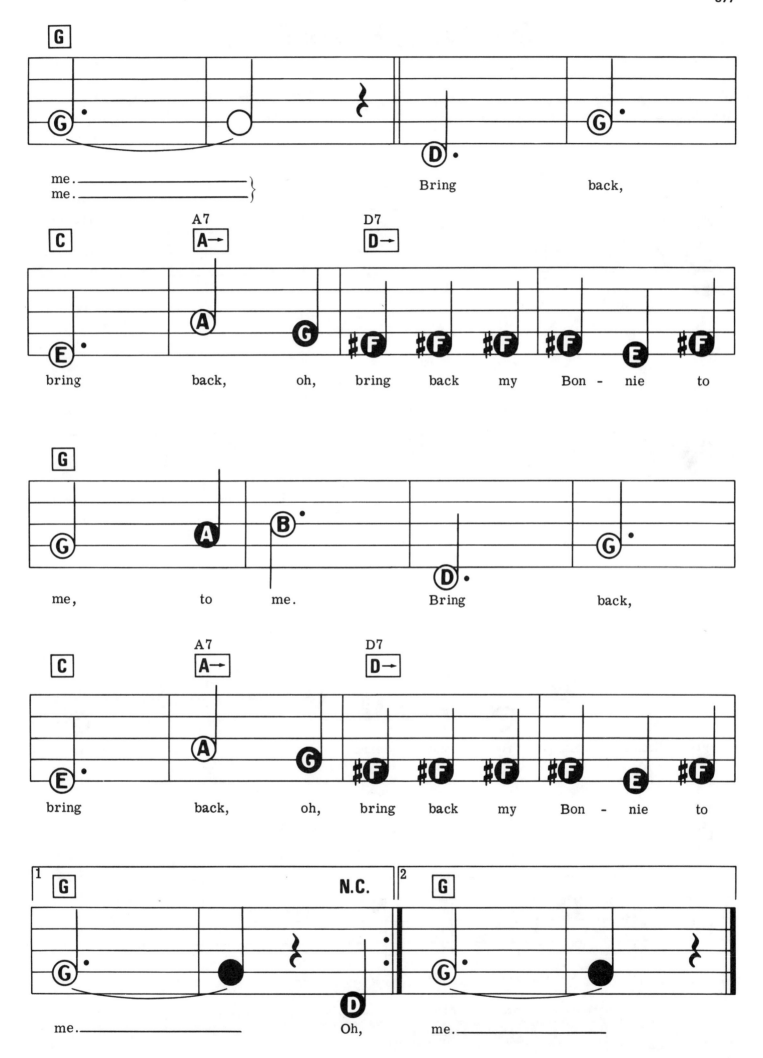

My Wild Irish Rose

Registration 2

Words and Music by
Chauncey Olcott

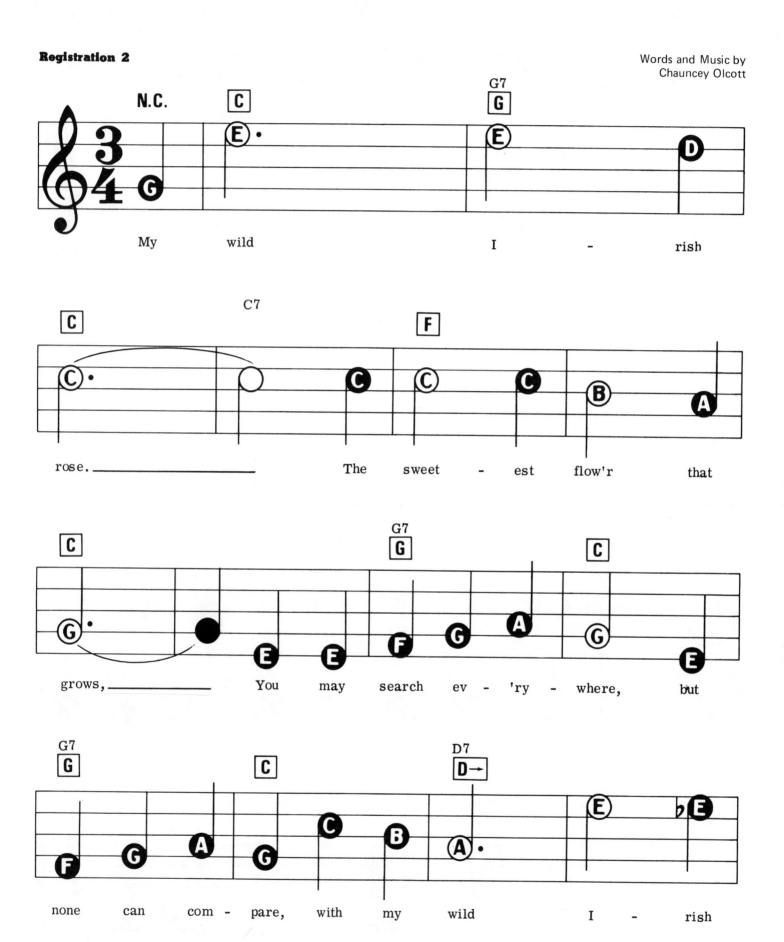

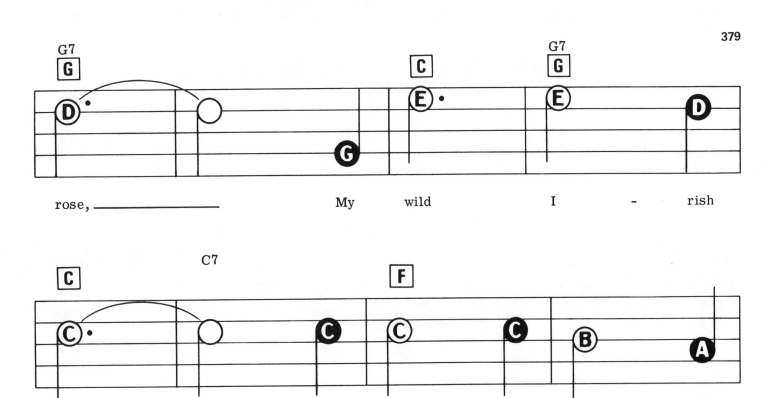

rose, _____ My wild I - rish

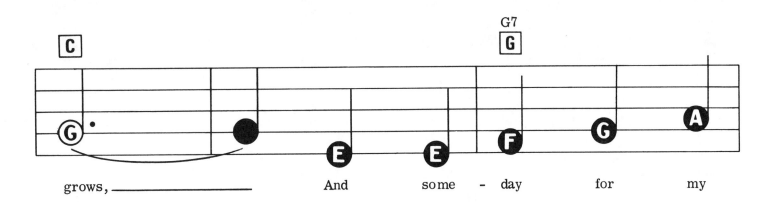

rose _____ The dear - est flow'r that

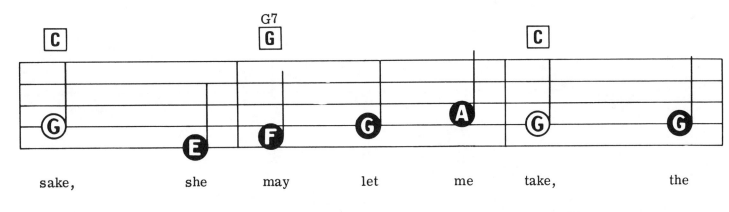

grows, _____ And some - day for my

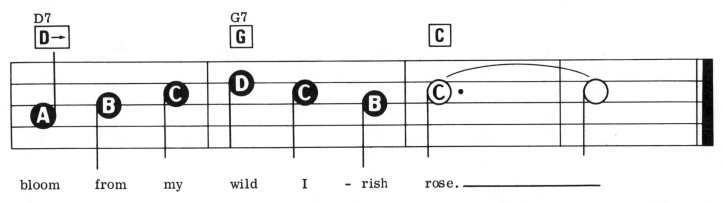

sake, she may let me take, the

bloom from my wild I - rish rose. _____

Oh My Darling Clementine

Registration 1

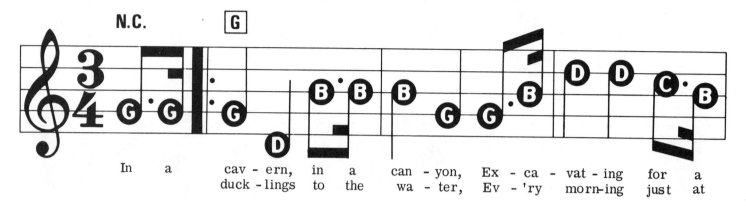

In a   cav - ern, in a   can - yon, Ex - ca - vat - ing for a
duck - lings to the wa - ter, Ev - 'ry morn - ing just at

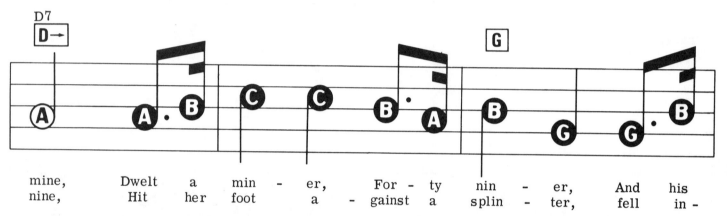

mine,   Dwelt a min - er,   For - ty nin - er, And his
nine,   Hit her foot a - gainst a splin - ter, And fell in -

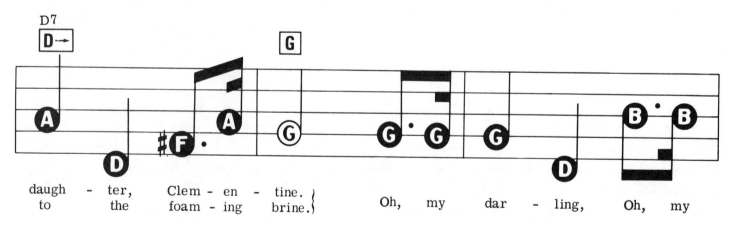

daugh - ter, Clem - en - tine. } Oh, my dar - ling, Oh, my
to the foam - ing brine. }

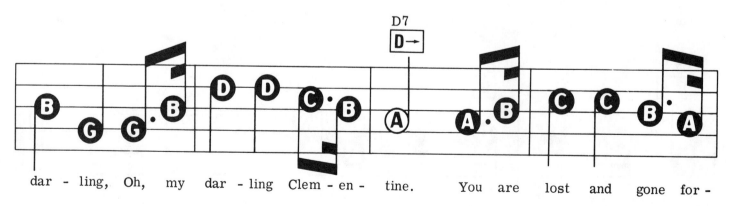

dar - ling, Oh, my dar - ling Clem - en - tine. You are lost and gone for -

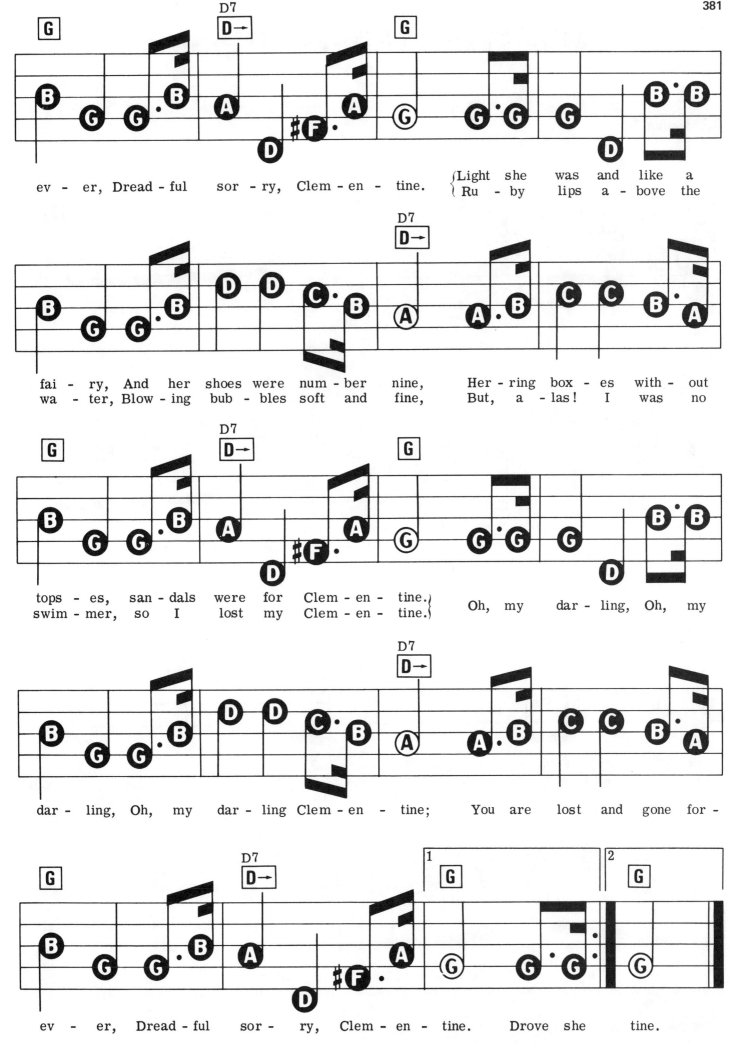

Oh, Them Golden Slippers

Registration 7

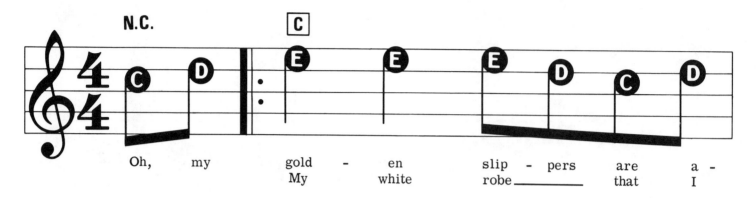

Oh,   my   gold - en   slip - pers   are   a -
My   white   robe _____ are   that   I

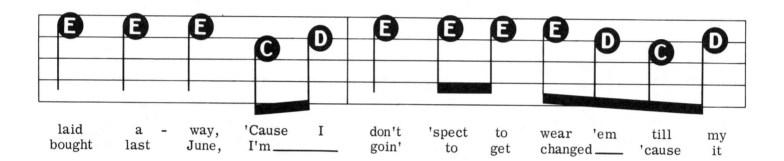

laid   a - way,   'Cause   I   don't   'spect   to   wear   'em   till   my
bought   last   June,   I'm _____ goin'   'spect   to   get   changed _____ 'cause   it

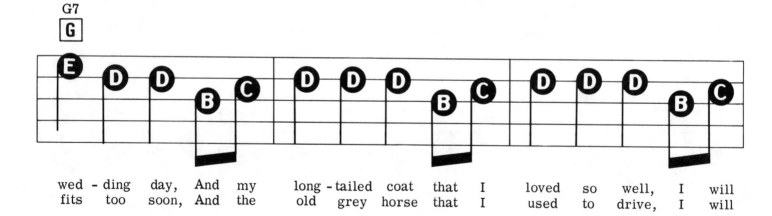

wed - ding   day,   And   my   long - tailed   coat   that   I   loved   so   well,   I   will
fits   too   soon,   And   the   old   grey   horse   that   I   used   to   drive,   I   will

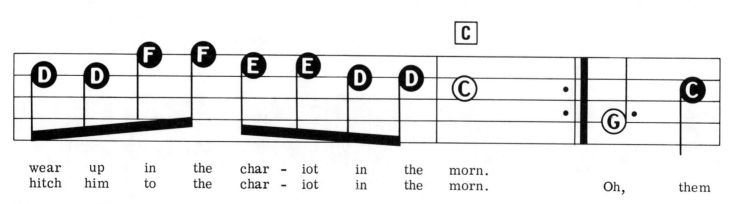

wear   up   in   the   char - iot   in   the   morn.
hitch   him   to   the   char - iot   in   the   morn.   Oh,   them

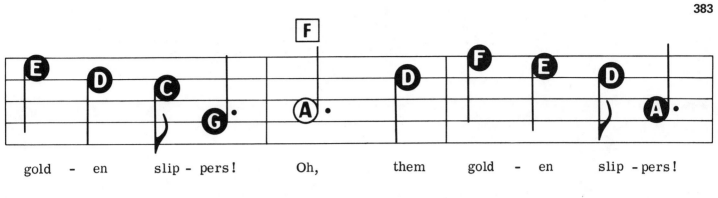

gold - en slip - pers! Oh, them gold - en slip - pers!

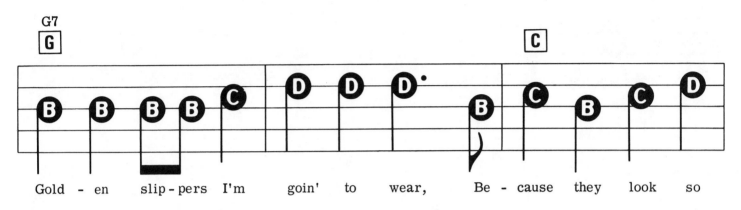

Gold - en slip - pers I'm goin' to wear, Be - cause they look so

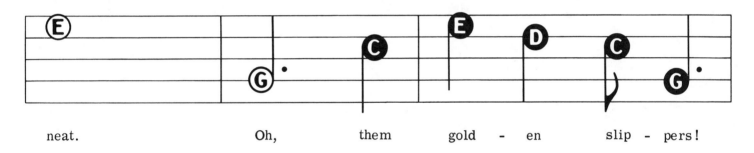

neat. Oh, them gold - en slip - pers!

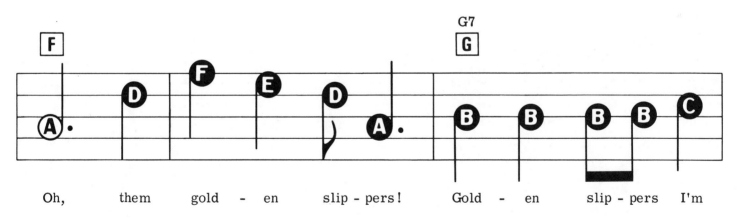

Oh, them gold - en slip - pers! Gold - en slip - pers I'm

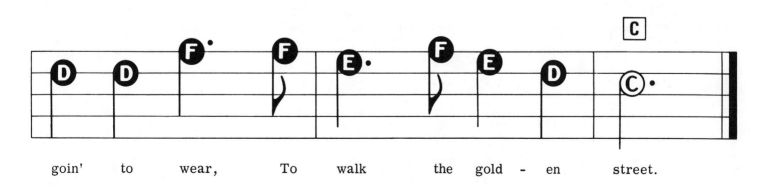

goin' to wear, To walk the gold - en street.

Oh! Susanna

Registration 3

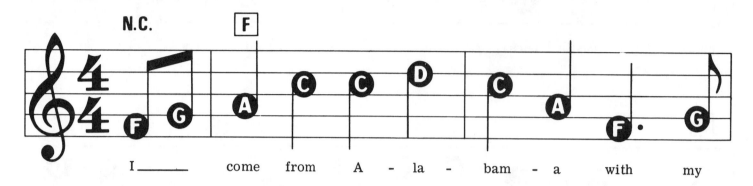

I____ come from A - la - bam - a with my

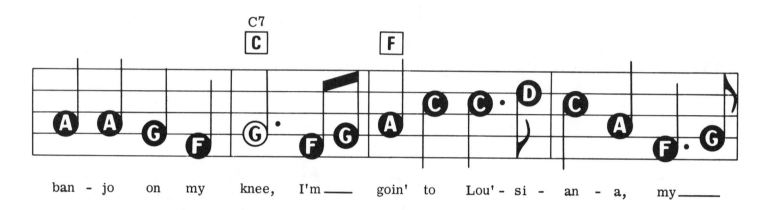

ban - jo on my knee, I'm____ goin' to Lou' - si - an - a, my____

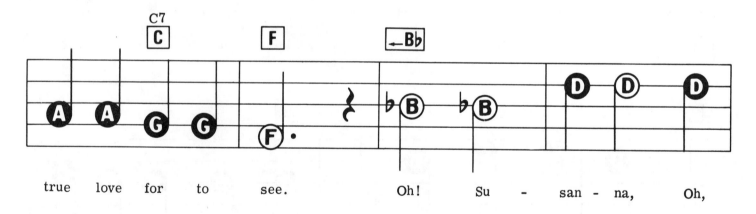

true love for to see. Oh! Su - san - na, Oh,

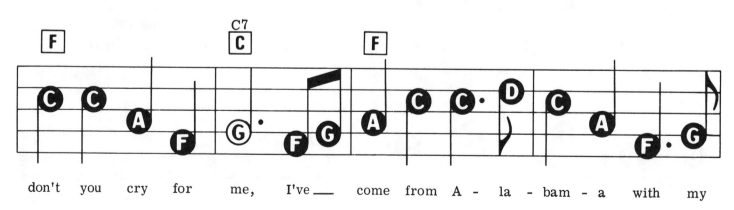

don't you cry for me, I've____ come from A - la - bam - a with my

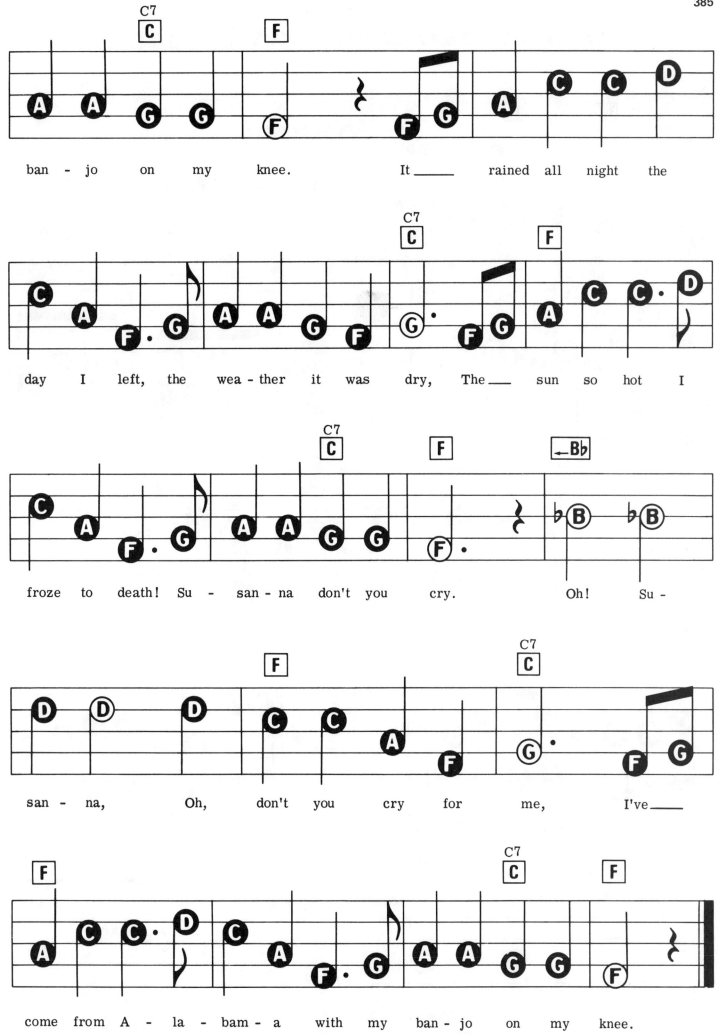

On The Banks Of The Wabash

Registration 5

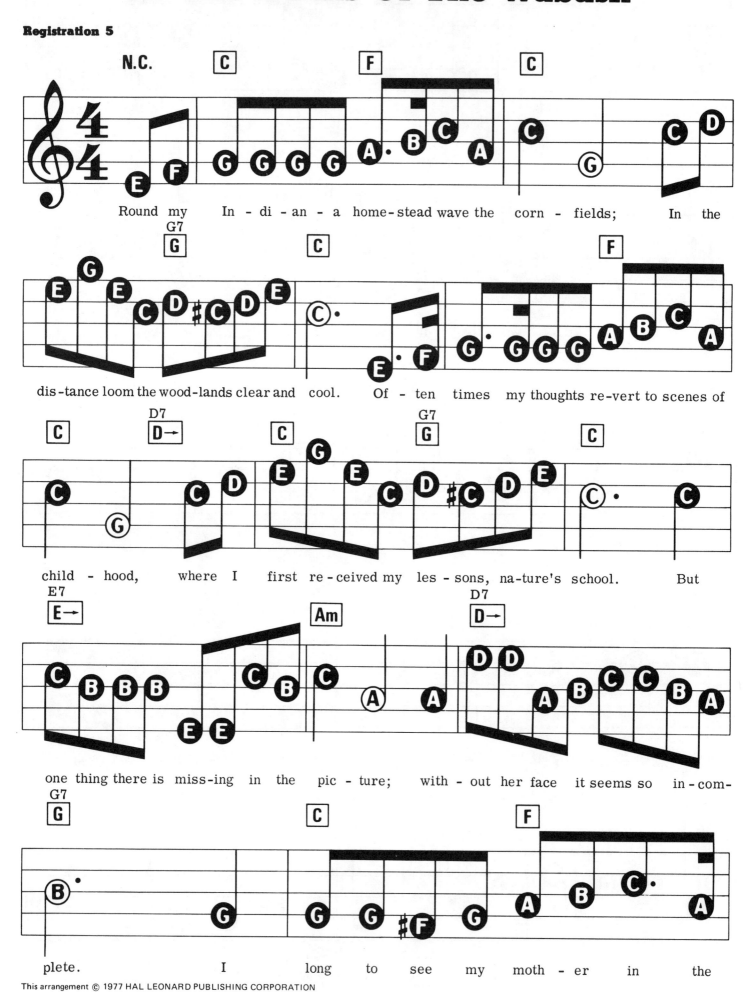

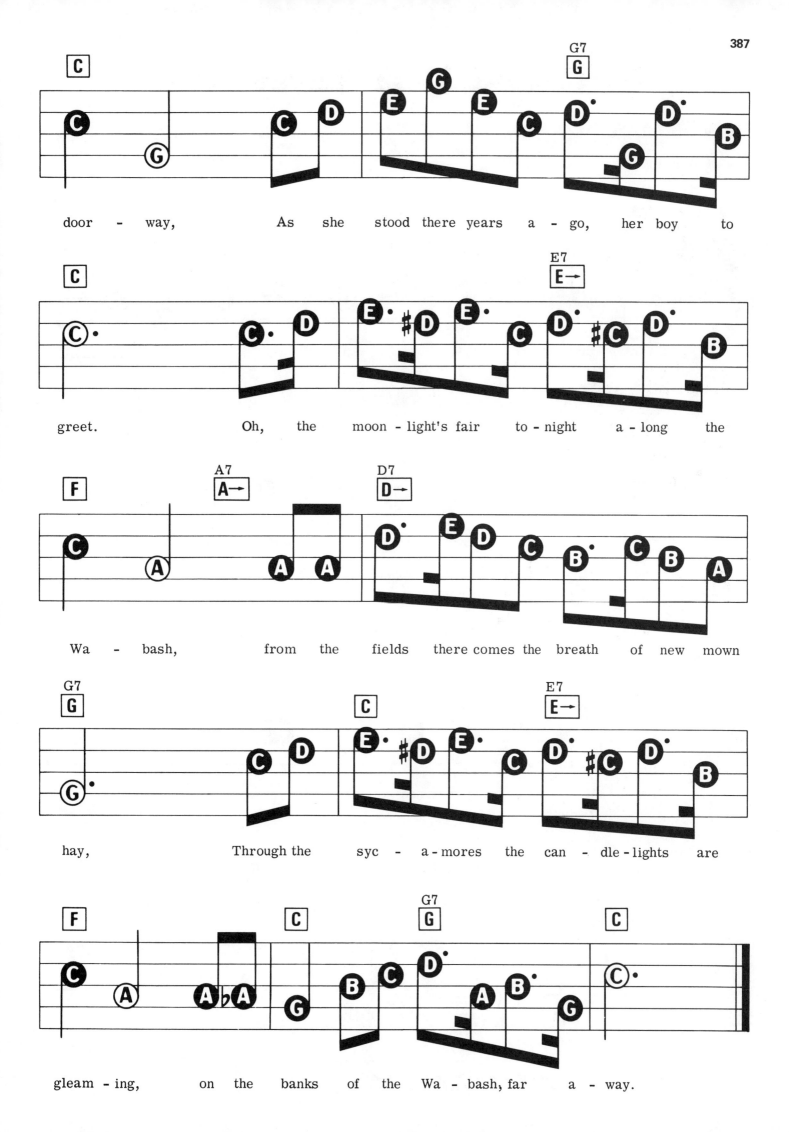

Red River Valley

Registration 4

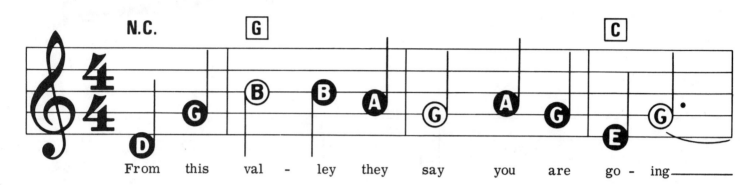

From this val - ley they say you are go - ing

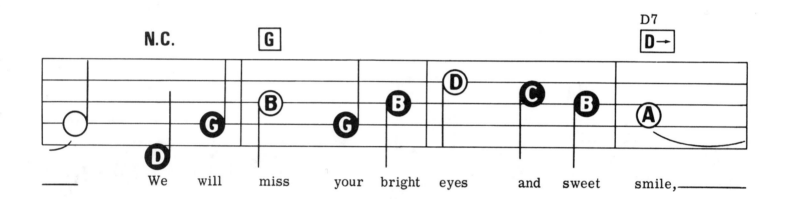

We will miss your bright eyes and sweet smile,

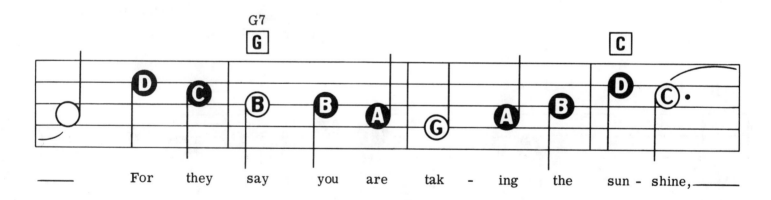

For they say you are tak - ing the sun - shine,

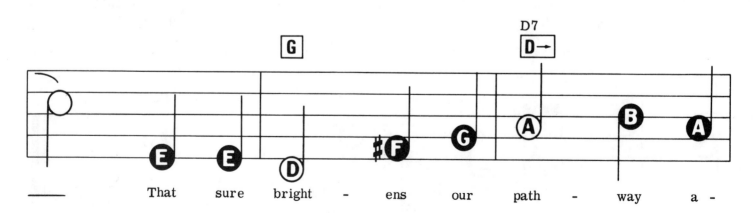

That sure bright - ens our path - way a -

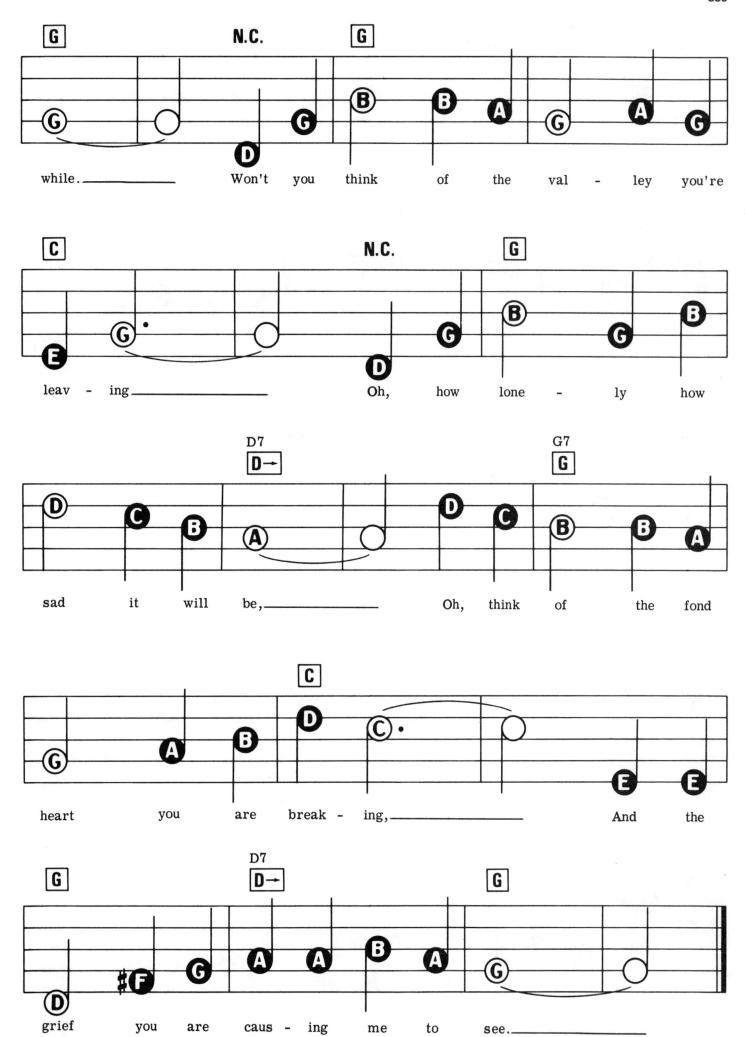

She'll Be Comin' 'Round The Mountain

Registration 8

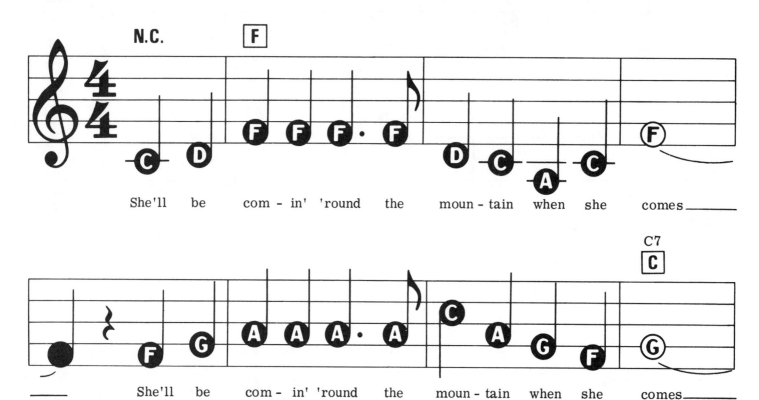

She'll be com - in' 'round the moun - tain when she comes____

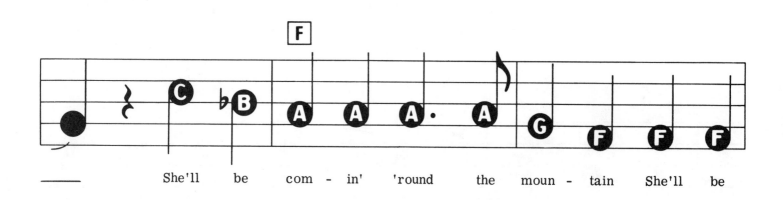

____ She'll be com - in' 'round the moun - tain when she comes____

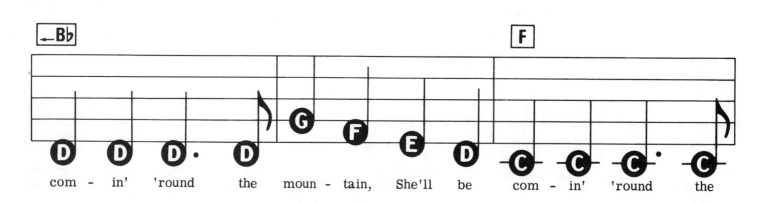

____ She'll be com - in' 'round the moun - tain She'll be

com - in' 'round the moun - tain, She'll be com - in' 'round the

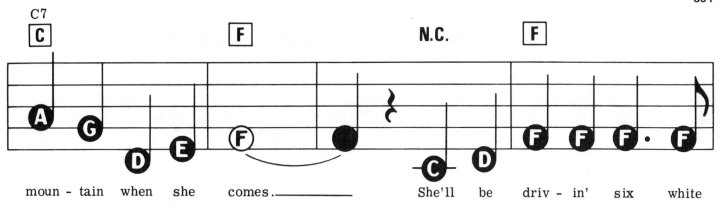

moun - tain when she comes._____ She'll be driv - in' six white

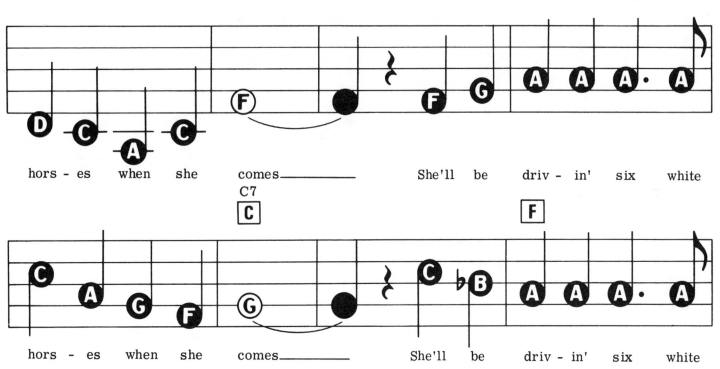

hors - es when she comes_____ She'll be driv - in' six white

hors - es when she comes_____ She'll be driv - in' six white

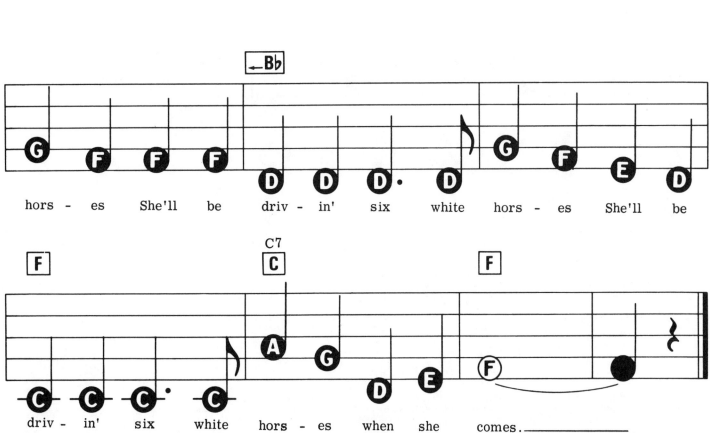

hors - es She'll be driv - in' six white hors - es She'll be

driv - in' six white hors - es when she comes._____

Sidewalks Of New York

Registration 3

Words and Music by Charles B. Lawlor and
James W. Blake

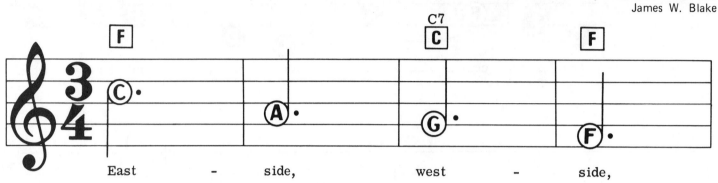

East - side, west - side,

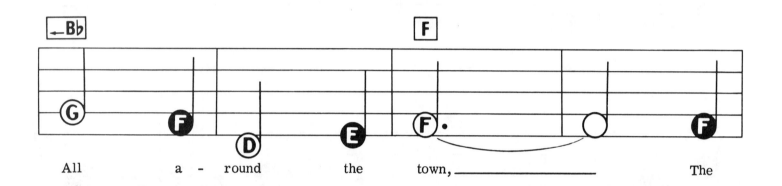

All a - round the town, _____ The

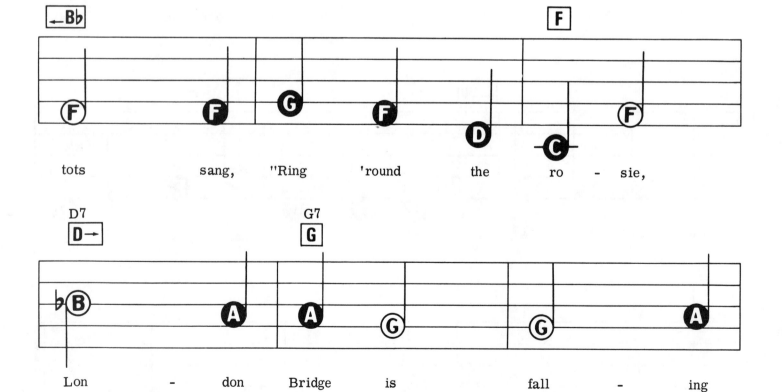

tots sang, "Ring 'round the ro - sie,

Lon - don Bridge is fall - ing

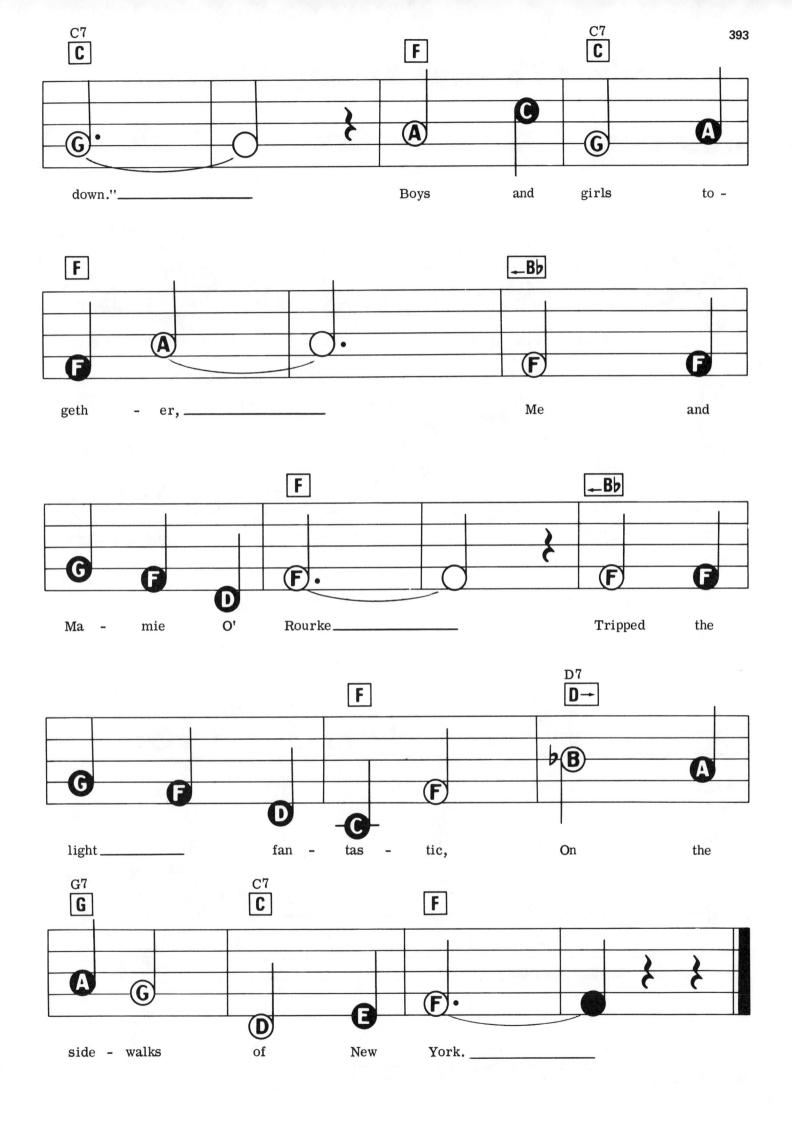

Silver Threads Among The Gold

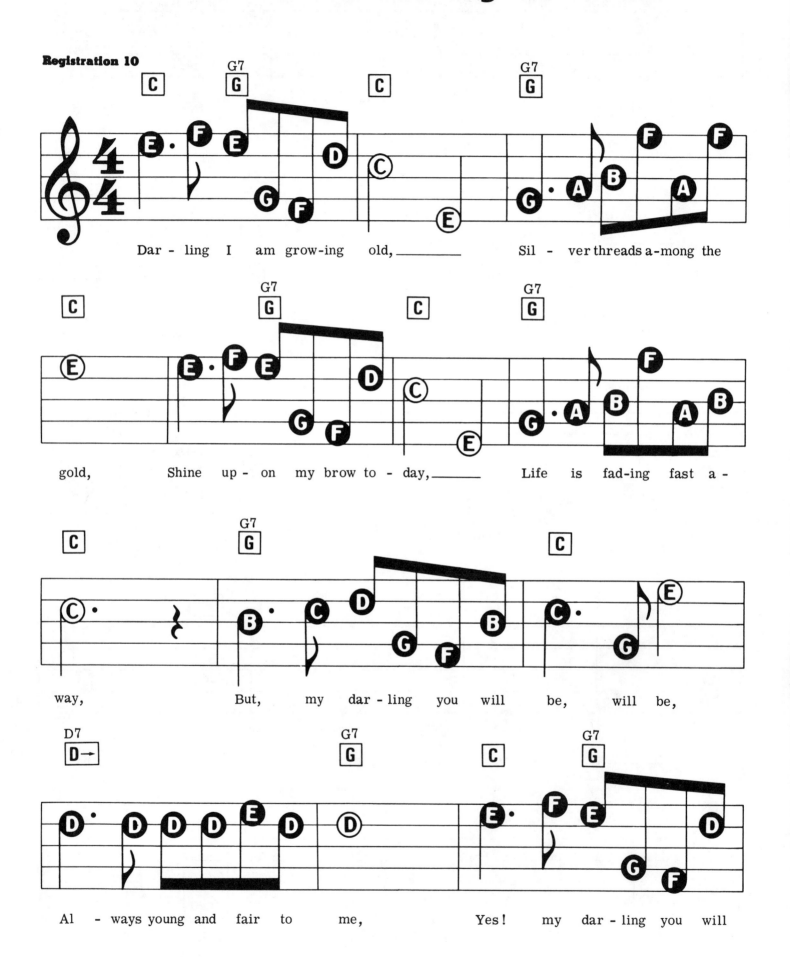

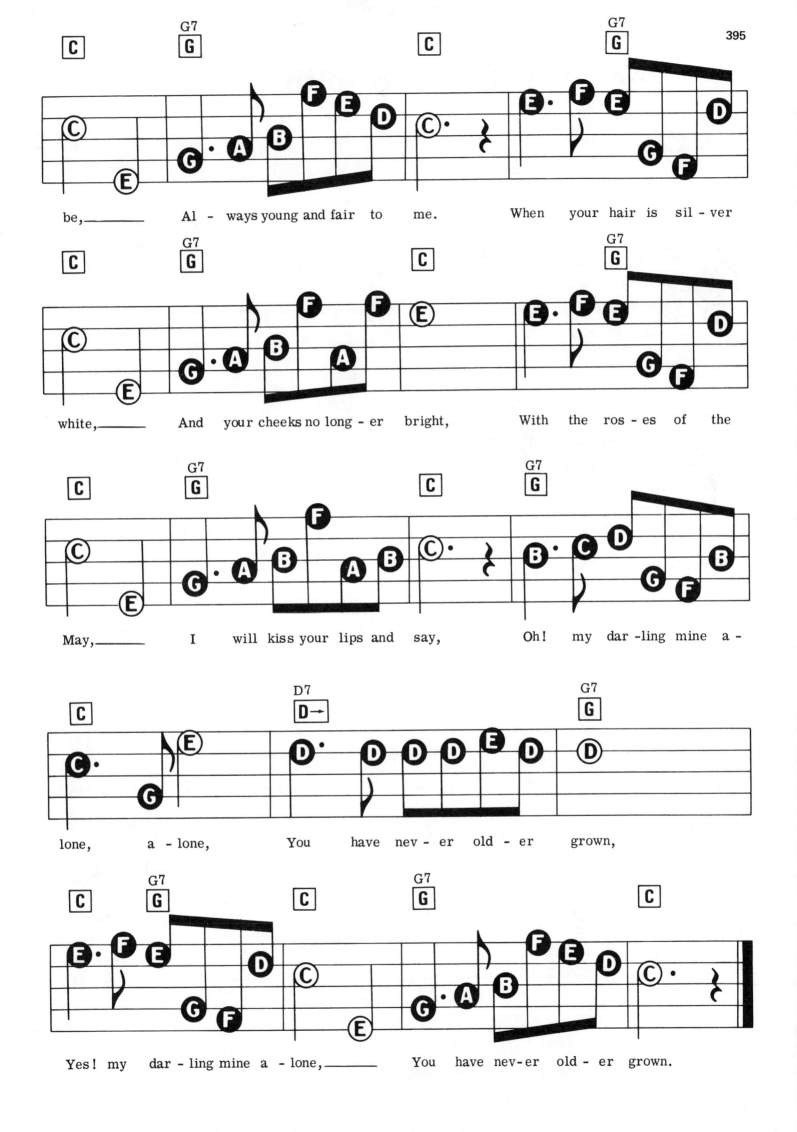

Sweet Adeline

Registration 4

Words and Music by Richard H. Gerard and Harry Armstrong

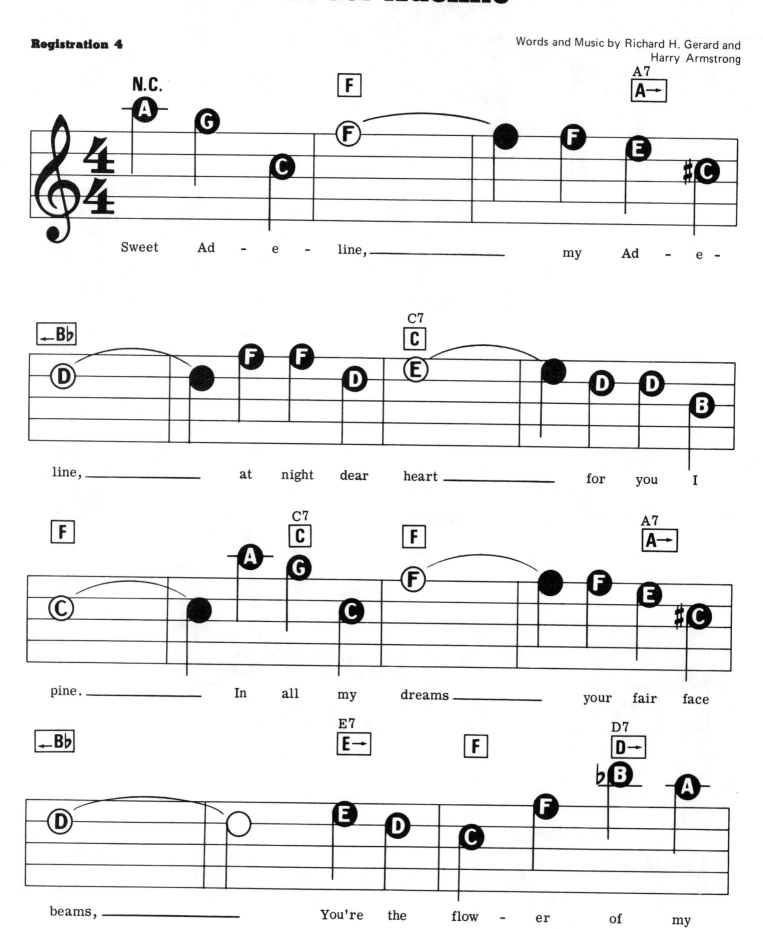

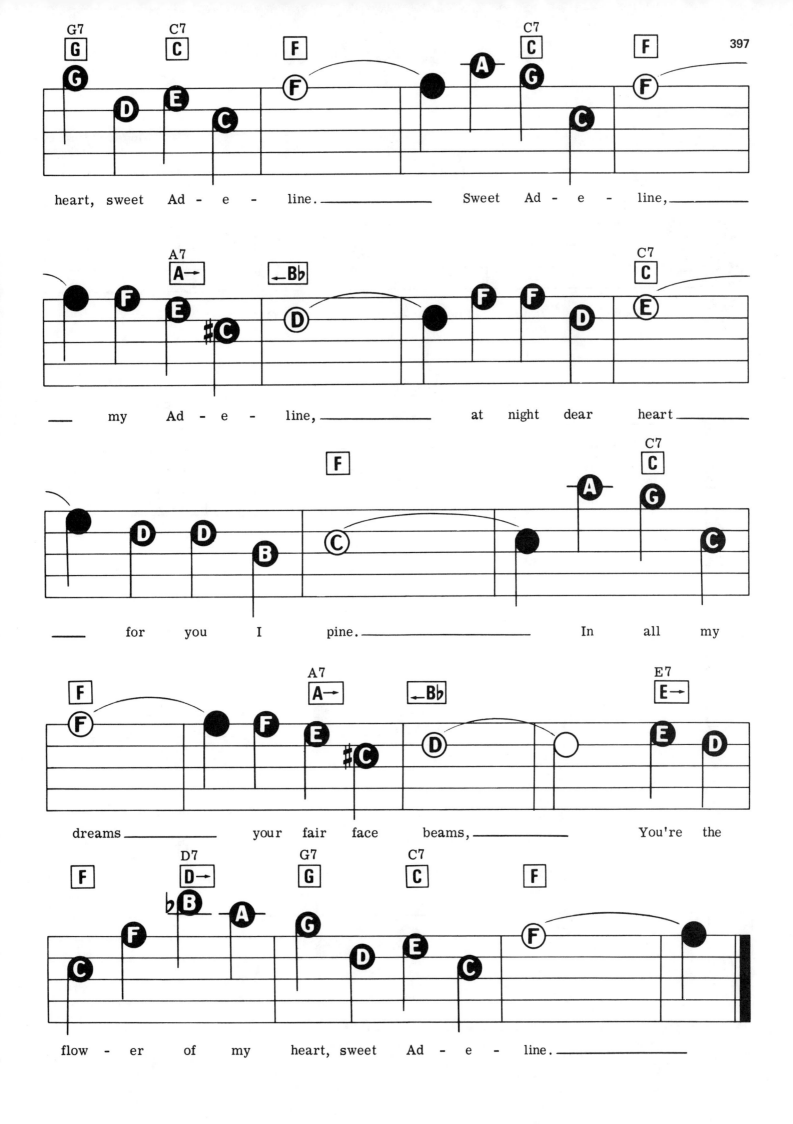

Sweet Rosie O'Grady

Registration 10

Words and Music by
Maud Nugent

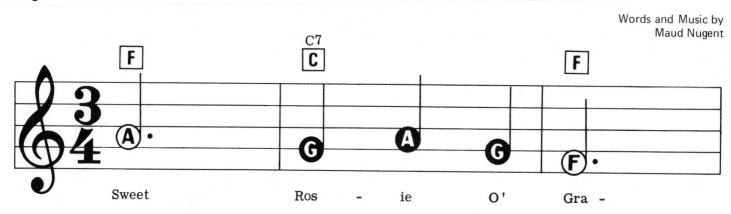

Sweet Ros - ie O' Gra -

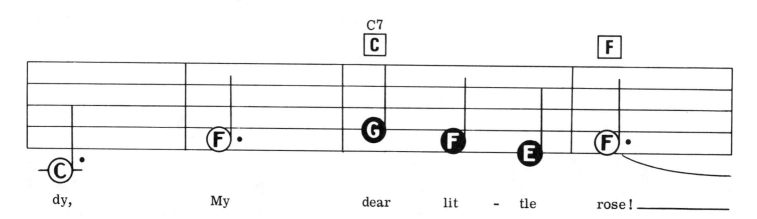

dy, My dear lit - tle rose! _____

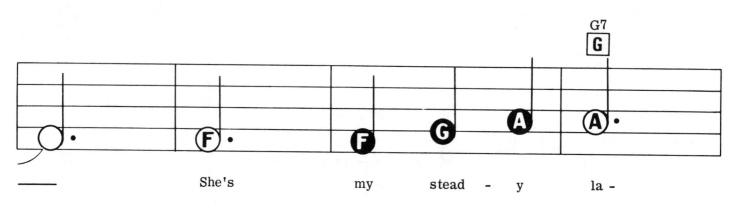

_____ She's my stead - y la -

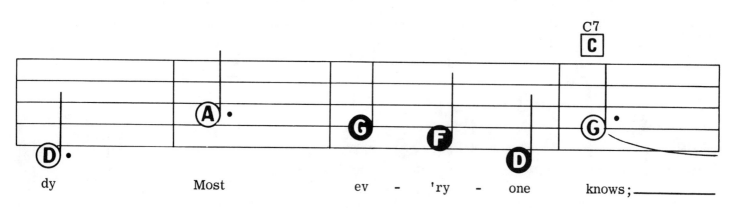

dy Most ev - 'ry - one knows; _____

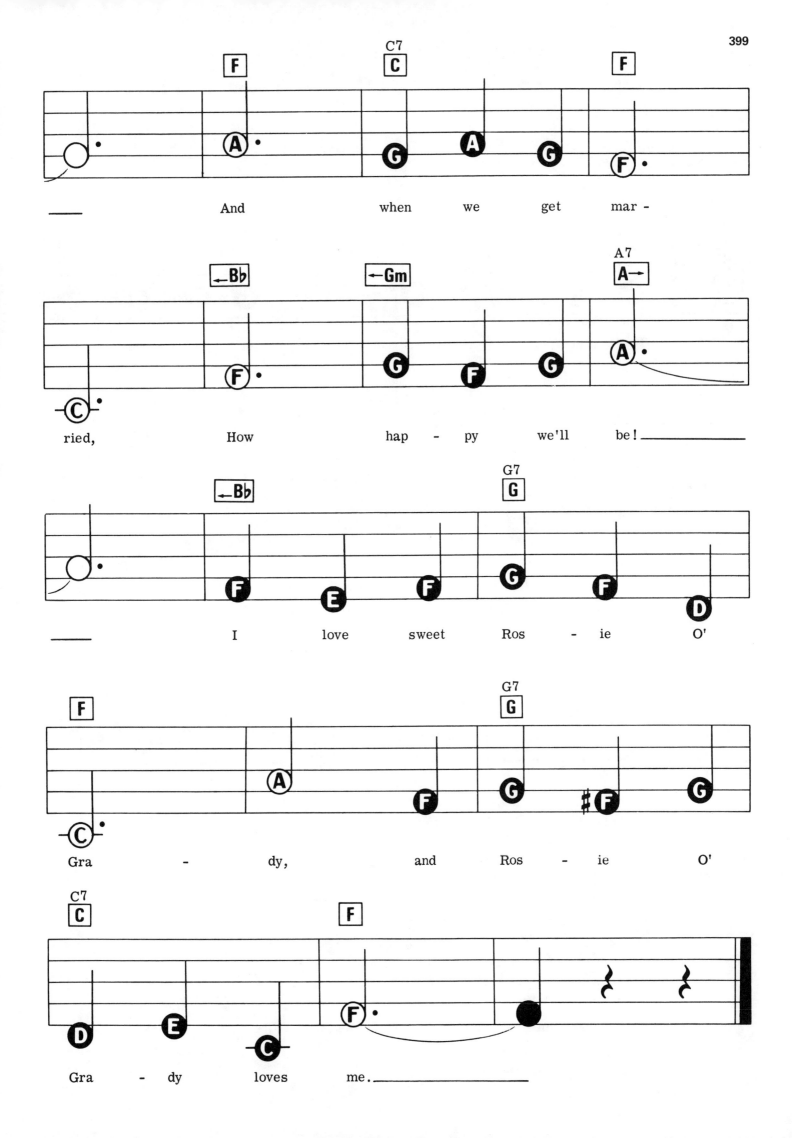

There Is A Tavern In The Town

Registration 8

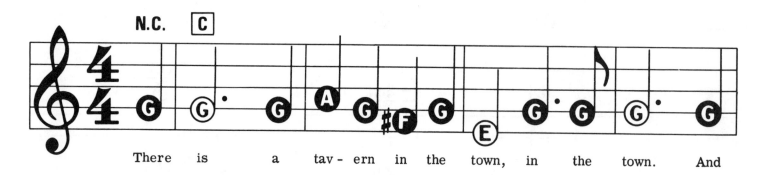

There is a tav - ern in the town, in the town. And

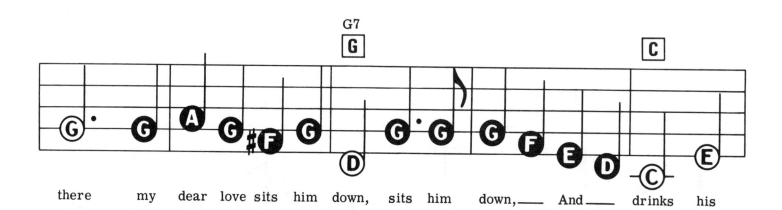

there my dear love sits him down, sits him down,___ And___ drinks his

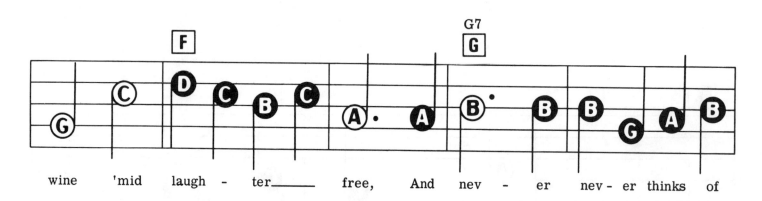

wine 'mid laugh - ter___ free, And nev - er nev - er thinks of

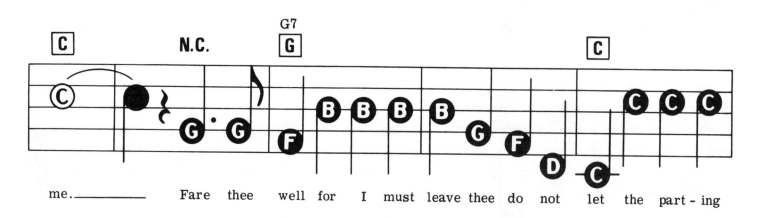

me._____ Fare thee well for I must leave thee do not let the part - ing

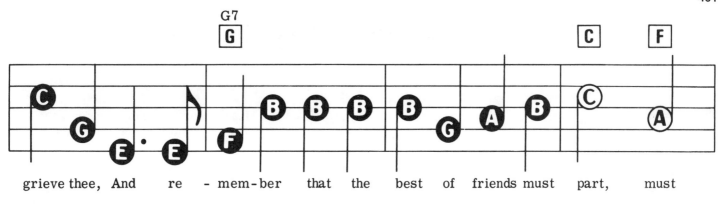

grieve thee, And re - mem-ber that the best of friends must part, must

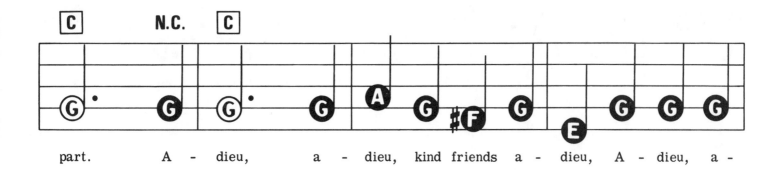

part. A - dieu, a - dieu, kind friends a - dieu, A - dieu, a-

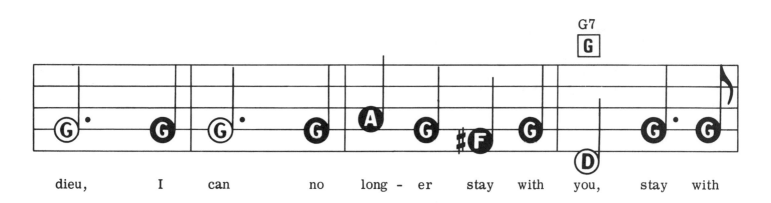

dieu, I can no long - er stay with you, stay with

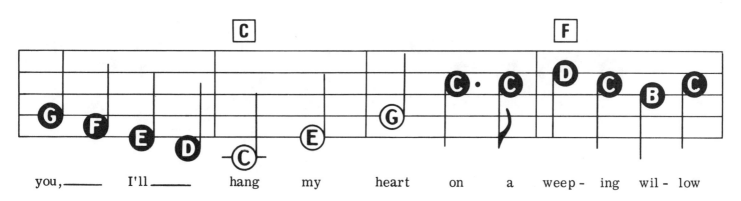

you,____ I'll____ hang my heart on a weep-ing wil-low

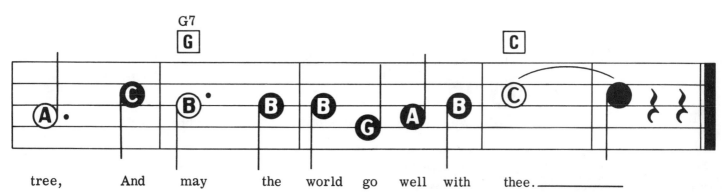

tree, And may the world go well with thee.____

Tom Dooley

Registration 8

Words and Music collected, adapted and arranged by
Frank Warner, John A. Lomax and Alan Lomax

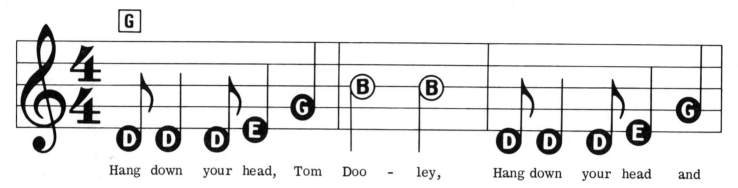

Hang down your head, Tom Doo - ley, Hang down your head and

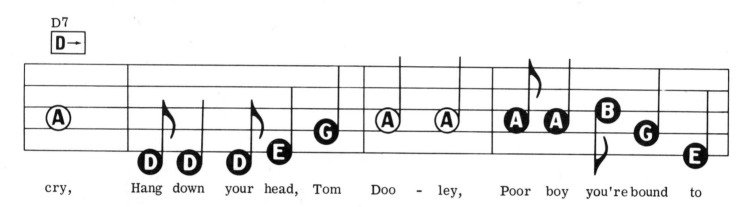

cry, Hang down your head, Tom Doo - ley, Poor boy you're bound to

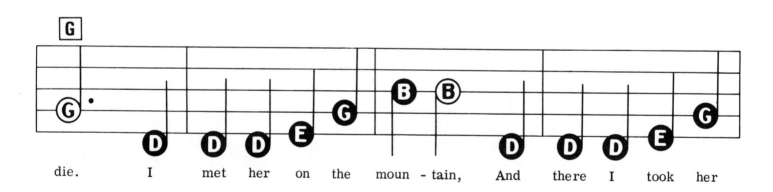

die. I met her on the moun - tain, And there I took her

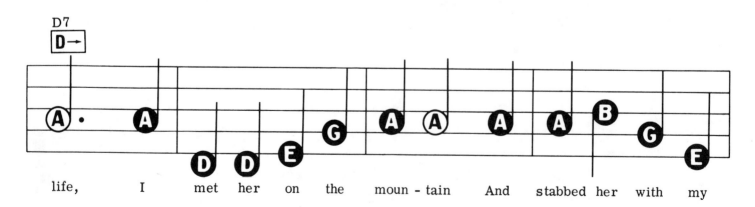

life, I met her on the moun - tain And stabbed her with my

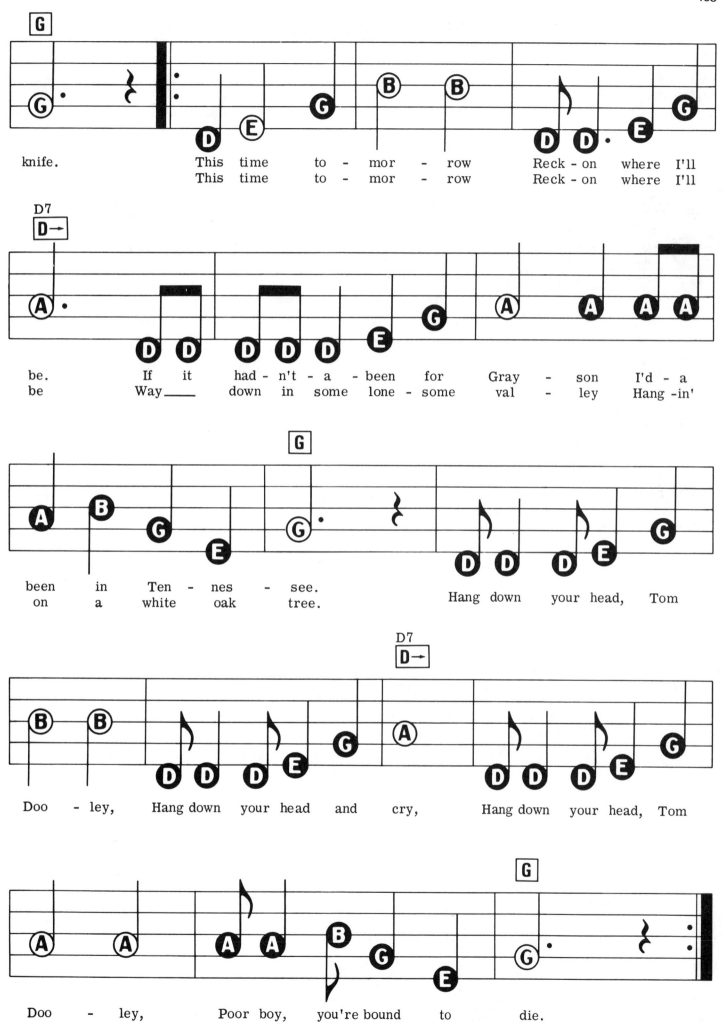

Wait 'Til The Sun Shines, Nellie

Registration 2

Words and Music by Andrew B. Sterling &
Harry Von Tilzer

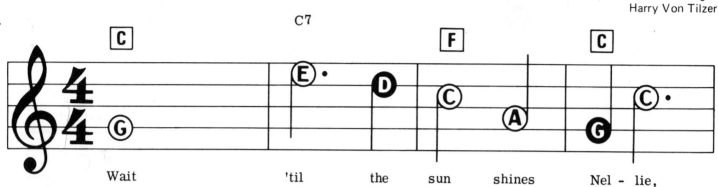

Wait 'til the sun shines Nel - lie,

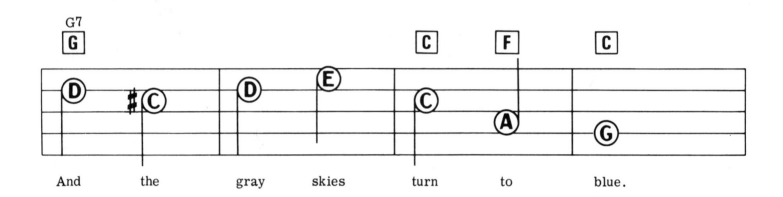

And the gray skies turn to blue.

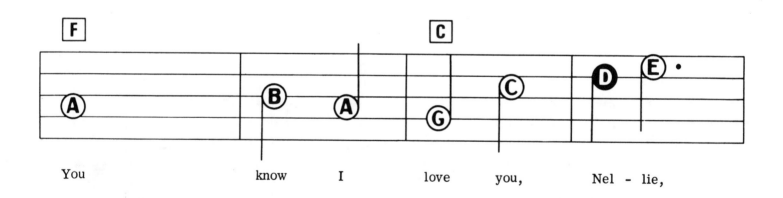

You know I love you, Nel - lie,

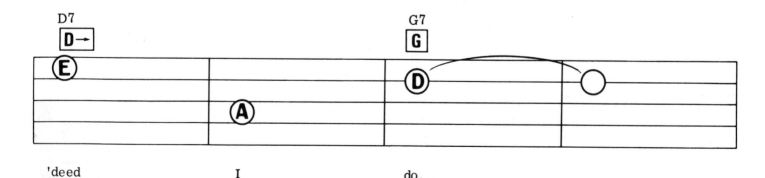

'deed I do. _____

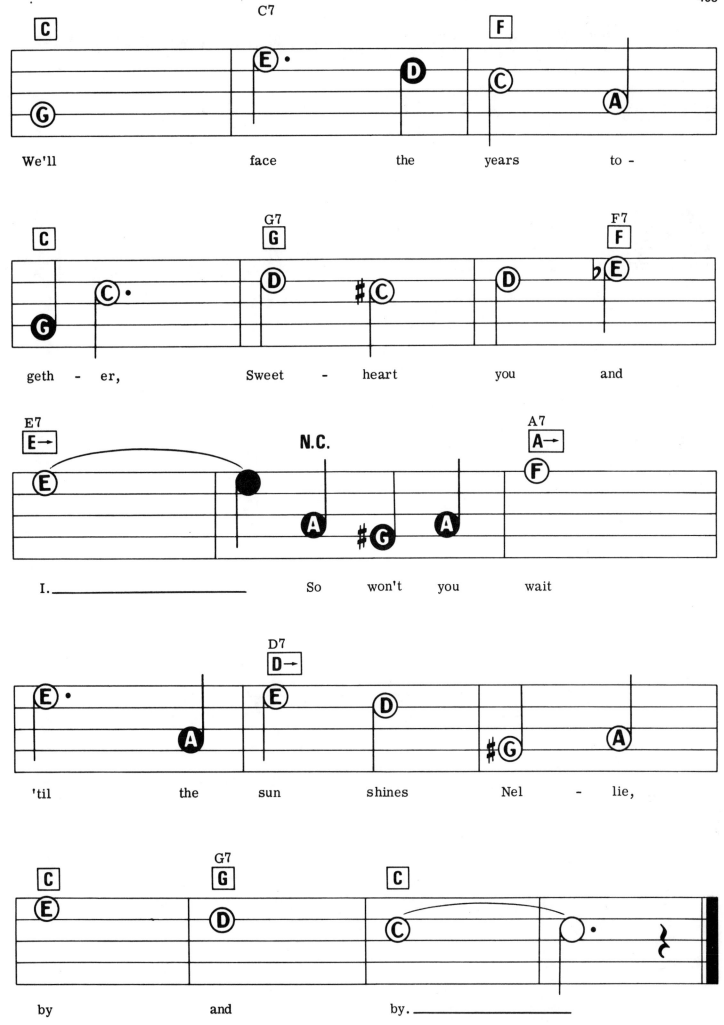

When You And I Were Young, Maggie

Registration 5

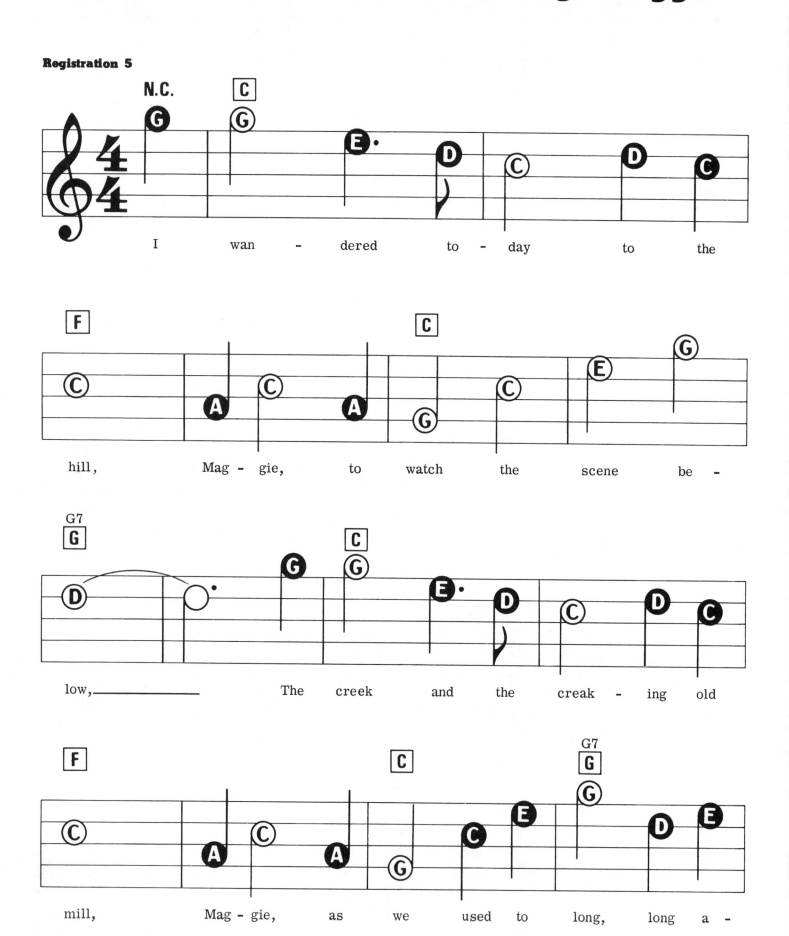

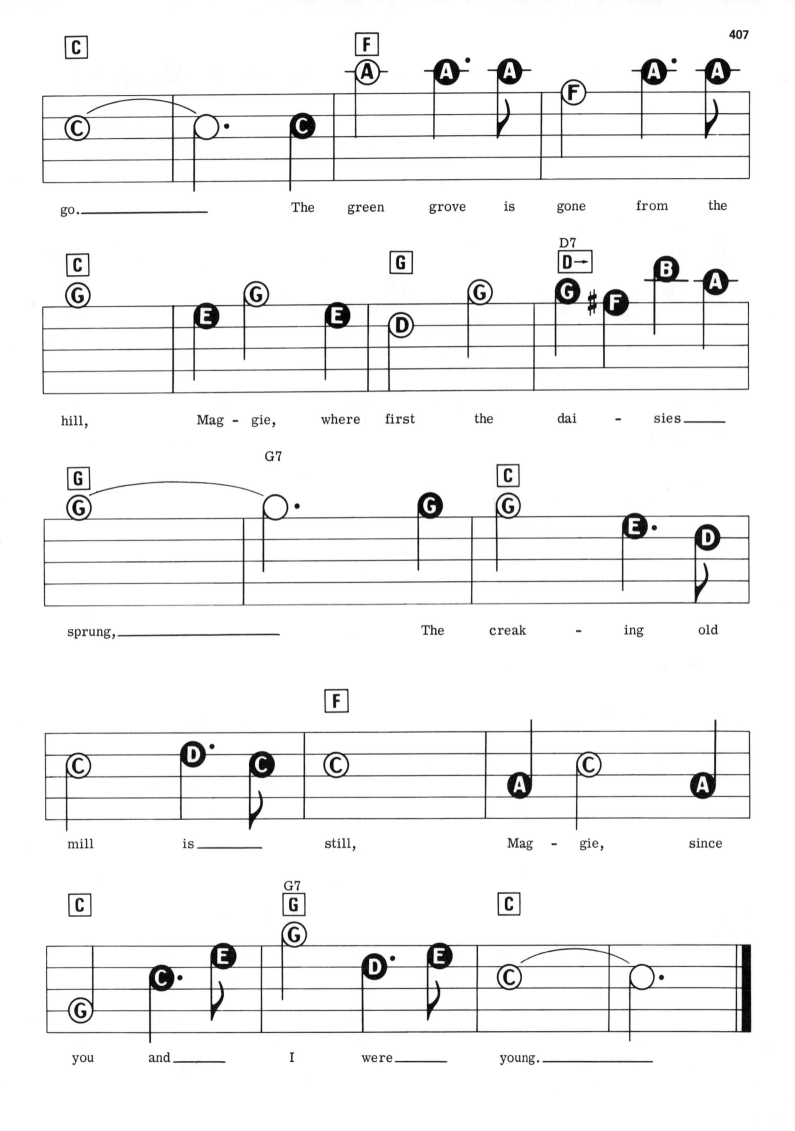

While Strolling Through The Park

Registration 2

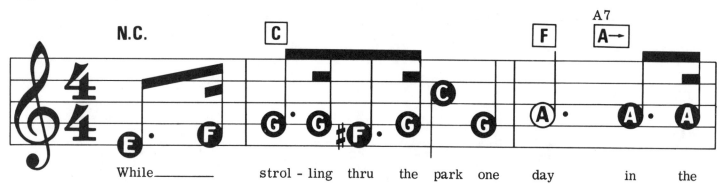

While_____ strol - ling thru the park one day in the

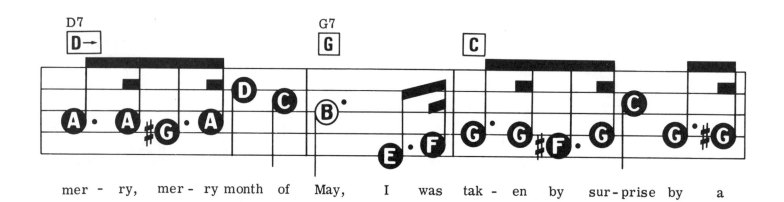

mer - ry, mer - ry month of May, I was tak - en by sur-prise by a

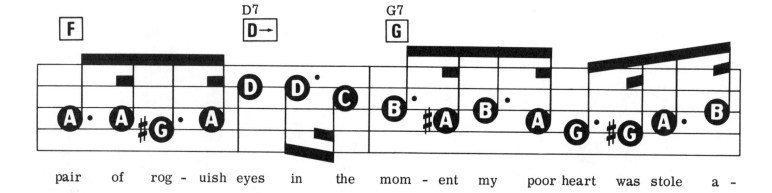

pair of rog - uish eyes in the mom - ent my poor heart was stole a -

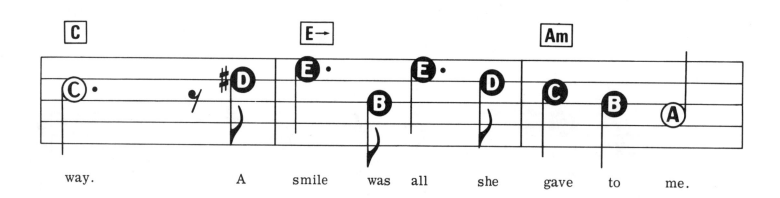

way. A smile was all she gave to me.

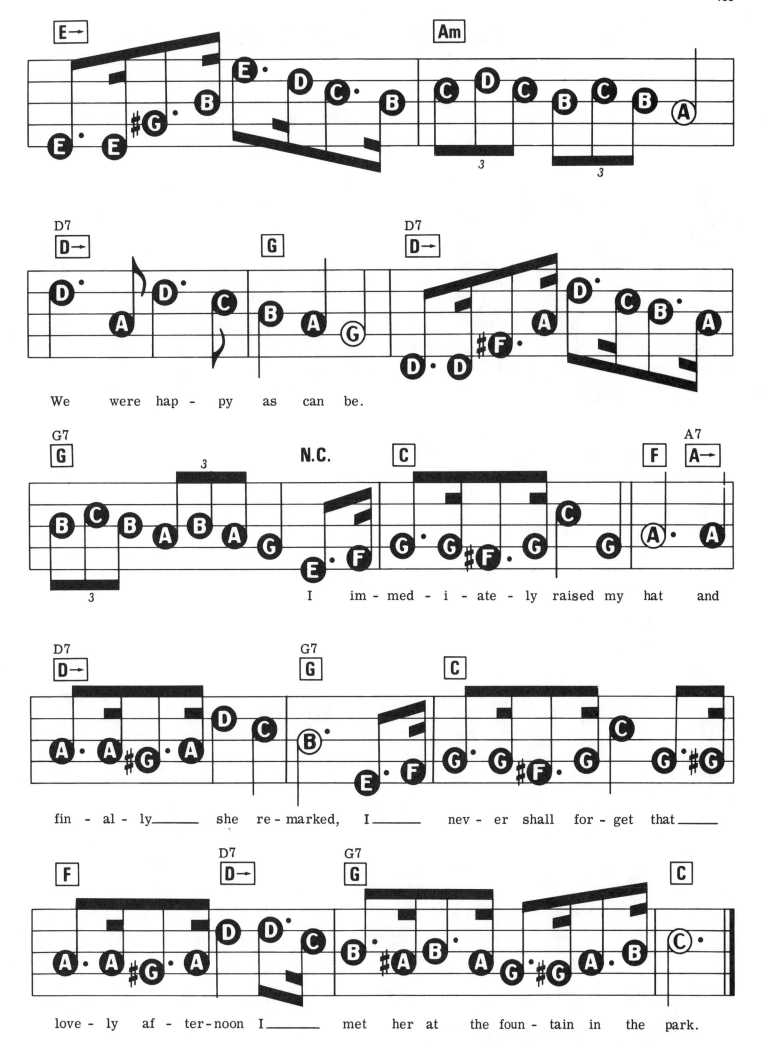

The Birthday Song

Registration 5

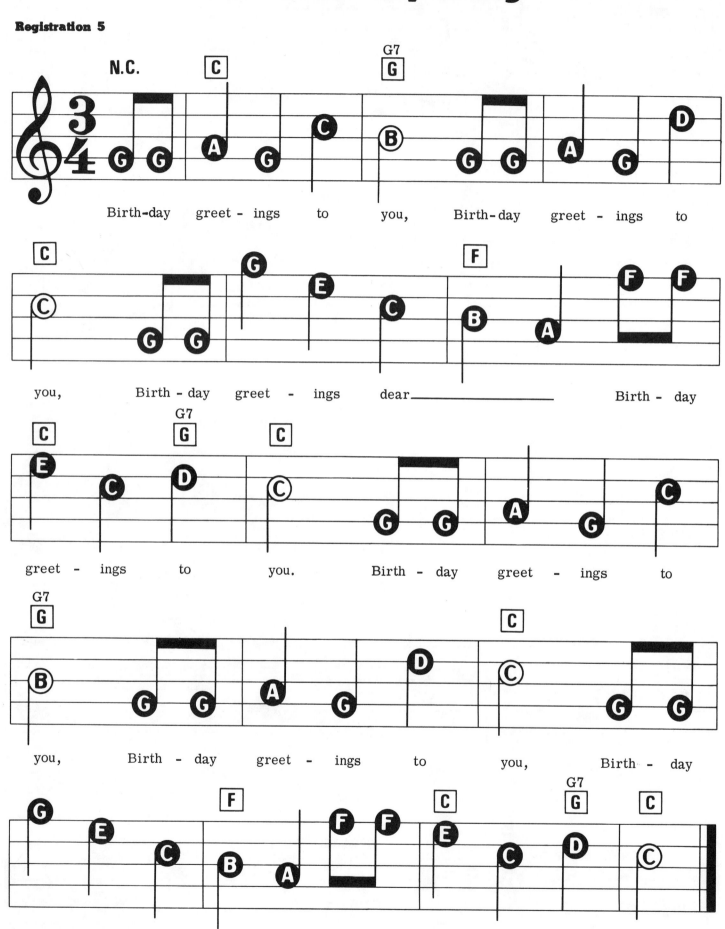

Hickory Dickory Dock

Registration 8

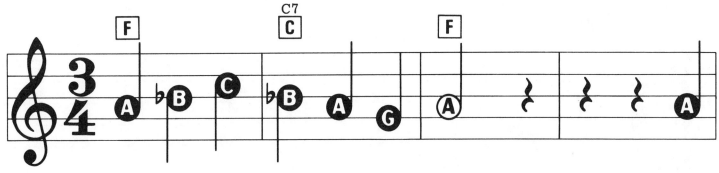

Hick - o - ry, dick - o - ry dock; The

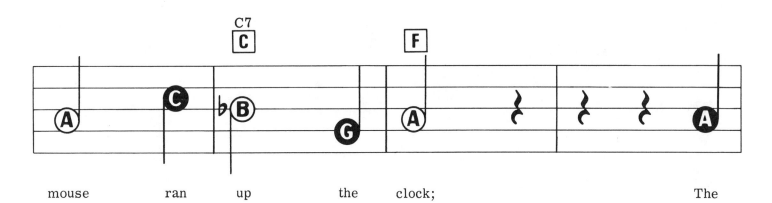

mouse ran up the clock; The

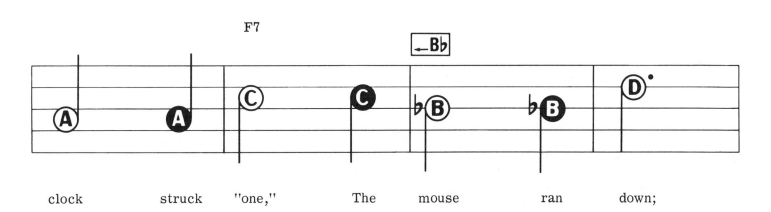

clock struck "one," The mouse ran down;

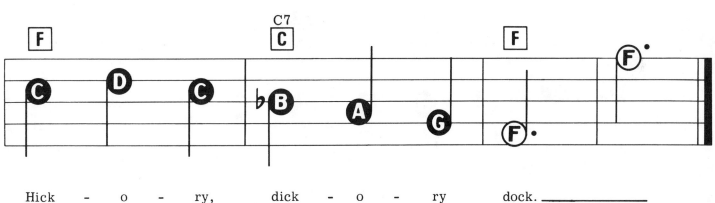

Hick - o - ry, dick - o - ry dock. _____

Humpty Dumpty

Registration 2

Little Miss Muffet

Registration 8

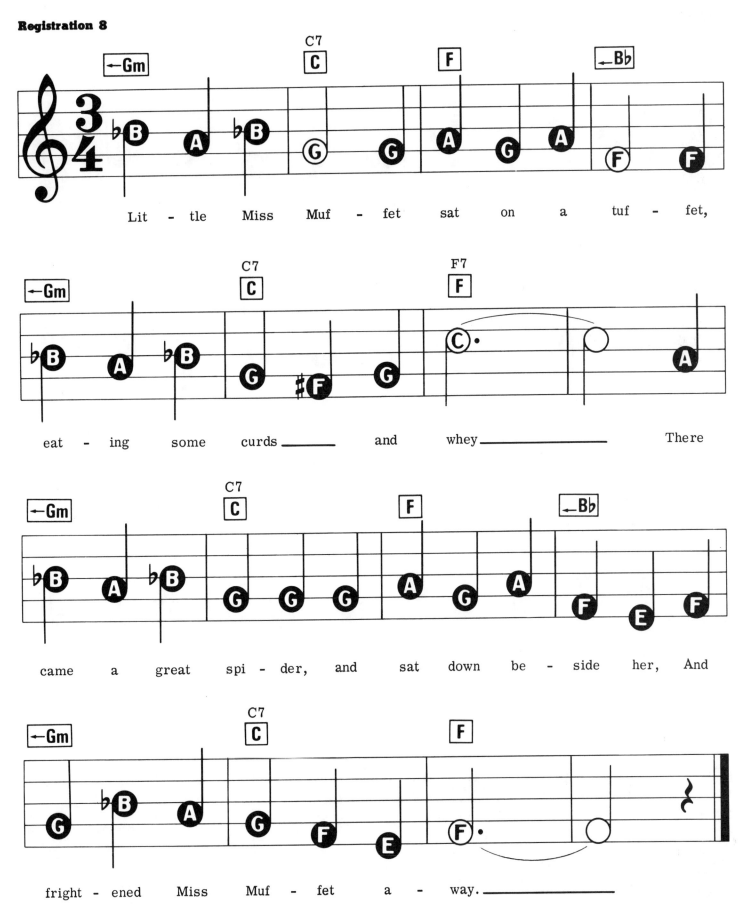

Oh Where Has My Little Dog Gone

Registration 5

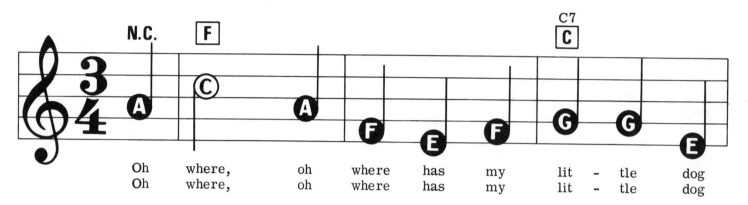

Oh   where,   oh   where   has   my   lit - tle   dog
Oh   where,   oh   where   has   my   lit - tle   dog

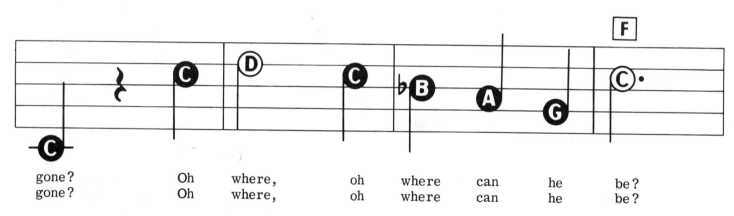

gone?   Oh   where,   oh   where   can   he   be?
gone?   Oh   where,   oh   where   can   he   be?

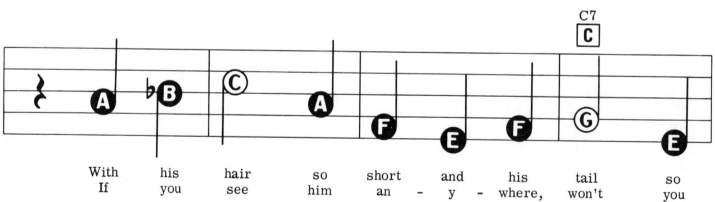

With   his   hair   so   short   and   his   tail   so
If   you   see   him   an - y - where,   won't   you

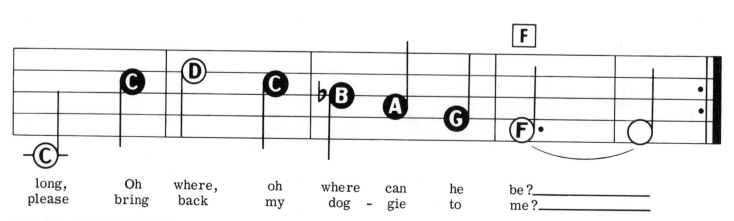

long,   Oh   where,   oh   where   can   he   be?_____
please   bring   back   my   dog - gie   to   me?_____

Old King Cole

Registration 4

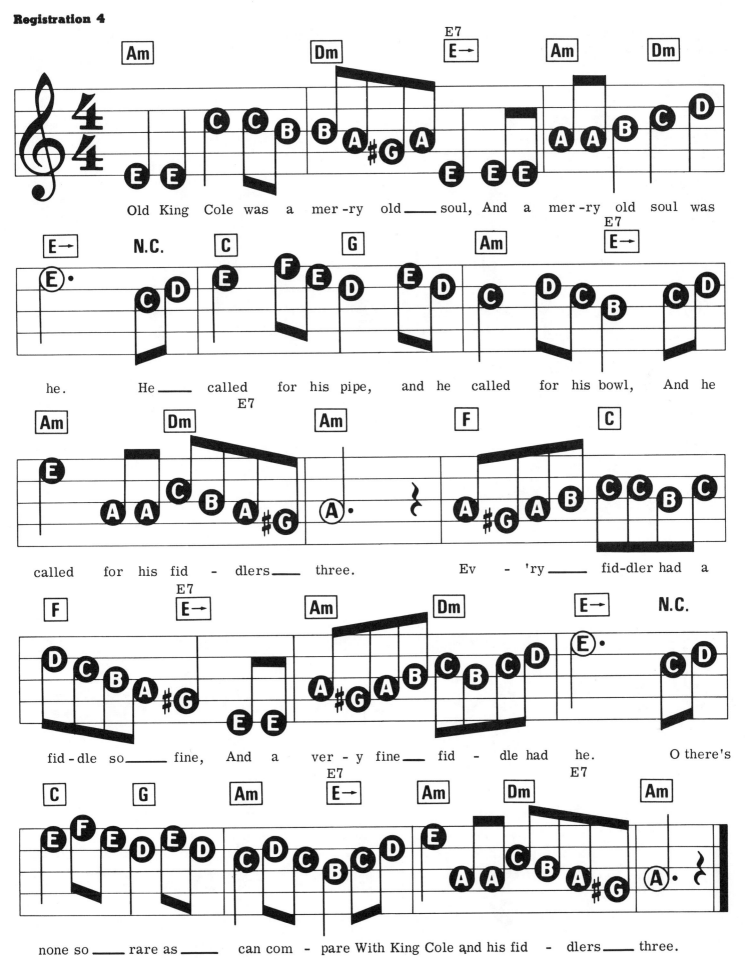

Old MacDonald Had A Farm

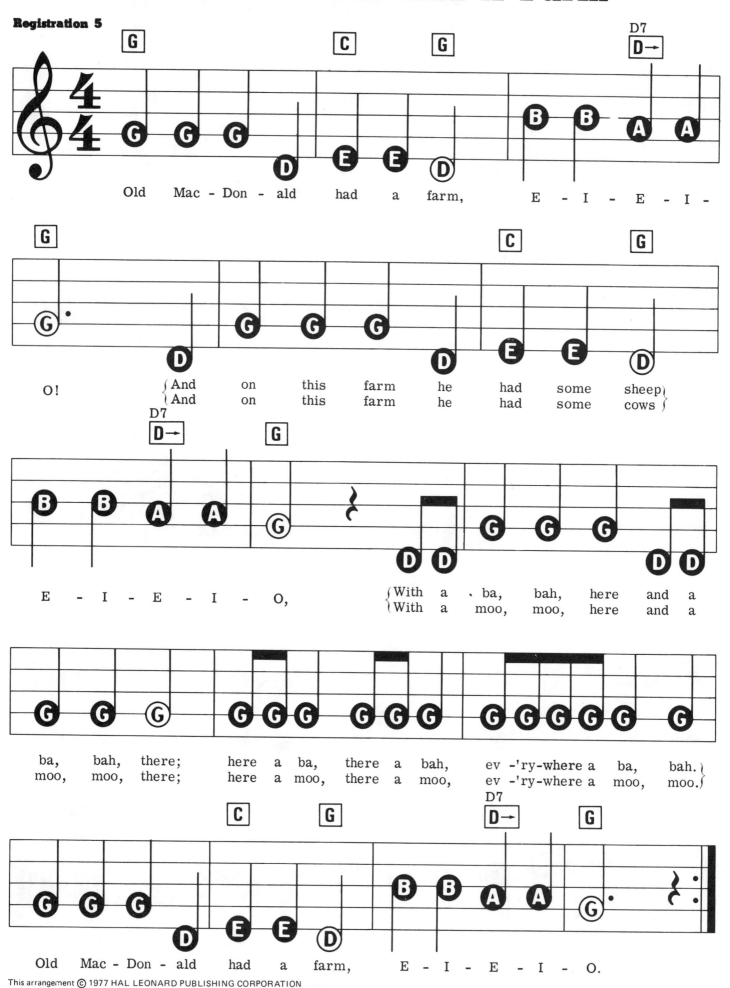

Pop Goes The Weasel

Registration 5

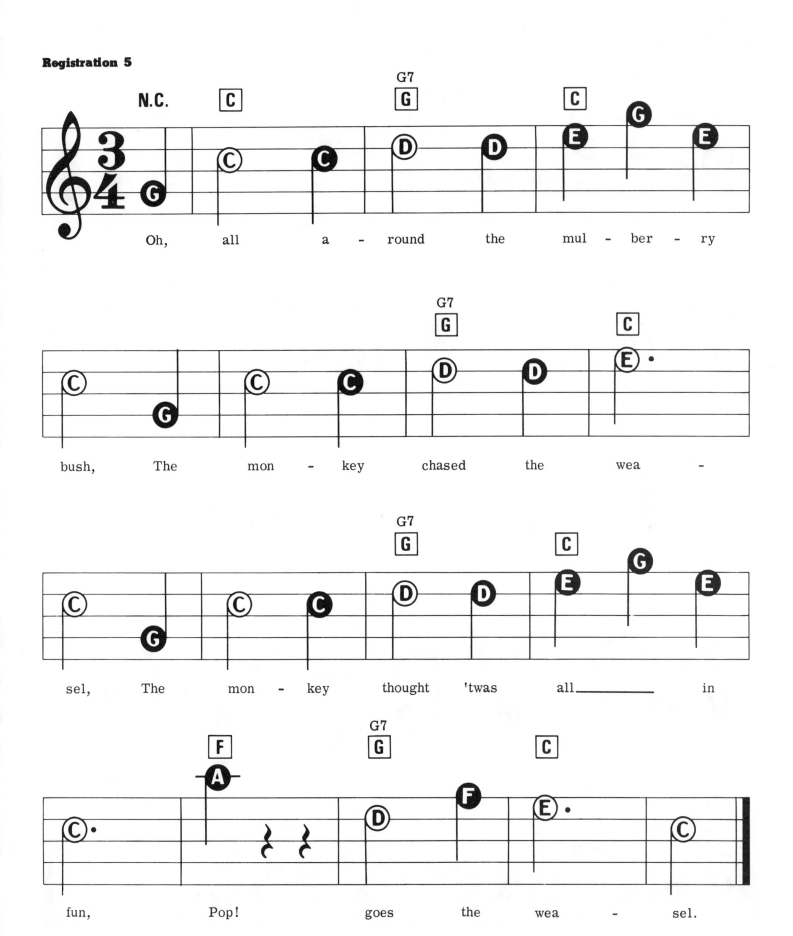

Skip To My Lou

Registration 10

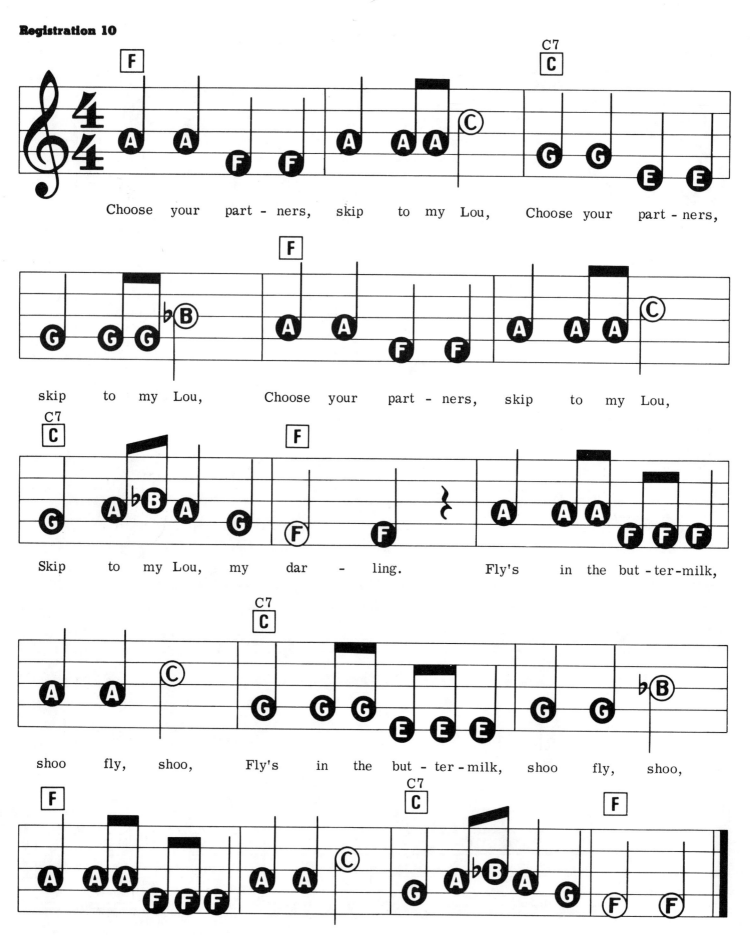

Choose your part-ners, skip to my Lou, Choose your part-ners,

skip to my Lou, Choose your part-ners, skip to my Lou,

Skip to my Lou, my dar-ling. Fly's in the but-ter-milk,

shoo fly, shoo, Fly's in the but-ter-milk, shoo fly, shoo,

Fly's in the but-ter-milk, shoo fly, shoo, Skip to my Lou, my dar-ling.

Turkey In The Straw

Registration 3

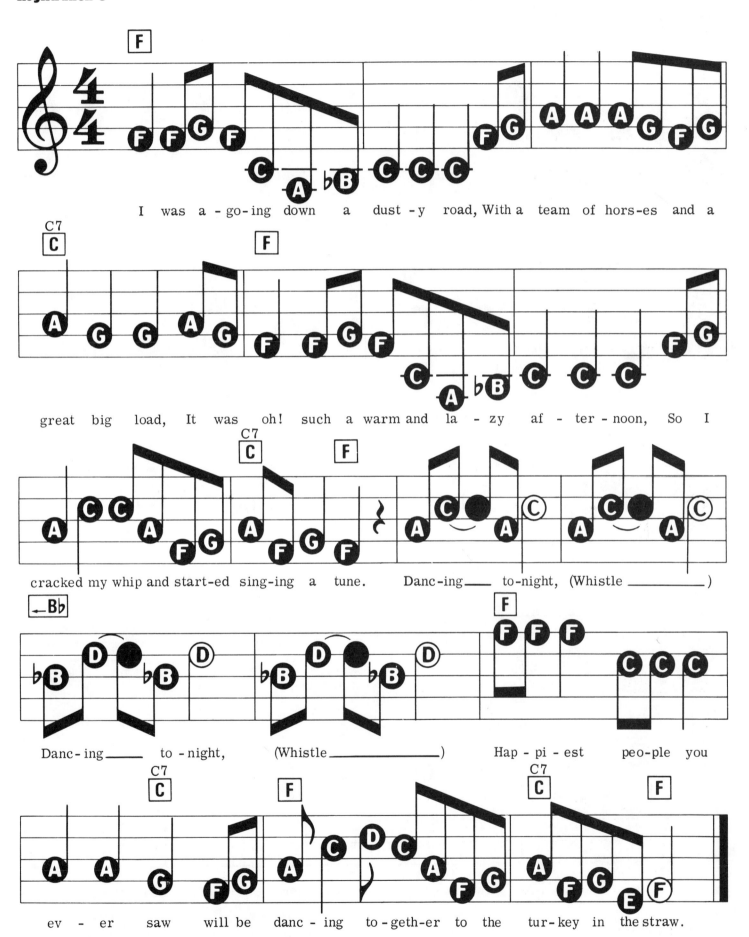

Twinkle, Twinkle, Little Star

Registration 1

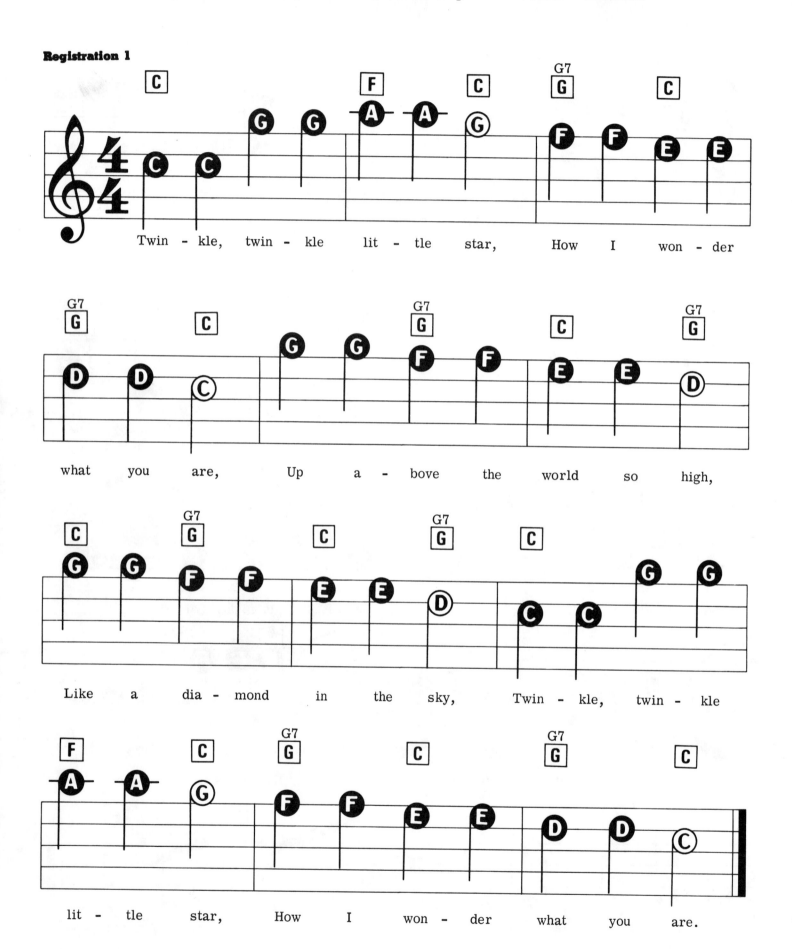

I Heard The Bells On Christmas Day

Registration 6

Angels From The Realms Of Glory

Registration 6

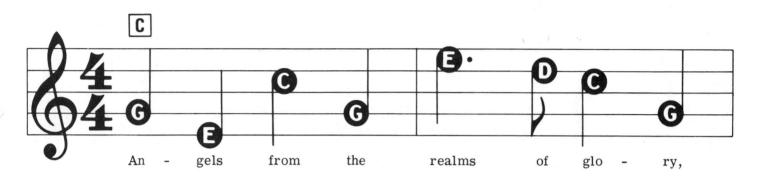

An - gels from the realms of glo - ry,

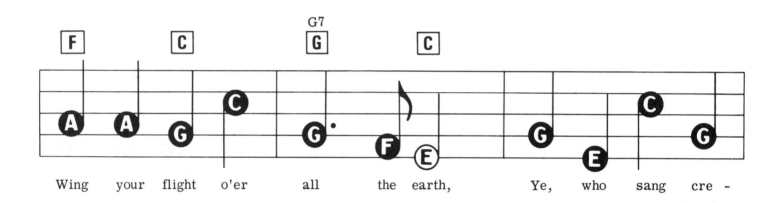

Wing your flight o'er all the earth, Ye, who sang cre -

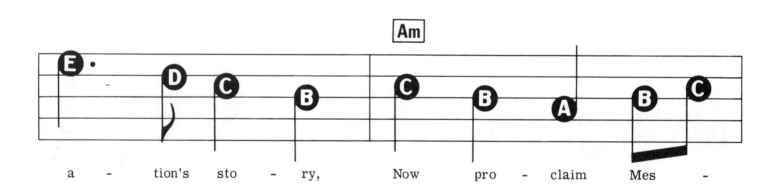

a - tion's sto - ry, Now pro - claim Mes -

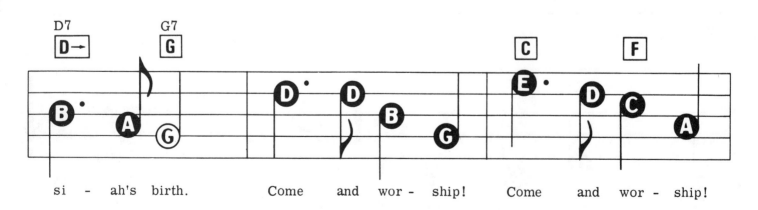

si - ah's birth. Come and wor - ship! Come and wor - ship!

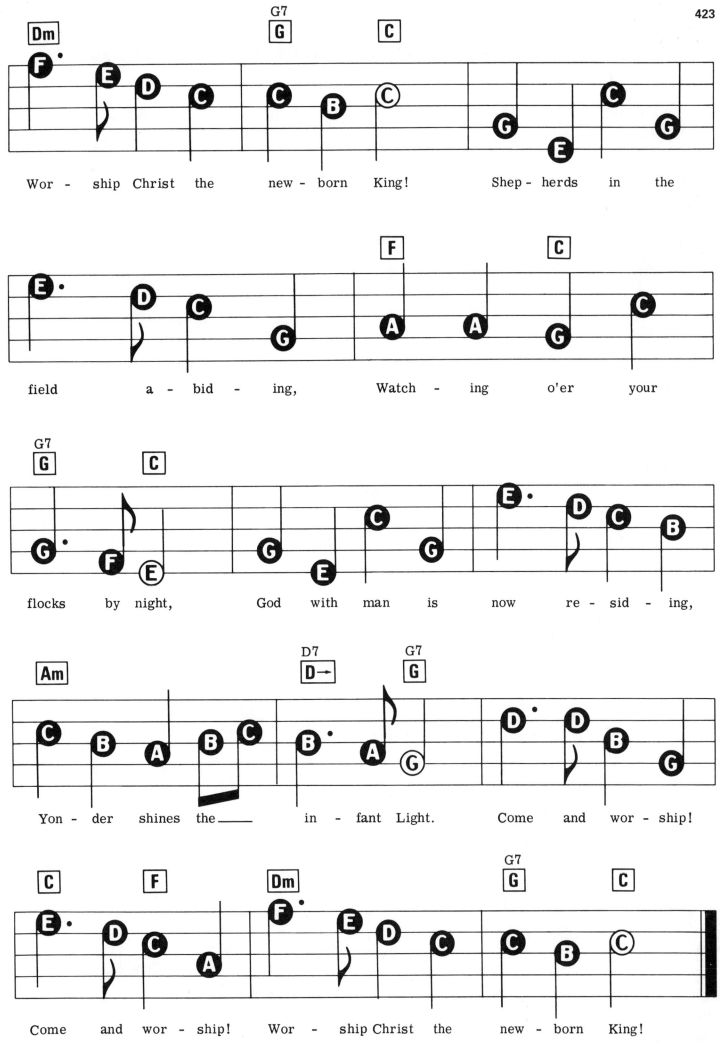

Angels We Have Heard On High

Registration 3

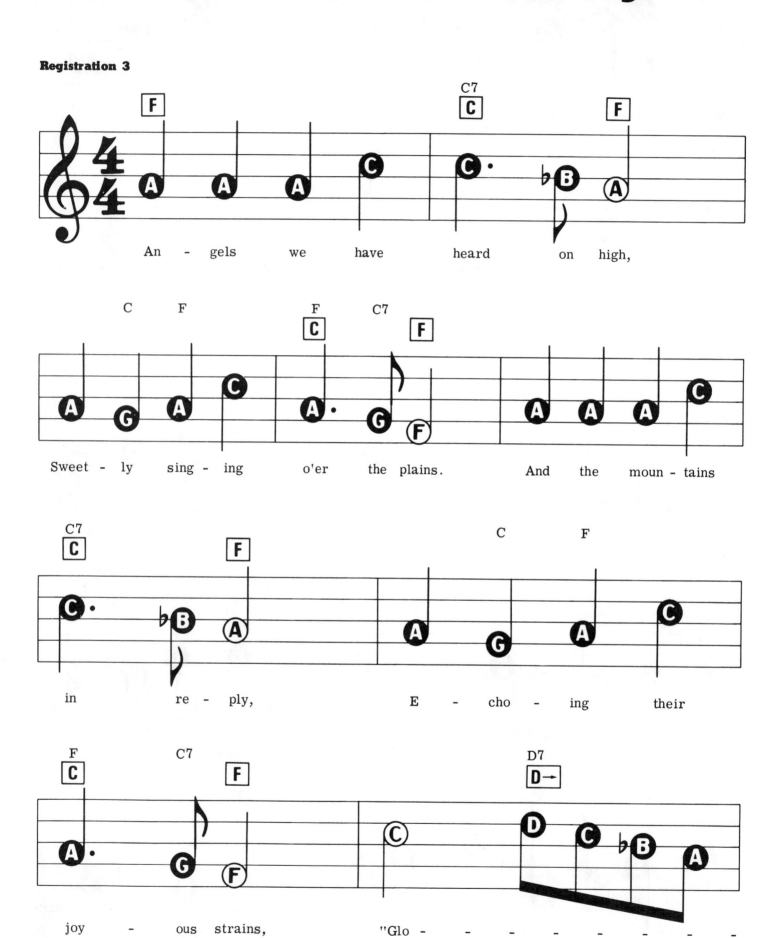

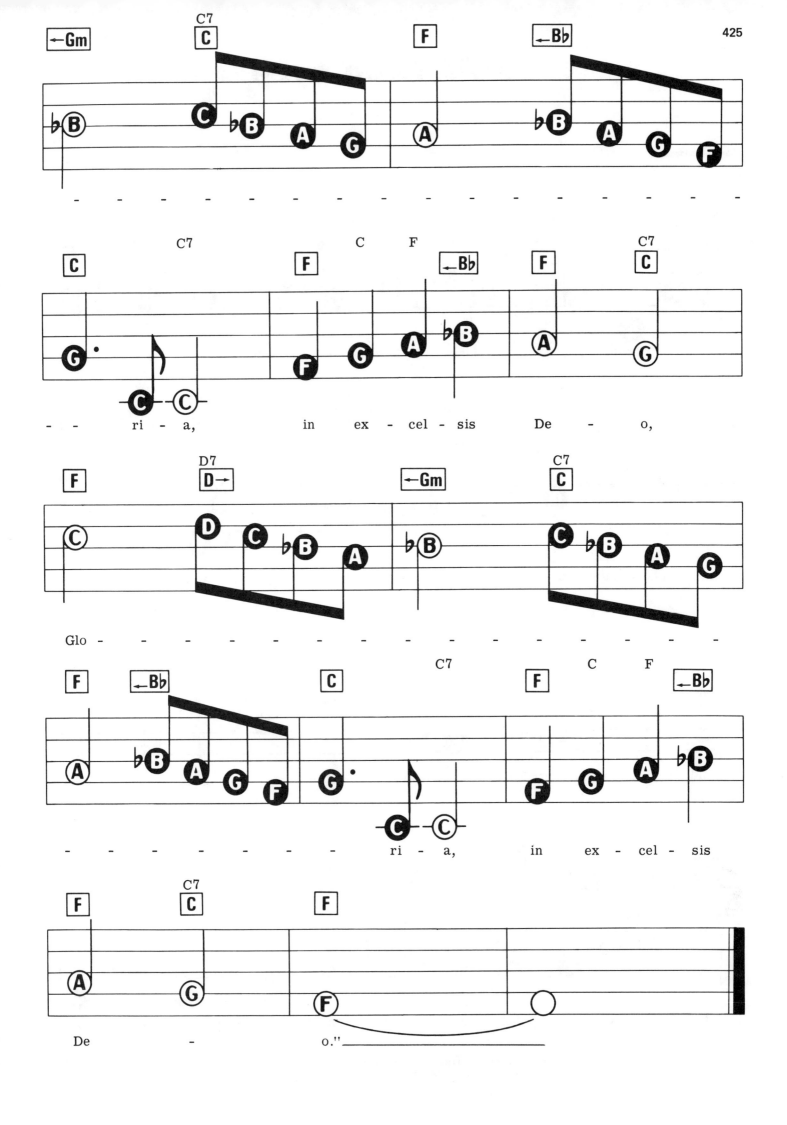

Auld Lang Syne

Registration 2

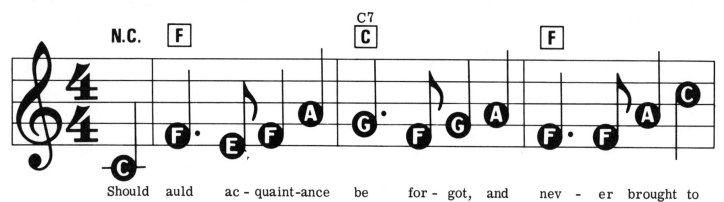

Should auld ac-quaint-ance be for-got, and nev - er brought to

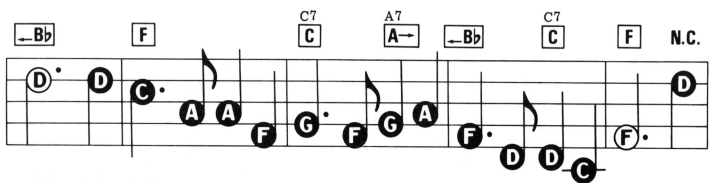

mind? Should auld ac- quaint-ance be for - got and days of Auld Lang Syne? For

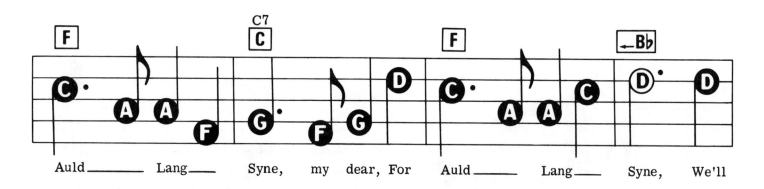

Auld_____ Lang_____ Syne, my dear, For Auld_____ Lang_____ Syne, We'll

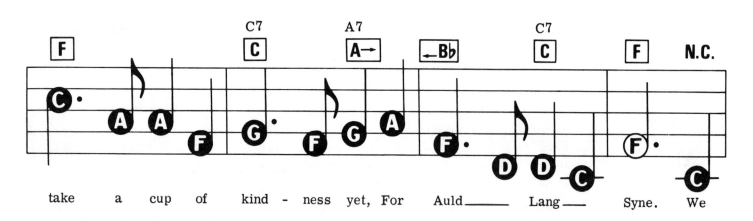

take a cup of kind - ness yet, For Auld_____ Lang_____ Syne. We

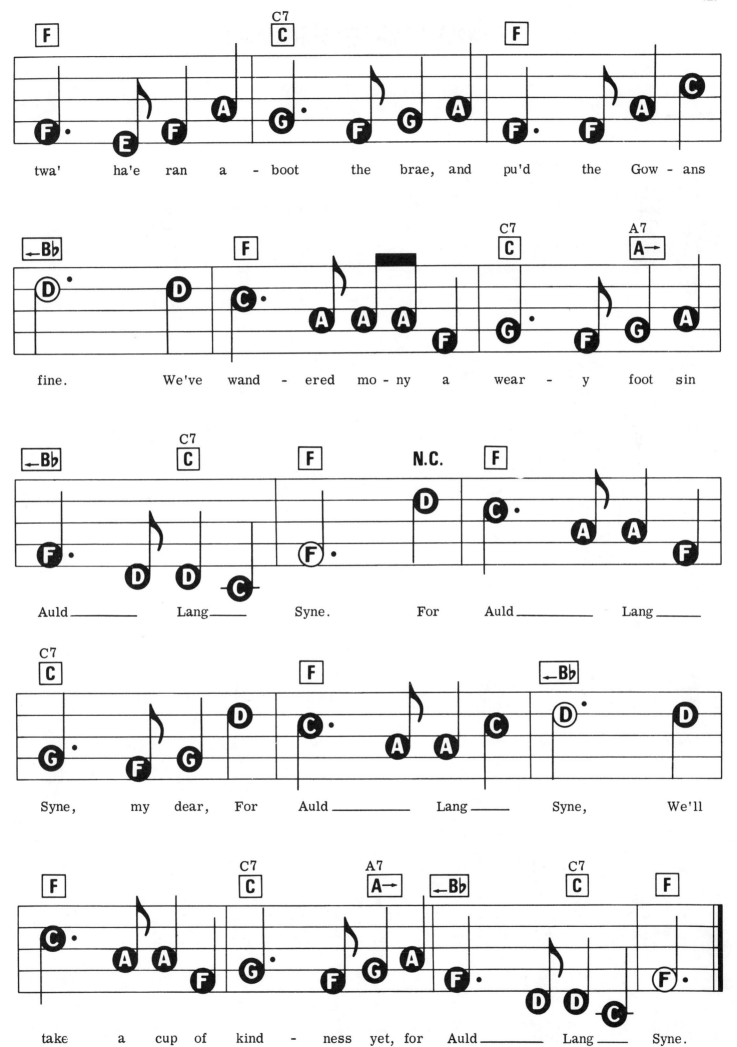

Away In A Manger

Registration 4

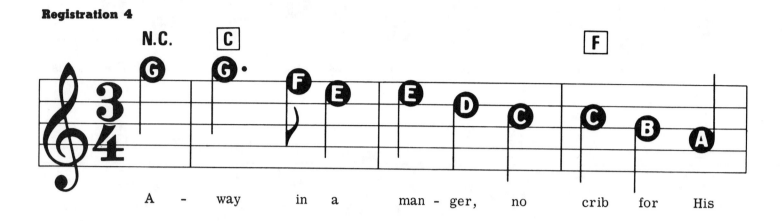

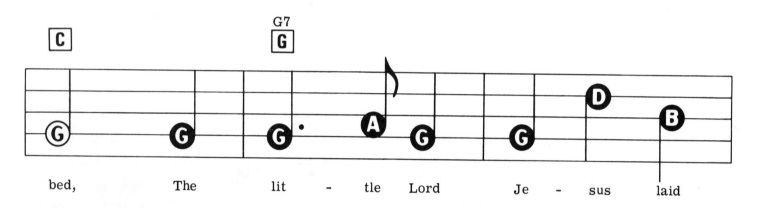

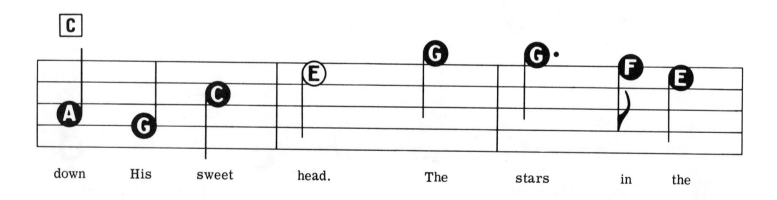

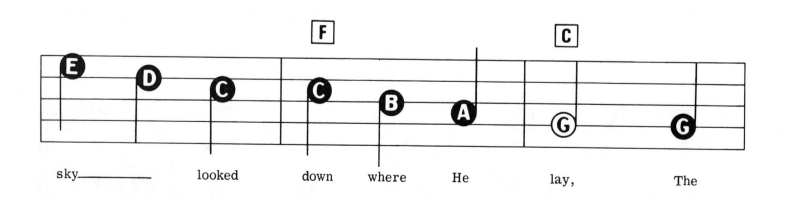

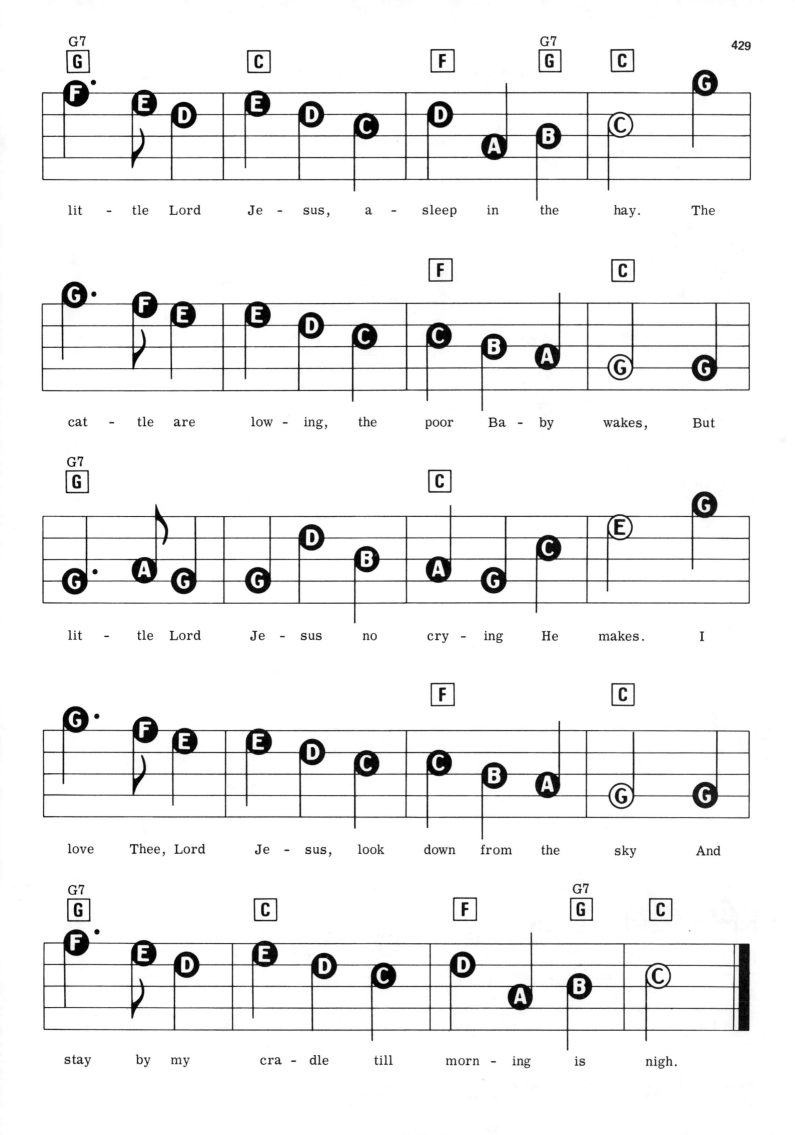

Bring A Torch, Jeannette, Isabella

Registration 3

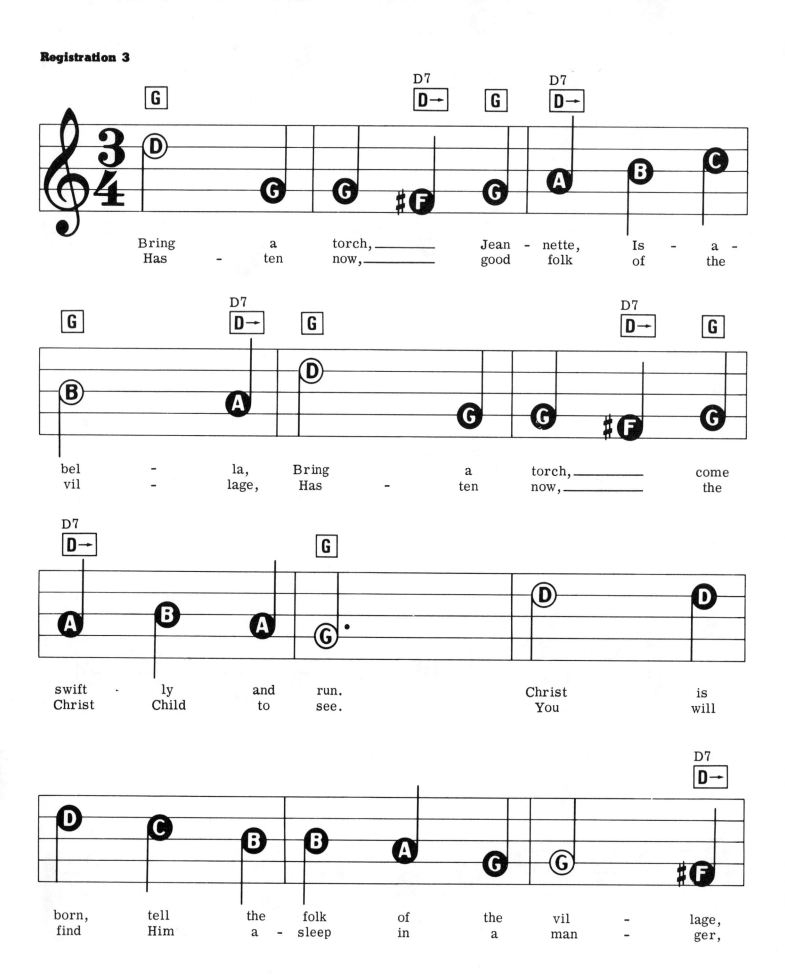

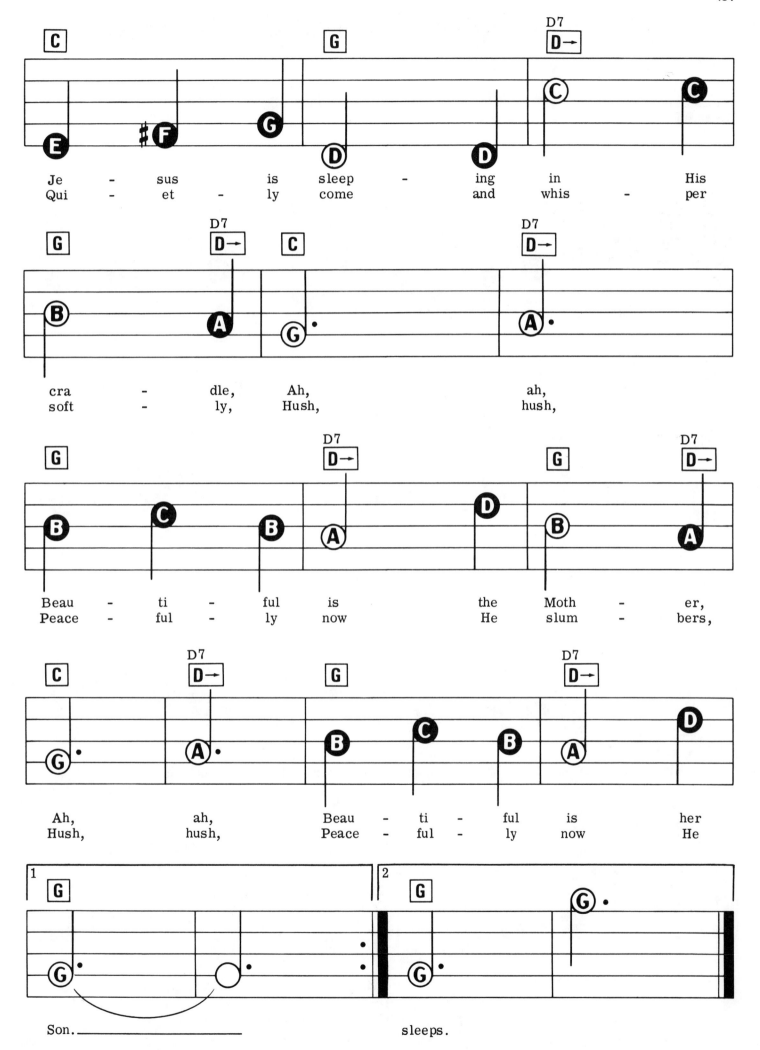

Deck The Halls

Registration 5

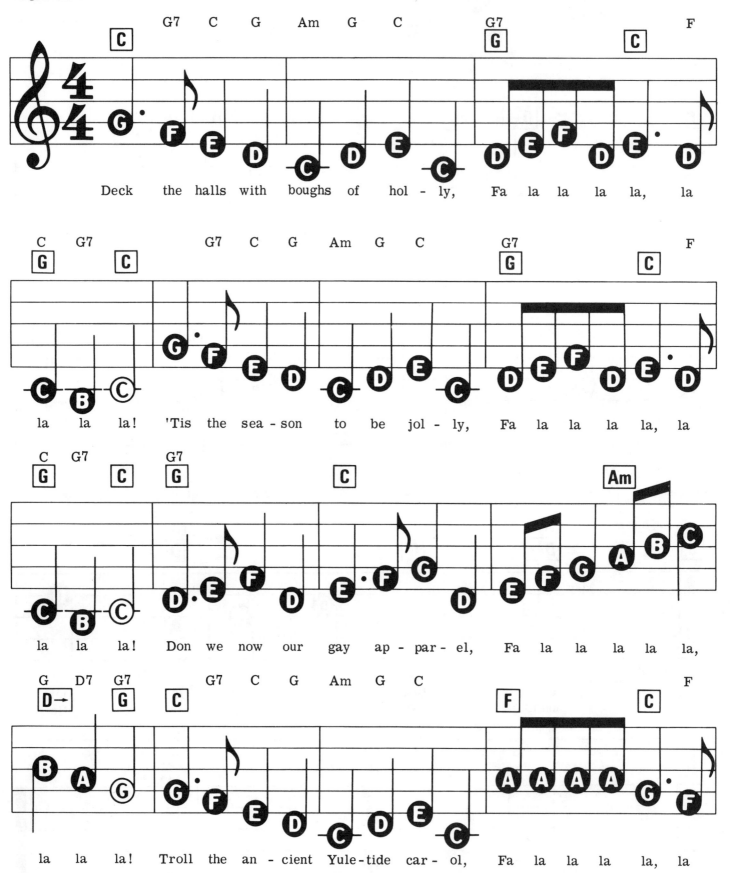

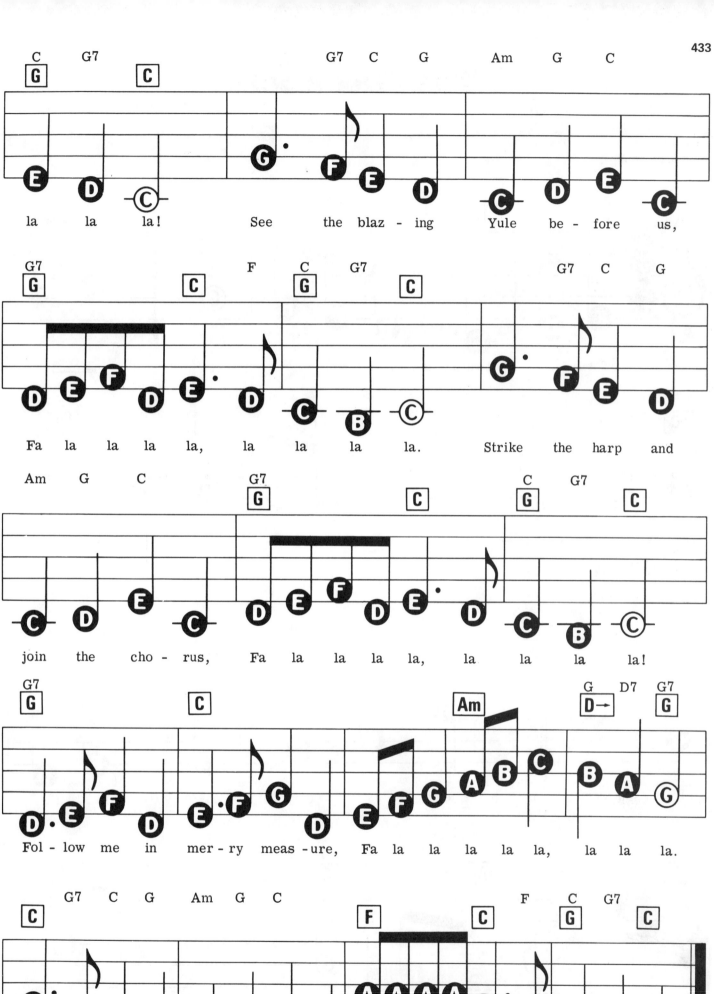

la la la! See the blaz - ing Yule be - fore us,

Fa la la la la, la la la la. Strike the harp and

join the cho - rus, Fa la la la la, la la la la!

Fol - low me in mer - ry meas - ure, Fa la la la la la, la la la.

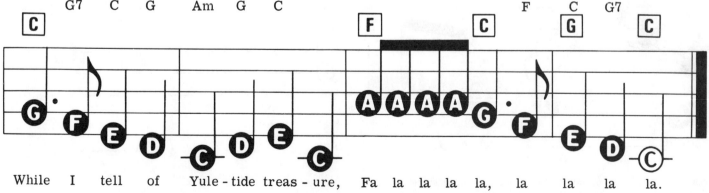

While I tell of Yule - tide treas - ure, Fa la la la la, la la la la.

The First Noel

Registration 9

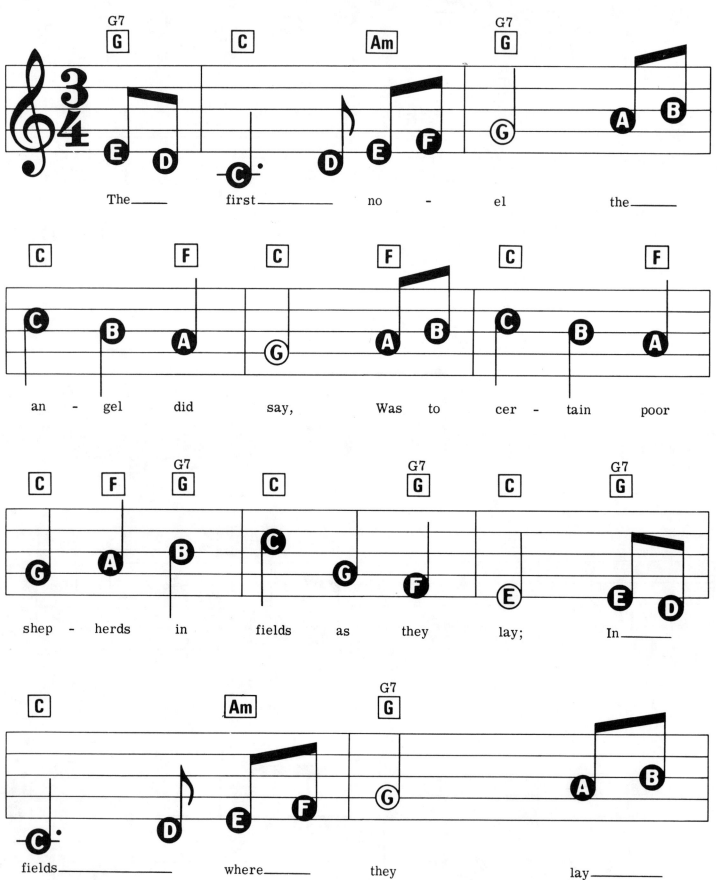

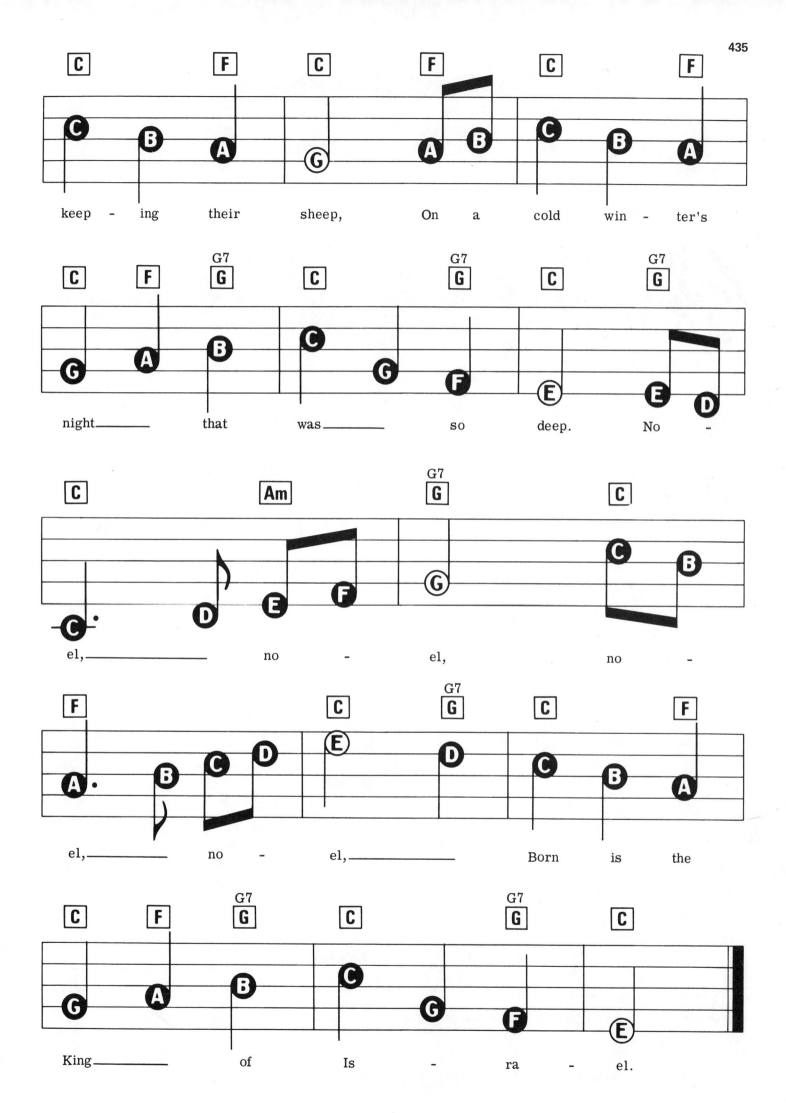

The Friendly Beasts

Registration 3

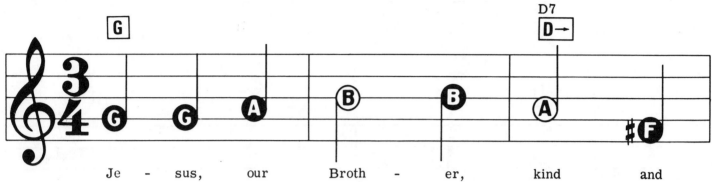

Je - sus,   our   Broth - er,   kind   and

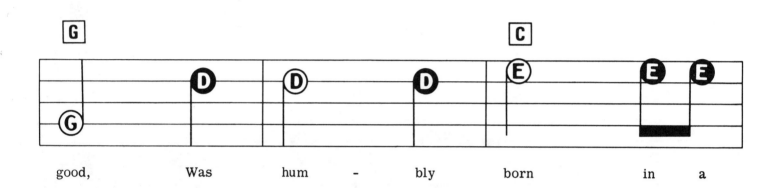

good,   Was   hum - bly   born   in   a

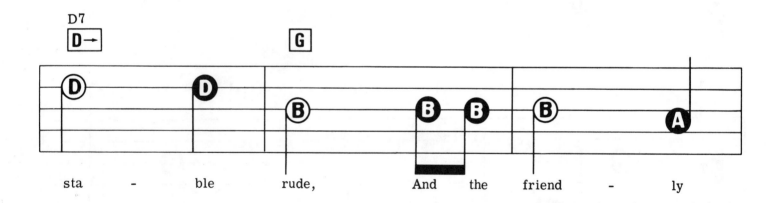

sta - ble   rude,   And   the   friend - ly

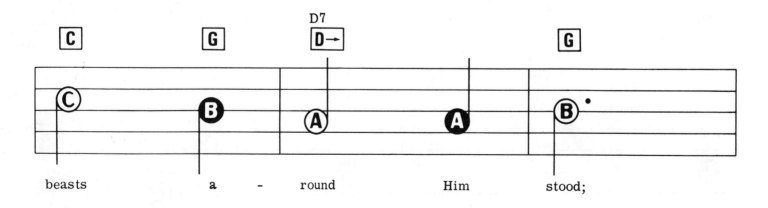

beasts   a - round   Him   stood;

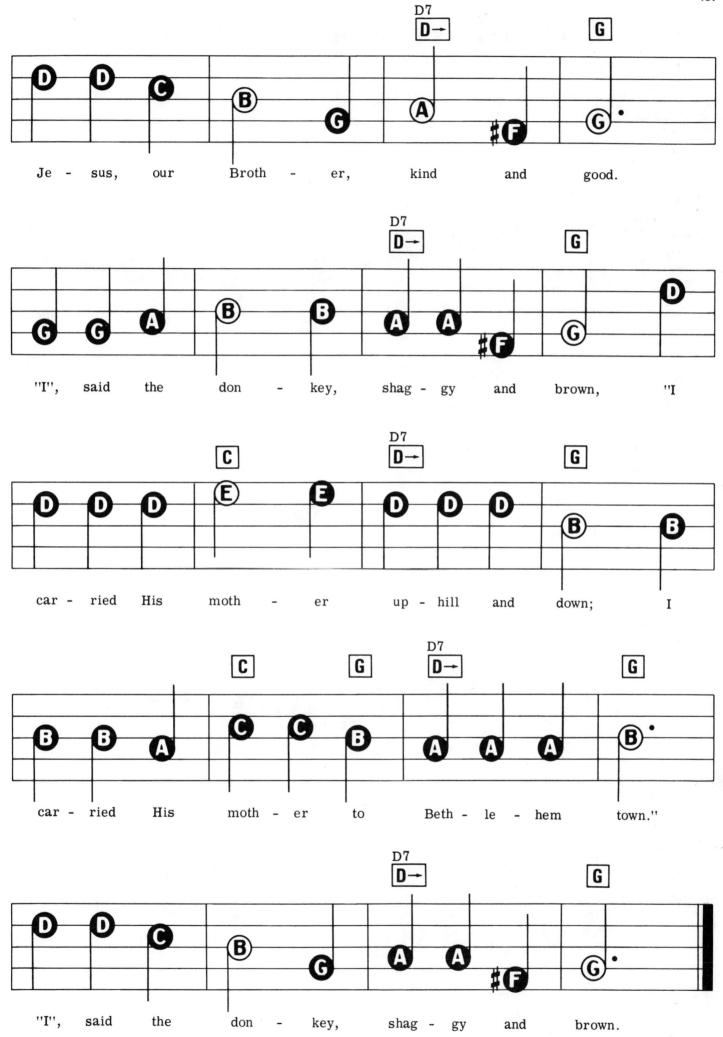

God Rest Ye, Merry Gentlemen

Registration 6

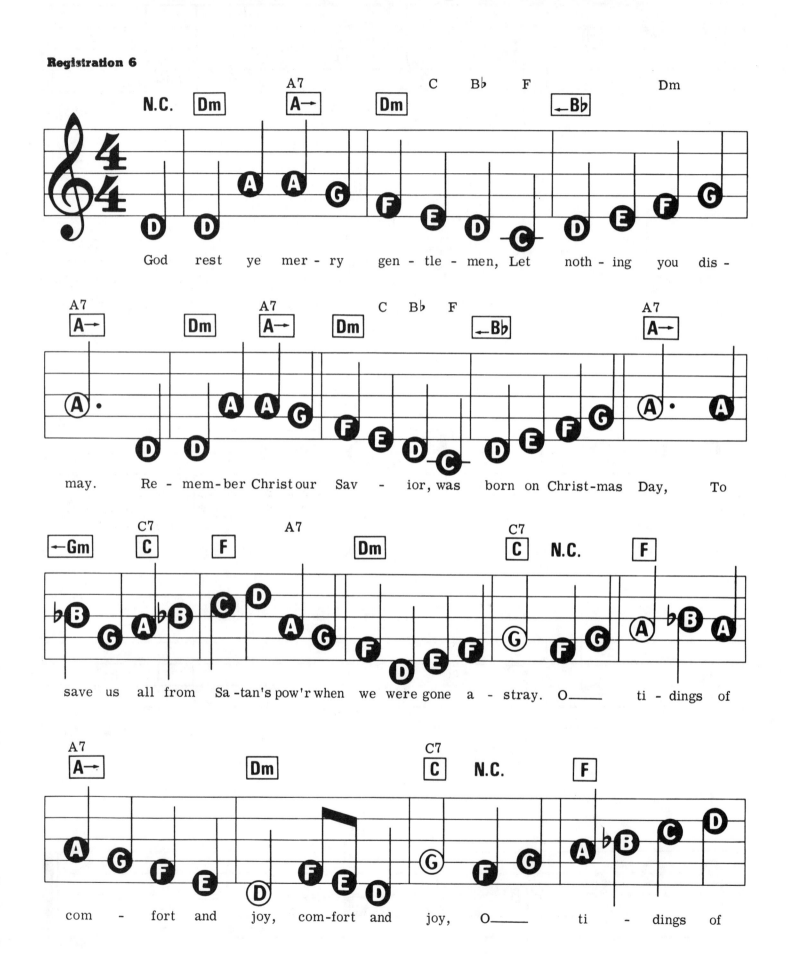

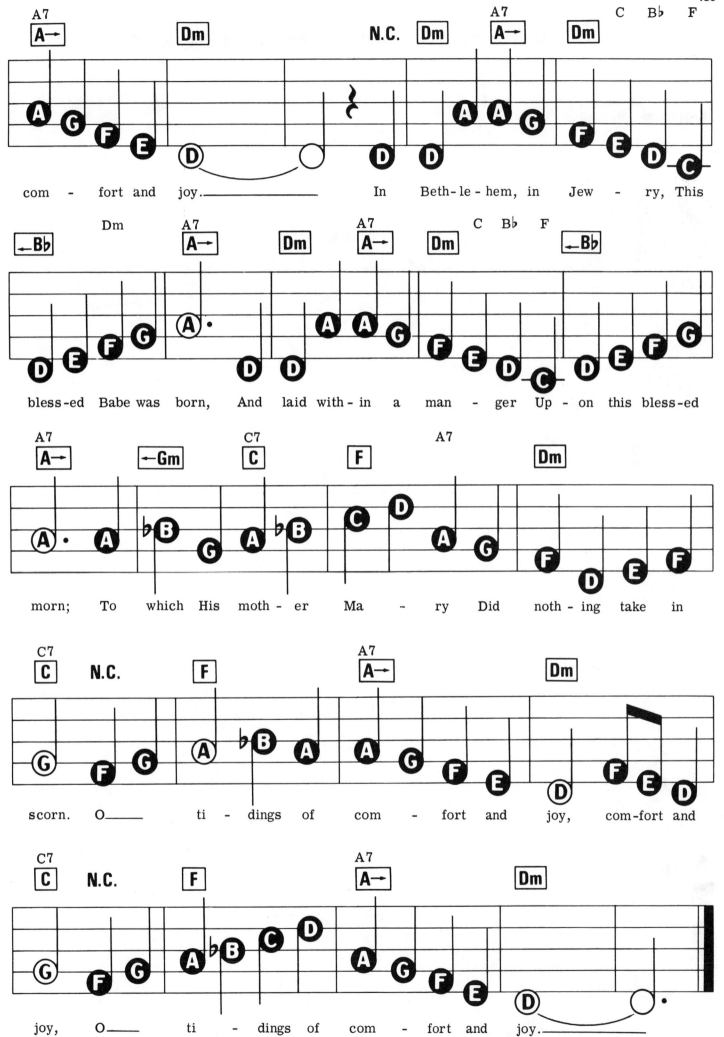

Good Christian Men Rejoice

Registration 6

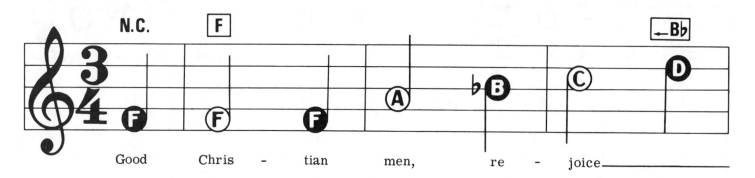

Good   Chris - tian   men,   re - joice

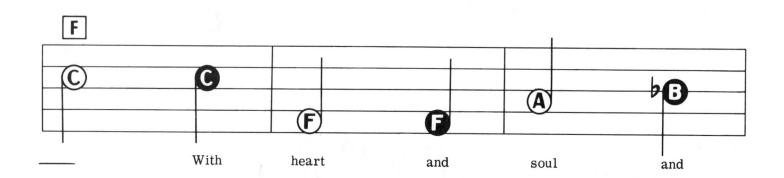

With   heart   and   soul   and

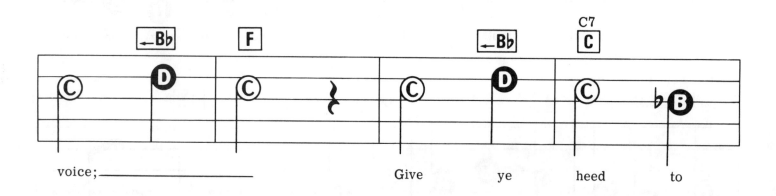

voice;   Give   ye   heed   to

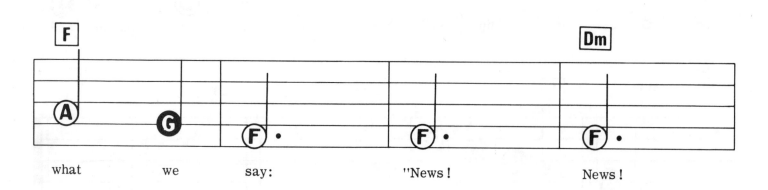

what   we   say: "News!   News!

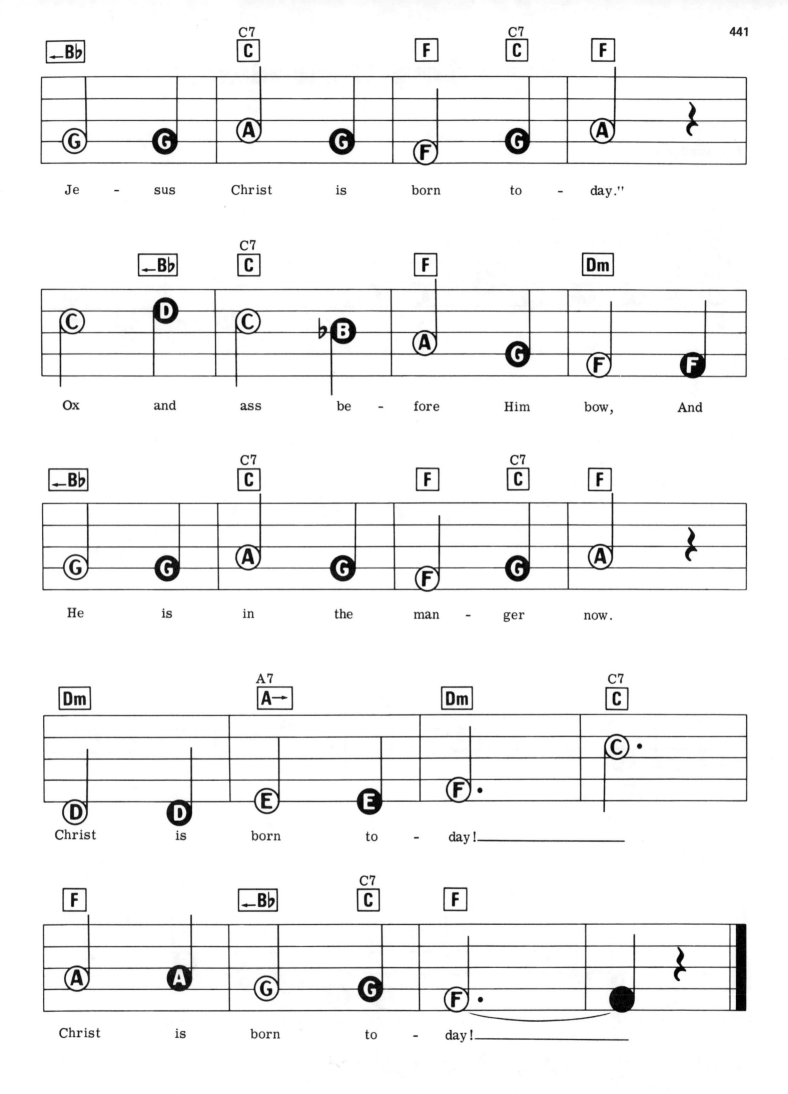

Good King Wenceslas

Registration 4

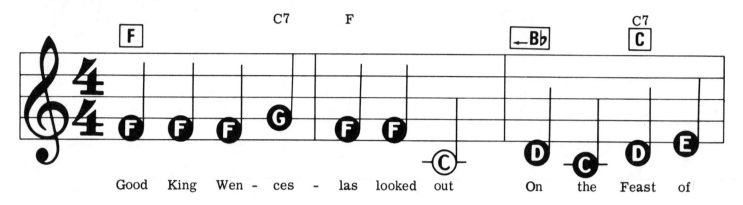

Good King Wen - ces - las looked out   On the Feast of

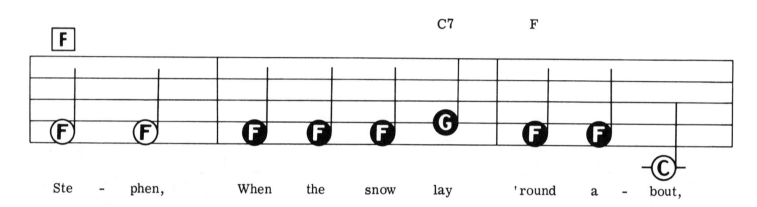

Ste - phen,   When the snow lay 'round a - bout,

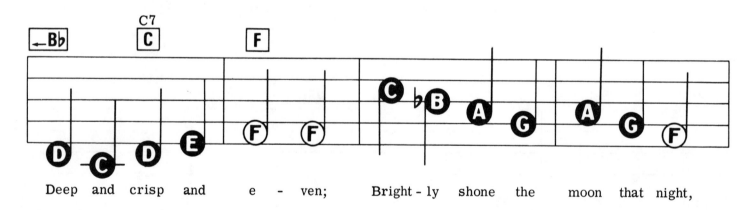

Deep and crisp and e - ven;   Bright - ly shone the moon that night,

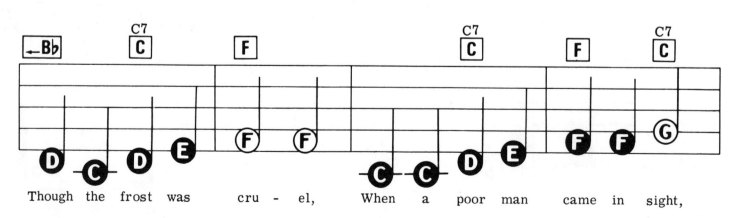

Though the frost was cru - el,   When a poor man came in sight,

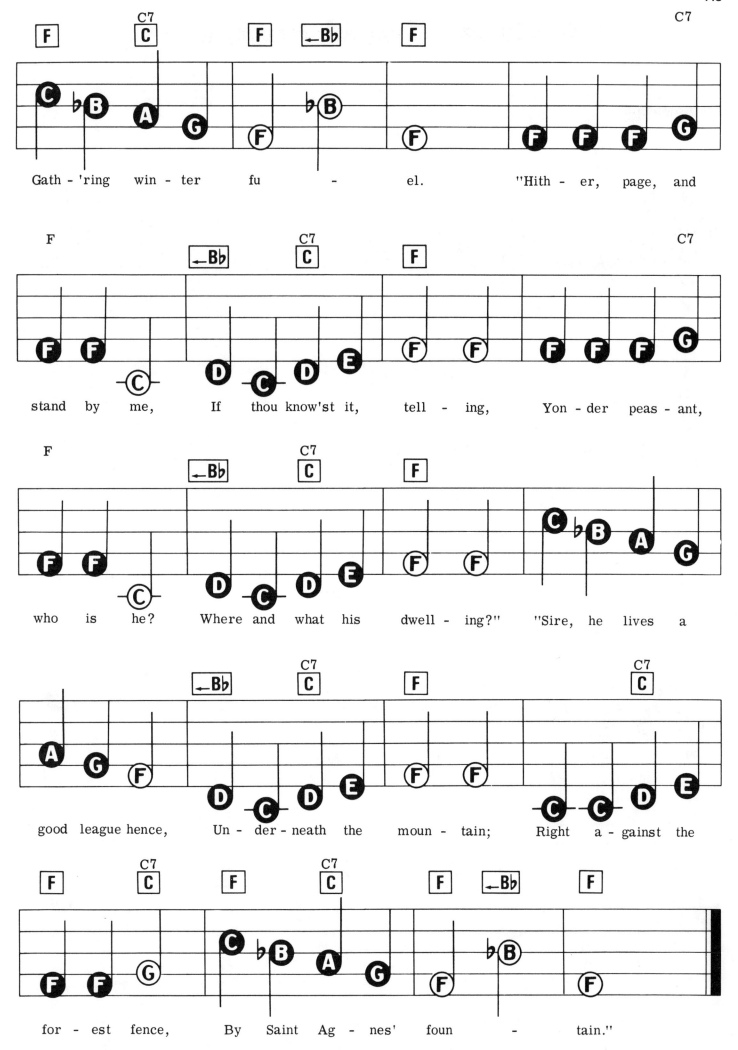

443

Hark! The Herald Angels Sing

Registration 5

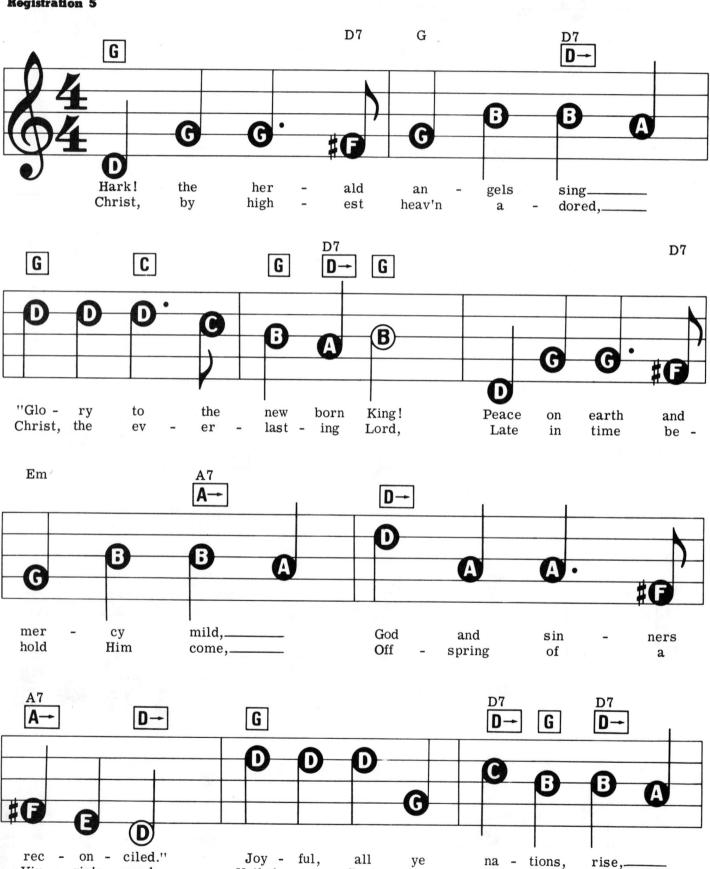

Join   the   tri - umph   of   the   skies.____
Hail   the in - car - nate   De - i - ty,____

With   an - gel - ic   host   pro - claim,
Pleased   as   Man   with   man   to   dwell,

"Christ   is____   born   in   Beth - le - hem."
Je - sus,____   our   Im - man - u - el!

Hark!   the   her - ald   an - gels   sing,
Hark!   the   her - ald   an - gels   sing,

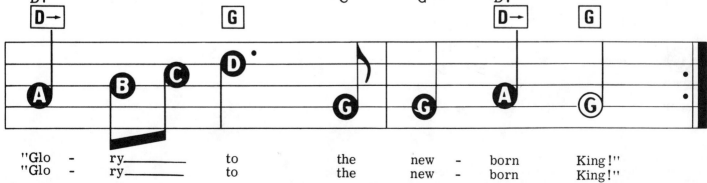

"Glo - ry____   to   the   new - born   King!"
"Glo - ry____   to   the   new - born   King!"

It Came Upon The Midnight Clear

Registration 1

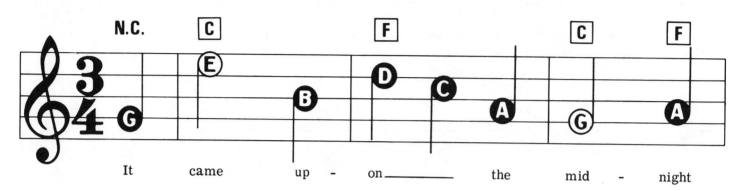

It   came   up - on _____ the   mid - night

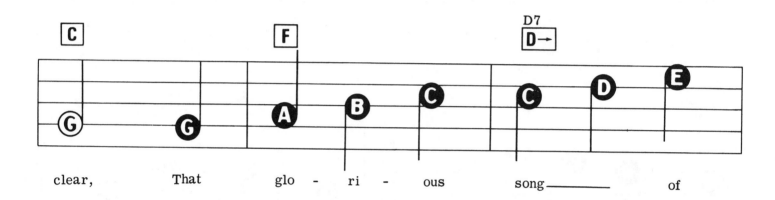

clear,   That   glo - ri - ous   song _____ of

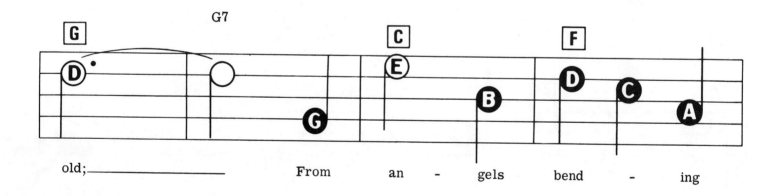

old; _____ From   an - gels   bend - ing

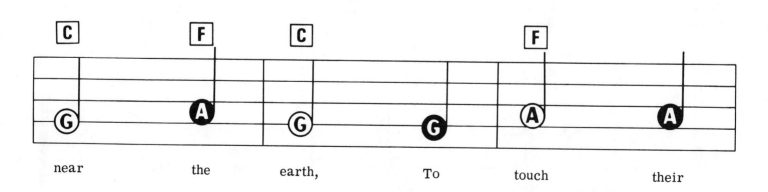

near   the   earth,   To   touch   their

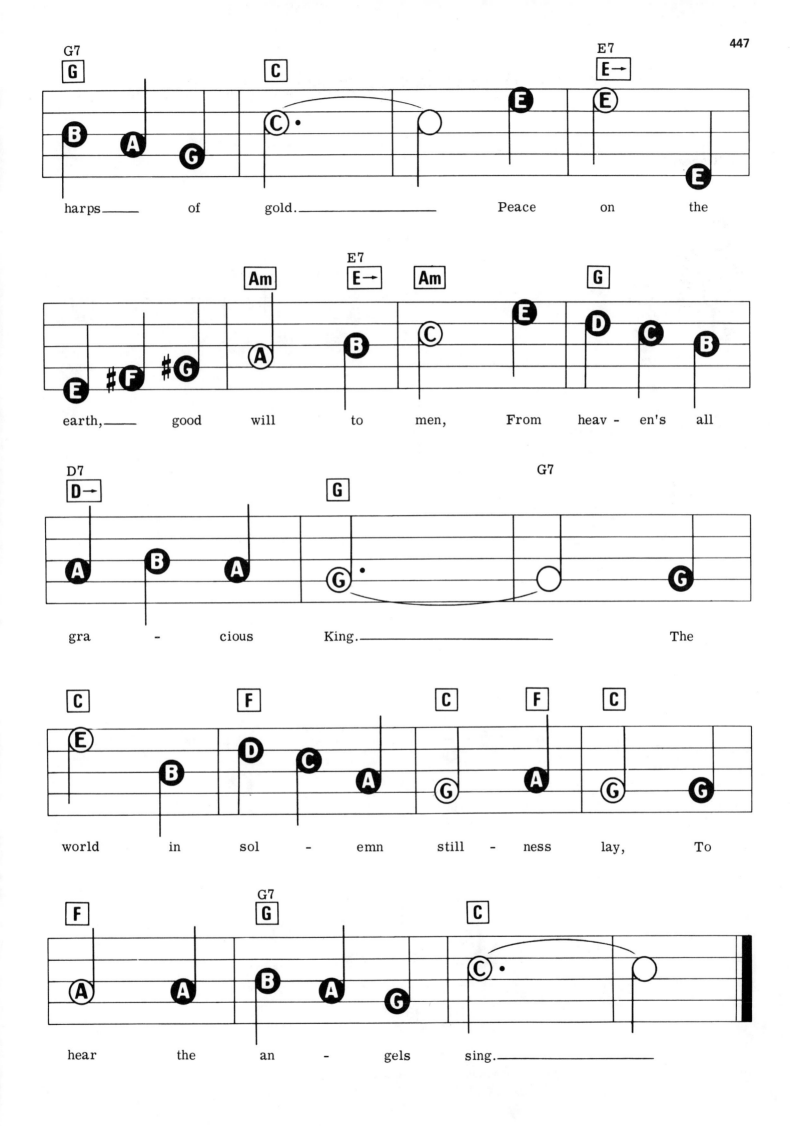

Jingle Bells

Registration 5

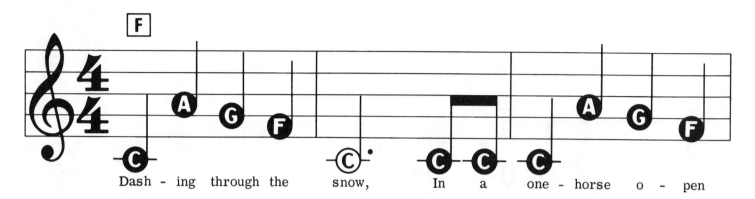

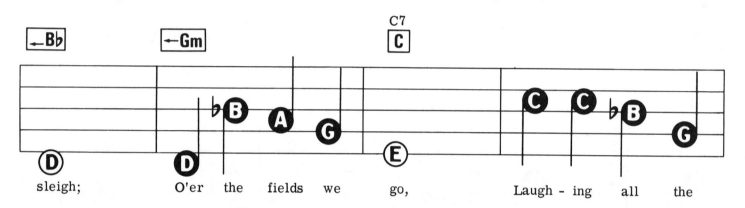

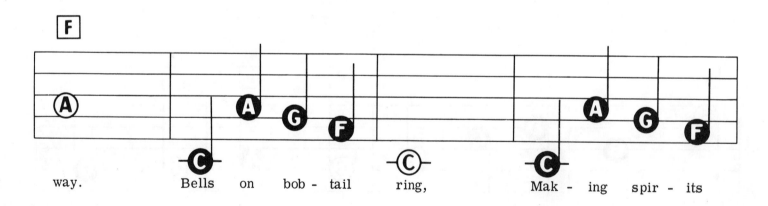

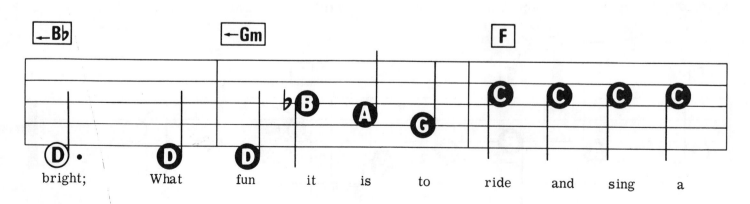

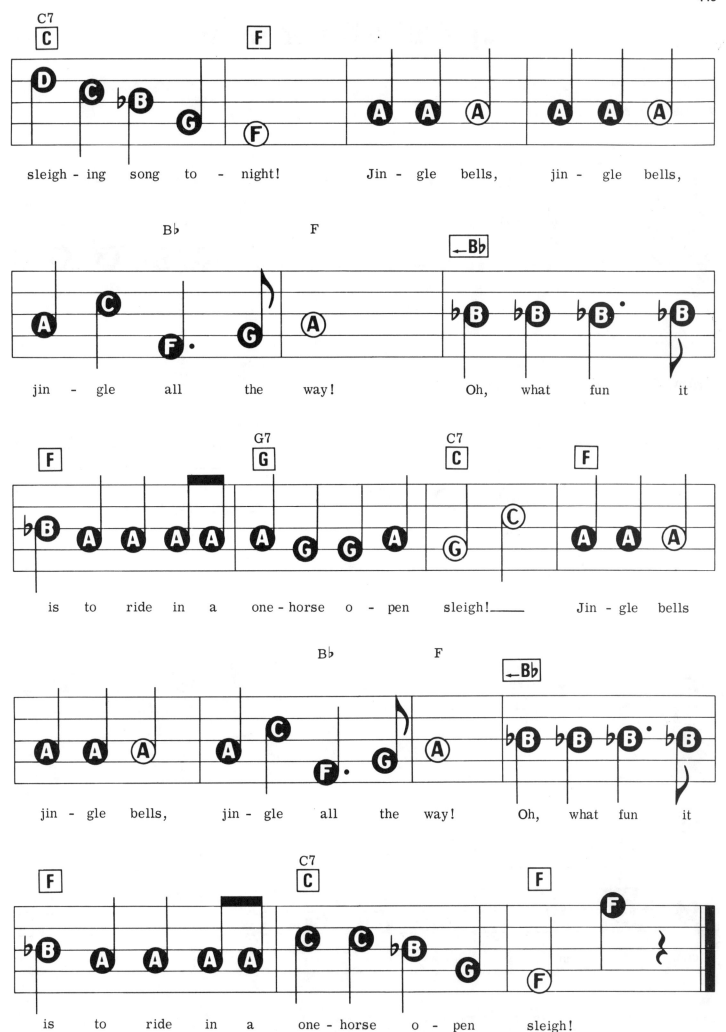

Jolly Old St. Nicholas

Registration 2

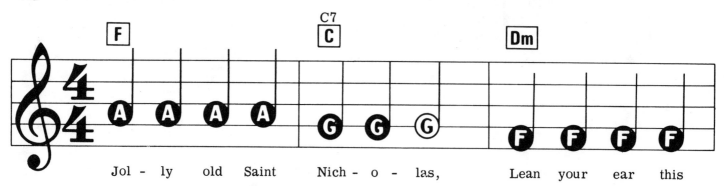

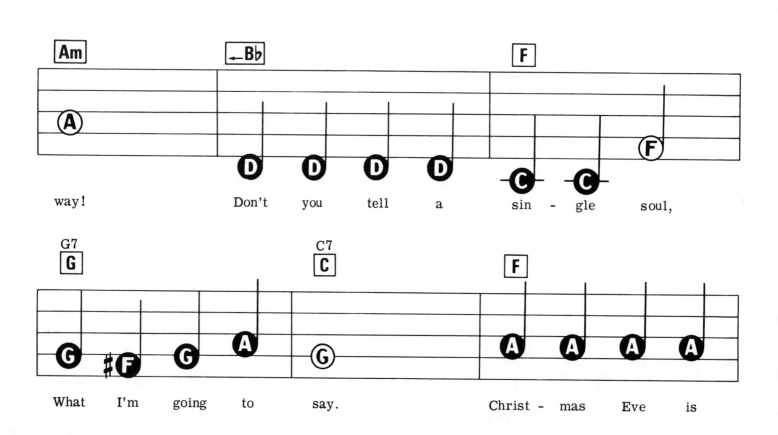

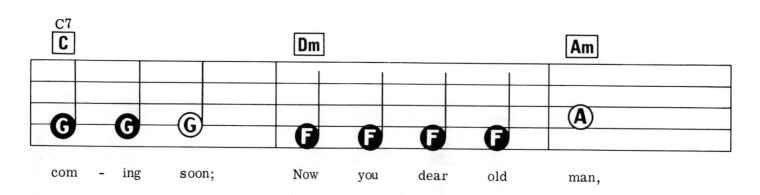

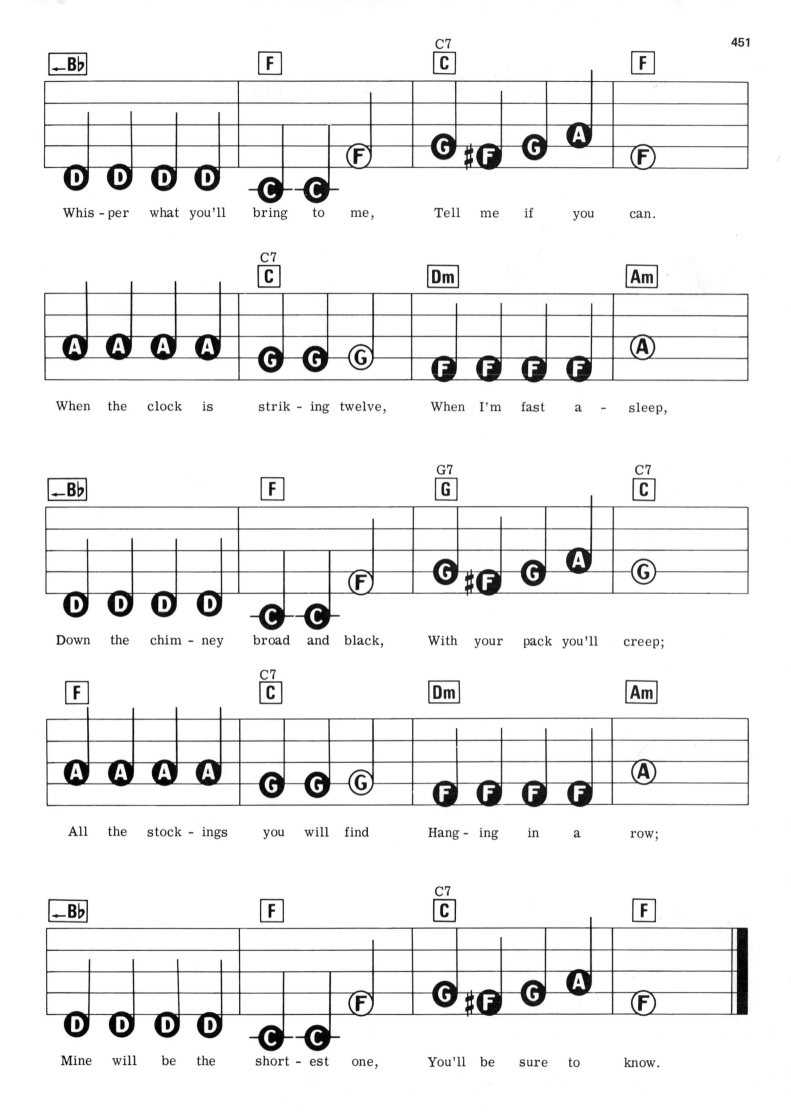

451

Joy To The World

Registration 2

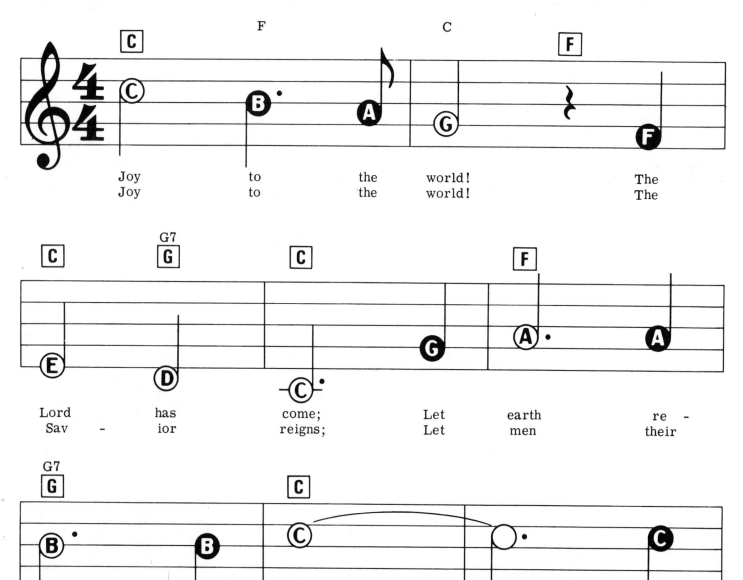

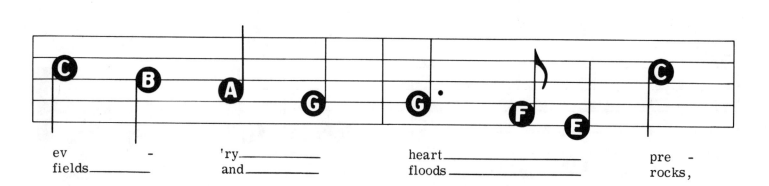

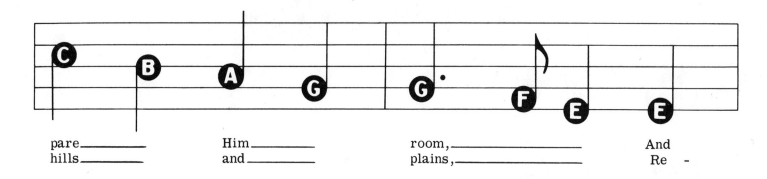

pare_____ Him_____ room,_____ And
hills_____ and_____ plains,_____ Re -

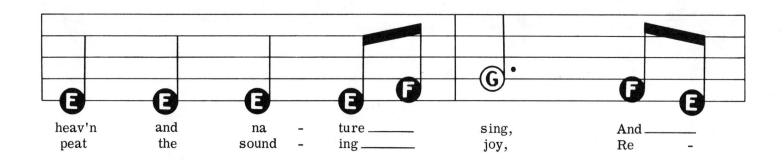

heav'n and na - ture____ sing, And____
peat and the sound - ing____ joy, Re -

G7

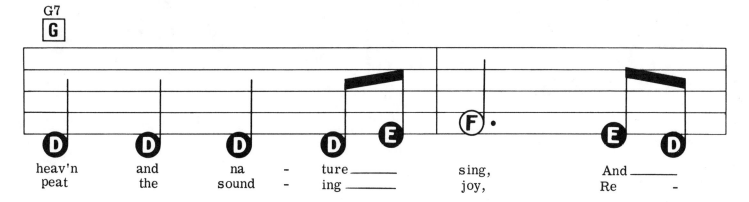

heav'n and na - ture____ sing, And____
peat and the sound - ing____ joy, Re -

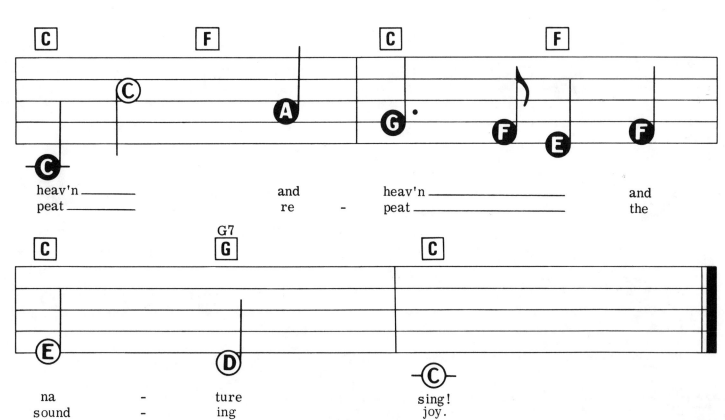

heav'n_____ and heav'n_____ and
peat_____ re - peat_____ the

na - ture sing!
sound - ing joy.

O Christmas Tree

Registration 3

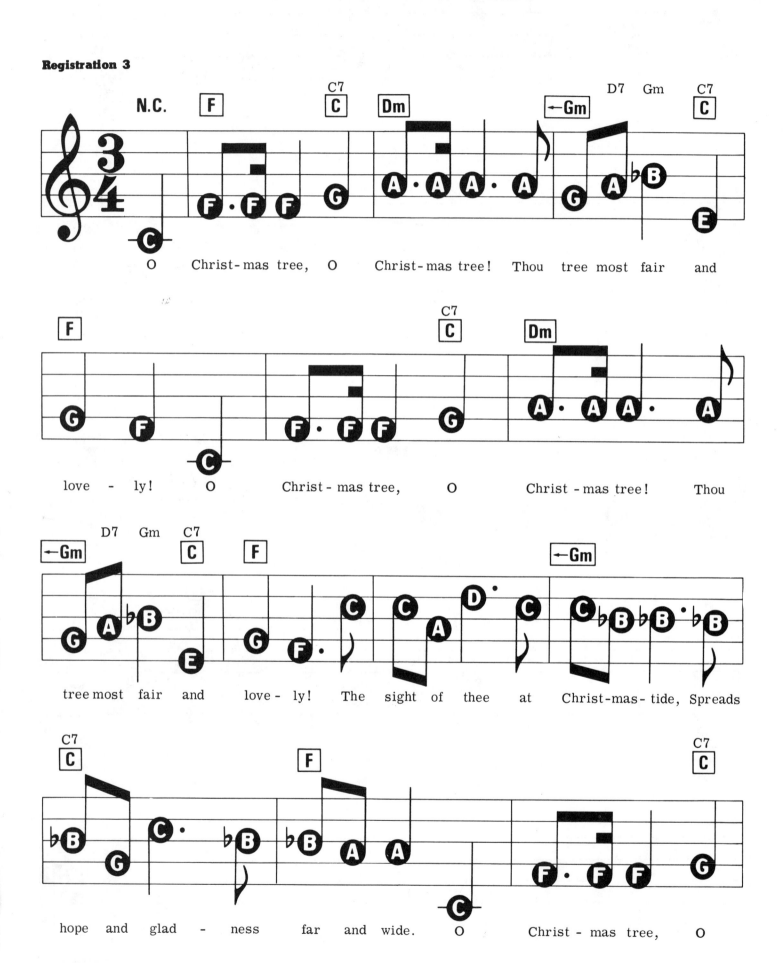

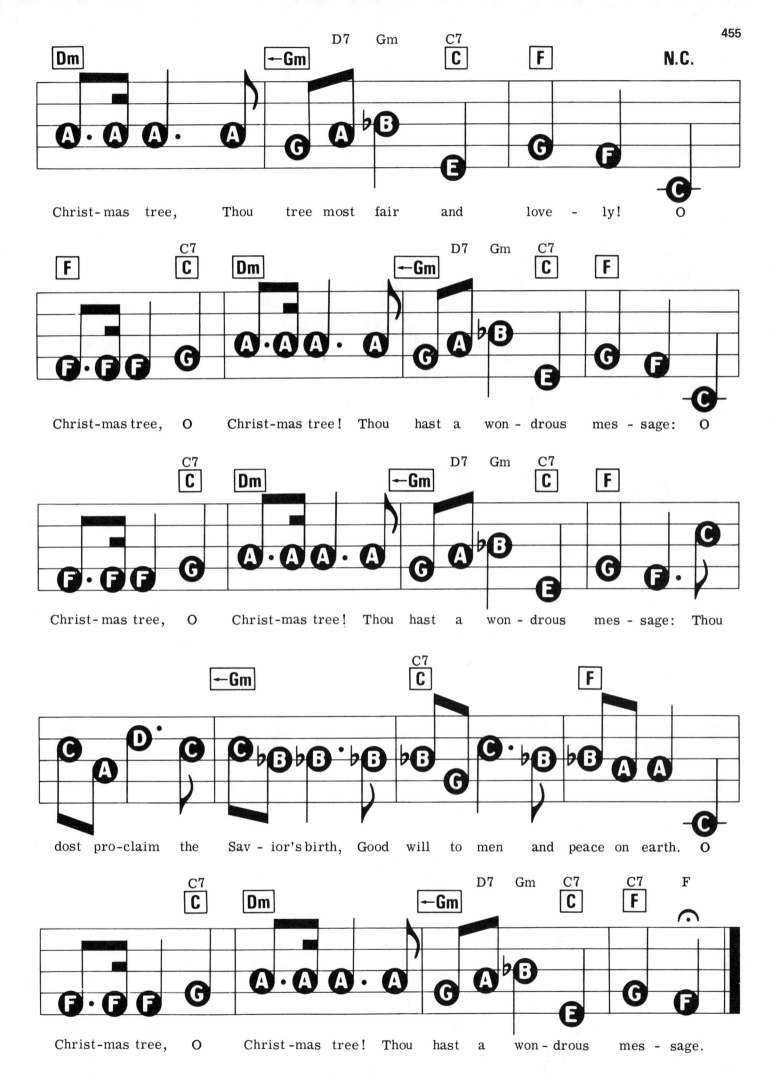

Christ-mas tree, Thou tree most fair and love - ly! O

Christ-mas tree, O Christ-mas tree! Thou hast a won - drous mes - sage: O

Christ-mas tree, O Christ-mas tree! Thou hast a won - drous mes - sage: Thou

dost pro-claim the Sav - ior's birth, Good will to men and peace on earth. O

Christ-mas tree, O Christ-mas tree! Thou hast a won - drous mes - sage.

O Come All Ye Faithful

Registration 6

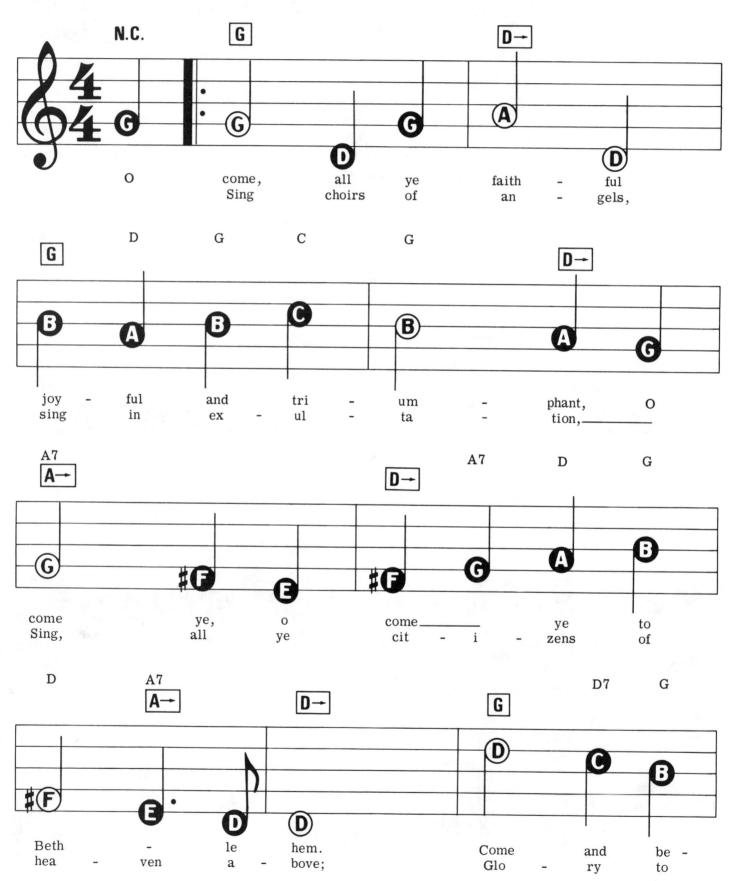

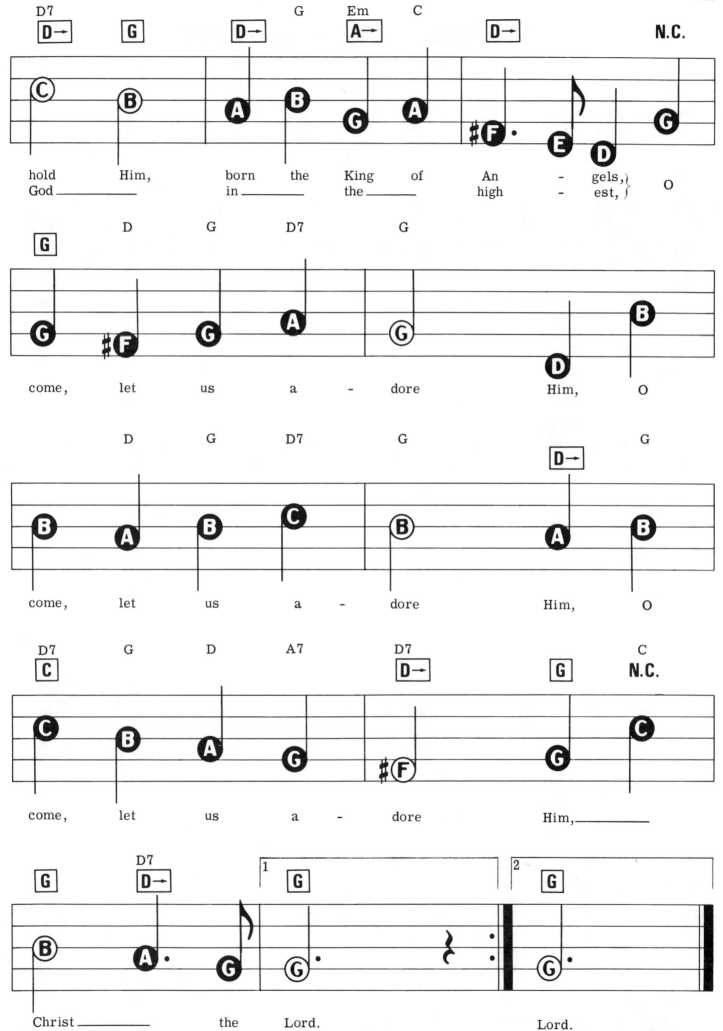

O Come Little Children

Registration 1

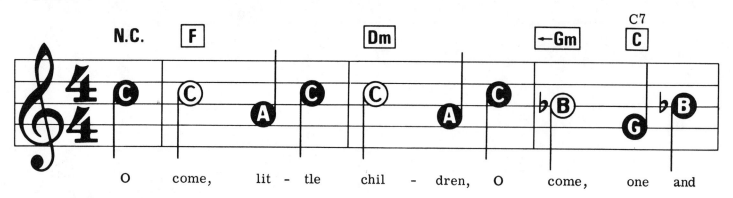

O come, lit - tle chil - dren, O come, one and

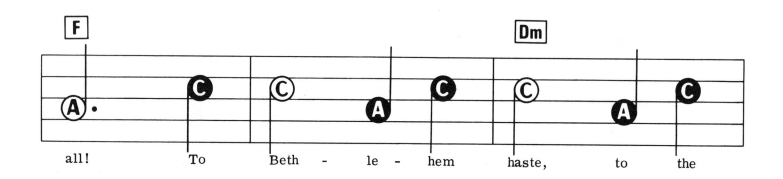

all! To Beth - le - hem haste, to the

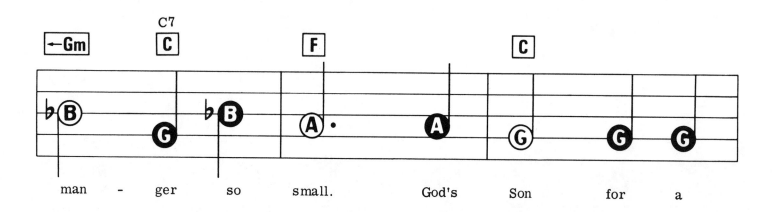

man - ger so small. God's Son for a

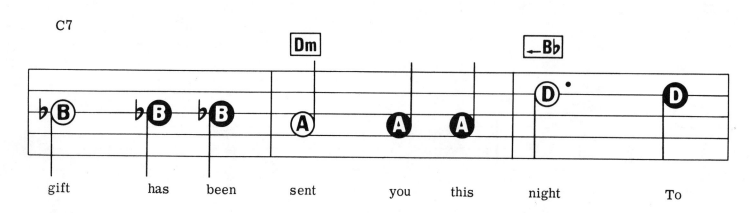

gift has been sent you this night To

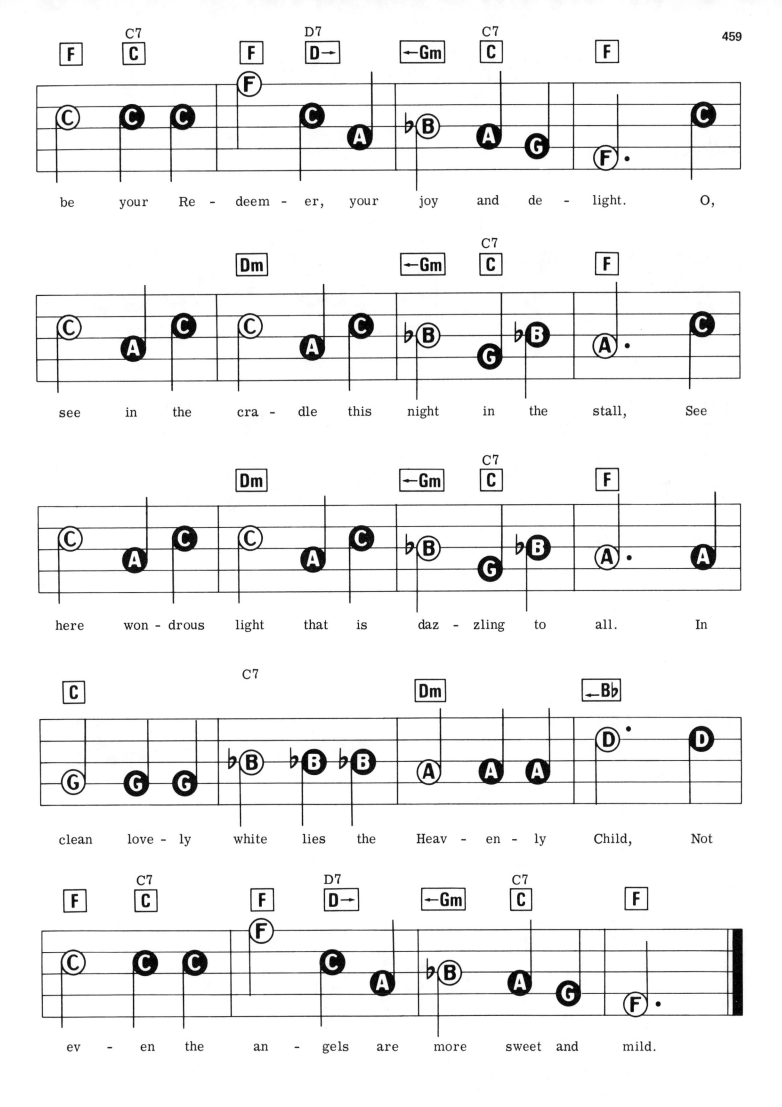

O Holy Night

Registration 6

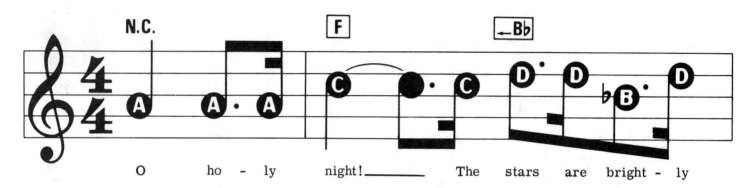

O ho - ly night!_____ The stars are bright - ly

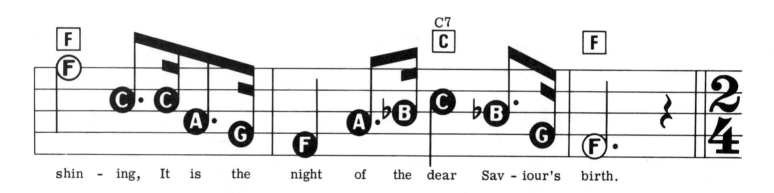

shin - ing, It is the night of the dear Sav - iour's birth.

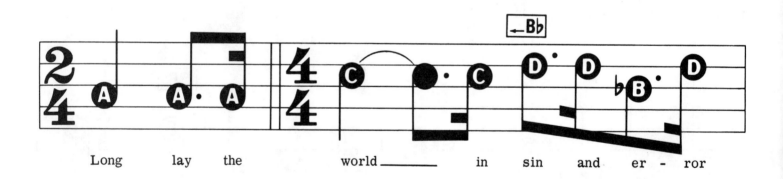

Long lay the world_____ in sin and er - ror

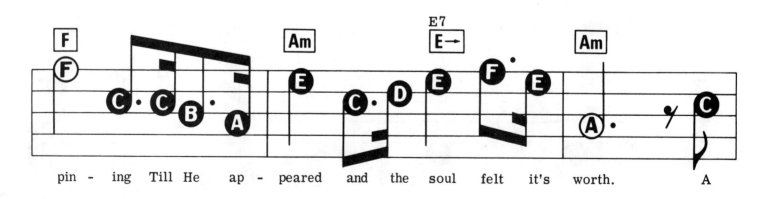

pin - ing Till He ap - peared and the soul felt it's worth.　　A

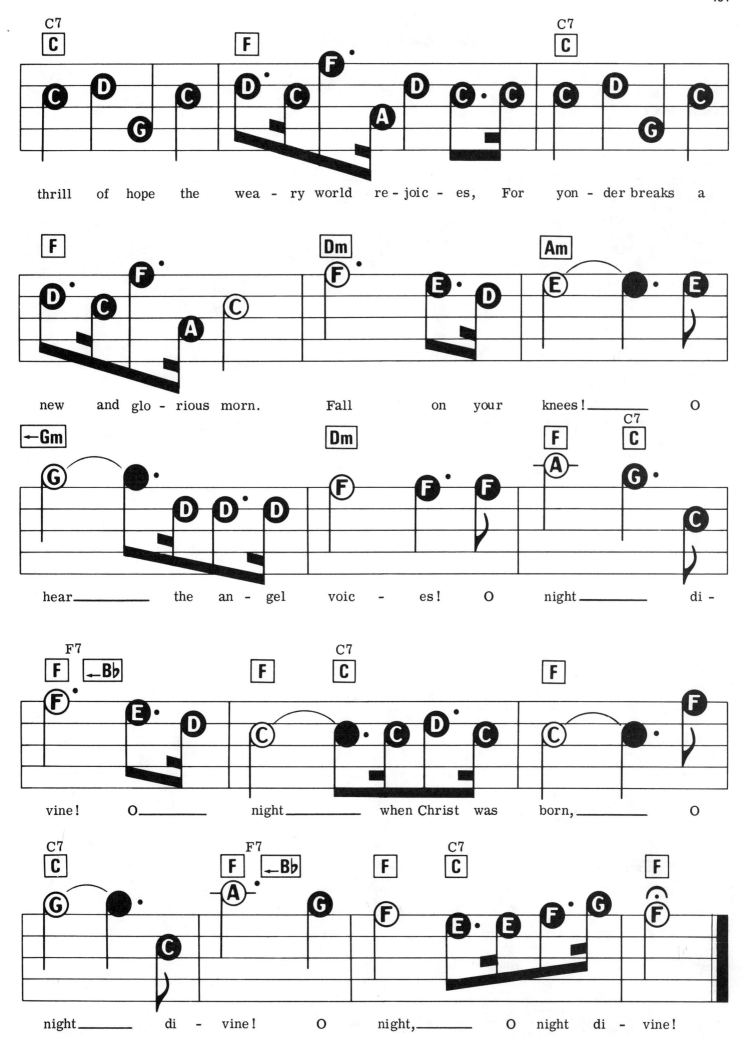

Silent Night

Registration 1

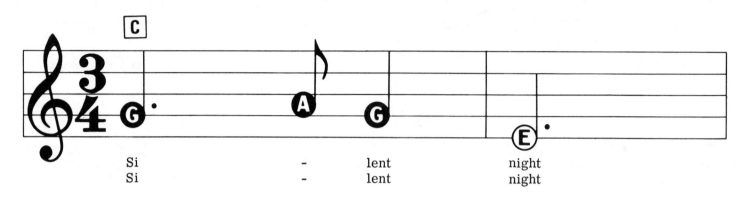

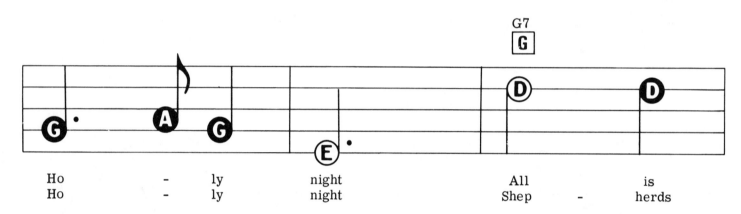

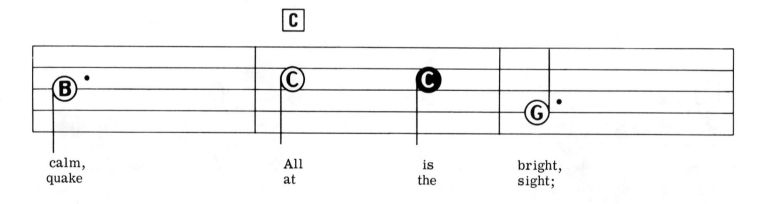

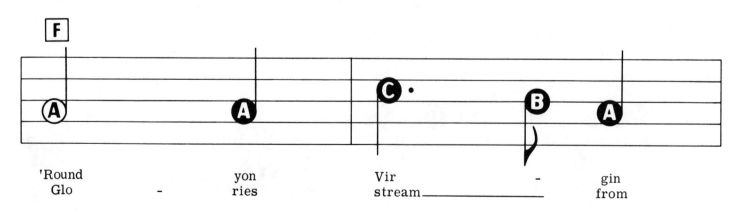

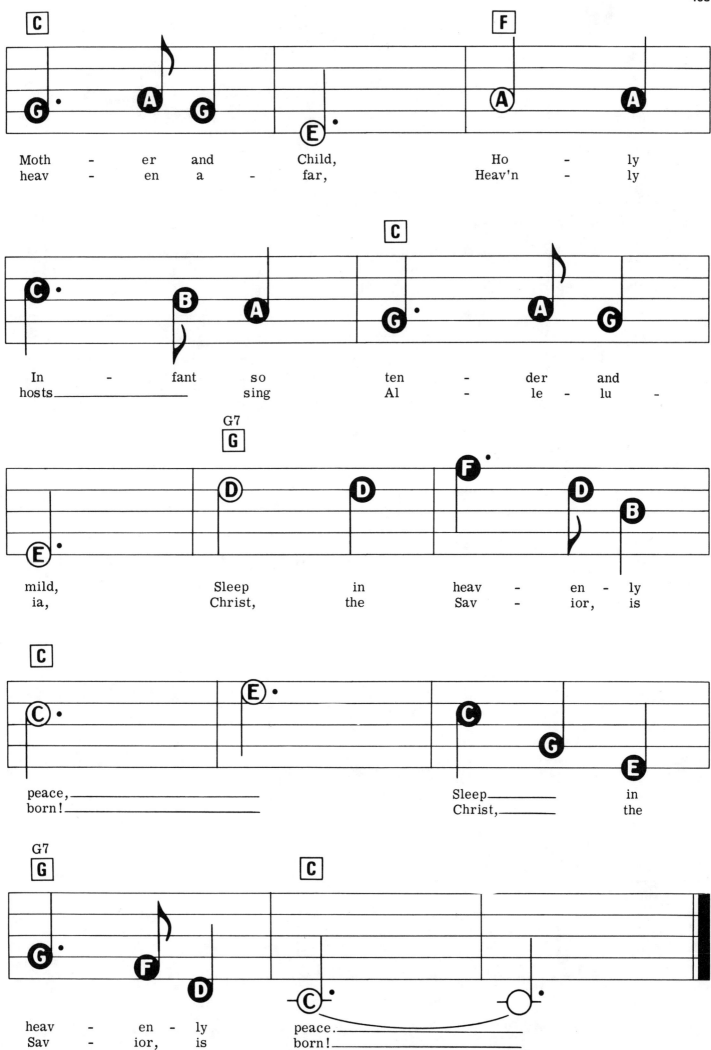

The Twelve Days of Christmas

Registration 5

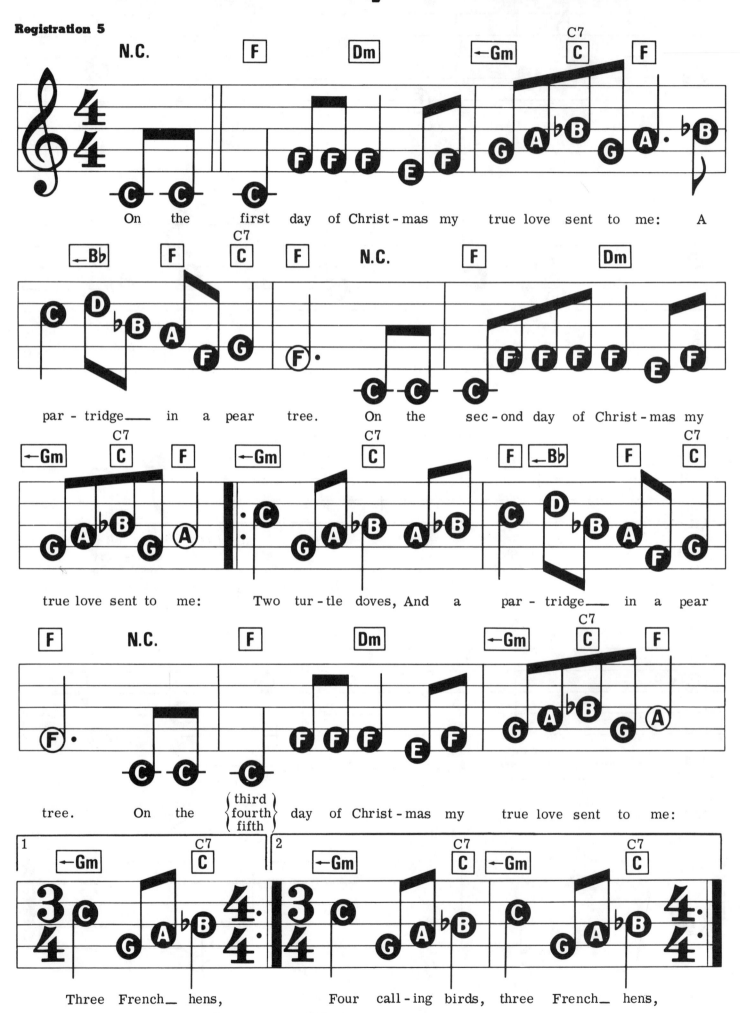

On the first day of Christ-mas my true love sent to me: A par-tridge___ in a pear tree. On the sec-ond day of Christ-mas my true love sent to me: Two tur-tle doves, And a par-tridge___ in a pear tree. On the { third fourth fifth } day of Christ-mas my true love sent to me:

Three French_ hens,

Four call-ing birds, three French_ hens,

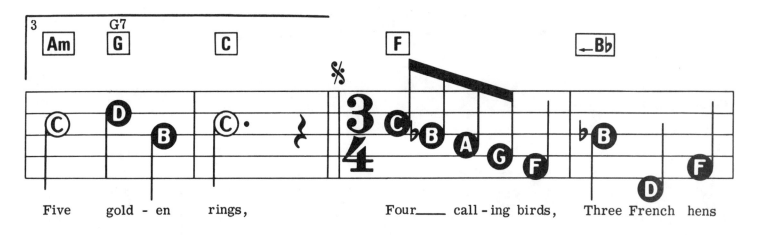

Five gold - en rings, Four___ call - ing birds, Three French hens

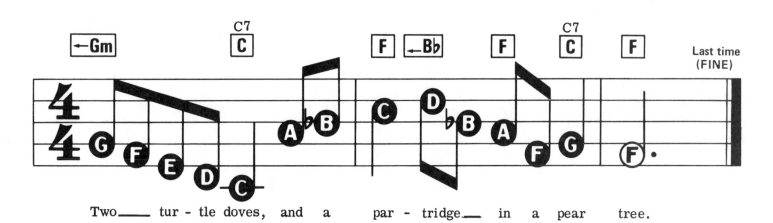

Two___ tur - tle doves, and a par - tridge___ in a pear tree.

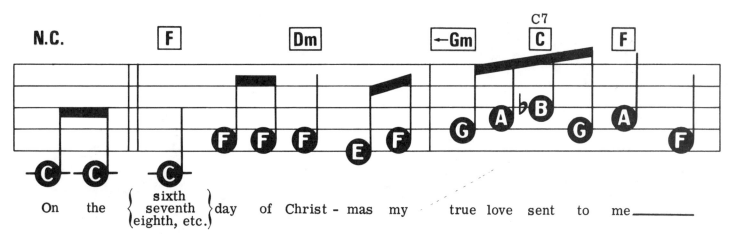

On the {sixth / seventh / eighth, etc.} day of Christ - mas my true love sent to me___

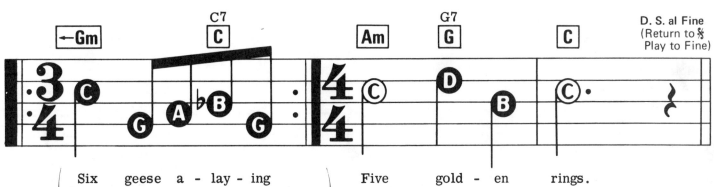

Six	geese	a - lay - ing
Seven	swans	a swim - ming (to 6)
Eight	maids	a milk - ing (to 7)
Nine	la - dies	danc - ing (to 8)
Ten	lords	a leap - ing (to 9)
Eleven	pi - pers	pip - ing (to 10)
Twelve	drum - mers	drum - ming (to 11)

Five gold - en rings.

Up On The Housetop

Registration 5

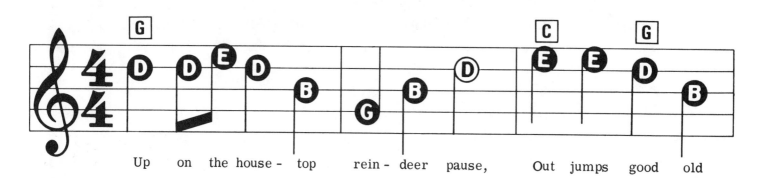

Up on the house-top rein-deer pause, Out jumps good old

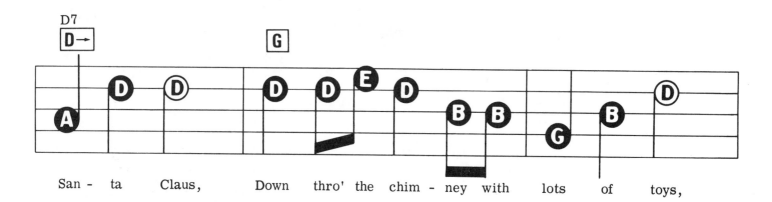

San - ta Claus, Down thro' the chim - ney with lots of toys,

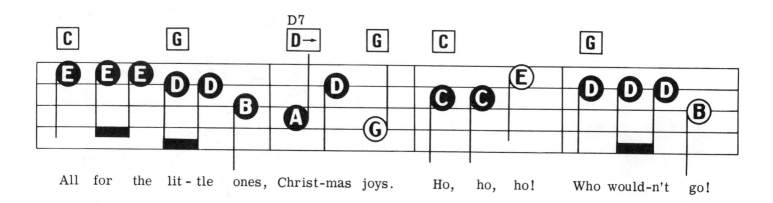

All for the lit - tle ones, Christ-mas joys. Ho, ho, ho! Who would-n't go!

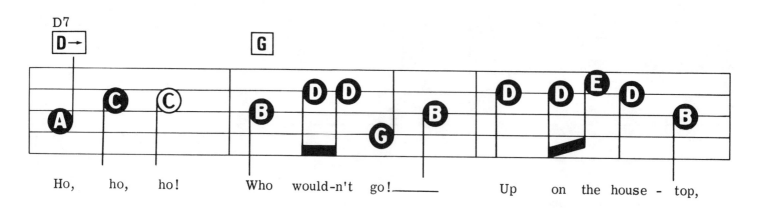

Ho, ho, ho! Who would-n't go!_____ Up on the house - top,

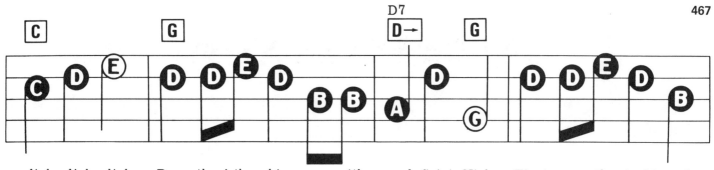

click, click, click, Down thro' the chim-ney with good Saint Nick. First comes the stocking of

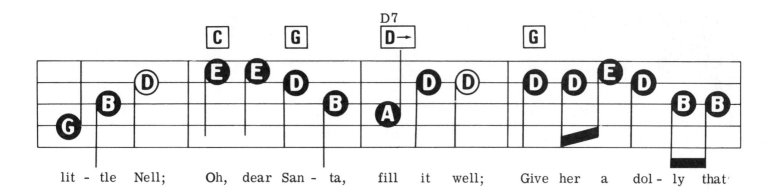

lit - tle Nell; Oh, dear San - ta, fill it well; Give her a dol - ly that

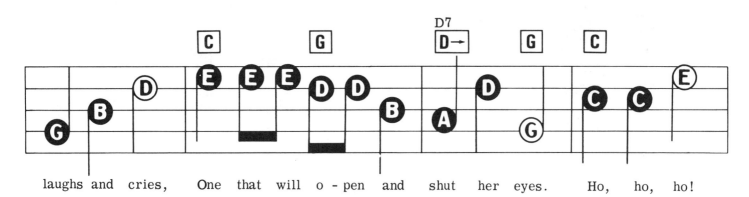

laughs and cries, One that will o - pen and shut her eyes. Ho, ho, ho!

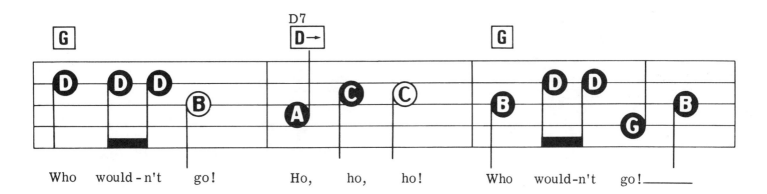

Who would-n't go! Ho, ho, ho! Who would-n't go!

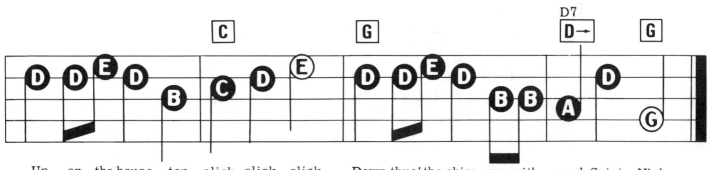

Up on the house - top click, click, click, Down thro' the chim -ney with good Saint Nick.

We Three Kings of Orient Are

Registration 9

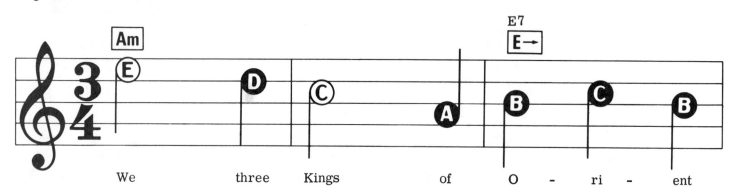

We three Kings of O - ri - ent

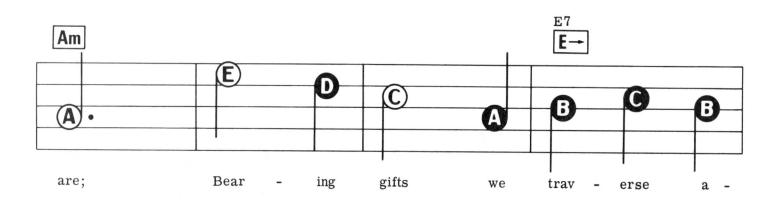

are; Bear - ing gifts we trav - erse a -

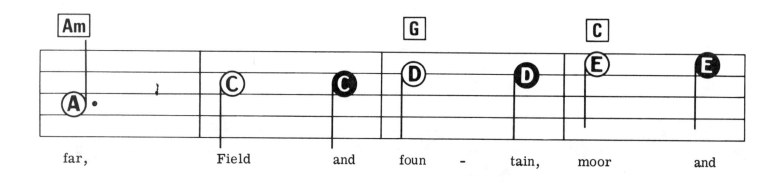

far, Field and foun - tain, moor and

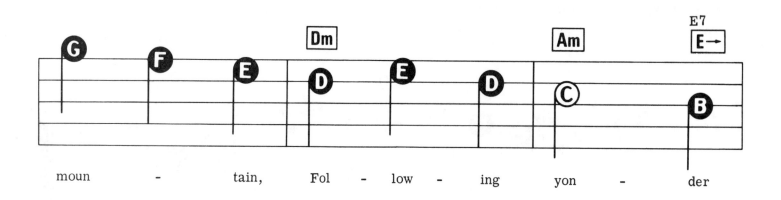

moun - tain, Fol - low - ing yon - der

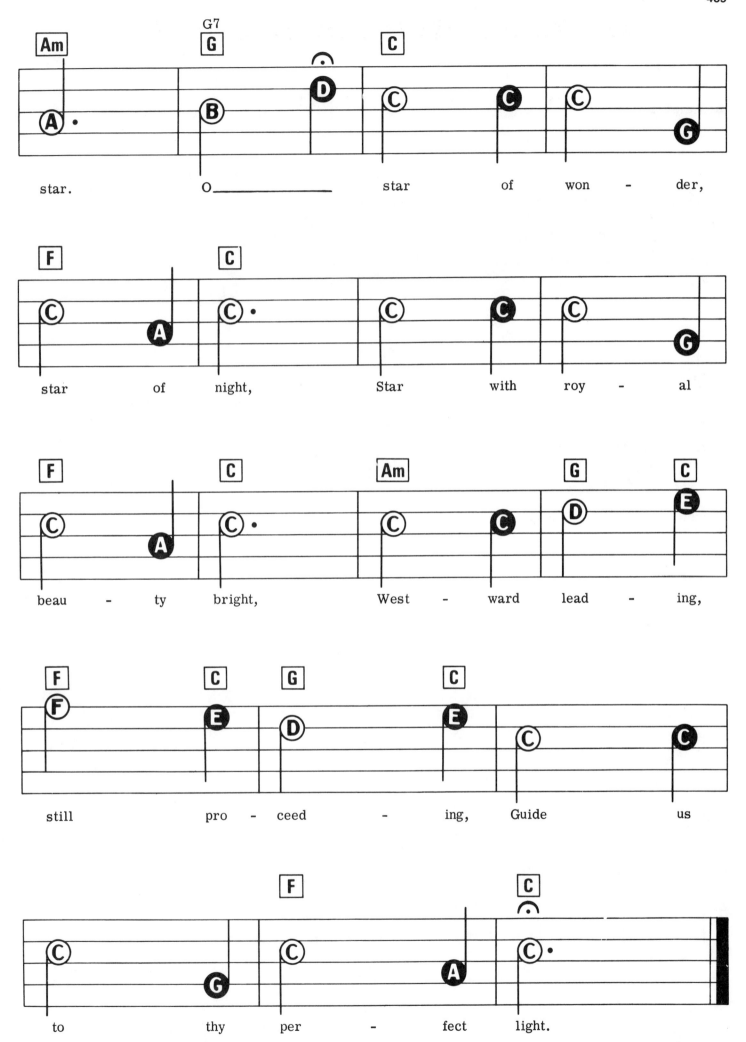

We Wish You A Merry Christmas

Registration 4

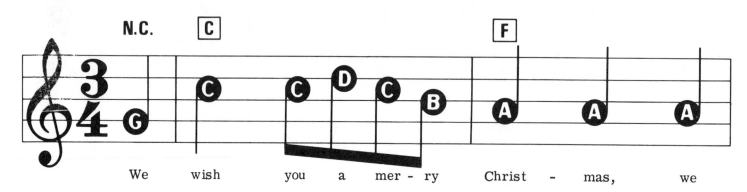

We wish you a mer - ry Christ - mas, we

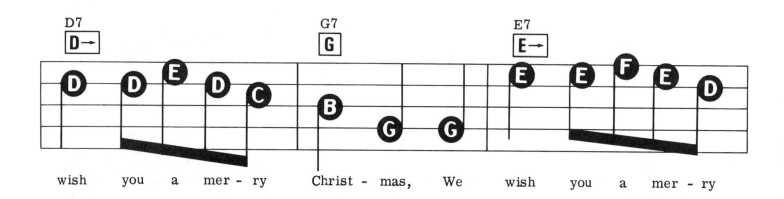

wish you a mer - ry Christ - mas, We wish you a mer - ry

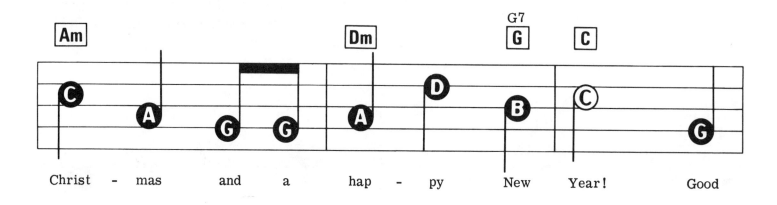

Christ - mas and a hap - py New Year! Good

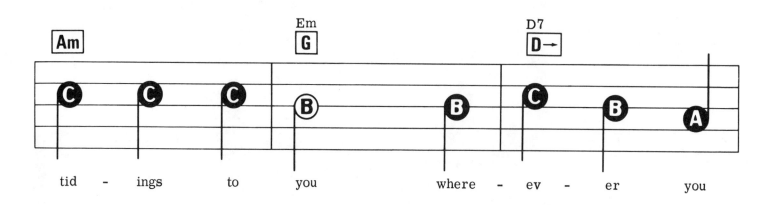

tid - ings to you where - ev - er you

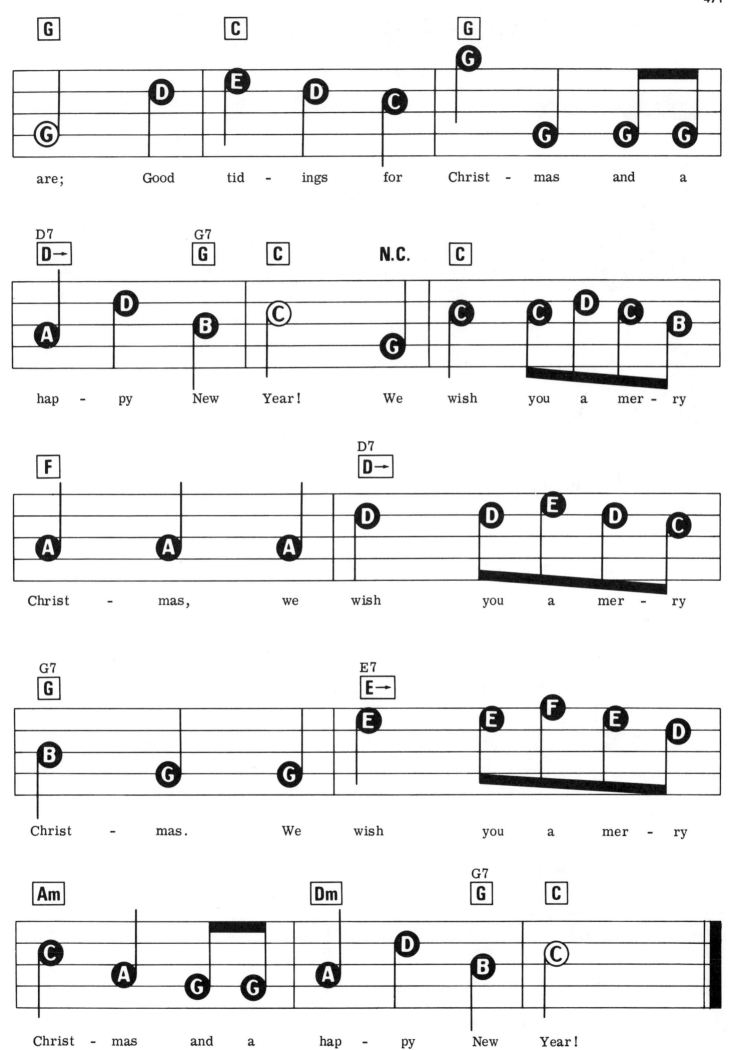

What Child Is This

Registration 10

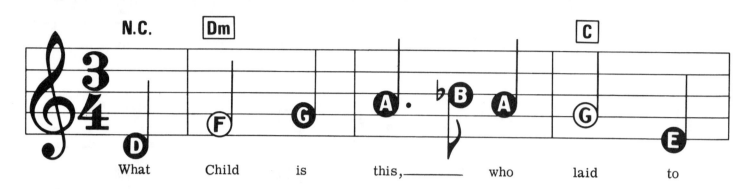

What Child is this,_____ who laid to

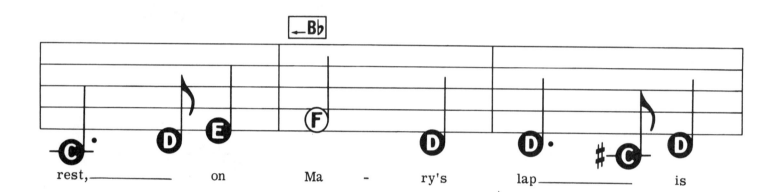

rest,_____ on Ma - ry's lap_____ is

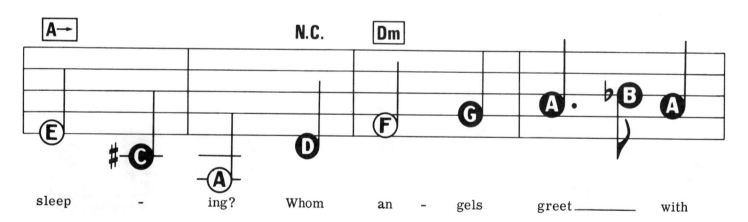

sleep - ing? Whom an - gels greet_____ with

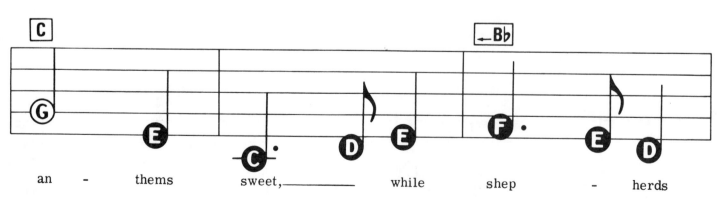

an - thems sweet,_____ while shep - herds

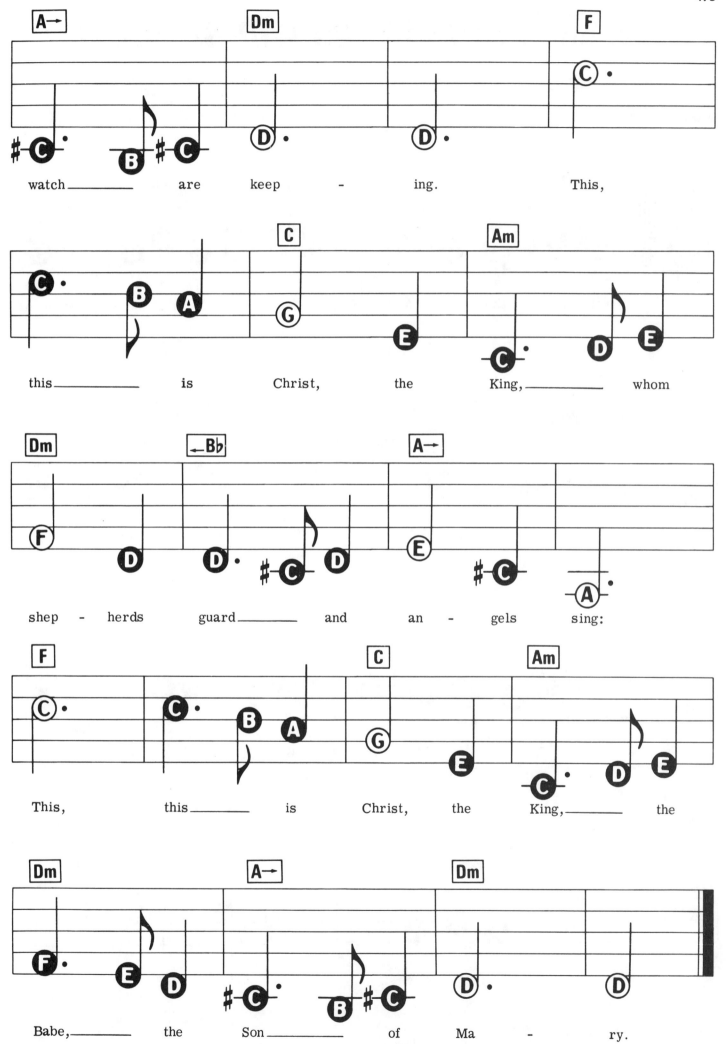

What Did I Say To Old St. Nick?

Registration 4

Words and Music by
Jim Cliff

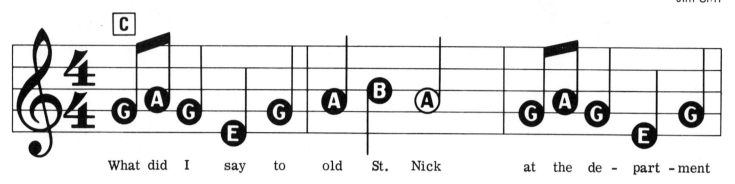

What did I say to old St. Nick at the de - part - ment

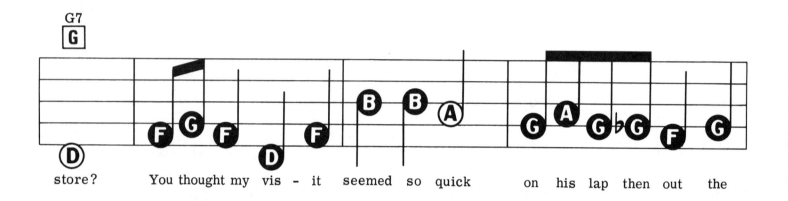

store? You thought my vis - it seemed so quick on his lap then out the

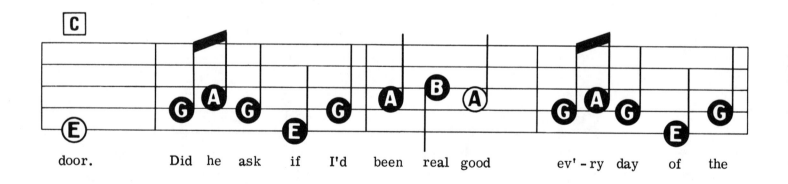

door. Did he ask if I'd been real good ev' - ry day of the

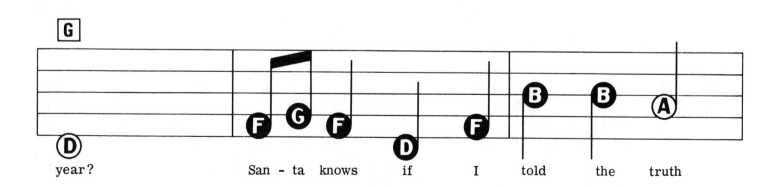

year? San - ta knows if I told the truth

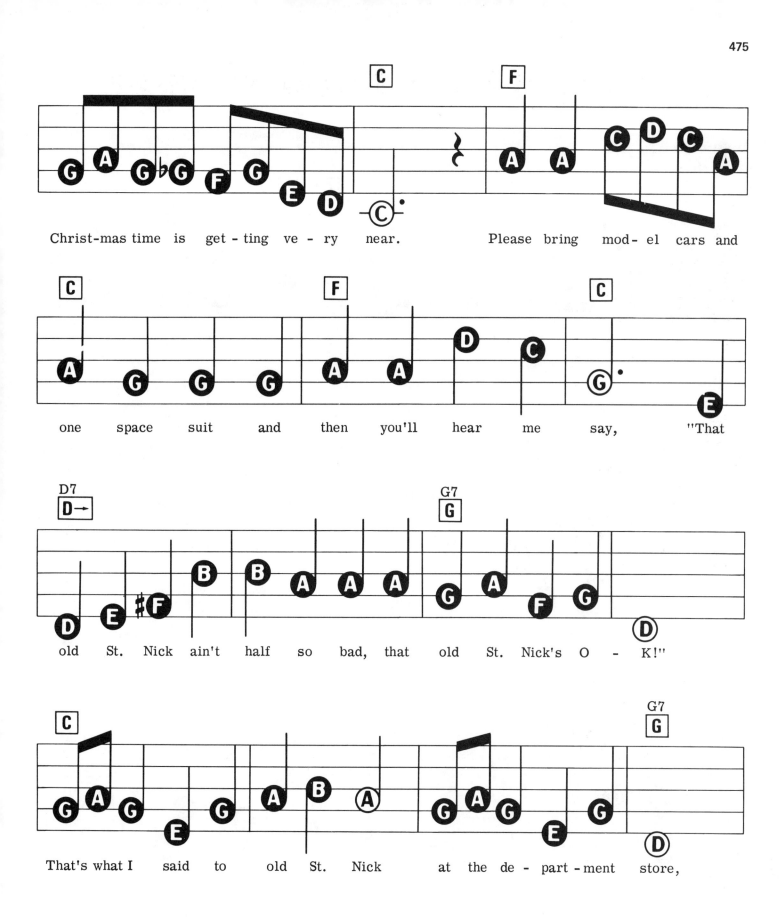

Christ-mas time is get-ting ve-ry near. Please bring mod-el cars and

one space suit and then you'll hear me say, "That

old St. Nick ain't half so bad, that old St. Nick's O - K!"

That's what I said to old St. Nick at the de - part-ment store,

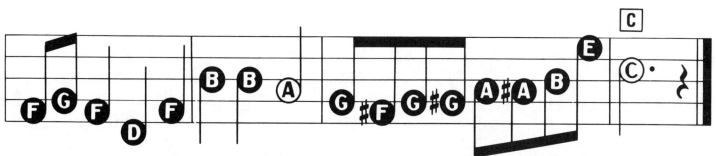

Did he say that he'd bring some toys? Ask me Christ-mas Day, I'll tell you more.

Bridal Chorus

Registration 6

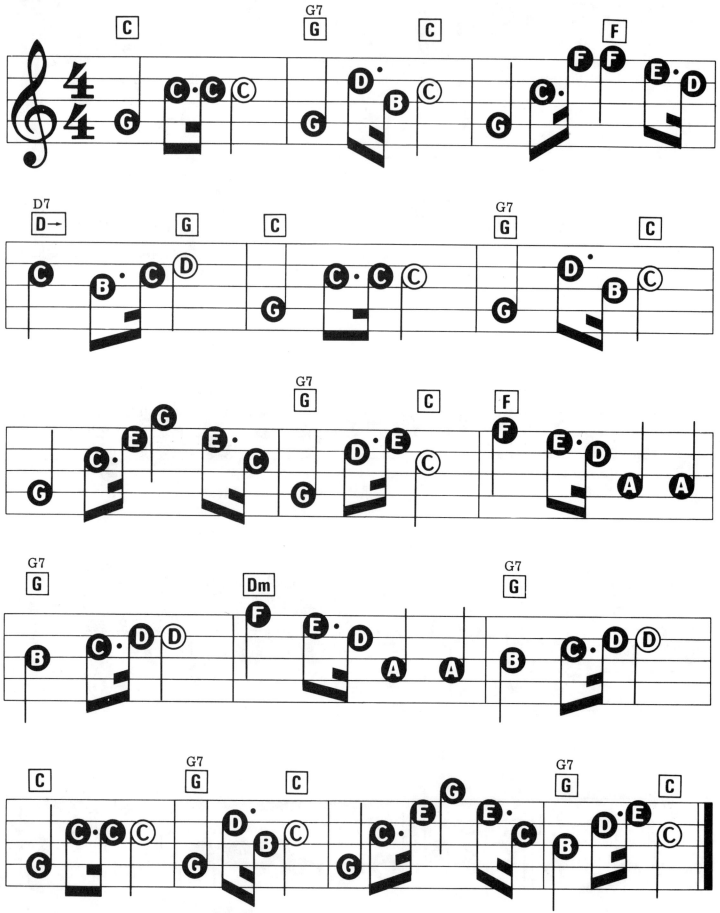

Ich Liebe Dich
(I Love Thee)

Registration 10

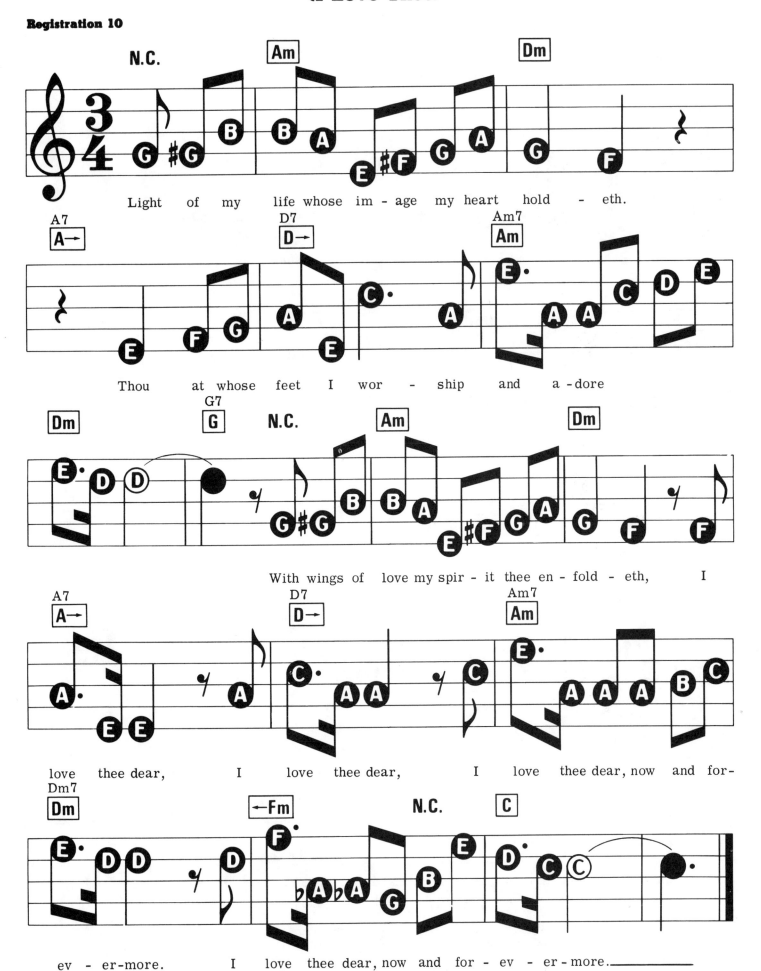

Just A Song At Twilight

Registration 1

Just a song at twi - light, when the lights are low;

And the flick - 'ring shad - ows, soft - ly come and go,

Tho' the heart be wear - y, sad the day and long, Still to us at

twi - light comes love's old song, comes love's___ old sweet___ song.

Wedding March

Registration 5

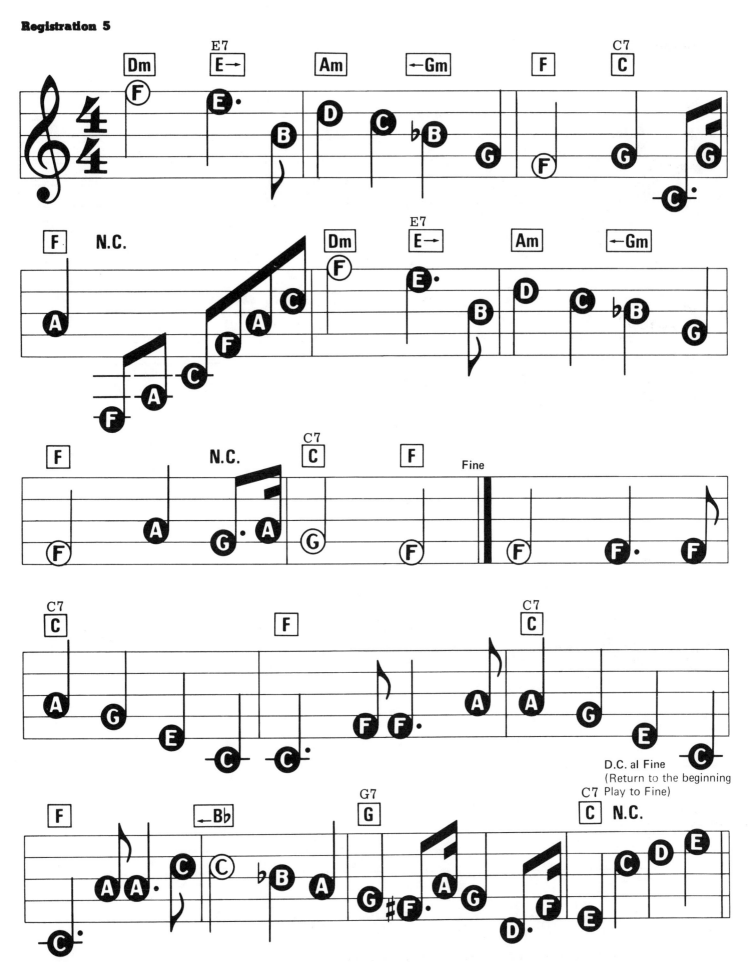

I Love You Truly

Registration 10

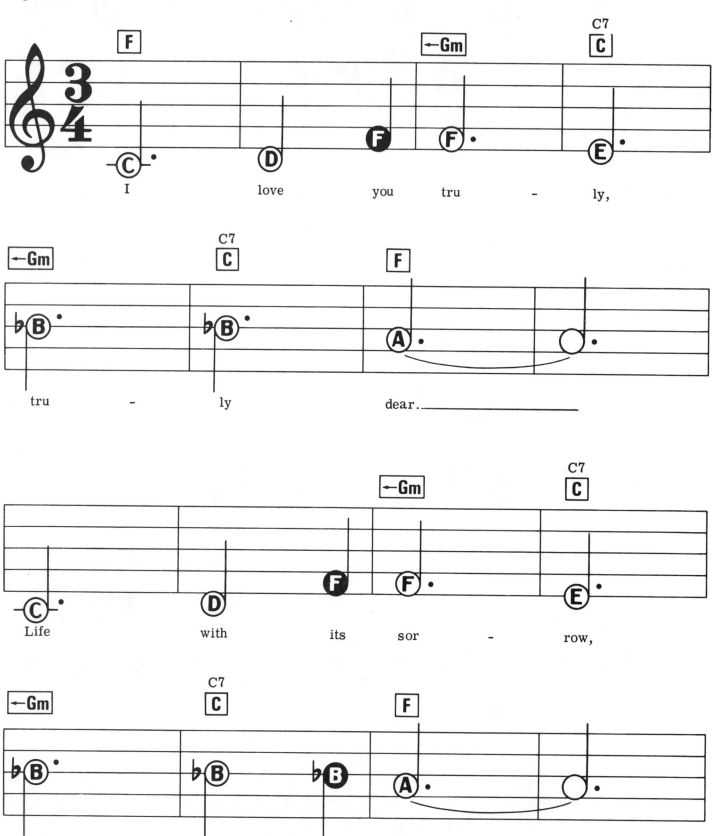

I love you tru - ly,

tru - ly dear.

Life with its sor - row,

Life with its tear.

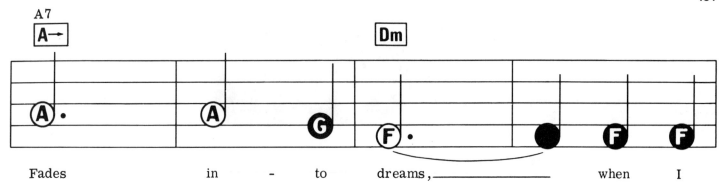

Fades   in - to   dreams,_____   when   I

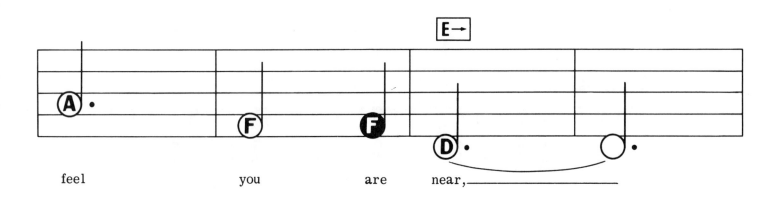

feel   you   are   near,_____

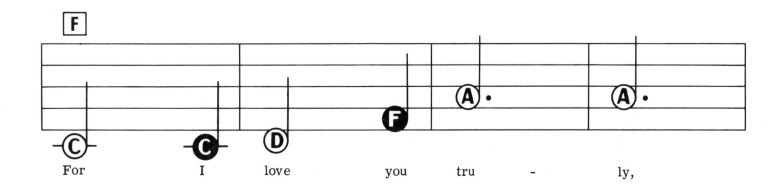

For   I   love   you   tru   -   ly,

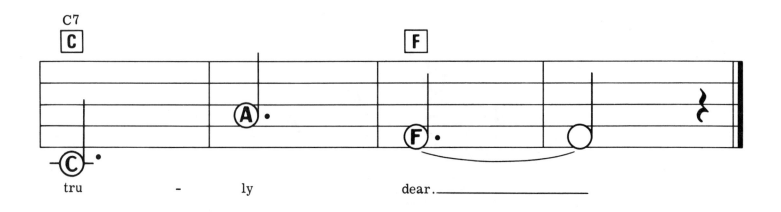

tru   -   ly   dear._____

GLOSSARY OF NOTATION AND TERMS

The following Glossary of Notation and Terms has been included for your reference. Some additional music fundamentals have been included which you may encounter in other songbooks in the E-Z Play TODAY music series.

NOTATION

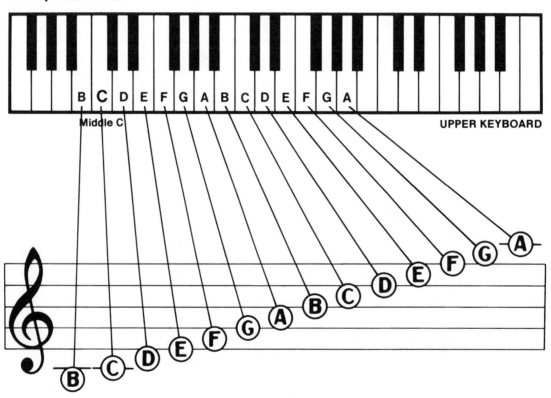

Time Signatures

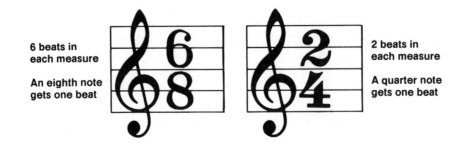

6 beats in each measure

An eighth note gets one beat

2 beats in each measure

A quarter note gets one beat

Note Values

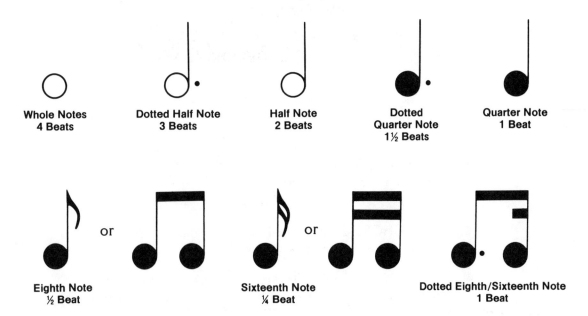

Whole Notes 4 Beats · **Dotted Half Note** 3 Beats · **Half Note** 2 Beats · **Dotted Quarter Note** 1½ Beats · **Quarter Note** 1 Beat

Eighth Note ½ Beat or · **Sixteenth Note** ¼ Beat or · **Dotted Eighth/Sixteenth Note** 1 Beat

A "triplet" is a group of three notes played in the same amount of time as two notes of the same time value. A triplet is indicated by the number 3 above or below the notes.

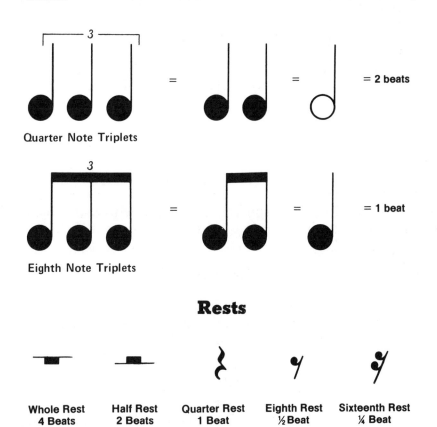

Quarter Note Triplets = = = 2 beats

Eighth Note Triplets = = = 1 beat

Rests

Whole Rest 4 Beats · **Half Rest** 2 Beats · **Quarter Rest** 1 Beat · **Eighth Rest** ½ Beat · **Sixteenth Rest** ¼ Beat

Chords

(ONE KEY or CHORD BUTTON)

| C | | D→ | | Dm | | E→ | | F | | ←Fm |

| G | | ←Gm | | A→ | | Am | | ↓B♭ |

- TRIAD CHORDS—Form all new chords according to the method introduced on page 6.

- STANDARD CHORD POSITIONS—Refer to the Chord Speller Chart on the next page for playing chords used in the E-Z Play TODAY music arrangements.

TERMS

Repeat Signs

D.S. al Coda—Return to 𝄋, play up to "To Coda," skip to "Coda" section.

D.S. al Fine—Return to 𝄋, play up through Fine (end of song).

D.C. al Coda—Return to the beginning and play to this sign ⊕. Then skip to the section marked "Coda."

D.C. al Fine—Return to the beginning and play to Fine.

Repeat and Fade—Repeat to beginning or to last repeat sign, and gradually fade out by decreasing the volume.

Fermata 𝄐

When a fermata sign appears above or below a note, it indicates that you may hold the note longer than its normal time value.

N.C.

This is an abbreviation for No Chord. Do not play a chord or pedal until the next chord symbol appears.

Chord Speller Chart
of Standard Chord Positions

For those who play standard chord positions, all chords used in the E-Z Play TODAY music arrangements are shown here in their most commonly used chord positions. Suggested fingering is also indicated, but feel free to use alternate fingering.

CHORD FAMILY Abbrev.	MAJOR	MINOR (m)	7TH (7)	MINOR 7TH (m7)
C	5 2 1 G-C-E	5 2 1 G-C-Eb	5 3 2 1 G-Bb-C-E	5 3 2 1 G-Bb-C-Eb
Db	5 2 1 Ab-Db-F	5 2 1 Ab-Db-E	5 3 2 1 Ab-B-Db-F	5 3 2 1 Ab-B-Db-E
D	5 3 1 F#-A-D	5 2 1 A-D-F	5 3 2 1 F#-A-C-D	5 3 2 1 A-C-D-F
Eb	5 3 1 G-Bb-Eb	5 3 1 Gb-Bb-Eb	5 3 2 1 G-Bb-Db-Eb	5 3 2 1 Gb-Bb-Db-Eb
E	5 3 1 G#-B-E	5 3 1 G-B-E	5 3 2 1 G#-B-D-E	5 3 2 1 G-B-D-E
F	4 2 1 A-C-F	4 2 1 Ab-C-F	5 3 2 1 A-C-Eb-F	5 3 2 1 Ab-C-Eb-F
F#	4 2 1 F#-A#-C#	4 2 1 F#-A-C#	5 3 2 1 F#-A#-C#-E	5 3 2 1 F#-A-C#-E
G	5 3 1 G-B-D	5 3 1 G-Bb-D	5 3 2 1 G-B-D-F	5 3 2 1 G-Bb-D-F
Ab	4 2 1 Ab-C-Eb	4 2 1 Ab-B-Eb	5 3 2 1 Ab-C-Eb-Gb	5 3 2 1 Ab-B-Eb-Gb
A	4 2 1 A-C#-E	4 2 1 A-C-E	5 4 2 1 G-A-C#-E	5 4 2 1 G-A-C-E
Bb	4 2 1 Bb-D-F	4 2 1 Bb-Db-F	5 4 2 1 Ab-Bb-D-F	5 4 2 1 Ab-Bb-Db-F
B	5 2 1 F#-B-D#	5 2 1 F#-B-D	5 3 2 1 F#-A-B-D#	5 3 2 1 F#-A-B-D

Guitar Chord Chart

To use the E-Z Play TODAY Guitar Chord Chart, simply find the **letter name** of the chord at the top of the chart, and the **kind of chord** (Major, Minor, etc.) in the column at the left. Read down and across to find the correct chord. Suggested fingering has been indicated, but feel free to use alternate fingering.

	C	Db	D	Eb	E	F
MAJOR						
MINOR (m)						
7TH (7)						
MINOR 7TH (m7)						

	F♯	G	A♭	A	B♭	B
MAJOR	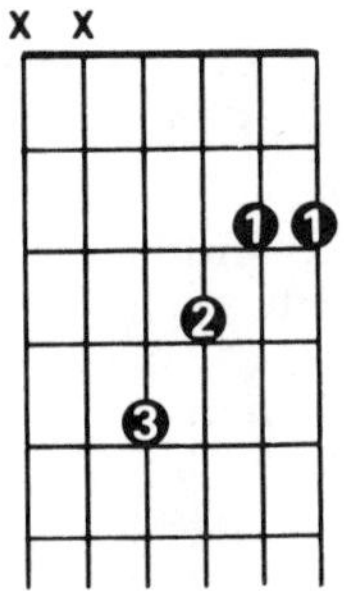	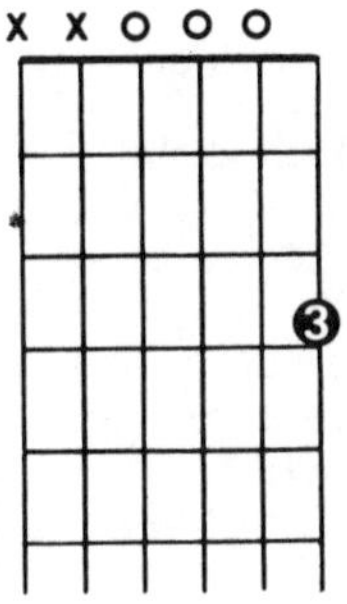	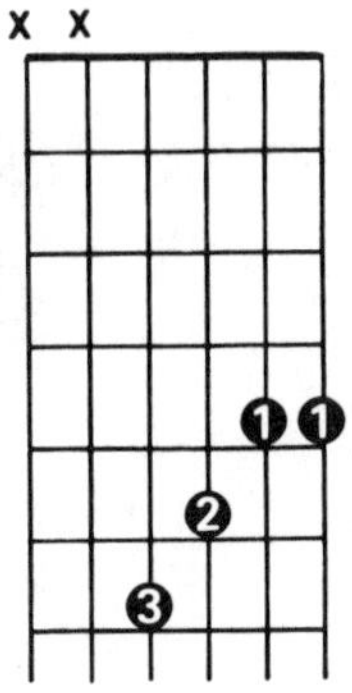	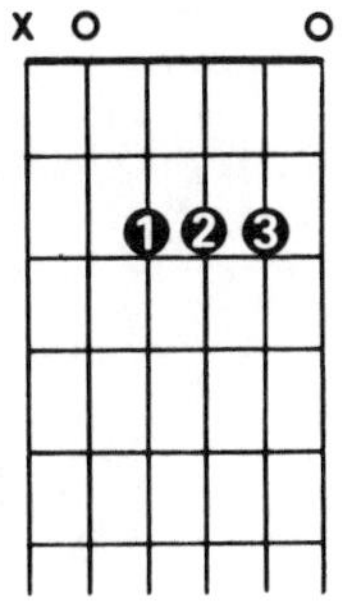	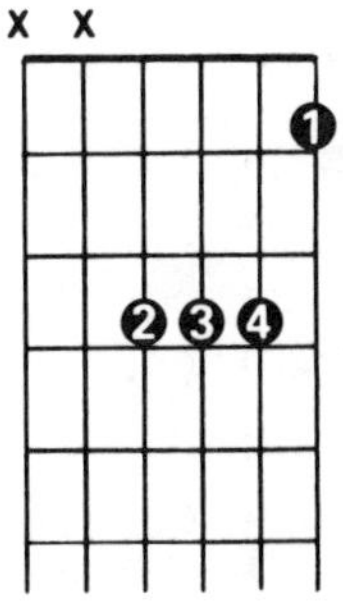	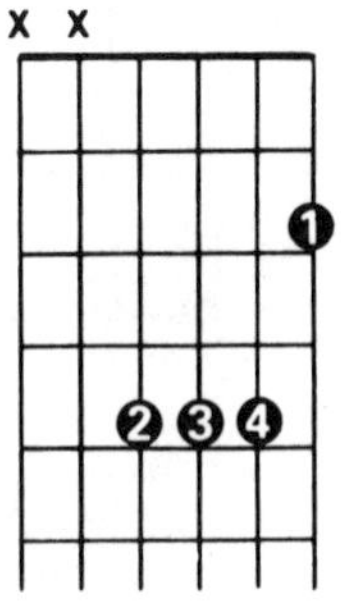
MINOR (m)	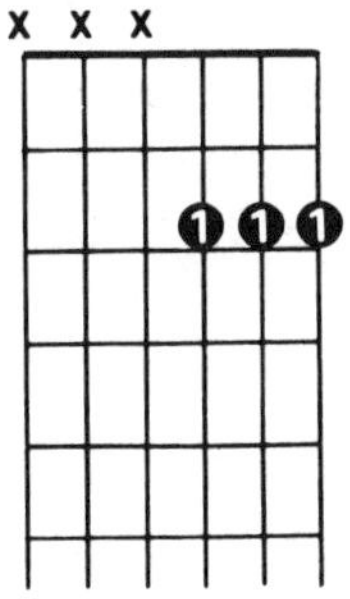	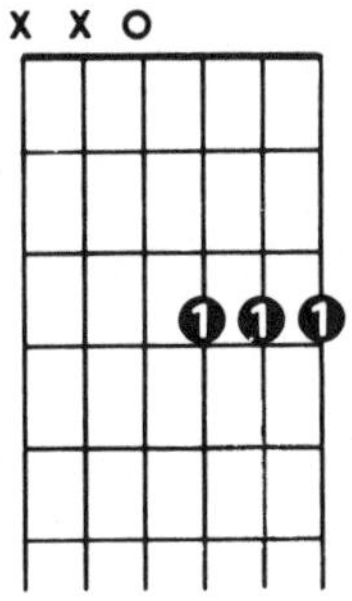	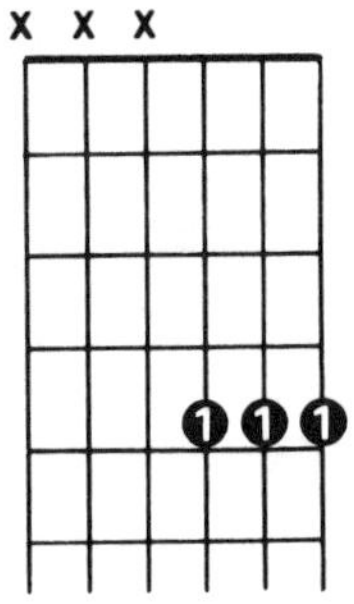	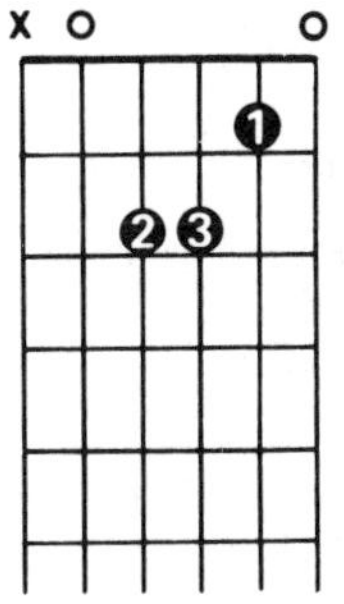	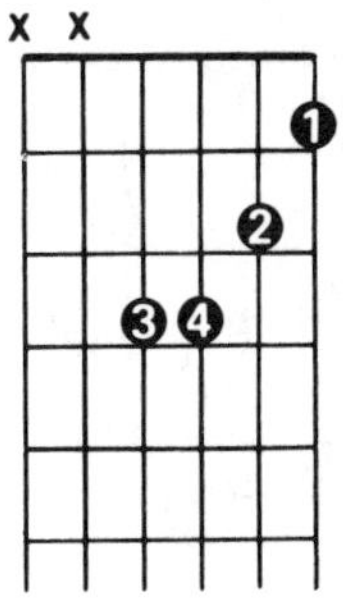	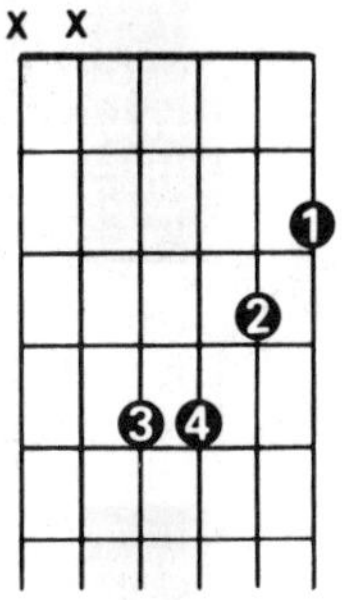
7TH (7)	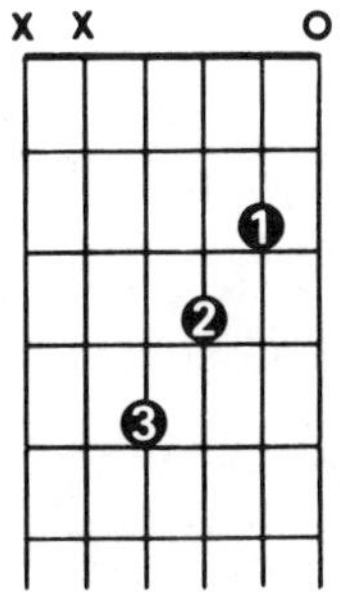	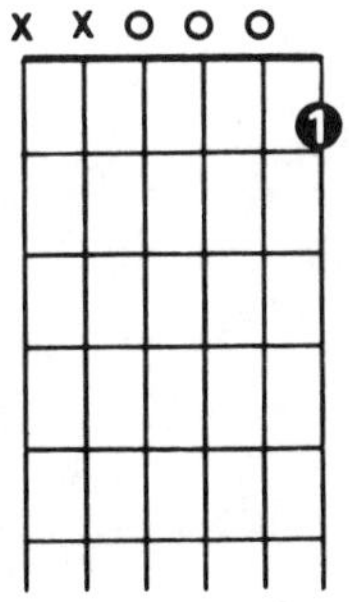	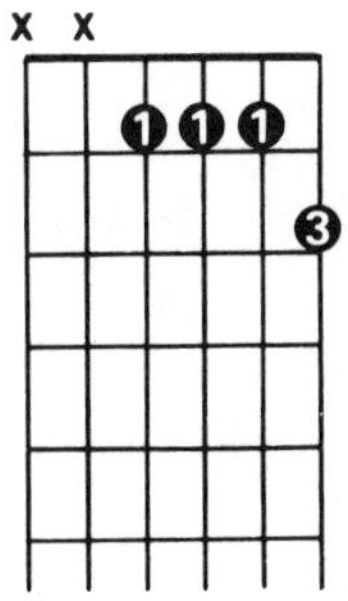	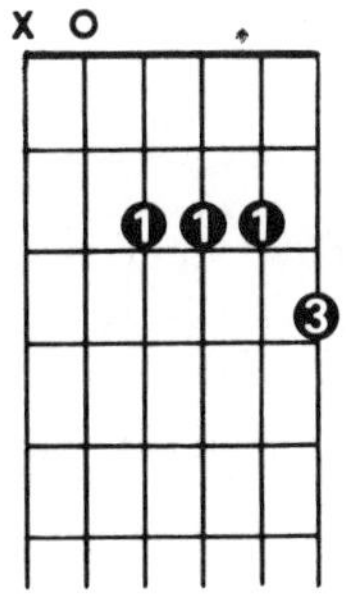	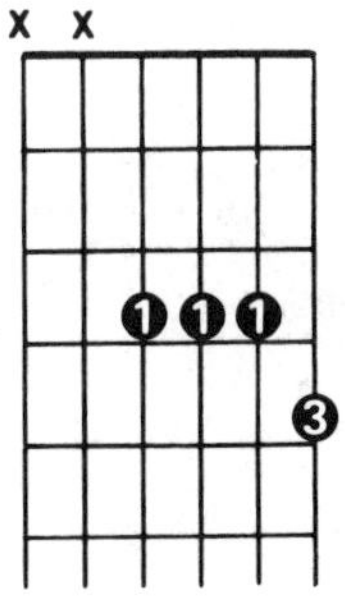	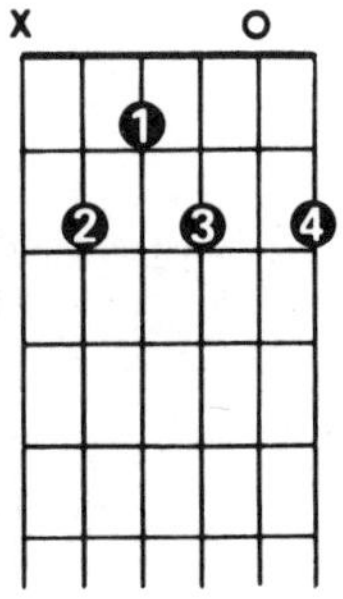
MINOR 7TH (m7)	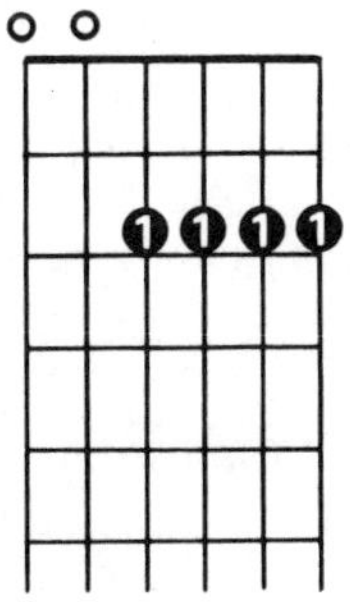	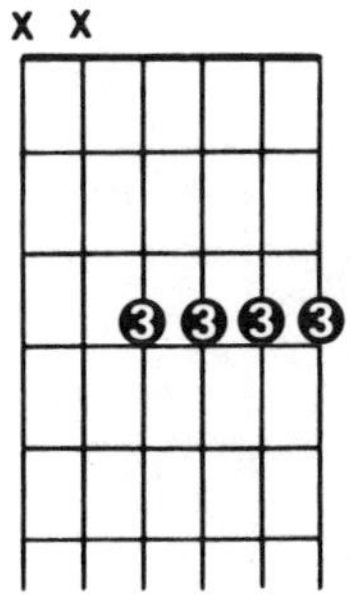	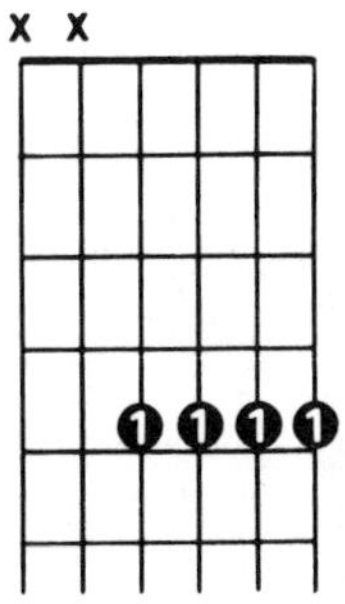	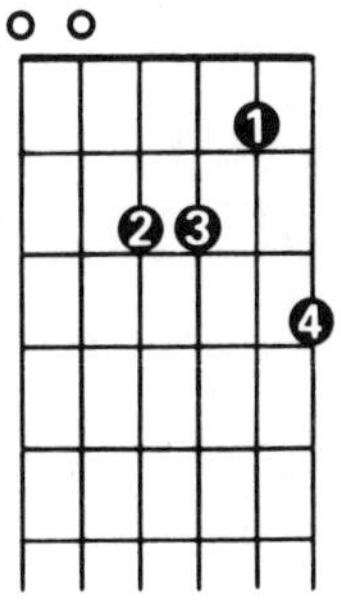	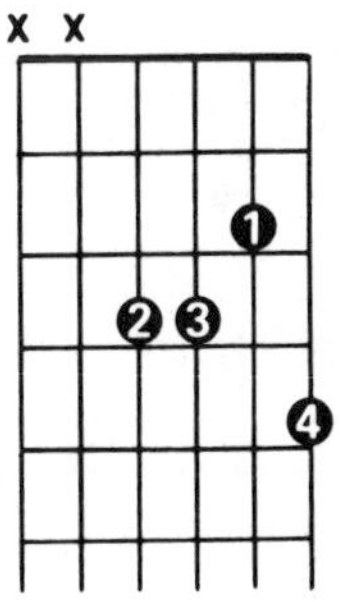	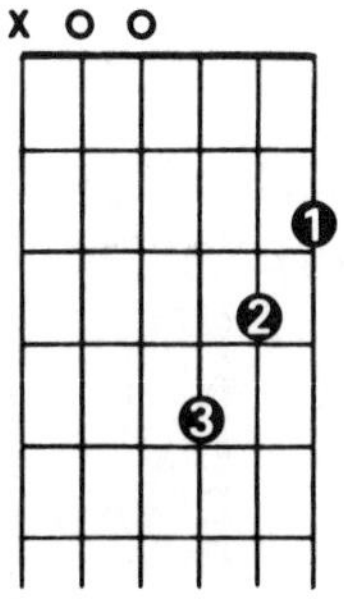